Sustainable Low-Carbon City Development in China

Sustainable Low-Carbon City Development in China

Edited by

Axel Baeumler, Ede Ijjasz-Vasquez, and Shomik Mehndiratta

THE WORLD BANK

ISBN: 978-0-8213-8987-4
eISBN: 978-0-8213-8988-1
DOI: 10.1596/978-0-8213-8987-4

Cover design: Naylor Design, Inc.

Library of Congress Cataloging-in-Publication Data

Sustainable low-carbon city development in China / edited by Axel Baeumler, Ede Ijjasz-Vasquez, and Shomik Mehndiratta.
    p. cm.
  Includes bibliographical references.
  ISBN 978-0-8213-8987-4 -- ISBN 978-0-8213-8988-1 (electronic)
  1. Sustainable urban development--China. 2. Energy policy--China. 3. Carbon dioxide mitigation--China. 4. Urbanization--Environmental aspects--China. 5. City planning--Environmental aspects--China. 6. Urban ecology (Sociology)--China. I. Baeumler, Axel. II. Ijjasz-Vasquez, Ede. III. Mehndiratta, Shomik.
  HT243.C6S87 2012
  307.1'2160951--dc23

                                                                      2011052340

Contents

BOXES

Figures

TABLES

Foreword

World Bank

Over the last 30 years, China has experienced unprecedented economic development, with annual growth averaging around 10 percent. China's economy is now the world's second largest. Accompanying this growth, modern energy, transport, and public service infrastructure is rapidly being built across the country to serve the Chinese people. Cities, of course, have been an important part of this development and are key elements in transitioning the country into a modern state. Currently, China has 665 million urban residents, up from 191 million just 30 years ago.

Although China's cities have modernized significantly in recent years, more needs to be done. The most significant challenge will be accommodating the 350 million new urban residents expected to migrate to cities in the coming 20 years. Every year, the equivalent of one megacity, such as Shanghai or Beijing, will be created in China. Rapid urbanization will be accompanied by significant pressure to provide jobs and economic opportunities, housing, public services, and improved quality of life. Meeting these needs will, in turn, require extensive efforts to solve current and future problems related to energy efficiency, transport and congestion, solid waste, and water and air pollution.

Adding to these already complex challenges is China's recent imperative of lowering the carbon intensity of its economy. President Hu Jintao has set a goal of reducing the economy's carbon intensity by 40 to 45 percent in 2020, compared to 2005. For the 12th Five-Year Plan period, a 17 percent reduction target for carbon intensity has been set. Given that cities contribute more than 70 percent of energy-related carbon emissions, addressing cities' emissions will be a crucial element of this planned reduction.

In the context of these development challenges, the World Bank is publishing *Sustainable Low-Carbon City Development in China*. This book provides many practical lessons on sustainable low-carbon development, based on World Bank experience and its long-term relationship with many Chinese provinces and cities. The book provides a framework for actions Chinese cities could and are already taking to promote both economic development and low-carbon growth.

The book starts from the premise that the imperative to reduce carbon intensity is only one of many competing priorities for government officials amidst unprecedented urbanization, modernization, and economic development. The book's main message is that actions to achieve both carbon emission reductions and local sustainable development are closely aligned: cities that embark on a low-carbon transformation will also become more livable, efficient, competitive, and ultimately sustainable.

Developing China's cities into livable and low-carbon cities with economic opportunities and a good quality of life is an important challenge for China. The World Bank appreciates its ongoing collaboration and partnership with China in addressing its low-carbon development challenges, and looks forward to a continued, effective collaboration on implementing this important development agenda.

Klaus Rohland
Country Director, China
The East Asia and Pacific Region
The World Bank

Foreword

National Development and Reform Commission

Climate change as a global issue is drawing close attention from the international community. In recent years, frequent extreme weather events such as extreme temperatures, droughts, and floods have negatively impacted the development of all countries. Because of this, actively addressing climate change and promoting low-carbon development are now a common goal across countries and a new development trend in the world.

China, as a large developing country in the midst of ongoing industrialization and urbanization, faces the complex challenge of simultaneously developing its economy, improving peoples' livelihoods, protecting the environment, and addressing climate change. To ensure not only China's but also global sustainable development, the Government of China not only attaches great importance to climate change, but also coordinates related domestic and international issues and uses addressing climate change as a key strategy for achieving socioeconomic development and as a major opportunity to speed up changes to China's economic development patterns and the restructuring of its economy. In addition, the Government of China actively advocates and promotes green and low-carbon development.

The 11th Five-Year Plan (2006–10) already called for a 20 percent reduction in energy intensity per unit of GDP. Over those five years, the

Chinese Government controlled greenhouse gas (GHG) emissions and adopted a series of major policy measures to mitigate and adapt to climate change, which lead to several significant results, including an annual average economic growth of 11.2 percent supported by an annual average energy consumption growth of only 6.6 percent. Energy intensity per unit of GDP decreased by 19.1 percent with energy savings reaching 630 million tonnes of coal equivalent (tce) or 1.46 billion tonnes of CO_2 reduced. The share of clean energy in primary energy further increased due to an ongoing nuclear power program, the installation of hydropower capacity as well as solar water heaters, and the use of rural biogas—all currently the largest programs of their kind in the world—along with the world's second-largest installed capacity for wind power. Moreover, by replanting 62 million hectares—the largest plantation effort globally—China's forest area has grown to 175 million hectares and its forest coverage has increased from 18.2 percent in 2005 to 20.36 percent in 2010. China also focused on climate change adaptation and disaster prevention and mitigation, resulting in a growing capacity to manage climate change challenges. Finally, also in 2010, China launched a low-carbon province and city project pilot and selected five provinces and eight cities to carry out pilot activities for green and low-carbon development.

Last year, in March 2011, China's National People's Congress passed the "12th Five-Year Plan for National Economic and Social Development." Relying on scientific development and increasingly rapid changes in economic development patterns, the plan calls for a reduction in energy intensity per unit of GDP of 16 percent by 2015 and a reduction in CO_2 emissions per unit of GDP by 17 percent in the same year, compared to 2010. It also provides further guidance for controlling total energy consumption and identifies key tasks for addressing climate change in the next five years.

As China's urbanization is accelerating—China's urbanization rate reached 47.5 percent in 2010 and is expected to increase to 51 percent by 2015—China's cities will play an increasingly larger role in socioeconomic development and in China's efforts to mitigate and adapt to climate change. The economic and technical roadmap for urban development will have important "lock-in effects" on China's future energy demand and GHG emissions, making it essential, in the process of urbanization, to accelerate shifts in economic development patterns; increase the use of low-carbon, energy-saving, and environmentally friendly technologies; and strengthen low-carbon and eco-city development.

In this context, *Sustainable Low-Carbon City Development in China* has significant value and can assist China in exploring and defining a green and low-carbon development path using the book's key information related to low-carbon development in Chinese cities, its in-depth analysis of future socioeconomic development challenges, and recommendations for practical policy measures to promote green and low-carbon development in Chinese cities.

China and the World Bank have engaged in a successful collaboration on climate change–related topics for many years, an effort that has greatly contributed to the formulation of China's low-carbon development policies and capacity building. The Government of China supports and encourages the World Bank to continue to contribute to China's and global efforts to address climate change.

Mr. Su Wei
Director General of Climate Change Department
National Development and Reform Commission

Preface

After 30 years of reform, China enters its 12th Five-Year Plan period facing many complex challenges. Paramount among them is continued urbanization and the need to transition to a less carbon-intensive form of economic development. The 12th Five-Year Plan includes two key targets in these areas: a reduction of carbon emissions per unit of GDP by 17 percent, and an increase in China's urbanization rate to 51.5 percent by 2015.

In recent years, the World Bank has actively supported sustainable urbanization in China. Many programs have been crucial to promote a low-carbon form of development. Generally, the low-carbon imperative reinforces elements at the core of the sustainable urbanization agenda, such as compact, public transport–focused growth and building and district heating reform. In some cases, however, the low-carbon agenda also refines the sustainable urbanization agenda, for example, by presenting new opportunities for "green" financing of urban development.

As China implements its 12th Five-Year Plan, it is opportune to summarize, through the specific lens of low-carbon development, the lessons of the World Bank's activities relating to sustainable urbanization in China. This edited book is the result of that stock-taking exercise.

This book is not intended to be a comprehensive compendium of global best practices. Rather, it builds on existing analytical work and investment project experience from the World Bank–financed portfolio in China. In areas of importance for the low-carbon city agenda where the World Bank does not have specific experience in China, this book brings lessons from other projects and analytical work implemented by the Chinese government or development partners. In a few cases where such experience is not available in China, relevant cases from other countries are used to illustrate current international practice.

As an edited book, the scope and depth of each chapter vary and depend on the experience available. The book brings together materials from a wide range of sources and areas of expertise, and, to allow for a diverse presentation that matches the depth of knowledge in each area, the editors did not seek full consistency across chapters. Moreover, while there is important overlap between the low-carbon urban growth agenda and sustainable urban development—and the book presents ample evidence of such an alignment of benefits—there are multiple important aspects of urban development that are not covered by this publication.

The intended audience of this edited book is government officials of municipalities, cities, and townships in China who will be defining policies and programs to achieve the disaggregated targets of economic growth and carbon emission reductions emerging from the 12th Five-Year Plan. Some of the lessons presented may also be of interest to other countries and development partners supporting low-carbon urban programs. The World Bank also expects to bring these lessons to counterparts preparing new lending operations in China.

Finally, this edited book has been prepared in a relatively short time frame to support actions at the municipal level to achieve the 12th Five-Year Plan targets, as well as to support some of the low-carbon city and regional pilots under preparation. Therefore, many questions and issues remain that need further research or would benefit from an extraction of lessons from the implementation of pilots. We intend to prepare a second edition of this edited book over the next 18–24 months to update the findings and lessons presented here.

Acknowledgments

This edited book, *Sustainable Low-Carbon City Development in China*, is the result of the collective effort of a World Bank team working on China's sustainable development challenges. The information and analysis in this book build on many years of World Bank experience working in partnership with cities and provinces across China. For this work, we gratefully acknowledge the collaborations with local, municipal, and provincial governments, as well as the active support of a range of central government ministries and institutions. In particular, the guidance provided by the Ministry of Finance and the National Development and Reform Commission is sincerely appreciated.

Sustainable Low-Carbon City Development in China was edited by Axel Baeumler, Ede Ijjasz-Vasquez, and Shomik Mehndiratta. Chapters were written by the editors and Anjali Acharya, Frederic Asseline, Noureddine Berrah, Henrike Brecht, Jie Cao, Mansha Chen, Stefan Csordas, Alexander Danilenko, Gailius Draugelis, Hua Du, Marielle Dubbeling, Ke Fang, Leticia Guimarães, Dan Hoornweg, Takao Ikegami, Kanako Iuchi, Paul Kriss, Steinar Larssen, Marcus Lee, Shawna Fei Li, Menahem Libhaber, Guido Licciardi, Li Liu, Zhi Liu, Junko Narimatsu, Jostein Nygard, Ximing Peng, Paul Procee, Monali Ranade, Andrew Salzberg, Jon Strand, Randeep Sudan, Lorraine Sugar, Hiroaki Suzuki, Xiaodong Wang, Jian Xie, and Dingsheng Zhang. Additional contributions were made by

Hyun-Chan Cho, Peter Cook, Said Dahdah, Gladys Frame, Matthew Gamser, Abhas Jha, Abed Khalil, Holly Krambeck, Chuck Peterson, Federica Ranghieri, Bob Taylor, Peggy Margaret Walsh, and Victor Vergara. This book would also not have been possible without the active leadership of Jim Adams, Klaus Rohland, and John Roome, who supported and guided the development of this book.

Peer reviewers were Marianne Fay, Jose Luis Irigoyen, Michael Toman, Ardo Hansson, and Dan Kammen. Additional technical reviews were provided by Om Prakash Agarwal, Veronique Bishop, Ranjan Bose, Julia Bucknall, Isabel Chatterton, Guang Zhe Chen, Kenneth M. Chomitz, Said Dahdah, Jane Olga Ebinger, Ronald N. Hoffer, Vijay Jagannathan, Marc H. Juhel, Ajay Kumar, Feng Liu, Aurelio Menendez, Lucio Monari, Ian Roy Noble, Neeraj Prasad, Robin Michael Rajack, Ashok Sarkar, Sudipto Sarkar, Jas Singh, Laura E. Tlaiye, Xiaolu Yu, Victor Vergara, Belinda Yuen, Wael Zakout, and Ming Zhang.

The Chinese translation was prepared by a team consisting of Haina Jin, Ying Li, Yong Li, Wenliang Liu, Lin Wang, Jinhong Yu, An Zhang, Wei Zhang, Xiuzhen Zhang, and Yinfeng Zhi. Lixin Gu, Peishen Wang, Wei Wang, Jun Xia, Rong Yu, and Yan Zong provided additional review of the Chinese translations.

Further support for this book was provided by Ying Fan, Vel Fernandes, Sukhbir Kalirai, Evelyn Bautista Laguidao, Guangqin Luo, Caroline Makram Milad, Teresita Ortega, Ruifeng Yuan, and Lu Zeng. Isabelle Cyr, Anna van der Heijden, and Charles Warwick provided technical editing for all chapters of this book. Bruce Ross-Larson contributed to the editing of the Overview.

The support of the Energy Sector Management Assistance Program (ESMAP) is gratefully acknowledged. ESMAP is a global knowledge and technical assistance program administered by the World Bank that assists low- and middle-income countries to increase know-how and institutional capacity to achieve environmentally sustainable energy solutions for poverty reduction and economic growth. ESMAP is funded by Australia, Austria, Denmark, Finland, France, Germany, Iceland, Lithuania, the Netherlands, Norway, Sweden, and the United Kingdom, as well as the World Bank.

About the Authors

Axel Baeumler is a senior infrastructure economist at the World Bank (abaeumler@worldbank.org).

Anjali Acharya is a senior environmental specialist at the World Bank (aacharya@worldbank.org).

Frederic Asseline is a senior energy specialist at the World Bank (fasseline@worldbank.org).

Noureddine Berrah is a consultant at the World Bank (nberrah@worldbank.org).

Henrike Brecht is a disaster risk management specialist at the World Bank (hbrecht@worldbank.org).

Jie Cao is an engineer at the Shanxi Environmental Information Center (jie39@sohu.com).

Mansha Chen is an operations analyst at the World Bank (mchen2@worldbank.org).

Stefan Csordas is a junior professional officer at the World Bank (scsordas@worldbank.org).

Alexander Danilenko is a senior water and sanitation specialist at the World Bank (adanilenko@worldbank.org).

Gailius Draugelis is energy sector coordinator at the World Bank (gdraugelis@worldbank.org).

Hua Du is a consultant at the World Bank (hdu@worldbank.org).

Marielle Dubbeling is a senior advisor in urban agriculture at the RUAF Foundation (m.dubbeling@etcnl.nl).

Ke Fang is a senior urban transport specialist at the World Bank (kfang@worldbank.org).

Leticia Guimarães is a consultant at the World Bank (leticiag@umd.edu).

Dan Hoornweg is a lead urban specialist at the World Bank (dhoornweg@worldbank.org).

Takao Ikegami is a senior sanitary engineer at the World Bank (tikegami@worldbank.org).

Kanako Iuchi is a consultant at the World Bank (kiuchi@worldbank.org).

Marcus Lee is an urban economist at the World Bank (mlee1@worldbank.org).

Shawna Fei Li is a junior professional associate at the World Bank (sli3@worldbank.org).

Menahem Libhaber is a consultant at the World Bank (mlibhaber@worldbank.org).

Li Liu is a scientist at the Norwegian Institute for Air Research (lli@nilu.no).

Paul Kriss is a lead urban specialist at the World Bank (pkriss@worldbank.org).

Steinar Larssen is an air quality expert (stlarssen@hotmail.com).

Guido Licciardi is an urban specialist at the World Bank (glicciardi@worldbank.org.)

Zhi Liu is a lead infrastructure specialist at the World Bank (zliu@worldbank.org).

Shomik Mehndiratta is a lead urban transport specialist at the World Bank (smehndiratta@worldbank.org).

Junko Narimatsu is a consultant at the World Bank (jnarimatsu@worldbank.org).

Jostein Nygard is a senior environmental specialist at the World Bank (jnygard@worldbank.org).

Ximing Peng is a senior energy specialist at the World Bank (xpeng1@worldbank.org).

Paul Procee is a senior urban environment and disaster risk management specialist at the World Bank (pprocee@worldbank.org).

Monali Ranade is a senior environmental specialist at the World Bank (mranade@worldbank.org).

Andrew Salzberg is an urban transport consultant at the World Bank (asalzberg@worldbank.org).

Jon Strand is a senior economist at the World Bank (jstrand1@worldbank.org).

Randeep Sudan is a lead ICT policy specialist at the World Bank (rsudan@worldbank.org).

Lorraine Sugar is a consultant at the World Bank (lsugar@worldbank.org).

Hiroaki Suzuki is a lead urban specialist at the World Bank (hsuzuki@worldbank.org).

Ede Ijjasz-Vasquez is a sector manager, China and Mongolia Sustainable Development Unit, the World Bank (eijjasz@worldbank.org).

Xiaodong Wang is a senior energy specialist at the World Bank (xwang1@worldbank.org).

Jian Xie is a senior environmental specialist at the World Bank (jxie@worldbank.org).

Dingsheng Zhang is a senior engineer at the Shanxi Environmental Information Center (zwzhang63@126.com).

Abbreviations

ADB	Asian Development Bank
AFOLU	Agriculture, Forestry, and Other Land Uses
AMI	Advanced Metering Infrastructure
APL	Adaptable Program Loan
AQM	Air Quality Management
ASTAE	Asia Sustainable and Alternative Energy Program
ATC	Area Traffic Control
AusAID	Australian Government Overseas Aid Program
AVL	Automatic Vehicle Location
BAU	Business as Usual
BEEC	Building Energy Efficiency Code
BIPV	Building Integrated Photovoltaic
BLS	Building Level Substations
BMS	Building Management System
BOB	Bank of Beijing
BOT	Build-Operate-Transfer
BRE	Building Research Establishment
BREEAM	Building Research Establishment Environmental Assessment Method
BRT	Bus Rapid Transit
CASBEE	Comprehensive Assessment System for Built Environment Efficiency

CASS	Chinese Academy of Social Sciences
CAUPD	Chinese Academy of Urban Planning and Design
CBEEX	China Beijing Environmental Exchange
CBD	Central Business District
CBRC	China Banking Regulatory Commission
CCRIF	Caribbean Catastrophe Risk Insurance Facility
CCS	Carbon Capture and Sequestration
CCX	Chicago Climate Exchange
CCZ	Congestion Charging Zone
CDM	Clean Development Mechanism
CEEC	Central and Eastern European Countries
CERs	Certified Emission Reductions
CHP	Combined Heat and Power
CHUEE	China Utility-Based Energy Efficiency Finance Program
CIF	Climate Investment Funds
CIP	Capital Improvement Plan
CNG	Compressed Natural Gas
CNMC	China National Monitoring Center
CNPC	China National Petroleum Corporation
CO	Carbon Monoxide
CO_2	Carbon Dioxide
COD	Chemical Oxygen Demand
COP-15	Conference of Parties, 15th Conference of Parties to UNFCCC
CPC	Communist Party of China
CPF	Carbon Partnership Facility
CRESP	China Renewable Energy Scale-Up Project
CSO	Combined Sewer Overflow
CSUS	Chinese Society for Urban Studies
CTF	Clean Technology Fund
CUD	Connected Urban Development
CWP	China WindPower
DFID	U.K. Department for International Development
DH	District Heating
DNA	Designated National Authority
DPL	Development Policy Loan
DRC	Development and Reform Commission (Beijing)
DRFI	Disaster Risk Financing and Insurance, a program of GFDRR
ECARU	Egyptian Company for Solid Waste Utilization

EDZ	Economic Development Zone
EE	Energy Efficiency
EEUs	Energy Efficiency Utilities
EFX	Electronic Freight Exchanges
EIA	U.S. Energy Information Administration
EMAS	European Eco-Management and Audit Scheme
EMC	Energy Management Company
EMCA	Energy Management Company Association
EMS	Energy Management System
EPs	Equator Principles
EPA	U.S. Environmental Protection Agency
EPB	Environmental Protection Bureau
EPC	Energy Performance Contract
ER	Emission Reduction
ERP	Electronic Road Pricing
ERPA	Emission reduction purchase agreements
ERU	Emission Reduction Unit
ESCO	Energy Service Company
ESMAP	Energy Sector Management Assistance Program
ETC	Electronic Toll Collection
ETS	Emissions Trading System
EU	European Union
EU-ETS	European Union Emissions Trading Scheme
EV	Electric Vehicle
FAR	Floor Area Ratio
FDI	Foreign Direct Investment
FDP	Federation of Disabled Persons
FIP	Forest Investment Program
FYP	Five-Year Plan
GBEC	Green Building Evaluation Committee
GBES	Green Building Evaluation Standard
gce/kWh	Grams of Coal Equivalent per Kilowatt Hour
GCIF	Global City Indicator Facility
GDP	Gross Domestic Product
GEF	Global Environment Facility
GER	Gross Energy Requirement
GFDRR	Global Facility for Disaster Reduction and Recovery
GGAS	Greenhouse Gas Reduction Scheme
GGFDP	Guangdong Green Freight Demonstration Project
GHG	Greenhouse Gas

GIS	Geographic Information Systems
GJ	Gigajoule
GPS	Global Positioning System
GRDP	Gross Regional Domestic Product
GS	Group Substation
GSHP	Ground Source Heat Pump
Gt	Gigatonne
$GtCO_2e$	Gigatonne of CO_2 Equivalent
GTZ	Deutsche Gesellschaft für Internationale Zusammenarbeit
GW	Gigawatt
GWh	Gigawatt Hour
HAN	Home Area Network
HDPE	High-Density Polyethylene
HFCs	Hydrofluorocarbons
HoB	Heat-only Boiler
HRBEE	Heat Reform and Building Energy Efficiency Project
IAP	Indoor Air Pollution
IB	Industrial Bank
IBNET	International Benchmarking Network
IBRD	International Bank for Reconstruction and Development
ICLEI	International Council for Local Environmental Initiatives, renamed ICLEI–Local Governments for Sustainability
ICT	Information and Communication Technology
IDA	International Development Agency
IEA	International Energy Agency
IFC	International Finance Corporation
I&G	China National Investment and Guarantee Company
IGCC	Integrated Gasification Combined Cycle
IMC	Intelligent Motor Controllers
IPCC	Intergovernmental Panel on Climate Change
IRR	Internal Rate of Return
ISWM	Integrated Solid Waste Management
ITDP	Institute for Transportation and Development Policy
ITS	Intelligent Transport System
JICA	Japan International Cooperation Agency
KPI	Key Performance Indicators
KRTC	Kunming Rail Transit Company

ktoe	Kilotonne of Oil Equivalent
kWh	Kilowatt Hour
LCA	Life Cycle Assessment
LCC	Low-Carbon City
LDPE	Low-Density Polyethylene
LECZ	Low Elevation Coastal Zone
LED	Light Emitting Diode
LEED	Leadership in Energy and Environmental Design (U.S. Green Building Council)
LEED-ND	Leadership in Energy and Environmental Design (LEED) for Neighborhood Development
LEGGI	London Energy and Greenhouse Gas Inventory
LFG	Landfill Gas
LGOP	Local Government Operations Protocol
LIEN	Large Industry Energy Network
LMCIP	Liaoning Medium Cities Urban Transport Project
LRAP	Local Resilience Action Plan
LRT	Light Rapid Transit; also Light Rail Transit
MDB	Multilateral Development Bank
MEP	Ministry of Environmental Protection
MIGA	Multilateral Investment Guarantee Agency
MJ	Megajoule
MOC	Ministry of Construction
MOF	Ministry of Finance
MoHURD	Ministry of Housing and Urban-Rural Development
MoT	Ministry of Transport
MRV	Measuring, Reporting, and Verification
MRT	Mass Rapid Transit
MSW	Municipal Solid Waste
Mt	Megatonne
Mtoe	Million Tonnes of Oil Equivalent
MW	Megawatt
MWh	Megawatt Hour
NAMAs	Nationally Appropriate Mitigation Actions
NDRC	National Development and Reform Commission
NGN	Next Generation Networks
NH_3	Ammonia
NMV	Non-Motorized Vehicles
N_2O	Nitrous Oxide
NO_2	Nitrogen Dioxide

NO_x	Nitrogen Oxides
NYCMO	New York City Mayor's Office of Long-term Planning and Sustainability
OECD	Organisation for Economic Co-operation and Development
PDI	Power Dissipation Index
PER	Process Energy Requirement
PFCs	Perfluorocarbons
PM	Particulate Matter
PMR	Partnership for Market Readiness
PoA	Program of Activities
PPCR	Pilot Program for Climate Resilience
PPP	Public-Private Partnership
PV	Photovoltaic
RBEED-95	Residential Building Energy Efficient Design Standards
RE	Renewable Energy
RECLAIM	Regional Clean Air Incentives Market
RFID	Radio Frequency Identification
RGGI	Regional Greenhouse Gas Initiative
RMB	Renminbi
ROW	Right-of-Way
RTRO	Real Time Route Optimization
SAR	Special Administrative Region
SCADA	Supervisory Control and Data Acquisition Systems
SCE	Standard Coal Equivalent
SCF	Strategic Climate Fund
SECSC	Shanghai Energy Conservation Supervision Center
SEEE	Shanghai Environment Energy Exchange
SEI	Sustainable Energy Ireland
SF_6	Sulfur Hexafluoride
SHEC	Shanghai Economic Commission
SILs	Specific Investment Loans
SMEPC	Shanghai Municipal Electric Power Company
SMEs	Small- and Medium-Size Enterprises
SO_2	Sulfur Dioxide
SOE	State-Owned Enterprise
SPDB	Shanghai Pudong Development Bank
SREP	Program for Scaling-Up Renewable Energy in Low Income Countries
SST	Sea Surface Temperature

SSTEC	Sino-Singapore Tianjin Eco-City
SWA	Shandong Provincial Water Association
SWC	Shanghai South Water Company
t	Tonne (1,000 kg or 1 metric ton)
TA	Technical Assistance
tce	Tonnes of Coal Equivalent
TCIP	Turkish Catastrophe Insurance Pool
tCO_2e	Tonnes of Carbon Dioxide Equivalent
TCX	Tianjin Climate Exchange
T&D	Transmission and Distribution
TDM	Travel Demand Management
TFL	Transport for London
TMG	Tokyo Metropolitan Government
TRV	Thermostatic Radiator Valves
TSP	Total Suspended Particles
TVEs	Township and Village Enterprises
TWh	Terawatt Hours
UCLG	United Cities and Local Governments
UDIC	Urban Development Investment Corporation
UNDP	United Nations Development Programme
UNEP	United Nations Environment Programme
UNFCCC	United Nations Framework Convention on Climate Change
UN-HABITAT	United Nations Human Settlement Program
USEPA	U.S. Environmental Protection Agency
VA	Value Added
VAT	Value Added Tax
VCS	Voluntary Carbon Standard
VDHC	Vilnius District Heating Company
VMT	Vehicle Miles Traveled
VOC	Volatile Organic Compounds
VOM	Volatile Organic Material
VSD	Variable-Speed Drive
WBCSD	World Business Council for Sustainable Development
WHO	World Health Organization
WPSB	Wuhan Traffic Police
WRI	World Resources Institute
WTP	Water Treatment Plant
WWTP	Wastewater Treatment Plant

Sustainable Low-Carbon Cities in China: Why it Matters and What Can be Done

Axel Baeumler, Ede Ijjasz-Vasquez, and Shomik Mehndiratta

Cities contribute an estimated 70 percent of the world's energy-related greenhouse gases (GHG). Their locations—often in low-elevation coastal zones—and large populations make them particularly vulnerable to the impacts of climate change. But cities often take steps, even ahead of national governments, to reduce GHG emissions. So it is with China's cities, which are well placed to chart a low-carbon growth path to help reach China's national targets for reducing the energy and carbon intensity of its economy.

At the onset of the 12th Five-Year Plan (FYP) for 2011–15, many Chinese cities are already on a high carbon-emission growth path. With China set to add an estimated 350 million residents to its cities over the next 20 years, the case for urgent action is strong. However, the imperative to reduce carbon intensity is only one of many competing priorities for government officials in the midst of unprecedented urbanization, modernization, and economic development. The good news is that the actions to achieve both globally relevant carbon emission reductions and local sustainable development are closely aligned: cities that embark on a low-carbon transformation will also become more livable, efficient, competitive, and ultimately sustainable. Low-carbon growth only adds another imperative to solve the immediate development concerns of Chinese cities.

China's cities will need to act on multiple fronts, in some cases scaling up elements of existing good practice, in others changing established ways of doing business. Actions affecting land-use and spatial development are among the most critical to achieving low-carbon growth as carbon emissions are closely connected to urban form. Spatial development also has very strong "lock-in" effects: once cities grow and define their urban form, it is almost impossible to retrofit them because the built environment is largely irreversible and very costly to modify. Furthermore, cities need energy-efficient buildings and industries. They need a transport system that offers alternatives to automobiles. They need to shift to efficient management of water, wastewater, and solid waste. And they need to incorporate responses to climate change in their planning, investment decisions, and emergency-preparedness plans.

Cities Are Key to Meeting China's Carbon Reduction Targets

China's cities continue to absorb about 13 million rural residents each year. Accompanied by high economic growth, this rapid urbanization puts tremendous pressure on all forms of public services: energy, water, transport, and waste. This pressure will continue during the 12th Five-Year Plan period (2011–15) with explicit targets for a 4 percentage point increase in urbanization to 51.5 percent and the creation of 45 million jobs in urban areas. That cities are responsible for about 70 percent of global energy-related GHG emissions adds an additional challenge for Chinese cities, given that China is already the single largest contributor of carbon emissions.

China's leaders have made ambitious commitments to reduce the carbon and energy intensity of the economy and transition to a low-carbon growth path. Consider President Hu Jintao's commitment to a 40–45 percent reduction in the carbon intensity of GDP by 2020, relative to 2005. The 12th Five-Year Plan includes, for the first time ever, an explicit target to reduce carbon intensity by 17 percent by the end of 2015.

Chinese cities can contribute to such change because the structure of government gives them a high level of autonomy. They are politically, financially, and administratively organized to act quickly and to realize national policy goals. Indeed, they have been the primary agents driving the economic transformation in the last three decades. Today, in response to the emerging focus on environmentally sustainable growth, many cities are already developing eco-city and low-carbon city initiatives. Such initiatives are expected to intensify as the implementation of the 12th Five-Year Plan unfolds. The National Development and Reform Commission recently announced that areas in five provinces and eight cities are to pilot low-carbon growth while specific plans are also being developed to pilot carbon-emissions trading schemes.

But despite this promising attention and activity, more work is needed to produce an integrated vision and action plan to shift China's cities onto a low-carbon path.

Low-Carbon Growth in Chinese Cities: Definitions and Visions

The first step in offering guidance on a low-carbon transition is to have a common understanding of the current carbon footprint of Chinese cities and to articulate a shared vision of what would constitute low-carbon growth.

What Is the Carbon Footprint of Chinese Cities Today?

Most assessments of carbon emissions are based on the location of economic activity, not on consumption of goods and services produced. On the basis of these assessments, many Chinese cities are already high emitters of carbon due to characteristics that distinguish them from other cities around the world. Chinese cities are important centers of industrial production of goods for national and global export markets. As a result, industry and power generation are major contributors to the carbon footprint of Chinese cities, especially so because the energy mix is dominated by coal. Data from Beijing, Shanghai, and Tianjin suggest that about 40 percent of their city emissions is from power generation and another 40 percent is from industrial activities (see figure 1). The remaining emissions, about 20 percent, come from transport, buildings, and waste. Overall, carbon emissions are likely to continue to grow quickly across all key sources—power, industry, buildings, transport, and waste—unless decisive measures are implemented to lower carbon intensity.

What Is a Low-Carbon City?

There is no universally applicable definition of a low-carbon city. There are two reasons for this. First, cities differ in their initial carbon endowments. Cities engaged in energy-intensive heavy industry, or those in colder, northern provinces requiring a lot of heating, will start with higher absolute carbon intensities than cities focusing on service and non-

Figure 1   Per Capita Carbon Emissions of Selected Cities

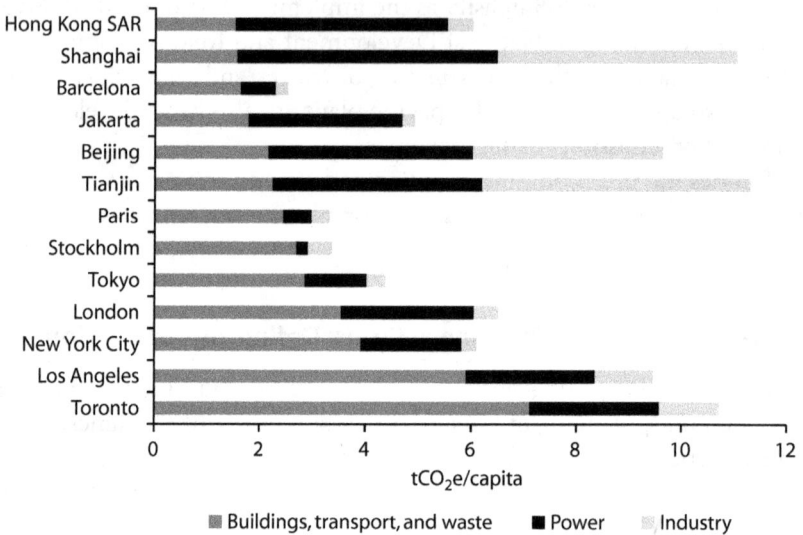

Source: World Bank 2010 (see also chapter 3).

energy-intensive industries or those in moderate climates with less need for heating or cooling. Second, the essential *raison d'etre* of cities is to provide economic opportunities and quality of life for its citizens—and not simply focus on carbon reductions. Actions that compromise on this fundamental fact risk undermining a city's long-term sustainability. Therefore, definitions of a low-carbon city should above all focus on how cities change their carbon emission *trajectories* independent of their initial carbon *endowments*, but in ways that do not compromise economic development and livability (see also box 1).

Box 1

Measuring Low-Carbon Cities

Standards for measuring a city's carbon performance are still a work in progress. Above all, a number of key accounting issues need to be resolved, especially on how to account for carbon emitted when activities and services are consumed in locations different from where the carbon is emitted. Furthermore, the relation-

(continued next page)

Box 1 *(continued)*

ship between carbon emitted in a city and its underlying drivers—the city's economic structure and GDP, energy mix, climate, population and urban form, transport and built infrastructure—is complex. This complexity makes it especially
hard to measure progress along specific dimensions: in many cases adequate indicators have simply not yet been identified. Nevertheless there is agreement that
low-carbon performance is about measuring and managing a city's trajectory
relative to its physical and economic endowment—in particular a trajectory that
maximizes low-carbon energy sources, enhances efficiency in delivering urban
services, and moves to lower carbon intensity for a given unit of GDP.

Source: Authors.

A central message emerging from the review of low-carbon city development is that there is, in fact, a strong alignment between low-carbon
and locally appropriate sustainable development strategies for cities. A
low-carbon city is therefore, above all, a sustainable, efficient, livable, and
competitive city. The low-carbon development angle adds an important
additional lens for evaluating a city's sustainable development objective.
Examples of the close alignment between local development and the
benefits of mitigating global climate change include (see figure 2):

Smart urban form and spatial development. Low-carbon cities need
compact urban form and smart spatial development. But related concerns
linked to the rapid expansion of cities such as congestion, local pollution,

**Figure 2   Alignment of Low-Carbon Growth and Sustainable Urban
Development Objectives**

Smart urban form and spatial development	Energy-efficient industry and buildings	Low-carbon vehicles and a public transport–oriented system	Low-carbon waste management and other services
• Preserved agricultural land • Reduced contingent financial liabilities • Improved rural land compensation and equity concerns • Limited encroachment into sensitive sites	• Reduced air pollution • Improved energy security • Enhanced energy efficiency and industrial competitiveness • Increased resource efficiency in buildings and heating	• Reduced congestion • Reduced air pollution • Improved traffic safety • Increased urban livability	• Improved solid waste management • Reduced air pollution • Increased efficiency water resource utilization and protection

Source: Authors.

and safety also increase when public transport becomes less competitive as a result of poor spatial growth. Rural agricultural land is over-consumed. Cities expand into areas with higher risks of disasters or higher ecological values. Contingent liabilities increase from off-budget borrowing linked to land expansion. And equity concerns arise over the compensation of rural land users on the urban periphery. Reforms in land-use planning, municipal financial frameworks, and changes in spatial development can address these concerns and promote low-carbon growth.

Urban energy use. Addressing local concerns relating to air pollution, energy security, and energy efficiency is also aligned with low-carbon growth. For example, reducing carbon emissions from heating by replacing small, decentralized, coal-fired boilers with more efficient, modern, larger, and cleaner central systems—accompanied by innovations in distribution and system management leading to consumption-based billing and better demand management—will lower the cost of service provision, improve the quality of heating services, and reduce local pollution. Similarly, enhanced energy efficiency results in not just a greener, lower-carbon industry, but a more competitive industry.

Urban transport. Local policy makers have to contend with congestion, accidents, safety, and equity implications of rapid motorization, which is also causing fast growth in carbon emissions. The broader sustainable urban transport agenda is aligned with the low-carbon agenda through concentrating development near public transport nodes; promoting walking, cycling, and public transport as alternatives to private automobiles; and managing demand to restrict automobile use.

Municipal services. Waste minimization, recycling, and modern disposal methods can lower carbon emissions of solid waste systems. For urban water and wastewater systems, holistic solutions to manage demand and to develop integrated waste, stormwater protection, and flood management systems also address water scarcity, service quality, and carbon emissions.

The close alignment between local and global benefits becomes less straightforward with respect to issues related to the overall economic structure of a city and the aggregate demand for energy from industry. Replacing energy-intensive manufacturing with relatively low-energy-intensive economic activities, such as services, sometimes offers a seemingly easy transition to a low-carbon economy. However, such strategies need to be considered carefully. Future GDP growth will be driven more by services and lower-carbon industries—both decisive for reducing the carbon intensity in many Chinese cities. For today's industrial centers, however, simply relocating higher-emission industries outside a city boundary to reduce the carbon footprint of that city—while reducing carbon emissions locally—would make little (if any) difference on larger spatial scales. But rapidly growing small and medium-sized cities may have the opportunity to leapfrog and bypass the polluting, high-carbon growth paths taken by an earlier generation.

What Needs to Be Done: A Framework for Action

To achieve low-carbon outcomes, city leaders will need to engage in a comprehensive set of actions. All key sectors under city management will have important roles, including land and spatial development, urban energy use for industry and buildings, transport, and municipal services. In some cases, elements of good practice need to be scaled up. In others, there is a need to significantly change existing ways of doing business and forge new partnerships. Moreover, policy themes that cut across sectors need to be addressed to provide a supportive environment to realize sectoral priorities. The combination of cross-cutting policy themes and sectoral priorities forms a framework for action to achieve low-carbon growth in China's cities (see figure 3).

Figure 3   A Framework for Action: Cross-cutting Policy Themes and Sectoral Priorities

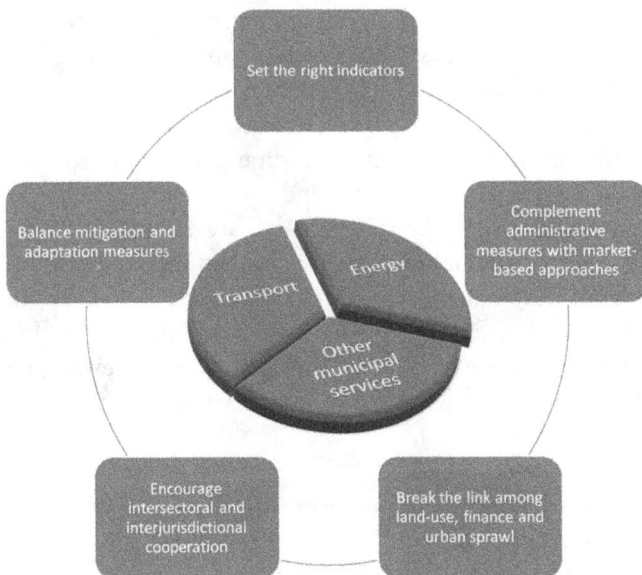

Set the right indicators

Complement administrative measures with market-based approaches

Balance mitigation and adaptation measures

Energy

Transport

Other municipal services

Encourage intersectoral and interjurisdictional cooperation

Break the link among land-use, finance and urban sprawl

Source: Authors.

Policy Imperatives and Key Cross-cutting Actions

What is needed for cities to become low-carbon cities? Many important cross-cutting actions relate to overarching policy directions and guidance provided to cities, incentives for low-carbon development, and efforts to overcome institutional constraints. Cities are the key units of action and accountability, but they are also part of a national effort, and the achievement of low-carbon city objectives will depend critically on national policies and reforms. Therefore, the central government will have a key role in providing an enabling environment for cities to implement low-carbon development strategies. Five key cross-cutting actions are described here, in line with the framework shown in figure 3.

Set the Right Indicators to Encourage Low-Carbon Growth

In China's institutional setting, local government leadership responds directly to quantifiable indicators for which they are held accountable by higher authorities. The target in the 12th Five-Year Plan—to reduce carbon intensity per unit of GDP by 17 percent—will therefore provide a strong administrative impetus for the formulation of local low-carbon development strategies. This aggregate target has to be translated into more detailed indicators to more closely track the carbon intensity of the economy and the performance of specific sectors.

While some of these indicators are straightforward, such as those related to electricity consumption, identifying appropriate indicators is more difficult in other sectors, such as urban transport and spatial development. An important first step for the national and local governments will be to determine appropriate indicators that can be easily tracked and that will provide the right incentives to lower the carbon emissions of specific sectors.

Early lessons suggest that output indicators, while important in their ability to measure easily tangible results, are sometimes not optimal. Indicators such as kilometers of urban rail laid or number of wind turbines installed may not in themselves be indicators of the desired outcomes—even if they are intermediate steps to measure the increase in public transport's share of trips or the increase in renewables' share of electricity used. Instead, identifiable and measurable outcome indicators will be required (see box 2).

Complement Administrative Measures with Market-Based Approaches and Tools

Administrative tools, critical to China's growth in the past three decades, will remain important in the short term. But gains can be achieved from

Box 2

Indicators Can Set the Right Administrative Incentives for Local Governments

Based on international and Chinese experience, the following low-carbon indicators may serve as an initial guide for further review and discussion:

- *Carbon emissions:* emissions per capita and emission intensity.
- *Energy:* energy consumption per capita, energy intensity, and share of renewable energy.
- *Green buildings:* energy consumption per square meter in commercial and residential buildings.
- *Sustainable transport:* share of green transport mode trips (percentage of citizens walking, cycling, or using public transport).
- *Smart urban form:* population density and mixed land use.

Quantitative indicators need to be complemented with qualitative indicators of policies, regulations, and standards. "Yes/No" indicators can help determine progress toward a comprehensive package of policies, ranging from land zoning and building codes, to energy efficiency and clean energy standards, and to green transport policies (congestion pricing, parking fees) and municipal finance frameworks that promote low-carbon urban growth. More research is needed in this area and future editions of this book will continue to compile and collect emerging knowledge.

Source: Chapter 3.

integrating policies and approaches based on market mechanisms whenever possible. Chinese governance places strong emphasis on government leadership and administrative guidance, and examples abound of how this tradition has helped to deliver energy efficiency outcomes. During the 11th Five-Year Plan period these included mandatory efficiency targets disaggregated at the local level, a focus on a smaller number of large entities to achieve gains, and holding local governments and enterprises accountable for achieving agreed targets. These types of measures will continue to play a vital role in the transition to a low-carbon economy. It is thus an ideal starting point that the 12th Five-Year Plan includes explicit targets—not only for energy efficiency but also for carbon intensity.

However, relying only on administrative tools will not be sufficient to realize the carbon emission targets or lead to the most cost-effective solutions. It can also have distortionary effects. Similarly, relying on market forces can sometimes bring major economic efficiencies, but this too is not sufficient in the Chinese development context. What is needed is a blend of the two sets of tools—administrative and market-based—with the emphasis on the market-based approaches increasing over time. Three key market principles and mechanisms are most relevant to low-carbon cities: setting appropriate prices, using market discipline, and introducing transparent competitive methods (see box 3).

Box 3

Three Market Principles for Low-Carbon Cities

Set appropriate prices. Prices send users a signal of value. Using price signals for public services to increase efficiency and reduce waste also supports low-carbon urban growth. Appropriate tariffs for water, wastewater, and solid waste can not only ensure cost recovery but also create a culture of conservation and promote recycling. Similarly, setting appropriate prices for fuel, parking, car ownership, and car use will help reflect the costs that drivers impose on others in congestion, accidents, and local pollution. Suitable energy pricing mechanisms are also essential to encourage residential and commercial consumers to adopt energy-efficient construction and operations. Perhaps the price signals that most urgently need correcting are those for land. Current land policy undervalues "rural" land on the urban periphery, creating incentives for overconsumption and inefficient use.

Use market discipline and market-based frameworks in providing urban services. In many ways, the spectacular development of China's cities in the last three decades reflects the success of market principles. In the transport sector, fiscal discipline and cost-recovery frameworks underlying the development of roads and bus networks have allowed those services to grow with the expansion of demand. In the energy sector, energy service companies were created with explicit financial incentives to deliver energy conservation. But there remain further opportunities for more consistent and accelerated use of market-based incentives in the delivery of urban services to achieve low-carbon goals.

(continued next page)

Box 3 *(continued)*

Introduce transparent competitive methods to increase efficiency of public subsidies. Subsidies and other forms of government monies, used across public services, support a range of objectives. Invariably, these objectives can be achieved more efficiently and more effectively by using transparent competitive methods. For industrial energy efficiency, linking public energy efficiency funds more closely to verifiable energy savings could make their use more effective. Similarly, competitive selection of operators to provide public transport could ensure that any subsidies to support such operations are efficiently used.

Source: Authors.

Break the Link between Land Use, Finance, and Urban Sprawl

A particularly important issue for Chinese leadership to consider is the spatial growth of Chinese cities and the links with municipal finance. Spatial growth patterns determine long-term carbon use in a city. Once cities grow and define their urban shape, it is almost impossible to change and retrofit them because their built form is highly durable, largely irreversible, and very costly to modify. There is almost no asset in the local economy as long lived as the urban form—with an asset life of more than 100 years. Cities that have spread over large areas and with fragmented land use are locked into high-carbon development paths.

Urban sprawl—with rapid growth of low-density areas at the urban periphery—can increase carbon emissions through three mechanisms. First, low-density development increases carbon emissions from urban transport through longer commutes and more private motorized trips. Second, low-density areas increase living space per person, and consequently lead to higher per capita emissions from home heating, cooling, and general power consumption. Third, low-density development produces infrastructure used less intensively than that in dense urban cores, such as suburban highway access roads, raising emissions per capita. Figure 4 shows that Chinese cities are starting from a good base of densities—but the financial incentives now in place undermine this advantage by promoting urban sprawl.

Many Chinese cities have more than doubled their built area in a 10-year period. The dynamics of urban spatial growth are closely linked to shortcomings in the municipal finance framework, with an imbalance

Figure 4   Alternative Futures: Urban Density or Urban Sprawl?

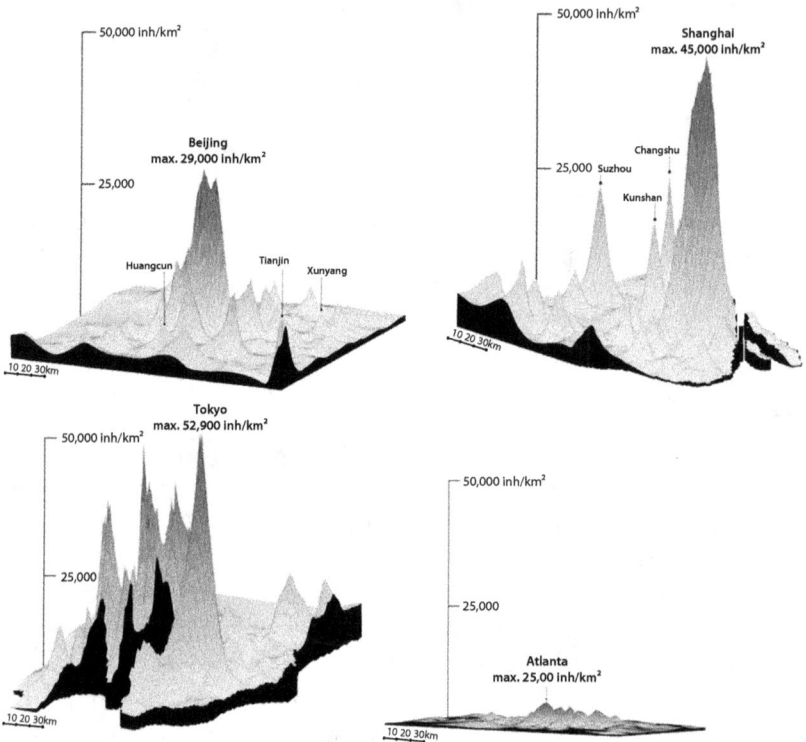

between the sources of finances available to Chinese cities and the demands for services and infrastructure. This mismatch, combined with possibilities for cities to derive potentially large revenue from sales of collectively owned rural land, in large part drives excessive land use and conversion in the urban periphery. In addition to "locking in" high-carbon land-use patterns, the practice creates contingent liabilities linked to the off-budget borrowings of land-backed, state-owned, urban investment companies.

The central government should therefore reexamine the financial incentives of municipal governments and curtail their ability to engage in excessive land conversion (see box 4). Specifically, the central government could offer cities an alternative sustainable financing framework, including through the ability to directly raise debt.

Box 4

Financing Structures for Cities Need to Be Fundamentally Rethought

Municipalities have significant responsibilities for local economic development and for providing a range of urban public services. But they have limited options to mobilize finance. Their share of the total tax base is not commensurate with their responsibilities, and they are not allowed to mobilize debt directly.

Assistance is needed to establish transparent, credible, and stable local revenue streams to help local governments to access capital markets. Currently, the bulk of urban financing is structured through off-balance-sheet government platforms that depend heavily on land sales and redevelopment for their revenue base. This creates incentives for land development inconsistent with low-carbon spatial forms.

National policy makers should create a sustainable and alternative financing paradigm for Chinese cities. Work on this complex issue is still in its developmental stages, but it will likely need to include tax reform, better access to debt and capital markets, and refined mechanisms to allow fiscal transfers from higher levels of government. The national government and cities will also have an opportunity to introduce innovative financing mechanisms that focus explicitly on supporting low-carbon development, such as carbon finance, environmental or green bonds, and various concessional finance programs.

Source: Authors.

Encourage More Intersectoral and Interjurisdictional Cooperation

Many of China's public service and infrastructure achievements come from the ability to hold specific elements of government accountable for specific outcomes. Agencies are empowered with an unusual level of decision-making authority and then held accountable for promised targets. While this has facilitated project execution, it has also lowered interest in and focus on cooperation across sectoral and jurisdictional boundaries. Authorities building an urban road may find it easier and quicker to avoid connecting with an inter-urban highway than to engage in potentially protracted discussions with a different municipal or provincial authority on how to facilitate such an interchange. For the same reasons, intermodal facilities between bus and urban rail, or between inter-urban and urban modes of transport, are often not adequately addressed and consequently never get programmed, allocated land, or implemented.

The result can be an infrastructure system with key pieces constructed in record time, but with suboptimal integration across elements managed by different agencies. While this is an issue for all leaders aiming to create livable and efficient modern cities, it is particularly important for low-carbon growth. Attracting car users to public transport requires road agencies, public transport agencies, and traffic and sidewalk management agencies to cooperate and provide seamless high-quality experiences. Managing scarce regional water resources and building energy- and cost-efficient waste systems will similarly require more cooperation among county, district, and sometimes municipal governments.

The challenge for Chinese cities will be to facilitate such cooperation across sectors and jurisdictional boundaries without significantly compromising the strong culture of implementation that has been at the core of economic development in the last three decades. Often in China, the best solutions will likely be local and context-sensitive pragmatic answers to particular issues rather than wholesale changes in approach. It will be important to identify such solutions as they emerge and find ways of mainstreaming them across cities.

Balance Mitigation and Adaptation Measures

China ranks among the most vulnerable countries exposed to climate change impacts and meteorological hazards. Projections show that it will be vulnerable to more frequent and intense rainfall and floods in the southwest, and while typhoons are predicted to fall in number, their intensity and impacts are projected to increase. China's water scarcity is also expected to become more severe, with arid areas at risk of increased desertification. And the 130 million residents of China's coastal cities are particularly vulnerable to rising sea levels.

Although the costs of adapting to climate change can initially be high, the costs of delaying action to integrate climate risk management into these investments and to ensure climate-smart growth could be much higher. Costs will result not only from direct damages but also from indirect impacts, including supply-line disruptions, productivity losses, and relocation costs. Prevention is cost-effective, and governments can take measures to build safer cities. The challenge for city governments is not merely to have a short-term view of policies but to adopt a long-term cost-benefit outlook, favoring measures for climate change adaptation and disaster prevention.

Adapting to climate risks builds on elements of sound urban planning, which are linked to successful adaptation and effective low-carbon city development (see box 5). The concept of "integrated climate risk management" captures this link and builds in adaptation measures that are flexible, spread the risk, and are integrated with city planning. Flexibility and resilience are particularly important for cities because impacts at the local level are expected but cannot yet be predicted with precision at the scale of a city.

Sectoral Priorities and Key Actions

The cross-cutting actions identified in the previous section help to create a favorable policy environment for low-carbon cities. To realize the desired low-carbon outcomes, however, actions will need to focus on addressing specific sectoral challenges, particularly those related to energy, transport, and other municipal services including water and waste management services (see figure 5 for a breakdown of carbon emissions

---

Box 5

Adaptation—Elements of an Integrated Climate Risk Management Approach

Investments in climate change adaptation link to successful urban planning and low-carbon city development. The following five elements characterize an integrated climate risk management approach:

- *Mapping risks:* understanding the vulnerable terrains and critical water flows.
- *Identifying vulnerable communities:* the poorest are often the greatest at risk.
- *Emergency preparedness:* using early warning systems to mitigate impacts and community-based approaches to respond speedily and effectively to climatic events.
- *Working with nature:* nonstructural strategies that "work with nature" need to complement traditional engineering solutions that "manage and control nature," especially in the context of flood plains and shore management.
- *Planning for response:* implementing a standard system of "safe" routes and facilities, establishing community-based response plans, and introducing official coordination and response plans.

Source: Authors.

Figure 5   Carbon Emissions per Capita in Beijing, Tianjin, and Shanghai (2006 estimates)

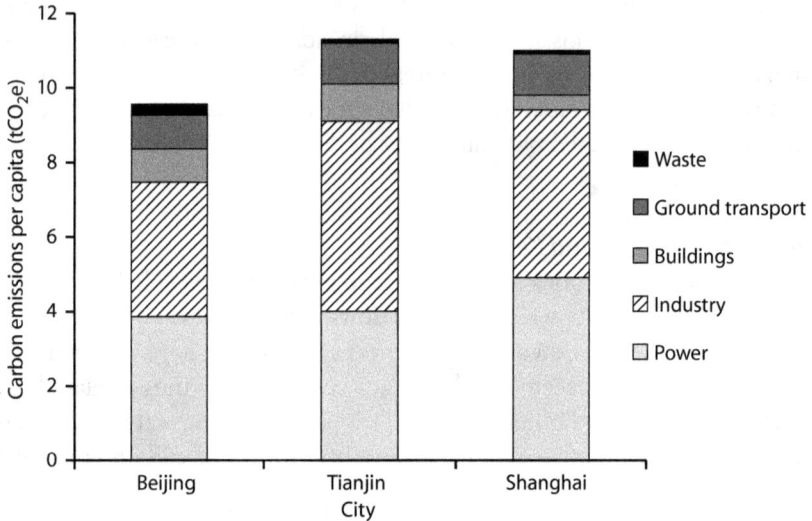

Source: Authors based on data from World Bank 2010 (see also chapter 3).

across sectors in three major Chinese cities). This section reviews key lessons and experiences for each of those sectors, based on the experience of Chinese cities and World Bank–supported programs.

Energy—the Key Driver of Carbon Emission across All Sectors

Encouraging a cleaner and greener supply of electricity. National and to some degree regional characteristics, together with associated national policies and trends, are the main determining factors influencing the eventual carbon footprint of a city's electricity consumption. At the national level, gains in reducing the carbon intensity of power generation have been overtaken by increases in aggregate demand (see figure 6). While no municipality in China has direct control over national policies and trends relating to electricity generation, municipalities still have some options to reduce their carbon footprint. For example, they can import power from sources that have lower emissions, generate green power locally, increase local renewable and other distributed sources of generation in the city mix, and provide end users with a choice of green electricity supply (see box 6).

Industrial energy efficiency—a story of success and continuing potential. Industrial plants in or near urban centers produce a large share of emis-

Figure 6   Carbon Emissions in the Power Sector in China

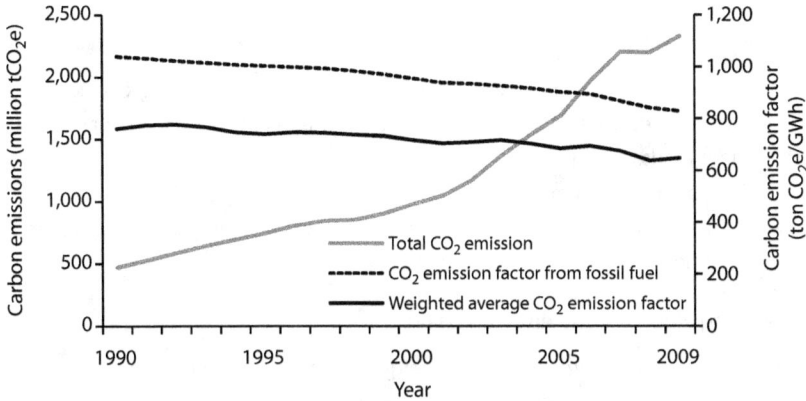

Source: Chapter 5.

Box 6

Key Energy Sector Recommendations

The 11th Five-Year Plan period yielded an impressive 19.1 percent reduction in the energy intensity of the GDP, which was achieved primarily by focusing on the industrial energy sector. Contributing factors included setting administrative targets for subnational governments, focusing on the energy efficiency potential of the largest enterprises, systematically incorporating energy assessments in new project appraisal, creating a system of incentives and requirements to eliminate inefficient capacity and plants, creating the Energy Services Company industry, and developing grant programs to encourage energy efficiency. To build on this recent success in the energy sector, leaders should consider the following actions:

Energy generation

- Maximize the use of renewable energy as well as technical options such as co-generation and tri-generation.
- Evaluate all choices to make and buy electricity. When possible, consider buying low-carbon electricity from outside the municipality.
- Develop programs that allow end users to voluntarily pay for the incremental costs of green electricity.

(continued next page)

Box 6 *(continued)*

Industrial sector

- Consider an enhanced role for market-based methods, including pricing energy to reflect externality costs and creating transparent competition for public grant funds.
- Support a financial market that provides credit for energy efficiency.
- Further support the energy service industry through benchmarking and peer learning.

Building efficiency and district heating

- Consistently implement building energy efficiency codes for new construction.
- Retrofit public buildings to achieve energy efficiency.
- Accelerate material labeling to encourage appropriate technologies.
- Switch to consumption-based billing to provide end users with an incentive to preserve energy and make their buildings more energy efficient.

Source: Authors.

sions in Chinese cities and were a major focus of the efforts to reduce the energy intensity of the economy during the 11th Five-Year Plan. Some critics have cited anecdotes of local officials being placed under pressure to meet energy efficiency targets by shutting down industries, schools, and even hospitals in the name of energy efficiency. Such unproductive and isolated events notwithstanding, the overall experience in terms of promoting industrial energy efficiency has been positive and sets the policy and program foundations for achieving more long-term energy savings.

The core elements of industrial energy efficiency reforms—administrative targets and incentives, a focus on the biggest emitters, and incentive programs to accelerate new-technology adoption—work well in the Chinese context. Strengthening market-based tools within this administrative structure would increase the effectiveness of this approach. This could include support for the nascent financial sector to provide credit for energy efficiency and for energy efficiency service companies that have a profit incentive linked to energy efficiency. Market thinking also remains relevant to enhancing policy effectiveness such as using transparent competitive approaches to allocate public funds and incorporating social and environmental costs into energy pricing policy.

Building energy efficiency and district heating—cost-effective options to mitigate carbon emissions. Buildings are a low-cost option to obtain significant reductions in carbon emissions. They account for one-third of global energy consumption, and a business-as-usual scenario could see close to a 50 percent increase in consumption by 2035 relative to 2007. With about 40 percent of China's 2030 building stock yet to be built, implementing building codes for energy efficiency can yield substantial results. China is among the first non-OECD countries to introduce such mandatory codes, but opportunities remain for municipalities to implement codes that are stricter and more comprehensive than the national standard—and for more effective monitoring and support to ensure compliance. An ongoing national initiative on labeling building materials can also improve new building standards by certifying the quality and sustainability of materials. Despite a concerted national effort to retrofit existing buildings, only limited progress has been achieved. The key challenge remains creating an institutional framework that encourages end users to actively participate. Public buildings may offer a good entry point for retrofitting efforts.

District heating reform should complement energy efficiency measures for buildings. A key element is consumption-based billing. Paying for heat according to the meter will provide a strong incentive to conserve energy for heating. District heating also gives cities the ability to switch to greener fuels with more flexibility than distributed solutions. And while most energy reduction programs are aimed at heating, there is good potential to conserve energy during the cooling seasons.

Urban Transport Policy—the Fastest Growing Source of Carbon Emissions

Transport produces about 26 percent of China's carbon emissions from fuel combustion. It is also the fastest growing consumer of fossil fuels and source of carbon emissions. Transport emissions result from a complex interplay of the economic activity in a city, the transport activity, and the way trips are split across modes. In general, there are three key strategic options for a city to reduce the carbon footprint of its urban transport, all highly relevant to Chinese cities (see box 7).

Changing the distribution of activities in space. A city can influence the distribution of activities in space—by changing land-use patterns, densities, and urban design and reducing the total level of transport activity. Better land-use planning and compact city development can lead to fewer or shorter motorized trips and to a larger share of motorized trips on public transport.

Box 7

Key Urban Transport Sector Recommendations

While Chinese cities have focused primarily on building out road networks to facilitate automobility and spatial expansion, some recent steps are consistent with low-carbon growth. These include a 2005 State Council directive to prioritize public transport, as well as the development, currently under way, of more than 5,000 kilometers of urban rail in 23 cities. Future efforts to develop a low-carbon transport growth path could include:

Walking and cycling

- Preserve and increase the contribution of walking and cycling.
- Improve the experience of walking/cycling by building smaller block sizes and developing secondary road networks; improving the quality of feeder roads, improving basic facilities such as toilets, lights, trees, and benches; and improving safety along key arterial corridors.

Public transport

- Enhance the quality of basic bus services with attention to planning, regulation, infrastructure improvements, and on-street priority.
- Develop a customer-oriented approach to attract users of choice, paying attention to the door-to-door customer experience and to intermodal facilities and services, including premium services.
- Focus on integration across modes and services, particularly schedules, fares, and physical facilities for buses and bicycles at rail stations.
- Integrate land-use and transport planning—improving urban planning to bring it in line with international best practice for transit development.

Addressing motor vehicles

- Consider policies to manage auto ownership and use, including taxation and fees for ownership, parking, fuel, and use.
- Enhance parking management, which is a simple and important way to manage auto demand.
- Use electric vehicles and other technologies, especially as the market matures and if the electricity grid becomes significantly greener.

Source: Authors.

Supporting low-carbon transport modes. A city can also improve the quality of relatively "low emission" modes, such as walking, cycling, and various forms of public transport. Even today, between 50 percent and 60 percent of trips in most Chinese cities are by walking or cycling. But in most Chinese cities the trend is negative, with bicycle use falling precipitously. To transition to a low-carbon growth path, Chinese cities should preserve, as far as possible, the trips using non-motorized means, and then, ultimately, again attract the pool of trip-makers who could consider these modes for some of their trips.

For public transport, even with the significant investments in urban rail, more attention is needed to improve bus services, which will remain the mainstay for most cities. Significant mass transit investments currently under way in urban rail provide opportunities for quantum improvements in service if the investments are properly integrated with the bus network. China also has some good bus rapid transit systems, which offer many of the benefits of urban rail at a lower cost. But they require careful attention to system performance, including operating plans, traffic management, and system integration.

Reducing emissions from private vehicle use. A city can directly influence what vehicles and how much private transport is used. Most of the transport-related carbon emissions in China's urban areas are generated by motorized passenger transport (see figure 7), and private cars have the

Figure 7   Autos Represent a Small Share of Trips but a Large Share of Transport Sector Emissions

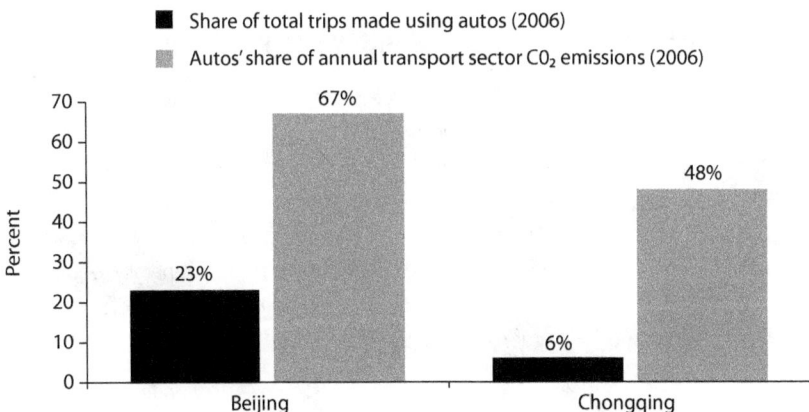

■ Share of total trips made using autos (2006)

Autos' share of annual transport sector CO_2 emissions (2006)

Source: Chapter 12.

largest transport-related carbon emissions per capita. Two approaches can reduce emissions from motorized vehicles. The first is to adopt technological measures—such as electric vehicles, energy-efficient technologies, or technologies to strengthen road freight logistics—that reduce the carbon emissions of motorized vehicles per unit of travel. The second is to adopt demand management measures that reduce the amount of automotive travel. Such measures include both nonpricing controls on vehicle ownership and use (such as restrictions on parking or days the car can be used) and pricing controls (such as fuel taxes, higher parking fees, and congestion pricing).

Other Municipal Services—Also Part of the Solution

Waste is another rapidly growing source of carbon emissions. Global estimates suggest that solid waste accounts for 5–10 percent of carbon emissions generated within a city boundary. If current rates of growth in waste generation are not tempered, residents of Chinese cities may become among the highest generators of urban waste globally. Regardless of the growth trajectory of waste, significant efforts will be needed by Chinese cities to address their waste management needs in coming years. Cities could effectively reduce carbon emissions related to the waste sector by developing an integrated sustainable waste management approach based on a hierarchical "reduce-reuse-recycle-compost-dispose" philosophy that minimizes the amount of waste disposed (see box 8).

Box 8

Key Water, Wastewater, and Solid Waste Recommendations

Chinese cities have increased both the access to and the sustainability of all their key municipal services. Almost all households are now connected to a 24-hour water supply, and in recent years China has implemented the world's largest-ever wastewater treatment investment program. Cities have also gradually moved in the direction of cost recovery tariffs. Many actions necessary to lower the municipal services' carbon footprint are now well understood and also generally required for optimal functioning of the respective sectors, independent of their carbon impact. Recommended actions include:

(continued next page)

Box 8 *(continued)*

Water supply

- Consider compact urban development patterns to minimize infrastructure needs and pumping costs.
- Reevaluate raw water intake strategies to minimize energy use requirements.
- Reevaluate advanced water treatment methods (for example, desalination) to minimize energy use.
- Enhance demand management, including through appropriate pricing strategies.

Wastewater/drainage

- Introduce holistic and integrated approaches to flood protection and natural wastewater purification, and expand wastewater provision using natural systems such as constructed wetlands.
- Consider decentralized methods of treatment as coverage is expanded to peri-urban areas.
- Consider low-energy, anaerobic treatments, particularly in smaller cities and towns.
- Minimize carbon emissions from sludge disposal.

Solid waste

- Promote waste minimization, waste segregation, composting, and recycling through a combination of pricing, increased awareness, and administrative control measures.
- Reduce the need for incineration and, if incineration is needed, ensure that emissions meet most advanced global standards.
- Ensure that landfills are designed and managed professionally and that methane gas is captured for energy generation where possible.

Source: Authors.

The water and wastewater sector also offers some opportunities for emission reductions. The sector does not, at first glance, offer obvious opportunities to reduce a city's carbon footprint. Estimates suggest that even in 2020 it will be responsible for less than 1 percent of China's carbon emissions. But there still are good reasons to focus on the sector, including the considerable overlap between low-carbon solutions and established good practice. In addition, some technical proposals to address water scarcity are potentially very energy intensive and need to be balanced with stronger demand management.

Finally, in addition to the reforms in the key urban sectors, city officials can introduce innovative reforms in other less obviously related sectors. Preserving and reusing historic built assets, for example, reduces the energy needed to build new buildings, while downtown regeneration goes hand-in-hand with livable, walkable downtown areas that support bicycle and pedestrian transport. Urban agriculture and forestry are both gaining momentum as innovative ways to reduce emissions and—in urban agriculture—also improve food security. Finally, developments in information and communication technology, such as smart grids and electric vehicles, will be an essential backbone for any low-carbon city development (see box 9).

Box 9

A Growing Role for Technology

Technology will be critical in the effort of Chinese cities to develop low-carbon economies. This includes renewable energy technologies currently under development or in an early stage of commercialization, technologies that reduce emissions from fossil-fuel generation, and other energy-saving transportation technologies. Equally important will be "smart" systems based on information and communication technologies to optimize system performance. These include "smart grid" technologies, systems applications to increase the efficiency of wastewater treatment processes, and software applications to benchmark industrial energy efficiency efforts.

Perhaps less obvious are some "lower tech" traditional technologies that can support the transition to a low-carbon growth path. In transport the core tested technologies that will create livable cities with low-carbon transport systems are bicycles and buses. Renovating and reusing old buildings, particularly those built before the 1920s, can be an energy-efficient alternative to rebuilding. For wastewater, anaerobic methods offer opportunities for less carbon-intensive treatment. For solid waste, well-constructed landfills complemented with recycling are an alternative to energy-intensive incineration.

Source: Authors.

Developing a Plan of Action

To realize low-carbon urban development and implement a comprehensive multisectoral policy agenda will require coordinated action from a range of stakeholders. Different levels of government in China will need to be actively involved, and complementary initiatives will be required from civil society. By focusing on "how," this section proposes recommendations to turn the outlined policy framework into an actionable set of priorities for key stakeholders.

National Government Leadership

The central government has to create an enabling environment. While cities are key units of action and accountability, the achievement of low-carbon city objectives needs clear national leadership. Most of the cross-cutting policy themes identified above lend themselves primarily to national government policy interventions, including setting low-carbon development indicators, complementing administrative with market-based approaches, breaking the link between municipal finance and urban sprawl, encouraging more intersectoral and interjurisdictional cooperation, and balancing mitigation with adaptation.

Some of these actions will require analytical policy guidance but may be relatively easy to implement, such as finding the right indicators to encourage low-carbon development or providing clear guidance to cities on the climate change adaptation agenda. Others, such as increasing the role of market-based approaches in the economy, essentially call for accelerating broader reform efforts long under way. But two reform areas will require a marked departure from business as usual. The first is the need to comprehensively reform existing municipal finance mechanisms and create stable and adequate revenue sources for cities that take away the incentive for excessive rural land conversion and urban sprawl. Without such a reform, complex as it might be, cities will continue to find it challenging to reduce their overreliance on land sales as a key source of city financing. The second is to promote an administrative culture that facilitates cooperation across intersectoral and interjurisdictional boundaries—essential for addressing the complex management challenges in introducing effective low-carbon development solutions.

Some sectoral priorities will also require action from the central government. In particular, the central government will need to continue to take the lead in greening the country's energy supply and in overall technological and industrial policy. Regulatory refinements will be needed to facilitate innovations in energy consumption (such as possibly giving cities flexibility in their sources of energy) and deployment of new transport technologies (such as electric vehicles). Finally, the central government will have to set priorities and provide targeted concessional finance for low-carbon initiatives—ranging from promoting public transport to developing decentralized renewable energy and wastewater treatment systems.

Local Government Leadership

Even with strong national leadership, cities will carry the bulk of responsibility for implementing the low-carbon city agenda. Chinese cities have significant autonomy to implement policy directives and a track record of implementing ambitious policy agendas effectively and with agility. City leaders are expected to be charged with quickly establishing a roadmap for action during the 12th Five-Year Plan to achieve low-carbon outcomes. From a *substantive* standpoint, this will require implementation of the sectoral agendas highlighted in the previous section and summarized in boxes 6, 7, and 8. From a *process* standpoint, city leaders will need to:

- *Determine the city's carbon footprint.* This requires establishing an accounting framework with baselines and benchmarks—based on a globally or nationally recognized inventory methodology—to measure progress. Conducting a citywide carbon emissions inventory requires a consistent methodology, robust data collection, and transparency. Knowledge of a city's footprint is critical to informing citizens and policy makers about the level and source of baseline emissions.
- *Develop a vision and set a low-carbon target.* This will require bottom-up analyses of options and a top-down articulation of a long-term vision from the city's officials. Establishing carbon emission targets at the city level would include four steps: determining the carbon reduction potential, including developing a city's carbon emission abatement cost curve (see box 10); developing the carbon emission abatement scenarios; defining the carbon emission vision and target for the city; and disaggregating the carbon emission target for the city, using quantifiable and monitorable indicators.
- *Implement a low-carbon city action plan.* A low-carbon city strategy and implementation plan will need to be developed and organized into a balanced and ranked set of cross-sectoral and sectoral actions—with each activity fully costed and with financing identified. The low-carbon-city action plans should clearly address institutional integration.

Box 10

When to Adopt Which Abatement Technology at What Cost

Cities must choose from a variety of possible actions to promote low-carbon development. Scientific approaches to balance actions—and identify priorities—across sectors can help. Analytical tools can provide quantitative fact-based analyses to help policy makers and business leaders identify and prioritize potential solutions across sectors. One such methodology is the GHG Abatement Cost Curve developed by the McKinsey Institute and applied by countries around the world, including China (McKinsey 2009).

The cost of an abatement technology reflects its resource (or techno-engineering) costs—its capital, operating, and maintenance costs—offset by any energy or other savings associated with abating one tonne of CO_2 equivalent (one tCO_2e) per year using this technology. For each sector, the abatement technologies can be arrayed from the lowest to the highest cost, and from this range the sector abatement cost curve can be constructed. The curves plot the estimated maximum technical abatement potential of each option and the realistic costs of implementing them. For Chinese cities, abatement options could be considered in at least four key emission-intensive sectors: industry, power, buildings, and transport. The analysis could be extended to cover other potentially important sectors, such as municipal services (solid waste, water, and wastewater), as well as actions with important co-benefits, such as those related to air pollution. Figure B10.1 shows the general schematic of a typical GHG abatement cost curve.

Figure B10.1   Marginal Abatement Cost Curve

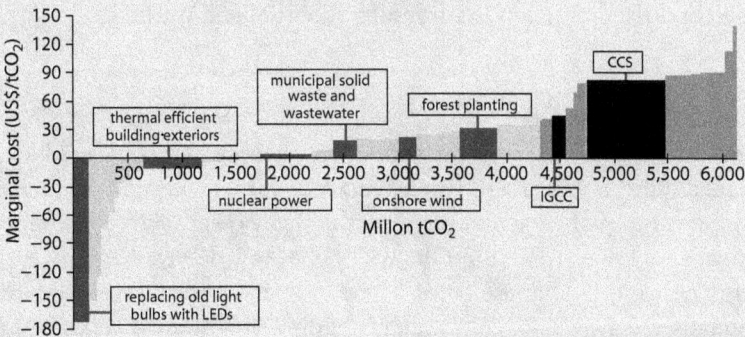

Source: Based on data from McKinsey & Company 2009 (see chapter 3).
Note: CCS = carbon capture and sequestration; IGCC = integrated gasification combined cycle.

(continued next page)

Box 10 *(continued)*

While the abatement cost curve has proved useful in undertaking the analysis, it is important to note its drawbacks. It does not cover transaction costs (the cost of designing the policies and programs and the institutional changes associated with them), and it focuses exclusively on GHG abatement technologies, leaving aside other "non-technology" GHG abatement options, such as urban form, public transport, and household and citizen behavior changes. Such interventions can often be the most transformative ones a city can undertake. As a result, the GHG abatement cost curve must be seen as only one among several analytical tools to help inform a broader strategy for low-carbon city development.

Source: Authors.

This is especially crucial given the strong interdependencies of many activities, particularly those for urban land use and transport. The action plans should also clearly identify the local economic development benefits.

• *Carefully monitor progress.* Monitoring, verifying, and reporting carbon emissions will ensure that the city is moving toward a low-carbon growth path and is on track to deliver sustainable development. A measuring and reporting system should again use a nationally or globally recognized inventory methodology, be based on a robust data collection system, and start with a solid baseline inventory that provides a benchmark for comparing subsequent inventories. Inventories should be conducted regularly, with results reported and verified.

What Citizens Can Do

Cities will also have to seek the support of their citizens and build a consensus around a resource-efficient and low-carbon lifestyle. With rising incomes and higher individual purchasing power and consumption demands, a low-carbon lifestyle will be a key determinant of future energy demand in Chinese cities. Some tools have been developed internationally to engage citizens in understanding their individual and household carbon footprints and in taking actions to reduce them. Similar partnerships at the city level can generate interest in Chinese households to improve the quality of their lives in less carbon-intensive ways.

Citizens should be made aware of the link between lifestyles, carbon footprints, and the global and local impact of these lifestyles. Citizens can then choose public transport and walk and cycle where possible. They can also choose to live close to work and along public transport corridors to reduce commuting distances and related emissions. They can reduce home energy consumption through the use of energy-efficient appliances. And they can support a low-carbon waste management system by recycling, composting, and generally reducing household waste. Informed, motivated, and proactive citizens will no doubt be essential for the success of any low-carbon city.

*   *   *

China is acutely aware of the need to reduce its carbon emissions and has made ambitious commitments to reduce carbon intensity. The development of low-carbon cities is the key to succeeding in this undertaking, making the timely adoption of a framework and action plan, such as the one outlined in this overview, crucial. In the upcoming 12th Five-Year Plan period and beyond, China has an opportunity to implement low-carbon strategies and approaches, ranging from innovations in new technology, to increased efficiency in existing industries, and to better management of the growth of cities. This will also make its future cities more sustainable, more efficient, more competitive, and more livable.

References

McKinsey & Company. 2009. "China's Green Revolution: Prioritizing Technologies to Achieve Energy and Environmental Sustainability." March 2009. http://www.mckinsey.com/locations/greaterchina/mckonchina/reports/china_green_revolution_report.pdf.

World Bank. 2010. *Cities and Climate Change: An Urgent Agenda.* Washington, DC: World Bank.

PART 1

Introduction to Low-Carbon Cities

CHAPTER 1

Cities and Climate Change: An Urgent Agenda

Dan Hoornweg

Overview

Cities are a key contributor of global greenhouse gas (GHG) emissions. This chapter establishes that cities are also natural partners to mitigate the impacts of climate change by reducing their GHG emissions. Moreover, there are significant co-benefits between becoming a low-carbon city and a livable, sustainable city with a high quality of life. Becoming a low-carbon city not only helps mitigate the impacts of climate change, but also brings about other advantages, such as cost-savings, cleaner air, and a generally higher quality of life. This chapter addresses the specific link between cities and climate change. Because of the dramatic increase in urban populations—in China and around the world—addressing urban GHG emissions is key. In addition to mitigating climate change, cities also have to prepare for the impacts of climate change through adaptation measures.

This chapter will first discuss the link between cities and climate change and why cities matter for climate change mitigation. Next, it will discuss estimates for city GHG emissions, links between emissions and city design, and possible actions to mitigate and adapt to climate change. A final section discusses available World Bank support for climate action in cities. This chapter is based on the World Bank Report, *Cities and Climate Change: an Urgent Agenda* (World Bank 2010).

Cities and Their Role in a Globalized World

Globalization is anchored through the growing connectivity of about 75 "global cities." The world's top 10 cities combined have an economy larger than the economy of all of Japan. In fact, out of the world's 100 largest economies, 53 are countries, 34 are cities, and the remaining 13 are large corporations.

In addition, the world's 50 largest cities (by population) and the C40, an association of 40 of the world's largest cities,[1] have combined economies larger than the economies of either China or Japan, and second only to the United States. Those 50 largest cities, with their more than 500 million urban citizens, generate about 2,600 million tonnes CO_2 equivalent (tCO_2e) GHG emissions, more than all countries apart from the United States and China. Table 1.1 highlights the enormous impact that a relatively few cities have on global GHG emissions. The top 10 GHG emitting cities alone, for example, have emissions roughly equal to all of Japan.

As significant contributors to GHG emissions, cities are natural stakeholders in all climate mitigation efforts. Due to the combination of their economic clout, concentration of skilled manpower, and often the relevant government authority to implement changes that would influence GHG emissions, cities are uniquely important partners to engage with on

Table 1.1   Top 10 Cities, Countries, C40 Cities (Combined), and the 50 Largest Cities (Combined), in Terms of Population Size, GHG Emissions, and GDP

Population (millions)	GHG emissions (million tCO_2e)	GDP (billion US$ PPP)
1. China: 1,192	1. United States: 7,107	1. United States: 14,202
2. India: 916	2. China: 4,058	2. 50 Largest Cities: 9,564
3. 50 Largest Cities: 500	3. 50 Largest Cities: 2,606	3. C40 Cities: 8,781
4. C40 Cities: 393	4. C40 Cities: 2,364	4. China: 7,903
5. United States: 301	5. Russian Federation: 2,193	5. Japan: 4,354
6. Indonesia: 190	6. Japan: 1,374	6. Top 10 GHG Cities: 4,313
7. Brazil: 159	7. Top 10 GHG Cities: 1,367	7. India: 3,388
8. Russian Federation: 142	8. India: 1,214	8. Germany: 2,925
9. Top 10 GHG Cities: 136	9. Germany: 956	9. Russian Federation: 2,288
10. Japan: 128	10. Canada: 747	10. United Kingdom: 2,176

Source: World Bank 2010.
Note: This table is for indicative purposes only. The years of data sources vary across countries and are determined by the last available UNFCCC reported country data. All China data refer to 1994, the last year when China reported its GHG emissions to UNFCCC.

climate mitigation issues. Cities are dynamic, offer scale, and can create a sense of urgency among residents and their local leaders, which can be focused for rapid and widespread action on climate change mitigation and adaptation. Large cities may also have a greater innate ability to learn from each other in the rapidly evolving area of climate change; for example, the carbon finance programming efforts being developed in São Paulo and Rio de Janeiro may be particularly relevant to Beijing and Shanghai.

Cities and Climate Change

Why Cities Matter for Climate Change Mitigation

In a world rapidly approaching a population of 9 billion people, 70 percent of whom will live in urban areas by 2050 (figure 1.1), cities must be efficient, well managed, and better at protecting their most vulnerable populations.

The International Energy Agency (IEA) estimates that cities in 2006 emitted 19.8 gigatonnes of CO_2e ($GtCO_2e$) from energy use, which was 71 percent of global energy-related GHG emissions. By 2030, this number is expected to increase to 30.8 $GtCO_2e$, or 76 percent of global energy-related emissions. Moreover, 89 percent of this 11 $GtCO_2e$ cumulative increase between now and 2030 will come from cities in countries

Figure 1.1   **Share of Urban and Rural Population in 2010 and 2050**

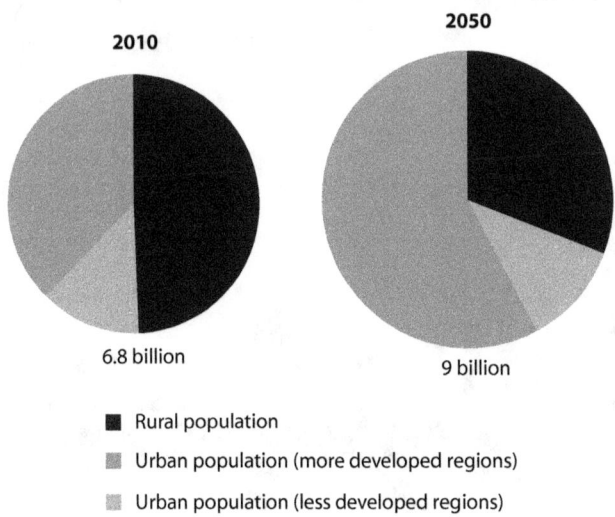

2010

2050

6.8 billion

9 billion

■ Rural population

▨ Urban population (more developed regions)

▨ Urban population (less developed regions)

Source: United Nations 2007.

not in the Organisation for Economic Co-operation and Development (OECD), mainly in rapidly urbanizing countries such as China and India (IEA 2008).

Cities meet approximately 72 percent of their total energy demand from coal, oil, and natural gas, the main contributors to GHG emissions. While cities also use about 70 percent of the energy generated from renewable sources, these sources still make up just a small share of total energy consumed.

Climate Change Impact on Cities

Cities not only contribute to climate change, they also are particularly vulnerable to its impacts. Their large population sizes and the fact that they—for historic and trade reasons—are located in low-elevation coastal areas, make them vulnerable to rising sea levels. In addition, cities can be affected by changed weather patterns and severe weather events.

Impacts of sea level rise. Approximately 360 million urban residents live in coastal areas less than 10 meters above sea level where they are vulnerable to flooding and storm surges (Satterthwaite and Moser 2008). Figure 1.2 shows countries with highest urban populations living in the low-elevation coastal zone, and figure 1.3 shows that 15 of the world's 20

Figure 1.2   Countries with Highest Urban Populations Living in the Low-Elevation Coastal Zone, 2000

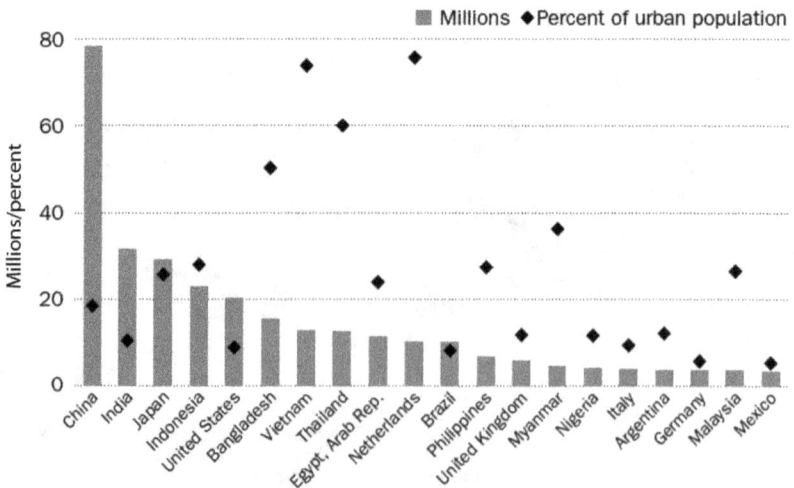

Source: World Bank 2010.

Figure 1.3   At Risk: Population and Megacities Concentrate in Low-Elevation Coastal Zones Threatened by Sea Level Rise and Storm Surges

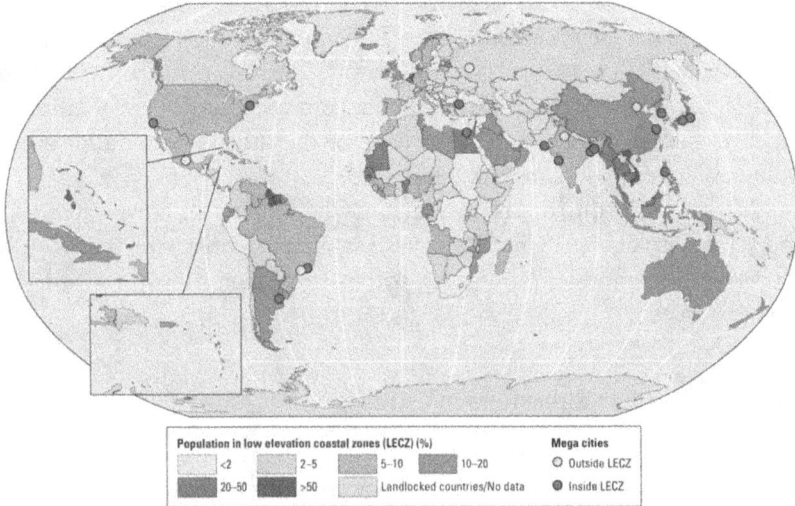

Population in low elevation coastal zones (LECZ) (%)

| <2 | 2–5 | 5–10 | 10–20 |
| 20–50 | >50 | Landlocked countries/No data | |

Mega cities
O Outside LECZ
● Inside LECZ

Source: World Bank 2009.

megacities are at risk from rising sea levels and coastal surges. The Intergovernmental Panel on Climate Change (IPCC) estimates that average sea level rose 0.17 meter in the 20th century and predicts a 1-meter rise over the next 100 years because of climate change (IPCC 2007).

This 1-meter rise in sea level over the next century is important because it affects the use of urban infrastructure. Much of the long-lived infrastructure such as flood protection works, major transportation systems, and large-scale energy plants (which are often located near water to have access to cooling water) are designed with service lives in excess of 60 years. For example, major infrastructure such as subways, sewers, and bridges located in cities like London, New York, and Paris is more than 100 years old. Building similar infrastructure in cities like Shanghai, Jakarta, Bangkok, and Rio de Janeiro where sea level may increase by a meter adds an enormous degree of complexity to an already challenging task.

Within the next decade, as greater certainty on the likely rate of sea level rise is available, some larger cities will begin to assess the need for strategic retreat and abandonment of key infrastructure and areas. This will represent an enormous loss of value in land and infrastructure and the largest transfer of economic wealth in human history. China's cities are particularly vulnerable to these changes, as shown in figure 1.3.

Weather events. Not only poor countries, but also rich ones are affected by anomalous climate events and trends (World Bank 2010). European cities such as Paris have recently experienced thousands of heat-related deaths from heat waves (Dhainut et al. 2004). In 2003 alone, more than 70,000 people died in Europe due to a severe heat wave (World Bank 2009). In most developing countries the ability of cities to adapt to climate change is most critical for the urban poor and for other vulnerable groups such as children and the elderly.

Cities depend on the security of their key inputs: energy, water, and food. Climate change, which is occurring concurrently with the world's largest degree of urbanization ever, will further strain supply networks of key resources.

Greenhouse Gas Emissions in Cities

Calculating a city's GHG emissions is not straightforward, but methodologies exist to provide numbers that can be compared to other regional and national inventories. This section discusses GHG inventories in cities and describes how emissions are linked to density and urban form, as well as to city resident lifestyle choices.

Greenhouse Gas Inventories in Cities

Accounting of urban GHG emissions is not yet standardized and not straightforward. Issues of inventory scope and inventory boundaries cause complications. The IPCC has published guidelines for calculating national or regional GHG emissions, which are used by national governments for emissions reporting. The methodology is specific regarding the activities that need to be included: all emissions related to energy consumption, industrial processes, agriculture, land use change, and waste production are included, as long as they occur within the country. Ideally, urban GHG inventories will follow a similar procedure, which will enable all city inventories to mesh with regional and national inventories. These inventories should be structured in a manner that is consistent with the IPCC and has maximum utility to cities.

Inventory scope. The scope concept, introduced by the World Resources Institute (WRI) and the World Business Council for Sustainable Development (WBCSD), addresses inventory scope for corporate and organizational inventories. As illustrated in figure 1.4, scope 1 emissions are those from sources under the direct control of the organization, such as furnaces, factories, or vehicles. Scope 2 emissions are from electricity

Figure 1.4   Scope of Urban Greenhouse Gas Emissions

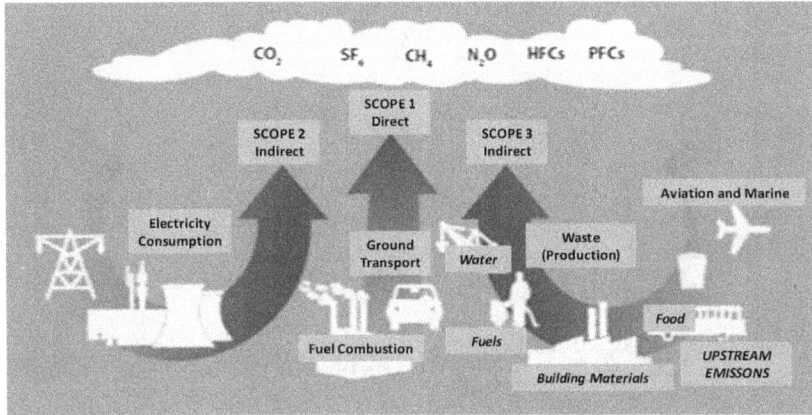

Source: Adapted from UNEP and UNEP SBCI 2009.

consumed by the organization, though emissions may be produced elsewhere. Finally, scope 3 emissions, also called upstream emissions or embodied emissions, are associated with the extraction, production, and transportation of products or services used by the organization. The scope concept of emissions attribution can also be applied to cities, giving cities the responsibility for emissions that are a consequence of all urban activity, regardless of whether or not they occur inside or outside of the city boundary.

Kennedy et al. (2009b) show that the inclusion of aviation and maritime emissions can result in a per capita increase of about 20 percent, depending on the connectivity of city residents. For example, London's aviation emissions alone are 3.12 tCO_2e per capita, more than the total 2.3 tCO_2e per capita emissions for Rio de Janeiro residents. Ramaswami et al. (2008) demonstrate that emissions in Denver increase by 2.9 tCO_2e per capita when the embodied emissions from food and cement are included.[2]

Density, Urban Form, and Greenhouse Gas Emissions

While the urban population is expected to double by 2030, the global built-up area is expected to triple during the same period (Angel et al. 2005). This "building out" instead of "building up" will dramatically increase energy requirements and costs of new infrastructure. As shown in figure 1.5, there is evidence that suggests that cities of lower density produce more emissions per capita.

Figure 1.5   City Densities and Their Greenhouse Gas Emissions per Capita

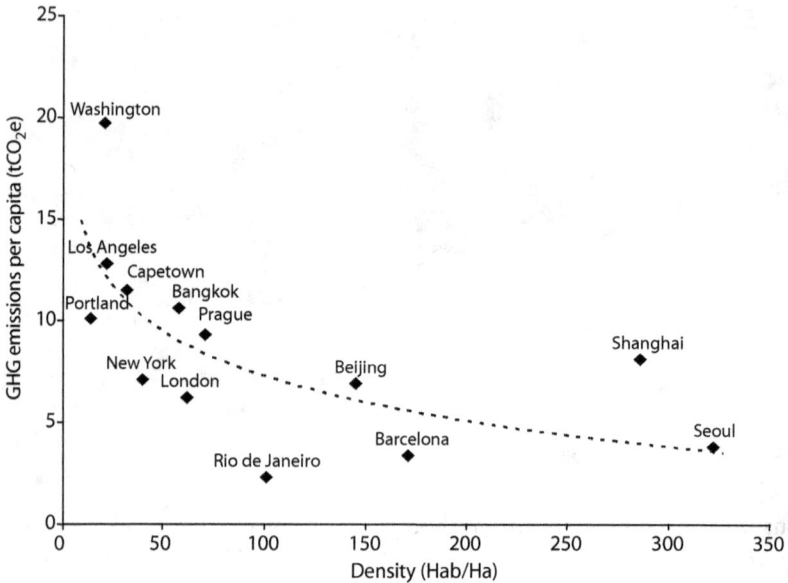

Sources: Density from Bertaud and Malpezzi 2003; GHGs from Kennedy et al. 2009a.

U.S. cities provide a clear example of how denser urban areas are the most efficient way to provide a high quality of life. Glaeser (2009) calculated that an "average household" in 48 major metropolitan areas generates up to 35 percent less GHG emissions when located in the city than when located in the corresponding suburb. The largest difference was seen in New York City where a Manhattan household generates 6.4 tCO_2e less than their suburban neighbors. In Toronto, detailed neighborhood GHG emissions inventories showed a variation from a low of 1.31 tCO_2e per capita in an area with multifamily units close to services and public transit, to a high of 13.02 tCO_2e per capita in a typical "sprawling" neighborhood with large single-family homes distant from all services and totally automobile dependent (VandeWeghe and Kennedy 2007).

Recent research suggests that simply increasing density in cities will not be enough. Gaigné et al. (2010) note that as density increases, emissions may rise more from traffic congestion and longer work trips than they are reduced from increasing efficiency in city-to-city transport. Consequently, city growth is not only about density but also about the smart planning of public transport networks, urban forms, and efficient water, wastewater, and solid waste systems.

Related to that, current research on urban form and density of cities reveals interesting patterns. Box 1.1 shows 4 of 16 images developed by the Neptis Foundation, emphasizing the urban form, density, and trans-

Box 1.1

Neptis Foundation Images Illustrating Metropolitan Indicators for Four World Cities

The following Neptis Foundation images illustrate metropolitan indicators (urban density, road length per capita, transportation mode share, metropolitan profile) for the cities of Houston and Denver (both in the United States), Madrid (Spain), and Vienna (Austria).

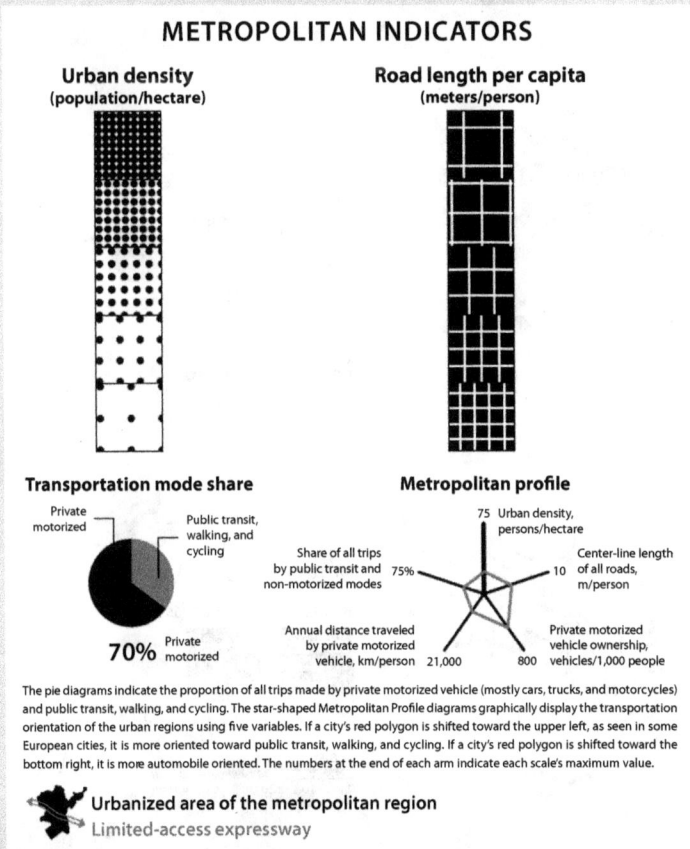

METROPOLITAN INDICATORS

Urban density
(population/hectare)

Road length per capita
(meters/person)

Transportation mode share

Private motorized

Public transit, walking, and cycling

70% Private motorized

Metropolitan profile

75 Urban density, persons/hectare

Share of all trips by public transit and non-motorized modes 75%

Center-line length 10 of all roads, m/person

Annual distance traveled by private motorized vehicle, km/person 21,000

Private motorized vehicle ownership, 800 vehicles/1,000 people

The pie diagrams indicate the proportion of all trips made by private motorized vehicle (mostly cars, trucks, and motorcycles) and public transit, walking, and cycling. The star-shaped Metropolitan Profile diagrams graphically display the transportation orientation of the urban regions using five variables. If a city's red polygon is shifted toward the upper left, as seen in some European cities, it is more oriented toward public transit, walking, and cycling. If a city's red polygon is shifted toward the bottom right, it is more automobile oriented. The numbers at the end of each arm indicate each scale's maximum value.

Urbanized area of the metropolitan region
Limited-access expressway

(continued next page)

Box 1.1 *(continued)*

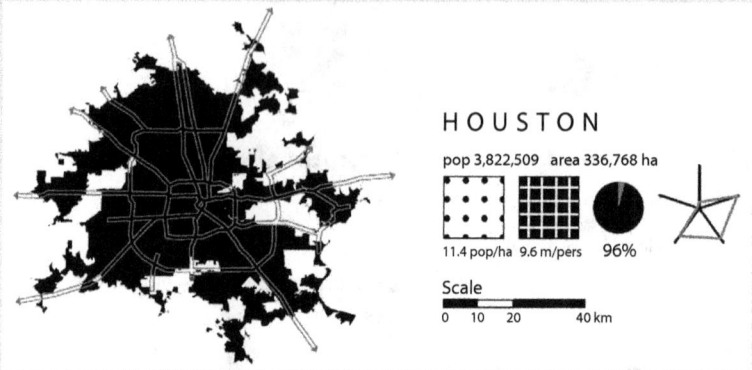

HOUSTON

pop 3,822,509   area 336,768 ha

11.4 pop/ha   9.6 m/pers   96%

Scale
0   10   20   40 km

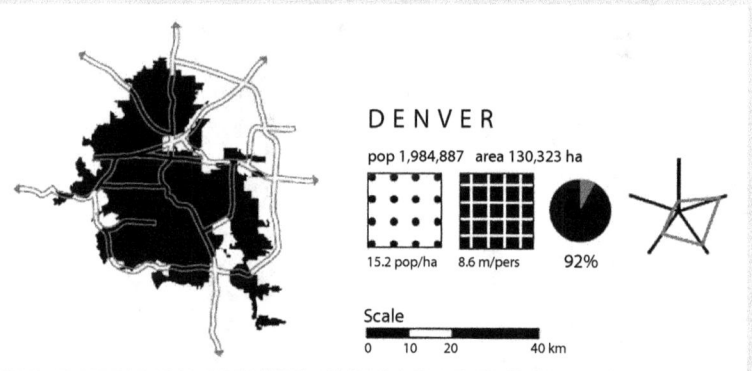

DENVER

pop 1,984,887   area 130,323 ha

15.2 pop/ha   8.6 m/pers   92%

Scale
0   10   20   40 km

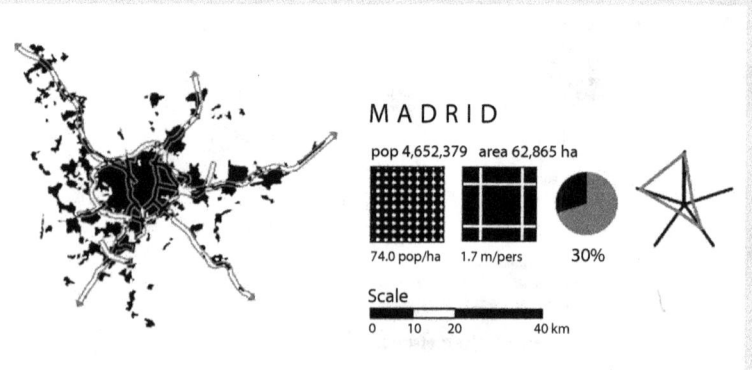

MADRID

pop 4,652,379   area 62,865 ha

74.0 pop/ha   1.7 m/pers   30%

Scale
0   10   20   40 km

(continued next page)

Box 1.1 *(continued)*

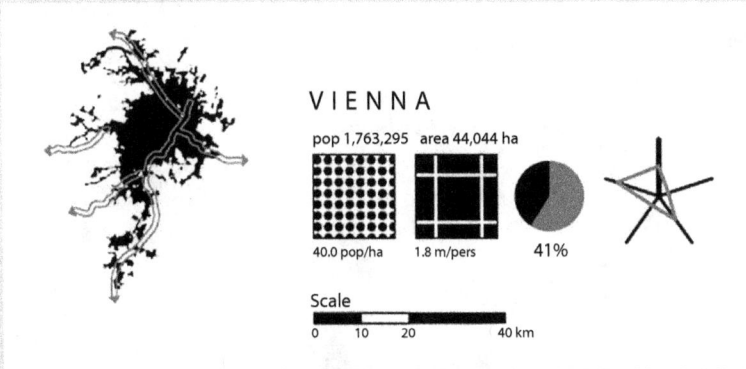

VIENNA

pop 1,763,295   area 44,044 ha

40.0 pop/ha   1.8 m/pers   41%

Scale

0   10   20   40 km

Source: Images were created by André Sorensen and Paul Hess, Department of Geography, University of Toronto with Zack Taylor and Marcy Burchfield (The Neptis Foundation) and Byron Moldofsky and Jo Ashley (The Cartography Office). © 2007 The Neptis Foundation.

portation characteristics of world cities. The images show that compact cities, such as Vienna and Madrid, have a significantly higher population density and higher use of public transport, compared to more sprawling cities, such as Atlanta and Houston.

Spatial population density figures produced by Chreod Ltd. also illustrate density distribution for different cities around the world (box 1.2). Population density is highest in the city core of compact Chinese cities, while spatial density variation is less pronounced in sprawling U.S. cities. Tokyo offers an interesting example: with many dense city neighborhoods, Tokyo's population density distribution is relatively spatially consistent throughout the city. Cities like Portland, Seattle, Barcelona, and Vancouver provide important lessons. In these cities, geography—oceans and mountains—limit the land available for development, and as a result these cities have developed "up" as much as "out" and ensured a commensurate enhancement in local quality of life.

One of the biggest challenges for cities is the tendency to "lock-in" the form that they grow into, as infrastructure investments quickly become long-term sunk costs. The transportation system that a city develops largely defines the final shape of the city, as influenced by local geography. Roads and public transit lines are the "bones" of a city, with water, wastewater, and power services fleshing it out. Once buildings grow

Box 1.2

Chreod Ltd. Images of Population Densities of Selected Metropolitan Regions, 2000

The images produced by Chreod Ltd. are three-dimensional representations of population densities (nighttime) in selected metropolitan regions. Data are for 2000 and, in some cases, 2001. Densities were calculated using 3D-Field software using geo-referenced, small-area population point data at the census tract scale.

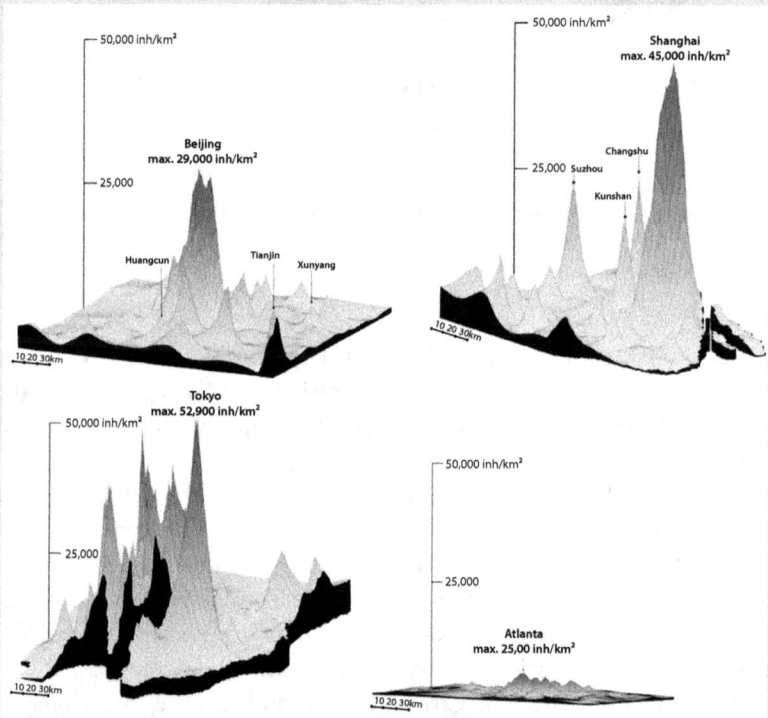

around transportation and service nodes, the form of a city is almost completely locked in.

Greenhouse Gas and City Resident Lifestyle Choices

Some argue that city-based attribution should only take into account contributions for which the municipality has jurisdictional responsibility, which is about 60 percent of a city's total emissions. However cities are home to urban customers, and their lifestyle choices have significant impacts on emissions. City governments can influence these choices. The urban infrastructure and mitigation policies in a city can directly influence lifestyle choices and impact GHG emissions. The lifestyle choices of individuals have significant impacts on emissions—from the choice to drive a car because of lack of public transit, to the necessity to burn biomass and charcoal due to the lack of kerosene or natural gas. Box 1.3 describes the carbon emissions of three individuals living in different cities. These examples illustrate the GHG intensities associated with various urban systems and activities, demonstrating how urban infrastructure, policy, lifestyle, and access to services are closely interrelated.

Related to box 1.3, an issue of interest is the amount of national emissions that should be apportioned to these citizens. The three countries—

Box 1.3

Greenhouse Gas Emissions and Urban Lifestyle: Three Personal Examples

Maria, a program assistant for a private company, lives in **Bogota City**. She shares a house with her husband and two children, and she loves to cook. To make her cooking easier, she has many electrical appliances in her kitchen, such as a rice cooker, blender, coffee machine, refrigerator, microwave, and stove. Apart from these appliances, she also has a TV set, DVD player, desktop computer, iron, washing machine, music player, video game, fixed telephone, digital camera, and two mobile phones, which she frequently leaves plugged in. Throughout the year, there is no need for her to have air conditioning or heating in her house. When it comes to her daily eating habits, Maria considers herself to be a heavy meat eater and likes having in her diet a combination of local and imported products. Maria has never traveled by plane, and she usually spends her vacation time in Bogota or its surrounding areas. For local transportation, she always commutes from home to the office on the "Transmilenio" bus rapid transport system. On average, her daily travel distance is 7.2 kilometers one way.

Maria's personal GHG inventory, considering her electricity use, transportation habits, and food consumption, is about **3.5 tCO_2e per year.**

(continued next page)

Box 1.3 *(continued)*

Further north, Nathan Tremblay, a **Toronto** citizen, is a vegetarian graduate student living in the suburbs. He lives with his parents in a detached house and owns a medium-size car that he uses to go to school. Every day, he drives about 25 kilometers per ride, and also travels by plane twice a year when he goes on vacation. The flights usually last between one and a half hours to three hours. Like many of his friends, Nathan cannot imagine himself without having his mobile phone, iPod, and laptop. In addition to these electrical devices, he also has at home a video camera, a digital camera, an electric razor, a printer, and a home theater, which are plugged in most of the time. Due to the weather conditions in Toronto, there are heating and cooling systems in his parents' house.

Nathan's personal GHG inventory, considering his electricity use, home heating needs, transportation habits, and food consumption, is about **11.5 tCO$_2$e per year**.

In contrast with the two urban residents mentioned above, Zuhura Ngan-yanyuka, a Tanzanian tailor who lives in **Dar es Salaam**, never has her electrical appliances plugged in unless she is using them. She is afraid that once the power comes on after one of the very common power cuts in the city, her TV, sewing machine, radio, refrigerator, water boiler, and table fan might overload due to the power fluctuations. Zuhura lives with her husband, three children, and two cousins in a typical Swahili house, composed of several rooms linked by a central corridor. Despite the permanent warm weather, there is no air conditioning system in her home. Every day she takes a "daladala" (minivan) for a 10-kilometer ride (one way) to go to work. Along with her relatives, she considers herself to be a moderate meat eater and generally buys local products.

Zuhura's personal GHG inventory, considering her electricity use, transportation habits, and food consumption, is about **1.8 tCO$_2$e per year.**

Source: World Bank 2010.

Colombia, Canada, and Tanzania—have very different levels of national commercial and industrial activity from which the urban citizens economically benefit. National commercial and industrial activity enables individual lifestyles by facilitating consumption activity, as well as informing the life-cycle carbon emissions associated with such activity. Aside from a detailed GHG life-cycle analysis of the economic and consumption habits of individuals, there is currently no pragmatic approach to apportion these national emissions to individual citizens. While further research is needed in this area, it is interesting to note the wide variations in the national per capita emissions for these three countries: 22.65 tCO_2e per capita in Canada, 3.84 tCO_2e per capita in Colombia, and 1.35 tCO_2e per capita in Tanzania.

City Actions on Climate Change: Mitigation and Adaptation

Cities can take action on both mitigation and adaptation to climate change. Mitigation aims to prevent further climate change; adaptation involves readjusting life to the reality that a certain amount of climate change will inevitably occur. While the distinction may initially appear to be a conflict of optimism versus pessimism, an effective approach to tackling climate change at the city level requires a synergy of both mitigation and adaptation. Cities are best placed to address climate change in an integrated manner that can address mitigation and adaptation simultaneously.

If addressed individually, the short- and long-term costs associated with mitigation and adaptation can be strikingly different. Adaptation strategies are usually less expensive in the short term, but they will become increasingly expensive as climate change intensifies and eventually become ineffective. In contrast, mitigation strategies are expensive in the short term because they are capital intensive and require fundamental changes to urban systems; however, over time, mitigation strategies are broadly sustainable and result in cost savings. These financial implications further emphasize the necessity for a balance between both adaptation and mitigation efforts.

Climate Change Mitigation

Climate change mitigation and urban development are not mutually exclusive; on the contrary, they are intricately related and can be accomplished concurrently. Sustainable infrastructure choices not only mitigate climate change, but they also make cities more accessible, improve air quality, and raise the standard of living for residents.

When analyzing GHG inventories from urban areas around the world, some important trends can be observed. Developing countries tend to have lower per capita emissions than developed countries; dense cities tend to have relatively lower per capita emissions—particularly those with good transportation systems (see also the section above, "Density,

Urban Form, and Greenhouse Gas Emissions"); and cities tend to have higher emissions if located in a cold climate zone. The most important observation is that there is no single factor that can explain variations in per capita emissions across cities; they are agglomerations of a variety of physical, economic, and social factors specific to their unique urban life. The details of each inventory and its ability to undergo peer review, however, are critical to the development and monitoring of an effective mitigation strategy.

Key urban policy initiatives can play an important role in addressing climate change mitigation and adaptation. Kamal-Chaoui and Robert (2009) emphasize that policy complementarities across urban sectors are essential for enhancing policy effectiveness. For example, they note that "congestion fees for driving during peak hours worked well in London because they were combined with improvements in management of the road network and substantial enhancements in bus service." These more progressive and far-reaching efforts will also require greater cooperation across different levels of government, as demonstrated in the case of New York where the state of New York rejected New York City's plan for traffic congestion charges.

As discussed in the previous section, urban infrastructure and policies can influence lifestyle choices, which in turn impact urban emissions. For example, a lack of efficient public transit and low parking prices encourage greater car use. City governments have the ability to influence lifestyle choices and reduce GHG emissions. Table 1.2 provides an array of policy tools that are being implemented by cities. Some examples of municipal government actions leading to reductions in emissions include congestion pricing (Singapore and Stockholm), dense and integrated land use (Barcelona and São Paulo), and provision of good public transit (Zurich and Curitiba).

Adaptation to Climate Change

Cities are complex systems with inherent strengths and resilience, and their citizens—given the chance—are innovative and resourceful. Climate change will require cities to increase their capacity to adapt. Responses to growing climate change vulnerabilities need to build on current experiences with disaster risk reduction. Climate change will place an even higher premium on municipal capacity and management structures. Based on current experiences of disaster risk reduction, social capital is a critical aspect for all urban communities. Cities with strong social networks are always better able to ameliorate the impacts of disasters.

Table 1.2   Policy Tools for Local-Level Action on Climate Change

Policy goals	Policy tools	Policy sector	Purpose	Mode of governance	Complementary with policy tools that:
Reduce trip lengths	Restructure land value tax to increase value of land closer to urban core, jobs, or services	Land-use zoning	Mitigation	Regulatory	• Increase mass transit use
	Mixed-use zoning to shorten trip distances	Land-use zoning	Mitigation	Regulatory	• Discourage vehicle use • Support non-motorized means of travel
	Transit-oriented development zones	Land-use zoning	Mitigation	Regulatory	• Increase mass transit use • Discourage vehicle use
	Restructure land value tax to increase value of land served by public transportation	Land-use zoning	Mitigation	Regulatory	• Increase mass transit use
	Tax incentives to developers near public transportation	Land-use zoning	Mitigation	Regulatory	• Increase mass transit use
Increase mass transit use	Improve quality of public transportation	Transportation	Mitigation	Service provision	• Discourage vehicle use
	Provide linkages with multiple modes of travel	Transportation	Mitigation	Service provision	• Discourage vehicle use • Support non-motorized means of travel
	Expand mass transit service	Transportation	Mitigation	Service provision	• Discourage vehicle use
	Employee transport plans	Transportation	Mitigation	Facilitative	• Improve quality of public transportation • Provide linkages with multiple modes of travel • Expand mass transit service

(Continued next page)

Table 1.2 *(continued)*

Policy goals	Policy tools	Policy sector	Purpose	Mode of governance	Complementary with policy tools that:
Discourage vehicle use	Traffic calming to discourage driving	Land-use zoning	Mitigation	Regulatory/ service provision	• Improve quality of public transportation • Provide linkages with multiple modes of travel • Expand mass transit service
	Driving and parking restrictions in certain zones	Transportation	Mitigation	Regulatory	• Improve quality of public transportation • Provide linkages with multiple modes of travel • Expand mass transit service
Support non-motorized means of travel	Traffic calming and increasing bike lanes	Transportation	Mitigation	Regulatory/ service provision	• Discourage vehicle use
Increase vehicle efficiency and alternative fuels use	Special parking privileges for alternative fuel or hybrid vehicles	Transportation	Mitigation	Regulatory	• Driving and parking restrictions in certain zones
	Purchase of fuel-efficient, hybrid, or alternative fuel vehicles for city fleet	Transportation	Mitigation	Self-governance	—

(Continued next page)

Table 1.2 *(continued)*

Policy goals	Policy tools	Policy sector	Purpose	Mode of governance	Complementary with policy tools that:
Increase building energy efficiency	Zoning regulation to promote multifamily and connected residential housing	Land-use zoning	Mitigation	Regulatory	• Increase attractiveness of higher density developments through policy tools that: • Increase neighborhood open space • Improve quality of public transportation • Provide linkages with multiple modes of travel • Expand mass transit service • Provide tree-planting programs
	Energy efficiency requirements in building codes	Building	Mitigation	Regulatory	• Coordination of public-private retrofitting programs • Stringent enforcement policies • National building codes
	Coordination of public-private retrofitting programs	Building	Mitigation	Service provision	• Energy efficiency requirements in building codes
Increase local share of renewable and captured energy generation	Building codes requiring a minimum share of renewable energy	Building	Mitigation	Regulatory	• Technical support to developers and property owners
	District heating and cooling projects	Building	Mitigation	Regulatory/ service provision	• Remove regulatory barriers to requiring connection to district heating/cooling system
	Waste-to-energy programs	Waste	Mitigation	Service provision	• Strictly regulate incinerator emissions • Remove recyclables from waste stream

(Continued next page)

Table 1.2 *(continued)*

Policy goals	Policy tools	Policy sector	Purpose	Mode of governance	Complementary with policy tools that:
Reduce vulnerability to flooding and increased storm events	Zoning regulation to create more open space	Land-use zoning	Adaptation	Regulatory	• Zoning regulation to promote multifamily and connected residential housing
	Retrofitting and improvements to mass transit systems to reduce potential damage from flooding	Transportation	Adaptation	Service provision	• Improve quality of public transportation • Provide linkages with multiple modes of travel • Expand mass transit service
	Designation of open space as buffer zones for flooding	Natural resources	Adaptation	Regulatory	• Zoning regulation to create more open space • Zoning regulation to promote multifamily and connected residential housing
	Building codes requiring minimum ground clearance	Building	Adaptation	Regulatory	• Designation of open space as buffer zones for flooding
Reduce urban heat island effects and vulnerability to extreme heat	Retrofitting and improvements to mass transit systems to reduce potential damage from extreme temperatures	Transportation	Adaptation	Service provision	• Improve quality of public transportation • Provide linkages with multiple modes of travel • Expand mass transit service
	Tree-planting programs	Natural resources	Mitigation and adaptation	Self-governance	• Increase attractiveness of higher density developments
	Building codes requiring design materials that reduce heat-island effects	Building	Adaptation	Regulatory	• Energy efficiency requirements in building codes
	Building codes requiring "green roofs" with vegetation or white surfaces	Building	Mitigation and adaptation	Regulatory	• Energy efficiency requirements in building codes

Source: Adapted from Kamal-Chaoui and Robert 2009.

Resilience typically encompasses robustness, readiness (or preparedness), recovery, and adaptation. Each of these aspects can be found in well-functioning cities, and they are readily compared to natural ecosystems. Building resilience in a city is similar to strengthening a body's immune system, and a few key initiatives can yield large results. Key focus areas for cities are:

- Robust decision making and incorporating broader-based cost and benefit assessments that include values, ecosystem services, risks, and longer time horizons
- Buttressing of key infrastructure—for example, increased robustness of water and power supply systems
- Social inclusion—for example, less pronounced differences between rich and poor
- Urban risk assessments
- Emergency preparedness, including preparedness practices, knowing where risks are likely, and making emergency preparedness information public
- Partnerships with other cities, agencies, and governments
- Increased adaptive capacity, through buildings and critical infrastructure (for example, metros) that can withstand increased climate variability
- Reduced social tensions
- Where practicable and cost effective, redundancy of key services and infrastructure
- Protection and integration of key ecosystem services.

Chapter 6 of this book will further discuss climate change adaptation in urban areas in China.

Co-benefits of Joint Action for Mitigation and Adaptation at the City Level

An integrated approach that considers mitigation, adaptation, and urban development is needed for cities. The improvement of city services is correlated to the ability of cities to adapt to climate change and reduce their GHG emissions. Cities with excellent services are resilient cities: advanced drainage systems can alleviate flooding during intense storms, health care services are equipped to respond in emergency situations, and warning systems and transportation infrastructure allow citizens to evacuate in response to risk. As cities develop, a focus on infrastructure and service improvements that promote climate change mitigation, adaptation, and poverty alleviation are essential.

Many urban service sectors simultaneously address climate change mitigation and adaptation, as well as improve access to services for the poor. Adaptation to and mitigation of climate change on a citywide scale can follow a similar integrated hierarchy:

- Full provision of basic health and environmental services
- Enhancing the resilience of community organizations
- Improving building quality, particularly for residential buildings
- Avoiding development in hazardous or sensitive areas
- Protecting buffering capacities of local ecosystems (for example, groundwater, mangroves, and wetlands)
- Ensuring food security (for example, evaluating relevance of local agriculture provision)
- Ensuring the security and resilience of water supply and quality and energy provision
- Strengthening citywide security nets and resilience planning
- Providing and regularly updating publicly available land-use or development plans
- Effectively integrating migrants
- Increasing the energy efficiency of buildings and transportation
- Identifying and, where possible, ameliorating local climate impacts such as urban heat islands
- Participating in regional and national programs to increase resilience
- Enhancing local economies
- Switching to low-consumption lifestyles
- Participating in global policy dialogues (for example, city influence on national and international policies such as agriculture and energy subsidies and the United Nations Framework Convention on Climate Change [UNFCCC] negotiations).

As cities are already taking integrated actions in response to climate change, the collection of examples of best practices in this area is growing. Examples are shown in table 1.3.

Cities Acting Together on Climate Change

Cities are an organic form of governance and often express the aspirations of their citizens more succinctly and quicker than higher levels of government. When citizens' voices are credibly articulated, their global impact

Table 1.3   Benefits of an Integrated Approach, Combining Mitigation, Adaptation, and Development

City	Action	Integrated value
Mexico City, Mexico	Infrastructure improvements for water supply pipes to reduce water losses and leaks	• Increases water supply • Reduces vulnerability to lack of water • Increases access of basic services to the poor
Dar es Salaam, Tanzania	Established a coastal and marine conservation project to plant mangrove trees along the coast	• Prevents beach erosion • Mangroves sequester carbon • Protects the city from storm surges • Maintains a healthy coastal ecosystem
Makati City, the Philippines	Introduced a major citywide tree-planting program, where 3,000 trees are planted each year	• Sequesters approximately 25,000 kilograms of CO_2e/year in GHG emissions • Reduces atmospheric pollution • Reduces the urban heat-island effect • Provides recreational space
Lviv, Ukraine	Energy efficiency program for buildings	• Reduces energy consumption for buildings • Reduces energy costs • Makes buildings, and their occupants, better able to withstand extremes in temperature and precipitation

Source: World Bank 2010, with input from (i) Summary of Mexico City Climate Action Program: 2008–2012, Secretaria del Medio Ambiente, Gobierno Del Distrito Federal; (ii) Community Infrastructure Upgrading Programme—Get to Know the Programme, currently implemented in Dar es Salaam City, Tanzania (2005–10); (iii) Climate Resilient Cities, World Bank: 2008 Primer; (iv) Energy Efficient Cities Initiative Practitioners' Roundtable, Workshop Proceedings Series, ESMAP, World Bank, November 2008.

is considerable; and this impact is currently growing. The global response to climate change is illustrative. In the United States, for example, 1,017 cities have signed on to meet or exceed Kyoto Protocol targets to reduce GHG emissions (U.S. Conference of Mayors 2008).

Climate change will require city administrations to develop more robust partnerships with their constituencies, especially in developing countries. The public needs to be an integral part of future responses to climate change and trust needs to be strengthened before specific actions are introduced. One way to achieve this is to regularly supply the public with credible, standardized information that encourages active debate but also outlines the need for scheduled concrete actions. However, despite these well-intentioned efforts to better include the public in municipal management, climate change will probably still require cities to lead initiatives that do not always have widespread public support. For example, the city of Bogota's initial plans to reduce car use were widely rejected (but are now broadly supported), as were Curitiba's initial pedestrian zone and bus rapid transit system.

With the growing importance of cities, many believe that they need to be better represented in international forums. For example, United Cities and Local Governments (UCLG) and ICLEI—Local Governments for Sustainability[3] presented a joint resolution at the Conference of Parties (COP-15) in Copenhagen requesting a greater voice for cities in the UNFCCC negotiating process.

The impacts of climate change will require cities to be managed more professionally, efficiently, and strategically. Worldwide, many cities have legislated against such items as plastic bags, disposable cups, and bottled water. While these initiatives may be important for social messaging, their environmental impact has so far been minimal. Cities need to focus on ways to bring the public on board with more strategic interventions such as congestion charging, incentives for greener buildings, premiums on residential locations requiring less automobile dependence, and incorporating carbon pricing in land taxes and development rights. Such broader, high-impact efforts require a more comprehensive cultural momentum to overcome entrenched lifestyle preferences that significantly contribute to climate change. These high-impact city-based policies also need to be developed within a clear national and international framework. Cities need to be part of "nested" national and international initiatives such as carbon taxes, emissions trading, setting of policy on targets, cap-and-trade, and GHG inventories.

World Bank Support for Cities in Climate Change Action

The world's urban areas are growing by an additional 3 million people every week. This unprecedented growth, which is happening almost entirely in developing-country cities, is occurring at the same time that cities are being forced to grow in a carbon-constrained world and are already being forced to adapt to a changing climate. Cities are tasked with responding to these two mammoth trends—urbanization and climate change—while they are already often overwhelmed with the existing task of supplying basic services to more than 3 billion people.

In November 2009, the World Bank launched its new Urban Sector Strategy. Recognizing the Bank's extensive experience and the current rate of urbanization and growing significance of cities, the Strategy outlines a more active role for the World Bank in the urban sector. Cities and climate change constitute an important component of the Bank's Urban Sector Strategy.

Many World Bank client cities have a program of financial support and analytical services much larger than countries. São Paulo, Jakarta, Mexico City, and Cairo, for example, have World Bank partnerships as comprehensive as most country support programs.

Even with the World Bank's full array of support targeted at specific cities, there obviously still is an urgent need for additional partners. Working with key partners such as the United Nations Environment Program (UNEP), UN-HABITAT, Cities Alliance, OECD, ICLEI, UCLG (Metropolis), World Economic Forum, World Business Council for Sustainable Development (WBCSD), the global engineering community, and client cities, the World Bank is developing a suite of standard tools and services for cities, including the following:

- *Urban Risk Assessment:* The World Bank recently released a template for a standard approach to assess risk and vulnerability in cities. The Urban Risk Assessment would facilitate prioritization of possible adaptation funds, enable cities to monitor their geophysical and climate-induced risks over time, and highlight specific neighborhoods of poor residents.
- *Greenhouse gas standard:* A proposed standard for cities to monitor their per capita GHG emissions was launched at the World Urban Forum in Rio de Janeiro in March 2010.
- *Energy Sector Management Assistance Program (ESMAP)—Rapid Appraisal Framework:* ESMAP has developed a user-friendly tool called TRACE (Tool for Rapid Assessment of City Energy), formerly known as the Rapid Assessment Framework. TRACE offers cities a quick and easy way to assess their energy efficiency and identify sectors to improve. This tool prioritizes sectors with significant energy savings potential and identifies appropriate energy efficiency interventions across six sectors—transport, buildings, water and wastewater, public lighting, solid waste, and power and heat. It is a simple, low-cost, user-friendly, and practical tool that can be applied in any socioeconomic setting. The tool is being deployed in several cities around the world, including

Gazientep (Turkey), Da Nang (Vietnam), Quezon City and Cebu (the Philippines), and Surabaya (Indonesia).

- *Eco² Cities:* Eco² is a framework for cities to integrate economic and environmental considerations. These efforts will be supported within the World Bank and integrated with other urban programming. (See also chapter 2.)
- *Global City Indicator Facility (GCIF):* For the last eight years the World Bank has been working with key partners such as UN-HABITAT, ICLEI, and Cities Alliance to propose a standard set of city indicators.[4] The GCIF is now sufficiently well established with more than 100 cities participating and a thorough vetting of the indicators now completed. The World Bank will encourage all client cities to join the GCIF and will also continue to serve as a Board member.
- *Knowledge platform:* Building on the success of a Metropolis' Cisco-supported listing of city experiences on mitigation and adaptation presented in December 2009, the World Bank, with program partners UNEP, UN-HABITAT, and Cities Alliance, will expand this database to ensure a "one-stop" location for cities and climate change experience.
- *Citywide Carbon Finance Methodology:* The World Bank's Carbon Finance Unit recently launched a citywide methodology for carbon finance. The methodology is based on a citywide GHG inventory and supports a broad array of interventions designed to reduce GHG emissions. The program is to be first piloted in Amman, Jordan. The World Bank will work to increase the number of cities that avail themselves of this new methodology. (See also chapter 24 about carbon finance and the citywide methodology.)

Conclusion

This chapter described the important role cities play related to climate change. Because of their large and growing populations and activities, cities across the world contribute an estimated 71 percent of energy-related GHG. At the same time, that large population, as well as their location—often in low-elevation coastal zones—makes them vulnerable to the impacts of climate change. Cities, however, are also taking active steps—sometimes ahead of national agreements—to mitigate and adapt to climate change. Recent research has demonstrated that a city's GHG emission level is closely connected to a city's density and urban form, suggesting cities need to not only grow smarter, but also denser, through public transport networks, good urban form, and efficient water, wastewater, and solid waste management. And as was described above in the section "Co-benefits of Joint Action for Mitigation and Adaptation at the City Level," cities with excellent city services and strong social networks are also resilient cities and more prepared for the adverse effects of climate change. Going forward, cities need to focus on high-quality basic service provision, social inclusion, and integration of climate change mitigation, adaptation, and emergency preparedness into their city planning. A broad selection of World Bank programs is available to assist cities on this path.

Notes

1. The C40 is an association of 40 of the world's larger cities, plus affiliate cities, focused mainly on GHG mitigation (see www.c40cities.org).
2. Denver's 2005 emissions were made up of commercial/industrial buildings (34 percent), residential buildings (14 percent), heavy and light trucks (12 percent), food (10 percent), cars (7 percent), fuel processing (7 percent), air travel (6 percent), commercial trucks (4 percent), city government buildings (3 percent), cement (2 percent), and transit (1 percent).
3. Formerly known as International Coalition for Local Environmental Initiatives (ICLEI).
4. These indicators are available at www.cityindicators.org.

Bibliography

Angel, S., S. Sheppard, and D. Civco. 2005. *The Dynamics of Global Urban Expansion.* Washington, DC: World Bank.

Bertaud, A., and S. Malpezzi. 2003. "The Spatial Distribution of Population in 48 World Cities: Implications for Economies in Transition." Wisconsin Real Estate Department Working Paper. http://www.bus.wisc.edu/realestate/docu-ments/Complete%20Spatial%20Distribution%20of%20Population%20in%2050%20World%20Ci.pdf.

Dhainut, J-F., Y-E Claessens, C. Ginsburg, and B. Riou. 2004. "Unprecedented Heat-Related Deaths during the 2003 Heat Wave in Paris: Consequences on Emergency Departments." *Critical Care* 8(1): 1–2.

Dhakal, S. 2009. "Urban Energy Use and Carbon Emissions from Cities in China and Policy Implications." *Energy Policy* 37(11): 4208–19.

Forbes. 2008. "The Global 2000." Forbes.com Special Report. http://www.forbes.com/lists/2008/18/biz_2000global08_The-Global-2000_Rank.html.

Gaigné, C., S. Riou, and J-F. Thisse. 2010. "Are Compact Cities Environmentally Friendly?" Working paper. Groupe d'Analyse et de Théorie Économique (GATE), Lyon St Étienne, France.

Glaeser, E. L. 2009. "Green Cities, Brown Suburbs." *City Journal* 19(1): 50–5. New York, NY: The Manhattan Institute.

Intergovernmental Panel on Climate Change (IPCC). 2007. "Summary for Policymakers." In S. Solomon, D. Qin, M. Manning, Z. Chen, M. Marquis, K. Averyt, M. Tignor, and H. Miller, eds., *Climate Change 2007: The Physical Science Basis. Contribution of Working Group I to the Fourth Assessment Report of the Intergovernmental Panel on Climate Change.* Cambridge, UK, and New York, NY: Cambridge University Press.

International Energy Agency (IEA). 2008. *World Energy Outlook 2008.* Paris: IEA.

Kamal-Chaoui, L., and A. Robert, eds. 2009. "Competitive Cities and Climate Change." *OECD Regional Development Working Papers No. 2.* Paris: OECD Publishing.

Kennedy, C., A. Ramaswami, S. Carney, and S. Dhakal. 2009a. "Greenhouse Gas Emission Baselines for Global Cities and Metropolitan Regions." *Proceedings of the 5th Urban Research Symposium* Marseille, France: June 28–30, 2009.

Kennedy, C., J. Steinberger, B. Gasson, Y. Hansen, T. Hillman, M. Havranek, D. Pataki, A. Phdungsilp, A. Ramaswami, and G.V. Mendez. 2009b. "Greenhouse Gas Emissions from Global Cities." *Environmental Science & Technology* 43(19): 7297–309.

Neptis Foundation, www.neptis.org.

Ramaswami, A., T. Hillman, B. Janson, M. Reiner, and G. Thomas. 2008. "A Demand-Centered, Hybrid Life-Cycle Methodology for City-Scale Greenhouse Gas Inventories." *Environmental Science & Technology* 42(17): 6455–61.

Satterthwaite, D., and C. Moser. 2008. *Pro-poor Climate Change Adaptation in the Urban Centers of Low- and Middle-Income Countries.* Washington, DC: World Bank.

United Nations. 2007. *World Urbanization Prospects: The 2007 Revision Population Database.* New York, NY: United Nations.

United Nations Environment Program (UNEP) and UNEP Sustainable Buildings and Climate Initiative (SBCI). 2009. "Common Carbon Metric for Measuring Energy Use & Reporting Greenhouse Gas Emissions from Building Operations." UNEP and UNEP SBCI. http://www.unep.org/sbci/pdfs/UNEPSBCICarbon Metric.pdf.

U.S. Conference of Mayors. 2008. *Climate Protection Agreement.* U.S. Conference of Mayors. http://usmayors.org/climateprotection/agreement.htm.

VandeWeghe, J., and C. Kennedy. 2007. "A Spatial Analysis of Residential Greenhouse Gas Emissions in the Toronto Census Metropolitan Area." *Journal of Industrial Ecology* 11(2): 133–44.

World Bank. 2009. *World Development Report 2010: Development and Climate Change*. Washington, DC: World Bank.

———. 2010. *Cities and Climate Change: an Urgent Agenda*. Washington, DC: World Bank.

CHAPTER 2

Eco-Cities and Low-Carbon Cities: The China Context and Global Perspectives

Axel Baeumler, Mansha Chen, Kanako Iuchi, and Hiroaki Suzuki

Overview

Over the past 20 years, China has developed and promoted "eco-cities." More recently, it has begun to apply low-carbon city development concepts, making Chinese cities part of a global trend in which cities take a lead role in incorporating ecological and low-carbon development considerations into their urban planning and management models. This is, of course, particularly urgent in China because of its unprecedented scale of urbanization and corresponding buildup of environmental pressures. With continued urban-led economic growth, much is at stake related to China's urban ecological footprint—not just for China, but for the world.

Since the early 1990s, China's central government, in particular the Ministry of Environmental Protection (MEP) and the Ministry of Housing and Urban-Rural Development (MoHURD), has attempted to guide cities toward greater sustainability, including by developing various eco-city standards and policies. In addition, many local and provincial governments have begun to develop eco-cities on their own or together with international partners. However, both the national-level policy guidance and the local-level eco-city initiatives have adopted a rather broad definition of ecological sustainability and, more important, have not yet articulated a clear vision of what successful low-carbon city development actually entails and would require.

The objective of this chapter is to review some of the lessons learned from China's eco-city experiences, compare them with global practices on sustainable urban development, and highlight what China's and international eco-city experiences imply going forward. Although some Chinese eco-cities have mixed track records and the existing eco-city indicators and national policy regulations do not provide clear guidance on low-carbon development, the fact that China actively develops eco-city initiatives could provide an entry point for future low-carbon city development. However, clearer policy guidance is required and global best practices must be applied.

Eco- and Low-Carbon City Development in China

Recognizing the various resource and environmental challenges of its existing development pattern, China is at a critical stage in shifting its policy framework to become more of a "resource-conserving and environmentally friendly society."[1] As climate change receives increasing attention in China's development policy agenda, Chinese leaders have made ambitious commitments to reduce the energy intensity of the economy and put it on a "low-carbon" growth path.

China's 11th Five-Year Plan (2006–10) set specific targets, including a 20 percent reduction in energy use per unit GDP from 2005 to 2010, while doubling per capita GDP between 2000 and 2010 (NDRC 2006). In 2009, prior to the COP-15[2] Climate Negotiations in Copenhagen, China expressed its intention to reduce the carbon intensity of its GDP by 40–45 percent by 2020 compared to 2005. The 12th Five-Year Plan (2011–15), for the first time, now contains explicit targets to reduce carbon intensity per unit of GDP by 17 percent, in addition to other targets to promote resource efficiency and environmental sustainability. Provinces and cities will be required to include corresponding indicators in their local Five-Year Plans. This reflects some progress on incorporating "green" elements into the long-standing GDP-oriented performance appraisal system of local governments.

While the targets set by the national government are promising, implementation at the provincial and city levels is a major challenge. The idea of sustainable urban development has gained momentum, but relatively little policy guidance exists at the national level to describe what this means in practical and operational terms, even though some degree of guidance is provided by the national standards on "eco-cities," developed by MEP and MoHURD.

MoHURD and MEP National Standards for Eco-Cities

MoHURD National Standards

In 2004, MoHURD created a National Standard for Eco-Garden Cities, which was based on the 1992 National Standards for Garden Cities (MoHURD 2004). Cities must first be approved as "Garden Cities" before they can qualify as "Eco-Garden Cities," and have to be recommended to MoHURD by the provincial Construction Bureaus. MoHURD annually reviews and selects eco-garden cities. The Eco-Garden City Standard consists of 19 quantitative indicators related to the natural environment, living environment, and infrastructure (table 2.1). While the Garden City

Table 2.1   Quantitative Indicators of the MoHURD National Standards for Eco-Garden Cities

No.	Indicator area	Indicative value
Natural environment		
1	Species diversity index	≥0.5
2	Local plant index	≥0.7
3	Proportion of pervious surface in roads and squares in built-up area (%)	≥50
4	Urban heat-island effect (°C)	≤2.5
5	Forestation coverage in built-up area (%)	≥45
6	Public green area per capita in built-up area	≥12
7	Green space coverage in built-up area (%)	≥38
Living environment		
8	No. of days per year in which ambient air quality meets or exceeds China's National Ambient Air Quality Grade II standard	≥300
9	Quality of water bodies meeting national surface water quality standard (%)	100
10	Quality of water from pipe network meeting national drinking water quality standard (%)	100
11	Noise pollution levels meeting national noise standard in built-up area (%)	≥95
12	Citizen satisfaction with environmental quality (%)	≥85

(continued next page)

Table 2.1 *(continued)*

No.	Indicator area	Indicative value
Infrastructure		
13	Infrastructure good condition index	≥85
14	Tap water coverage (%)	100, 24-hour hot water supply
15	Sewage treatment rate (%)	≥70
16	Treated water utilization rate (%)	≥30
17	Domestic solid waste non-toxic treatment rate (%)	≥90
18	No. of hospital beds per 10,000 people	≥90
19	Average vehicle speed of major and secondary roads (km/h)	≥40
Updated indicators from National Standard for Garden Cities (2005 revised)		
	Proportion of energy-efficient buildings and green buildings	≥50
	Proportion of trips by public transport	≥20% in big cities ≥15% in medium cities

Sources: MoHURD 2004, 2005.

Standard focuses heavily on landscape and green space coverage, the Eco-Garden City Standard places more stringent requirements on the quality and coverage of cities' public infrastructure services and pollution control. In 2005, the National Standards for Garden Cities were updated to incorporate requirements on green buildings and public transport, reflecting MoHURD's recognition of the importance of energy efficiency in cities (MoHURD 2005).

MEP National Standards
Since 1997, MEP has named 63 cities and five districts as National Environment Protection Model Cities/Districts (MEP 1997). The qualification is based on 26 comprehensive indicators, both quantitative and qualitative, covering socioeconomic development, environmental quality, environmental infrastructure, and environmental management. The indicators are updated every few years (last updated in 2007), and all qualified cities are reviewed every three years to ensure their performance meets the updated requirements. In December 2007, MEP announced revised Indices for Eco-County, Eco-City, and Eco-Province, which introduced stricter standards, particularly for energy consumption, water consumption, and pollutant emissions (MEP 2007). The standards target a

city's entire jurisdiction and require the development of an Eco-County, City, and Province Construction Plan. MEP's Eco-City Standard has 19 quantitative indicators related to economic development, environmental protection, and social development (table 2.2), of which 15 are obligatory and 4 are indicative. Only a city already qualified as a National Environment Protection Model City can become an Eco-City.

Table 2.2 MEP Indices for Eco-County, Eco-City, and Eco-Province

No.	Indicator area	Indicative value	Type
Economic development			
1	Rural net annual income per capita (RMB)		Obligatory
	In developed areas	≥8000	
	In underdeveloped areas	≥6000	
2	Share of tertiary industry in GDP (%)	≥40	Indicative
3	Energy consumption (tonnes Standard Coal Equivalent [SCE] per RMB 10,000 GDP)	≤0.9	Obligatory
4	Fresh water consumption (m^3 per RMB 10,000 industry Value Added [VA])	≤20	Obligatory
	Efficiency coefficient of irrigation water	≥0.55	
5	Passing rate of enterprises that are required for clean production (%)	100	Obligatory
Environment protection			
6	Forestation coverage (%)		Obligatory
	In mountainous area	≥70	
	In hilly area	≥40	
	In plain area	≥15	
	Forest-grass coverage in cold area and meadow area (%)	≥85	
7	Proportion of protected area in total land area (%)	≥17	Obligatory
8	Ambient air quality	Meeting stipulated standard for different functional zones	Obligatory
9	Quality of water bodies	Meeting stipulated standard for different functional zones, no lower than Grade V	Obligatory
	Quality of water bodies in coastal area		

(continued next page)

Table 2.2 *(continued)*

10	Major pollutant emission (kg per RMB 10,000 GDP)		Obligatory
	COD	<4.0	
	SO$_2$	<5.0	
11	Quality of centralized drinking water sources meeting national surface/groundwater Grade III standard (%)	100	Obligatory
12	Urban sewage centralized treatment rate (%)	≥85	Obligatory
	Industrial water reuse rate (%)	≥80	
13	Noise pollution levels	Meeting stipulated standard for different functional zones	Obligatory
14	Urban domestic solid waste nontoxic treatment rate (%)	≥90	Obligatory
	Industrial solid waste treatment rate (%)	≥90, no hazardous waste	
15	Urban public green space per capita	≥11 m^2	Obligatory
16	Environmental protection investment in GDP (%)	≥3.5	Obligatory
Social development			
17	Urbanization rate (%)	≥55	Indicative
18	Central heating coverage in heated region (%)	≥65	Indicative
19	Citizen satisfaction with environment quality (%)	>90	Indicative

Source: **MEP 2007.**

Figure 2.1 shows all cities and counties that have been awarded an "eco-city" status by MEP and MoHURD. Until now, MEP has designated 11 counties, districts, and cities as "eco-cities," including Miyun county and Yanqing county in Beijing; Taicang city, Zhangjiagang city, Changshu city, and Jiangyin city in Jiangsu province; Rongcheng city in Shandong province; Yantian district in Shenzhen; Minhang district in Shanghai; and Anji county in Zhejiang province. MoHURD's National Eco-Garden Cities include Shenzen, Qingdao, Nanjing, Hangzhou, Weihai, Yangzhou, Suzhou, Shaoxing, Guilin, Changshu, Kunshan, and Zhangjiagang.

By setting ecological indicators at levels above current practices in many cities, the central government provides incentives for local govern-

Figure 2.1   Map of MEP and MoHURD Eco-Cities

Source: MEP and MoHURD.

ments to benchmark, monitor, and improve cities' urban development in more environmentally friendly and resource-saving ways. However, MEP's and MoHURD's indicators are limited in the way they capture and encourage true ecological and sustainable development and do not explicitly relate to the low-carbon development agenda. The indicators essentially focus on physical construction targets for basic urban infrastructure, such as wastewater treatment ratios and the provision of green space, or focus on even broader, less directly relevant measures like the urbanization rate. While some targets for the construction of physical infrastructure are important for sustainable development, meeting those targets alone does not ensure eco- and low-carbon development. Aware of these shortcomings, MoHURD is in the process of updating its eco-city standards, which is an opportunity to strengthen the central government's guidance on eco- and low-carbon city development.

National Pilot Programs for Low-Carbon Cities

Just as for the development of eco-cities, no integrated vision exists at the national level on how to transform cities into low-carbon cities. National standards and an official accounting system for carbon emissions, both of which could guide development at the city level, are lacking. In addition, local governments often do not have the capacity to operationalize the directives from the central government. In response to this, the National Development and Reform Commission (NDRC) and MoHURD have both selected a few cities and provinces on a pilot basis to explore pathways to low-carbon development.

Under the NDRC pilot, provinces and cities are asked to design low-carbon development plans, as well as policies and specific measures to reduce carbon emissions. The NDRC guidance focuses on low-carbon technology innovation, a shift to industries that are less carbon intense, and encouraging the adoption of a low-carbon lifestyle (box 2.1).

MoHURD has also since January 2010 entered into agreements with several cities, including Shenzhen city in Guangdong province, Wuxi city in Jiangsu province, Chongqing municipality, and four new districts in the municipalities of Tangshan, Shijiazhuang, Cangzhou, and Qinhuangdao in Hebei province, to support their low-carbon city development. MoHURD will assist these cities by establishing a low-carbon city indicator system, testing the latest policies and technology standards, and developing demonstration projects related to low-impact development, green transporta-

---

Box 2.1

NDRC Pilot on Low-Carbon Province and City Development

In August 2010, NDRC launched a pilot program for national low-carbon province and city development. The program will be implemented in five provinces (Guangdong, Liaoning, Hubei, Shaanxi, and Yunnan) and in eight cities (Tianjin, Chongqing, Shenzhen, Xiamen, Hangzhou, Nanchang, Guiyang, and Baoding). According to NDRC, the selected pilot provinces and cities will incorporate climate change into their local 12th Five-Year Plans and formulate specific low-carbon development plans, including in the following areas: (i) developing low-carbon urban planning incorporating economic structural changes, low-carbon energy mix, and energy conservation considerations; (ii) establishing low-carbon policies to encourage energy conservation and renewable energy; (iii) accelerating innovation and R&D for low-carbon industries; (iv) establishing GHG emission database and management systems; and (v) encouraging green lifestyles changes.

Source: People's Daily Online, August 19, 2010.

tion, green utilities, green buildings, and renewable energy. MoHURD has also sponsored comprehensive research programs on low-carbon eco-city development to better support the selected pilot cities (box 2.2).

Box 2.2

MoHURD Initiatives on Low-Carbon Eco-City Development

The China Low-Carbon Eco-City Strategy was launched in October 2009 by the Chinese Society for Urban Studies (CSUS) under MoHURD. The strategy recommends a move toward integrated public transport systems, green buildings, clean energy technology, and cleaner manufacturing—incentivized by targeted concessional finance programs. The strategy also includes guidelines for low-carbon city planning with a focus on the design of the living environment, mixed land use, and public and non-motorized transport. Key indicators proposed in the low-carbon city planning guideline include (i) population density; (ii) connectivity of pedestrian and bicycle lanes; (iii) public transit's share of total trips; (iv) proximity of transit stations; (v) availability of public facilities, housing, and jobs; (vi) block size; (vii) average commuting time and distance; and (viii) regulation of parking lots provision.

CSUS and the United Technologies Corporation also launched the multiyear Eco-City Assessment and Best Practices Program in July 2009. The first component is to establish an Eco-City Indicator System, which will be used to measure China's eco-city planning and development as well as existing eco-city practices. The assessment identified 61 key performance indicators, which incorporate the various eco-city standards by MEP and MoHURD. Additional indicators that have an explicit low-carbon focus were also included, such as CO_2 emissions per capita, water consumption per capita, energy consumption per capita, proportion of renewable energy, proportion of green transport, and proportion of green buildings. The second component of the program is to publish a best practices report on China's eco-cities at the end of each program year, and propose policy and development strategies for China's eco-city planning and development.

Thirteen pilot cities and districts have been identified, including Sino-Singapore Tianjin Eco-City, Caofeidian International Eco-City, Beichuan New Town in Sichuan province, Tulufan city (new district) in Xinjiang autonomous region, Miyun county and Yanqing county in Beijing, Dezhou city in Shandong province, Baoding city in Hebei province, Anji county in Zhejiang province, Changsha city in Hunan province, and Shenzhen city and Dongguan city (eco-industrial park) in Guangdong province.

Source: China.org.cn 2009.

Local Level Eco- and Low-Carbon City Initiatives

National indicators and pilot programs have a positive impact on local governments striving for official recognition by reaching the specified eco-city goals or being selected as pilot cities. Active and healthy competition among cities can spur local entrepreneurial activities and advance the environmental sustainability agenda. More than 18 provinces and 150 counties and cities are estimated to have started planning for some form of ecological development.[3] More recently, several "low-carbon" city initiatives, which explicitly target low-carbon development, have been under development. However, as there are no agreed definitions, integrated standards, or well-accepted methodologies for ecological or low-carbon city development, cities—national pilots or not—are using different approaches on different scales (box 2.3). Some of these initiatives appear similar in nature to the previous generation of eco-cities, and thus share similar shortcomings. Overall, however, it is still too early to assess emerging lessons from the city initiatives that have a clear and explicit low-carbon focus.

Box 2.3

Emerging Low-Carbon City Initiatives in China

Shenzhen. In January 2010, MoHURD and the Shenzhen government signed a framework agreement, making Shenzhen China's first low-carbon eco-demonstration city. Shenzhen is also one of the eight low-carbon pilot cities under NDRC's plan. In October 2010, Shenzhen put in place the Shenzhen National Low-Carbon Pilot City Implementation Scheme (2010–20), which lays out a comprehensive plan for low-carbon development. The city is also developing an indicator system for low-carbon projects, which will be integrated into the environmental impact assessment and approval processes for new projects.

Wuxi. In July 2010, Wuxi signed a framework agreement with MoHURD to jointly develop Wuxi Taihu Lake New City as a low-carbon eco-demonstration city. The planning area of the new city is 150 square kilometers, including the 2.4-square-kilometer Sino-Swedish Low-Carbon Eco-City. In October 2010, Wuxi municipality approved the Wuxi Taihu Lake New City Planning Indicator System and Implementation Guideline (2010–20). Among the 62 key performance indicators, which cover land-use planning, green transport, energy and resource efficiency, eco-

(continued next page)

Box 2.3 *(continued)*

logical environment, green building, and social development, key targets are to ensure that the new city's carbon emissions per capita are lower than 4.28 tonnes per year by 2020, and that the proportion of renewable energy reaches 20 percent by that same year.

Guiyang. Guiyang, a third-tier city in southwest China, has a target to reduce the carbon intensity of GDP by 40–45 percent by 2020, compared to a 2005 baseline. The Guiyang municipal government in July 2010 issued an Action Plan for Low-Carbon Development in Guiyang City (2010–20), which identified 10 priority areas, including the development of a low-carbon tourism industry, a shift to low-carbon industrial structures, evaluation of enterprise performances on energy efficiency, adjustment of energy supply structure, development of a low-carbon transport system, low-carbon green building, and management of forests as carbon sinks. The government issued a series of preferential policies on capital investment, taxation, and market access to support the implementation of the action plan.

Baoding. As one of the eight NDRC low-carbon pilot cities, the Baoding municipal government has released a development guide and roadmap for its low-carbon development. It aims to reduce the carbon intensity of GDP by 35 percent by 2015 and 48 percent by 2020, compared to a 2005 baseline. The focus areas are retrofitting buildings to meet energy efficiency, renewable energy, and greening of communities. The city of Baoding, in the northern Chinese province of Hebei, has since 2006 been a center for clean and energy-saving technology, including solar PV, wind, biomass, solar thermal energy, and energy efficiency.

Hangzhou. Hangzhou, capital of east China's Zhejiang province, aims to reduce carbon intensity by 35 percent by 2015 and 50 percent by 2020 compared to a 2005 baseline. In December 2009, Hangzhou municipality released the Resolution on Construction of a Low-Carbon City and has since developed several low-carbon emission campaigns in a bid to become a model low-carbon city. One notable initiative is that Hangzhou has spent about RMB 300 million on establishing a public bicycle rental system, including 50,000 bicycles in 2,000 rental spots, to reduce its reliance on cars. In addition to promoting non-motorized transport, the length of the metro system will be extended to 278 kilometers, the modal share of buses is planned to exceed 50 percent, and 25 percent of the bus fleet will be energy efficient.

Sources: People's Daily Online 2010 and Reinvang et al. 2008.

A notable trend is that some cities, especially those experiencing fast demographic and economic growth, are focusing on developing new urban areas in sustainable ways. Given the lack of experience in advanced eco-city development and the high initial capital investment associated with large-scale new developments, these new eco-city initiatives often ask international partners for support, mainly on integrated approaches to eco-city planning and management, advanced environment-related technologies, and financial investment. New eco-city projects that have gained international attention include the Sino-United Kingdom Dongtan Eco-City in Shanghai, Caofeidian International Eco-City in Tangshan, Sino-Swedish Wuxi Low Carbon Eco-City, Sino-Finland Mentougou Eco-Valley in Beijing, and the Sino-Singapore Tianjin Eco-City (SSTEC).

In addition to these relatively high-profile projects, international cooperation has also supported small-scale eco-community developments, such as the Huangbaiyu Eco-Village project in Benxi. However, some of these eco-city projects have revealed mixed results, given the complexities in large-scale greenfield development. Some projects were difficult to implement and some were put on hold, as happened in Dongtan (Shanghai) and Huangbaiyu (Benxi); see box 2.4. A key lesson from these abandoned projects is that it is important for eco-city projects to have strong support from local governments and local communities, so that plans can be translated into real development.

Box 2.4

Abandoned Eco-City Developments in China

Dongtan Eco-City, Shanghai. Dongtan is located on Chongming Island (Shanghai), the third largest island in China at the mouth of the Yangtze River. Dongtan Eco-City was scheduled to provide a home for 50,000 people by 2010 and 500,000 by 2040. The urban area was supposed to occupy one-third of the site's 86 square kilometers, with the remaining land retained for agriculture and as a buffer zone of managed wetland between the city and the natural wetland. Dongtan would produce its own energy from wind, solar, bio-fuel, and recycled city waste. Clean technologies such as hydrogen fuel cells were to power public transport, and a network of bicycle paths and footpaths was to help the city achieve close to zero vehicle emissions. Farmland within the Dongtan site was expected to use organic

(continued next page)

Box 2.4 *(continued)*

farming methods to grow food and buildings were to be energy efficient. However, while the plan was devised in 2005 and the first phase of construction was expected to be completed by the Shanghai Expo in 2010, the project was put on hold and almost nothing has been built on the site to date. This illustrates that even high-profile projects can face implementation challenges, particularly because of financial constraints, changing local government priorities, and environmental concerns. Key environmental concerns for Dongtan included the site selection, which was close to an important wetland and implied extended commuting distances for residents to the core urban area of Shanghai.

"Ecologically Sustainable"Village in Huangbaiyu, Benxi, Liaoning province. Huangbaiyu is a poor village in northeast Liaoning province, chosen in 2003 as a site for one of China's "ecologically sustainable model villages."The objective of this project was to cut energy costs by building new homes out of hay and pressed-earth bricks, a new technology developed in the United States. The designs were to incorporate full southern exposure, complete insulation, rooftop solar panels, radiant heat floors, and pipes to transport cooking gas produced by a nearby methane biomass plant. A total of 370 households scattered across the village were planned to be centralized, and their farmlands were to be consolidated with additional land made available for farming and development. As of 2009, only 42 houses had been constructed, and most in unplanned ways. This failure resulted mainly from a deficient understanding of local conditions. Farmers refused to live in the new houses as the new yards were not large enough to raise animals and sustain livelihoods; and some homes were built with garages, although no villagers can afford cars. Another problem is the lack of oversight on costs and the construction process. Due to cost overruns and lack of government subsidies, house prices rose to US$20,000, an amount villagers cannot afford.

Source: Larson 2009.

World Bank Support to Eco- and Low-Carbon Cities in China

The World Bank is interested in the eco-city agenda for a number of reasons, including because addressing the issues of sustainable and low-carbon city development will require a more integrated approach across the key urban sectors. China's eco-city experiments, which attempt to look at sustainability in a more integrated manner, could provide opportunities to advance this agenda. In this context, the World Bank partnered with the Chinese Academy of Urban Planning and Design (CAUPD) to conduct a stocktaking and extract lessons from China's eco-city experiences so far. The study looked at eco-city development in 22 cities across different regions, which represent most of the national pilot eco-cities thus far recognized by the MEP and MoHURD. In addition to some of the lessons discussed above, key findings emerging from the study are highlighted in box 2.5.

Box 2.5

Key Lessons from a Stocktaking Analysis of Eco-City Initiatives and Regulations in China

In 2009, the World Bank and CAUPD conducted a study to take stock of China's eco-city experiences. The study looked at eco-city development in 22 cities of various scales and identified the following key lessons learned:

Lack of integrated and sound planning. Eco-city planning in China is at the initial stage, lacking clearly specified principles and techniques. Most cities tend to mistake "eco-city planning" for "city green planning" and mainly focus on beautification projects of the natural environment without due attention to the local natural and social characteristics or a more comprehensive vision of what constitutes environmental sustainability.

Lack of a comprehensive management system. A supportive institutional structure for the construction, assessment, and supervision of an eco-city is not yet in place in many cities. Individual city line departments only control some aspects of eco-city development, although a multisectoral effort with participation from different municipal bureaus, such as planning, construction, environment, trade and industry, finance, and water resources, is required. Such coordination mechanisms are rarely established, and the degree of collaboration and sharing of information among different departments is very limited.

Need for increased public awareness. The concept of eco-cities is not widely understood. Even among city officials, eco-city development is at times seen as the opposite of their economic development priority. Increased awareness of the link between sustainable development and eco-city development is necessary, as is the need to ensure public participation.

(continued next page)

Box 2.5 *(continued)*

Lack of advanced research and weak capacity to apply eco-technologies.
Because the "eco-city concept" is still emerging in China, relatively few in-depth
research programs exist to support the planning for and application of eco-city
technologies. The lack of sound technical research, shortage of technically qualified staff, and weak capacity to deploy affordable eco-technology create obstacles for the development of eco-cities.

Insufficient funding and financing mechanism. The main financing sources
include city budgets, central government transfers, and loans from commercial
banks or the China Development Bank. However, the demand for financing is
larger than the supply and there is a need to develop special financing mechanisms to fund the development of eco-cities. In addition, cities should explore
innovative financing mechanisms (such as issuing environmental bonds) and
adopt a diversified investment and financing strategy.

Source: CAUPD 2009.

Sino-Singapore Tianjin Eco-City Project
The World Bank was also requested to operationally support one specific
eco-city initiative: the Sino-Singapore Tianjin Eco-City Project (SSTEC).
Because of the complexity of the project and the fact that it was the
World Bank's first engagement in eco-cities in China, it was agreed to
review the master and sector plans of the Sino-Singapore Tianjin Eco-
City Project at an early stage of project implementation in the form of a
Technical Assistance (TA) report, and to contextualize the project in the
larger eco-city context in China. In addition, a Global Environment Facility
(GEF) project was recently approved to deepen the World Bank's operational support to SSTEC decision makers (see also boxes 2.6 and 2.7).
    The SSTEC project is one example of a project implemented through
international partnerships, in this case in the form of a Sino-Singaporean
joint venture. Located in nonarable land and deserted salt pans with a
total area of 34.2 square kilometers, SSTEC is envisioned to become a
model eco- and low-carbon city replicable by other cities in China. To
guide the implementation of the project, a set of binding key performance indicators (KPIs) were developed. Compared to the existing eco-
city standards developed by MEP and MoHURD, SSTEC's key

Box 2.6

Urban Design Challenges for the SSTEC Project

The overall spatial density in the Sino-Singapore Tianjin Eco-City Project (SSTEC) is relatively high, with about 10,000 people per square kilometer. At an aggregate level, such densities provide a sufficient economic demand base to efficiently provide infrastructure services, such as public transportation. The overall urban form and density gradient fully support transit-oriented development, with 100 percent of the population living within 400 meters of some form of public transportation such as metro, light rail, or bus.

However, much of the eventual success of introducing a higher share of walking, cycling, and public transportation depends on the micro-level urban design. Good urban design can contribute to creating the conditions for walkable and vibrant neighborhoods that reinforce the public transport system, pedestrian modes, and bicycle use. Though SSTEC's urban design has some notable features, including plans to have mixed-use communities that will provide citizens with easy access to various destinations within a 300-to-500-meter walking distance, a risk is posed by SSTEC's decision to use the relatively large 400 by 400 meter block design rather typical of new urban development in China (even though the blocks are further subdivided by access roads). Using this block design as the basis for the city's layout may not create the envisioned walkable communities, especially if these blocks are separated by large roads. Achieving the KPI of 90 percent green transport (walking, cycling, and the use of public transport) may then become a challenge.

B2.6.1   Schematic View of the Tianjin Block Structure Compared to a New York City Area of the Same Perimeter (1,600 meters)

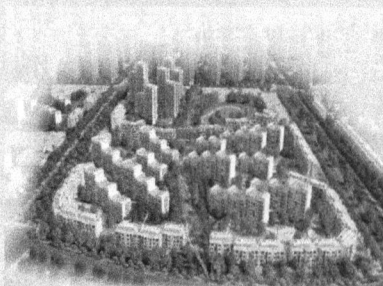

Sources: SSTEC and Google Earth 2010.

Source: Baeumler et al. 2009.

performance indicators are broader in scope, and in part more ambitious. While some indicators refer to existing national standards, for example, stipulating access to quality tap water, maintaining the quality of water bodies, and ambient air quality, others imply a shift toward a potentially more ecological urban development pattern, including the following (targets to be achieved by 2020):

- KPI 5: Carbon emissions per unit of GDP: ≤150 tonnes of carbon per 1 million US$ GDP
- KPI 7: Proportion of green buildings: 100 percent
- KPI 11: Per capita domestic waste generation: ≤ 0.8 kg per day per capita (by 2013)
- KPI 12: Proportion of green trips: 90 percent
- KPI 13: Overall solid waste recycling rate: 60 percent
- KPI 19: Renewable energy usage: 20 percent
- KPI 20: Water supply from nonconventional sources: at least 50 percent.

The SSTEC project has some notable features. For example, in addition to setting up ambitious KPIs, including explicit ones on carbon intensity, the master plan calls for high population density, transit-orientated development, a mixed land-use plan, an explicit local working/living ratio, and the provision of affordable housing—all necessary conditions for eco- and low-carbon city development. The project, however, also confirms some lessons from the broader assessment of China's eco-cities as described above in box 2.5, and in addition points to the need to complement technological solutions with economic incentives, to manage the balance between commercial and public interests, to ensure affordability to create socially inclusive, vibrant communities, and to avoid the mistakes made in other countries that embarked on large-scale "new town" experiments where too much was built too quickly. One particular lesson, relating to land use and urban design, stands out, as it is central to many of the objectives set for an eco-city, in particular for sustainable transport development (see box 2.6).

In addition to the World Bank's work with CAUPD and SSTEC policy makers, the Bank also explicitly supports the low-carbon city development agenda through a broader set of activities. Most of those activities are part of TA or GEF projects and have as a common thread a focus on measuring low-carbon city development objectives and taking an integrated, strategic view on how best to help cities achieve their low-carbon objectives. In addition, project interventions provide specific support, in particular in the energy or transport sectors, and an opportunity to test innovative reforms in practice. Box 2.7 summarizes the various activities. All are at an early stage—either in preparation or having just commenced implementation.

Box 2.7

World Bank Support for Integrated Low-Carbon City Initiatives

Sino-Singapore Tianjin Eco-City GEF Project. In 2010, a GEF project was approved to provide policy advice to help the eco-city become a resource efficient and low-carbon emission city. The project provides overall advice on project implementation and on policy, regulation, and institutional issues, in part through a newly established advisory council. Also, pilot investments and advice on public transport and green and energy efficient buildings will be provided.

Beijing GEF Project. This project uses GEF grant savings to support studies and analyses of sustainable climate change mitigation models and low-carbon economic development approaches. Three specific clusters are supported: crosscutting policies for supporting low-carbon development, low-carbon strategies for key urban infrastructure, and specific low-carbon development demonstration projects.

Beijing Proposed IBRD Project. The proposed Beijing Energy Efficiency and Emission Reduction Demonstration Project aims to implement a low-carbon development approach by financing several pilot projects in Beijing. The proposed project would concentrate on (i) high energy efficiency supply and smart grid systems, (ii) low-carbon building demonstration and green public transport systems, (iii) ecological water recycling and utilization systems, and (iv) utilization of solar energy.

Shanghai Technical Assistance. The World Bank is providing advice to Changning District in Shanghai on a pilot low-carbon district. The work is focusing on transferring international knowledge and best practices, as well as applying the McKinsey marginal abatement cost curve at the municipal/district level. The World Bank is also in discussions with Shanghai on a possible GEF project on Green Energy Schemes for a Low-Carbon City in Shanghai which would pilot

(continued next page)

Box 2.7 *(continued)*

green energy schemes, in particular in buildings (retrofitting existing buildings and piloting new zero-emission buildings) and by supporting the use of a low-carbon energy mix (on-site clean energy generation for power and heat and purchase of green electricity).

Wuhan Technical Assistance. The World Bank, with funding from the Swiss government, is helping to develop a partnership program between government and local enterprises to reduce carbon emissions from the transport sector in urban areas. The program focuses on three major transport-related carbon emitters: industry transport users (such as manufacturers and retailers), individual transport users (such as residents living in a large suburban residential area), and transport carriers (such as public transport operators, freight carriers, or freight logistics operators). The program aims to increase awareness of the transport-related footprints of these users and help them develop strategies to reduce carbon emissions from their transport activities.

Source: World Bank project documents.

Global Perspectives on Eco- and Low-Carbon Cities

This section provides an overview of global perspectives on eco-city and low-carbon city experiences, with the objective to better understand how China's development discussed above compares to global best practices.

Eco-City Definition and Key Approaches

As in China, no universally recognized global definition of "eco-city" exists. The term, however, is frequently used by policy makers, urban planners, environmentalists, civil society activists, and development experts, often in the context of sustainable cities. A typical observation is that eco-cities enhance the well-being of citizens and society through integrated urban planning and management that harnesses the benefits of ecological systems and protects and nurtures these assets for future generations. An eco-city also creates value and opportunities for citizens, businesses, and society by efficiently using the tangible and intangible assets of cities and enabling productive, inclusive, and sustainable economic activities, while promoting social equity. A recent trend is to include energy and resource efficiency and GHG emission reduction dimensions, given that cities consume about 70 percent of energy-related GHG emissions.

Highlights of Key Approaches

Among the key approaches currently adopted in eco-city developments with an emphasis on low-carbon emissions, three areas are widely recognized as best practices. They are the adoption of (i) integrated approaches, (ii) smart land use, and (iii) energy and resource efficiency. Some of these approaches and corresponding good practice examples are captured in a recent World Bank publication, *Eco² Cities: Ecological Cities as Economic Cities* (box 2.8).

Integrated approach. Integrated approaches link land use with infrastructure planning, and funding with delivery. At the planning stage, this means coordinating spatial development (land use and urban design) with the planning of infrastructure systems. Urban form and spatial development establish the location, concentration, distribution, and nature of demand nodes that serve as important parameters for the design of infrastructure system networks. On the other hand, new development can be directed to those locations with a surplus of water, energy, and transit. How these two systems are integrated has tremendous implica-

---

Box 2.8

Eco² Cities: Ecological Cities as Economic Cities

The Eco² Cities initiative is an integrated part of the new World Bank urban strategy to help cities in developing countries achieve a greater degree of ecological and economic sustainability. The four main principles of Eco² Cities are:

- A city-based approach
- An expanded platform for collaborative design and decision making
- A one-system approach
- An investment framework that values sustainability and resiliency.

The Eco² Cities initiative builds on the lessons learned from global good practice cities such as Curitiba, Stockholm, Singapore, Yokohama, and Brisbane. The Eco² Cities book provides the operational and analytical framework of the Eco² concept, its methodology and tools, and various case studies including those presented in this section. The book is available at www.worldbank.org/eco2 .

Source: World Bank 2010.

tions for resource use efficiency. At the implementation stage, an integrated approach means sequencing investments so that the city sets the correct foundation by addressing the long-lasting, cross-cutting issues first. This also means creating a policy environment that enables coordinating a full range of policy tools, collaborating with stakeholders to align key policies, and targeting new policies to reflect the different circumstances between urbanization in new areas and improving existing urban areas. In this regard, the efforts of Stockholm, Sweden, in integrated planning, detailed below, offer a best practice example.

Smart land use. This approach aims to promote compact and efficient land-use patterns and contain urban sprawl to maximize energy and resource efficiency and minimize possible pollutant and GHG emissions. It promotes higher population density and mixed land use that are integrated with key public transport networks. It also aims to reduce car dependency by creating an environment that is conducive to walking and cycling and by introducing efficient and affordable public transport. It places a focus on preservation and promotion of green space through preservation of forests as a carbon sink, increasing green coverage, and promoting urban agriculture and rooftop or vertical greening. It also adopts low-impact development approaches to retain and promote infiltration of rainwater at the source through vegetated basins (such as rain gardens, bio-soils, and constructed wetlands) and minimize impermeable areas using green roofs and porous pavement, thus minimizing the flooding and environmental impacts of storm water. Good examples for this type of development are the cities of Curitiba in Brazil and Freiburg in Germany, as mentioned below.

Energy and resource efficiency. Energy and resource efficiency consists of improved efficiency in all key urban sectors, such as transport and buildings, cross-sectoral use of energy and other resources, the use of renewable energy, and the recycling of waste and resources. Of all these, the integrated and cross-sectoral use of energy and resources is the most important. A good example is co-generation and the use of wastewater sludge for collecting biogas and bio-soils as, for example, practiced in Stockholm. Also, renewable energy is gaining momentum as the cost of the technology declines, in part as a result of incentive mechanisms such as feed-in tariffs provided by many developed countries. The 3Rs concept—Reuse, Reduce, and Recycle—is another traditional yet powerful approach. More recently, the "5Rs" go beyond the 3Rs with activities related to "refining" materials and "retrieving" energy. Overall, the goal of recycling is to have a minimal, and eventually zero, production of waste by using these three or five rules of action. Below, the case of Yokohama, Japan, shows how the city achieves waste reduction and related economic benefits by promoting the 3Rs.

Examples of Global Good Practices
Around the world, cities are implementing sustainable development and low-carbon emission concepts using the approaches discussed above. The experiences of Stockholm, Freiburg, and Curitiba are summarized below.

Stockholm, Sweden
Stockholm's Hammarby Sjöstad District in Sweden has demonstrated how integrated and collaborative planning and management can transform an old inner-city industrial area into an attractive and ecologically sustainable district. Since 1995, Stockholm has been redeveloping a southern city district called Hammarby Sjöstad. When planning this redevelopment, the city council aimed to be twice as sustainable as Swedish best practices on a range of indicators, most notably, energy efficiency per square meter. Hammarby Sjöstad also has targets for, among others, water conservation, waste reduction and reuse, emissions reduction, reduced use of hazardous materials in construction, use of renewable energy sources, and integrated transportation solutions. Because success in such a project depends on coordination among key stakeholders, the city incorporated the project team into the city's Department of Roads and Real Estate (now called the Development Department), under which key representatives from different city departments, including planning, energy, waste, real estate, traffic, and water and sewage, were assembled and led by a project manager and an environmental officer. As a result, the city departments of waste, energy, and water and sewage collaboratively came up with the Hammarby Model, illustrated in figure 2.2. This model streamlines various systems of infrastructure and urban service delivery and provides the blueprint for achieving many of the sustainability targets outlined above. Some of the initial results have been a 30 percent reduction in non-renewable energy use and a 41 percent reduction in water use.

Freiburg, Germany
The city of Freiburg, Germany is well known as one of the world's top eco-cities and has, since the 1970s, developed a reputation as Germany's ecological capital. In 1986, the city created a vision for a sustainable city reliant on an ecologically oriented energy supply. In 1996, the city passed a resolution, the Climate Protection Concept, to reduce CO_2 emissions

Figure 2.2   The Hammarby Model, Stockholm: An Example of Integrated Planning and Management

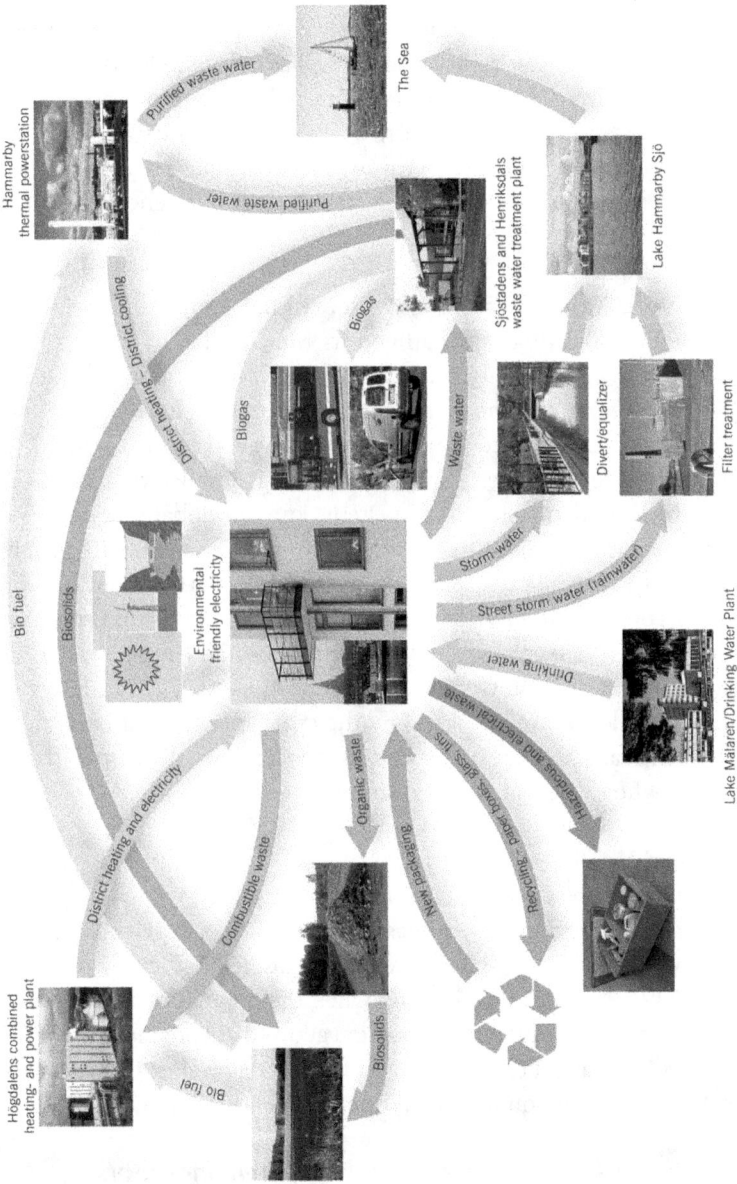

The Sea

Hammarby thermal powerstation

Purified waste water

Purified waste water

Biogas

Sjöstadens and Henriksdals waste water treatment plant

Lake Hammarby Sjö

Biogas

Bio fuel

Biosolids

District heating — District cooling

Biogas

Waste water

Divert/equalizer

Filter treatment

Environmental friendly electricity

Storm water

Street storm water (rainwater)

Lake Mälaren/Drinking Water Plant

Drinking water

Hazardous and electrical waste

District heating and electricity

Organic waste

New packaging

Recycling — paper, cans, glass, tins

Combustible waste

Högdalens combined heating- and power plant

Bio fuel

Biosolids

Source: World Bank 2010.

to 25 percent below the 1992 level by 2010. With this resolution in effect, Freiburg has experienced a CO_2 emissions reduction of more than 10 percent per capita over the last 10 years, while having a 100 percent increase in public transport use. Freiburg, a typical compact city with a relatively high population density in mixed land use, has successfully adopted transit-oriented development, with more than 35 percent of the population choosing not to own a car. Freiburg is also known for its efforts in reducing per capita waste generation through its recycling programs, as well as various initiatives to promote the installation of solar energy systems.

Curitiba, Brazil

The city of Curitiba, Brazil, also successfully adopted transit-oriented development. Curitiba first outlined its Master Plan in 1965, aiming to limit the growth of the city center and encourage commercial and service sector development along transportation arteries. The Master Plan also included strategies for economic development and local community self-sufficiency with livable city spaces. The city is public-transport oriented and its bus rapid transit (BRT) system, known globally as the "surface metro," carries 50 times more passengers than it did 20 years ago. Additionally, Curitiba's gasoline use per capita is 30 percent below that of eight comparable Brazilian cities. It also has lower greenhouse gas (GHG) emission levels, less traffic congestion, and more livable urban spaces. Particularly noteworthy is that Curitiba adopted an incremental approach to development, whereby the city procured the basic rights of way for critical transport infrastructure systems, but developed the infrastructure when demand justified supply.

Yokohama, Japan

Yokohama, Japan's largest city, has demonstrated how an integrated approach to waste management based on the 3Rs concept—Reuse, Reduce, and Recycle—combined with stakeholder engagement, could reduce solid waste by 39 percent during a period when the population actually grew by 170,000. This significant waste reduction allowed Yokohama to save US$1.1 billion, which was otherwise required for the renewal of two incinerators, as well as US$6 million in annual operation and maintenance costs.

Measuring Progress: Sustainable Development Indicators

To promote urban sustainability, cities need to know the current state of their economy, environment, and society to be able to make improvements, monitor progress, and compare with other cities. Without a globally recognized definition of urban sustainability or eco-cities, however, no globally recognized standard indicators to measure a city's sustainability or an eco-city's performance are available.

Various entities, however, are developing their own sustainable development indicators for local governments. The most significant efforts are being made by municipal associations, such as Local Governments for Sustainability (ICLEI), or by local governments themselves, either individually or collectively within the framework of Local Agenda 21.[4] In Liverpool, United Kingdom, for example, the public and the city council have drawn up their own indicators measuring the success of sustainable development (City of Liverpool 2005). ICLEI-USA is currently developing a nationwide standardized sustainable index for local government, called the STAR Community Index, addressing the three intertwining facets of sustainability: economy, environment, and society (ICLEI-USA 2010; see also box 2.9). The World Bank, together with other partners, is

Box 2.9

STAR Community Index

The STAR Community Index that ICLEI-USA is currently developing includes 81 sustainability goals and 10 guiding principles, collectively defining community-scale sustainability. The index presents a vision of how communities can become more healthy, inclusive, and prosperous across eight specific categories. Its environment goals include the three categories of natural systems, planning and design, and energy and climate.

Environment		
Natural Systems	*Planning and Design*	*Energy and Climate*
• Natural Resource Planning and Inventory • Green Infrastructure • Land Use in Watersheds • Water Quality and Supply • Agriculture and Aquaculture • Resource Lands • Biodiversity and Invasive Species • Ambient Noise and Light • Waste Minimization	• Comprehensive Planning • Excellence in Design • Interconnected Land Use • Compact and Complete Communities • Design for People • Housing • Public Spaces • Transportation and Mobility • Land Conservation • Historic Preservation and Cultural Heritage • Code Barriers • Public Engagement and Participation	• Greenhouse Gas Mitigation • Climate Adaptation • Energy Supply • Energy Use • Resource Efficient Buildings • Alternative Fuels and Infrastructure • Industrial Sector Energy Use • Agricultural Climate Impacts

Source: ICLEI-USA 2010.

developing the Global City Indicators Program, which provides an established set of city indicators with a globally standardized methodology that allows for global comparability of city performance and knowledge sharing. The program is structured around 22 "themes" that measure a range of city services and quality of life factors.

In general, these sustainable development indicators are usually measuring environmental, social, institutional, and economic dimensions of sustainable development. Indicators to measure environmental sustainability, for example, often include energy, transport, air quality, noise, drinking water, green space, waste, and ecosystems and heritage. Attempts to measure sustainability of energy systems in the urban area are also emerging. This area of indicators aims to include measuring "satisfying" level of energy consumption, secure environmental protection, ensure the reliability and sufficiency of energy resources, and assess budget limitation and economic efficiency. Last, current measurement of low-carbon cities often relies on the carbon intensity per person or per unit GDP.

Another often-applied monitoring mechanism is an independent "eco-audit." An eco-audit would start by monitoring the key performance indicators and gradually adopt independent auditing and verification of performance. The latter activities would strengthen measurement, credibility, and compliance with the overall ecological vision and development. Eco-audits exist in a variety of forms and are increasingly applied at the urban level. The European Eco-Management and Audit Scheme (EMAS) is one such example (see box 2.10).

Conclusion and Key Policy Recommendations

The above analysis of China's and global experiences with low-carbon city development points to a number of key messages for China's low-carbon city agenda. China's relatively vibrant and bottom-up approach to eco-city development provides the potential to continue to explore and evaluate approaches to promote low-carbon city developments. The recent call to cities by NDRC and MoHURD to implement low-carbon development strategies provides additional impetus for the agenda, which is likely to be reinforced by the resource/energy efficiency and low-carbon development targets in the 12th Five-Year Plan. However, the national government, as well as provincial and city-level officials, should incorporate some of the lessons learned from China's initial eco-city development experiments, in particular in the following areas:

Box 2.10

The European Eco-Management and Audit Scheme (EMAS)

EMAS is an initiative established by European Regulation 1836/93 (later replaced by Council Regulation 761/01) to help public and private organizations—including cities—evaluate, report, and improve their environmental performance.

To register for EMAS, an organization must take five actions: (i) develop an environmental policy, (ii) establish an environmental management system, (iii) carry out an internal environmental audit, (iv) develop an environmental statement, and (v) obtain validation by an EMAS verifier and become registered. Each EU country has a national Competent Body that is responsible for the registration of EMAS organizations, an Accreditation Body that is responsible for EMAS verifiers, and EMAS verifiers that are independent of the organization being verified. The verifiers certify that the organization's environmental policy, environmental management system, internal audit, and environmental statement comply with EMAS regulation.

Participation in EMAS is voluntary. However, with growing concern and demand for environmentally friendly services and products, demonstration of environmental performance and sustainability is becoming important for organizations. As of April 2009, 4,319 organizations, including public entities or local/district councils in 28 European countries, are registered in EMAS.

The Leicester City Council in the United Kingdom (population 280,000) has applied for EMAS. The City Council uses EMAS to manage and improve its environmental performance to achieve its sustainable development goals. The City Council focused on improving the performance of its public works, to ensure waste minimization and prudent use of energy, water, and natural resources. The Council also focused on environmental training for City Council employees, contractors and suppliers, and local students and teachers, which was accomplished by extending the EMAS scheme to local schools and education programs. As a result, the City Council achieved improved environmental outcomes; increased share of electricity from renewable sources; decreased water consumption by the City Council; increased use of bicycles; reduced CO_2 emissions from Council vehicles; reduced paper consumption; and so on. Every year, the City Council produces an Environmental Statement with an assessment of its performance toward environmental targets, which is checked by an independent UK verifier to ensure that the Environmental Statement complies with the EMAS standard. Annual independent EMAS verification of the Environmental Statement ensures that the City Council's environmental performance is transparent and credible.

Source: EMAS 2010.

Updated indicators: Given that the existing indicators fall short in defining sustainability and low-carbon development, the eco- and low-carbon city development indicators—either those used by MEP, MoHURD, or others—need to be updated. The indicators that have been articulated for cities such as the Caofeidian Eco-City or the Sino-Singapore Eco-City are generally more advanced and could guide any revision of the national standards.

- *Integrated approaches:* China's rapid pace of urbanization provides an opportunity to advance integrated planning approaches that take into account the interlinkages between key urban sectors, especially land use and transportation planning. The potential of integrated planning is rarely explored, and once the urban form (both macro-densities and micro-level designs) is determined, cities are often locked into a prede-termined development pattern.
- *Balance of new towns vs. retrofitting:* While developing new towns pro-vides interesting opportunities, existing urban areas should not be ne-glected. There appears to be a tendency to focus on new towns at the expense of existing urban areas. Also, often these greenfield experi-ments do not sufficiently incorporate the many important lessons learned on failed "new town" developments, especially from the 1960s and 1970s in Europe and Japan.
- *Incentives and market mechanisms:* It is important that cities not rely too heavily on administrative controls to reduce pollution, or on meeting physical infrastructure construction targets, but that they complement these efforts with market-based mechanisms and economic incentive schemes to change behaviors, for example, through water tariff and congestion pricing.
- *Social inclusion and affordability:* Because some envisioned low-carbon city developments are very ambitious and potentially expensive (also in light of a technology-focused development approach), the risk exists that the eco- and low-carbon cities will be developed at the cost of social inclusion. To create vibrant and living communities, project develop-ments will need to pay attention to affordability and social inclusion.

Notes

1. This concept was put forward by Hu Jintao, General Secretary of the Central Committee of the Communist Party of China (CPC), during the fifth plenary session of the 16th Central Committee of the CPC in October 2005.

2. 15th Conference of Parties to the United Nations Framework Convention on Climate Change (UNFCCC).

3. Cities pursuing an eco-city agenda, beyond those formally recognized by MEP and MoHURD, include Shanghai, Tianjin, Harbin, Chongqing, Changzhou, Chengdu, Qinhuangdao, Rizhao, Guiyang, Tangshan, Xiangfan, Changchun, and Changsha, among others. Provinces such as Hainan, Jilin, Shanxi, Fujian, Shandong, Anhui, Jiangsu, and Zhejiang have also set the goal of building eco-provinces, and started the planning process (Xinhua News Agency 2008).

4. Local Agenda 21 is a local government-led, community-wide, and participatory effort to establish a comprehensive action strategy for environmental protection, economic prosperity, and community well-being in the local jurisdiction or area. Local Agenda 21 is an integral part of Agenda 21, adopted in the 1992 Rio Summit.

Bibliography

Baeumler, A., M. Chen, A. Dastur, Y. Zhang, R. Filewood, K. Al-Jamal, C. Peterson, and M. Ranade. 2009. "Sino-Singapore Tianjin Eco-City (SSTEC): a Case Study of an Emerging Eco-City in China." World Bank TA Report, November 2009. World Bank, Washington, DC.

China.org.cn. 2009. "China Maps Out Low Carbon Eco-City Strategy." http://www.china.org.cn/environment/2009-10/23/content_18757609.htm.

Chinese Academy of Urban Planning and Design (CAUPD). 2009. "Stocktaking Analysis of Eco-City Initiatives and Regulations in China." In collaboration with the World Bank. September.

City of Liverpool. 2005. Liverpool's Sustainable Development Plan 2006–2009 (November 2005). http://www.liverpool.gov.uk/Images/tcm21-63907.pdf.

EU Eco-Management and Audit Scheme (EMAS). 2010. EMAS Website. http://ec.europa.eu/environment/emas/index_en.htm.

Hammarby Sjöstad, City of Stockholm. 2010. Hammarby Sjöstad Website. http://www.hammarbysjostad.se.

ICLEI–USA (Local Governments for Sustainability). 2010. "STAR Community Index: Sustainability Goals & Guiding Principles." http://www.icleiusa.org/library/documents/STAR_Sustainability_Goals.pdf.

Jovanovic, M., N. Afgan, and V. Bakic. 2010. "An Analytical Method for the Measurement of Energy System Sustainability in Urban Areas." Energy 35(9): 3909–20.

Larson, C. 2009. "China's Grand Plans for Eco-Cities Now Lie Abandoned." Yale Environment 360. April 6.

Ministry of Environmental Protection (MEP). 1997. "National Environment Protection Model City and Model District." Beijing.

———. 2007. "Indices for Eco-County, Eco-City and Eco-Province." Beijing.

———. 2008. "2007 National Urban Environment Management and Comprehensive Treatment Annual Report." Beijing.

Ministry of Housing and Urban-Rural Development (MoHURD). 2004. "National Standards for Eco-Garden City." Beijing.

———. 2005. "National Standards for Garden City (revised)." Beijing.

National Development and Reform Commission (NDRC). 2006. "China's 11th Five-Year (2006–2010) Plan for National Economic and Social Development." Beijing.

People's Daily Online. 2010. "Shenzhen Becomes China's First Low Carbon Eco-Demonstration City." http://english.people.com.cn/90001/90778/90862/6871885.html.

Reinvang, R. (ed.), C. Dongmei, S. Henningsson, L. Hongpeng, L. Junfeng, L. Minglian, M. Lingjuan, D. Pamlin, and W. Ying. 2008. "Baoding. A Global 'Electric Valley' for Sustainable Energy Production? A Litmus Test for the World's Commitment to Renewable Energy." Published by the WWF China Programme Office, in cooperation with China Renewable Energy Industry Association (CREIA), and China Wind Energy Association. April 2008. http://assets.wwf.no/downloads/baoding_intro_report_final_2008.pdf.

World Bank. 2010. Eco2 Cities—Ecological Cities as Economic Cities. Washington, DC: World Bank. http://www.worldbank.org/eco2.

Xinhua News Agency. 2008. Article in the Economic Information Journal of July 16.

CHAPTER 3

Low-Carbon Cities in China: Characteristics, Roadmap, and Indicators

Xiaodong Wang, Noureddine Berrah, Ximing Peng, Lorraine Sugar, and Hua Du

Overview

This chapter addresses two key questions related to low-carbon cities: (i) what constitutes a low-carbon city and what are its characteristics and indicators, and (ii) how can a city get started on a path to becoming a low-carbon city. The chapter presents a roadmap that cities can use to reduce their emissions and guide their transition to becoming low carbon, and then outlines concrete steps for this transition. These steps include measuring a city's carbon footprint by assessing greenhouse gas (GHG) emissions; developing a vision and determining low-carbon targets; setting key sector indicators based on GHG abatement cost curves and scenarios; designing and implementing an action plan; and measuring progress through monitoring, reporting, and verification.

Low-Carbon Cities in China: Background and Initial Strategies

China, despite having lower emissions per capita than industrialized countries, has become, partly by the sheer size of its population, the largest GHG emitter in the world. GHG emissions in China have the potential, if left unchecked, to reach unsustainable levels. There is a national consensus that China cannot sustain its current carbon-intensive economic growth. To avoid embarking irrevocably on a high-carbon growth path, the central government has been designing and implementing strategies to decouple growth from CO_2 emissions by setting a national target to reduce carbon intensity by 40–45 percent between 2005 and 2020.

Over the next 20 years, as a projected 300 million people will migrate to urban areas, energy demand for buildings and transport will increase rapidly. Energy demand and its related CO_2 emissions are expected to triple for buildings and appliances, and more than quadruple to meet the population's mobility needs, accommodating a 10-fold increase in the vehicle fleet over the next two decades (McKinsey 2009). The speed and scale of urbanization in China are a momentous challenge, but also present an unrivaled opportunity to build low-carbon cities today.

As described in chapter 2, many municipal governments in China are already developing and implementing eco-city or low-carbon city initiatives. Low-carbon cities are, in fact, a subset of eco-cities, which aim to more broadly develop in a "sustainable" way.[1] The local-level drive to develop low-carbon cities has recently received new impetus from the National Development and Reform Commission (NDRC) announcement that five provinces and eight cities had been selected to pilot low-carbon growth (see box 2.1).

Low-carbon strategies from Chinese cities have become increasingly comprehensive and sophisticated over the last two years and are characterized by six focus areas: (i) driving energy efficiency in industrial processes; (ii) restructuring the local economy to favor low-carbon business, including development of low-carbon industrial parks; (iii) making new and existing buildings more energy efficient; (iv) making low-carbon transport widely available and improving access to public transport; (v) increasing the share of renewable energy generation; and (vi) reducing the impact of consumption (The Climate Group 2010).

For many decades, China's economic reform and modernization have been marked by incremental change. However, today, urgent action is required as scientific evidence about climate change and its negative impact is now largely accepted and the window of opportunity to act is closing quickly. Urban infrastructure has a long lifetime—buildings and roads last for decades and urban forms endure for a century or more—so emissions through 2050 and beyond will be largely determined by the new urban infrastructure constructed over the next decade. Introducing efficient low-carbon technologies into new urban infrastructure today can lock cities into a low-carbon path for decades to come.

Defining Low-Carbon Cities

The overall objective of a low-carbon city is to significantly reduce its carbon footprint in ways that do not compromise a city's economic development potential. What exactly constitutes a low-carbon city, however, is difficult, if not impossible, to define, despite extensive research. This is because a city's carbon footprint—defined as its GHG emissions per capita—is dependent on the city's GDP, energy intensity, and energy mix. Energy intensity, in turn, is contingent on a city's economic structure, climate, population density, transport infrastructure, energy efficiency, and way and quality of life.

Two major contributors to the carbon footprint of Chinese cities are industry and power[2] (see figure 3.1). These two sectors also significantly contribute to the GDP and job creation in cities, as the tertiary and services sectors, as well as other low-carbon industries, are still underdeveloped. While a city may consider relocating its higher-emission industries outside its city boundary to reduce its carbon footprint, this strategy—while effective in reducing local GHG emissions—makes little difference on larger spatial scales at the national level (Bai et al. 2009). The differ-

Figure 3.1   Industry and Power Dominate CO_2 Emissions per Capita in Chinese Cities

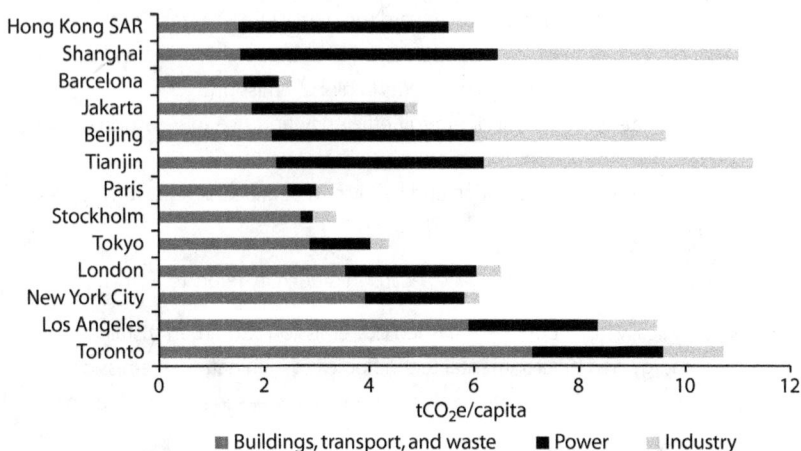

Source: Adapted from World Bank 2010a.

ences in underlying economic structures and the significant role of industry and power sectors in Chinese cities make the comparison of emissions per capita between developed and developing cities and the establishment of universal benchmarks difficult.

Chinese and international literature on low-carbon cities includes a wide diversity of definitions of low-carbon cities (see selected ones in box 3.1). However, taking into consideration the typical emission sources and characteristics of Chinese cities *and* the determinant factors of GHG emissions, it is clear a low-carbon city would at least take the following characteristic actions:

Box 3.1

Selected Definitions of a Low-Carbon City

Definitions of low-carbon cities vary considerably, although all address the need for carbon reductions and are related to social aspects, such as jobs, income, or quality of life.

Dai (2009) stresses that in a low-carbon city, the pattern of city construction and social development is aimed at reducing carbon emissions and changing city residents' ideas and behavior related to consumption without compromising their overall quality of life.

Skea and Nishioka (2008) describe the consensus that a low-carbon city should:

- Take actions that are compatible with the principles of sustainable development, ensuring that the development needs of all groups within society are met
- Make an equitable contribution toward the global effort to stabilize the atmospheric concentration of CO_2 and other GHG at a level that will avoid dangerous climate change, through deep cuts in global emissions
- Demonstrate a high level of energy efficiency and use low-carbon energy sources and production technologies
- Adopt patterns of consumption and behavior that are consistent with low levels of GHG emissions.

Finally, Wang (2010) says that a low-carbon green city refers to a city that:

- Is ecologically innocuous with slashed CO_2 emission and urban sustainability
- Uses energy and environmental technologies to eliminate CO_2 emission and thus gains economic benefits which will lead to increased jobs and income.

Source: Authors, based on Dai 2009, Skea and Nishioka 2008, and Wang 2010.

- Sharply reduce GHG emissions by having targets that, at a minimum, comply with the national targets of energy efficiency, renewable energy, and carbon intensity and would contribute to reversing the country's growing trend of GHG emissions.
- Rely on energy efficient and low-carbon energy resources and production technologies.
- Build efficient and integrated public transport infrastructure that supports green modes of transport.
- Achieve a compact urban form.
- Educate and increase awareness of citizens to support low-carbon consumption patterns.

Roadmap for a Low-Carbon City

Chinese cities aspiring to become a low-carbon city need to focus on a comprehensive multisector approach to reduce their GHG emissions and progress toward sustainability, with clear priorities based on their specific conditions. Figure 3.2 presents a roadmap with five components to help cities become low carbon.

Figure 3.2   Low-Carbon City Roadmap

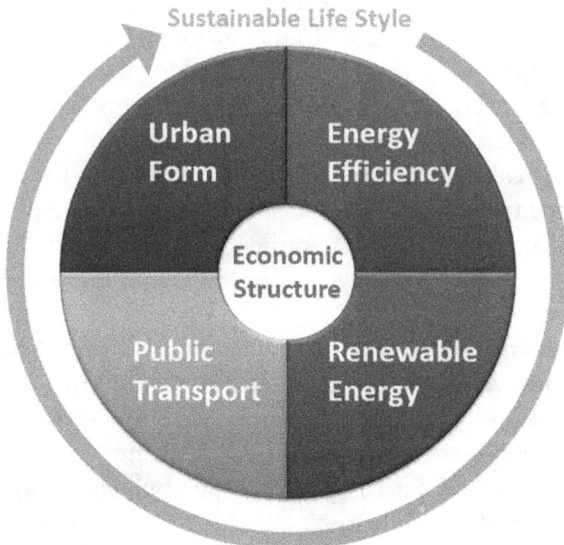

Source: Authors.

First, cities should make a consistent effort to reduce carbon emissions by sustaining demand-side energy efficiency measures—particularly in the industrial, power, heating, and buildings sectors. This should be combined with a focus on increasing the use of clean, renewable sources of energy.

Second, cities should minimize emissions from the transport sector through the adoption of new technologies and the provision of high-quality public and non-motorized transport.

Third, cities need to carefully direct their spatial growth and urban form. Cities with higher densities emit less GHG (see also chapter 1). Cities will need to grow not only denser, but also *smarter*, through public transport networks and compact urban forms.

Fourth, cities should seek the support of their citizens and build a consensus around a resource-efficient and low-carbon lifestyle. With rising income and higher individual purchasing power and demands, a low-carbon lifestyle will be key to lowering future energy demand in Chinese cities. Box 3.6 describes the CoolClimate Network, a university-government-industry partnership in California that develops practical tools to help citizens understand and reduce their individual and household carbon footprint. Similar partnerships at the city and neighborhood levels in China could contribute to less carbon-intensive households.

Finally, cities will need to address their economic structure, as future GDP growth will increasingly be driven by a city's services and lower-carbon industries, both decisive factors for reducing carbon intensity in many Chinese cities. However, simply relocating higher emission industries outside a city boundary to reduce that city's carbon footprint—while reducing GHG emissions locally—would make little, if any, difference on larger spatial scales. In general, the guiding principle for all cities will therefore need to be to develop strategies to lower their respective carbon footprints relative to the existing carbon intensity baseline. In particular, the less industrialized cities have an opportunity to leapfrog into a lower carbon trajectory from the outset.

Of all these measures, urban planning, public transport, and building energy efficiency are traditionally within a municipal government's authority. In addition, while the national government is usually better positioned to rebalance economic structure, mandate industrial energy efficiency (particularly for large SOEs), issue building energy efficiency codes, and support the shift to renewable energy, each province or city also has its own top industrial enterprises programs and can provide additional regulations and financial incentives for energy conservation in these enterprises. Municipal governments also have the capacity to implement more stringent building codes than the national level.[3] Given the wide variation in GDP, economic structure, population, resource endowment, and carbon emission profiles among Chinese cities, a "one size fits all" approach to allocate the same low-carbon target has its limitations and sometimes a heavy cost. Instead, Chinese cities should have an opportunity to determine their own best approach based on their city profile. In addition, they could consider engaging in carbon cap and trade or at least trade in energy savings certificates or purchase green electricity, all of which can substantially reduce the costs of meeting low-carbon objectives. Purchase of green electricity, for example, is important for cities with a relatively limited supply of on-site renewable energy within the city boundaries. Developing green electricity trading schemes through imports of renewable electricity is essential to achieve a low-carbon energy mix, and can spur large demand for green electricity.

The city of London, through its actions, has provided an example of a roadmap that can help a city progress toward becoming low carbon (see also box 3.2). Such a roadmap, which will be expanded upon in the sections below, would entail the following steps for Chinese cities:

- *Step One—knowing the city's carbon footprint:* This requires establishing an accounting framework and baseline or benchmark against which progress will be measured. Knowledge of the city's carbon footprint is critical to inform citizens and policy makers about the level and source of baseline emissions.
- *Step Two—developing a vision and setting a low-carbon target:* This step begins with careful and comprehensive analyses of a city's GHG reduction potentials and their costs, along with decisive and visionary leadership from the city's officials. As part of this process, the city can use national GHG reduction targets and examine experiences from other Chinese and international cities. A bold vision is a key characteristic of a low-carbon city and would ensure not only *decoupling* growth from carbon emissions (consistent with the central government's target to reduce carbon intensity by 40–45 percent from 2005 to 2020) but also *reversing* the upward GHG emission trend within 15–20 years. The vision should be complemented with clear indicators and targets for actions that combine the highest potential to reduce GHG emissions with the lowest costs.
- *Step Three—implementing a low-carbon city action plan:* A comprehensive low-carbon city strategy and implementation plan will lead the city

Box 3.2

London's Low-Carbon Action Plan: From Vision to Action

London has set itself the target of becoming "a world leading low-carbon capital by 2025." To fulfill this vision, the city has taken several steps to develop a detailed low-carbon climate action plan that can guide its transition to a low-carbon economy.

Step 1: Developing a baseline GHG inventory. No city could formulate a climate action plan without knowing its carbon footprint. Therefore, in 2002, London set up the London Energy and Greenhouse Gas Inventory (LEGGI), a database with city-level information about energy use and GHG emissions within the Greater London area. The database informs policies by geographically showing the level and source of emissions.

Step 2: Establishing a GHG reduction goal. Next, an ambitious emission reduction target is required to demonstrate the aspiration and commitment to transform into a low-carbon city. Aligning with the U.K. government's commitments to the Kyoto Protocol, the mayor of London has set the ambitious targets of achieving a 60 percent reduction in CO_2 emissions by 2025, and at least an 80 percent reduction by 2050 relative to the 1990 level.

Step 3: Formulating policies and supporting actions. To achieve the committed emission reduction targets, a Climate Change Mitigation and Energy Strategy was prepared for London, proposing 17 policies and supporting actions. If implemented successfully, these policies would contribute to 40 percent of the required emission reduction targets. The proposed policies and programs cover many areas, ranging from maximizing economic opportunities of transitioning to a low-carbon economy to securing a low-carbon energy supply and reducing CO_2 emissions from building and transport sectors.

Step 4: Monitoring and reporting of CO_2 emissions. Recognizing the importance of monitoring and verification of CO_2 emission reductions, London will on an annual basis maintain and update its emission inventory of direct and indirect CO_2 emissions. The LEGGI 2008 is currently being published online at the London Datastore. The city will also produce an annual summary report with updated information on CO_2 emissions and progress of mayoral climate change mitigation programs, illustrating the progress that London is making toward its 2025 target.

Source: City of London 2010.

to achieve its overall GHG emission reduction objective. It requires effective innovative policies and targeted financing to make a low-carbon city a reality.

- *Step Four—carefully monitoring progress:* Monitoring, verification, and reporting of carbon emissions will ensure that the city remains on a low-carbon growth path and toward a sustainable way of life.

Step One: Knowing a City's Carbon Footprint

Measuring a city's GHG emissions is an important first step toward becoming low carbon. This section discusses measuring emissions and also presents emission sources and determinant factors of GHG emissions in Chinese cities.

Measuring GHG Emissions of a City

While different approaches to assessing GHG emissions of a certain area have been proposed, most current and globally accepted assessments attribute emissions to an area based on the location of production, not consumption.

The Intergovernmental Panel on Climate Change (IPCC), for example, has issued guidelines to calculate national GHG emissions that include all emissions produced within the boundaries of a given country and a similar methodology could be used to measure emissions at the city level, which would also facilitate comparability and aggregation at the national level. Compared to national inventories, however, city GHG emission inventories face two additional complexities—the *scope* of the emissions being measured and the *boundaries* of the city unit.

To address the issue of scope, the World Resources Institute (WRI) and the World Business Council for Sustainable Development (WBCSD) have introduced three levels of scope that can be considered for calculating GHG emissions from cities:

- *Scope 1: Direct* emissions produced *within* the city boundary.
- *Scope 2: Indirect* emissions produced *outside* the city boundary, which are a direct result of activities within the boundary; that is, electricity consumption from a power plant located outside the city.
- *Scope 3: Upstream* or embodied emissions produced *outside* the inventory boundary and associated with the extraction, production, and transportation of products and services used within the city boundary. Specifically, Scope 3 includes emissions from aviation or marine fuels

used for air and sea transport, out-of-boundary waste decomposition, and electricity transmission and distribution losses. Embodied emissions from energy, water, building materials, and food may be reported as additional items but are not included.

Building on these approaches, the United Nations Environment Program (UNEP), the United Nations Human Settlements Programme (UN-HABITAT), and the World Bank jointly developed the International Standard for Reporting GHGs from Cities (UNEP et al. 2010). This standard follows the principles promoted by the IPCC, while accommodating the Scope 2 and Scope 3 emissions inevitably connected to cities. The standard also specifically addresses the issues of boundary and attribution of emissions and establishes that:

- City emissions include major emissions from consumption within a city, as well as major upstream emissions that are attributable to city residents.[4]
- City boundaries are defined by a city's metropolitan or functional limit, which, especially for larger cities, is considered the best scale to use (World Bank 2010a).

ICLEI has also developed an International Local Government GHG Emissions Analysis Protocol (ICLEI 2009). As this methodology does not include most of the embodied emissions produced outside the city boundary from upstream production, it inherently penalizes cities with energy-intensive industries. Potential future work should consider including consumption-based emissions at city level.

GHG Emissions in Chinese Cities—Determinants and Recent Trends

As discussed, the majority of GHG emissions in Chinese cities come from the industrial and power sectors (Sugar et al. 2012). Data from Beijing, Shanghai, and Tianjin (see figures 3.1 and 3.3) indicate that about 35 percent of city emissions relate to power consumption and about 45 percent to industrial activities within the city boundaries. This distribution of emissions is representative of two important characteristics of these cities. First, industry and power generation activities within city boundaries account for as much as 70 percent of energy consumption. Second, the energy mix is dominated by coal. While emissions per capita relating to transport and buildings are still relatively low in Chinese cities com-

Figure 3.3   Industry Emissions Dominate in Chinese Cities: Ground Transportation Emissions Dominate in Los Angeles and Toronto

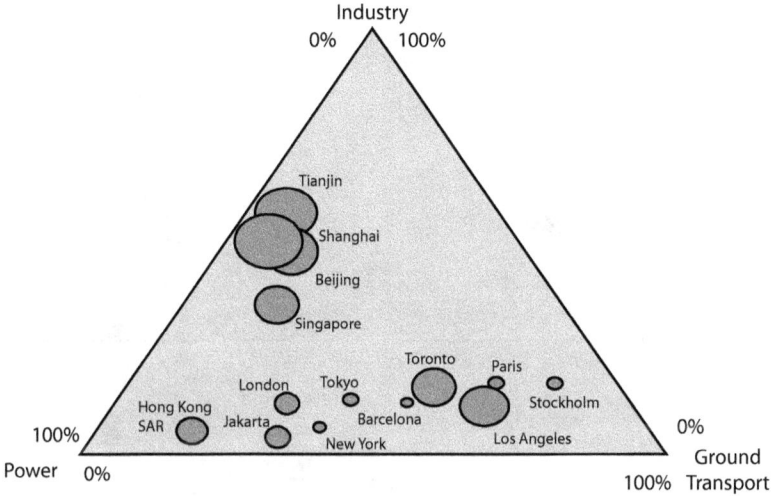

Industry
0%   100%

Tianjin
Shanghai
Beijing
Singapore
Toronto   Paris
London   Tokyo
Hong Kong   Stockholm
SAR   Jakarta   Barcelona
New York   Los Angeles

100%   0%
Power   0%   Ground
100%   Transport

Sources: Based on data from Sugar, Kennedy, and Leman 2012 and World Bank 2010a.
Note: Points reflect actual size of emissions per capita.

pared to developed cities, with rising incomes, these emissions will inevitably grow rapidly, unless measures are taken to keep them in check.

The key challenge for Chinese cities will be to achieve gains in energy intensity of GDP and improve the energy mix to counter the inevitable increases in emissions resulting from a higher GDP. GHG emissions in a city are a product of the city's GDP, the energy intensity of the GDP, and the carbon intensity of the energy mix used by the city. With likely continued strong GDP per capita growth across Chinese cities, actions for low-carbon growth will need to focus on the other two determinants of GHG use, namely, by (i) reducing energy intensity and (ii) shifting the energy mix toward low-carbon energy resources. As cities have only limited opportunities[5] to significantly impact the energy mix they use—considerably changing the parameters of this mix is largely the responsibility of the central government—this section focuses primarily on key trends and determinants related to the energy intensity of transport and buildings.

Overall, it is important to note that so far in China, gains in energy intensity have not been adequate to counter the strong aggregate impact of GDP growth on total GHG emissions. Figure 3.4 shows that in the last

Figure 3.4   Carbon Emissions per Capita in Major Chinese Cities over the Past Two Decades

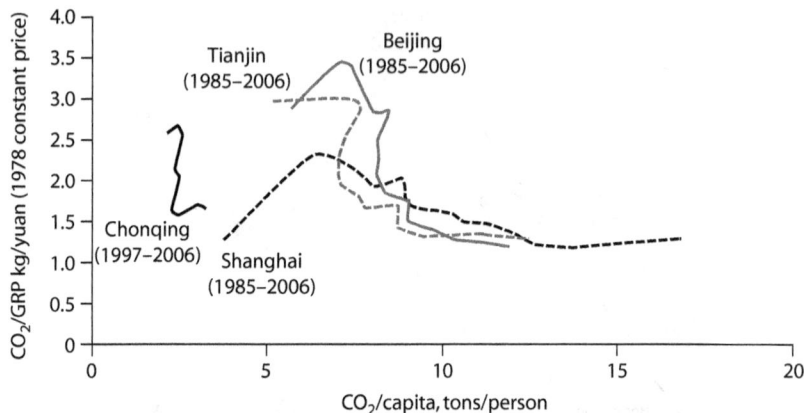

Source: Dhakal 2009.

two decades, as Chinese cities have become wealthier, their GHG emissions per capita have continuously increased, even while achieving dramatic reductions in carbon intensity.

The energy intensity of a city depends on a variety of factors, including the economic structure, climate, population density, transport infrastructure, energy efficiency, and the characteristics and quality of life. Therefore, any effort to reduce energy intensity needs to focus on these determinant factors.

Experiences in the transport sector show how policy choices can affect energy intensity. While transport emissions are currently relatively low in Chinese cities, they are growing rapidly. Motorized private vehicles are the key drivers of transport emissions and inevitably, as incomes rise, the number of motorized trips and consequent emissions will only increase. Emission levels and development patterns, however, will not be the same for all cities. Figure 3.5 illustrates that even just among Chinese cities a range of potential trajectories for carbon emissions per capita in relation to economic development exist. This is because factors such as a city's urban form and spatial development patterns, policies regarding motorization, and quality of public transit are also important.

Shanghai, for example, with a very dense, walkable core and various restrictions that discourage car ownership and driving, along with one of the longest public transport networks in the world in absolute length, has

Figure 3.5   Potential CO$_2$ Pathways for Urban Transport with Respect to Economic Output

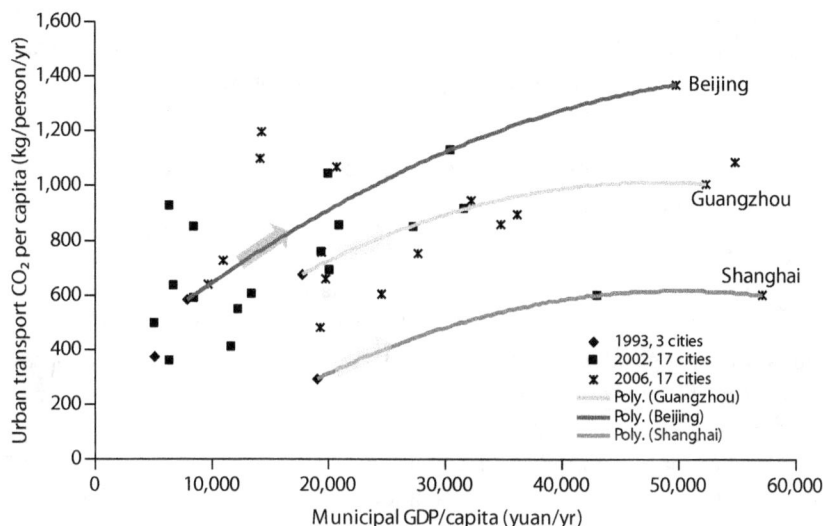

Source: Darido et al. 2009.

significantly fewer cars and a much lower level of emissions than Beijing, despite comparable levels of income. Beijing has many more cars, trips are generally longer (in part because the historic center does not in itself attract a lot of trips), and the city is not as easy to serve with public transport because of an urban development pattern developed around the city's ring roads, which, while still dense, is harder to serve competitively with public transport. Chinese cities that create walkable urban forms around public transport nodes and prioritize high-quality public transport over cars will be able to maintain relatively low emissions in the transport sector (see also chapter 4 on spatial development and chapters 9, 10, and 11 on urban transport).

Policy choices in the building sector have demonstrated they can effectively counter the effect of initial endowments, such as a cooler climate. The variation in energy efficiency and energy consumption patterns among international cities, even among those with a similar climate, suggests that cities can achieve low energy intensity, even when starting from quite extreme circumstances. Although cities in a colder climate generally have higher building emissions per capita, energy conservation in buildings has proven to have an even larger impact on emissions. The city of

Stockholm, for example, is generally much colder than Toronto, but has about one-third of the emissions per capita as a result of aggressive building energy conservation measures. Similarly, Chinese cities can also overcome a colder climate and keep building emissions low by improving building energy efficiency and reducing energy consumption.

Step Two: Developing a Vision for a Low-Carbon City and Setting a Low-Carbon Target

Establishing a vision and setting objectives begins by conducting careful and comprehensive analyses to establish abatement potentials and costs, and then developing scenarios to inform target setting. Defining GHG emission targets at the city level includes the following steps, further described in the sections below:

- Determining the city's GHG abatement cost curve (with abatement potentials, abatement cost of each identified option, and barriers to its implementation)
- Developing GHG abatement scenarios
- Defining the GHG target for the city
- Disaggregating the GHG target into low-carbon city indicators and targets.

Determining the City's GHG Abatement Cost Curve

The GHG abatement cost curve has been developed by the McKinsey Institute to determine GHG abatement potential and cost at the global level. The methodology has also been applied at the country level in many countries around the world, including China (McKinsey 2009). The GHG abatement cost curve is a useful analytical tool to provide a quantitative, fact-based analysis to help policy makers and business leaders identify and prioritize potential solutions. It outlines *when* to adopt *which* abatement technology at *what* costs. The GHG abatement cost curve also provides an analytical underpinning to allow indicators to be set for key sectors.

While the GHG abatement cost curve has proved to be useful for this kind of analysis, it is important to note it also has drawbacks. Some of its most significant shortcomings include covering neither transaction costs (the cost of designing the policies and programs and the institutional changes associated with them) nor barriers to implementation. The methodology also focuses exclusively on GHG abatement technologies, leaving aside other GHG abatement options such as those related to urban form, public transport, and household and citizen behavior changes, which are not necessarily based on technology.

To overcome one of these shortcomings, improvements are being considered by McKinsey and other users to incorporate the feasibility or ease of implementation as a key criterion, in addition to abatement cost and potential, for prioritizing investments. The investments with low abatement costs and easy implementation are "no-regret" options that should be implemented first. The investments with moderate cost and implementation barriers should be piloted and implemented over the medium term (prior to 2020). The investments with high cost, but also high potentials, and with significant implementation challenges should be explored and assessed, and implementation should be planned for only after 2020 to meet a city's target.

The cost of an abatement technology reflects its resource (or techno-engineering) costs—that is, capital, operating, and maintenance costs—offset by any energy or other savings associated with abating one tonne of CO_2e per year using this technology, calculated based on the following formula:

$$\text{Abatement cost} = \frac{[\text{Full cost of abatement option}] - [\text{Full cost of baseline option}]}{[CO_2e \text{ emissions from baseline solution}] - [CO_2e \text{ emissions from abatement option}]} .$$

When using this formula, the time value of all financial flows should be considered using a social discount rate, thereby allowing the technical potential to reduce emissions below the baseline scenario to be estimated. This depends on optimal government support, the applicability, and maturity of the technology, as well as the supply and talent constraints (McKinsey 2009). For each sector, the abatement technologies can be arrayed from lowest to highest cost and a sector abatement cost curve can be constructed. The abatement cost curves plot the estimated maximum technical abatement potential of each option and the realistic costs of implementing them (see figure 3.6). In the context of Chinese cities, abatement options could be considered in four key emissions-intensive sectors: industry, power, transport, and buildings. An example is shown for Shanghai in the next section, "Developing GHG Abatement Scenarios."

Developing GHG Abatement Scenarios

Cities could consider beginning with the development of at least the following three scenarios:

Figure 3.6   Marginal Abatement Cost Curve

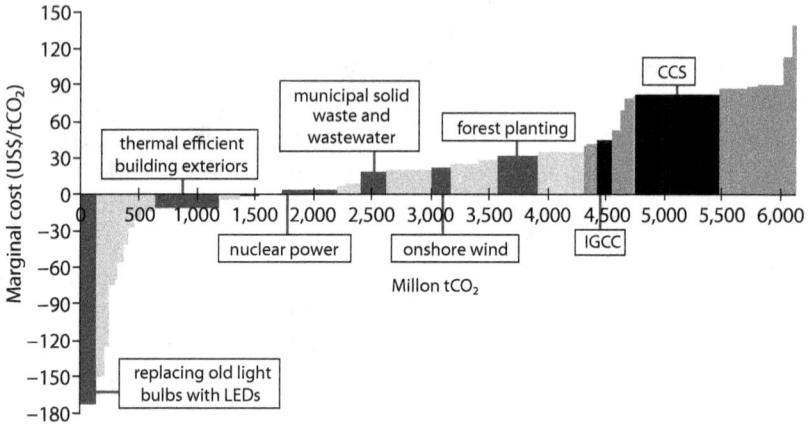

Source: Based on data from McKinsey & Company 2009.
Note: CCS = carbon capture and sequestration; IGCC = integrated gasification combined cycle.

- *Frozen technology scenario:* This scenario shows the cost of no action, when existing technologies are not further deployed and no new technologies will be adopted.
- *Baseline scenario:* This scenario includes all actions to meet the national government's objectives.
- *Full potential abatement scenario:* This scenario taps the maximum technical potential constrained only by technology applicability, maturity, and supply. Ideally, this scenario should set a target of emissions peaking and then starting to decline within 15 to 20 years.

Cities can construct scenarios to determine abatement objectives in the domain between the baseline scenario (all cities have to meet the target assigned to them by the national government) and the full potential scenarios (maximum achievable potential). It must be noted that these scenarios should be periodically updated as the national target and the technological environment evolve.

All scenarios should be technically feasible. Decision makers should therefore base their target determination on the affordability and cost effectiveness of the investments. The Changning district in Shanghai has adopted this methodology and developed one of the first abatement cost curves at a district level in China to identify abatement potentials and costs of each technology and set the district's low-carbon target (see box 3.3).

Box 3.3

Changning District, Shanghai: Initial Results of a GHG Abatement Cost Curve at City District Level

The Shanghai municipal and Changning district governments are committed to building a low-carbon city. In particular, the Changning district government envisions learning from international best practices, adapting successful schemes to the district's specific conditions, and becoming a leading low-carbon district in Shanghai as well as in China during the 12th Five-Year Plan period. Following the Changning district government's request for assistance, a World Bank team is working closely with the Shanghai Energy Conservation Supervision Center (SEC-SC) to help determine carbon emission reduction targets for the district.

To get started, the SECSC conducted a complete survey of energy use, building envelope, and electric appliances for all buildings—commercial, residential, and schools—in the area. Next, the center analyzed energy saving potentials and costs for each abatement technology in the power, building, transport, and waste sectors, as well as options related to carbon sinks and behavior changes. The SECSC then ranked the ease of implementation of all the identified abatement options in four categories from readily achievable to having significant barriers. Finally, they developed an abatement cost curve.

The SECSC also developed three scenarios up to 2020 to determine the district's low-carbon target. Intermediary scenarios are currently under development with the assistance of the World Bank team and will be submitted to the district government for discussion.

Source: Authors.

Defining the Low-Carbon Objective and GHG Target for the City

Chinese cities and metropolises should, as good international practice indicates, be in the forefront of combating climate change by transitioning to sustainable development and adopting sustainable lifestyles. Most of these cities have the ambition, means, and thus the opportunity to be a key part of China's efforts to avoid a high-carbon growth path, while also pursuing ways to improve the quality of life of its citizens.

A low-carbon city in China should at least comply with its assigned city-level target to ensure that the national target of reducing carbon intensity by 40–45 percent between 2005 and 2020 can be reached. Achieving this target will already require concerted efforts and consensus from the public and private sectors as well as civil society. Cities that want to earn the "low-carbon" label should aim higher than these targets assigned by the government. Reduction in GHG emissions above the government target should be determined by potentials of abatement options, technical feasibility, and affordability. While international experience is useful, Chinese cities should aim to lead and not follow, by avoiding the high-carbon paths followed by the developed cities at their early development stages. Chinese cities have the opportunity to adopt best urban practices and progress immediately to the most advanced technologies. Emission reduction targets should therefore be bold, ensuring not only delinking growth from carbon emission (a reduction in carbon intensity) but also reversing the upward emissions trend within 15 to 20 years.

Disaggregating the GHG City Target into Low-Carbon Indicators

After determining low-carbon targets, a city can set sector-level and measurable indicators to establish specific goals and measure progress.

International Experience with Low-Carbon City Indicators

Low-carbon indicators are included in most of the recently developed sustainability indexes, such as the Global City Indicators, the Low-Carbon Cities Development Index, the City Sustainable Development Index, as well as indexes developed by UN organizations, the United States, Europe, Australia, Japan, and others. These indicators generally focus on four different but overlapping objectives—sustainable cities, green cities, eco-cities, and low-carbon cities—and attempt to define benchmarks to determine whether or not cities have reached this particular goal. This section will not attempt to present a structured differentiation among these proposed categories, as they emphasize different but overlapping aspects of sustainable and livable cities. Rather, this section will focus on low-carbon city indicators, while noting that there are many other definitions and indicators available for the sustainable development of cities. It will also build on some of the city-level indicators that already exist in China, including those developed by the Ministry of Environmental Protection (MEP) and the Ministry of Housing and Urban-Rural Development (MoHURD). Chapter 2 presents a review of these indicators, their limitations, and areas for further development.

Another index, the Low Carbon Cities Development Index, cited in the *Copenhagen Declaration*, has been recently created to support cities in developing monitoring indicators based on global best practices. The index focuses on three areas: (i) policies that the city has in place to reduce direct and embedded emissions and how these are linked to exports and imports of low-carbon solutions; (ii) emissions, including direct emissions and embodied emissions; and (iii) investments made by the city to enable future reductions, ranging from infrastructure investments to education.

Low-carbon cities indicators usually focus on the key sectors that can contribute to emission reductions in cities. Box 3.4 presents two index systems to illustrate different approaches to developing indicators. Given the nature of compact cities in Europe, for example, the European Green City Index focuses on a small number of tangible and measurable indicators at city level, but does not include indicators for land-use planning and urban form. The U.S. Leadership in Energy and Environmental Design for Neighborhood Development (LEED-ND), however, does provide good indicators for compact urban planning and mixed land use.

Box 3.4

European Green City Index and LEED for Neighborhood Development

Index systems can take different approaches to the development of indicators, as illustrated by these examples of the European Green City Index and the LEED-ND standard.

European Green City Index

The European Green City Index ranks the environmental performance of 30 major European cities. The methodology was developed by the Economist Intelligence Unit and Siemens, with feedback from an independent group of urban sustainability experts.

The index was developed by looking for underlying factors that have allowed some cities to perform better in certain environmental areas than other cities. Results suggested a strong correlation between wealth and a high overall ranking in the index, as wealthier cities tend to invest more heavily in energy-efficient infrastructures and can afford environmental managers. The index shows little correlation between city size and performance, though the leading cities tend to be smaller. Public funding and consumer behavior, however, are important factors.

(continued next page)

Box 3.4 *(continued)*

The study connected to the index compared European cities in eight catego-ries: (i) CO_2 emissions, (ii) energy consumption, (iii) buildings, (iv) transport, (v) water, (vi) waste and land use, (vii) air quality, and (viii) environmental governance. The overall ranking of each city was determined by aggregating scores of each indicator with assigned weightings by each category. About half of the 30 indica-tors are quantitative, the others qualitative. The key indicators of this index rele-vant to low-carbon cities are as follows:

- *CO_2 emissions:* CO_2 emissions per capita, and CO_2 intensity
- *Energy:* Energy consumption per capita, energy intensity, and share of renew-able energy in primary energy supply
- *Buildings:* Energy consumption per square meter and building energy effi-ciency policies
- *Transport:* Percentage of citizens traveling by public transport, walking, or cy-cling to work, length of public transport network, and existence of congestion reduction policies.

LEED for Neighborhood Development

The LEED-ND rating system is a set of standards, designed by the U.S. Green Build-ing Council, for evaluating the performance of the planning and development of neighborhoods. The rating system builds on the combined principles of smart growth, new urbanism, and green infrastructure and buildings.

The LEED-ND system emphasizes the creation of compact, walkable, vibrant, and mixed-use neighborhoods with good connections to nearby communities. Its goal is to establish a national leadership standard for assessing and rewarding environmentally superior green neighborhood development practices.

LEED-ND evaluates a neighborhood development project on five dimensions: (i) smart location and linkage, (ii) neighborhood pattern and design, (iii) green infrastructure and buildings, (iv) innovation and design, and (v) regional priority credit. The rating system contains a number of mandatory prerequisites and op-tional criteria for which credits can be earned. The criteria related to low-carbon development are summarized below.

The project must satisfy all prerequisites and earn a minimum of 40 points to become LEED certified. The project may qualify for LEED Silver, Gold, and Platinum with higher scores, depending on which threshold point each level of certifica-

(continued next page)

Box 3.4 *(continued)*

tion holds. The Smart Location and Linkage prerequisites require a new project to be located adjacent to an existing community and not on environmentally sensitive land. The Neighborhood Pattern and Design prerequisites require development of a neighborhood with compact design, high levels of connectivity, and walkable streets. The Green Infrastructure and Buildings prerequisites disqualify a project with poor energy and water efficiency buildings. Key LEED-ND indicators are:

- *Land Use:* Compact development, mixed-use neighborhood center, walkable streets, and access to open space or recreational facilities
- *Buildings:* Number of certified green buildings, minimum building energy efficiency, district heating and cooling, on-site renewable energy sources, and solar orientation for building blocks.
- *Transport:* Reduced parking footprint, transportation demand management, bicycle network and storage, and transit facilities.

Sources: European Green City Index 2009 and U.S. Green Building Council et al. 2009.

Possible List of Low-Carbon Indicators for Chinese Cities

Based on international and Chinese experience with low-carbon city indicators and based on Chinese cities' emission sources and determinant factors, it is possible to determine a list of low-carbon indicators that may serve as an initial guide for review and discussion. While more research and experience are needed in this area and later editions of this book will continue to compile the emerging knowledge, the following indicators can determine progress toward a low-carbon trajectory:

- *Carbon emissions:* emissions per capita and emission intensity
- *Energy:* energy consumption per capita, energy intensity, and share of renewable energy
- *Green buildings:* energy consumption per square meter in commercial and residential buildings
- *Sustainable transport:* share of green transport mode trips (percentage of citizens walking, cycling, or taking public transport)
- *Smart urban form:* population density and mixed land use.

The indicators match the key sectors identified in the initial pilots of GHG abatement cost curves in China, cover the main determinants for cities' carbon footprints, and are in line with Chinese government and city priorities. Data for monitoring these indicators are generally available or relatively easy to collect through periodic surveys or focus groups.

These quantitative indicators need to be complemented with a series of qualitative indicators dealing with policy, regulations, and standards. Table 1.2 in chapter 1 presents a list of policy tools for local-level action on climate change, and to determine the progress of a low-carbon city action plan, "Yes/No" indicators for each of the selected policy tools could be used. These policies range from land zoning and building codes, to energy efficiency and clean energy standards, as well as green transport policies (congestion pricing, parking fees) and municipal finance frameworks that promote low-carbon urban growth.

Comparison of Low-Carbon Indicators in Chinese and International Cities

To better understand where Chinese cities stand today among global leading cities in terms of the low-carbon cities' indicators selected above, and to set realistic expectations for the future, table 3.1 compares the value of these indicators in different cities around the world.

Step Three: Designing and Implementing a Low-Carbon City Action Plan

After cities develop a vision and set low-carbon targets and indicators, effective and innovative policies and implementation strategies are needed to make them a reality. This will need to involve an integrated multisector approach promoting green energy on demand and supply sides, sustainable transport, and compact urban design.

The following chapters of this book will discuss in greater detail the experiences, lessons, and key recommendations for a number of sectors including energy (consumption and production), transport, urban design, municipal services (district heating, water, wastewater, and solid waste), and buildings. This section will therefore not attempt to present specific examples of low-carbon policies and programs. In general, however, a low-carbon city action plan would have the following characteristics:

- Have a multisectoral perspective on low-carbon development based on a quantitative analysis of the city's abatement potential in all key sectors of urban life.

Table 3.1   Comparison of Chinese and International Cities Using Selected Low-Carbon City Indicators

Category	Key low-carbon city indicators	Chinese cities		Global cities	
CO_2	CO_2 emissions per capita (tCO₂e/capita)[a]	• Chongqing:	3.7	• Stockholm:	3.6
		• Beijing:	10.1	• Tokyo:	4.9
		• Tianjin:	11.1	• Singapore:	7.9
		• Shanghai:	11.7	• London:	9.6
				• New York:	10.5
	CO_2 intensity (tCO₂e/million US$)[a]	• Chongqing:	535	• Stockholm:	71[b]
		• Shanghai:	1,063	• Copenhagen:	95[b]
		• Beijing:	1,107	• Hong Kong SAR:	102
		• Tianjin:	2,316	• Tokyo:	146
				• London:	162
				• New York:	173
Energy	Energy consumption per capita (gigajoules/capita)[c]	• Beijing:	80	• London:	78[b]
		• Tianjin:	90	• Copenhagen:	81[b]
		• Shanghai:	93	• Oslo:	95[b]
				• Stockholm:	105[b]
				• New York:	129
	Energy intensity (megajoules/US$)[c]	• Shanghai:	8.5	• London:	1.3[b]
		• Beijing:	8.8	• Copenhagen:	1.4[b]
		• Tianjin:	18.7	• Stockholm:	2.0[b]
				• New York:	2.1
				• Singapore:	6.3
	Share of renewable energy [d]	• Beijing: 4% by 2010		• Oslo:	65%[b]
		• Tianjin Binhai Eco-city: 20% by 2020		• Stockholm:	20%[b]
		• China national average: 8% now and 15% by 2020		• Copenhagen:	19%[b]
				• London:	1.2%[b]
Transport	Share of green transport mode (percentage of citizens walking, cycling, or taking public transport to work)[d]	• Shanghai:	56%	• Stockholm:	93%[b]
		• Beijing:	64%	• Hong Kong SAR:	84%
		• Tianjin:	92%	• Copenhagen:	68%[b]
				• São Paulo:	66%
				• London:	63%[b]
Land use	Population density (people/hectare)[e]	• Shanghai:	286	• Seoul:	322
		• Tianjin:	228	• Singapore:	107
		• Beijing:	145	• New York:	80
				• London:	62

Sources: a. World Bank 2010a; b. European Green City Index 2009; c. Authors' calculation based on World Bank 2010a, Sugar et al. 2012, City of New York 2010, and Singapore Department of Statistics 2010; d. Baeumler et al. 2009; and e. Bertaud and Malpezzi 2003.

- Use a balance between investments and policies, as some of the most effective actions at the city level depend on clear regulations and signals to the market and individuals that would lead them to greater resource efficiencies and lower carbon footprints.
- Use an interagency coordinating platform, to ensure that both actions at the sectoral level and cross-sectoral programs are implemented effectively and with clear line agency responsibilities.
- Be fully costed and have a clear financing plan indicating local, national, and international sources (see also chapters 24 and 25).
- Be integrated into other planning documents and programs, including the city's Five-Year Plan, its urban master plan, and sectoral agency plans and programs.
- Be widely disseminated in a manner that builds a coalition of action for low-carbon growth with private enterprises and city residents.

Step Four: Measuring Progress: Monitoring, Verification, and Reporting

To follow their low-carbon action plans and successfully achieve low-carbon targets, cities should establish mechanisms to measure and track GHG emissions. Monitoring, verification, and reporting of GHG emissions require institutional systems at the city, national, and—in some cases—international levels.

Conducting regular citywide inventory of GHG emissions requires a consistent methodology, robust data collection, transparency, and inventories that must be replicable and consistent over time for effective longitudinal comparisons. Specific recommendations for an institutional measuring and reporting system are to:

- *Use a globally recognized inventory methodology:* Many organizations have published methodologies for citywide GHG inventories, and some have online tools to assist with calculations (see Bader and Bleischwitz 2009; Kennedy et al. 2009). While each methodology has benefits and drawbacks, following a globally recognized methodology ensures long-term consistency and transparency.
- *Set up a robust data collection system:* This is one of the most important aspects of a measuring and reporting system because a GHG inventory is only as good as the data used in calculations. Working with energy and municipal service providers is an effective way to obtain quality activity data, such as electricity consumption, fossil fuel consumption,

and waste production. Consistency in data collection over time ensures consistency in inventory calculations.

- *Conduct a baseline inventory:* A baseline inventory provides a benchmark to which subsequent inventories are compared. It can also provide insight into which sectors to target for emissions reduction strategies and sustainability goals.
- *Conduct inventories regularly:* Conducting GHG inventories every year or every two years will highlight progress on sustainability targets. If applicable, variations in methodology or data collection from year to year must also be reported to ensure long-term accurate comparisons.
- *Report and verify inventory results:* Inventories should be open to verification and academic review by the international community.

Many cities around the world have started to conduct initial baseline inventories (Kennedy et al. 2009). Some, such as New York City, have made sustainability a top priority and their city governments have instituted policies mandating the regular measuring and reporting of GHG emissions (box 3.5). Tokyo has even gone a step further: the city government has established a mandatory monitoring, reporting, and cap-and-trade system for high-emitting commercial buildings. In the United States, California has developed a calculator tool to allow individuals, households, businesses, and cities to calculate, benchmark, and take action on their carbon footprints (see box 3.6).

Box 3.5

New York: An Example of GHG Inventory and Reporting

The New York City Mayor's Office of Long-term Planning and Sustainability (NYC-MO) is responsible for measuring, updating, and reporting New York's GHG emission inventory. The inventory is based on the draft International Local Government GHG Emissions Analysis Protocol, the draft Local Government Operations Protocol (LGOP), and the Greenhouse Gas Protocol of the World Resources Institute and World Business Council for Sustainable Development.

To gather the data, the NYCMO collects original activity data from utility companies and municipal agencies, and the city also hires consultants to compile and process data. NYCMO staff calculate final emission data with assistance from ICLEI.

(continued next page)

Box 3.5 *(continued)*

The methodologies that are used have been reviewed and endorsed by the U.S. Environmental Protection Agency, by Consolidated Edison (or ConEd), and by the New York Power Authority. In addition, the NYCMO also developed its own vehicle fuel economy coefficients to better reflect the actual fuel economy of automobiles registered in New York City. Since GHG emissions accounting is an evolving process, the NYCMO updates its protocols each year, revising methodologies and improving the accuracy of data to improve the quality of its GHG emissions inventory.

In early 2008, New York passed the Local Law 22, which mandates annual updates of the inventory. Since the first release of the inventory in 2007, three annual updates have been released and made available online. The inventory assists New York City in tracking progress toward achieving its emission reduction targets and also helps inform policies to more effectively and efficiently reduce city-level GHG emissions.

Source: City of New York, *Inventory of New York City Greenhouse Gas Emissions, September 2010*, by Jonathan Dickinson and Rishi Desai. Mayor's Office of Long-Term Planning and Sustainability, New York, 2010.

Box 3.6

The CoolClimate Network: A University-Government-Industry Partnership Developing Carbon Footprint Management Tools

The CoolClimate Network Consortium is a membership program within the Renewable and Appropriate Energy Lab at UC Berkeley supporting research and development of advanced carbon footprint management tools for households, small businesses, and communities in the United States and internationally.

The CoolClimate program includes a variety of projects ranging from the CoolClimate Calculators to the Climate Action Widgets. The CoolClimate Calculators are the first and still some of the only online carbon footprint calculators to include benchmarking, carbon footprint estimates, and quantified recommendations. The CoolClimate Calculator measures carbon impacts of specific transportation choices and energy use, but also includes impacts related to water, waste,

(continued next page)

Box 3.6 *(continued)*

food, goods, and services for both households and businesses. These indirect sources of emissions account for more than 50 percent of the total carbon footprint of a typical household in the United States.

Benchmarking is an important underlying feature in all CoolClimate tools, as it shows users how their level of emissions compared to groups of similar size or character. Without meaningful comparisons among households or businesses, even the best footprint analysis is just a collection of numbers.

For mayors and policy makers, location-specific benchmark values rank emissions from each category—transportation, housing, food, goods, and services—for each city or region. This is essential for good carbon management, as the size and composition of carbon footprints can vary dramatically from place to place. For example, in California, with its moderate climate and relatively clean electricity production, household electricity accounts for only about 5 percent of total average household carbon footprints, while motor vehicles account for nearly 40 percent. In other U.S. states, emissions from electricity and other forms of household energy are larger than emissions from motor vehicles. Within each region, emissions profiles also vary from one household to the next. For high-income households, air transportation is an important source of emissions, while for low-income households food is a bigger overall contributor. This means that different actions should be prioritized for different target groups, based on the analysis, if policy makers and program developers want to have the greatest impact.

Differences in households' carbon footprints are even more pronounced between different countries. A Brazilian version of the CoolClimate calculator being developed by *Amigos da Terra* shows that meat consumption, due to its relationships with Amazonian deforestation, is the single largest contributor to household carbon footprints, far greater than household energy or transportation.

Source: http://coolclimate.berkeley.edu.

In addition to city-level inventories, global cooperation in reporting and verification of GHG emissions is necessary for coordinated efforts towards sustainability. While the United Nations Framework Convention on Climate Change (UNFCCC) hosts a verification and reporting system for GHG emissions from nations, a global system for cities does not yet exist. The International Standard for Reporting GHG Emissions from Cities (UNEP et al. 2010) is a first step toward it.

Conclusion

The characteristics, indicators, and roadmap presented in this chapter can serve as guidance for Chinese cities seeking to become low carbon. To avoid the high-carbon paths pursued by developed cities during their early development stages, Chinese cities should adopt best urban practices and a comprehensive multisector approach, and progress to using the most advanced technologies. Chinese cities that want to earn the "low carbon" label should aim higher than the national government's targets to reduce their carbon intensity, and have the ambition to even reverse the current upward emissions trend within 15 to 20 years. The window of opportunity is closing fast.

Most important, a city should know its own carbon footprint. This provides a baseline against which progress can be measured and helps direct an effective action plan by providing information on the level and source of emissions. Next, a city should develop an overall vision and set a low-carbon target. An ambitious vision is a key characteristic of a low-carbon city and can ensure not only decoupling growth from carbon emissions but also, relatively quickly, reversing the upward GHG emission trend. A city must also develop and implement a low-carbon city action plan with effective innovative policies and targeted financing. Finally, a city must carefully monitor progress to ensure it remains on track and the low-carbon city becomes a reality.

Notes

1. Sustainable development here is defined as the "ability to use natural resources in order to meet the essential needs of people for the present and future generations, improving life quality" (UN WCED 1987).

2. The analysis of the city-level emission profiles in this section is based on the International Standard for Reporting GHGs from Cities developed by UNEP, UN-HABITAT, and the World Bank. This methodology primarily accounts for production-based emissions, rather than consumption-based emissions (see section 4.1) and thereby inherently penalizes cities with energy-intensive industries.

3. In Rizhou, for example, 99 percent of households in the central district installed solar water heaters due to a mandatory municipal requirement.

4. In most cases, four categories of emissions are required to be reported: (i) energy (including stationary and mobile fossil fuel combustion), (ii) industrial processes, (iii) agriculture, forestry, and other land uses (AFOLU), and (iv) waste.

5. Chapter 5 presents options for a city to "green" its energy supply.

Bibliography

Australian Conservation Foundation. 2010. Sustainable Cities Index-Ranking Australia's 20 Largest Cities in 2010. http://www.acfonline.org.au.

Bader, N., and R. Bleischwitz. 2009. "Study Report: Comparative Analysis of Local GHG Inventory Tools." Veolia Environment Institute. http://www.institut. veolia.org/ive/ressources/documents/2/491,Final-report-Comparative-Analysis-of.pdf.

Baeumler, A., M. Chen, A. Dastur, Y. Zhang, R. Filewood, K. Al-Jamal, C. Peterson, and M. Ranade. 2009. "Sino-Singapore Tianjin Eco-City (SSTEC): a Case Study of an Emerging Eco-City in China." World Bank TA Report, November 2009. Washington, DC: World Bank.

Bai, X., A. Wieczorek, S. Kaneko, S. Lisson, and A. Contreras. 2009. "Enabling Sustainability Transitions in Asia: The Importance of Vertical and Horizontal Linkages." *Technological Forecasting & Social Change* 76(2): 255–66.

Bertaud, A., and A. Malpezzi. 2003. "The Spatial Distribution of Population in 48 World Cities: Implications for Economics in Transition." Wisconsin Real Estate Department Working Paper. Madison.

Business Courier. 2010. "US Green City Index." *American City Business Journals.* http://www.bizjournals.com/cincinnati/datacenter/green_cities.html.

China Dialogue. 2010. "From Sham to Reality," an article by Liu Jianqiang basd on an interview with Jiang Kejun. November 3. http://www.chinadialogue. net/article/show/single/en/3916-From-sham-to-reality.

Chinese Society for Urban Studies. 2010. *China's Low Carbon Eco-City Development Strategy.* Edited by Chinese Society for Urban Studies, published by China City Press.

City of Copenhagen. 2009. *The Copenhagen Climate Plan: The Short Version Draft.* http://www.c40cities.org/docs/ccap-copenhagen-030709.pdf.

City of Issaquah. Issaquah Sustainable City Indicators. http://www.ci.issaquah. wa.us/Page.asp?NavID=1852.

City of London. 2010. *Delivering London's Energy Future: The Mayor's Draft Climate Change Mitigation and Energy Strategy for Consultation with the London Assembly and Functional Bodies.* February 2010. http://www.london. gov.uk/climatechange/sites/climatechange/staticdocs/Delivering_Londons_ Energy_Future.pdf.

City of New York. 2010. *PlaNYC Progress Report 2010.* New York, NY: Mayor's Office of Long-Term Planning and Sustainability. http://www.nyc.gov/ planyc2030.

The Climate Group. December 2010. *China Clean Revolution Report III: Low Carbon Development in Cities.* http://www.theclimategroup.org/publications/2010/12/6/china-clean-revolution-report-iii-low-carbon-development-in-cities/.

Coplák, J. 2003. "The Conceptual Framework of the EU Project ECOCITY." *ALFA-SPECTRA* 2(10). http://www.ecocity.szm.com/framework.html.

Dai, Yixin. 2009. *Analysis on the Necessity and Management Pattern of Emerging Low Carbon City in China.* China Population Resource and Environment, March 2009 (in Chinese).

Darido, G., M. Torres-Montoya, and S. Mehndiratta. 2009. "Urban Transport and CO_2 Emissions: Some Evidence from Chinese Cities." Working paper. World Bank, Washington, DC.

Dhakal, S. 2004. "Urban Development and Transportation Energy Demand: Motorisation in Asian Cities." Used in a presentation by Naoko Doi, 22 August 2005. APERC Workshop at the EWG30: APEC Energy Future. http://www.ieej.or.jp/aperc/pdf/urbanisation.pdf.

———. 2009. "Urban Energy Use and Carbon Emissions from Cities in China and Policy Implications." *Energy Policy* 37(11): 4208–19.

Dickinson, J., and R. Desai. 2010. *City of New York, Inventory of New York City Greenhouse Gas Emissions, September 2010.* New York, NY: Mayor's Office of Long-Term Planning and Sustainability.

Energy Efficiency Office of the Electrical and Mechanical Services Department, Hong Kong SAR, China. 2010. "Consultancy Study on the Development of Energy Consumption Indicators and Benchmarks for Selected Energy-consuming Groups in Hong Kong." http://202.155.228.28/energy2/introduction.htm.

Esty, D., M. Levy, T. Srebotnjak, and A. Sherbinin. 2005. *Environmental Sustainability Index: Benchmarking National Environmental Stewardship.* New Haven: Yale Center for Environmental Law & Policy.

Forum for the Future. 2008. *The Sustainable Cities Index—Ranking the Largest 20 British Cities.* http://www.forumforthefuture.org.

Gatewood, R. 2009. "America's First Eco-Sustainable City Destiny, Florida." *AIP Conference Proceedings* 1157: 174–83.

Global City Indicators Facility, www.cityindicators.org.

Hawksworth, J., T. Hoehn, and A. Tiwari. 2009. "Which Are the Largest City Economies in the World and How Might This Change by 2025?" In PwC (PricewaterhouseCoopers), *UK Economic Outlook November 2009*: 20–34. http://www.bus.wisc.edu/realestate/documents/Complete%20Spatial%20Distribution%20of%20Population%20in%202050%20World%20Ci.pdf.

Intergovernmental Panel on Climate Change (IPCC). 2006. *2006 IPCC Guidelines for National Greenhouse Gas Inventories.* The National Greenhouse Gas Inventories Programme. Japan: IGES.

International Association of Public Transport (UITP). 2005. *Mobility in Cities Database (2001).*

Jing, F., and T. Yu. 2008. "Half of New Buildings Fail Energy Standards." *China Daily,* January 2008.

Kennedy, C., A. Ramaswami, S. Carney, and S. Dhakal. 2009. "Greenhouse Gas Emission Baselines for Global Cities and Metropolitan Regions." Commissioned research paper presented at the 5th Urban Research Symposium, June 28–30, 2009, Marseilles, France. World Bank, Washington, DC.

Lam, S., and T. Toan. 2006. "Land Transport Policy and Public Transit in Singapore." *Transportation* 33(2): 171–88.

Langdon, D. 2007. *Cost of Green Revisited: Reexamining the Feasibility and Cost Impact of Sustainable Design in the Light of Increased Market Adoption.* http://www.davislangdon.com.

Lee, H., A. MacGillivray, P. Begley, and E. Zayakova. 2010. *The Climate Competitiveness Index 2010: National Progress in the Low Carbon Economy.* AccountAbility. http://www.climatecompetitiveness.org/images/CCI_Download_Main_Report_PDF/cci-exec-summary.pdf.

Local Governments for Sustainability (ICLEI). 2009. *International Local Government GHG Emissions Analysis Protocol (IEAP), Version 1.0 (October 2009).* http://www.iclei.org/index.php?id=ghgprotocol.

Low Carbon Cities Development Index. http://www.lowcarbondevelopmentindex.net.

McKinsey & Company. 2009. *China's Green Revolution: Prioritizing Technologies to Achieve Energy and Environmental Sustainability.* http://www.mckinsey.com/locations/greaterchina/mckonchina/reports/china_green_revolution.aspx.

New York City Department of City Planning Transportation Division. 2010. *Peripheral Travel Study.* New York, NY. http://www.nyc.gov/html/dcp/html/transportation/td_peripheral_study.shtml.

Padeco. 2010. *Cities and Climate Change Mitigation: Case Study on Tokyo's Emissions Trading System.* Report prepared for the World Bank. http://siteresources.worldbank.org/INTURBANDEVELOPMENT/Resources/336387-1226422021646/Tokyo_ETS_Padeco.pdf.

Schipper, L. 2007. *Automobile Fuel, Economy and CO_2 Emissions in Industrialized Countries: Troubling Trends through 2005/6.* Washington, DC: EMBARQ, the World Resources Institute Center for Sustainable Transport.

Shields, K., and H. Langer. 2009. *European Green City Index.* Economist Intelligence Unit. www.eiu.com.

Siemens AG. Green City Index. http://www.siemens.com/greencityindex.

Singapore Department of Statistics. 2010. Gas and Electricity Sales, *2010 Yearbook of Statistics Singapore.*

Singapore General Household Survey. 2005. "Statistical Release 2: Transport, Overseas Travel, Households and Housing Characteristics." http://www.sing-stat.gov.sg/pubn/popn/ghsr2.html.

Skea, J., and S. Nishioka. 2008. "Policies and Practices for a Low-carbon Society." Editorial. National Institute for Environmental Studies. *Climate Policy* 8 (2008) S5–S16. http://www.earthscan.co.uk/Portals/0/Files/Sample%20 Chapters/9781844075942.pdf.

Stanley, C., and T. Yip. 2008. *Planning for Eco-Cities in China: Visions, Approaches, and Challenges.* International Society of City and Regional Planners (ISOCARP), 44th Congress, Dalian, China, September 19–23.

STAR Community Index. ICLEI. http://www.icleiusa.org/sustainability/star-community-index.

Sugar, L., C. Kennedy, and E. Leman. 2012. "Greenhouse Gas Emissions from Chinese Cities." *Journal of Industrial Ecology*, under review.

Sustain Lane. 2008. U.S. City Rankings 2008. http://www.sustainlane.com/us-city-rankings.

Sustainable Development Indicators. 2010. http://www.defra.gov.uk/sustainable/ government/progress.

Tokyo Metropolitan Government. 2010. "Tokyo Cap-and-Trade Program: Japan's First Mandatory Emissions Trading Scheme." http://www2.kankyo.metro. tokyo.jp/sgw/e/data/Tokyo-cap_and_trade_program-march_2010_TMG.pdf.

United Nations Environment Program (UNEP), The United Nations Human Settlements Programme (UN-HABITAT), and the World Bank. 2010. "International Standard for Determining Greenhouse Gas Emissions." World Urban Forum, Brazil, March 2010.

United Nations Division for Sustainable Development. 2007. *Indicators of Sustainable Development: Guidelines and Methodologies.* http://www.un.org/ esa/sustdev/natlinfo/indicators/guidelines.pdf.

United Nations World Commission on Environment and Development (UN WCED). 1987. *Our Common Future (Brundtland Report).* New York, NY: United Nations.

Urban China Initiative. 2010. *City Sustainable Development Index: a New Tool for Measuring Chinese Cities.* 2010. http://urbanchinainitiative.typepad.com/ files/usi.pdf.

U.S. Green Building Council, the Congress for the New Urbanism, and Natural Resources Defense Council. 2009. *Leadership in Environmental and Energy Design (LEED) for Neighborhood Development.* http://www.cnu.org/leednd.

Wang, K. 2010. *A Low-Carbon Green City Project in Korea.* Korea Research Institute for Human Settlement. http://unpan1.un.org/intradoc/groups/public/documents/UNGC/UNPAN041663.pdf.

Williams, B. 2007. "Statement by Brian Williams, Chief Energy and Transport Section, Nairobi, Kenya" To: UN-HABITAT, United Nations Human Settlements Programme, UN Commission on Sustainable Development, 15th Session, New York, 30 April–11 May 2007. http://www.unhabitat.org/downloads/docs/4756_78604_STATEMENT%20FOR%20CLIMATE%20CHANGE%20.pdf.

Willoughby, C. 2001. "Singapore's Motorization Policies 1960–2000." *Transport Policy* 8(2): 125–39.

World Bank. 2009a. *World Development Report 2010: Development and Climate Change.* Washington, DC: World Bank.

———. 2009b. *World Development Indicators 2009.* Washington, DC: World Bank.

———. 2010a. *Cities and Climate Change: An Urgent Agenda.* Washington, DC: World Bank.

———. 2010b. *A City-Wide Approach to Carbon Finance.* Washington, DC: World Bank.

———. 2010c. *City GHG Emissions per Capita Table.* Washington, DC: World Bank.

World Wildlife Fund (WWF) Living Planet Index. http://wwf.panda.org/about_our_earth/all_publications/living_planet_report.

CHAPTER 4

Developing Low-Carbon Cities in China: Local Governance, Municipal Finance, and Land-Use Planning—The Key Underlying Drivers

Zhi Liu and Andrew Salzberg

Overview

This chapter addresses three important topics related to the development of low-carbon cities—local governance, municipal finance, and urban land-use planning. In China, the interaction of these three systems creates dramatic, unique challenges for the low-carbon city agenda. Crucially, the system of municipal finance developed over the last 15 years—where land concessions form an important source of off-budget revenues—has created strong financial incentives for local governments to develop excessive quantities of scattered urban land, at low densities, exceeding the level justified by demand. Addressing these challenges will form an essential element of any successful low-carbon city agenda in China.

Introduction

The three topics described in this chapter are closely interrelated, and all contribute in shaping China's urban form. Consequently, this chapter treats these three topics together, focusing on their interrelationships and their crucial links to the development of low-carbon cities in China.

The first topic is local governance. Low-carbon cities are a global public good, but they also have the potential to generate significant public benefits at the local level, in the form of increased energy efficiency, reduced environmental degradation, and improved quality of urban life. The role, responsibilities, and effectiveness of local public institutions are indispensable to achieving these outcomes. These institutions work by setting objectives; building consensus; making policy; developing, financing, and implementing strategies and plans; enabling the beneficial activities of the free market; coordinating with stakeholders; managing risks; safeguarding public interests; and monitoring the achievement of objectives.

Municipal finance—the second topic—is also significant, in that it underpins the institutional capacity for public policy implementation. The development of low-carbon cities will require extensive long-term public interventions. However, this will not be possible without sustainable municipal finance mechanisms. In China, municipal finance has over the last 15 years interacted with urban development in a unique and sometimes dramatic fashion. The conversion of farmland to urban use has been driven by more than simply rapid urbanization; this process has also served as a crucial extrabudgetary source of municipal revenues. As a result, farmland conversion through land concessions has created strong financial incentives for local governments to develop excessive quantities of scattered urban land, at low densities, well beyond the level justified by demand.

Finally, the third topic, urban land-use planning, also plays an important role. Planning practice in China today is often overwhelmed by the rapid pace of development: approval of a master plan can take many years, by which time it is already well out of date. In addition, the existing system of checks and balances is generally insufficient to ensure that master plans, when approved, are not arbitrarily modified by local government officials.

The interaction of these three factors has major consequences for China in a number of areas, especially the effect on the development of urban form. This is crucial to the low-carbon city agenda. Empirical evidence from international and domestic studies suggests that differing urban forms (measured in terms of residential densities, job concentration, and mix of land uses) require different amounts of land for accommodating similar levels of population and activities, result in different levels of energy consumption, and generate widely varying CO_2 emissions per capita. Overall, our analysis argues that the existing system of Chinese municipal governance, finance, and planning has a detrimental effect on the development of low-carbon urban form. A successful low-carbon city agenda in China will need to include reform of this system.

Municipal Governance, Finance, and Planning in Chinese Cities

The Role of Governments

A low-carbon city involves a range of choices: what economic goods and services a city produces, what municipal infrastructure services are provided, and what goods and services are consumed by urban households. While businesses, households, and individuals are all involved, governments will play a major role in guiding the process.

The role of the Chinese central government is to establish broad national policies and targets. National policies for urbanization, rural-to-urban land conversion, energy saving, and CO_2 emission reduction all are relevant to the development of low-carbon cities.

The central government also has crucial review and guidance roles essential to support this development. The central government reviews and approves urban master plans for major cities, mega-investment projects, and applications for rural-to-urban land conversion. Moreover, the central government provides technical guidelines and standards for cities in specific areas such as public transport and public utility services. Direct financial support is limited to intergovernmental transfers to provincial and municipal governments, primarily in less-developed provinces.

At the local level, municipal governments are all-purpose governments. Unlike traditional Western local governments, they are responsible for the local economy and employment, as well as the provision and management of municipal services. Their wide-ranging responsibilities make them well positioned to lead the development of low-carbon cities, although obstacles remain. The past two decades of urban development experience have demonstrated that most Chinese cities have the capacity to make decisions and implement them quickly. However, a number of institutional deficiencies have also been exposed in the difficult trade-offs between short-term economic growth and long-term environmental sustainability. Experience to date demonstrates that short-term economic growth is often given priority over long-term environmental sustainability. Developing low-carbon cities in China will pose a major challenge for China's urban institutions.

Some critical questions need to be addressed. Do cities have the right incentives to make strategic decisions that do not compromise the long-term interests of their citizens, the country as a whole, and the international community? Is there an adequate governance mechanism to ensure that strategic decisions that are aligned with these interests are made and implemented? Are the available financial means adequate and sustainable in the long term? Is current city planning practice adequate for addressing the issues stemming from rapid urbanization in a low-carbon framework? The following sections will examine these questions in the context of China's decentralized government framework.

Decentralization, Local Incentives, and Accountability

China's urbanization over the last 30 years, during which hundreds of millions of people migrated to cities, is unprecedented in human history. During this same period, demand for urban services has grown rapidly with the increase in personal income of urban dwellers. Overall, most municipal governments have accommodated the new urban population and met this rapidly increasing demand for urban services. Almost all cities—large and small—have gone through a dramatic transformation and modernization of their cityscape within the short span of only a generation. High-rise office buildings, industrial parks, modern residential compounds, shopping malls, wide boulevards, landmark structures, ecological parks, artificial lakes, and wastewater treatment plants are now common urban landscapes across the country. However, many problems have also emerged throughout the process—wasteful investment, excessive conversion of agricultural land for urban construction, degradation of the environment, and neglect of adverse social impacts, to name only the most prominent. All of these will have to be addressed if cities are ultimately to transfer to a low-carbon development path.

Both China's spectacular achievements and significant challenges in the area of urban development are closely connected to the country's decentralized governance structure, which has devolved a range of functional and fiscal responsibilities from the national to subnational governments, particularly municipalities. Decentralization was essential to China's economic reform as it progressed from its formerly rigid centralized management system. Under the decentralized system, urban development is considered a local concern, and municipal governments assume primary responsibility—both functional and fiscal—for it.

The responsibilities of the national government are limited to the review and approval of urban master plans and large urban infrastructure investment projects, setting technical standards and policy guidance, promoting knowledge exchange, and facilitating capacity building.[1] However, the increasingly rapid economic and spatial changes at the local level are making it increasingly difficult for the national government to exercise guidance and control in a timely manner. The effectiveness of the national government in policy management is seriously compromised by the limited national budget available for urban development. Given the large number of localities, central monitoring and supervision is often inadequate at the local level where policy implementation is carried out. To some extent, this situation creates an institutional void in addressing the spillover effects of urban development, such as energy security and CO_2 emissions, which are largely national and even international concerns more than they are strictly local.

The existence and growth of these spillover effects justify a reconsideration of the role of the national government in urban development. The development of low-carbon cities forms part of a national agenda. The co-benefits at the local level alone—such as energy saving, reduced environmental degradation, and better quality of urban life—will not be sufficient to warrant cities taking action on their own to develop low-carbon cities. Given the extra effort required at the city level to mitigate CO_2 emissions, additional momentum from the central government will be required. The central government has a strong track record for leading national policy implementation on other issues, but its role will have to be strengthened to fill this institutional void.

Significantly more will also have to be achieved at the municipal level. Decentralization is a long process and remains largely unfinished. Due to their transitional nature, municipal governments face a number of unprecedented management problems. Unlike mayors in many other countries, Chinese mayors are held accountable not only for the provision of urban public services, but also for the performance of the urban economy, investment, and employment. They all face difficult choices between rapid GDP growth and a more balanced, sustainable urban development.

Until very recently, the performance of mayors has been judged almost exclusively by annual urban GDP growth (see box 4.1). Since its economic reform that started in 1978, China's economic growth has relied heavily on exports and investment. As a result, cities compete fiercely for foreign direct investment (FDI) by improving urban infrastructure and offering land concessions. The incentive to rapidly improve urban infrastructure conditions is so strong that consideration of environmental sustainability and other long-term interests of city residents are seriously compromised. It is now well understood that the single-minded pursuit of GDP growth has caused substantial damage to the environment. A case in point is the excessive conversion of farmland that contributes to excessive urban sprawl, which will be discussed later in this chapter. Fortunately, this is beginning to change, due in part to the "green GDP" and "people-centered development" concepts recently promoted by the central government.[2] However, with the expected continuing pressure for GDP growth, there will be a time lag before cities incorporate these new concepts into on-the-ground practice.

Municipal Finance and Land Concessions

Over the last 15 years, China has experienced explosive urban growth and rapid increases in the demand for urban services. At the same time,

---

Box 4.1

Incentives for the Performance of Municipal Leaders

At the top of the leadership in every Chinese municipality are the municipal Communist Party secretary and the mayor. Both are mostly technocrats, rising to their positions through a merit-based promotion system. The party secretary is often appointed by the higher-level party organizations, and the mayor is nominated, elected, and confirmed by the local People's Congress. In general, the party secretary oversees the implementation of broad policy directions and intervenes when necessary, while the mayor is responsible for day-to-day executive functions. They are often drawn from technical and managerial backgrounds and have experience in line departments. Due to their technical competence, the publicity associated with good performance, and the opportunity for further promotion based on performance and tangible results, there is a strong sense and culture of competition—between leaders in a province or a region as well as across time. Mayors experience pressure to perform better than both preceding mayors and neighboring mayors. Successful municipal leaders are promoted quickly to positions of higher responsibility and seniority, creating strong incentives for performance. When performance is mainly measured by GDP growth, these incentives have led to a single-minded focus on GDP growth—a focus which is only now slowly beginning to change.

Source: Authors.

decentralization has shifted much of the responsibility for providing these services to local governments. In 1994 China adopted a Tax Sharing System that provides separate tax-collection powers for the central government and subnational governments over certain categories of taxes. Crucially, two main sources of municipal fiscal revenues for many countries—residential property tax and land value incremental tax—have not yet been widely imposed in China.[3]

The system is asymmetrically designed in the assignment of fiscal power and expenditures. The ratio of subnational revenues to the total revenues has averaged around 50 percent, while the ratio of local fiscal expenditures to the total remains high at about 70 percent. Local governments increasingly face the burden of rapidly growing expenditures without the power to raise tax revenues on the required scale.

This gap between limited municipal budgetary revenues and growing expenditures is generally filled by two sources of funds, depending on the economic status of the localities. One source of funds is fiscal transfers from the central government. One category of these transfers is general purpose transfers including revenue-sharing transfers and tax rebates (Shah and Shen 2006). These transfers are normally predictable by the localities. Another category is specific-purpose transfers mainly provided to a limited number of designated poor and rural localities. For most localities, all local revenues including central transfers are not sufficient to meet the expenditure needs, especially capital expenditures needed for urbanization and industrial development. The estimated needs for these capital expenditures could be excessive as they are mainly aimed at attracting business investments and jobs. The gap is then filled using off-budget funds. These include revenues from land concessions, borrowing through a municipal government-owned urban development investment corporation (UDIC), municipality-imposed surcharges, and, to a much lesser extent, public-private partnership (PPP) financing arrangements, or build-operate-transfer (BOT) schemes.

Under the Chinese Budget Law, municipal governments are allowed to borrow from commercial banks or raise funds from the capital market only under tightly controlled and limited circumstances.[4] To bypass this legal constraint, municipal governments establish UDICs, which are legally permitted to borrow. Many UDICs are given parcels of public land as starting assets. With these as collateral, UDICs are able to borrow on behalf of the municipal governments for infrastructure investments, some with revenue flows (such as tolled roads) and others without (such as urban streets). Some UDICs are created as a majority shareholder company for several municipally owned urban utility companies (that provide services such as water supply, district heating, and cooking gas supply) and thus generate cash flows. Others are simply fiscally backed, "empty-shell" companies that borrow for the municipal governments. The UDICs obtain commercial loans from commercial banks or policy loans from the China Development Bank. To date, banks have been more than willing to lend, as UDICs represent a large stream of business and municipal governments are assumed to be providing an implicit guarantee.

These off-budget funds have been instrumental in financing urban infrastructure and urban development over the last decade. However, rapid urbanization and income growth, compounded with market speculation, continue to drive up demand for housing and land. The municipal governments are increasingly under tremendous pressure to mobilize extra resources for the delivery of urban services. To meet financing needs, municipal governments mainly rely on the only sizable local resource available to them for appropriation—rural land within municipal boundaries.

Most Chinese municipalities cover a sizable geographic area, within which much of the land is rural. A typical municipality consists of a central city built-up area along with several suburban districts or suburban counties. Given that urban development is occurring so rapidly, these suburban districts and counties are a source of rural land for urban development needed to meet growing demand. Viewed from a different perspective, however, this land represents an enormous opportunity for municipal governments to generate off-budget revenues from land concessions under the guise of addressing urban development needs.

There are two ways to convert farmland into urban use. Both are related to the structure of land ownership in China. Urban land is state owned, with land-use rights transferrable through the market. Rural land is collectively owned by the villages and can be leased to other users.

One method of converting farmland into urban land is through land acquisition as part of a land acquisition plan based on an urban master plan. This process is closely monitored and supervised by the national government through the central Ministry of State Land and Resources. Municipal governments acquire rural land at low prices set by the state based on agricultural revenues and relocations costs, improve the land with urban infrastructure, and then sell or auction the serviced land to developers for property development. The revenues from land concessions are considerable, as the financial costs of land acquisition are low and the sale prices of serviced land-use rights are high. According to the

Ministry of Land and Resources, total revenues from land concessions nationwide amounted to RMB 2.7 trillion in 2010, or RMB 2,000 (or US$300) per capita.[5] This sizable revenue stream creates an enormous incentive for municipal governments to develop land, often on a scale that far outpaces real demand. This imbalance is far worse for smaller cities as they are not closely monitored by the central government (see also box 4.2). Recent media reports demonstrate the results of this with astounding pictures of ghost towns—completed but empty apartments and office complexes—built by some smaller municipalities (see figure 4.1).

The inflated expectation of property developers and investors in future increases in the value of developed land and properties—which fuels land development and concessions—also contributes to this process. It is understandable that developers become optimistic when they have witnessed sustained rapid growth in urban population, incomes, and property prices over the last two decades. Although the topic is still actively debated, a consensus is emerging that this has led to a significant bubble in Chinese real estate prices.[6] The optimism is also mirrored by the city master plans: the previous round of master plans of 99 major cities developed 10 years ago together had projected a total urban population of 2 billion by 2010 and 3 billion in 2020 (Wang and Tang 2005).

Box 4.2

Land Purchase and Disposal Cost Differentials

Compensation for land purchases from farmers is not provided at market values and is often much lower than the expected value and the income of local governments from the disposal price. Estimates based on the World Bank's "Sustainable Development on the Urban Fringe" study (World Bank 2007) suggest land is disposed, on average, at six to eight times the compensation cost, although multiples of 20–30 are not unusual and the number can be as high as 75. The report highlighted the specific case of Ganjingzi, which was to be incorporated into the Dalian urban boundaries. The land was resold between 1.2 and 7 times the compensation cost given to farmers. With the differential potentially so large, it is no coincidence that in many cities, land release provides a major part of municipal governmental incomes (around 30–60 percent or even more in some rapidly developing regions).

Source: World Bank 2007.

Figure 4.1   Empty Corridor in a Mostly Vacant Shopping Mall in the South of China

Source: Wikimedia Commons 2011.

This phenomenon is also driven by the fact that the performance of mayors is primarily measured by the rate of annual urban GDP growth, which in turn creates perverse incentives for land development. Due to the drive for GDP growth, the primary concern for mayors is attracting investment (especially FDI) and creating jobs. Every mayor has the same goal, and competition for FDI among cities is fierce. Cities race for infrastructure investment and provide various local incentives to investors. Infrastructure development is perceived by nearly every city as a win-win strategy. A good business environment for FDI requires quality infrastructure, and infrastructure development can be profitable for cities, not through direct revenues (such as user fees) but through associated land transactions and concessions. Enticed by improved infrastructure, FDI in manufacturing leads to new factories, industrial parks, and development zones, all requiring land.

It is now well understood that the widespread combination of land concessions and infrastructure investments through UDICs has helped generate significant amounts of local debt. These outstanding debts were estimated to be RMB 7 trillion in 2009.[7] This has caused serious concern about the potential impact of local debt to lead to financial crises, and prompted the central government to put a halt to the operations of the fiscally backed UDICs. Local debt management capacity is being developed in an increasing number of cities, some of which is supported by World Bank–funded technical assistance. It is hoped that UDIC reform and better local debt management can at least help to cool down wasteful land concessions and infrastructure investment.

The second method of converting rural land into urban land is through leasing rural land directly by suburban villages for residential or industrial development.[8] Many villages are located in the peripheries of urban built-up areas but outside planned and approved development zones (see box 4.3). With high demand for industrial and residential land, these villages become willing to lease their farmland for industrial and residential development. This development occurs outside of the urban land acquisition plan and outside of the supervision and monitoring of the municipal government. As such, the development is often fragmented and mostly unregulated. According to the analysis of the government, this type of farmland conversion contributes significantly to excessive, inefficient land use (Qiu 2008). This is a serious issue that needs to be addressed through broad land policy reform.

In summary, local governments' excessive reliance on off-budget funds is creating a wide range of problems. Lack of transparency and the resultant hidden financial liabilities are a major concern to the national gov-

---

Box 4.3

In-Situ Urbanization

Evidence of the "leapfrog" nature of urban development is the degree to which people become "urbanized" without relocating—known as "in-situ" urbanization. This occurs when existing villages are absorbed into expanding municipal boundaries. Estimates based on the World Bank's "Sustainable Development on the Urban Fringe" study (World Bank 2007) suggest that in-situ urbanization accounted for almost 40 percent of the growth in China's urban population during the 1990s. Given that the natural population increase in cities (the amount by which births exceed deaths) accounted for around 33 percent of this growth, "true" rural-urban migration accounted for only around 27 percent of the increase in urban population in the past decade.

Source: World Bank 2007.

ernment. In addition, for local governments, relying on off-budget funds such as land concessions is clearly not sustainable—the current rate of urban expansion that sustains this process cannot continue indefinitely. New and more stable sources of local revenues are needed. Unfortunately, property taxes, betterment charges, and municipal borrowing—important sources of funding for infrastructure in many developed cities—are either in their infancy or not permitted by law. In addition, private sector participation in infrastructure financing is still limited and is present in only a few sectors including water supply, wastewater treatment, and solid waste disposal.

Given the dramatic impact of this financing system on the nature of urban development in China, addressing these issues is essential to the ultimate creation of a planning and implementation framework that can support low-carbon growth in Chinese cities. The World Bank is currently providing technical assistance for local debt management. Clearly, however, this issue is national in scope and has an impact on many core aspects of Chinese urban policy. As such, addressing the issue of municipal finance goes beyond the scope of any single project, whether World Bank financed or otherwise. The current system of municipal finance is hindering efforts aimed at supporting low-carbon development, in both the short and long term.

Chinese Urban Planning Practice and Implementation

Compared with many developing countries, China has, in theory, a relatively rigorous urban planning process. However, it is far looser in implementation. Most master plans are not fully implemented within the time frame of the plan, which is usually 20 years. This is caused by two issues, both specific to China. First, cities have been growing at an unprecedented rate and most face major challenges in overcoming the inherent rigidity of the urban master plan to provide the flexibility necessary to accommodate the rapid population growth as well as the demand for urban services. Currently, the urban planning process produces a 20-year urban master plan, a 5-year implementation plan, and a number of associated sectoral master plans and implementation plans for a given planning area, defined by jurisdiction. But urbanization has occurred so rapidly that the actual urban population often exceeds the planned population target for the entire time horizon of the master plan (that is, 20 years), and the actual urban functional area expands beyond jurisdictional boundaries. Amendments to the approved master plan are often needed just a few years after the initial approval, but they are usually lengthy to prepare and take even longer for review and approval. In addition, despite the effort and time required, many newly inaugurated mayors seek to amend master plans to serve their new priorities.

This search for flexibility raises a second major issue—the lack of effective checks and balances to ensure municipal decisions take into consideration the long-term interests of urban residents and the national interest in low-carbon development. Currently, there is no viable system to hold decision makers responsible for the social and environmental consequences of their decisions. While planners diligently carry out their work, mayors often use the rapid pace of urban growth as a reason to deviate from the master plan to accommodate additional urban GDP growth. Rapidly growing demand for urban services invariably creates a sense of urgency, encouraging municipal governments to make decisions and take action quickly. Due to the lack of effective checks and balances, they often succeed in deviating from the master plan.

In theory, the urban planning and implementation process in China is kept in check by higher levels of government and the People's Congress of the city. However, higher level authorities—especially provincial governments—often share the cities' interest in GDP growth and the same sense of urgency for urban development, as provincial GDP comes mostly from cities. It is rare that the higher level authority directly confronts deviations from the master plan, especially in decisions related to business investment. The People's Congresses in many cities are increasingly fulfilling a supervisory role by checking the actions of the municipal government against plans, but they have neither sufficient technical capacity nor sufficient representation from all stakeholders to intervene. There is also no existing procedure for expert witness testimony over issues relating to the public interest in urban planning.

In recent years, the planning and implementation process has increasingly been opened up for inquiry and monitoring by the general public. This has helped, but more openness is critical. Increased transparency will not only help safeguard the interests of society, but also prevent uncontrolled rent-seeking behavior that frequently occurs in urban land use and real estate markets with undesirable consequences such as overspeculation and wasted resources. In short, it is essential to improve the current system of checks and balances to ensure sensible decisions are made on a broadly informed, transparent basis, and that sound plans are duly implemented. These challenges need to be addressed before low-carbon development can effectively be mainstreamed into the Chinese urban master planning process.

CO_2 Implications of Inefficiencies in China's Urban Land Use

As has been widely documented, the configuration of urban form can have a considerable impact on the generation of greenhouse gases (see figure 4.2 and box 4.4). In general terms, evidence suggests that urban sprawl— the rapid growth of low-density areas at the urban periphery—can lead to larger emissions through a variety of different mechanisms. First, low-density development tends to increase CO_2 emissions from urban transport through longer trip distances and a higher proportion of private motorized trips.[9] Second, low-density areas tend to provide a higher amount of living space per person, leading to higher emissions from home heating, cooling, and general power consumption (Norman MacLean, and Kennedy 2006). Finally, low-density development tends to produce infrastructure that is less intensively used than in dense urban cores, for example suburban highway access roads, thereby raising emissions per capita.

To a degree, this description of "sprawl" describes the economic aspirations of urban dwellers in developing countries, and the economic reality for many living in developed countries: a private home and the freedom of movement provided by a private automobile. However, large gaps between the emission profiles of cities in developed countries—Hong Kong SAR, London, New York, and Houston—suggest that high incomes

Figure 4.2   Urban Density and per Capita CO_2 Emissions from Transport

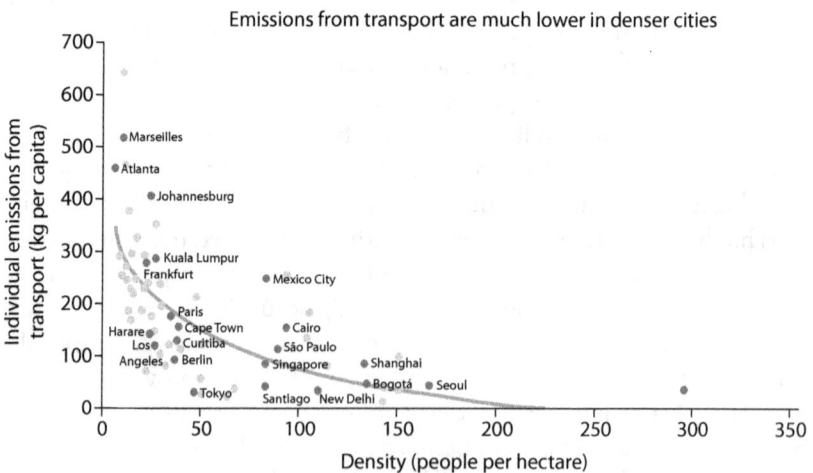

Emissions from transport are much lower in denser cities

x-axis: Density (people per hectare)
y-axis: Individual emissions from transport (kg per capita)

Source: World Bank 2009a.

Note: The figure does not correct for income because a regression of transport emissions on density and income reveals that density, not income, is a key factor. Data are for 1995.

Box 4.4

Empirical Evidence Regarding Urban Forms and CO_2 Emissions

A growing number of empirical studies on urban form (including density, land-use mix, public transport supply, and commuting distance, among other variables) and CO_2 emissions have been carried out. Although debate continues on some important points, a broad consensus is emerging that urban form can play a key role in mitigating GHG emissions. The findings of several studies are highlighted below.

According to an OECD study report edited by Kamal-Chaoui and Robert (2009), global city data show that a higher urban density (population per square kilometer) is generally associated with lower per capita electricity consumption.

Using a different city data set from the one used for figure 4.2, the same OECD study shows the similar pattern that higher urban density is associated with lower per capita transport CO_2 emissions.

A study by Brown and Logan (2008) examines the residential energy and carbon footprints of the 100 largest U.S. metropolitan areas and found that relatively more compact metropolitan areas have lower per capita residential carbon footprints.

A study by Magalhaes and Duran-Ortiz (2009) compares the fuel consumption and light vehicle carbon footprints between Brasilia and Curitiba. Brasilia was planned as a symbolic capital, with low densities, segregated land use, spatial stratification, and satellite towns. Curitiba is perhaps the world's best-known transit-oriented city. The study shows, unsurprisingly, that Curitiba has significantly lower annual average CO_2 emissions from light vehicles than Brasilia.

Evidence has also been produced comparing different neighborhoods within a given city. Evidence from Toronto (VandeWeghe and Kennedy 2007) suggests that residential emissions per capita in Toronto vary by as much as an order of magnitude between urban and suburban areas.

There remains some debate about the effect of moving from a monocentric to polycentric employment pattern on overall commute length and hence overall emissions. This debate is notably summarized in Jencks et al. (1996). In China, while there is clear evidence that peripheral employment locations have the potential to reduce commute times overall, they also induce a mode shift away from public transport. These effects have opposite effects on emissions—but the likely combined effect, in the opinion of the authors, is markedly increased emissions. Further research is needed on this topic in the Chinese context.

(continued next page)

Box 4.4 *(continued)*

Figure B4.4.1   Residential CO$_2$ Emissions in Toronto Vary by an Order of Magnitude from Central City to Suburb

| East-York, 1.3 tCO$_2$e/cap (residential only) | Etobicoke, 6.62 tCO$_2$e/cap (residential only) | Whitby, 13.02 tCO$_2$e/cap (residential only) |

Source: VandeWeghe and Kennedy 2007, images from Google Maps 2011.
Note: tCO$_2$e/cap = tonnes of CO$_2$ equivalent per capita (residential only).

Source: Authors.

and economic opportunity do not necessarily lead to uniform outcomes as measured by greenhouse gas (GHG) emissions per person.

The large difference in emissions between these cities certainly does not suggest that Houston can ever be transformed into Hong Kong SAR (or that its citizens would support such a change). Indeed, the largely fixed and irreversible nature of urban development suggests that increasing the density of new development in cities in the United States would have only a marginal impact on their overall energy consumption and emissions (TRB 2009). This evidence from U.S. cities, however, does not diminish the argument for dense development in Chinese cities. If anything, it argues for immediate action, while urban development is occurring rapidly and patterns are being set that will endure for the foreseeable future.

Indeed, Chinese cities are growing at an unprecedented rate, and how these cities are built now will have a long-lasting impact. Many cities have more than doubled their built-up area between 1990 and 2000, and the trend continued strongly in the 2000s. This expansion is likely to continue as the level of urbanization is projected to increase from 43 percent in 2005 to almost 60 percent by 2030. This translates into the addition of over 300 million people to the urban population in 25 years.

Unfortunately, urban growth in Chinese cities is occurring in a haphazard, inefficient, and unsustainable way, particularly at the urban periphery. The World Bank carried out an analysis of China's rapid spatial growth at the urban periphery in 2009 (World Bank 2009a). Due to the importance of this development to the achievement of low-carbon growth in Chinese cities, the major conclusions and evidence from this work have been summarized below.[10]

Several factors are leading to rapid growth at the Chinese urban periphery. First, a large number of urban migrants are moving to cities and settling at the urban fringe, where housing prices are more affordable than in central locations. Second, living standards are increasing rapidly and residential floor space per person has increased dramatically in large Chinese cities, forcing development outward. Third, the restructuring of the urban economy in response to globalization has broken down the self-contained *danwei*—live-work unit—creating a modern central business district and separate residential areas. Fourth, a rapid change from non-motorized and public transport modes to the private vehicle has pushed development outward. Finally, many industries have relocated from central districts to economic zones located at the fringe of urban areas.

Box 4.5

Urban Design Regulations in Chinese Cities: Taking a New Look

Chinese municipalities and the Chinese national government would benefit from a fresh but critical review of the urban land-use and design regulations at the municipal level, to identify practices that are not consistent with, or even detrimental to, low-carbon city development. In many Western countries, debates around sustainable land-use planning typically revolve around increasing densities (residents per square kilometer). In general, in Chinese cities, densities remain higher than all but the densest Western cities, even for new development. The primary issues then are related to design. The width and density of streets; the layout of buildings, lots, and sidewalks; and the design of other key features tend to reinforce a move away from walking as a convenient way for getting around, hampering efforts to lower overall carbon emissions.

One notable example of this type of regulation is building setback requirements. The setback is the required distance from the edge of a transport right-of-way (ROW) to the front edge of a permanent structure, such as an office, an apartment, or a retail building, outside of ROW. Different setbacks have been justified

(continued next page)

Box 4.5 *(continued)*

at different times for different purposes. Some early incarnations in the United States were designed to allow sufficient light and air into dense city blocks. In modern China, setbacks are often mandated in order to maintain a sufficient safety buffer zone from the transport infrastructure in case of natural disasters such as earthquakes, although most planners agree that there are engineering solutions to overcome these problems. In general, there are no clear technical guidelines for setting the size of setbacks. Municipal governments determine what is appropriate for their cities and specify the setback requirements in local regulations.

In the past, Chinese cities generally mandated setbacks ranging from 5 to 15 meters. In recent years, however, some cities have proposed setback requirements as large as 40 meters or more for primary arterial roads. There is no doubt about the kind of urban design that a setback of 40 meters creates: an urban environment that favors private car driving and that is unfriendly to public and non-motorized transport. As a point of reference, a typical Beijing *hutong,* many of which serve as thriving modern commercial arteries today, are no more than 5 to 6 meters across—from building face to building face. The comparable number for a large street with 40-meter setbacks would be well over 120 meters, a 20-fold increase. A critical examination of such land-use regulations is necessary and urgent at a time when high-density compact city development is much desired in China. Indeed, many American cities are beginning to eliminate their setback requirements altogether and replace them with "build-to" lines—where buildings are *required* to be close to the sidewalk to favor active streets and promote walking and cycling.

Figure B4.5.1   Setback Examples

Source: Wikimedia Commons, Geoff McKim.
Commercial street in Beijing with very small setbacks.

Source: Wikimedia Commons, Chen Si Yuan.
Successful American shopping street with very minimal setbacks.

Source: Authors.

In addition to these trends, a series of current policies is also hindering the efficient development of cities. They include the rigid protection of basic farmland (despite the policy's good intentions), incentives for municipalities to convert land to urban uses, limits on building intensity in central cities, and a lack of coordination between transport and land-use planning (see box 4.5). Each of these factors was examined in greater detail by the World Bank in the 2009 work (World Bank 2009a) and is summarized below.

- *Rigid protection of basic farmland:* This first factor relates to a key national government policy. The Chinese national government has strictly enforced a national policy on the preservation of basic farmland, designed to prevent the rapid loss of agricultural land. Unfortunately, this policy does not adequately distinguish between land contiguous to existing urban areas and isolated agricultural areas. As a result, farmland is converted in a haphazard manner, with leapfrog development often leaving large swaths of agricultural land between high-density urbanized pockets (see figure 4.3).
- *Incentives for converting land to urban uses:* As described above, the system of municipal finance provides strong incentives for cities to con-

Figure 4.3   Fragmented Urban Land Use at Zhengzhou Periphery

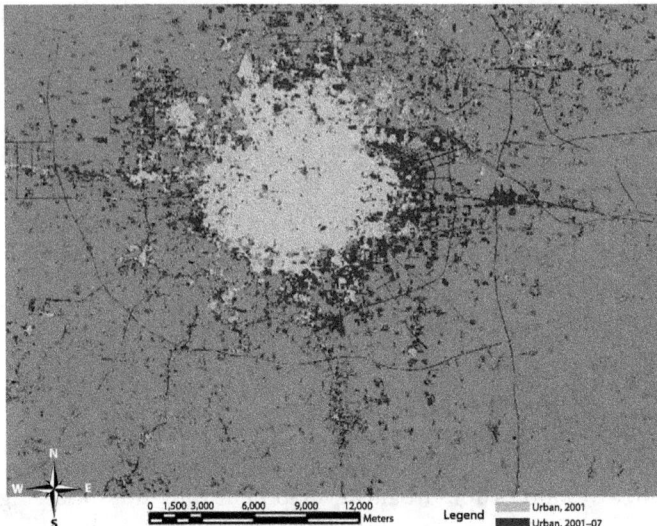

Source: World Bank 2009a.

vert agricultural to urban land. This creates substantial perverse incentives in terms of over-requisitioning. For example, a 2006 World Bank report concluded that the area of economic development zones in 2004 exceeded the total existing built-up area of the country (World Bank 2006). Industrial zones, which allow land to be taxed, are often provided in amounts far greater than what an efficient land market would supply—sometimes two to three times the industrial land area of cities with comparable economic bases. These sprawling land claims rapidly expand the urban periphery.

- *Limits on building intensity:* Contemporary Chinese planning practice also contributes to land-use inefficiencies. Density regulations have not been used effectively or to their full potential by most Chinese municipalities to encourage the efficient development of urban areas. In general, floor area ratio (FAR)—a measure of building density—is applied at the individual block or parcel level but often lacks a clear strategic policy direction. In general, density restrictions are too rigid in center cities, forcing development to the urban periphery and reinforcing the trends described above.

- *Lack of coordination between transport and land-use planning:* Planning practice also suffers from insufficient integration between land use and transport planning. Most noticeably, municipalities do not vary land-use density allocations in relation to infrastructure. For example, a rational land-use policy would ideally allow for higher density development near transit nodes, allowing the land market to capture the benefit of reduced travel times. This is not yet generally the case in China, although some cities are beginning to move in this direction.

These trends suggest that Chinese cities are currently on a path that does not support the overall goals of a low-carbon city. These policies are mutually reinforcing and move the city toward a more dispersed and less efficient urban spatial structure. Given that built form is highly durable, largely irreversible, or very costly to modify, existing trends could generate unsustainable costs in the future.

Agenda for Reforms

As the above diagnostic analysis indicates, China's cities are generally able to mobilize resources for urban development, but the emerging complexities of the urban economy and related demand for low-carbon development require forward-looking institutions that are adaptive to changes and capable of managing a sustainability and low-carbon agenda for their cities. At this stage of rapid development and social transformation, institutions are paramount. The issues analyzed above are, in general, well known to the Chinese central government. The institutional weaknesses—namely the institutional gulf between the national and municipal levels, and the inadequacies of incentives, accountability, municipal financing, and land-use planning at the local level—have been long recognized, but have not been systematically addressed through policy and institutional reforms. All these issues will need to be addressed if China is to succeed in accelerating low-carbon city development. Each is discussed below.

Strengthening the Role of Central Government
Within the decentralization framework, the central government may wish to strengthen its role in low-carbon city development to provide policy direction and reward good practice. This is an essential step to realign the incentives of municipal governments so that the long-term interests of the urban dwellers and the country as a whole are appropriately considered in the local decision-making process. While urban development should remain the primary responsibility of the local government, national budget support should be considered to encourage and reward best practices at the local level. Rewards from the central government—either moral or financial—can be a powerful tool for realigning the incentives of the municipal governments. In relation to the incentives created by the central government, a benchmarking and evaluation system for low-carbon urban development among cities should be established to monitor how cities are performing in urban development.

The central government could initiate and guide the deepening of municipal finance reform (especially the expansion of the local revenue base) and help create supportive conditions for municipal borrowing. Moreover, the national government has the opportunity to play a stronger role in creating and overseeing a low-carbon city planning process (content, procedure, consultation, and so forth) that is fully integrated into the existing urban master planning process. The national budget support proposed in this section should be linked to the successful implementation of the agreed planning process.

The central government may also consider developing a national low-carbon city development strategy, as a vehicle to finalize the details of the above recommendations and build a nationwide consensus on policy directions. It should be formulated in line with the national land, environment, and energy strategies. The strategy should be comprehensive, clarifying the key elements of low-carbon urban development and addressing issues relating to the roles and responsibilities, incentives, financing, implementation, monitoring, and enforcement mechanisms. It should also suggest specific policy directions for related urban development issues, including urban planning, land conservation, energy efficiency, building codes, urban transport, and motor vehicle CO_2 emission standards. The policy directions and the strategy could then be formally adopted after wide consultation, especially with a variety of municipal governments.

For the central government to assume a more effective role, it might consider supporting pilot demonstration programs at the local level.[11] The program would be based on a central/local partnership. The national government may develop technical guidelines for low-carbon cities under the framework set by the national low-carbon urban development strategy. A few cities could be selected to develop and implement their city-specific strategy, institutional reforms, and development projects in line with the national low-carbon city development strategy and policy directions. The program would be a test ground to demonstrate how low-carbon results can be achieved at the local level. National budget support for the program will be an important lever to encourage buy-in from the selected cities.

Improving Incentives and Accountability of Municipal Governments

Clearly, there is scope for improving the incentive structure of municipal governments. The performance of a city should be evaluated more comprehensively, not only in terms of GDP, FDI, and employment growth, but also in terms of environmental quality, urban livability, local capacity building, and level of CO_2 emission reduction. Existing national reward programs such as the Human Settlement Environment Award are helping to realign incentives to some extent, but a deeper improvement of the local governance structure is the foundation for aligning incentives. An effective system of checks and balances must be in place.

A comprehensive set of performance indicators should be adopted at the city level. In addition, the performance of the municipal government should be monitored not only by higher level authorities, but also by a local institution that represents the long-term interests of city residents and that is empowered to safeguard the due procedures for conflict resolution. Under the current political structure of local governance in China, the local People's Congress is well positioned to assume this role. Some local People's Congresses are already actively involved in the development and enforcement of local laws and the review and approval of key municipal appointments.

The openness of the municipal decision-making process through public participation, consultation, and monitoring is another important element of the local governance structure for low-carbon city development. Public participation throughout the decision-making process should be made mandatory and ensured by law. It would be desirable if public participation is organized by the local People's Congress, instead of the municipal government and its associated agencies. Independent expert witness testimony should be introduced into the process. Other channels for direct feedback from the public to the municipal government and local People's Congress, such as the mayor's hotline, the Internet, town hall meetings, and local mass media, are being increasingly adopted by cities, and should be further encouraged.[12]

Developing Sustainable Municipal Finance Mechanisms

As analyzed earlier, the lack of sustainable financing mechanisms does more than simply financially constrain China's cities; it also creates perverse incentives that result in adverse social and environmental consequences. After more than a decade of rapid growth in off-budget financing for urban development, cities need to develop sustainable municipal finance mechanisms that move away from a reliance on land concessions. This should commence with a clear municipal infrastructure finance framework. The self-financing discipline of the public entities such as UDICs that provide infrastructure services should be emphasized and strengthened. Infrastructure assets are designed and built to last for the long term, often 30 years or more. Clearly, long-term debt instruments are needed to help ensure that infrastructure with a long lifespan is paid for by users over its entire useful life.

Municipal governments are taking on debt via UDICs, with highly mixed results. Local debt enables municipalities to finance needed infrastructure, but also creates debt management problems. While it is unclear if municipal governments will be allowed to borrow directly in the near future, short- to medium-term actions should focus on reforming the UDICs to improve transparency and introduce mandatory rating of credit worthiness. With assistance from the World Bank, credit rating has been piloted for some UDICs. This should be introduced as a common practice for all UDICs as soon as possible. Perhaps more importantly, given the presence of a number of fiscally backed UDICs, credit rating for municipal governments has become necessary and should be introduced and piloted. Local debt management capacity should also be developed in every city.

Moreover, comprehensive actions should be started immediately to introduce more stable local revenue bases (such as a property tax and land-value incremental tax), improve the quality of municipal financial management, harden budget constraints, make municipal finance transparent, and build up creditworthiness. As the extra-budgetary fund process is expected to continue in infrastructure financing, it should be formalized and made transparent. It should be made an integral part of the municipal financing plans.

It is also expected that off-budget funds from land concessions will become increasingly restricted. Given limited resources, cities have to prioritize their urban development expenditures. This should be based on careful assessment of the demand for funds. It is first necessary to understand the magnitude of urban development that a local government will require and how it can fund them. Cities should adopt a planning process that establishes funding priorities and rations them in favor of the most cost-effective investments. One of the most critical steps is the capital improvement plan (CIP), which is used in some developed countries but not yet implemented rigorously in China. Such a plan prioritizes urban improvements by sector (for example, transport, water and sewerage, power, recreation, education). It is necessary to determine resource allocation priorities among sectors, while maintaining the city's fiscal integrity and the hard budget constraint.

The cities should also produce a multiyear financial plan that demonstrates how it will fund the priority development investments, and what sources of revenue are available for these improvements. The plan—consisting of the multiyear operating plan and multiyear capital improvement plan—will demonstrate to lenders how the city expects to maintain its creditworthiness in the period matching the likely duration of commercial bank loans (that is, over 5–10 years). Each year the city will revise the multiyear financial plan based on annual outcomes: the actual level of revenues received versus forecasted revenues and operating and capital expenditures. The multiyear financial plan can also be used in the annual budgeting process in an iterative fashion to confirm that sufficient operating and capital revenues are available in the medium term to maintain city services and expand its infrastructure base while protecting its fiscal health.

To prevent aggregate overspending by local governments, the national government has long controlled the size of local investment through its review and approval process. However, this control has proven to be ineffective as overspending has tended to occur periodically. This is partly because the approval process has applied to megaprojects only, instead of each city's whole CIP. The introduction of CIP, along with the hardening of the budget constraint at the local level, would help the national government keep the potential risk of local financial liabilities in check.

Strengthening Physical Planning to Improve the Efficiency of Urban Land Use

This chapter suggests that China's land planning and development system still contains many significant elements that lead to inefficient spatial development. World Bank analysis on Chinese land development suggests at least two lessons from international experience that could be applied to the Chinese case to address these inefficiencies.

The first is that density regulations should be used to enable positive outcomes rather than attempting to prevent negative outcomes. Experience from Seoul and Tokyo summarized in the World Bank (2009a) report suggests that placing barriers such as greenbelts in the path of development tends only to push development farther to the edges of urban areas. A better approach is to enable the land market to create efficient development patterns by encouraging development where it best serves efficiency objectives, notably near transit stations. Additional focus is also needed at the level of neighborhood design (see box 4.6).

A second lesson is that the sequencing of urban development can play a major role in determining final outcomes. Urban development at the fringe of large cities developed in advance of public transport infrastructure can precipitate patterns of urban commuting that are hard to break, even if high-quality infrastructure is later provided. Chinese cities currently investing billions in metro systems in areas that were poorly served by public transport for many years are witnessing this issue firsthand.

Preliminary estimates from World Bank work conducted in 2009 indicate that progress in these areas could yield significant benefits. This work estimated that average carbon emissions per person could be as much as 10 percent lower with feasible increases in density. Chinese cities have grown rapidly over the last 25 years, but the urban boom is far from complete. The World Bank remains committed to working with client cities in China to address these issues in all urban development projects, seeking wherever possible to employ best practice on efficient and low-carbon growth now and into the future.

Box 4.6

Low-Carbon Neighborhood Design in China

Most Chinese urban dwellers have not yet locked in patterns of consumption with high-carbon emission implications, as is the case in many Western countries. This provides China with a possible advantage in pursuing low-carbon development.

To take advantage of this opportunity, China must support innovations in urban land-use and transport planning to help shape a low-carbon urban lifestyle. As described above, allowing density regulations to vary to support transit accessibility and central city growth is an excellent macro-level strategy. Micro-level design is also an area worthy of further examination. Neighborhood design to support environmentally friendly growth has long been a goal of many groups in developed countries (notably the New Urbanists in the United States) and some of the principles of ecologically friendly neighborhood planning were recently codified in the Leadership in Energy and Environmental Design for Neighborhood Development (LEED-ND) guidelines by the U.S. Green Building Council.

Figure B4.6.1   Traditional Grid of Back Bay, Boston (left), Compared with a Cul-de-sac Layout

Source: Wikimedia Commons 2011, Rick Berk.   *Source:* Wikimedia Commons 2011.

As in other countries, in-home energy use and personal travel are the two main forms of household energy consumption in China. With income growth and urban expansion, households demand bigger homes, more appliances, and private cars. Neighborhood design can help mitigate these effects, though it acts in complex ways. Residents of neighborhoods arrive in new neighborhoods with their own habits and desires, and their behavior is impacted by their surroundings,

(continued next page)

Box 4.6 *(continued)*

the habits of their neighbors, and their adaptation over time. It is not always easy to assign a given effect to a particular design characteristic (Crane and Crepeau 1998).

There is limited research on this topic in Western countries, and as far as the authors know, little or no research on this topic in the Chinese context. Understanding the impact of neighborhood design on patterns of energy consumption in Chinese urban areas appears to be a fruitful avenue for further research. At least one researcher has begun work on this topic, exploring the decision-making dynamics of households' residence and vehicle purchases, home energy use habits and travel behaviors, attitudes toward lifestyle, and how they are impacted by neighborhood design.

Source: Authors.

The institutional and financial elements of urban planning in Chinese cities must be addressed systematically before the conditions for true low-carbon physical planning can be enabled. These reforms will not by themselves ensure low-carbon development—as the experience of many developed countries shows. However, without reform of the current financing and institutional reward structures of municipalities, true low-carbon development is not likely to occur. In the interim, a variety of efforts, including those described in this section, can improve the efficiency of urban land use at the margin—and these have been and will continue to be supported by the World Bank.

Political Commitment to Reform Actions

Political commitment to reform is key to success. Implementation of the above recommended actions will not be easy. In addition to the continuing pressure for income growth, there are various powerful business interests (such as the automobile, real estate, and banking industries) supporting the current urban land-use and consumption patterns, which could make the development of low-carbon, compact cities difficult. Reforms of fiscal systems and intergovernmental fiscal relations to harden the local budget constraint are urgent but will also be difficult. Capacity development for city planning and financial planning to serve low-carbon city development will take time. All of the above point to a need for a strong political commitment to take immediate action.

Conclusion

This chapter discussed the closely interrelated topics of local governance, municipal finance, and urban land-use planning and their influence on the potential for the development of low-carbon urban form in China. Municipal finance is a crucial element of this story and its reform—in particular, shifting away from inefficient and wasteful farmland conversion—will be integral in developing a system of long-term financing that can support low-carbon growth.

Urban form locks in long-term consequences. Careful planning and effective implementation are therefore vital. This chapter demonstrates that for the low-carbon city agenda to succeed, a comprehensive reform of China's existing system of local governance, municipal finance, and urban planning is needed.

Notes

1. Although this paper focuses on the Chinese master plan which governs land use, China has three separate processes that cover different yet interrelated aspects of planning. In addition to master plans, they include socioeconomic development five-year plans and state land resource utilization plans, which require approval by the higher level governments. The three plans are inter-related. In practice, these plans are developed by three different agencies and can sometimes set targets and goals that are inconsistent or even contradictory. Nevertheless, these plans are considered necessary by Chinese officials for guiding local socioeconomic and spatial development while safeguarding the national interest in land resources.

2. Green GDP is a concept proposed in China in 2004 that attempts to factor the environmental consequences of economic growth in the accounting of national GDP. Although it is not yet formalized in national accounting, the idea reflects a new policy emphasis that more environmentally friendly GDP growth is needed to replace the single-minded pursuit of GDP growth at the cost of the environment. People-centered development is another concept that emphasizes the ultimate goal of GDP growth as the real improvement of the well-being of the people instead of merely the expansion of material wealth. It was first proposed as a development approach by the Central Committee of the Chinese Communist Party in 2003.

3. In a potential sign of things to come elsewhere, residential property tax collection was piloted in Shanghai and Chongqing in early 2011.

4. In recent years, the Ministry of Finance has issued local government bonds on behalf of a limited number of local governments. The total size of the bonds is tightly controlled by the central government.

5. The number was revealed in the speech of the Minister of Land and Resources in the National Land and Resources Working Conference held on January 7, 2011. It was then widely reported by the Chinese mass media. According to the Ministry data, the revenues from land concessions amounted to RMB 0.7 trillion in 2006, RMB 1.3 trillion in 2007, RMB 0.96 trillion in 2008, and RMB 1.59 trillion in 2009 (http://cq.people.com.cn/news/201118/20111885626.htm).

6. The degree to which Chinese real estate is overvalued is a topic of much recent debate. A survey published in a report on the housing market in China, recently released by the Chinese Academy of Social Sciences (CASS), estimated the average "bubble" (the percent by which the current market price of real estate exceeds its estimated underlying value) in 35 major Chinese cities at 29.5 percent—with some major cities reaching 50 percent (Jia 2010).

7. The number was from the China Banking Regulation Commission and widely reported by the media in May 2009.

8. Officially, villages are not allowed to develop or lease land for nonvillage-based uses. However, villages are able to develop land for industrial or commercial purposes for local township and village enterprises (TVEs). The process of village urbanization described in this chapter has often occurred "informally" through the unofficial lease of TVE land to outside groups. Given its informal nature, only limited information is available on this process.

9. One or both of these effects may be present. In some cases, low-density areas may have shorter average commutes than areas with dense urban cores—for example, Houston has a shorter average commute than New York—but the overwhelming dominance of the private automobile in these areas leads to overall higher emissions per trip. In many cases, sprawling areas experience both longer commutes and increased use of private motorization—with both effects increasing emissions.

10. The unpublished analysis is based on case studies in Tianjin, Zhengzhou, and Shanghai.

11. See chapter 2 on China's eco- and low-carbon cities for an overview of pilot programs.

12. As can be seen in some high-income countries, government transparency is by no means guaranteed to encourage low-carbon development. This is especially the case when households are already locked into a high-carbon lifestyle. In China, however, households have not yet attained a locked-in high-carbon lifestyle. Aside from the need to support greater government openness for its own substantial merits, the authors believe greater transparency can also support the low-carbon agenda in China.

Bibliography

Brown, M., and E. Logan. 2008. "The Residential Energy and Carbon Footprints of the 100 Largest U.S. Metropolitan Areas." Working Paper 39, School of Public Policy, Ivan Allen College, Georgia Institute of Technology.

Chapman, R. 2008. "Transitioning to Low-Carbon Urban Form and Transport in New Zealand." *Political Science* 60(1), June.

Crane, R., and R. Crepeau. 1998. "Does Neighborhood Design Influence Travel? A Behavioral Analysis of Travel Diary and GIS Data." *Transportation Research Part D: Transport and Environment* 3: 225–38.

Daily Mail Online. 2010. "The Ghost Towns of China: Amazing Satellite Images Show Cities Meant to be Home to Millions Lying Deserted." December 18. http://www.dailymail.co.uk/news/article-1339536/Ghost-towns-China-Satellite-images-cities-lying-completely-deserted.html.

Darsch, B. 2005. "Urban Transport Finance in China." Unpublished background paper prepared for the World Bank China transport team. World Bank, Washington, DC.

Dhakal, S. 2009. "Urban Energy Use and Carbon Emissions from Cities in China and Policy Implications." *Energy Policy* 37(11): 4208–219.

Jenks, M., E. Burton, and K. Williams, eds. 1996. *The Compact City: A Sustainable Urban Form?* Spon Press.

Jia, C. 2010. "Cities See a New Spike in Real Estate Bubble." *China Daily Online,* December 12. http://www.chinadaily.com.cn/china/2010-12/09/content_11673788.htm.

Kamal-Chaoul, L., and A. Robert, eds. 2009. "Competitive Cities and Climate Change." OECD Regional Development Working Paper No. 2. http://www.forum15.org.il/art_images/files/103/COMPETITIVE-CITIES-CLIMATE-CHANGE.pdf.

Magalhaes, F., and M. Duran-Ortiz. 2009. "Low Carbon Cities: Curitiba and Brasillia." 45th ISOCARP Congress 2009. http://www.isocarp.net/Data/case_studies/1492.pdf.

Norman, J., H. MacLean, and C. Kennedy. 2006. "Comparing High and Low Residential Density: Life-Cycle Analysis of Energy Use and Greenhouse Gas Emissions." *Journal of Urban Planning and Development* 132(1): 10–21.

O'Toole, R. 2009. "The Myth of the Compact City: Why Compact Development Is Not the Way to Reduce Carbon Dioxide Emissions." *Policy Analysis* 653, November 18.

Qiu, B. 2008. "Responding to Opportunities and Challenges: Key Issues and Policies for Urbanization Strategies in China." *China Architecture Industry Press* (in Chinese).

———. 2010. "Application of Eco-City Planning Policy in Post-Quake Reconstruction of Yushu." *City Planning Review* 10.

Shah, A., and C. Shen. 2006. "The Reform of the Intergovernmental Transfer System to Achieve a Harmonious Society and a Level Playing Field for Regional Development in China." Policy research working paper. World Bank, Washington, DC.

Transportation Research Board (TRB). 2009. "Special Report 298: Driving and the Built Environment: The Effects of Compact Development on Motorized Travel, Energy Use, and CO_2 Emissions." Washington, DC: Transportation Research Board. http://www.nap.edu/catalog.php?record_id=12747.

VandeWeghe, J., and C. Kennedy. 2007. "A Spatial Analysis of Residential Greenhouse Gas Emissions in the Toronto Census Metropolitan Area." *Journal of Industrial Ecology* 11(2): 133–44. http://dx.doi.org/10.1162/jie.2007.1220.

Wang, J., and M. Tang. 2005. "The Romance of the Three Kingdoms in the Formulation of City Master Plans." (In Chinese.) *The Outlook Newsweek* (Liao Wang Xin Wen Zhou Kan), November 7.

Wikimedia Commons. 2011. http://commons.wikimedia.org.

World Bank. 2006. "China: Building Institutions for Sustainable Urban Transport." Working Paper No. 4, Transport Sector Unit, Infrastructure Department, East Asia and Pacific Region. World Bank, Washington, DC.

———. 2007. "EAP Sustainable Development on the Urban Fringe." World Bank, Washington, DC. http://siteresources.worldbank.org/INTEAPHALFYEARLY UPDATE/Resources/550192-1175629375615/EAP-Update-April2007-sp-focus.pdf.

———. 2009a. "The Spatial Growth of Metropolitan Cities in China: Issues and Options in Urban Land Use." Urban Development Sector Unit, East Asia and Pacific Region. Unpublished working paper. World Bank, Washington, DC.

———. 2009b. "World Bank Urban Strategy." World Bank, Washington, DC.

PART 2

Sectoral Action for Low-Carbon Cities: Energy

CHAPTER 5

Low-Carbon Electricity for Cities

Ximing Peng

Overview

This chapter discusses the potential reduction of carbon emissions associated with electricity generation for Chinese cities. Decisions and policies can support this reduction on three levels: on the national, municipal, and end-user level. National (and to some degree regional) characteristics, along with national policies and trends, are the main determining factors for the carbon footprint of a city's electricity consumption. The chapter presents an overview of China's current electricity generation system and briefly highlights key policies and trends. Next, the chapter describes options for municipalities to reduce the carbon footprint of their electricity consumption. This includes exploring the trade-offs in importing versus generating power locally, importing power from sources that have lower emissions, as well as ways to increase the role of local renewable and other distributed sources of generation. Finally, the chapter discusses the potential to present an end user with a choice of electricity supply. Shanghai's pilot green electricity scheme, which gives end users the option to lower the carbon emissions associated with their own electricity consumption by purchasing "green" or low-carbon electricity for a higher price, is described and analyzed. The chapter finishes with a summary of recommended next steps.

Overview of the National Power System and Associated Greenhouse Gas Emissions

National Power System

In April 2002, with the release by the State Council of a comprehensive reform program,[1] China initiated the reform of its power sector from a monopoly single buyer model to a competitive regional power market model.

Generation capacity. By the end of 2009, the total generation capacity of the national power system was 874 gigawatts (GW). This included 197 GW of hydro, 651 GW of coal- or gas-fired thermal, 9 GW of nuclear, and 17 GW of other sources, such as wind power. Although more than 4,000 companies generate electricity, the 5 largest generation companies—Huaneng, Huadian, Guodian, Datang, and China Power Investment Corporation—have a combined installed capacity of about 48 percent of the national total. Other generation companies include those owned by either the central or provincial governments, as well as independent power producers such as private and joint venture companies.

Transmission and distribution. Also by the end of 2009, the national power system included 69,217 kilometers of transmission lines and 371,000 megavolt amperes of transformer capacity. A national power grid has been established that transfers power from west to east, and from the coal-producing provinces of Shanxi, Shaanxi, and Inner Mongolia to provinces that are net consumers of energy. The prevailing model is a single buyer/supplier, and pilots have been launched allowing certain industrial customers to choose their electricity suppliers. The electricity tariff is strictly regulated by the government. Two transmission companies—State Grid Corporation (5 regions and 26 provinces) and South China Grid Corporation (5 provinces)—have been provided exclusive authorization for operations in their respective territories.

Governance. Major government agencies are responsible for the regulation of the power sector. These are (i) the National Development and Reform Commission (NDRC)/National Energy Administration, responsible for planning, approval of major investments, and approval of electricity tariffs at generation, transmission, and retail levels, as well as daily operation management, and (ii) the State Electricity Regulation Commission, responsible for certification, inspection of safety management, tariff implementation, environmental protection, and pilots relating to power market reform.

Greenhouse Gas Emissions of Electricity Generated in China

Based on an estimate by the International Energy Agency (IEA), the total CO_2 emissions in China in 2007 exceeded 6,000 million tonnes, about 21 percent of global CO_2 emissions. Emissions by the electricity and heat generation sector have increased significantly since 1990, representing about 50 percent of those emissions in 2007 (see figure 5.1).[2]

Also since the early 1990s, electricity consumption in China has maintained a high growth rate, parallel to China's economic development. In 1990, electricity consumption was 612.5 terawatt hours (TWh), which increased to 3,643.0 TWh in 2009. This represents an average annual growth rate of 9.8 percent, only marginally lower than the average annual GDP growth rate of 10.5 percent during the same period.

While emissions and electricity consumption have increased, the overall efficiency of the power sector has improved. The average generation efficiency (gross, LHV[3]) was 31.3 percent (392 grams of coal equivalent per kilowatt hour or gce/kWh) in 1990. This increased to 38.4 percent (320 gce/kWh) in 2009, although the national average efficiency of thermal power was still below levels in industrialized countries. Transmission losses were also reduced—line losses decreased from 8.06 percent in 1990 to 6.72 percent in 2009.

Figure 5.1 CO_2 Emissions by Sector in China

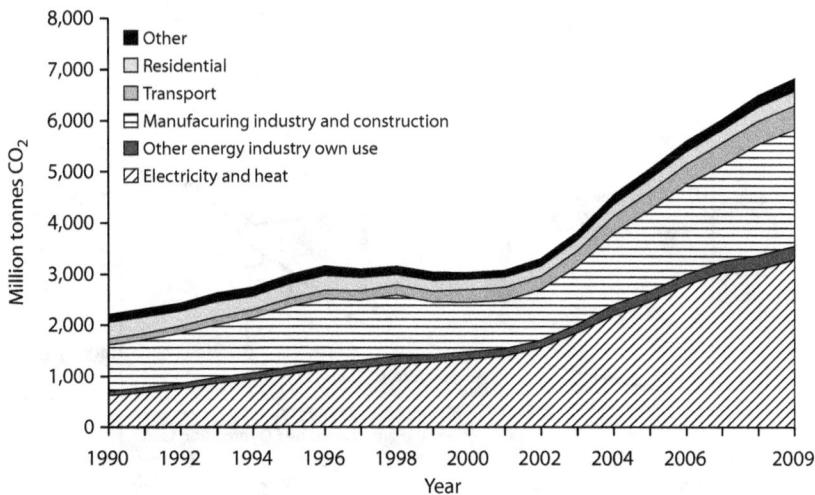

Legend:
- Other
- Residential
- Transport
- Manufacuring industry and construction
- Other energy industry own use
- Electricity and heat

y-axis: Million tonnes CO_2 (0 to 8,000)
x-axis: Year (1990, 1992, 1994, 1996, 1998, 2000, 2002, 2004, 2006, 2009)

Source: © OECD/IEA 2011.

National-Level Targets

The central government has publicly committed to two targets. The first is a reduction in carbon emissions per unit of GDP—or a reduction in "carbon intensity"—of about 40–45 percent by 2020 compared to the 2005 level. The second target is an increase in the share of nonfossil fuels in China's total energy consumption to 15 percent by 2020, from about 7.8 percent in 2009.

China is currently developing its New Energy Plan. Based on information collected from diverse sources, the anticipated development targets of non-fossil fuels technologies are summarized in table 5.1.

With the improvements in efficiency over the past decades, the carbon emissions per kWh of power generation have been reduced. As shown in figure 5.2, the weighted average carbon emission factor for China's generation mix has decreased from about 760 tonnes of CO_2 equivalent

Table 5.1   Anticipated Development Targets of Non-fossil Fuels in China

Non-fossil fuel technologies	Existing capacity in 2010 (GW)	Targets in 2020 (GW)
Nuclear power	10.8	70–80
Hydropower	213.4	300–350
Wind power	31.1	120–150
Biomass power	5.0	15–30
Solar photovoltaic	0.6	20–30

Source: Select speeches by Chinese authorities in 2010.

Figure 5.2   Carbon Emissions in China's Power Sector

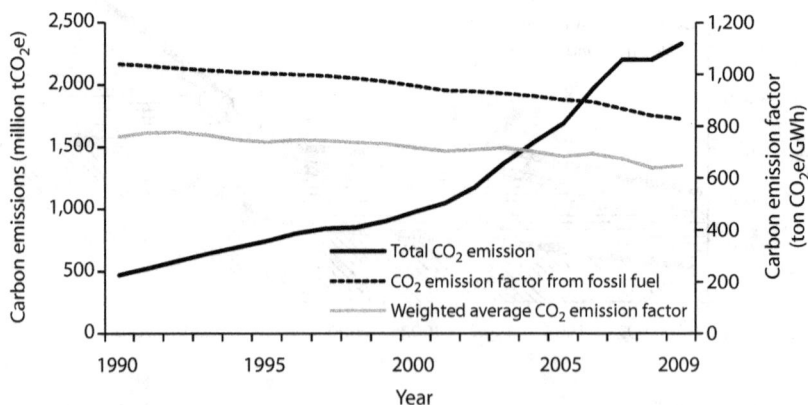

Source: Estimated by author.

(tCO$_2$e) per gigawatt hour (GWh) of electricity produced in 1990 to about 640 tCO$_2$e/GWh in 2009.[4] However, with total carbon emissions from power generation increasing from about 470 million tCO$_2$e in 1990 to 2,300 million tCO$_2$e in 2009, the impact of the reduction of this emission factor has been marginal and overall emissions have increased considerably.

China is already taking several important mitigation measures to reduce carbon emissions in the power sector. Current actions include (i) the closure of inefficient small power plants; (ii) the utilization of advanced generation technologies, including wide adoption of supercritical and ultra-supercritical technology for newly commissioned coal-fired power plants, as well as ongoing pilots to test the use of integrated gasification combined cycle (IGCC)[5] technologies; (iii) the development of nuclear power, hydropower, wind power, and other non-fossil fuel technologies to replace coal consumption; (iv) the establishment of a more robust national power grid to transmit power from west to east and enhance the cross-provincial or regional power transmission to optimize the cross-region resource use; (v) the rehabilitation of the urban and rural distribution networks to reduce line losses; and (vi) the development and application of state-of-the-art technologies to improve system efficiency and maximize the integration of renewable energy (RE), such as smart grids and new energy storage methods (see also box 5.1).

Box 5.1

Technologies of the Future

Electric vehicles (EV) and the "smart grid" are two examples of innovations that are receiving widespread public and governmental attention. Broader application of these technologies could further reduce carbon emissions.

Electric vehicles: China is competing with industrialized countries in developing EV technology, and significant progress has been made in the field of battery technology. Of particular interest is the potential to use EV batteries as part of a demand-side management strategy at the city level. Optimal management of battery charging in a city could maximize the use of off-peak electricity and would also store the energy in batteries, which is widely recognized as a potential future

(continued next page)

Box 5.1 *(continued)*

energy storage technology. The batteries, by serving as buffers, could also help provide stable streams of power from sources such as wind power and solar photovoltaic (PV).

Smart grid technology: Similar to EV technologies, smart grid technologies, which use digital technologies to improve electric grid operations, also offer significant potential to improve the operations of the power industry. For generators, such technologies can help the grid to better adjust to their generation profile, which could result in more electricity sold, and also enable more dynamic real-time management. For grid operators, these technologies can lead to a more robust power network, guaranteeing better capacity for both power transmission and distribution. For consumers, smarter grids should mean a more reliable power supply and a greater choice of suppliers, enabling them to lower their electricity bills. Finally, at the city level, the technology could be used for smart metering of both distributed generators and electricity consumers.

Source: Author.

Making Smart Electricity Generation Choices at the City Level

While the status of the national power system and national decisions and policies are important, municipalities can make individual choices to reduce carbon emissions from their electricity consumption. This can include choices about the amounts and sources of electricity imported from outside a municipality's boundaries, or efforts to optimize the amount of electricity produced internally.

Carbon Footprint of Imported Power

When accounting for a municipality's carbon emissions, emissions associated with the generation of imported power—power purchased from outside the municipality's boundaries—also need to be included, even though the emissions themselves occur outside those boundaries. A city might assess these additional carbon emissions by a systems analysis of the sources of the purchased power. Alternatively, if detailed data are not available, a system-weighted average emission factor for the regional or even the national grid can be used as the benchmark emission factor for the power import. For example, Shanghai in 2010 imported about one-third of its electricity from the East China Power Grid (Jiangsu and

Anhui) and the Central China Power Grid (hydropower). By appropriately weighting the average emission factors of these two grids, it is possible to calculate the emissions associated with Shanghai's "power import."

A city may be able to choose the source of its imported power, depending on technical and regulatory restrictions, and different purchase options would lead to different levels of carbon emissions for the city. However, economic and technical constraints—such as the availability of resources, transmission limitations and losses, peaking capacity and load following, reliability requirements, and cost-benefits, as well as other factors (employment, industry development, and fiscal impact)—would need to be taken into consideration.

City-based Low-Carbon Energy Mix

In some cases, a portion of the electricity used by the city is generated within the municipal boundaries. A city may find that increasing the portion of electricity generated within its boundaries can actually reduce the carbon footprint of its electricity consumption. Two key opportunities for municipalities to create a low-carbon energy mix within their boundaries are (i) maximizing the use of co-generation or tri-generation (both considered "poly-generation") technologies for power, heating, and cooling from natural gas, and (ii) increasing the use of renewable energy sources.

Poly-generation technologies. Poly-generation technologies,[6] when viable, tend to have a higher efficiency than a "power only" technology. Co-generation is a popular option when a demand for heating or steam is guaranteed. A growing number of tri-generation projects are being developed in large and medium-size cities, especially for commercial buildings.

Renewable energy. Renewable energy technologies can be viewed as technologies that control virtually all pollutants. Rather than installing controls for each pollutant, the use of renewables simultaneously reduces emissions of sulfur dioxide, nitrogen oxides, particulates, toxics, and greenhouse gases. Their use also avoids problems related to solid waste disposal and extensive water use associated with electricity generation from non-renewable sources. The Chinese government has already launched several programs to promote the installation of solar PV (for example, the national Golden Sun Program) or to encourage the application of geothermal power for heating in cities. Before the use of such distributed technologies can be scaled up, however, the government will need to overcome two key issues by (i) creating mechanisms to pay for the incremental cost of generating renewable energy and (ii) developing grid connections for distributed generation.

Grid connections. The key to successful grid connections will be to ensure open access for all eligible generation sources. Existing problems will need to be solved with efficient solutions, and it is expected that these issues will be addressed as part of the broader sector reforms over the coming years.

Costs. Although costs remain an obstacle, costs of renewable generation have been reduced significantly over the last decade and the advent of many Chinese manufacturers in the sector has been an important contributor. Despite recent price reductions, however, the financial costs of wind power and solar PV are still significantly higher than those for conventional coal-fired generation. Technologies for producing electricity from renewable resources have only been commercialized for a short time and lack the historical development and price supports for fossil fuels.

The most common policies to pay for the incremental cost of renewable energy are a mix of incentives and mandates. Incentives include tax credits, buy-down programs to decrease installation costs for consumers, and accelerated depreciation. Mandates can be used to create markets for renewables by introducing a legal obligation to develop, sell, or buy renewable energy. Under a legal obligation, the incremental cost of renewable energy is passed on to all end users. If these increased tariffs would be undesirable for certain categories of end users, such as the poor or selected industries, these groups can be protected.

An alternative method to promote the development of renewable energy is for utilities or other vendors to introduce a green electricity program. Green electricity programs allow end users to voluntarily purchase green electricity, usually at a premium, and thus promote their own values related to the environment, economy, and national security. Current experiences with these programs will be the focus of the next section.

Green Electricity Programs—Enabling End Users to Make Green Choices

Under green electricity programs, utilities purchase or generate electricity from renewable resources and offer it as a distinct product to consumers. The customers then have the option to purchase some or all of their electricity from these green sources. A voluntary green electricity program can be implemented instead of or even in addition to a legal obligation. Governments generally have been supportive of green electricity programs because they contribute to the development of renewable electricity without increasing prices for consumers who are not willing to pay. Utilities have been supportive for similar reasons, but also because the costs of renewable resources are not subject to the same volatility as fossil fuel prices, thereby providing a measure of price stability.

Considerations for Designing Green Electricity Programs

From international and national experience, several lessons have emerged for the design and implementation of green electricity programs. Essentially, there are three types of green electricity programs:

- In a *contribution-based program*, electricity consumers contribute voluntarily to a fund from which renewable electricity projects are financed. There is no relation between the contribution and the electricity generated from renewable resources or the installed capacity to generate renewable electricity.
- In a *capacity-based program*, electricity consumers pay extra for the installation of a certain renewable electricity-generating capacity. In this program, there is a direct link between the contribution and the additional installed capacity to generate renewable electricity. For example, in the United States, utilities have offered to install an additional 100-watt PV capacity for consumers for a monthly premium of US$6.00.
- In an *energy-based program*, electricity consumers pay a certain premium for any kWh of renewable electricity they agree to purchase. The agreed amount can be a fixed percentage of their electricity consumption or a fixed amount per month. The energy-based green electricity programs are, by far, the most popular among electricity consumers and vendors. The Shanghai municipal government has piloted such a program and their experience is discussed below.

Green electricity consumers buy green electricity on a voluntary basis, making a conscious choice to contribute to the improvement of the environment. It is purely a market-based transaction. However, to protect consumers and provide them the necessary assurances, legal and regulatory frameworks have been established to manage the market. Frameworks can be established by the government—through law or regulation—or by third parties certifying or labeling green electricity products. The extent of the framework varies among participants and locations but usually includes most of the following specifications:

- *Type of renewable energy source:* By specifying the types of renewable energy that are included, undesirable or controversial resources can be excluded if they are socially or environmentally unacceptable.
- *Location of production:* The framework can specify whether renewable electricity must be produced locally—and what is defined as local—or whether imports are allowed.
- *Age of the production facility:* This specification may restrict the use of old, established facilities to assure consumers that participation in the green electricity scheme will result in the development of new—additional—renewable electricity capacity and new production.
- *Minimum content of "new" renewable electricity:* If renewable electricity from older, established facilities is included, the share of this "old" renewable electricity is normally limited by specifying the minimum amount of "new" renewable electricity in green electricity. This minimum amount of new renewable electricity is often increased over time to slowly phase out any "old" renewable electricity and encourage the construction of new facilities.
- *The one-for-one requirement:* This requirement specifies that for each kWh of renewable electricity sold in a green electricity product, one kWh of renewable electricity is produced or purchased by the vendor. An independent party normally verifies this requirement.
- *Settlement period:* The settlement period specifies the time frame in which the one-for-one requirement must be met.
- *Method of balancing:* The amount of renewable electricity bought, generated, and sold during the settlement period—assumed to be a calendar year—will normally fluctuate. This fluctuation will make it virtually impossible to sell exactly the same amount as is purchased and generated. Accordingly, a method is defined to balance the surplus or deficit of the green electricity.
- *Additionality:* This is the stipulation that only renewable electricity beyond any legal requirement can be included in green electricity products.
- *"Minimum renewable energy content" requirements for green electricity products:* This is the specification of a required minimum content of renewable electricity for the utilities and vendors.
- *Requirements for information and product disclosure to consumers:* For full transparency, consumers must not only receive enough information to make an informed decision about the purchase of green electricity, but also they must, at least annually, be assured of the content in their product. Information about the exact nature of a product, environmental attributes, and product ownership and trading rights should be shared.

- *Product name and use of framework name and logo:* The product name should be a clear and identifiable name specific to the product sold and indicative of an environmentally friendly program or product. A framework name and logo can also strengthen the marketing of the product.
- *Requirements for verification and certification:* An independent verification of green electricity products ensures that products meet the requirements of the framework. This information, such as details about the sources and amounts of electricity purchased and sold, along with supporting evidence, must be made available to the independent verification body.

Shanghai's Experience with a Green Electricity Scheme

In 2005 Shanghai introduced its first, voluntary electricity scheme. Plans for this pilot program for green electricity generation within the city began in June 2003, when the mayor of Shanghai instructed the Shanghai Economic Commission (SHEC) to design the pilot and submit a proposal to the municipal government. SHEC then invited the World Bank to assist and entrusted the Shanghai Energy Conservation Supervision Center (SECSC) with designing the subsequent new scheme, which became the Jade Electricity Program.

With assistance from the World Bank and others, Shanghai integrated international experience into its design of the green electricity scheme, which was eventually implemented by the Shanghai Municipal Electric Power Company (SMEPC) under the aegis of the Shanghai Economic Commission and the Shanghai Development and Reform Commission. The voluntary green electricity scheme, together with the mandatory government-approved tariffs and subsidies, covers the incremental cost of generating renewable energy, and the approach is replicable at the national and regional levels in China.

Jade Electricity uses both wind and PV electricity generated in Shanghai. From 2003 to 2009 three onshore wind farms were established in Shanghai, with a total installed capacity of 39.4 megawatts (MW) and an estimated annual generation of 78.8 GWh. The first offshore wind farm was commissioned in Shanghai in July 2010, with an installed capacity of 100 MW and annual generation of about 267 GWh. Photovoltaic capacity is still limited in Shanghai. The total green electricity generation is about 0.4 percent of the total generation in the city. The incremental cost of Jade Electricity is RMB 0.53 per kWh. This price has been regulated and has remained unchanged since the start of the program.

Since 2005, the electricity product of the program has been offered to households and large non-household consumers. Consumers need to buy a minimum amount depending on their category. Table 5.2 summarizes the program's annual sales between 2005 and 2010. The table shows that the market for green electricity in Shanghai boomed in the first three years but has decreased dramatically since 2008. One interesting finding is that about 65 percent of the non-household customers are foreign companies or joint ventures.

Implementation barriers. SECSC, which worked with the World Bank to design and oversee the electricity scheme's implementation, identified four major barriers to the successful implementation of the scheme:

- *Inadequate financial incentives:* While the green electricity customers received a certificate of participation, which was helpful for the image of their enterprises, customers were not offered any direct or indirect financial incentive to participate in the program. With the global financial crisis in 2008, many of the scheme's customers left or reduced the amount of green electricity they purchased.
- *Inadequate marketing and dissemination efforts:* After a one-time initial promotion in the media when the green electricity purchase agreement was signed, neither the government nor the power company took any systematic or sustained actions to raise public awareness of the scheme.
- *Insufficient governmental attention:* The program is implemented primarily by SMEPC; more support from the municipal government for the power company could have encouraged greater participation from the public and the city's enterprises.

Table 5.2   Sales of Green Electricity in Shanghai during 2005–10

Year	Number of customers		Purchased green electricity (MWh)	
	Non-household	Household	Non-household	Household
2005	22	27	12,540	7.0
2006	7	6,847	2,220	964.0
2007	8	414	2,658	67.0
2008	3	6	182	0.7
2009	6	8	1,500	1.2
2010	3	1	1,320	0.1
Total	49	7,303	20,420	1,040.0

Source: Shanghai Energy Conservation Supervision Center.

- *Complicated administrative procedures:* The procedures for purchasing green electricity are complicated and require detailed information from consumers as part of the application process. This appears to have been detrimental, and there are indications that these requirements and procedures have prevented households from participating in the scheme.

In addition to these concerns, it should be noted that the program design did not link the revenues from this scheme directly to investments in renewable energy. Consequently, producers of renewable energy do not rely on revenues from this scheme to cover their incremental costs, which are covered in part by government subsidies and preapproved tariffs. This reduced the incentives for the power company to ensure the success of this scheme.

Lessons learned. The five years of implementation of the green electricity scheme have provided several lessons for the implementation of future projects. Three key lessons are as follows:

- The *government should play a more proactive role* if such schemes are to be replicated in other cities or provinces. Ideally, a program should be integrated with other national or provincial policies or regulations related to renewable energy. A stand-alone showcase is unlikely to be successful.
- *Public awareness* is critical. A professionally managed marketing and dissemination effort is a necessary component of a green electricity scheme.
- *Financial incentives:* In addition to a certificate of participation, other incentives should be considered, including financial compensation for the certificate holders, inclusion of the purchased green electricity in its renewable energy quota (if a quota mechanism is to be applied), or trade of the certificate. Additional research in this area is required.

Nongovernmental third parties could also be important partners in this program, as they could help increase public awareness and support and supervise the implementation effort.

Next Steps

As Chinese cities work to reduce the carbon intensity of their GDP, in line with national policies and targets, several actions could reduce the carbon emissions associated with the consumption of electricity. Building on the discussion in this chapter, specific suggestions include the following:

- *Facilitating and encouraging the trade of carbon emission credits* among cities or provinces to reduce the joint costs of carbon intensity reduction. Cities, and other entities being held to carbon intensity targets, should be allowed to trade carbon emission credits. The ideal mechanism would provide an incentive for (i) electricity generators (cities, provinces, and power producers) with the ability to generate low-carbon power to optimize production and to export their power, and for (ii) energy consumers (cities, provinces, and enterprises) to purchase power from nonlocal power producers in other provinces and cities with the lowest carbon footprint (see also chapter 24 for further information about cities and carbon finance).
- *Developing local distributed renewable energy* as a major supplemental measure in addition to establishing energy efficiency improvements.
- *Developing and establishing green electricity programs.*
- *Increasing public awareness* on issues related to energy efficiency and renewable energy.
- *Piloting new technologies* with both administrative and market instruments, including smart grid technologies, EVs, and carbon capture utilization and storage technologies.
- *Promoting pricing reform* together with efforts by both central and provincial government authorities to make the price signal effective and efficient.
- *Establishing a transparent and accountable carbon emission measurement/calculation, reporting, and verification system*, as well as a sound statistics system.
- *Developing policies to provide incentives and penalties* toward achieving the carbon intensity target.

Conclusion

This chapter addresses the pressing need to reduce the level of carbon emissions associated with generating the electricity consumed by a Chinese city. The national trend suggests that while significant progress is being made to lower the carbon intensity of the national grid, this progress is largely being overwhelmed by the rapid increase in aggregate demand: the last two decades have seen a dramatic increase in total carbon emissions from power generation in China. The chapter discusses possible remedies available to a municipality to lower the carbon footprint of the power it consumes by focusing on developing local low-carbon distributed generation and by carefully choosing the amounts and origin of imported power. The chapter also emphasizes the potential of green electricity programs that provide end users with the opportunity to express their preference for this option.

Notes

1. Document 2002/No. 5.

2. All carbon emissions data in this section are referred to in *IEA Statistics: CO$_2$ Emissions from Fuel Combustion—Highlights 2009 Edition* (IEA 2009).

3. Lower heating value: a property of a fuel, defined as the amount of heat released by combusting a specified quantity (initially at 25°C or another reference state) and returning the temperature of the combustion products to 150°C.

4. For comparison, the carbon emission factor of coal-fired thermal has decreased from about 1,000 tCO$_2$e/GWh in 1990 to about 830 tCO$_2$e/GWh in 2009. The figures are estimated based on the Chinese electric power industry's efficiency.

5. A technology turning coal into synthesis gas for generating electricity, resulting in lower sulfur dioxide, particulates, and mercury.

6. Poly-generation refers to technologies that can produce not only one product (electricity) but also other products such as heating, cooling, and chemical products. Some common poly-generation technologies include co-generation (producing electricity and heating/steam) and tri-generation (producing electricity, heating, and cooling).

Bibliography

OECD/IEA. 2009. *IEA Statistics: CO$_2$ Emissions from Fuel Combustion—Highlights 2009 Edition*. Paris, France: OECD/IEA.

———. *CO$_2$ Emissions from Fuel Combustion 2011*. Paris, France: OECD/IEA.

Shanghai Energy Conservation Supervision Center, http://www.sh-ec.org/jatpage/home.xml.

CHAPTER 6

Industrial Energy Efficiency

Gailius Draugelis

Overview[1]

Industrial plants are often located in or near urban centers, and undoubtedly addressing the emissions from industry will be a critical element of a city's low-carbon growth strategy.[2] The industrial sector has also been an important focus of China's efforts to reduce the energy intensity of the economy during the 11th Five-Year Plan (2006–10). This chapter starts by describing some important approaches and tools that have been used to improve energy efficiency to date, listing successes and lessons learned. The chapter then discusses ways to further strengthen energy efficiency efforts—in particular by expanding the use of market-based tools and emphasizing the quality of program implementation. The final section recommends short- and medium-term actions for accelerating adoption of industrial energy efficiency measures.

The role of China's provinces and municipalities. Although industries are located within the administrative boundaries of municipalities, many high energy–consuming enterprises fall under the jurisdiction of provincial or central governments. Therefore, low-carbon strategies addressing such companies rely on good intergovernmental policy and program coordination. On the one hand, national-level government institutions promulgate new national regulations and policies (such as industrial restructuring policies and new taxation regulations), set national targets, establish new national standards and codes (such as national minimum energy efficiency equipment standards and building codes), design and oversee implementation of a series of national-level programs (such as programs for energy conservation renovation in existing buildings), and allocate resources from the central government budget. On the other hand, China's provincial and (for certain programs within their jurisdiction) municipal governments have been at the core of program implementation. Working with the central government, they have put new systems into operation to allocate and supervise mandatory energy conservation targets for key energy-using industries and to provide technical and financial support to help these industries achieve their targets. Provincial and municipal governments have added specific local policies and policy interpretations, issued local standards and regulations, set local targets, allocated additional budget resources, and implemented large new programs to eliminate particularly wasteful industrial plants and assess the energy efficiency characteristics of proposed new large projects. They have helped strengthen enforcement of national energy efficiency codes and standards. Provinces have also set up new, public energy efficiency funds and implemented policy adjustments for energy pricing. In addition, many have undertaken programs to further develop local energy efficiency service enterprises.

While this chapter focuses on provinces, implementing energy conservation programs and achieving energy intensity targets is a joint effort between the central government, provinces, and municipalities. Experiences and lessons learned at the provincial level described below can inform municipal-level practitioners involved in local energy efficiency programs.

Recent Achievements, Approaches, Tools, and Lessons

China's leadership set an ambitious target in late 2005 to reduce energy use per unit of gross domestic product (GDP) by 20 percent during 2006–10. This challenging target required a sharp reversal in the trend of increasing GDP energy intensity during the previous five years of industry-led growth. To achieve the goal, targets were subdivided and assigned both to provinces and lower administration levels and to administrators of key national programs, with clear accountabilities for delivery. Quantitative results were disappointing in the first year. However, the government of China maintained that delivery against the goal was essential. The program commenced with a level of attention among all groups at all levels on how to achieve energy conservation results that has never before been witnessed in China. The drive has yielded a wealth of new ideas, development of a host of new major programs, promulgation of many new and relatively advanced regulations, and a massive organization effort with great human and financial investment.

Energy intensity reductions. The latest comprehensive statistics show a reduction in China's energy intensity per unit GDP of 12.45 percent over the 2006–08 period.[3] At the end of 2010, China had achieved a cumulative reduction of 19.1 percent in energy intensity toward the 11th Five-Year Plan target.[4] This suggests that even with strong industrial growth, gains in physical energy efficiency appear to have made a truly impressive contribution during this five-year plan (FYP). Moreover, this comprehensive energy conservation drive has succeeded in both delivering strong results and, perhaps most important, laying policy and program foundations for achieving more long-term energy savings.

Institutional gains. The achievement of solid energy savings is important, but perhaps an even more significant result of the national energy conservation program has been the institutional gains. The new legal and regulatory foundations established design and implementation experience in a large number of new major programs, capacity building at all levels, and generation of innovative new approaches—all of which can serve China well in the future. Cities can learn from these lessons to plan for lower-carbon growth programs. The following sections provide a summary of recently developed practices, as well as lessons learned, that have contributed to reducing energy consumption in the industrial sector. The sections will describe (i) enterprise energy-saving programs, (ii) structural adjustments in the industrial sector, (iii) ideas for developing the energy efficiency service industry, and (iv) fiscal incentive programs and pricing.

Key Enterprise Energy-Saving Program

One of the most important new program areas for energy conservation involves mandatory energy savings targets and associated support initiatives for China's key energy-consuming enterprises. China's Energy Conservation Law, revised in 2007, defines key energy-consuming enterprises as enterprises that consume more than 10,000 tons of coal equivalent (tce) per year.[5] Of the more than 15,000 key enterprises operating in China, the vast majority are industrial enterprises.

Responsibility contracts for enterprise energy savings. The national Top-1000 Energy-Consuming Enterprises Program (or 1000 Enterprise Program), launched in 2006, established a new system for government-enterprise agreements on specific enterprise energy savings targets, moni-toring, and supervision of compliance. The central government designated the top 1,008 energy-consuming enterprises in the country for participa-tion. Together they account for about one-third of China's total energy use. Agreements on various enterprise energy conservation measures and energy savings targets for the FYP are established in energy savings responsibility contracts. National agencies have set the objectives, targets, scope, and implementation guidelines. Provincial governments are in charge of most of the details of implementation. Progress in each enter-prise is evaluated annually. Initial estimates show that the program is well on track to meet and perhaps surpass its aggregate goal of saving some 100 million tce over the five-year period.

Provinces and prefectures also signed energy savings responsibility contracts with thousands of additional key energy-using enterprises, espe-cially during 2007–08. In Shandong Province, for example, key energy-consuming enterprises responsible for about 70 percent of the province's total energy consumption have entered into energy savings responsibility contracts with various levels of government (see also box 6.1).

Additional and associated measures. While the enterprise targeting system focuses attention on achieving quantified results, the enterprise energy savings responsibility system also provides a platform for regular and sustained public sector and enterprise interaction on a host of energy

---

Box 6.1

Targeting Large Energy–Consuming Enterprises to Meet FYP Energy Intensity Reduction Obligations

The governments of Shanxi, Shandong, and Jiangxi Provinces and Nanchang Pre-fecture have developed programs modeled after the national 1000 Enterprise Program to target large energy–consuming enterprises within their local jurisdic-tion to enter into specific energy savings responsibility contracts. This is part of their overall efforts to meet the FYP energy intensity reduction obligations. In addition to including enterprises that are part of the national program, these re-gional programs also mandate an expanded list of designated enterprises to re-duce their energy intensity.

Source: Taylor et al. 2010.

conservation initiatives. Some particularly important areas now being developed include (i) training of enterprise energy managers and organization of related technical assistance; (ii) rollout of new, standardized enterprise Energy Management Systems (EMSs); (iii) development of comparative unit energy use benchmarking to assist enterprises in assessing savings potential; (iv) supervision and support for compliance with minimum energy efficiency performance standards and other key regulations; and (v) identification, packaging, and arranging of some types of financing support for energy efficiency investment projects.

Monitoring and supervision. Provincial and prefectural governments have the main responsibility for monitoring and supervising the key enterprise energy savings programs (although the central government also oversees the 1000 Enterprise Program). As of mid-2008, 19 provinces had established provincial-level supervision units to undertake this function, with authority broadly established by the Energy Conservation Law. A key task for the near term is the development and operation of new systems for data collection and reporting of enterprise energy use. To ensure enterprise compliance with agreements, provincial and local governments can at their discretion use their broad permitting and regulatory powers relating to enterprise operation and new project approvals.

Structural Adjustments in the Industrial Sector
Recently, China has emphasized sectoral adjustments in its overall industrial policy, aiming to encourage development characterized by "low input, low consumption, lower emissions, and high efficiency." To achieve this goal, current policies focus on (i) energy efficiency assessments for new capacity, (ii) elimination of energy-inefficient industrial capacity, and (iii) developing high- and new-technology industries and the service sector.

Energy efficiency assessments for new capacity. China's National Development and Reform Commission (NDRC) now requires energy conservation assessments as part of new energy-intensive project proposals under its purview. Many provinces now have similar requirements, establishing new systems as part of their project-permitting process (see also box 6.2). Project reviews aim both to question more rigorously the benefits and costs of large new energy-intensive capacity expansion and to evaluate the energy efficiency of the technologies that are proposed.

Elimination of inefficient industrial capacity. One of the largest programs of China's current energy conservation drive is the national effort to close down old, small-scale, and particularly inefficient energy-intensive industrial capacity. The program focuses mainly on the thermal

Box 6.2

Beijing's Fixed Assets Investment Appraisal and Examination Method

Beijing municipality has been one of the leaders in carefully assessing the energy efficiency characteristics of new projects that are seeking local government approval. In 2007, the municipality developed a Fixed Assets Investment Appraisal and Examination Method, with specific energy conservation assessment elements, to be carried out by a specialized energy efficiency appraisal agency. Beijing's Development and Reform Commission (DRC) will not register or approve a new project unless the required energy conservation assessments are included and approved. Large new building construction and enterprises must undergo energy conservation assessments and examination, while other smaller-scale projects must register for energy conservation management. Beijing's DRC and other authorities will also supervise the project throughout its development.

By the end of 2008, Beijing had conducted energy conservation assessment and examinations for 151 projects, with estimated energy savings of 129,000 tce of energy or 13.1 percent compared to energy consumption under a business-as-usual scenario.

Source: Taylor et al. 2010.

power, iron and steel, cement, electrolytic aluminum, ferroalloy, coke, and calcium carbide industries, and is implemented by provincial and local governments. The main measures include (i) policies to "replace the small with the large" by linking investment approval for new larger-scale projects to progress achieved in the same locality in eliminating inefficient capacity;[6] (ii) price surcharges on electricity consumed by inefficient plants; (iii) allocation of special funds to compensate for financial loss and unemployment impacts, and to provide awards for early success; and (iv) other administrative measures. Although the provision is difficult to implement, subsector reports indicate that the program is having a large impact. In Shanxi Province, for example, successful closure of particularly wasteful capacity is estimated to have accounted for about 60 percent of the total energy savings in the province's large industrial sector during 2006–08 (see box 6.3).

While the policy of eliminating inefficient capacity has significantly contributed to energy intensity reduction, it can cause economic, fiscal, financial, and social challenges for local governments, especially in the

Box 6.3

Shanxi's Special Compensation Fund for Eliminating Inefficient Capacity

In Shanxi Province, a special compensation fund has been used successfully to eliminate particularly wasteful capacity. The compensation began in 2006.

Financing Sources

Financing for the fund comes from the central government allocation, the province's Coal Sustainable Development Fund (paid for by a resource tax on coal production), its Electricity Construction Fund, and the provincial government fiscal budget.

Major Uses

The main uses of the fund include the following:

- Compensation to enterprises that are to close down and demolish their inefficient production equipment. If an enterprise is eligible for this compensation, the enterprise needs to demolish the equipment and clean up the site; if an enterprise does not demolish the inefficient capacity according to the schedule, the fund will be used for mandatory demolition of the equipment.
- Mandatory demolition of targeted equipment in those cases where enterprises do not meet the deadline.
- Site clearance and restoration.

Principles

- Early elimination of inefficient capacity is especially encouraged. If the targeted production line is closed one year earlier than required, the enterprise receives 10 percent extra compensation; if it is closed two years earlier than required, the enterprise receives 20 percent extra compensation. If the targeted production line is not closed by the required schedule date, the government will provide no compensation and will ensure demolition.
- The government provides no compensation in the following cases: (i) the enterprise does not demolish the inefficient equipment, but instead uses it for other purposes; (ii) the enterprise does not demolish the inefficient capacity within the predetermined schedule; (iii) the closed capacity will be replaced

(continued next page)

Box 6.3 *(continued)*

with new, larger-scale capacity; (iv) assets were built illegally or did not comply with regulations; or (v) asset construction was completed without proper environmental assessment.

Examples of Compensation

- Iron and steel industry:

Asset life	Blast furnaces			Steel converters	
	<100 m³	*100–200 m³*	*200–300 m³*	*<15 tons*	*<20 tons*
>5 years	0	RMB 1.8 million	RMB 3.0 million	0	RMB 0.5 million
<5 years	0	RMB 2.8 million	RMB 3.5 million	0	RMB 1.0 million

- Thermal power: No provincial compensation is provided for capacity targeted for closure in the national power generation corporate groups; compensation of RMB 0.2 million/MW is provided for other small thermal power plants targeted for closure.

Source: Taylor et al. 2010.

near term. The construction of new plants that replace inefficient capacity mitigates some of these issues, but even then the elimination of the inefficient plants has a major impact on employment as fewer employees are needed at more centralized sites. To achieve sustained good results in the restructuring of energy-inefficient enterprises, exit mechanisms that address post-elimination issues related to reemployment and compensation for former workers at the eliminated enterprises are key, as well as compensation to the enterprises. Many provinces have already established special compensation funds for this purpose. Local governments have also adopted favorable policies to provide laid-off workers employment priority in similar sectors or encourage them to start small businesses. Some local governments have also attempted to recover and reuse the land of eliminated units, aiming to increase its value, which in turn can become a funding source for compensation.

Development of high- and new-technology industries and the service sector. Encouraging development of high- and new-technology industries and the service sector is another important aspect of the structural adjustment policy. Favorable income tax policies were issued in 2006 to mobilize investment in research and development and the establishment of high- and new-technology industries. In 2007, the State Council issued an *Opinion on Promoting Service Industries* in an attempt to further efforts to accelerate the development of service industries, and to support the 11th FYP's target of having a five percent increase in GDP from the service industry by 2010 compared to 2005. Several provincial and municipal governments have followed the central government's policy to promote high- and new-technology industries and the service sector. This includes:

- Liaoning Provincial Government prioritized the development of low energy use, advanced equipment manufacturing, and agricultural processing industries, which resulted in an increase in output of 32 percent in 2007.
- Hubei Provincial Government focused on financial, technical, and human resources in the development of electronic information, biomedical, and new materials industries, which led to a GDP increase from these industries of 26.3 percent in 2007.
- Beijing Municipal Government adopted a policy of *one strict and one loose* (yi song yi jin), which (i) restricts development or requires closure of highly energy-intensive and highly polluting industries, and (ii) encourages high- and new-technology industries and the service sector. In 2007, growth in the service sector accounted for 71 percent of a 12.3 percent increase in Beijing's GDP. The expansion of high- and new-technology industries and the service sector policy, which are significantly less energy intensive, also helped Beijing to reduce its overall energy intensity by 6 percent in 2007.

Developing the Energy Efficiency Service Industry

In addition to energy savings programs, regulations, and structural adjustments, enterprises focused on energy efficiency services are needed to support many new activities. Many provinces have taken measures to foster development of local energy efficiency service entities to undertake such critical market functions as energy auditing and testing, consulting, energy efficiency technology dissemination, energy efficiency project design and appraisal, project construction management and maintenance, training, detailed energy use monitoring tasks, and assistance in arranging project financing. Many energy efficiency service entities also have become engaged in the energy performance contracting business (see also box 6.4). Nationwide, energy efficiency investments using energy perfor-

Box 6.4

Energy Performance Contracting to Promote Energy Efficiency

Energy performance contracting (EPC) provides an energy consumer, or "host fa-cility," with a range of services related to the adoption of energy efficient products, technologies, and equipment, carried out by an energy service company (ESCO). It is an energy efficiency investment model in which ESCOs sign a contract with the host enterprise and use cost savings from the reduced energy consumption to cover the project's full investment cost.

The EPC approach is generally characterized by (i) offering a complete energy efficiency service, including design, engineering, commissioning, and operations and maintenance of the energy efficiency measures, as well as training and mea-surement and verification of the resulting energy and cost savings; (ii) providing or arranging financing to help customers pay for the energy services with a por-tion of the actual energy cost savings achieved; (iii) guaranteeing performance for the entire project based on the level of energy or cost savings; and (iv) bearing most of the technical, financial, construction, and performance risks that are part of the EPC (Singh et al. 2010). The EPC mechanism in China has been structured in three models—shared savings, guaranteed savings, and outsourcing.

The concept of EPC was introduced in China by the World Bank/GEF-financed China Energy Conservation Project. Three pilot ESCOs, part of the project, focused mostly on the industrial sector, which represents the biggest energy savings po-

Figure B6.4.1   Annual CO$_2$ Emission Reduction by Pilot ESCOs

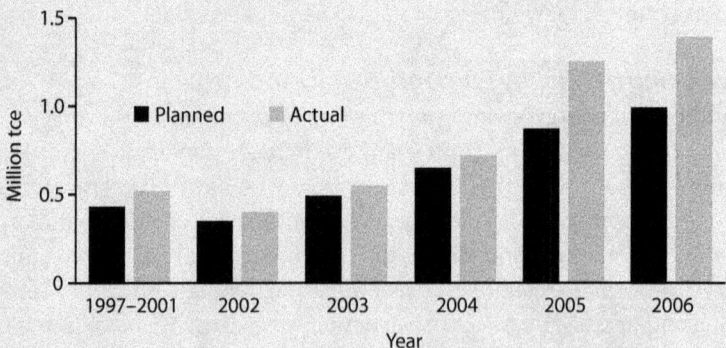

Source: Project Management Office of NDRC/WB/GEF China Energy Conservation Project 2010.

(continued next page)

Box 6.4 *(continued)*

tential. The success achieved by these early ESCOs demonstrated that the EPC mechanism has great potential for expansion in China and that China's ESCO industry can have a prosperous future. By the end of the project in 2006, the three pilot ESCOs implemented 475 energy performance contracts, resulting in an energy saving of 1.49 million tce per year and a CO_2 emission reduction of 1.39 million tce per year.

In April 2004, encouraged by the work and achievements of the World Bank/ GEF China Energy Conservation Project and with critical financial support from the U.K. Department for International Development (DFID), the ESCO Committee of the China Energy Conservation Association, commonly known as the Energy Management Company Association (EMCA), was established to further promote the EPC mechanism offered by ESCOs. EMCA has served as the implementation agency of the Second World Bank/GEF China Energy Conservation Project. While continuing to promote the EPC mechanism in China and foster growth of the energy service industry, EMCA also provides technical assistance for new or potential ESCOs to help them get established in the sector, develop new business opportunities, and improve operations capacity.

With support from this Second Energy Conservation Project, EMCA became self-supporting in 2008. By 2010, the ESCO (and energy management company— EMC) market is accelerating and dynamic with EPC investment amounts totaling US$4.24 billion, similar to volumes seen in the United States. By the same year, EMCA membership had increased to 560, with 428 members completing at least one EPC project.

Sources: Project Management Office of NDRC/WB/GEF China Energy Conservation Project 2010; Sun et al. 2011.

mance contracting totaled about US$1.5 billion in 2008—rivaled internationally only by the United States. This business is expected to grow even further in the coming years.

Fiscal Incentive Programs and Pricing
Fiscal programs at different levels of government could provide an incentive for energy efficiency if they are well designed. In addition, it is recognized that energy pricing is a critical and perhaps the most effective tool in stimulating interest in energy efficiency. The provincial programs

usually include energy conservation special funds, investment subsidies, energy pricing (within the province's jurisdiction), and tax incentives.

Energy conservation special funds. The central government, most provinces, and some prefectures have established special funds for energy conservation and emission reduction through annual allocations from the government budget. While the main use of the funds can vary, the most common uses include providing subsidies for energy efficiency investment projects (payable upon project commissioning) and subsidies for research and development, for technology demonstration, for information dissemination, and for various types of energy conservation awards (see also box 6.5). The central government's fund allocations for all aspects of energy efficiency and emission reduction were about RMB 105 billion in total during 2007–09, of which allocations for energy efficiency were only one part.

Investment subsidies. Different government levels have a variety of concessional financing programs that enterprises can tap into for energy efficiency investments. Assistance in arranging concessional finance is one of the key supportive measures that supervising authorities can provide as part of their new relationship on energy efficiency with key energy-consuming enterprises. For example, the central government has a large RMB 200–250 award program per tce of qualified savings generated from

---

Box 6.5

Rewarding Outstanding Energy Conservation Achievements

Many provinces have established annual awards to local government units, organizations, enterprises, and individuals for outstanding energy conservation achievements.

In 2007, Shandong Province implemented an Energy Conservation Rewarding Method, which includes "Outstanding" and "Excellence" awards of RMB 1 million and RMB 50,000, respectively, for organizations, enterprises, and projects. For the "Outstanding" award, the recipient must meet the national leading level in energy intensity for two consecutive years, and must achieve a minimum of 40,000 tce in energy savings annually. In 2007, five enterprises and five projects received the "Outstanding" awards.

Source: Taylor et al. 2010.

pre-agreed energy efficiency projects. For this program, local supervising authorities also play an important role in monitoring and evaluating to verify whether the planned savings have been achieved.

Energy pricing. Generally, average prices for the main energy types in China reflect the financial costs of supply. However, most prices do not reflect the additional, externality costs, such as long-term supply security issues or environmental concerns. Broad pricing policies are the mandate of the central government, but provinces can make certain adjustments, and some prices, such as for heating, are set by municipal authorities within national guidelines. Shanxi Province, for example, has instituted a resource tax on coal production, which is a major source of financing for its energy efficiency special fund and for compensation for eliminated inefficient industrial capacity. Some provinces also have added small across-the-board electricity surcharges or use revenues from electricity load management and energy saving programs. Finally, provinces have followed central government guidance and implemented large increases in electricity prices for wasteful industrial capacity that is identified for closure.

Tax incentives. Although some readjustments were made after the global financial crises, tax rebates for many energy-intensive product exports were reduced at the outset of the 2006–10 energy-saving program. Favorable taxation policies also have been instituted to encourage the purchase of highly energy-efficient equipment and to attract high- and new-technology industries. To attract those same industries and encourage investments in energy efficiency, provincial governments have also offered fiscal incentives, such as income tax reductions or exemptions, certain tax rebates, and the allowance of accelerated depreciation for specified investments or purchases. Shandong Province offered some of these tax incentives to enterprises that engage in energy- and water-conserving manufacturing and business practices.

Meeting the Challenges of the Future

Improving energy efficiency will continue to be a central part of China's efforts to build a resource-saving society for the foreseeable future. To build on the foundations established, especially over the past five years, China's provincial and municipal agencies will need to play an even greater role. To meet the challenges, however, attention is needed in some key areas. These are (i) improving the balance between administrative and market-based tools for improving energy efficiency, (ii) strengthening quality in administrative program implementation, (iii) expanding the role of markets in delivering energy efficiency (including developing the energy efficiency services industry), (iv) further improving energy efficiency in key energy enterprises, and (v) developing market-based approaches for use of public energy efficiency funds.

Improving the Balance between Administrative and Market-Based Tools

China needs both administrative and market-based measures to achieve the best long-term energy efficiency results. In this respect, China is not unique. Other countries that have implemented successful energy efficiency programs also have used mixes of both tools. In China, however, government guidance and leadership are especially important. Administrative measures, such as mandatory targeting and regulations, codes, and standards aimed at achieving minimum performance requirements, have certainly played key roles in the energy efficiency gains achieved in the 11th FYP. Yet they also pose difficulties in realizing the full potential for savings, and such measures can create economic distortions. Reliance on market forces brings major economic efficiency advantages, but also brings various practical difficulties in trying to capture the full potential for energy efficiency gains. A blend of the two sets of tools—administrative and market based—is needed. In this blend, a greater emphasis on market-based tools is recommended to provide a better balance and to foster greater synergy between the two. Areas worthy of increased emphasis include greater use of energy pricing and fiscal incentive tools, increased support for the development of the energy efficiency service industry (also discussed in the next section), and increased collaboration with financial sector institutions to foster market-based investment. In addition, good potential exists for increased reliance upon market-based programs as implementation mechanisms for public sector programs, as is effectively employed by many countries abroad.

Furthermore, China's energy pricing policy should go beyond covering the financial costs of energy supply and should better align with the government's goals and policies to create a less energy- and resource-intensive society. Environmental, indirect, and supply security externality costs that are clearly stated as important aspects of energy pricing policy should be reflected in the actual energy prices. However, aggressive energy pricing could aggravate existing barriers that hinder energy efficiency investments. Many energy efficiency projects in China would be highly profitable, even at current prices, but to date they remain unimplemented. Additional barriers include lack of information, prejudice against operating cost-saving investments in favor of revenue-generating investments, initial high transaction costs, and others. Serious market failure exists, particularly in aspects of the building energy efficiency sector, which often require regulation in addition to the use of market forces. Due to these barriers, other countries with successful energy conservation programs have taken approaches that do not rely solely on pricing and laissez-faire market forces. European and North American countries also made great efforts in program design and implementation methods that emphasize the delivery of energy efficiency investments and results, in order to capture as many market forces as possible.

Strengthening Quality in Administrative Program Implementation

Capacity-building needs. Success in achieving ambitious energy efficiency goals through both market-based and administrative efforts will require a massive and continuing capacity-building effort at provincial, prefectural, and even county levels of administration, as well as within tens of thousands of enterprises and all types of energy efficiency service institutions. Government monitoring and supervision units need to play central roles to ensure that the increased number of government oversight requirements is handled effectively. Current staffing numbers and qualification levels, especially in units below the provincial level, are seriously inadequate. It is important for government units' staff to possess basic technical knowledge and to have an understanding of current programs and regulations, but it is also important, especially for the future, for them to have a good understanding of business economics and possible innovative approaches.

Development of enterprise energy-use data reporting systems. Development and rollout of key enterprise energy-use data collection, reporting, validation, and analysis systems is a major and important task for the coming years. Access to internally consistent, comparable, accurate, and timely data is essential if government units are to play a productive role in monitoring and supervision and to devise policies and programs that can best meet the actual needs of enterprises. Careful design of the new data collection systems at the outset is critical. Standard approaches to the complexities of enterprise energy and output accounting are needed, so that data can be usefully compared. Continued national-level guidance on accounting and measurement protocols would be of great assistance. Up-front emphasis is needed on maintaining data quality control and determining exactly how the government will validate data entered by enterprises. Additional issues for attention include data security measures, a clear definition of institutional responsibilities, and development of phased plans for piloting prior to scaling up.

Expanding the Role of the Market in Delivering Energy Efficiency

Having bolstered enterprise interest in energy efficiency investments through administrative measures, provincial governments need to do more to ensure that local enterprises can actually undertake the investments requested of them. While the government provides some concessional finance to encourage investment, by far the largest portion of financing for investment projects must come through the market. Currently, however, many enterprises face serious difficulty in packaging projects in ways that can be accepted by financiers and in securing finance. As a result, many financially attractive potential projects remain unimplemented. Except for a limited number of cases where enterprises possess all the necessary financing and expertise, three key actors are required to deliver energy efficiency project investment through the market: the enterprise, energy efficiency technical and project expert groups, and financiers such as banks. To bring together these three actors, the following areas need to be addressed: (i) developing the energy efficiency industry, (ii) increasing the collaboration with financial sector institutions to foster market-based investment, and (iii) expanding the use of energy pricing tools. Experience in China and elsewhere has shown that rapid development of the energy efficiency service industry and engagement of financial institutions in the energy efficiency business will not just automatically happen. Steady support and targeted assistance are required.

Developing the energy efficiency service industry. While independent institutes and companies involved in the details of identifying, appraising, and implementing energy efficiency projects form a vibrant industry in some parts of China, this industry remains very underdeveloped in others, creating a blockage to rapid progress. Improving the capacity of local companies in technical energy efficiency work, such as auditing, technology assessment, project design, procurement, and commissioning, is crucial. Also important, however, is development of associated business expertise for packaging projects so that enterprises and financiers can accept them, and for helping to bring projects to financial closure. Provincial governments, and, to a large extent, municipal governments, can help with formal policy support and legitimization of the industry, including the EPC business, by using government contracting and contracting procedures to bolster the industry (see the section "Public Buildings" in chapter 7), by fostering training and information exchange, and by supporting development of local energy efficiency service industry associations where appropriate. Standard approaches to improve services can also generate energy savings. For example, governments can organize competitive bidding among third-party companies to take over the operation and maintenance of energy-related services, such as district heating. A key criterion is to require the winning bidder to provide improved service at a lower overall cost. This approach, known as *chauffage*, was introduced over 60 years ago in France. Other well-known models such as concessions and leasing arrangements can have elements of energy savings in utility services, involving the energy efficiency service industry.

Developing energy efficiency lending in the banking sector. Most local banks are unfamiliar with the technology and business of energy efficiency. Financing projects in which benefits are described as projected operating cost savings is not conventional for most banks, which are more used to projects that create new production assets. Many banks are concerned about potentially high transaction costs. Experience in China and elsewhere shows that banks and the energy efficiency community do not naturally interact, and efforts to help them mutually understand and benefit from each other are needed to help move energy efficiency investments.

The World Bank has worked with the national and provincial governments and financial institutions on three main product areas: energy efficiency banking, providing loan guarantees for energy service company investments, and, soon, energy efficiency leasing (see box 6.6). All are useful tools that need appropriate adaptation to local circumstances. In

---

Box 6.6

Energy Efficiency Leasing Concept

In this concept, the lessor is neither a supplier nor vendor of the equipment; the lessor purchases the equipment only for the purpose of leasing it. The lease term and payment may be determined or structured according to the energy savings of the energy efficiency investment subproject. The leasing company will provide services required in designing and implementing an energy efficiency subproject at the client's (otherwise known as "host enterprise") facility, arrange project financing through financial leasing, pay the equipment supplier, and provide support to the host enterprise.

Source: Author.

addition, each may be more suitable for different market segments. For example, large banks may have good relations with established clients and can provide energy efficiency loans as a "value added" service. Under current accounting rules, financial leasing may be more attractive to small and medium enterprises that find collateral requirements of banks onerous, especially for energy savings projects, and accounting treatment of leases favorable.

Promoting equity investments in ESCOs could also help address banking concerns about lending to ESCOs. Due to the nature of their business, ESCOs in particular are traditionally undercapitalized. In response to new government initiatives for promoting EPC contracts, various investment companies or large corporate groups have started forming ESCOs. Unlike previous ESCOs, which mainly employed engineers, ESCOs in China have evolved over their 15-year history and now possess greater financial skills. Promoting equity investments in promising ESCOs is a possible, relatively unexplored area that, if done correctly, could address the problem of undercapitalization of ESCOs and attract much larger flows from commercial banks.

Provincial governments can help mobilize lending for energy efficiency investments from the banking sector by (i) convening regular forums on energy efficiency project financing; (ii) helping to arrange technical assistance on how to develop energy efficiency lending businesses; (iii) cost-sharing of preparation and appraisal costs for certain energy efficiency projects; and (iv) possibly facilitating the use of government energy efficiency investment awards as a form of loan security. Municipal governments could, in cooperation with provincial governments, support further information exchange and encourage participation of local enterprises in demonstration projects where appropriate.

Expanding the use of energy pricing tools. Select surcharges to consumer energy prices can effectively signal to consumers the true costs of their energy consumption to the nation. Revenue from the surcharges can often be returned to consumers through public financial support for energy efficiency measures, thereby minimizing or even completely negating the impact of higher prices on the energy bills of consumers. Provincial governments should review the areas where they have permission to adjust energy prices or add specific energy surcharges, and undertake such adjustments where they can further improve market incentives without unduly compromising vulnerable groups. Although they should be aware of the pricing policies, municipal governments most likely have limited, if any, authority in this area.

Improving Key Enterprise Energy Savings Responsibility Systems

More than 15,000 enterprises with energy consumption of more than 10,000 tce per year are designated as key energy-using enterprises under the Energy Conservation Law, with requirements for data submission and government supervision of their staffing, plans, and progress in energy savings. A further 12,000 may be designated at the discretion of government agencies. These enterprises account for the biggest share of China's total energy consumption. Platforms already put in place to guide and encourage greater energy efficiency in these enterprises will need to be further improved during the next FYP so that steady, continuing energy savings can be achieved.

The use of mandatory enterprise energy savings targets in China has been helpful in focusing attention on achieving energy efficiency results. However, during the 11th FYP, the method to establish quantitative energy intensity reduction targets was inexact. Attention within the Chinese energy efficiency community is now addressing the question of how to customize targets that are consistent with the actual enterprise energy savings potential during the 12th FYP. One possibly useful solution, aspects of which are currently being used in both Europe and Japan, is to follow a sector approach. This involves assessment of unit energy consumption variations, technology development and penetration patterns, and energy savings potential in specific energy-intensive industrial subsectors. The assessment is followed by agreement on overall subsector and enterprise energy savings targets.

Ultimately, however, the key for realizing energy savings in line with cost-effective potential lies with the efforts of enterprises themselves. Increased emphasis needs to be placed on assisting enterprises to plan, manage, and implement energy efficiency measures as part of their own internal systems, with the government playing a more indirect, but important, role monitoring the process, recording agreed enterprise-specific targets, and supervising results.

Supporting competence in enterprise energy managers. Japan's system of government supervision of the energy conservation work of key enterprises, implemented over three decades, places a strong emphasis on ensuring that enterprises have the competence to manage energy efficiently. With requirements for designation of key enterprise energy managers in China's Energy Conservation Law that are similar to those in Japan, China now aims to implement the very necessary major training programs for enterprise energy managers. Success in this effort will be critical to improve enterprise energy savings responsibility systems. It would be very useful to develop and implement one standardized national examination and licensing system for the required energy managers. If the system is established, encouragement of local enterprises by municipalities to participate in the energy managers program is recommended.

Adoption of standardized energy management systems. China's new national Energy Management System (EMS) standard became effective for voluntary implementation on November 1, 2009. EMSs are a set of detailed procedures and practices that enterprises can use to set specific energy efficiency targets and goals cutting across the whole enterprise, to make detailed operational adjustment programs and investment plans accordingly, to assess and quantitatively report on results achieved, and to make further adjustments for continuing future work. By their nature, EMSs are dynamic systems and are highly customized to the individual circumstances of enterprises. Application focuses on achieving steady progress over the short, medium, and long term. Proper application can yield many advantages, including reduction of enterprise energy costs, a solid basis for energy savings targeting, a systematic means to assess compliance with regulations, and an excellent method for identifying attractive investment projects. Rigorous and sustained adoption of standardized EMSs by enterprises provides a systematic way for enterprises to identify and implement energy savings measures of greatest benefit to them (see also box 6.7).

Box 6.7

EMSs and Energy Agreements Program in Ireland

Facilitated by Ireland's national energy agency, Sustainable Energy Ireland (SEI), the Irish industry has been operating a Large Industry Energy Network (LIEN) since the early 1990s. The aim of the network is to reduce energy costs for its members, as well as to gain associated environmental and reputational benefits. Participation is voluntary. To be eligible to participate, companies must be participants in the country's 2006 Energy Agreements Programme or have annual energy expenditures in excess of €1 million. By the end of 2008, LIEN had about 120 members.

In 2005, Ireland issued one of the first EMS standards in the world, IS 393. This standard has been one of the models for Europe's new EN 16001 EMS standard. The IS 393 EMS standard includes typical requirements for energy efficiency man-

(continued next page)

Box 6.7 *(continued)*

agement, planning, targeting, and reporting. As of September 2009, close to 100 enterprises had adopted the voluntary standardized EMS, representing about four-fifths of industrial energy use in Ireland. After the first year of EMS adoption, these companies reported an average energy-related cost savings of about 7 percent. Correct adaptation of the EMS in each enterprise is certified by an independent entity.

In May 2006, SEI launched a new Energy Agreements Programme. Industrial enterprises entering into these Agreements must commit to (i) obtaining certification of proper adaptation of the IS 393 EMS within three years and (ii) complete three "special investigations." In return, SEI guarantees support through (i) assignment of an enterprise-specific agreements support manager to provide both general and technical advice and support; (ii) assistance in overcoming any gaps for certification of EMS standard compliance; (iii) support for identifying topics for special investigations; (iv) financial support for special investigations; (v) workshops, training networking, and other "special initiatives" events; and (vi) publicizing the participation of members in the program as leaders in managing energy and reducing emissions.

The required "Special Investigations" are an important feature of the Energy Agreements Programme. These investigations are enterprise-specific, focusing on assessment of the viability of new energy efficiency technologies for the client enterprise or implementing changes to core processes in energy-intensive areas. SEI provides financial support for the investigations, which are undertaken with assistance from energy efficiency service entities. Host enterprises are not obligated to implement any identified projects, but are required to host the activities and devote management attention to the recommendations.

More than 60 major industrial companies signed onto the Energy Agreements Programme in the first 18 months.

Source: SEI, http://www.seai.ie.

Implementation of EMSs is the most effective when senior enterprise management becomes involved and is held accountable for results. If implemented well, the standardized EMS can also become a very good platform for government-enterprise relationships on energy conservation. Proper adoption of standardized enterprise EMSs can (i) help enterprises customize their own energy conservation actions to provide the greatest overall benefit to themselves; (ii) provide an excellent framework for incorporating compliance with key requirements of the Energy Conservation Law into enterprise practice, which can make the job of provincial and local governments to supervise implementation provisions under the law more efficient and more effective; and (iii) provide a steady and systematic mechanism for identification of priority energy efficiency investment projects. However, to be effective, standardized EMSs cannot be adopted in a lackluster manner. During the current launching phase in China, it is essential for central and provincial governments to provide strong leadership and to set the right tone on high-quality implementation to avoid the possibility that enterprises will perceive the standardized EMS as just another transitory, "in vogue," voluntary management standard. Thus, it is crucial for governments to stress the quality in adoption of the new EMS standard, and not to overemphasize the quantity of enterprises reportedly adopting new systems.

Shandong Province piloted application of its own EMS standard in eight enterprises beginning in 2008. After completing an evaluation of results in 2009, the province is moving to further dissemination. China's central government issued a national EMS standard in 2009, and is strategizing implementation. An international voluntary EMS standard—the ISO 150001—is being developed, with Chinese authorities and experts as active participants.

Trading of energy conservation certificates. Many countries, including China, have entered into agreements with enterprises obligating them to achieve specified energy savings targets, such as the agreements between U.S. regulators and power utility companies, and agreements between European governments and industrial enterprises. In these examples, outside of China, provisions for trading of "certified energy savings," generally known as certificates or credits, are key aspects of these programs. Enterprises have the choice of meeting their obligations fully through their own efforts or purchasing these certificates on the market to meet the gap. The trading scheme of these energy savings certificates or credits can offer great advantages in terms of increased fairness and increased economic efficiency, if implemented effectively. Given the experiences and successful international applications, the institution of consistent methodologies for determining actual energy savings from enterprise energy efficiency investments and completed action plans, backed up with suitable data, should be made a priority in China. Energy savings calculations need to be reliably comparable across enterprises and projects. Consistent calculations are needed to assess enterprise target compliance properly, to assess the contribution of various projects to target achievement, and to assess the results of public energy efficiency fund expenditures. Calculations pose challenges, since energy savings that cannot be directly measured as savings represent the *absence* of energy use.

Experimental pilots with a predefined limited scope could assess the practical potential and implementation possibilities under Chinese conditions. Cities should be aware of this tool, but, because of its complexity, the adoption in China will depend mainly on national government initiatives and provincial government support. Provinces could be a more ideal level for experimentation, perhaps involving a small group of enterprises in a similar line of business and for technical measures where the definition of energy savings is relatively straightforward.

Market-Based Approaches for Use of Public Energy Efficiency Funds

The energy efficiency special funds created by provinces during the 11th FYP are indispensable policy and program support mechanisms. To obtain the greatest energy efficiency results from these funds and put fund financing on sustainable, multiyear footings, attention should be paid to (i) monitoring and verification, (ii) energy efficiency utilities and other performance-based programs, (iii) increasing leverage, and (iv) attaining greater sustainability.

The importance of monitoring and verification. When considering how to get the best results, policy makers and fund administrators might ask, "How can we buy the most energy savings with the limited public funds available?" When shopping for the best deal, it is critical to know the amount of energy savings that has been delivered per RMB of special fund expenditure in different past and current programs. Monitoring and verification are key to estimating how much energy savings may be delivered per RMB from program alternatives in the future, and to monitor the accuracy of these estimates in practice to allow for adjustments.

Energy efficiency utilities and other performance-based programs. An increasingly popular approach among governments worldwide is to engage a third-party entity to deliver energy savings in the most cost-effective way possible under a performance contract with the government. One of a variety of approaches that may be of interest to provincial governments is the creation of new energy efficiency utilities (EEUs), as adopted by several state governments in the United States. These are new institutions, unrelated to electric power or other energy supply utilities, whose sole purpose is to realize energy savings requested by governments as effectively and cheaply as possible. EEUs prepare programs for investment project promotion, targeted subsidies, awareness-building activities, community organizing, and technical assistance, with an overriding objective of maximizing energy savings per unit expenditure. The legal entities that operate the EEUs are issued performance contracts, typically following competitive procurement procedures. The performance contracts tie compensation to energy savings levels validated by the state government. EEUs may be revenue earning or not (see also box 6.8). For Chinese

Box 6.8

Vermont's Energy Efficiency Utility

The state government of Vermont, located in the northeastern part of the United States, approved the establishment of a new EEU program in 1999. The EEU, called "Efficiency Vermont," is now well known among the state's residents and businesses. The objective of the utility program is to supply the maximum amount of electricity savings with the least amount of public funding. The utility program is implemented by an independent corporation, the Vermont Energy Investment Corporation, under a contract with the state's electric power regulatory agency, the Vermont Public Services Board. The contract was awarded following competitive bidding. The contract is for three years but can be renewed for an additional three years. Every six years, a new competitively bidding procedure must be followed for awarding the contract, according to state law.

The Public Services Board hires a Contract Administrator who oversees all details of the contract and EEU implementation. The contract is financed by an electricity sales surcharge amounting to 2.82 percent of consumers' total electricity payment. The surcharge funds are then transferred to the EEU contractor according to the terms of a contract by a Fiscal Agent, who is also hired by the Public Services Board. Rigorous and detailed monitoring and verification of the actual electricity savings achieved by the EEU program is undertaken by the state's Department of Public Services. The results of the independent verification of the savings achieved serve as an important factor in determining the payment of the EEU contractor's performance-based fee.

In recent years, the state government has used the EEU as a vehicle to implement several additional special programs to deliver specific electricity savings in regions experiencing serious congestion in the power grid. Recently, the state government authorized the EEU to undertake new programs to deliver fuel savings through improvements in home heating efficiency to alleviate the high heating costs due to rising oil prices.

Source: Efficiency Vermont (2009) and www.efficiencyvermont.org.

provinces and municipalities, the EEU concept could be a useful mechanism to achieve high energy savings rates with a portion of special energy efficiency public funding. The main objective may be to provide validated energy savings at an attractively low cost—at least well below the levels provided in current energy efficiency investment award programs, with rigorous monitoring and verification. A permanent legal entity could be established or assigned to implement the EEU through a performance or time-based contract with the government. Governments can also assign specific markets for concentration, either narrow or broad, as well as determine the legal status of the EEU. In some cases, especially for public buildings (see chapter 7), a SuperESCO approach may be attractive, in which the EEU, in exchange for a substantial share of the profits, provides financing for energy performance contracts developed by ESCOs in the province. This would serve to both foster development of the local ESCO industry and yield energy savings at low (or even negative) cost.

Increasing leverage. Another set of options for maximizing energy savings results is to establish partnerships with other financing institutions or sources to increase the leverage of public energy efficiency funds in fostering investment. Operation of loan guarantee facilities and development of new energy efficiency investment funds are two among a variety of possibilities (see boxes 6.9 and 6.10).

Box 6.9

Global Environment Facility Funding for China's ESCO Loan Guarantee Program

The Global Environment Facility (GEF) provided a grant to implement a partial-risk guarantee program for new loans from Chinese banks to emerging ESCOs in China. The objective was to help Chinese ESCOs develop project financing channels with local banks, and thereby help foster the growth of Chinese ESCOs. A grant of US$22 million was used to create and operate a reserve fund to back the guarantees issued by China National Investment and Guarantee Company (I&G) during the project's six years, which ended in December 2009.

Based on provisional tallies, I&G issued more than RMB 500 million in guarantees for 142 projects developed by 41 ESCOs during the first five years and nine

(continued next page)

Box 6.9 *(continued)*

months of the program. Energy performance contracting investment totaled about RMB 870 million, generating an annual energy savings capacity of about 520,000 tce. Over the life of the assets generated by the investment, total energy savings may be about 5.5 million tce.

US$21.2 million out of the US$22 million reserve fund were retained, with payouts made to only four project defaults (most of which have been recovered). Under the program, the net public financing outlay amounted to only about RMB 3 per tce of expected energy savings directly from projects supported by the guarantee program. The program also introduced many of China's emerging ESCOs to the financial community, creating new financing relationships. The Chinese government has decided to continue to provide long-term support to energy efficiency investments, using the same fund and similar types of guarantee mechanisms.

Source: World Bank project documents.

Box 6.10

The International Finance Corporation's China Utility-Based Energy Efficiency Finance Program (CHUEE)

Financing energy efficiency is an integral part of a strategic focus by the International Finance Corporation (IFC) on sustainability and climate change. The IFC-financed CHUEE program, which started in 2006, is aimed at stimulating energy efficiency investments in China through two main instruments: (i) bank guarantees for energy efficiency loans and (ii) technical assistance to market players, including utilities, equipment vendors, and energy service companies, to help implement energy efficiency projects.

CHUEE features loan guarantees for partner commercial banks, giving them incentives to lend to support energy efficiency projects. World Bank lending would then be supported by IFC's guarantees. The guarantee facility was designed to partially compensate participating banks for losses from this line of business. For example, 75 percent of the first 10 percent loss of the principal loan

(continued next page)

Box 6.10 *(continued)*

amount would be guaranteed by CHUEE, and the remaining 25 percent of the loss would be covered by the participating banks. For the remaining portfolio of energy efficiency lending (90 percent), IFC was to cover 40 percent of the losses and the participating banks were to cover the remaining 60 percent. The purpose of the risk-sharing facility was to provide incentives for participating banks to experiment with energy efficiency financing, as well as to build their capacity to undertake this kind of business as a standard business line.

As of June 2009, the program's participating banks provided loans, totaling RMB 3.5 billion (US$512 million), for 98 energy efficiency projects, such as heat and gas recovery power generation and the introduction of efficient production systems. The steel, chemical, and cement industries are the largest beneficiaries. It is estimated that these investments reduced greenhouse gas (GHG) emissions by 14 million tons of CO_2 per year, exceeding the program's original target. This reduction amounts to 40 percent of the annual emissions of the largest emitter of CO_2 among China's power plants.

Source: World Bank 2010.

Achieving greater sustainability. Achievement of the best results from public energy efficiency funds requires sustained effort over a number of years, which in turn requires predictable and steady financial support. This usually requires earmarking of some types of specific public revenues to energy efficiency funds. A common option internationally, which also has been adopted by some provinces and can be further considered by others, is the allocation of a portion of certain energy production or use surcharges.

China's provinces and cities should consider what options for development of multiyear earmarked financing for energy efficiency programs might best suit their conditions, and select one or two for implementation. In developing and processing proposals, it is also recommended that strong emphasis be placed on (i) specific monitoring and verification methods, procedures, and responsibilities to ensure that provincial governments can clearly see the actual energy savings results from fund expenditures, and (ii) specific mechanisms and the adoption of specific evaluation and adjustment procedures to allow a clear and credible focus on achieving maximum energy savings per unit of public investment.

Recommendations for Enhancing Industrial Energy Efficiency Programs in the Medium Term

The policies, program concepts, and implementation platforms created over the last four years will assist China to achieve further energy conservation results during the next five-year planning cycle, and will help the country achieve its target to reduce the carbon intensity of its economy by 40–45 percent by 2020. However, much work remains to be done to improve, adjust, and strengthen the programs further, and to continue to interject new and creative solutions.

Recommendations for provincial governments to consider for the upcoming 12th five-year planning cycle are outlined below, focusing mainly on improving the quality of provincial program implementation and increasing the use of market-based tools.[7] (Also see box 6.11 for an overview of the World Bank's support for industrial energy efficiency in

---

Box 6.11

World Bank Support for Industrial Energy Efficiency in China

The World Bank's long-standing support for industrial energy efficiency in China started with the introduction of key energy efficiency project concepts. Initially, the Energy Conservation Project provided GEF grant and World Bank loan support to three of China's first Energy Management Companies (EMCs, also commonly known as ESCOs; see also box 6.4). This project helped to buy down costs of the first EPC projects and demonstrated that EPCs can be a viable business. At this early stage of market development, the World Bank lending provided assured financing of good EPC projects under strict criteria.

The Second Energy Conservation Project, which started in 2004, provided a partial credit guarantee for commercial loans to ESCOs to encourage lending to the new market. This was the first time that GEF funds were used to set up a reserve fund backstopping a guarantee instrument. The US$22 million reserve fund covered about US$63 million in loans to 42 ESCOs for 148 EPC projects totaling US$123 million. The project supported a domestic guarantee company and focused exclusively on EPC projects. Shortly after, the IFC of the World Bank Group introduced the CHUEE Program with a similar first-loss guarantee scheme, which yielded US$512 million in investments in a broad range of energy efficiency projects. The Second Energy Conservation Project also supported the newly estab-

(continued next page)

Box 6.11 *(continued)*

lished EMCA, which was set up to promote the EPC mechanism offered by ESCOs, by providing funds to carry out dissemination and training, helping it gain operational experience and credibility in the market (see also box 6.4).

World Bank support for energy efficiency in China continued at the start of the 11th FYP (2006–11), which for the first time included binding energy intensity reduction targets assigned to provinces and the top 1,000 energy-consuming enterprises. Over this FYP period, the World Bank lent US$300 million to three banks (China Exim, Huaxia, and Mingsheng) for a wide range of energy efficiency investments—not just EPC investments—focusing mainly on medium-size enterprises. The Bank also mobilized an additional GEF grant that, among other things, provided start-up support to the National Energy Conservation Center under NDRC to help build institutional capacity to disseminate, monitor, and support the ever-growing range of programs and policies in energy conservation. During this time, the Bank also mobilized carbon financing through the Clean Development Mechanism with several industrial energy efficiency projects. This basically provided a "platform of support" in which repeater projects, with adjustments to promote innovations and incorporate lessons, are approved to support mainstreaming energy efficiency banking. These projects also accelerate energy efficiency investments to help meet energy intensity reduction targets. The system that eventually evolved to supervise achievement of these targets is maturing into a sophisticated regulatory framework, which will in the future rely more on the market to deliver energy savings.

World Bank support was maintained at the start of the 12th FYP. This plan, which continues energy intensity reduction efforts and includes new binding carbon intensity reduction targets, builds on the earlier platform approaches and will focus on implementation support at provincial and local levels to help augment capacities needed to undertake larger and more sophisticated energy conservation efforts. It also helps the markets and regulatory framework achieve the right balance to ensure a cost-effective and optimal achievement of energy savings. This approach has already included, in 2011, the approval of the GEF Provincial Energy Efficiency Scale Up Program (covering Shanxi, Shandong, and Jiangxi Provinces); the Shandong Energy Efficiency Project (supporting "Energy Efficiency Leasing," that is, financial leasing for energy savings projects following EPC principles); and the GEF Industrial Energy Efficiency Promotion Project (supporting training for energy management at the enterprise level). The Bank is also assisting China's efforts to develop a carbon cap-and-trade regime.

Source: World Bank project documents and Sun et al. 2011.

China.) While not all recommendations may be directly applicable to cities, the list highlights issues and options that provide a broader context to city-level energy efficiency efforts.

Improving Quality in Provincial Program Implementation

The quality of provincial program implementation can be increased by:

- *Strengthening local human infrastructure for energy conservation program delivery:* Staffing levels and skills must be upgraded at all levels, both within and outside of government.
- *Developing improved data reporting systems for enterprise energy use:* Systems need to be carefully planned and systematically rolled out.
- *Supporting innovation at local levels:* In the northern provinces, local experimentation and piloting are especially needed to implement consumption-based heat billing and energy efficiency renovation of existing buildings, as well as other areas.
- *Reviewing options for further expanding energy savings results from provincial energy conservation special funds:* Scientific assessments of energy savings achieved from current fund use need to be followed up with development of future strategies.
- *Considering how to develop multiyear, sustainable financing sources for provincial energy conservation special funds:* Further improvements in key energy-consuming enterprise energy savings agreements and associated initiatives could provide among the largest energy savings results during the 12th FYP. Three important areas for focus include:
  - *Increasing customization in enterprise energy savings targeting:* Completion of industrial subsector energy savings assessments may be one useful tool.
  - *Supporting competence in enterprise energy managers:* A standardized national examination and licensing system for designated energy managers is recommended.
  - *Fostering the adoption of rigorous and standardized EMSs in key enterprises:* Effective and high-quality implementation of standardized EMSs may be a crucial foundation for long-term, sustainable energy efficiency gains.

Increasing Use of Market-Based Tools

Expanding the use of market-based tools will accelerate and deepen energy efficiency efforts. Their role can be expanded through:

- *Expanding use of energy pricing tools:* In addition to increasing incentives to reduce energy costs, revenue from surcharges can be explicitly returned to energy-using taxpayers as concessional financing for energy efficiency measures.
- *Fostering development of local service industries for energy efficiency:* Local institutes, centers, and energy efficiency companies play critical technical and project packaging roles and need more support.
- *Encouraging the expansion of energy efficiency lending by local financial institutions:* Energy efficiency project lending rarely falls into standard loan categories for local banks and usually requires special efforts.
- *Moving to commodification of energy savings:* Measures to ensure consistent and credible calculation of energy savings from projects is a first step to making energy savings a tradable commodity.
- *Piloting trade in energy savings certificates:* Fairness and economic efficiency in the enterprise targeting system could be improved by allowing trade in certified energy savings, beginning with local experiments.
- *Developing possible new programs to expand results from provincial government energy conservation funds:* Two options include establishing provincial EEUs and partnering with other financial institutions to increase fund leverage.

Notes

1. This chapter is an edited excerpt from the June 2010 publication by Robert Taylor, Gailius Draugelis, Yabei Zhang, and Alberto U. Ang Co., *Accelerating Energy Conservation in China's Provinces.* The author also gratefully acknowledges research assistance for this chapter by Shawna Fei Li, World Bank junior professional associate.

2. According to analyses by Dhakal (2009), the industrial sector has historically dominated CO_2 emissions in the municipalities of Beijing, Chongqing Shanghai, and Tianjin. Although recent data show a declining trend of CO_2 emissions from the industrial sector, 60–70 percent of total CO_2 emissions in Chongqing, Shanghai, and Tianjin are from industries.

3. In December 2009, China's National Bureau of Statistics announced that the reconciliation of past series of energy consumption, GDP, and energy intensity statistics with the results of the massive 2008 National Economic Census had been completed. Previously reported energy consumption and GDP statistics are being revised accordingly.

4. Data and official announcement of the National Bureau of Energy and National Bureau of Statistics.

5. The law also allows relevant agencies to designate enterprises consuming between 5,000 and 10,000 tce per year as key energy-consuming enterprises.
6. In China, these industries are referred to as "backward." For the purposes of this chapter, we use "inefficient."
7. The recommendations in this section are based on the World Bank report, *Accelerating Energy Conservation in China's Provinces*. For more detailed information about these recommendations, please see the full report by Taylor et al. 2010.

Bibliography

Dhakal, S. 2009. "Urban Energy Use and Carbon Emissions from Cities in China and Policy Implications." *Energy Policy* 37 (11): 4208–19.

Efficiency Vermont. 2009. *Year 2008 Annual Report*. October 2009. Burlington, VT: Efficiency Vermont. http://www.efficiencyvermont.com/docs/about_efficiency_vermont/annual_reports/2008_Efficiency_Vermont_Annual_Report.pdf.

Project Management Office of NDRC/WB/GEF China Energy Conservation Project. 2010. "Energy Performance Contracting in China. The Growing Up of ESCO Industry in China 1998–2010." Project brochure.

Sustainable Energy Ireland (SEI). http://www.seai.ie/.

Singh, J., D. Limaye, B. Henderson, and X. Shi. 2010. "Public Procurement of Energy Efficiency Services, Lessons from International Experience." Washington DC: World Bank.

Sun, X., L. Zhu, and R. Taylor. 2011. "China's ESCO Industry: Saving More Energy Everyday through the Market." Unpublished manuscript, May 9. http://ryan-schuchard.files.wordpress.com/2011/06/chinas-esco-industry-2010.pdf.

Taylor, R., G. Draugelis, Y. Zhang, and A. U. Ang Co. 2010. *Accelerating Energy Conservation in China's Provinces*. Washington DC: AusAID/World Bank. http://www.worldbank.org/research/2010/06/12720925/accelerating-energy-conservation-chinas-provinces.

World Bank. 2010. "Energy Efficiency Finance: Assessing the Impact of IFC's China Utility-Based Energy Efficiency Finance Program." World Bank, Washington, DC.

CHAPTER 7

Energy Efficiency in Buildings

Gailius Draugelis and Shawna Fei Li

Overview

In general, buildings contribute to a large portion of total CO_2 emissions. For example, buildings in the United States contribute 37 percent of the country's total CO_2 emissions (U.S. Dept. of Energy 2005). Energy-efficient buildings are seen by climate change experts as one of the least-cost approaches to mitigating greenhouse gas (GHG) emissions. This chapter deals specifically with the Chinese experiences of energy efficiency measures that can be implemented at the building level. In addition to experience gained in World Bank projects and studies, the authors rely heavily on a recent World Bank report by Feng Liu, Anke Meyer, and John Hogan (2010), titled "Mainstreaming Building Energy Efficiency Codes in Developing Countries—Global Experiences and Lessons from Early Adopters." This chapter summarizes the achievements in the Chinese building sector to address the global problem of energy efficiency. It also proposes solutions to further develop the capacity of this sector and encourages further use of market-based and performance-based approaches, especially for government facilities. The chapter focuses mainly on thermal energy efficiency, an area where the Bank has extensive experience. Other building energy consumption aspects, such as appliances, lighting, and energy intensity of building materials, are also important parts of building energy consumption, but the Bank, thus far, has less experience with those in China.

Introduction

In China, building energy efficiency and district heating sector reform are essential elements of a low-carbon development strategy in the 16 cold-climate provinces where heating is a legal requirement. Building energy efficiency and heating sector reform go hand in hand. In 2001, the World Bank started working on the issue by providing technical assistance to investigate options for building energy efficiency. Subsequently, the World Bank has worked closely with the Ministry of Housing and Urban-Rural Development (MoHURD, formerly the Ministry of Construction, or MOC) and other ministries on preparing suggestions for a two-part heat tariff, studies on the social impacts of heating sector reform, and new heating sector regulations. As partners with MoHURD, the World Bank mobilized grant funds from the Global Environment Facility (GEF) and started the Heat Reform and Building Energy Efficiency Project (HRBEE) in 2005. Demonstration projects for consumption-based billing and building energy efficiency are being implemented in Urumqi, Tianjin, Tangshan, and Dalian, covering about 3.6 million square meters. The World Bank also is providing loan support for heating modernization—for example, in Beijing during the preparation of the 2008 Olympics and in Liaoning Province starting in the same year. In total, the World Bank is working with about 16 cities through GEF grant and World Bank loan projects.

If implemented well, district heating reform and building energy efficiency can generate important local and global benefits by improving air quality and reducing coal consumption. By reducing the energy needed to heat and cool a home or an office building, building energy efficiency measures and green building standards can also make renewable energy for heating and cooling more affordable. Technologies such as net zero energy buildings also exist, but they rely on different approaches to siting, design, and application of technologies than are commonly used today. When consumption-based billing is implemented, paying for heat according to the meter will provide a strong incentive to conserve energy for heating. This is the key to unlocking the full potential of building energy efficiency in the northern provinces.

In the future, siting and building design will need to take into greater account their influence on modes of transport, especially if buildings will be a source of energy for plug-in electric vehicles and other advanced low-carbon technologies.

Building Energy Efficiency

Background on the Chinese Building Sector in Cold and Severe-Cold Climates

About one-third of global energy consumption is for the provision of energy services in residential, commercial, and public service buildings. Building energy services include all the energy consumption associated with a building, such as heating and cooling,[1] ventilation fans, lighting, refrigeration, cooking, water heating, elevators and escalators, as well as operation of electric and electronic equipment.

China is among the first developing countries to introduce mandatory Building Energy Efficiency Codes (BEECs) and has achieved significant success in compliance enforcement. Government inspections indicate that in a few dozen large cities, about 80 percent of residential buildings completed in 2008 complied with the applicable BEECs, compared to about 20 percent in 2005 and 6 percent in 2000 (Liu, Meyer, and Hogan 2010). Much of the progress in compliance has been attained only in the past five years, benefiting from the convergence of several factors due to government reform efforts and economic growth. The national campaign to achieve the 20 percent energy intensity reduction goal of the 11th Five-Year Plan for 2006–10 has been critical for stepping up city-level enforcement of BEEC compliance. This is notable since it is estimated that 40 percent of the building stock in China by 2030 will be constructed after 2010 (Liu, Meyer, and Hogan 2010). In essence, because the rate of new building construction is so high in China, the level of building energy efficiency a decade from now will be heavily determined by the energy efficiency characteristics of buildings being constructed today.

China's cities of the future can continue a legacy of innovation with advanced building energy efficiency codes, designs, and technologies. Cities such as Tianjin have pioneered advanced building energy efficiency codes that are now replicated in other cities. National building energy efficiency codes should be considered a minimum requirement, and low-carbon cities are encouraged to exceed this requirement based on local circumstances and climatic conditions.

Building energy consumption patterns are heavily influenced by climate conditions because of the demand for heating and cooling, with heating being the single largest source of energy use in buildings for countries in a cold climate. These consumption patterns are equally and significantly affected by income levels, which underpin energy access and affordability.

Existing residential BEECs in China cover large urban residential constructions in three distinct zones: cold and severely cold zones, a hot-summer and cold-winter zone, and a hot-summer and warm-winter zone. Together these account for 97 percent of the residential building stock of the country (see box 7.1). Urban residential buildings in the temperate

---

Box 7.1

Climate Zoning for Building Thermal Designs in China

Building energy efficiency codes for the various climatic conditions were developed at the national level between 1995 and 2005. Municipalities may elect to adopt stricter standards, as, for example, Tianjin municipality has done. About 550 million people live in China's cold and severe-cold zones with about 43 percent of the urban residential and commercial stock; about 500 million people live in the hot-summer and cold-winter zone with about 42 percent of the urban stock; and about 160 million people live in the hot-summer and warm-winter zone with about 12 percent of the urban stock. About 3 percent of the residential building stock is found in the temperate-zone.

Figure B7.1.1   Map of China's Climate Zones

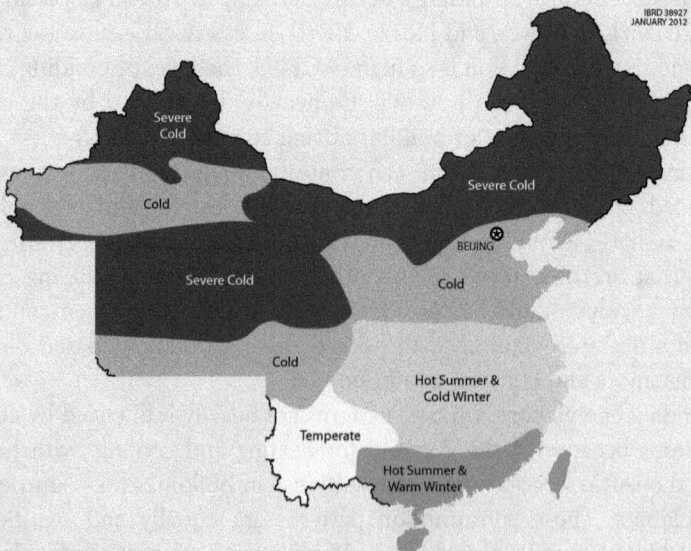

Source: Liu, Meyer, and Hogan 2010.

zone, about 3 percent of the total urban building stock, are not subjected to a mandatory residential BEEC. In contrast, the BEEC for public and commercial buildings covers all climate zones. Climatic conditions in China are varied and generally severe: winter is cold and summer is hot. Humidity levels are also high in eastern and southeastern regions. These conditions make for high heating and cooling requirements.

The main focus of municipalities regarding building energy efficiency includes the development and enforcement of energy efficiency codes for new residential and commercial buildings, the promotion of energy efficiency retrofits for existing buildings, and the development and implementation of heating reforms in northern provinces. MoHURD and its provincial- and municipal-level affiliated construction commissions have primary responsibility for these agendas within the government, and are responsible for government oversight of the heating industry. Municipal governments are responsible for program implementation, code enforcement, and setting heat prices. MoHURD and provincial governments provide policy guidance, coordination, and support.

As the 11th Five-Year Plan has progressed, increasing attention is also being devoted to new initiatives to improve energy efficiency in government-owned public buildings. In August 2008, the State Council issued a national *Regulation on Energy Conservation by Public Institutions* that, for the first time, establishes responsibilities, accountabilities, and targeting and monitoring requirements to increase energy efficiency in government facilities. While initial implementation focuses on central government facilities, this and other initiatives have set the stage for expanded efforts at provincial levels as well.

The International Energy Agency's reference scenario in the *2010 World Energy Outlook*, which assumes continuation of current policies and no major technological breakthroughs, indicates a 46 percent increase in building energy consumption, from 426 million tonnes of oil equivalent (Mtoe) in 2007 to 622 Mtoe in 2035 (IEA 2010).

The Residential Building Energy Efficient Design Standards, effective in 1996 (RBEED-95), specifically target new residential buildings with centralized heat supply in cold and severe-cold climates. Other codes include adjusted standards to cover hot-summer and cold/warm-winter zones (2001, updated in 2003), and a Public Building Energy Conservation Design (2005). The goal of these standards is to reduce the space-heating energy consumption by 50 percent compared to 1986 levels, primarily by improving the thermal integrity of the building envelope. To help strengthen consistency in compliance enforcement and to standardize procedures, the National Code for Acceptance of Energy Efficient Building Construction was promulgated in 2007. In addition, some municipalities have issued more stringent building energy efficiency codes, such as Tianjin municipality, calling for a reduction in consumption by 65 percent compared to 1986 levels. MoHURD is expected to promulgate a revised national residential standard for cold climate zones in 2010, with a similar energy savings target of 65 percent.

Overall, the improved compliance of new building designs with these energy efficiency codes has been a major achievement in recent years. Compliance was reported at only 30 percent in 2003, but has since risen to a reported 98 percent in 2008 (Cai et al. 2010). This effort has required strong organization and focus throughout the government system. However, while building energy efficiency codes were introduced early, and while their success is measured by high design compliance, other elements are required to make the BEECs more comprehensive. In fact, to be even more effective at reducing global building energy consumption patterns, the BEECs could introduce design solutions that are beyond simple energy efficiency criteria and integrate green building solutions, continue to improve code enforcement, and accelerate credible labeling for energy efficient building materials.

Green Buildings

Green buildings,[2] also labeled as green construction or sustainable buildings, is a shorthand term commonly used to describe the practice of creating structures and using processes that are environmentally responsible and resource efficient throughout a building's lifecycle: from siting to design, construction, operation, maintenance, renovation, and demolition. This practice expands and complements the classical building design concerns of economy, utility, durability, and comfort.

By definition, the term *green building* is a broad approach of resource conservation applied to construction, while the term *building energy efficiency standards* focuses more narrowly on energy consumption for space conditioning (heating and cooling). There are several prominent green building evaluation standards internationally. One example, Leadership in Energy and Environmental Design (LEED), a standard developed by the U.S. Green Building Council, is considered an important international benchmark and has been applied in China. Furthermore, in 2006 MoHURD issued the Green Building Evaluation Standard (GB 50378-2006) (GBES) and detailed technical rules to establish an evaluation system for green buildings. The structure of the GBES includes (i) land conservation and outdoor environment, (ii) energy conservation and utilization of energy resources, (iii) water conservation and utilization of water resources, (iv) materials conservation and utilization of materials resources, (v) indoor environment quality, and (vi) operation and maintenance. Each of these sections has quantitative as well as qualitative items. Performance standards are classified into three parts: prerequisite, general elective, and preferred elective. Based on general elective and preferred elective criteria, a green building can be rated as one-star, two-star, or three-star.

There are many sources of information on technical requirements, and it is difficult to cover all available information exhaustively. The GBES of the Sino-Singapore Tianjin Eco-City (SSTEC) in Tianjin municipality will be presented here as an example to highlight some topics and suggestions when considering local application of the green building concepts.

Municipalities should be encouraged to introduce evaluation criteria stricter than the national standard. This stricter standard, if designed well, encourages innovation and development of design and technical applications in the built environment.

Given that LEED is well known and has been used in China, it is used here as an example for more detailed comparison with SSTEC's GBES. Structurally, SSTEC's GBES is similar to major international building rating systems. Compared to LEED, SSTEC's GBES shares the same categories, except that it has an additional category on operations and management, which is a very important area for sustainable buildings in China. In terms of processes, the following four aspects are worthy of discussion.

Time of rating. Based on SSTEC's GBES, a rating can be awarded only after one year of property operation, while the LEED Core and Shell system allows developers to submit their designs and achieve "pre-certification" before buildings are built. The post facto certification system in SSTEC's GBES ensures that the predicted energy savings are actually achieved. This is especially important since compliance with building codes in China remains a challenge. The "pre-certification" system, however, allows developers to capture some of the benefits of going green by getting higher financial return, higher rents and real estate prices, quicker leases, and faster sales, and ultimately drives more developers to build green. The two systems can work together and complement each other, so SSTEC's GBES may also consider adding a "pre-certification" system.

Administration of the rating system. In the LEED system, LEED-accredited professionals help to administer the design and construction, while an "unknown" third party evaluates the submitted LEED documentation. SSTEC's GBES notes that the quantitative items will be evaluated by a third party certified by the SSTEC Green Building Evaluation Committee (GBEC) and the final award will be determined by the GBEC. However, it is not clear who will be responsible for the evaluation of qualitative items or how the quality of the evaluation is ensured. Evaluating and certifying all aspects of SSTES GBES will require significant skilled labor. One reason that China has uneven building code compliance is that the local government does not have sufficient staff to oversee compliance, especially for the energy efficiency component (discussed later in this chapter).

Energy commissioning. Energy commissioning is required in LEED, while no such requirement has been defined in SSTEC's GBES. While there is an acceptance standard for building energy efficiency elements, the concept of energy commissioning is used more broadly to verify that the project's energy-related systems are installed and calibrated to perform according to the project requirements, basis of design and construction documents. Energy commissioning has multiple benefits including reduced energy use, lower operating costs, fewer contractor callbacks, better building documentation, increased occupant productivity, and improved system performance verification. A recent study in China (Baeumler et al. 2009) shows that projects with a comprehensive approach to commissioning attained nearly twice the overall median level of savings and five times the savings of the least thorough projects. Adding this process to SSTEC's GBES is especially important not only because it helps ensure that the basic requirements for green buildings are met, but also because this process is a risk-management strategy to detect and correct future and possibly costly maintenance problems or safety issues.

Energy performance requirements for major energy end uses. For energy efficiency, besides building envelope and central heating, SSTEC's GBES does not have clearly defined requirements for other energy systems. This is especially true for residential buildings. Criteria may need to be developed for at least the following: (i) lighting, (ii) air conditioning, (iii) water heating, (iv) appliances, and (v) controls. The following are examples of the specific requirements used for LEED certification. Similar specific requirements for major energy end uses, suitable to SSTEC condition, could also be developed:

- Lighting standard: 0.7 watt/square foot to 1.0 watt/square foot
- Air conditioning: seasonal energy efficiency ratio of 12.0 to 15.0
- Water heating: instantaneous gas—over 90 percent efficient
- Tank heater: at least 80 percent efficient.

Box 7.2 describes an example of a new community implementing green building standards.

Hurdles to Improved Building Energy Efficiency

Various barriers exist to improving building energy efficiency in China. Box 7.3 describes a World Bank/GEF project that focused on overcoming these interwoven barriers. More information about these barriers can also be found in a series of specific World Bank study reports completed during 2001–09 and analysis and reports associated with the World Bank/ GEF Heat Reform and Building Energy Efficiency Project (World Bank 2001; Ping et al. 2002; World Bank 2005; Meyer and Kalkum 2008; Liu et al. 2006, and Liu, Meyer, and Hogan 2010) and the Eco^2 Cities report (Suzuki et al. 2010).

New Residential and Commercial Buildings

Building energy efficiency can be understood as a process of reducing energy consumption at each step of the building design, construction, and use. Improvements in building codes are only one step in the process. When designing building energy efficiency programs, the process can be further broken down into the urban plan and site plan (siting), the building envelope, the internal heat network, and the heating system. In addi-

---

Box 7.2

GEF's Huayuan Borui New Community: Combining Green Building and Heating Supply Reform

In 2005, the World Bank mobilized a GEF grant to support the MoHURD in promoting heat reform and building energy efficiency. One subcomponent of this project is to support the municipal government of Urumqi in developing the Huanyan Borui building energy efficiency demonstration project. The project was built using the "65%" building energy efficiency standard, which had not yet been formally adopted by the city. It implemented consumption-based billing for district heating and also included the use of solar hot water, water recycling, and other technologies. The Huayuan Village Project applied for a two-star rating under the national green building evaluation standard and received a national award from the China Real Estate Association. The project also was labeled in the *Xinjiang Daily News* as "the first large-scale green residential district of Urumqi."

Source: Authors.

Box 7.3

World Bank/GEF–Supported Heat Reform and Building Energy Efficiency Project

Recognizing the interwoven barriers that are hindering higher efficiency levels in heat supply and consumption in China, the World Bank and GEF mobilized a grant to provide technical assistance. This grant was extended to help China address the barrier in advancing the government's agenda in heat reform, through modernization of heat supply and improvement in building energy efficiency. The project, which is still under implementation, consists of three components:

- *Introducing modern heat supply and energy efficient building design and construction in the Tianjin municipality:* The project selected several new, large housing developments in Tianjin to pilot the reform measures to reduce heat loss by 30 percent below the previous building energy efficiency standard in Tianjin. This demonstration project supports the municipal government to integrate a heat supply system that is demand driven. Rapid expansion of Tianjin's individual metering and consumption-based billing program on a household level is also supported. One subproject includes geothermal district heating supply.
- *Supporting the central government in developing comprehensive policies in heat reform and building energy efficiency:* The project ensures that adequate expertise is available in the central government to monitor and evaluate progress and results of policy implementations by the provincial and local governments.
- *Promoting the development of heat system restructuring, billing and pricing reform, and building energy efficiency in four to six additional municipalities:* The project will apply lessons learned from the Tianjin pilot and incorporate new national-level policies to expand heat sector reform in designing and implementing additional local projects and policy support.

Source: World Bank project documents.

tion to thermal integrity of the building, energy efficiency gains can be achieved through broader planning and design measures. Building location and orientation, as well as distance to other buildings to prevent shadows in winter, are measures that can promote passive solar gains and lower energy use. Substantial energy efficiency gains can therefore be achieved at very low or zero cost by considering potential solar gains and heat loss reduction in building orientation (by using an optimal integration to sun and wind patterns, including window orientation and size, solar shading during summer, and making use of natural ventilation) and from optimal building shape coefficients (by optimizing the ratio of floor to wall area, see box 7.4). Realization of these potential gains, however, would require specific attention by developers and municipal authorities before site plans *(konggui)* are approved. Box 7.5 presents an example of such early planning for energy efficiency.

Box 7.4

Considering the Building Shape Coefficient

In architecture, exterior walls are often referred to as the building envelope. They are a critical point in the design of a building, shielding it from the weather and protecting its inhabitants. As the building envelope is directly in contact with the exterior, this is the main area where heat can be transmitted. Consequently, less exterior wall area can translate into less energy losses. However, in some instances, some building requirements, non-energy related, may contradict or even hamper building energy efficiency objectives. For example, a local building code or bylaw may require a window in the main bathroom. This would require a more complex layout, and possibly an increased amount of exterior wall space to achieve the requirement—resulting in larger energy losses. The following example demonstrates how the same building can be designed with a more optimal building shape without cost increases but with increased energy savings capacity.

Figure B7.4.1   Simplified Example of Building Shape Coefficient

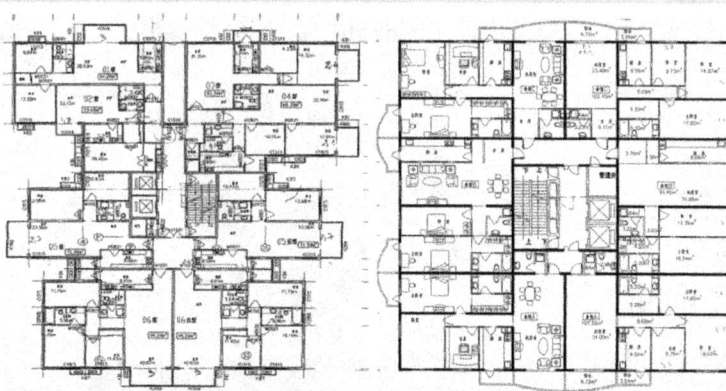

Main washroom with exterior window: Main washroom without exterior window:
Complex plan and increased building envelope.   Simpler plan, reduced building envelope.

Source: Bellanger 2009.

Box 7.5

Early Planning for Energy Efficiency: the Site Plan

Building orientation is one of the most determinant factors when trying to save energy. Indeed, correctly orienting a facade can maximize solar energy gains, thus allowing for savings in the use of the building systems. In a cold climate, a maximum of southern exposures will be ideal, while the reverse is true in a hot climate. Comparing the two options in this example, an optimized site plan could allow for 20–35 percent more solar energy. This could translate into energy savings of 4 to 8 percent during the winter.

Figure B7.5.1   Site Plans with Different Building Orientation

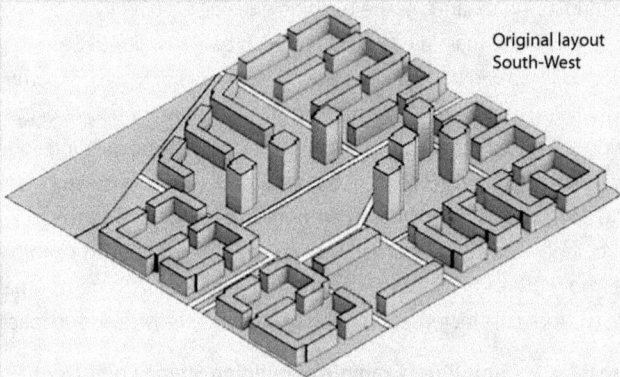

| 65,000 |
| 74,400 |
| 83,800 |
| 93,200 |
| 102,600 |
| 112,000 |
| 121,400 |
| 130,800 |
| 140,200 |
| 149,600 |
| 159,000 |
| 168,400 |
| 177,800 |
| 187,200 |
| 196,600 |
| 206,000 |
| 215,400 |
| 224,800 |
| 234,200 |
| 243,600 |
| 253,000 |
| 262,400 |
| 271,800 |
| 281,200 |
| 290,600 |
| W/m² |

Days total, Sum on hours, TOTAL Energy

Original layout
South-West

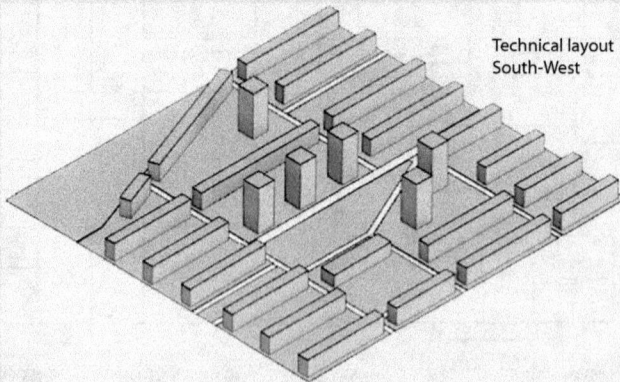

Days total, Sum on hours, TOTAL Energy

Technical layout
South-West

Source: Bellanger 2009.

Public Buildings

In August 2008, the State Council issued a National Regulation on Energy Conservation by Public Institutions, which for the first time established responsibilities, accountabilities, and targeting and monitoring requirements for increasing energy efficiency in government facilities. This regulation lays a critical framework for a series of energy efficiency initiatives targeting public buildings. According to the regulation, whether at county level or above, all state-funded entities must supervise their internal energy use and perform an audit of their own energy consumption. In addition, reports on energy use must be submitted annually to energy management authorities. These state-funded entities must make annual energy-saving plans, which will serve as the baseline to monitor progress in energy savings. There are also new regulations mandating not only the procurement of energy efficiency products but also the construction of new buildings (and building renovation projects) according to energy efficiency standards. The regulation endorses the potential use of energy performance contracts (EPC) by government entities through energy service companies (ESCOs). The opening of the energy efficiency market in the government sector will further stimulate China's growing ESCO industry.

Box 7.6 presents the federal buildings initiative program in Canada. Other programs exist in Europe and in the United States (see the Federal Energy Management Program in box 7.7 and an example of an energy efficiency utility below and in chapter 6, box 6.8).

Use of government contracting. Governments around the world have used different measures to attract investors to the energy efficiency market. Many local governments in other countries use competitive market principles when using public energy efficiency funds, as they try to attain maximum energy savings with minimum expenditure. Competitive procurement of energy savings, once the rules are established, is an excellent method for local governments to bring investors into new markets for energy efficiency, especially for public facilities (Singh et al. 2010).

Lead by example. One of the most effective methods is for governments to directly engage in energy savings practices, thus opening new markets to the energy efficiency services industry. While encouraging private enterprises to become more energy efficient, the U.S. and European governments lead by example by investing in their own assets, such as schools, hospitals, and office buildings, to reduce energy consumption.

Governments can also sign **indefinite quantity contracts.** When the government has multiple agencies that are responsible for their own

Box 7.6

Federal Buildings Initiative Program in Canada

In 1991, the Treasury Board of Canada authorized federal agencies to enter into multiyear EPCs under a program called the Federal Buildings Initiative. This is a voluntary initiative that offers the various departmental agencies a framework for updating their facilities with energy-saving technologies and practices, while the EPCs provide a source of funds outside of the administrative budget for carrying out energy efficiency projects. Prequalified private sector ESCOs are contracted by the Initiative's energy management service to implement two types of EPCs:

- First-out EPCs—the ESCO retains 100 percent of the actual energy savings either until the project is fully paid for, or until the end of the contract, whichever occurs first.
- Shared-savings EPCs—both the ESCO and the agency receive an agreed-upon percentage or amount of the savings over the life of the contract.

To date, this program has facilitated over 85 retrofit projects, attracting Can$320 million in private sector financing, resulting in over Can$40 million in annual energy savings in more than 7,500 buildings across Canada, covering 35 percent of the agency building stock.

Source: Singh et al. 2010.

assets, each agency would need to procure individual ESCOs to implement energy savings measures. These individual procurements would then all have to individually be in accordance with public procurement procedures. The lengthy and duplicative procurement process might not be cost effective and could lead to quality problems. However, an ESCO that is implementing a large EPC, known as a SuperESCO, can subcontract with smaller ESCOs on a competitive basis to actually complete the work (see box 7.7). This approach can help to stimulate the private market for ESCOs, while creating an artificial separation between the contractor and the client. However, this approach would make allocation of project performance risk from the SuperESCO to the subcontractors difficult.

Another more sophisticated approach is the **energy efficiency utility**, such as the one introduced in the state of Vermont in the United States. The government can establish a utility that is unrelated to electric power or other energy supply utilities and whose sole purpose is to implement

Box 7.7

SuperESCO for Federal (Central Government) Facilities Energy Efficiency in the United States

To accelerate the contracting process for its agencies, the U.S. federal government developed a system in which an ESCO is competitively selected, based on its qualifications and capacity to provide an energy savings project for federal (central government) facilities, to execute an umbrella EPC. The selected firm then is required to contact the Department of Energy contracting officer before submitting initial proposals to agencies. Upon approval, "delivery orders" or "task orders" under the umbrella EPC can be issued. The Department of Energy established this process to make EPCs a more practical and streamlined tool for agencies to use. Additionally, the structure of this process would allow the primary ESCO with the umbrella EPC to act as a SuperESCO to subcontract to smaller ESCOs with lesser credentials to gain entry into the market, while shielding the federal government from the risks of working with these smaller ESCOs.

Implementation of such contracts is under strict supervision, with energy savings verified and guaranteed. In the United States the payment to ESCOs must be less than the energy cost savings. These Indefinite Quantity Contracts are usually extended or reprocured each three to five years.

Under the SuperESCO model, it is important to ensure open and transparent competition during the public procurement process. Since the umbrella contract is awarded to one ESCO that will be responsible for implementing multiple "delivery orders" or "task orders" for various agencies without rebidding, the capacity and qualifications of all bidders of the umbrella contract should be carefully evaluated before the final contract is awarded. If an unqualified ESCO was ultimately selected, the quality of all energy efficiency project implementations could be severely compromised, resulting in time delay and financial loss.

Source: Singh et al. 2010.

energy saving measures. This utility has a performance contract with the government. It organizes tenders for energy savings projects and buys energy savings at the lowest cost per unit of energy savings (see also box 6.8 in chapter 6).

Building Elements and Code Compliance

While at the design level building code compliance has improved, especially in cold and severe-cold zones, improvements are still advisable to ensure compliance with the BEEC. The frequency of building inspections made to ensure the proper implementation of energy efficiency measures as specified in designs varies substantially. In some localities, no site inspections of energy efficiency aspects are undertaken at all.

Code compliance supervision focuses on two milestones: one at the beginning of the project with the design approval stage, and one at the end of construction with the building commissioning, or acceptance stage. However, it is very difficult to correct deviations at commissioning. Greater attention during construction may help solve problems in a cost-effective and efficient manner, as opposed to trying to find solutions at the commissioning stage. For example, the technical offer of a construction company should be strenuously reviewed by the developer, engineers, and especially the architect to ensure that the technical offer complies with approved technical specifications and construction drawings approved at the design stage. Interviews suggest that technical offers can deviate from technical drawings for various reasons. Materials should be checked to ensure that they can reliably meet thermal performance requirements. Involving experts is especially important if new technologies are proposed. Labeling, discussed below, is also an important tool to assist in ensuring that effective materials are used (see also box 7.8 about code enforcement).

Construction workers and construction supervisors could receive training on installation of energy efficient elements by the city quality inspection stations. Some localities have adopted checklists as part of the acceptance procedures, which are completed during key moments of the

---

Box 7.8

Building Energy Efficiency Code Enforcement: Stakeholders and Responsibilities

Tianjin municipality was a pioneer in integrating BEEC compliance into the regular housing construction cycle. As in other cities, a housing development project in Tianjin is required to go through a five-phase project approval cycle. At each stage of the project, the developer needs to interact with government oversight agencies, mainly various departments of the Tianjin Construction Commission (TJCC), Tianjin Development and Reform Commission (TJDRC), Tianjin Environ-

(continued next page)

Box 7.8 *(continued)*

mental Protection Bureau (TJEPB), and Tianjin Urban Planning Bureau (TJUPB), to obtain necessary government approvals. Technical engineering firms, architects, tendering companies, and contractors are all third-party entities who also provide important services to the developers that allow them to comply with basic requirements needed for those approvals.

The responsibilities of government oversight agencies for BEEC compliance are well defined and, in general, are followed by concerned agencies throughout the construction cycle. TJCC, through its functional divisions, is the designated line agency involved in the entire construction cycle. This includes the overall supervision and coordination (Building Energy Conservation Office), design review due diligence (Construction Design Management Department), tendering and contracting due diligence (Tender and Contract Management Office), compliance enforcement during construction (General Station for Building Construction Quality Supervision), and overall technical and administrative support (Tianjin Building Wall Reform and Energy Conservation Management Center). The role of this management center has been critical to ensure BEEC compliance because it has been the main repository of local BEEC technical competence and also acts as the municipal government's BEEC inspector.

Figure B7.8.1   Responsibilities for BEEC Enforcement in Tianjin

Housing construction cycle developer	Municipal oversight agencies	Third parties involved
Project Registration	TJDRC, TJEPB, and TJCC Approval of Project Feasibility Studies	Technical/engineering firms or institutes
Project Design and Construction Permit	TJUPB and TJCC Approval of Site Plans, Detailed Designs, Drawings, and Permits	Architecture and engineering design firms or institutes Drawings review entity
Project Tendering and Contracting	TJCC Tendering and Contracting Due Diligence	Tendering company
Project Construction	TJCC Construction Quality Inspection	Construction contractors Construction supervision entity Testing and certification entities
Project Completion Acceptance	TJCC Construction Quality Evaluation	Project design entities Construction contractors Construction supervision entity Acceptance inspection entities

Source: Liu et al. 2010.

construction cycle. Vancouver, Canada, provides an example of good practice. The city has municipal inspectors responsible for building energy efficiency, focusing on one building element at a time. For example, at current staffing and resource levels, it is not possible to comprehensively supervise building energy efficiency elements. The cooperation of the entire construction industry is required, including developers, suppliers of energy efficiency building elements, construction supervisors, construction companies, and workers. Inspectors can emphasize one building element, such as insulation or windows, during their regular inspections until compliance is improved. Once satisfied with compliance, they can move on to the next element and so forth. This can be accompanied by special training for all participants in the chain and especially construction supervisors and workers responsible for installations.

Green buildings. When dealing with the concept of green buildings in China, significant upgrading of skills is required throughout the building development cycle. It is suggested that municipalities ensure that they oversee a green building program with properly trained personnel since the programs' standards are rigorous. If not carefully supervised, the green building standard could be loosely applied and lead to the "green washing" of projects, meaning that the projects only superficially apply the green standards, yet still claim the benefits.

It may be useful for national authorities to encourage the adoption of an accreditation system similar to the LEED Accredited Professionals program. To reduce the risk of underperformance, municipal authorities could also consider mandating the participation of internationally accredited professionals to perform the inspections and participate in acceptance.

MoHURD has also initiated the labeling of building materials. During implementation of the HRBEE project, interviews with developers suggested that perhaps developers have experienced difficulty finding reliable information about good-quality building materials with advanced building energy efficiency technologies. A material labeling program, such as the one launched by MoHURD, should be accelerated so that such products could be used ubiquitously at the city level.

Under MoHURD's initiative to develop labeling of building energy efficiency, potential real estate buyers are able to compare the energy efficiency characteristics of buildings, thereby providing developers with greater incentives to build in an energy efficient way. Under MoHURD's pilot program, labels are given to rate the energy efficiency performance of a completed project, including use of renewable energy, from one to five stars. There are two stages of labeling: (i) the first after the commissioning stage, when a prelabeling is made based on the actual (revised) construction drawings submitted to the municipal authorities; and (ii) a second, final labeling, within one to five years after building commissioning, following testing and appraisal by certified laboratories such as the China Academy of Building Research. Developers pay for participation, including a fee to get a prelabel design review based on final construction drawings and some monitoring and verification, depending on the size of the building. However, MoHURD also has a green building standard with its own star rating system, the GBES. As discussed before, this standard takes into account other sustainable building practices similarly to other internationally recognized sustainable building initiatives, such as LEED. Even if the GBES and the energy efficiency labeling are commendable initiatives, they appear to overlap, and some type of integration may be worth considering.

More consideration could also be given to the heating and cooling cycle. Currently, building energy efficiency codes in cold and severe-cold zones calculate energy savings based on heating load only. However, in summer, air conditioning is often used, even in cold and severe-cold regions. Measures to improve building thermal integrity using current codes can also help save energy during cooling seasons; however, this is not calculated by these codes. There may also be a need for strengthened energy efficiency regulations for public and commercial buildings, as well as for residential buildings in two climate zones.[3] These codes cover both heating and cooling energy and present a 50 percent reduction target of the overall heating and cooling energy use. Indeed, it is appropriate to consider that greater energy savings targets can also be achieved in the warmer regions. Moreover, there should be clear guidance on how to further accelerate the integration of green building design principles, as they include much broader concepts than thermal integrity of buildings.

Building Renovation

MoHURD's 11th Five Year Plan includes a target to retrofit at least 150 million square meters of existing buildings in 16 northern provinces to achieve higher building energy efficiency. Each province was allocated a portion of this target. Technical guidelines for building renovations have been issued at the municipal level. The central government established a formula-driven subsidy, taking account of the various climatic zones, levels of reconstruction, and estimated energy conservation and implementation progress.[4] Central government support has been about RMB 45–55 per square meter, depending on the location. Although useful experiences have been achieved, the scope of the program has been limited and the pace is slower than originally hoped.

The introduction of energy efficiency measures in renovation projects, especially in existing centrally heated residential buildings, is a particularly difficult task and an area where administrative measures have only limited usefulness. The key issue is less technical and more institutional: homeowners must be actively and enthusiastically involved, requiring both incentives and effective local organization. The government's original targets will likely be difficult to reach. Addressing these challenges, MoHURD worked with the German development agency Deutsche Gesellschaft für Internationale Zusammenarbeit (GTZ) in Tangshan and other cities to demonstrate effective technical building renovation measures, leading to the creation of several guidelines on building renovation (the project in Tangshan dealt with buildings made of precast concrete panels).

Incentive issues. It is only with the implementation of consumption-based heat billing that homeowners can gain some financial benefit from energy efficiency retrofits—and in cases where apartments are currently very cold, they may also gain comfort benefits. However, some municipalities require that retrofitting should be undertaken *before* consumption-based billing can proceed, arguing the unfairness to saddle residents of older and poorly insulated apartments with higher heat bills. However, this post-retrofit billing tends to exclude a possible source of motivation from the program, as a pre-retrofit billing could easily demonstrate the needs for energy saving measures by highlighting the possible benefits and value of retrofit measures. The current post-retrofit billing creates an impasse that tends to slow down progress on both programs. In principle, government subsidies may provide financial incentives to help bridge this problem. However, if government subsidies are the only source of financial incentives to homeowners, the amounts of subsidy needed to foster the levels of organization and enthusiasm required for real success are likely to be exorbitant. Implementation of consumption-based billing and retrofitting might best be closely linked and completed as a package within a reasonable time frame. However, this places even greater requirements on the effectiveness of local organization.

Organizational issues. In other countries, including Eastern European countries with Soviet-era heating systems, successful efforts in energy efficiency retrofits are typically realized with the close involvement of local homeowners, building management, or other grassroots organizations. Involvement of such organizations is usually critical to achieve the needed homeowner support. To achieve effective results, a degree of customization of the actual technical conditions and institutional situation is often required. Even when buildings are of similar types and age, structural differences and substantial variations in heat demand and other conditions often exist, as well as different perceptions and desires among homeowners, making retrofitting projects different from one another. It is advisable to introduce flexibility in government retrofit programs— which tend to have uniform criteria, including uniform measures and estimated savings and subsidy amounts without the needed level of flexibility—to allow greater customization to the actual conditions in different building. In other countries, a common implementation approach is to have energy efficiency service companies working with homeowners, usually through local organizations, to develop customized packages from a menu of options that are supported by overall city programs. These companies have energy auditing skills and experience packaging investments with reasonable payback periods. Because energy efficiency services are their business, these companies also have specialized experience communicating the benefits of their technical proposals to homeowners and to building managers who may not have the technical background.

Additional organizational challenges. These challenges arise in buildings that retain traditional vertical heat piping systems. Radiators in older buildings are connected in series by vertical hot water pipes. Thus, there may be two or more vertical pipes connecting radiators of one apartment to those above and below it. If water flow is restricted to the radiator, it also restricts the flow of water to the radiator in the apartment below. Thus, it is impossible to control room temperature. It is also impossible to install apartment-level meters, which has been the preferred metering method for heating. In recent years, many Chinese cities have replaced this vertical pipe system by connecting apartments to one set of transmission pipes newly installed in the building stairwells. Horizontal pipes connect the apartment's radiators to the transmission pipes. This horizontal piping retrofit has been unpopular with many residents for a variety of reasons including poor workmanship. As an alternative to this heavy form of retrofit, cities could consider a less intrusive retrofit and a different billing method to accelerate incentives for energy efficiency. For example a bypass valve could be installed at each radiator at the inlet of a radiator's flow control device (that is, a thermostatic radiator valve). By connecting the inlet and outlet pipes of the radiator, the bypass valve allows water to flow to the next radiator even if the flow of water is restricted to that radiator by a flow control device. Also, billing based on a building meter could be adopted. Internationally, several methods are used to proportionally allocate building heat bills to individual apartments such as (i) apartment floor area, (ii) data from heat cost allocators (devices that measure the heat emitted by each radiator), and (iii) a combination of these two methods. The use of allocators is common in countries such as Austria, Denmark, Germany, Poland, and Switzerland, where individual heat metering is required by national regulations (JP Building Engineers 2002). Only in a few West European countries and in the Republic of Korea is individual metering of heat the dominant metering option as compared with building level metering (JP Building Engineers 2002).

Leading by doing. In many countries, governments are leading by example by making investments in their own buildings. Municipalities could consider paying closer attention to improving building energy efficiency in schools, hospitals, government office buildings, and other facilities within their administrative jurisdiction. Such programs could also include benefit-sharing schemes that would allow for savings to be shared, for example, between the school (for more educational materials) and the municipality energy-bill payers. In other countries, ESCOs are very active in supporting government initiatives in their own facilities. In addition, building energy efficiency in government facilities also raises awareness. For example, in Serbia, a World Bank project encouraged schools that had undertaken energy efficiency retrofits to prepare lessons about energy efficiency for their students. Similarly, the impact of energy efficiency measures is experienced by parents, doctors, nurses, patients, and others who work in and use efficient facilities. Box 7.9 presents an example of a "green school" in the Tianjin Eco-City project.

Conclusion

This chapter has presented an overview of the World Bank's ongoing activities in the building industry, in terms of energy efficiency. Overall, China has understood very early the importance of providing regulations to include energy efficiency measures in the building process. While BEECs are a good beginning, they could be further improved to ensure that the new building stock is addressing all possible avenues in terms of CO_2 emission reduction. Equally, initiatives such as the GBES are relevant to promote the integration of green building concepts into new buildings, while further attention could be given to elements such as the timing of rating, responsibility of qualitative evaluations, energy commissioning, and energy performance requirements. Other measures to

Box 7.9

Green Schools

The World Bank/GEF–financed Tianjin Eco-City project includes a component on piloting green building investments in public buildings. A middle school in the Tianjin Eco-City development was selected as the pilot project. The school has a total floor area of 35,000 square meters and will host 1,620 students. GEF will finance the incremental costs for energy/water efficiency and renewable energy use, which will exceed the minimum requirements of the GBES. Key GBES baseline indicators include (i) 50 percent heating and cooling energy efficiency for public buildings, as compared to buildings built in early 1980s; (ii) 5 percent of renewable energy use for public buildings; and (iii) the national standard for lighting. For certain energy and water efficiency measures, when there are no minimum requirements currently listed in the GBES, the national standard or normal practice will be used as the baseline.

International consultants for the project conducted a technology screening and review of green building solutions that are technically sound and commercially available in China. These enhancement options were then evaluated based on their lifetime cost effectiveness and replicability, and presented to GEF for its final decisions to provide incremental financing. For replicability, a five-point scoring system was used to evaluate the proposed measures. The list of proposed measures that met the selection criteria include high-efficiency windows, higher-efficiency wall insulation, improved roof insulation, lighting control systems, energy efficient lighting, improved or more efficient HVAC, an indoor stadium ventilation system, a solar water heating system, water-saving features, an intelligent metering system, natural light for parking areas, and a solar heating system.

Source: World Bank project documents.

increase energy efficiency and green buildings solutions—whether proper planning and siting, solar gains, and reduction of building envelope—can allow for substantial energy gains without extra costs.

Recently, a national Regulation on Energy Conservation by Public Institutions was issued, setting a standard for energy consumption monitoring at the national level. Such a regulation addresses issues related to energy efficiency code compliance inspections, accreditation programs, material labeling, and stakeholders' divided responsibilities during a project cycle. Finally, this chapter discussed energy efficiency retrofits, especially in residential buildings, and described what measures could support their implementation in residential buildings as well as in government facilities.

China has made substantial progress regarding building energy efficiency, and this will serve it well as it incorporates lessons and strengthens its programs to achieve higher energy savings and keep pace with urbanization.

Notes

1. In the text, heating and cooling refers to space heating and space cooling.
2. Sections on green buildings draw heavily from Baeumler et al. 2009.
3. These are the hot-summer cold-winter zone and the hot-summer warm-winter zone.
4. The formula is:

    $$B = b \times [\Sigma (0.6 \times R_1 + 0.3 \times R_2 + 0.1 \times R_3) \times 70\% + R \times E_c \times 30\%] \times P_c,$$

    where B is the final subsidy; b is the benchmark subsidy based on climate (severe-cold zone: RMB 55/m²; cold zone RMB 45/m²); R_1 is the reconstructed area of enclosed structure; R_2 is the reconstructed area of the indoor heating system; R_3 is the reconstructed area for temperature control; R is the total reconstructed area; E_c is an energy efficiency coefficient ranging from 0.8, 1, and 1.2 for 15–20%, 20–30%, and > 30 or >40% energy efficiency, depending on whether it is measured from the heat source or the substation; and P_c is a progress coefficient, that is, reconstruction completed before 2010 = 1.2, finished on 2010 = 1, and after 2010 = 0.8 (Cai et al. 2010).

Bibliography

Baeumler, A., M. Chen, A. Dastur, Y. Zhang, R. Filewood, K. Al-Jamal, C. Peterson, and M. Ranade. 2009. "Sino-Singapore Tianjin Eco-City (SSTEC): a Case Study of an Emerging Eco-City in China." World Bank TA Report, November 2009. World Bank, Washington, DC.

Bellanger, M. 2009. "Discussion of Building Energy Efficiency in China." Presentation with Gailius Draugelis at the World Bank Office, Beijing. December 10.

Cai, W., Y. Wu, Y. Zhong, and H. Ren. 2010. "Corrigendum to 'China Building Energy Consumption: Situation, Challenges and Corresponding Measures'." *Energy Policy* 38(1): 688.

Gochenour, C. 2001. "District Energy Trends, Issues and Opportunities: The Role of the World Bank." Technical Paper 493. World Bank, Washington, DC.

International Energy Agency (IEA). 2010. *World Energy Outlook*. Paris: IEA.

International Finance Corporation (IFC), China Utility-Based Energy Efficiency Finance Program (CHUEE). 2008. "Co- and Tri-generation and Heating Systems Policy Report and Market Research." Pöyry. http://www.poyry.com/.

JP Building Engineers, Center for Energy Efficiency in Buildings. 2002. "Heat Metering and Billing: Technical Options, Policies and Regulations: Chinese Demonstration Projects and International Experiences." World Bank Consultant Trust Fund Report. Espoo, Finland; Beijing, China. http://www.worldbank.org.cn/English/content/heat.pdf.

Liu, F., A. Meyer, and J. Hogan. 2010. "Mainstreaming Building Energy Efficiency Codes in Developing Countries—Global Experiences and Lessons from Early Adopters" World Bank Working Paper, No. 204. Washington, DC: World Bank.

Liu, F., X. Zhang, M. Bellanger, and M. Hassam. 2006. "Economic Analysis of Energy Efficiency Measures for New Residential Buildings in Northern China." Washington, DC: ASTAE, World Bank.

Meyer, A., and B. Kalkum. 2008. "China: Development of National Heat Pricing and Billing Policy." ESMAP Report. March 2008. World Bank, Washington, DC.

Ping, L., F. Liu, L. Younong, V-M Makela, A. Meyer, E. Toivanen, A. Han, and R. Taylor. 2002. "Heat Metering and Billing: Technical Options, Policies and Regulations. Asia Sustainable and Alternative Energy Program." Washington, DC: ASTAE/World Bank. http://www.worldbank.org.cn/english/content/heat.pdf.

Singh, J., D. Limaye, B. Henderson, and X. Shi. 2010. "Public Procurement of Energy Efficiency Services, Lessons from International Experience." Washington, DC: World Bank.

Suzuki, H., A. Dastur, S. Moffatt, N. Yabuki, and H. Maruyama. 2010. *Eco^2 Cities—Ecological Cities as Economic Cities*. Washington, DC: World Bank.

Taylor, R., G. Draugelis, Y. Zhang, and A. Ang Co. 2010. "Accelerating Energy Conservation in China's Provinces." Washington, DC: AusAID/World Bank. http://www.worldbank.org/research/2010/06/12720925/accelerating-energy-conservation-chinas-provinces.

U.S. Department of Energy–EERE (Energy Efficiency and Renewable Energy). 2005. *Buildings Energy Data Book 2005*. Washington, DC: U.S. Department of Energy–EERE.

Weiss, W., and F. Mauthner. 2008. "Solar Heat Worldwide: Markets and Contribution to Energy Supply." 2010 ed. International Energy Agency Solar Heating and Cooling Programme. Graz, Austria. http://www.iea-shc.org/publications/downloads/Solar_Heat_Worldwide-2010.pdf.

World Bank. 2001. "China, Opportunities to Improve Energy Efficiency in Buildings." Asia Alternative Energy Programme and Energy & Mining Unit East Asia and Pacific Region. World Bank, Washington, DC.

———. 2005. "Project Appraisal Document on a Proposed Global Environment Facility (GEF) Grant of US$18 Million to the People's Republic of China for the China Heat Reform and Building Energy Efficiency Project." Report Number 30747. World Bank, Washington, DC.

———. 2010. "Fuel Supply Handbook for Biomass-Fired Power Projects." World Bank ESMAP (Energy Sector Management Assistance Program) Report, May 2010. Prepared by BTG Biomass Technology Group BV.

CHAPTER 8

District Heating Reform

Gailius Draugelis and Shawna Fei Li

Overview

District heating is a system to meet residential and commercial heating requirements by distributing heat that is generated in a centralized location. District heating is mainly used for space heating and water heating. Currently in China, district heating is mostly produced by fossil-fuel-based boilers and heat and power cogeneration plants, although it offers the flexibility to switch to cleaner fuels as they become available. As coal is the dominant district heating fuel, a priority for the industry is to improve energy efficiency and reduce environmental impacts. However, technologies are advancing to a level where a wider use of renewable or cleaner energy alternatives to coal can be considered for district heating. In addition, alternatives to district heating itself, such as distributed generation (including gas furnaces, heat pumps, and so forth) can now be applied under certain circumstances.

The World Bank is currently supporting a heat reform program consisting of the promotion of demand-side measures including building energy efficiency, consumption-based billing, and the modernization of district heating supply systems. The program is financed by a Global Environment Facility (GEF) grant supporting the Heat Reform and Building Energy Efficiency Project (HRBEE), World Bank heating modernization loan projects, and donor and World Bank–supported technical assistance and policy support. HRBEE demonstration projects for consumption-based billing and building energy efficiency are being implemented in Urumqi, Tianjin, Tangshan, and Dalian, in total covering about 3.6 million square meters. Overall, the World Bank is working with about 16 cities through the GEF grant and World Bank loan projects. For cities in China's 16 cold climate provinces where heating is required by law, district heating reform is a critical part of a low-carbon strategy because it introduces incentives to use the fossil-fuel-based heating energy wisely.

This chapter draws on experience from these World Bank projects and other policy support activities. It focuses primarily on choices available to municipalities to improve district heating energy efficiency while addressing alternatives to coal-based systems. After an overview and background on the heating sector and heat reform initiatives, the chapter describes specific measures that could be implemented to strengthen the heat sector reform and provide heat to consumers in a cost-effective and energy-saving way. The chapter also reviews the viability of district heating and presents alternatives to the use of coal in district heating systems.

The Chinese Heating Sector and Heat Reform Initiative

Background on the Heating Sector and Heat Reform Initiatives

Since 2003, when the central government clearly defined the key directions of district heating reform, the district heating sector has represented about 5.3 to 6.1 percent of total coal consumption in China. In 2008, the heating sector consumed 145.4 million tons of raw coal—about 91 percent of the total energy supply to the sector, followed by petroleum products (5 percent) and natural and other gas (about 4 percent) (State Statistics Bureau 2010). Coal consumption may be underreported because it does not include amounts used by combined heat and power plants (CHPs) (accounted for in the national statistics as thermal power generation) or quantities used by small distributed boilers. Due to the seasonal nature of heating, its dependence on fossil fuels, and its low level of efficiency and environmental controls, wintertime air pollution in cold climate cities is usually far more severe than summertime air pollution. As the accelerated pace of urbanization continues and quality of life improves for most, the effort to minimize the carbon intensity of district heating is an essential part of low-carbon development strategies in China. This is most relevant for cities in China's 16 northern provinces where heating is required by law. In 2008, out of China's 655 cities, about 329 were equipped with district heating facilities.

In July 2003, eight central government ministries and commissions jointly issued a Government Circular calling for each of the 16 northern provinces to implement heat system reforms in several pilot municipalities, according to the guidelines specified in the document ("Heat Reform Guidelines"). The principles of these Guidelines are the commercialization of urban heating, the promotion of technical innovation of heating systems, the application of energy-saving building construction, and the improvement of living standards.

The objective of the heat reform program is to reduce energy use in district heating by:

- Reforming the system of payment. This is the first step. While currently some employers are still paying for the heating bill, households will become responsible for paying their heating bills and former in-kind wages will be transformed into a transparent payment for heat that will be added to the wage. Heat prices will be set locally to recover costs and would not be used to subsidize households. Targeted subsidies will instead be provided to low-income households.
- Creating incentives for end-use efficiency by introducing heat metering and consumption-based billing. The aim is to monetize and commercialize, or *commodify*, heating.
- Promoting new wall construction materials and energy-saving construction technologies and technological reform of heating facilities. This complements billing reform and enhances the efficiency of heat utilization through the heating supply chain up to the end user. The measures would consequently improve the air quality of urban areas.
- Developing and optimizing economic, safe, clean, and highly efficient urban heating systems based on centralized heating, along with other methods.
- Accelerating the development of a commercial heating sector, to introduce competition mechanisms, and foster and standardize the urban heating market.

A significant number of governmental agencies[1] have established a coordinating team to lead the implementation of the pilot reforms. A system of interministry joint conferences was created to coordinate the reform work and related policy research.

The assignment of heating bills to individual households has been largely successful, with only the last 35 percent still to be transferred. However, only 400 million square meters of floor area have been metered, of which only 150 million square meters are being billed by the meter. The consolidation of enterprises is ongoing, but the district heating industry remains highly fragmented. In Beijing, for instance, there are nearly 2,800 different district heating companies, while in Western and Eastern Europe, each city typically has only a few such companies and occasionally only one. Comparisons with international benchmarks suggest that while China's market is the fastest growing district heating market in the world, its efficiency and energy use are not comparable to European systems. Energy use per unit of floor area is at least double that of buildings located in similar cold climates in Western Europe or North America, and frequently with far less comfort. Market-based reforms in China's urban district heating sector are essential to tap the energy efficiency potential of the sector.

Toward a Sustainable Development of the District Heating Sector

Urban central heating has been called one of the last vestiges of China's welfare state. It is not surprising that potential reform is technically and institutionally complex, and especially socially sensitive. Although the assignment of individual responsibility of the heating bill has advanced considerably, a series of heating sector reforms in billing, pricing, and enterprise reform are still to be implemented. These and many other industry challenges have been left largely to municipalities to solve, simply because, in terms of energy conservation efforts, district heating does not attract the same attention as the industrial sector or the power sector. Nonetheless, while it remains a small percentage of the total national primary energy consumption—between 5.3 and 6.1 percent of the total coal consumption is from heating in the northern provinces—it is a significant regional concern. If not managed carefully, district heating could increase its share of coal consumption.

Achieving energy efficiency involves not only the installation of advanced technologies and designs, but also requires improving management of the sector and individual companies. Without this, district heating will not be able to transition to a sustainable development path. The following is a selected list of eight measures cities can implement or support. Putting these measures in place, and thus accelerating district heating reforms, is a major implementation and organizational challenge that will also require substantial financial inflows for investment in heat supply systems and for targeted social assistance. The financial burden on government budgets could lessen if the implementation of these measures is successful in attracting good-quality private capital, and creating incentives to reduce supply costs.

Measure 1: Metering Heat at Least at the Building Level
Metering heat at the building connection level or at the consumer door allows consumers to control consumption and pay according to use. Currently, the popular trend is for apartment-level metering. However, there are several challenges to installing heat meters at each apartment, including management of billing systems for such a large customer base, calibration requirements, and problems associated with heat transfer between walls. Municipalities could consider metering at the building or staircase level as an alternative in some cases. Implementing building and staircase metering has the following advantages:

- With fewer meters per building, there will be a lower initial investment and lower operating costs. According to regulations such as in Tianjin, meters must be calibrated only every three years.
- Building meters capture the heat used in common areas such as staircases, resulting in costs being more easily distributed among apartment owners. Apartment-level metering requires the heat price to be adjusted to take into account estimated heat losses.
- Building meters are easier to install in older, existing buildings. Apartment-level meters require a heavy retrofit of the internal piping system and are therefore more costly.

Box 8.1 provides an example of promoting metering in old, existing buildings in Central and Eastern Europe.

Measure 2: Completing the Heat Price System Reform
Completing the heat price system reform should be based on the recovery of reasonable costs with a fair profit margin, and with tariffs specific for each district heating provider. When possible, pricing regimes should incorporate performance targets and efficiency incentives, encouraging companies to improve their investments and operations. The principles and general methodologies for tariff setting should be established by a national agency and apply to all district heating providers. Concurrently, municipalities can implement the temporary guidelines of the two-part heat tariff issued by the Ministry of Housing and Urban-Rural Development (MoHURD) in 2007. With its component dealing with energy, this two-part

Box 8.1

Promoting Metering in Old, Existing Buildings in Central and Eastern Europe

Many Central and Eastern European countries (CEEC) have old and inefficient building stock, usually made of precast concrete panels and even older low-rise brick structures. Since the very early stages of the economic transition, about 18 years, heating in these buildings has been billed according to the meter. As with similar buildings in China, the radiators in these buildings are connected vertically in series with apartments below and above. If a shut-off valve is installed in a radiator, it cuts off hot water to the radiator in the apartment below.

As part of their heating demand-side management programs, many of the CEEC opted for installing either building or staircase meters. In addition, they installed Thermostatic Radiator Valves (TRVs) for each radiator. To solve the problem of vertically connected radiators, a "bypass valve" was installed between the inlet and outlet of the radiator to ensure a flow of hot water even if the radiator valve was shut off. While in many places in China the entire piping system might have been replaced in this situation, in the CEEC that was considered too costly and complex as it would require civil works inside each apartment.

The distribution of heating costs among apartments varies among the CEEC. Some countries, such as Lithuania, allow the building owners to decide how to distribute the bill. In most cases the building heat bill is distributed according to the floor area. While this is an easy solution, it limits the incentive for energy savings. This solution could, however, be considered as a first step to more sophisticated methods, such as using heat cost allocators. These devices, placed on each radiator, measure the amount of heat emitted by the radiator. Advanced devices can even be read remotely, and the data are used to distribute the building or staircase heat bill. Some German cities even use compensation factors to account for the heat transfer between walls, as, for example, a middle apartment needs less energy for heating because it is surrounded on five sides by interior walls. To distribute heating costs, municipalities can start with simple approaches and later move toward more sophisticated ones.

Source: Authors.

tariff provides incentives for energy conservation to consumers while, through its capacity component, reducing the revenue risks associated with a fluctuating demand for the district heating providers. Box 8.2 describes Tianjin's experience with heat prices and consumption-based billing.

Box 8.2

Tianjin District Heating Consumption-Based Billing

The Municipality of Tianjin is one of the cities in China supported by the World Bank through grant funds from the Energy Sector Management Assistance Program (ESMAP). The project is aimed at developing methodologies to determine heat prices for a regulated industry that are affordable for consumers and cost-recoverable for service providers. The methodology developed by the Tianjin Working Group has been accepted and adopted by other municipality regulators. It is also supported by the World Bank/GEF/MoHURD Heat Reform and Building Energy Efficiency Project.

Tianjin has accumulated extensive experience in this area and is now applying a two-part heat tariff for consumption-based billing in several large developments with buildings conforming to Building Energy Efficiency Codes (BEEC). The results from years of piloting heat metering and billing show that the actual heat consumption is, on average, substantially below the norm consumption assumed by the heating companies. This demonstrates that estimation of real heat demand can provide high value added in developing a tariff that balances the interests between enterprises and society.

Source: Meyer and Kalkum 2008.

Several municipalities have adopted two-part heat tariffs but have not yet implemented them. While detailed technical guidance cannot be provided in this chapter, municipalities could consider the following when preparing implementation of a two-part heat tariff:

- Implement a metering regime for one entire heating season or, alternatively, use a reasonable estimate of heating demand based on real measurements. This is important because if the price per gigajoule (GJ) consumed is not set properly, either the consumer or the heating company suffers.
- Resolve ownership and calibration responsibilities for the heat meter. Ensure that heating companies are satisfied with heat meter specifications if they are not owners of the meter.
- Strongly promote use of commercial accounting principles, following Ministry of Finance guidelines for heating companies so that uniform accounting rules can be applied when calculating heat prices.

- Become familiar with the relevant accounting issues, including how to determine justified and unjustified costs and how to split costs between fixed parts and variable parts. MoHURD can provide expert guidance on this issue. The World Bank has also produced the report, *China: Development of National Heat Pricing and Billing Policy* (Meyer and Kalkum 2008).
- Consider having more than one price in a city. Under the principle of cost reflective pricing, the heat price should reflect as closely as possible the real forecasted costs. A single heat price cannot achieve this principle simply because small and large district heating companies have different cost structures.

Measure 3: Strengthening the Working System for District Heating Regulation

Strengthening the working system for district heating regulation through a clear allocation of responsibilities and functions, strengthening the authority to execute those responsibilities, and building capacity to adequately perform these functions are required actions for successful reform. The government has issued a number of regulations and guidelines for regulatory functions in the sector, dealing with various issues such as planning, pricing, and franchise. However, because implementation of the guidelines varies across cities, local approaches are not fully harmonized with national guidelines. The success of the reform depends on political will, at both the national and local levels. Further, there are many issues requiring the attention of provincial and central government authorities, including the need for a National District Heating Regulation[2] that would help provide legal guidance to harmonize national initiatives with local implementation. Among the many issues that need to be addressed, two of the most important for cities are as follows:

- **Ensuring that institutional barriers are removed for heat reform and innovation.** For example, the municipality could consider whether the property boundaries between the district heating company and property owner are preventing the innovation and promotion of heat reform. Currently, heating networks connecting the substation to the buildings are constructed by the real estate developer and are popularly understood to be owned by the property owners. Ownership issues are not fully or consistently clarified. Substations are sometimes owned by property owners, and sometimes by heating companies. However, when such district heating assets are not owned by heating supply companies, they are usually not well maintained and depreciate quickly, wasting resources and energy by leaking heat and water. These can also be impediments to the introduction of new and advanced energy efficient technologies (see box 8.3).

- **Strengthening qualifications requirements for heating suppliers.** National guidance on qualification of district heating companies and licensing is needed. While these recommendations are being developed, municipalities could strengthen the qualification requirements of heat-

---

Box 8.3

Impediments to Energy Efficiency Innovations: Building Level Substations Example

Building level substations (BLS) are an advanced energy efficiency technology used widely in European district heating systems. Rather than constructing a substation that supplies heating for a block of apartment buildings, BLS are installed inside each building. The basic technology and operating principles are the same, but the differences are:

- Significantly lower space requirement (0.2 MW substation occupies space of 0.9 m^2)
- Prefabricated—no on-site assembly required
- Improved energy efficiency
- Better suited to China's real estate development pace.

Figure B8.3.1   Comparison of Group and Building Level Substations

Source: Arto Nuorkivi, World Bank Consultant, and Gailius Draugelis.

(continued next page)

Box 8.3 *(continued)*

The figure illustrates an example of a Chinese building complex supplied by 1 group substation (GS) or by 18 BLS. The GS needs much larger pumping power to supply all 18 buildings. Because the pump is farther away from the buildings, the heating supply is slower to respond to changes in the apartment thermostats. BLS are much closer to their heat load and do not need to pump as much. Although initial investment is higher, installation of BLS saves electricity and heat and improves heating quality by responding more quickly to changes in building heating needs. Moreover, BLS is modular and can be connected immediately as buildings are constructed. By contrast, a GS has to be constructed for the first buildings and wait for the rest of the load to be built.

In addition, with BLS, the total investment in piping is saved. Primary networks connecting the heat source to the GS are smaller in diameter than those of secondary networks. Secondary pipe diameters need to be larger because they carry lower temperature water compared to primary networks. When BLS is installed, the primary network is extended to the building and practically no secondary network is needed.

Problem of incentives: Implementing BLS is an organizational and logistical challenge because the secondary network (the pipes between the GS and the building) is usually constructed by the real estate developer. Therefore, benefits from lower pipeline, pumping, and energy costs are not equally shared between the property owner and the heating supply company. The municipality could change this practice by allowing the heating supply company to own the network all the way to the building inlet valve. This would not only improve maintenance of the network but would also encourage the implementation of new technologies like BLS.

Source: Arto Nuorkivi, World Bank Consultant, and Gailius Draugelis.

ing suppliers in part by requiring them to obtain a license. The qualification requirements should cover technical experience to effectively and safely operate district heating assets as well as financial capacity to invest, operate, and maintain these assets. Commercialization of heating suppliers, separating them from government, is especially important.

Due to the monopolistic nature of the heating industry, the heating service providers can potentially exploit their market power. Although many heating service providers are owned by the government, their operations have been commercialized and effective regulatory control needs to be established to oversee the price and quality of services. It will also be necessary to address the possibility that new centralized heating may not automatically remain optimal relative to the old boiler houses that will eventually need replacing. Therefore, in the medium term, there is a need to monitor the technical quality and standards of the new systems.

However, replacing small boilers with centralized heating systems will not automatically improve service quality substantially. A World Bank survey was conducted in Liaoning Province in 2007 to ascertain perceptions of heating reform (see box 8.4 and figure 8.1). It was found that the level of general satisfaction among consumers connected to "quality" centralized heating systems is not high; yet among consumers there was the expectation that changing the small boiler houses would improve the quality of their heating. Interviews with heating companies and officials

Box 8.4

Consumer Satisfaction and Service Quality Even More Important with Consumption-Based Billing

In 2007, the World Bank conducted a survey of 2,000 households in five cities to collect facts about the current situation of heating reforms in Liaoning Province. This helped to inform a Bank loan project for district heating modernization. A report was prepared which assessed the impacts of reforms, especially changes to billing and pricing, the necessity of social assistance for heating, the consumer's consumption patterns and, importantly, public perceptions and awareness of heating reforms.

When consumers pay for heat themselves, they become more sensitive to service quality. The study found that while people are very supportive of consumption-based billing and tend to prefer district heating to alternatives, district heating still needs to greatly improve its customer service (see figure 8.1). Only about 35 percent of households were satisfied generally, and only 25 percent were satisfied with the room temperature. While this perception could be attributed to many factors, it does point to the need to improve service quality. International experience suggests that customer service becomes a higher priority when using consumption-based billing systems.

Source: Draugelis and Wu 2009.

Figure 8.1   General Satisfaction Level between "Quality" Central Heating System and Small Boiler

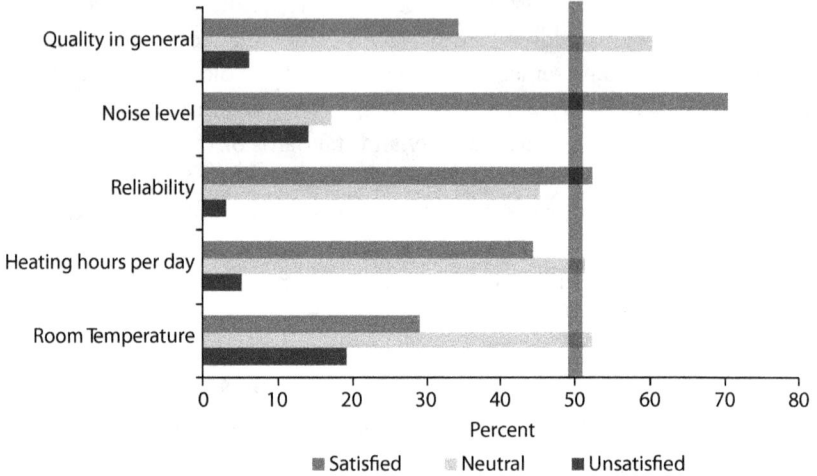

Source: Liaoning Social Analysis Survey, included in Draugelis and Wu 2009.

in several other provinces suggest a similar perception. Clearly, heating providers face a technical challenge to bridge the gap between expectation and current satisfaction.

Measure 4: Rationalizing the Sector

Rationalizing the sector by basing municipal heat planning on economic least-cost and environmental principles, as well as harmonizing district heating provider qualifications, are other required steps for this reform. Each city should have fewer heating networks of larger scale, as well as integrated networks operated by financially stronger providers. Box 8.5 presents the example of Urumqi.

Measure 5: Modernizing District Heating Assets and Management

Modernizing district heating assets and management to strengthen heat supply security and achieve efficient costs through the introduction of proven financial and management processes, in addition to new and efficient technologies, are also required steps to ensure the success of this reform. District heating providers should continue to evolve into corporate entities with the ability to access financing for new investment, introduce technologies compatible with heating reform (that is, based on demand-driven operating and resource-saving principles), and modernize

Box 8.5

Urumqi: Combining Rationalization of the Sector to Accelerate Modernization and Reform

Urumqi recently initiated a major effort to improve its air quality. The city program is to close down small and large boilers in urban areas and to connect the areas to an integrated district heating network with CHP plants as the main heat source and large heat-only boilers (HoB) as the peak load source. In areas where it is uneconomic to extend the district heating network, gas heating could be used. While it is not yet fully implemented, this approach presents several useful initiatives that can be taken into account when planning sector rationalization.

Due to economies of scale, the combined use of CHP for base load and HoBs for peak load can provide a more affordable heating supply alternative in dense urban areas like Urumqi. To use CHP is usually uneconomic because the extraction of steam for heating reduces the electricity output. Typically, a CHP plant provides the base heat load. During peak times, a peak load HoB adds heat to raise the supply temperature to the required level. The marginal cost of heat from CHP increases as its share in the total heat load increases because the power lost from steam extraction for heating increases. Assuming that the marginal cost of heat is determined by the value of the lost electricity output, if the share of CHP in the total heat load is increasing, its marginal cost will also exceed that of a heat-only boiler. Typically, the optimal share of CHP is between 40 and 60 percent.

Alternatives could include gas-fired peak load boilers, which can be more easily turned on than coal-fired boilers and significantly reduce environmental impacts. However, their heat supply will be more expensive than coal at a given demand.

Finally, the integration of heat sources requires commercial negotiations between the municipality and existing heat suppliers. In some cities, with either smaller systems or larger resources, municipalities have purchased the existing district heating assets. In Urumqi, the existing heat suppliers agreed to close down their heat source and buy heat from the new integrated district heating network based on a meter rate and a price set by the municipality. Peak-load boiler operators also use a revised price of heating based on the reduced heat supply requirement for peak load generation.

Source: Authors.

operations and management practices. In the process of introducing modern management methods, city master plans should be made consistent with national energy plans and policies, especially as the district heating sector is a large energy consumer (see also box 8.6).

Measure 6: Introducing Competition

Introducing competition for market entry, when feasible and economically possible—for example, by supplying heat to new housing developments—will also contribute to a successful reform. Competition involves using open and transparent bidding processes, following a process to qualify bidders, and requiring bidders to comply with all applicable regulations and government policies. Open competition, especially for new areas in the heating sector, would help raise the qualification level of heating suppliers. In addition, energy service companies (ESCOs) have recently shown interest in using energy performance contracting (EPC) to support energy efficiency investments in the heating boilers and network. Competition should also be grounded in good planning.

Box 8.6

Liaoning Medium Cities Infrastructure Project: Example of Generating Energy Efficiency and Environmental Benefits

In 2008, the World Bank approved a US$191 million loan to the Liaoning Provincial Government to modernize district heating services in nine cities. The objective was to improve the environmental performance and energy efficiency of district heating services. The project replaces hundreds of small boilers in urban areas with larger district heating networks supplied by CHP plants, large boilers, or industrial waste heat.

The province agreed to gauge success by measuring environmental performance and energy use per connected floor area of district heating. The indicators are provided below, with blue indicating the baseline and red the planned results after investment. The results demonstrate clearly that emissions, fuel consumption, electricity, and water use are all significantly reduced.

The project also demonstrated the use of BLS as an advanced energy efficiency technology and implemented heat metering at the heating source, each substation, and at the building level (on a pilot basis).

(continued next page)

Box 8.6 *(continued)*

Figure B8.6.1   Project Indicators and Targets for Environmental Performance and Energy Consumption in the Liaoning Medium Cities Infrastructure Project

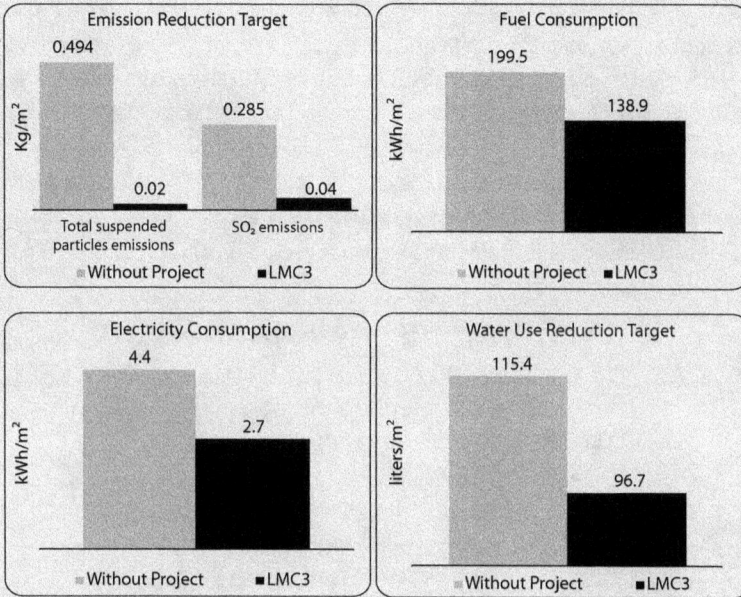

Source: World Bank, Liaoning Third Medium Cities Infrastructure Project.

Master planning can take into consideration how district heating and distributed alternatives are to be organized in a city to provide least-cost services while minimizing environmental impacts. Some cities in Germany have rules that establish district heating zones and, for example, natural gas heating zones. This reduces overall infrastructure costs because natural gas lines are not permitted in district heating zones (cooking is with electricity) and vice versa. Box 8.7 describes how competition was introduced in Vilnius, Lithuania.

Measure 7: Completing the Transfer of Payment Responsibilities to Consumers

Completing the shift of responsibility for full payment of heating bills to consumers while providing a safety net for low-income consumers

Box 8.7

Introducing Competition Together with Price Regulation in Vilnius, Lithuania

Vilnius municipality, the capital of Lithuania with a population of about 600,000, selected a private operator with significant foreign interest to lease the entire Vilnius District Heating Company (VDHC), which owned CHP sources as well as network installations. After it was signed, the contract was posted on the Vilnius municipality's website. In this lease contract, a "price cap" formula was agreed to determine the price of heating for the city, and an initial tariff was approved for a period of five years. In addition to general inflation, almost all cost drivers were indexed. Efficiency improvements that would reduce price increases were not included in the formula:

$$P1 = Px[0.416\ (G1/G) + 0.05\ (M1/M) + 0.018\ (K1/K)$$
$$+ 0.096\ (V1/V) + 0.169\ (S1/S) + 0.241\ (1 + ir/100),$$

where

P = initial heat price	P1 = new heat price
G = initial natural gas price	G1= new gas price
M = initial gas transport price	M1=new gas transport price
K = initial gas distribution price	K1 = new gas distribution price
V =initial cold water price	V1 = new cold water price
S = initial average salary	S1 = new average salary
Ir = official inflation rate	

The winning bidder brought new management to the company and improved customer relations. At the time, VDHC was losing market share to retail gas heating suppliers. Customer service was not the only determinant for improved market performance. The city also differentiated city zones for district heating and for gas.

Source: Meyer and Kalkum 2008.

through a targeted subsidy scheme are also recommended steps of this reform. There are no incentives for households to save energy for heating without the responsibility to pay the bill. Therefore, to accelerate district heating sector reform, the transfer of responsibilities should be completed as soon as possible. In support of the transition, government agencies could lead by example.

In addition, cost-reflective heating tariffs should be complemented by a financial support scheme to ensure low-income groups continue to have access to basic, clean, and affordable heating services. Subsidies to the financially vulnerable should be covered by the government. A World Bank survey in 2007 showed that low-income subsidy schemes could be further developed to address low-income groups other than the poorest (known as *dibaohu*) (Draugelis and Wu 2009).

The same study revealed that subsidy amounts tend to be smaller when subsidies are directly given to households compared to other distribution methods. In 2007, households eligible for direct subsidies received, on average, only RMB 426 in heating subsidies, while households that paid first and were then reimbursed could potentially obtain RMB 1,347 in heating subsidies. This disparity suggests that some employers may have reduced their financial obligations for heating subsidies when they directly gave the subsidies to employees in the form of a cash allowance.

Another indication that employers may be attempting to reduce their financial obligation in heating subsidies is apparent when comparing subsidies received against the percentage of subsidies that should be given. On average, households received 77 percent of the subsidies to which they are entitled. In one municipality, households responding to the survey obtained less than one-third of the amount of subsidies for which they were eligible.

Poor households, and especially the "near poor," spent a significant portion of their income on heating. Table 8.1 shows that, on average, heating alone demands more than 20 percent of the annual income for households in the first quintile (the poorest). However, if heating subsidies are excluded, poor households still make out-of-pocket payments of about 10 percent of their annual income. Interestingly, while the share of heating bills as a percentage of income is the same for *dibaohu* and households

Table 8.1   Out-of-Pocket Expenditure, by Quintile

Quintile	Heating bill as % of total income	Out-of-pocket expenditure for heating systems as % of total income
Dibaohu	20.6	6.5
1st quintile	22.8	10.0
2nd quintile	9.3	5.8
3rd quintile	7.1	3.8
4th quintile	6.1	3.7
5th quintile	4.2	2.4

Source: Draugelis and Wu 2009.

in the first quintile, the share of out-of-pocket payments for heating is actually lower for *dibaohu* than for households in the first quintile. This strongly suggests that the "near poor" might, in real terms, be in a worse condition financially than the *dibaohu* because they are not entitled to the same level of subsidy allocated to low-income families.

Measure 8: Implementing a National District Heating Regulation
Implementing a National District Heating Regulation, including the implementation of a data collection and monitoring system, separate from district heating providers' commercial interests, operations, and management is a further recommendation for successful reform. The National District Heating Regulation would provide guidance to provincial and city or local government agencies for preparing local regulations, and should define the roles of municipal and other agencies. Also, if possible, it could emphasize the necessary staffing and qualifications required to deliver those functions. The regulation should be transparent and balance the interests of consumers and investors in a fair manner.

Municipalities could implement new regulations for city-level benchmarking, which is one of the most important missing elements of the reform. Benchmarking is a tool that compares the performance of different heating enterprises, using various key performance indicators for service quality, cost effectiveness, safety, and others. These data could enable pricing bureaus and heating offices to compare unit costs, service quality, and other aspects across different companies, which could be extremely valuable as they monitor the development of the industry. Examples of the application of benchmarking include:

- Evaluation of the technical situation of the main assets of the district heating companies. Benchmarking could call for an assessment of the management quality of companies, providing information that could be helpful for planning.
- Analysis of energy efficiency. This information could be important for estimating the performance and quality of the district heating systems.
- Assessment of rehabilitation and demand for investments. This could signal future financing requirements for the district heating company.
- Assessment of the financial performance of the district heating company. This will be an essential input for heat tariff and price setting.

It is recommended that the benchmarking function be considered for a provincial-level institution. A benchmarking system led by a provincial-level institution would facilitate the comparison of benchmarking data within a province, helping to monitor and supervise the energy consumption, cost effectiveness, service quality, safety, and other factors within that same province. This provincial institution would help disseminate information to municipalities so they could learn more about nearby experiences with the implementation of reforms, experiences that may be more relevant to their local situation than experiences from farther away. As an initial step, methodologies, procedures, instructions, and survey forms could be developed. However, it is important to require enterprises to provide this information reliably and in a timely manner. Collected materials could be approved by the chief executive officer of a district heating company and should be subject to verification by the municipality. Final data could be published annually to illustrate trends in the district heating sector in the municipality and provinces.

Viability of District Heating

Numerous studies have shown that district heating is the most cost-effective heating system in densely populated urban areas with high heat loads. The break-even point is typically in the range of 2 to 4 megawatt (MW) per kilometer of network length. In China, the average heat load density is about 3 MW per kilometer, varying from 1.5 in Tianjin and 2.4 in Heilongjiang to 4.7 in Beijing.[3] District heating is clearly a viable heating option in the densely populated urban areas of China's severe-cold region. Several additional reasons favoring district heating in China are:

- Raw coal is the most common fuel used for heating. Burnt in individual stoves and small building boilers, coal consumption is a major contributor to serious pollution problems in the winter. Coal can be burnt with high efficiency and low emission levels in large boilers or CHP plants which provide, together with district heating networks, economies of scale in emission avoidance and heat supply.
- Under current pricing, the cleaner grid-bound alternative, natural gas, is expensive compared to coal, and also has a limited availability. For example, in Beijing, the cost to provide one GJ of natural gas compared to one GJ of coal was reportedly about three times higher even a few years ago.

Box 8.8 describes a World Bank project helping Yingkou municipality use carbon offsets to finance parts of its district heating system.

Box 8.8

Integrating Carbon Offset Benefits in Financing for District Heating Systems in China

Energy conservation is a high priority for China's government, while demand for cleaner, modern heating services continues to increase as urban areas place emphasis on more sustainable urban energy services. The Yingkou Economic Development Zone (EDZ), located in Yingkou Municipality in Liaoning Province, has a large number of small coal-fired boilers as its primary heating technology, representing 56 percent of the total heating supply area of the city. Many of the heating systems are in urgent need of modernization. Due to their lower efficiency, the small boilers consume excess amounts of coal and hence emit relatively significant amounts of CO_2 to the atmosphere.

The World Bank, through the Liaoning Third Medium Cities Infrastructure Project, is assisting Yingkou EDZ Huayuan Heating Company, a municipal state-owned enterprise (SOE), with financing the installation of a new centralized heating system, which will replace an estimated 79 inefficient and polluting boiler plants, operating with 132 boiler units, in heating areas in Yingkou. Once the project is implemented, a modernized heating system will improve the energy efficiency and environmental performance of heating services in the Yingkou EDZ, resulting in a reduction of CO_2 emissions. To turn this reduction into additional revenue, the World Bank is helping the heating company to prepare a carbon offset project under the auspices of the Clean Development Mechanism (CDM). The sale of emission reductions (ERs) will generate additional revenue and enhance the project's financial viability.

The World Bank will directly purchase the first 860,021 ERs, while the remaining ERs can be purchased by other buyers that need to fulfill their obligations to reduce CO_2 emissions during the Kyoto Protocol commitment period. Once registered, the project is expected to generate about 3,337,390 ERs during the 10-year crediting period. (See also chapter 24 for more information about carbon finance and CDM.)

Source: Authors.

Alternatives to Coal and to District Heating

Alternatives to coal-based district heating can either be (i) distributed alternatives (for example, natural gas furnaces at the building level) or (ii) fuel alternatives. The following sections present a range of technologies that can be considered substitutes for district heating, and which can be an alternative provided they are technically and economically feasible. This list is not intended to be exhaustive but provides illustrative examples of potential alternatives.

Distributed Alternatives

Conventional geothermal space heating. In 2007, this technology provided district heating for 17 million square meters $(Mm^2)^4$ in China, including 12 Mm^2 in Tianjin, 1.64 Mm^2 in Xianyang, 1 Mm^2 in Xian, and about 2 Mm^2 in Beijing (Zheng 2008). Conventional radiators or floor heating systems are typically used. Geothermal waters with temperatures higher than 80°C are first used in radiator systems, after which the return water is used for floor heating. Finally, heat pumps are used to extract more heat from the secondary return water for additional space heating (Zheng 2008).

According to the statistics of the Geothermal Professional Committee of the China Energy Research Society, China is leading the world in utilizing geothermal energy for direct use. With a total of 12,605 GWh/year in 2005 and 18,900 GWh/year in 2007, the rate of direct use geothermal development has increased by about 10 percent annually in recent years. In China, the development and utilization of geothermal energy are concentrated in metropolises, such as Beijing, Tianjin, Xian, Zhengzhou, and Anshan (Zheng 2008). At present, about 3,000 geothermal wells have been completed in China to provide more than 445.7 Mm^3 of hot water for direct use.

Ground Source Heat Pumps (GSHPs). GSHPs are used when the temperature of the heat source is too low for direct application such as district heating. Although research on GSHPs began in the 1950s and 1960s in China, its actual application did not commence until the end of the 1990s. Due to its potential for high efficiency, energy savings, CO_2 emission reductions, and wide application potential, GSHPs have experienced a rapid growth in recent years. Although some challenges remain, according to the statistics of the *Report on China Ground-Source Heat Pump* (Xu 2008), the GSHP market began to expand dramatically in 2005. By the end of 2007, GSHPs were heating about 80 million square meters. The rapid growth of GSHP activities in China since 1998 is shown in figure 8.2, while box 8.9 describes a GSHP demonstration project in Shenyang.

Natural gas furnaces. In several countries, including those in North America, natural gas is abundant and many customers prefer to install natural gas furnaces in individual homes or apartment buildings for space

Figure 8.2   The Growing Application of GSHP in China

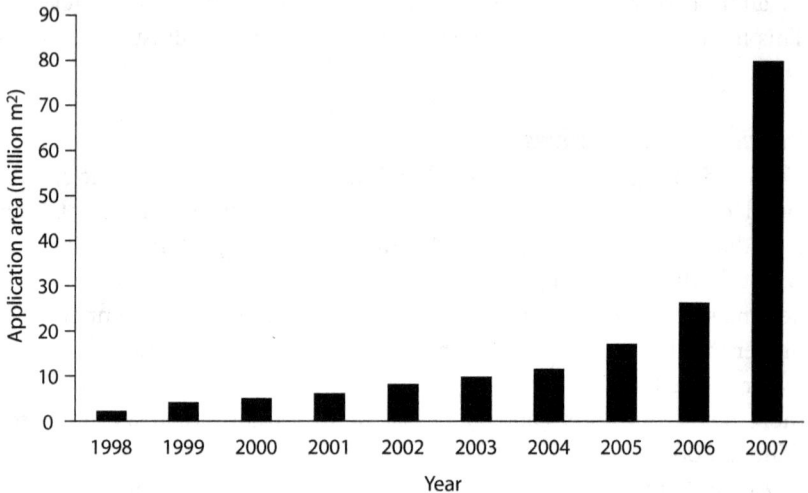

Source: Xu 2008.

Box 8.9

Ground Source Heat Pump Demonstration Project in Shenyang

Shenyang was recognized as a Demonstration City by the China Construction Ministry in 2006 for its effort to popularize ground source heat pumps (GSHPs). Shenyang's heating season lasts six months, and similar to other Chinese municipalities, the city provides heating only between the predetermined dates of October 15th and April 15th. By using a large-scale demonstration project, the city attempted to expand the GSHP market.

In August 2006, based on GSHP technology and its application across China, the provincial government authorized its "Particular Blueprint for Geothermal Source Heat Pump Application" in the 11th Five-Year Plan in Shenyang, as well as "Administrative Measures for Construction and Operation of Geothermal Source Heat Pump System in Shenyang." Through these orders, the government announced that, in principle, GSHPs will be installed in all buildings within 455 km^2 of the city's "third ring." Of this area, about 409 km^2 was deemed suitable for groundwater and about 46 km^2 would require bore heat exchangers.

(continued next page)

Box 8.9 *(continued)*

Other favorable policies were issued to complement the GSHP orders, including an exemption on a surcharge on residential electricity consumption. Furthermore, administrative units were established at all levels: in city, district, and county governments. In December 2006, the Association of Geothermal Source Heat Pump and Expert Research Group was founded in Shenyang, by which a series of scientific research projects was executed to explore related topics, such as technical specifications, reinjection of underground water, sedimentation, and an underground water environment survey.

Source: Authors.

heating and hot water production. Customers prefer this option because it is convenient; they can start heating when desired, rather than waiting for a heating season to begin. Further, in less dense areas, this option can be more economical and cleaner than coal-fired district heating. When comparing this alternative to coal-fired district heating, however, it is important to include the network expansion costs for natural gas. In addition, ensuring a secure supply is a particular concern in cold climate regions.

Micro-CHPs. Micro-CHPs are small units that generate electricity and waste heat to supply small homes and commercial buildings. These units are usually fired by gas and can be provided with the application of net metering. Net metering allows for the micro-CHP to sell surplus power to the grid. Net metering calculates the bill based on the balance between purchased and supplied electricity. This technology has potential in areas where smart grid technologies will be implemented and gas supply is secure.

Solar energy systems. China is the world's leader in the use of solar water heaters for production of domestic hot water, and using the same energy for heating could also be considered. Solar energy systems can produce domestic hot water and space heating. In most cases, pumps are necessary to circulate hot water through internal building radiator systems (Weiss and Mauthner 2008).

Storage. Heat storage is an increasingly important feature in alternative systems, even for electric heating, which is considered the most expensive form of heating and not the cleanest (if coal-fired power generation is used). Storage can also be considered in large district heating systems. It adds flexibility when heat energy is produced and consumed. As technologies mature, it should be further researched and piloted, either as part of distributed systems or as part of district heating systems.

Fuel Alternatives

Energy storage. Heat energy can be stored and this stored energy can be used to support energy saving measures in certain circumstances. In particular, when either electricity or heat demand does not allow a CHP plant to run optimally, the stored heat can be used as an alternative to running the plant.

Natural gas district heating. When a secure natural gas supply and sufficient heat load densities are present, natural gas–fired district heating is a much cleaner alternative to coal-fired district heating. Beijing switched off many coal-fired units in preparation for the 2008 Olympics, replacing them with gas-fired ones. Urumqi also has identified areas where coal-fired district heating is uneconomical and has extended gas networks to provide heating. Municipalities considering developing district heating systems based on CHP may wish to explore the use of gas-fired peak-load boilers rather than coal-fired peak-load boilers. Peak-load boilers are necessary for extreme cold weather when an incremental supply from CHP is unavailable or uneconomical. Although each case should be studied carefully, the advantages of gas are (i) a faster response to peak-load demand and emergencies, as gas-fired heat-only boilers (HoBs) can start operation much more quickly than coal-fired HoBs, and (ii) less air pollution, as gas-fired HoBs have fewer emissions (no total suspended particles [TSP], no SO_2 emissions) than coal-fired HoBs due to fuel characteristics and combustion efficiencies (that is, 94 percent efficiency for gas compared with 78 to 80 percent for coal).

Biomass district heating and CHP. Biomass energy can be used for district heating, especially for CHP. Wood chips, sawdust, various types of waste wood, straw, and agricultural waste (for example, cornstalks) can be used as a renewable energy resource for heating. However, the economics of biomass energy development depend on the sustainable supply of biomass fuels. The World Bank recently issued a study on fuel supply for biomass coal-fired power projects that identifies important considerations for the selection of fuels and supply chain management (World Bank 2010).

Tri-generation. Tri-generation refers to the production of electricity, heating, and cooling. There are two types of tri-generation: (i) decentralized production (for example, chillers at the building level and hot water/steam provided by the district heating network); and (ii) centralized production of cooled water distributed via a network. The emerging concept of district cooling has some distinct advantages including (i) greater use of CHP production (as it would be used year round, not only in the winter), (ii) a reduction in electricity peaks, and (iii) more business opportunities for district heating companies. However, if CHP continues to be largely based on coal, local air pollution impacts during the summer must be considered. District cooling has been used in Beijing, Qingdao, and Shanghai.

Central solar heating. Central solar heating plants produce hot water that is pumped through a district heating network. Some European countries have piloted this kind of approach, including Sweden and Germany. However, this remains a small share of the total district heating market. Most solar energy in Europe is used for domestic hot water systems.

Box 8.10 compares the use of heat pumps, heat-only boilers, and CHP.

Box 8.10

Comparison of CO_2 Emissions of Heat Pumps, Heat-Only Boilers, and CHP

Using figures from the preparation of a district heating modernization project, table B8.10.1 summarizes the estimated annual CO_2 emissions of heat pumps (the baseline), HoBs combined with district heating, and CHP with district heating. Calculations are based on the following scenarios:

Heat pumps (baseline): In the baseline scenario, 2,376 MW of peak-load heating is used for a period of 1,200 hours per year. The emission coefficient for coal is selected to represent a typical and rounded value, 320 grams/kWh of coal. Electricity generation is assumed to take place with coal in large condensing power plants, in which the fuel-to-power ratio is assumed to be 3, and where there is CHP.

Heat-only boilers: As an alternative to the heat pumps, the large heat-only boilers using coal as fuel and connected with the district heating network would provide the same amount of heat energy to customers as the heat pumps, taking into account network losses and boiler efficiency.

CHP: The CHP and district heating system firing local coal was simplified to assume it is the sole source of heating in the community. The electric power of CHP generation is assumed to be 60 percent of the CHP generated heat.

(continued next page)

Box 8.10 *(continued)*

Table B8.10.1   Estimated CO$_2$ Emissions of Heat Pumps, HoB, and CHP

Options	CO$_2$ emission per year (million tonnes)	Change (%)
Heat pumps	2.580	
HOBs with district heating	2.855	11%
CHP with district heating	1.770	−31%

The table illustrates that in the short term the heat-pump base case is more environmentally competitive than the HoB option. However, HoBs allow the heating system to be developed toward the CHP option, which is superior in general terms. CHP allows the most optimal use of fuel, including renewable fuel such as biomass and biogas, compared to any other technology, especially given its high efficiency of 90–94 percent. The application of CHP plants, however, is limited to regions and areas with existing heating loads (for example, district heating network or industrial steam consumption).

Source: Arto Nuorkivi, World Bank Consultant.

Conclusion

Low-carbon development in the built environment in cold climate regions starts with the buildings and continues to the heating source. The costs of using green alternatives are usually higher than the costs of using coal. To promote low-carbon technologies in the built environment and the systems that provide heating to this environment, energy demand first needs to be reduced to make low-carbon alternatives more affordable; if consumers use less energy for heating, they can afford higher priced, but greener alternatives. Such an approach would eventually make alternatives more viable. In addition, green electricity schemes could open new doors to low-carbon approaches to heating. In China, ground-source heat pumps, for example, are only marginally advantageous under certain conditions because of coal's dominance in the country's electricity generation, other conditions related to the technology such as coefficient of performance, and heating requirements. If technologies and mechanisms emerge that allow cities to purchase green electricity, the carbon intensity of such technologies could be reduced significantly.

District heating provides cities with the ability to switch to greener fuels with more flexibility than distributed solutions. As alternative technologies improve and the grid can deliver more green electricity, reliably and affordably, integration of greener options should be investigated. "Smart heat grids" also could be envisioned, whereby intermittent green energy sources could be integrated gradually with district heating. Integrated district heating networks using CHPs to supply the base load and HoBs for peak load, dispatched based on economic principles, is one example. District heating (perhaps also district cooling) has a bright future in the low-carbon city. However, district heating companies need to significantly improve their ability to serve customers with high-quality service, as consumers are now seeking a higher quality of life and on-demand heating. This is significant when consumers start to pay the heat bill themselves and can control costs through metered consumption. Finally, when looking at current district heating systems and approaches, heating supply sector reform is closely linked with building energy efficiency measures, creating both incentives for district heating and solutions for owners.

Notes

1. The Ministry of Commerce, the National Development and Reform Commission, the Ministry of Finance, the Ministry of Personnel, the Ministry of Civil Affairs, the Ministry of Labor and Social Security, the State Taxation Administration, and the State Environmental Protection Administration.

2. This regulation would have the force of law and is called "*Tiaoli*" in Chinese.

3. Based on 2004 data from the *2005 China Energy Statistical Yearbook* (State Statistics Bureau 2005).

4. Mm^2 corresponds to mega square meters, or 10^6 m^2.

Bibliography

Asia Sustainable and Alternative Energy Program (ASTAE), World Bank. 2001. "China Opportunities to Improve Energy Efficiency in Buildings." May. Washington, DC: ASTE/World Bank.

DHC Technology Platform. 2009. "District Heating & Cooling. A Vision towards 2020-2030-2050." May. Brussels. www.dhcplus.eu/Documents/Vision_DHC.pdf.

Draugelis, G., B. Jablonski, B. Kalkum, and V. Lukosevicius. Forthcoming. "Enhancing the Institutional Framework for District Heating Regulation in China." World Bank Technical Assistance Report. ESMAP/World Bank, Washington, DC.

Draugelis, G., and X. Wu. 2009. "Social Analysis of Heating Reforms in Liaoning Province." November 2009. ASTE. ASTE/World Bank, Washington, DC. http://siteresources.worldbank.org/EXTEAPASTAE/Resources/Liaoning-Report.pdf.

Gochenour, C. 2001. "District Heating Trends, Issues and Opportunities: the Role of the World Bank." March. World Bank Technical Paper No. 493. World Bank, Washington, DC.

Heat Reform and Building Energy Efficiency Project (HRBEE), Government of China. 2006. "Ground Sources Heat Pump Technology Application in China; Summary Report." Government of China, Beijing.

International Finance Corporation (IFC), China Utility-Based Energy Efficiency Finance Program (CHUEE). 2008. "Co and Trigeneration and Heating Systems Policy Report and Market Research." Pöyry. http://www.poyry.com/.

JP Building Engineers, Center for Energy Efficiency in Buildings. 2002. "Heat Metering and Billing: Technical Options, Policies and Regulations: Chinese Demonstration Projects and International Experiences." World Bank Consultant Trust Fund Report. August 2002. World Bank, Washington, DC. http://www.worldbank.org.cn/English/content/heat.pdf.

Liu, F., X. Zhang, M. Bellanger, and M. Hassam. 2006. "Economic Analysis of Energy Efficiency Measures for New Residential Buildings in Northern China." ASTAE. ASTAE/World Bank, Washington, DC.

Liu, F., A. Meyer, and J. Hogan. 2010. "Mainstreaming Building Energy Efficiency Codes in Developing Countries—Global Experiences and Lessons from Early Adopters." Working Paper No. 204. World Bank, Washington, DC.

Meyer, A., and B. Kalkum. 2008. *China: Development of National Heat Pricing and Billing Policy*. ESMAP Formal Report 330/08, World Bank Report Number 44988. March 2008. World Bank, Washington, DC.

Ping, L., F. Liu, L. Younong, V-M Makela, A. Meyer, E. Toivanen, A. Han, and R. Taylor. 2002. "Heat Metering and Billing: Technical Options, Policies and Regulations." ASTAE. ASTAE/World Bank, Washington, DC. http://www.worldbank.org.cn/english/content/heat.pdf.

State Statistics Bureau, Government of China. *2005 China Energy Statistical Yearbook*. China Statistics Press. Beijing.

———. 2010. *China Energy Statistical Yearbook 2009*. China Statistics Press.

Taylor, R., F. Liu, and A. Meyer. 2001. "China: Opportunities to Improve Energy Efficiency in Buildings." ASTAE Report. May. ASTE/World Bank, Washington, DC.

Taylor, R., G. Draugelis, Y. Zhang, and A. U. Ang Co. 2010. "Accelerating Energy Conservation in China's Provinces." AusAID/World Bank, Washington, DC. http://www.worldbank.org/research/2010/06/12720925/accelerating-energy-conservation-chinas-provinces.

Weiss, W., and F. Mauthner. 2008, "Solar Heat Worldwide: Markets and Contribution to Energy Supply." 2010 ed. International Energy Agency Solar Heating and Cooling Programme, Graz, Austria.

World Bank. 2005. "Project Appraisal Document on a Proposed Global Environment Facility (GEF) Grant of US$18 Million to the People's Republic of China for the China Heat Reform and Building Energy Efficiency Project." Report No. 30747. World Bank, Washington, DC.

———. 2008. "Project Appraisal Document, Liaoning Third Medium Cities Infrastructure Project." World Bank, Washington, DC. http://web.worldbank.org/external/projects/main?pagePK=64283627&piPK=73230&theSitePK=40941&menuPK=228424&Projectid=P099224.

———. 2010. "Fuel Supply Handbook for Biomass-Fired Power Projects." World Bank Energy Sector Management Assistance Program (ESMAP) Report May 2010. Prepared by BTG Biomass Technology Group BV. World Bank, Washington, DC.

Xu, W. 2008. Report on China Ground-Source Heat Pump. 1st ed. Beijing: China Architecture & Building Press.

Zheng, K. 2008. "Geothermal Resources and Use for Heating in China." Proceedings from Workshop for Decision Makers on Direct Heating Use of Geothermal Resources in Asia, organized by the Geothermal Training Programme of the United Nations University (UNU-GTP), Geothermal Management Department at Tianjin Bureau of Land, Resources and Real Estate Management (TBLRREM), and Tianjin Bureau of Geology and Mineral Exploration Development (TBGMED), in Tianjin, China, 11–18 May, 2008. http://www.os.is/gogn/unu-gtp-sc/UNU-GTP-SC-06-03.pdf.

PART 3

Sectoral Action for Low-Carbon Cities: Urban Transport

CHAPTER 9

Introduction: Urban Transport and Climate Change

Shomik Mehndiratta

Urban Transport and CO_2

Reducing CO_2 emissions is a growing challenge for the transport sector. Transportation produces roughly 23 percent of the global CO_2 emissions from fuel combustion. More alarmingly, transportation is the fastest growing consumer of fossil fuels and the fastest growing source of CO_2 emissions. With rapid urbanization in developing countries, energy consumption and CO_2 emissions by urban transport are increasing rapidly.

These growing emissions also pose an enormous challenge to urban transport in China. As a recent World Bank study of 17 sample cities in China indicates, urban transport energy use and greenhouse gas (GHG) emissions have recently grown between 4 and 6 percent a year in major cities such as Beijing, Shanghai, Guangzhou, and Xian (Darido, Torres-Montoya, and Mehndiratta 2009). In Beijing, CO_2 emissions from urban transport reached 1.4 tonnes per person in 2006. The numbers could be considerably higher in 2011. A national estimate suggests that in 2006 GHG emissions from urban transport in China were 290 million tonnes, or 700 kilograms per capita, and 26 percent of the total GHG emissions from all transportation in the country and about 15 percent of the CO_2 emissions per capita in China in the same year.[1]

Opportunities for Low-Carbon Urban Transport

Despite the trend toward increasing emissions, opportunities exist for low-carbon urban transport development in China. Figure 9.1 provides a schematic of the drivers of emissions from urban transport and indicates entry points for urban transport policy interventions to save energy and reduce CO_2 emissions.

The six entry points in figure 9.1 all relate to the fact that, in essence, GHG from transport are emitted from the fuel used on motorized trips. The figure shows that increases in the level of *economic activity* in a city usually result in an increase in the total number of trips; that is, the aggregate level of *transport activity*. These trips are distributed across the range of available modes (referred to as the *modal split*), depending on the competitiveness of the alternatives for any given trip maker. Every motorized trip emits GHG emissions and the amount of emission depends largely on the amount and GHG intensity of the fuel used, or the efficiency of the *vehicle fleet* and the *energy intensity of the fuel used*. Finally, *driver behavior* impacts the fuel use; after certain threshold speeds, fuel consumption becomes significantly higher. While this complex and distributed nature in which GHG emissions are generated makes transport a particularly hard sector in which to dramatically reduce emissions, there are several strategy options for a city looking to reduce the carbon foot-

Figure 9.1   Entry Points for Energy Saving and CO_2 Reduction

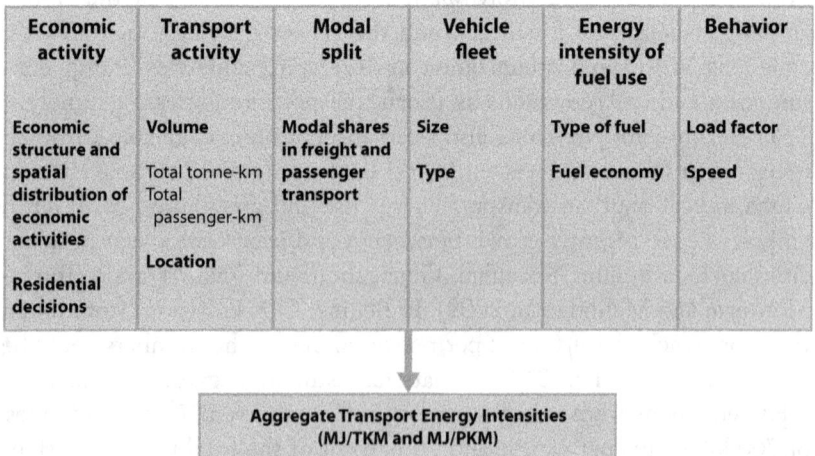

Economic activity	Transport activity	Modal split	Vehicle fleet	Energy intensity of fuel use	Behavior
Economic structure and spatial distribution of economic activities Residential decisions	Volume Total tonne-km Total passenger-km Location	Modal shares in freight and passenger transport	Size Type	Type of fuel Fuel economy	Load factor Speed

Aggregate Transport Energy Intensities (MJ/TKM and MJ/PKM)

Source: Authors.
Note: MJ = megajoules; TKM = tonne-kilometer; PKM = passenger-kilometer.

print of its urban transport sector, all of which are very relevant to Chinese cities today:

- *Changing the distribution of activities in space:* For any given level of economic activity, if a city can influence the distribution of activities in space (for example, by changing land-use patterns, densities, and urban design) it can have an impact on the total level of transport activity. Better land-use planning and compact city development can lead to fewer or shorter motorized trips and a larger share for public transport of motorized trips. Chapter 4 laid out the issues, structural challenges, and a way forward to address this challenge.
- *Supporting low-carbon transport modes:* A city can also influence the way transport activity is realized in terms of choice of modes. Chapters 10 and 11 will discuss improving the quality of relatively "low emission" modes such as walking, cycling, and various forms of public transport. Such steps can help a city attract trip takers to these modes and lower their carbon emissions per trip.
- *Affecting vehicle use:* Finally, a city can take a range of measures that directly influence what vehicles are being used and how much private transport is being used. Chapter 12 will describe two approaches to reduce emissions from motorized vehicles. One is the adoption of technological measures that reduce the carbon emissions of motorized vehicles per unit of travel. The other is the adoption of demand management measures that would reduce the amount of automotive travel. This includes both non-pricing controls on vehicle ownership and use (for example, restrictions on parking or days the car can be used), and pricing controls such as fuel taxes, higher parking fees, and congestion pricing.

Experience internationally and in China suggests that there is no easy solution to reduce GHG emissions from transport. A comprehensive approach is required that simultaneously seeks to (i) reduce the demand for total motorized transport activity through appropriately designed urban places; (ii) promote the use of "low-emission" transport modes such as walking, cycling, and public transport; and (iii) use the most efficient fuel-vehicle technology system possible for all trips. Box 9.1 presents the case of Singapore, illustrating the benefits of a comprehensive approach in this respect. While cities will need to find the right mix of strategies to suit their particular circumstances, the following general approaches apply:

- As cities grow in population and expand their spatial footprint, perhaps their most important priority is to ensure that their spatial footprint is compatible with strong, competitive public transport.
- As incomes increase, creating viable alternatives to the use of cars for those who have a choice will be absolutely critical in almost all of China's cities to keep them livable and functioning efficiently. For the larger cities, actively managing automobile use will increasingly be a necessary option to consider and develop.
- Technology will need to complement these two fundamental strategies—and in that role can provide significant GHG reductions and other related environmental benefits.

Box 9.1

Singapore: A Role Model for Urban Planning and Transport

Singapore is a model of the most transformative urban development in the world. The city-state has made a remarkable transition from a city afflicted by poverty to a wealthy, bustling metropolis—all in less than 40 years. Adherence to strong planning practices and transport policies has made Singapore an attractive place to live and work, as well as a desirable location for foreign investment.

With only about 650 square kilometers of land area and nearly 5 million inhabitants, Singapore is characterized by a high population density and efficient transport systems. This success is achieved through a multifaceted transport and land-use strategy consisting of three key components:

- *Integration of town and transport planning:* Industrial, residential, and social infrastructure is placed within walking distance of bus stops and mass rapid transit (MRT) stations. Road networks are designed to make bus service accessible from residential areas, and pedestrian walkways are covered to provide protection from rain and extreme weather. A mixed-use planning strategy puts work and home closer together, moderating the demand on transport systems. These strategies serve to minimize the levels of motorized transport activity associated with any given level of economic activity.
- *Improvements in public transport:* The far-reaching, multimodal public transit network consists of four major systems: MRT, light rapid transit (LRT), buses, and taxis. The transit systems have integrated operating institutions, service net-

(continued next page)

Box 9.1 *(continued)*

works, and fare schemes. The stations are situated in or near commercial and office developments and are designed to facilitate efficient transfers between modes. Public transit is regulated to maintain its reliability, affordability, and efficiency. These strategies serve to make public transport attractive even to relatively high-income users.

- *Management of vehicle ownership and usage:* Ownership of personal vehicles is limited by a government-controlled quota (Vehicle Quota Scheme) and a tax on new vehicle registrations (Additional Registration Scheme). Usage of personal vehicles is deterred by a congestion charge for vehicles entering a designated restricted zone during certain hours (Electronic Road Pricing). The city is also careful to limit total road length to what it considers "optimal levels" and ensures that all road construction and maintenance is supported directly by revenues from road users.

The planning and policy measures to deter driving and encourage public transit have reduced congestion and pollution, which is a major draw for international business and investment (Willoughby 2001). Over time, Singapore's planning strategies have contributed to an increase in GDP per capita to a level higher than some already developed countries, all while maintaining a low level of energy consumption in the road sector (see figure B9.1.1). Singapore has set a precedent for sustainable policy development, ensuring that low-carbon land use and sound transport planning practices are part of its future.

Figure B9.1.1   Singapore and Europe: Ground Transport Energy Consumption

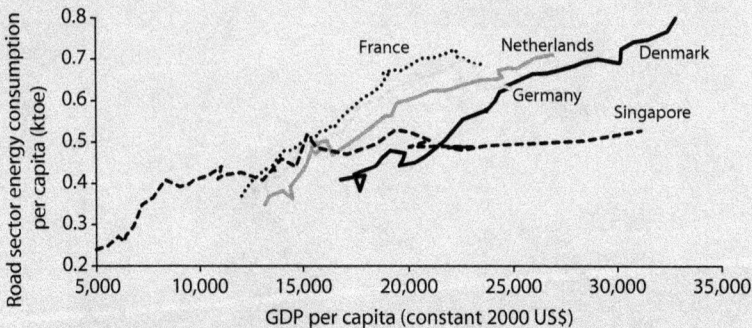

Sources: Lam and Toan 2006; Willoughby 2001; World Bank Development Indicators Databank.
Note: ktoe = kilotonne of oil equivalent.

Notes

1. This preliminary internal estimate made by the World Bank team is based on data from the Darido, Torres-Montoya, and Mehndiratta (2009) study and publicly available data from China National Bureau of Statistics (2008) and IEA (2008).

Bibliography

China National Bureau of Statistics. 2008. *China Statistical Year Book for Regional Economies.* Beijing.

Darido, G., M. Torres-Montoya, and S. Mehndiratta. 2009. "Urban Transport and CO_2 Emissions: Some Evidence from Chinese Cities." World Bank Working Paper. World Bank, Washington, DC.

International Energy Agency (IEA). 2008. "Selected 2006 Indicators for China, Peoples Republic of." Paris: IEA.

Lam, S., and T. Toan. 2006. "Land Transport Policy and Public Transit in Singapore." *Transportation* 33(2): 171–88.

Willoughby, C. 2001. "Singapore's Motorization Policies 1960–2000." *Transport Policy* 8(2): 125–39.

CHAPTER 10

Cycling and Walking: Preserving a Heritage, Regaining Lost Ground

Shomik Mehndiratta

Overview

Bicycling and walking are important aspects of city life, and this chapter summarizes the issues and challenges related to strengthening the bike and pedestrian accessibility of urban road networks in China. The chapter makes the case that apart from the greenhouse gas (GHG) benefits from avoiding motorized trips, cycling and walking are critical to well-functioning urban environments. After describing the current situation of pedestrian and bicycle access to China's urban centers, the chapter highlights the factors that have influenced current policies and discusses their consequences. Viable solutions to the current situation are discussed under four main categories: network issues, last-mile quality, basic facilities, and the safe corridor concept. Project descriptions and case studies highlight practical aspects related to these categories. The chapter concludes by summarizing the main challenges and presenting recommendations for moving forward.

This chapter is based on practical experience from a range of World Bank–financed projects in China, as well as a number of surveys and related research projects. The analysis draws extensively on work published in a series of working papers, including Y. Chen and Mehndiratta (2007), Tao et al. (2010), Jiang et al. (2012), and W. Chen and Mehndiratta (2007).

Introduction: Cycling and Walking as Critical Elements of an Urban Environment

Walking and cycling are not only true low-carbon urban mobility choices; they are also critical elements of any modern urban mobility system. From a planner's perspective, walking and cycling trips are space efficient, require low investments, and offer mobility without imposing external costs of noise, pollution, congestion, or accidents. In dense urban environments, walking and cycling often can be the most efficient modes of urban mobility. For users, they offer mobility at low cost, with the potential of health and lifestyle benefits. In all cities, these modes are the mainstay for short trips and often the only sources of mobility for the poor. In addition, walking and cycling are critical for providing last-mile access and connecting to public transport networks.

Though many cities globally—from New York and Buenos Aires to Paris and Copenhagen—actively promote and support cycling and walking as essential elements of their transport strategies, most would be envious of the situation in Chinese cities in terms of the share and importance of these modes. Chinese cities have a long and important tradition of cycling and walking. Even today, between 50 percent and 60 percent of trips in most Chinese cities are made on foot and by bicycle (see figure 10.1a). However, in most Chinese cities the trend is negative, and as shown in figure 10.1b, bicycle use in particular has been decreasing precipitously in recent years. China, as late as the 1980s, was often referred to as the "Bicycle Kingdom," with bicycles dominating traffic in cities across the country. That is no longer the case, and economic growth, changing cultural perceptions, rapid motorization, spatial growth, and changes in trip patterns have all resulted in sharp declines in cycling and walking. Walking and cycling, however, remain important modes and the challenge for Chinese cities now is how to at least preserve, and perhaps increase, the share of trips made using these non-motorized modes.

Conditions for both pedestrians and cyclists, however, have been deteriorating across Chinese cities in the last few years. This is due to a combination of factors, including the lack of policies prioritizing these users (see box 10.1), cities sacrificing space for non-motorized traffic to be used for motorized traffic, the spatial growth of cities resulting in longer trips, and specific difficulties related to the big arterial roads of a typical Chinese city. While the primary focus of this chapter is on actions cities can take to improve conditions and preserve the quality of infrastructure

Figure 10.1a   Walking and Bicycling as Percentage of Total Trips. While bicycling and walking remain an important mode of transport...

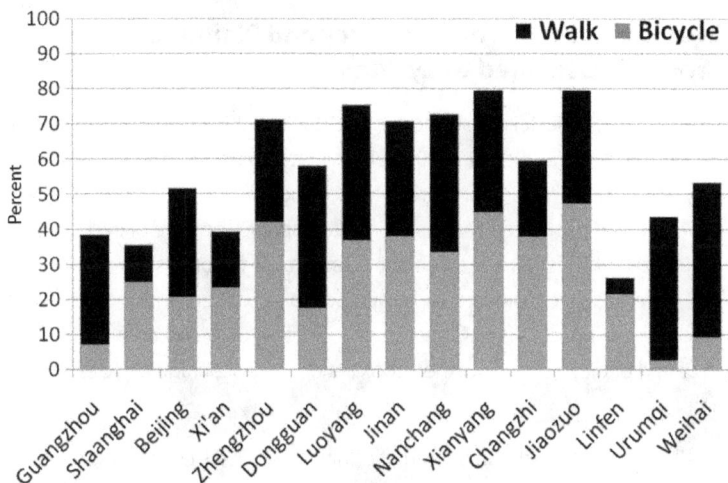

Source: Darido et al. 2009.

Figure 10.1b   Use of Bicycles Has Fallen Considerably in Many Large and Small Cities

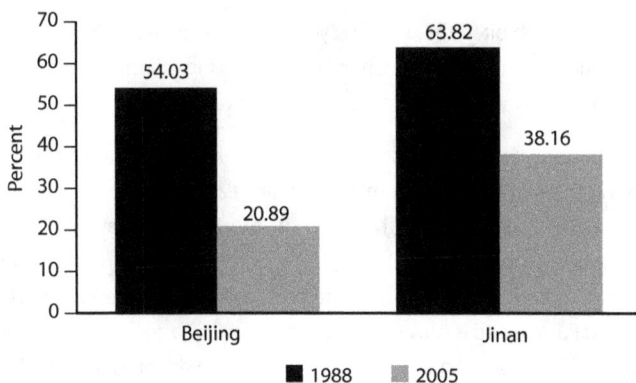

Source: Darido et al. 2009.

for cyclists and pedestrians, an overarching issue in this respect is the need to obtain strong policy-level support and guidance from the national government supporting and emphasizing the role of cycling and walking as part of the sustainable transport solution in China's cities.

Box 10.1

Evolution of Government Policy and Planning Procedures Related to Cycling

After a period of sustained support in the 1970s and 1980s, government policies in the 1990s and early 2000s demonstrated a negative attitude toward bicycles. While all World Bank projects focusing on urban transport have encouraged and supported various actions to improve the state of cycling, nonmotorized vehicles were often perceived as a cause of congestion and conflict and were widely considered to be symbols of a past era with no place in a modernized, industrialized China. Several cities actually had an official policy to get rid of bicycles. Many others took actions to discourage bicycles. For example:

- Zhengzhou, with its "Smooth Traffic" initiative in 2004, changed some bicycle lanes into motor vehicle lanes and combined bicycle lanes with pedestrian lanes on sidewalks at both sides of the road. Moreover, in 2004, the Zhengzhou Bureau of Education prohibited primary school students from bicycling to school. Middle schools also restricted the number of students cycling to school.
- Shanghai prohibited the use of bicycles on trunk roads in 2007.
- Shenzhen, in the 1997 Shenzhen Urban Planning Standards, removed bicycle lanes to increase the capacity of motor vehicle lanes.

While national policy now seems to recognize the importance of bicycles, the view at the city level is still mixed. For city leaders, cyclists and their concerns are often secondary to the concerns of motorized traffic. In terms of planning, one problem is that the formal four-step transport modeling framework used to evaluate transport investments, which originated in the United States and Europe and is now used extensively in China, focuses on motorized traffic only. The modeling process, however, can be adapted to explicitly account for cyclists, as has been done as part of World Bank appraisals of urban transport projects in Guangzhou, Wuhan, and Liaoning. In the Liaoning project, doing so helped prioritize investments in secondary streets, which disproportionately benefited cyclists. Estimates have since indicated that cyclists reaped 45 percent of the total economic benefits from the investments.

Source: Author.

Improving Cycling and Walking Infrastructure

To transition to a low-carbon growth path, the critical agenda for Chinese cities is to preserve, as far as possible, the trips currently made using non-motorized means, and then, ultimately, to attract the pool of trip makers who could consider these modes for some of their trips. Fundamentally, policy support is needed to create cities that encourage and enable walking and cycling as valid transport choices for all trip makers.

Recent experience suggests that four kinds of complementary improvements are needed to improve the quality of cycling and walking infrastructure in Chinese cities:

- *Addressing network issues:* Designing cities and road systems to better serve cyclists and pedestrians
- *Improving the quality of the "last mile":* Improving the often atrocious condition of the secondary and tertiary roads, as these are needed to access origins and destinations once trip makers get off the primary roads
- *Providing basic facilities and street furniture:* Providing toilets, trees, benches, bollards, and street lighting
- *Designing and operating safe arterials:* Systematically addressing safety issues on the most critical traffic corridors.

Addressing Network Issues

Networks, rather than individual links or roads, are the essential elements of urban mobility. Thus, the primary effort of all World Bank interventions in the urban transport sector in China has been to improve the performance of road, public transport, and non-motorized transport networks. A key gap in the development of Chinese road networks in the last two decades has been the lack of good quality tertiary and secondary roads.

In the last 30 years, as Chinese cities have dealt with motorization at a pace never seen before, the primary response of city leadership has been to engage in a frenzy of road-building. By some accounts, the total annual investment in the urban road sector in China is a staggering US$35 billion. An overwhelming majority of this investment, however, is focused on a network of wide primary roads. Much of this new primary road network was needed to accommodate the growth in population and incomes in the last 30 years, even though it is not always clear that the road design, in terms of width, is optimal for an urban environment with mixed traffic. Optimally, however, these investments in the primary network should be complemented by increased investments in secondary and tertiary roads that can serve non-motorized and local and short-distance trips, and as such take some pressure off the arterial road system. Currently, many primary roads have to perform incompatible mixed functions, such as providing for through traffic, local traffic, and other nontraffic functions such as shopping and local activities.

This weakness in the road networks has negative impacts on all modes of transport, but particularly so on walking and bicycling. In the case of cyclists, it is often the secondary and tertiary roads that form the core of a city's bicycle network. In the absence of this network, cyclists have no choice but to use the primary road network, where speeds are the highest, conflicts at intersections are the most severe, and, consequently, safety is the biggest concern. In addition to encouraging cities, such as cities in Liaoning, Wuhan, and Luan in Anhui, to address this gap in their secondary and tertiary road networks, World Bank projects have made a particular effort to support improvements in bicycle networks. This has included the identification of a priority cycle network in Shanghai, the design of routes primarily for bicycles in Shijiazhuang, extensive support for segregated bicycle lanes in the cities of Liaoning and in Wuhan, and the integration of cyclists with pedestrians in traffic-calmed zones in Guangzhou and Xian (see figure 10.2) (Frame 2004).

Figure 10.2   Integrating Cyclists with Pedestrians Using Different Colored Pavement in Xian

Source: World Bank.

In the case of pedestrians, the lack of a "thick" network of secondary streets fundamentally limits *accessibility*, the "walkability" of a city. Analytical work that compares pedestrian access to jobs and commercial opportunities in the central business districts of Beijing, London, and New York has been used to illustrate the issue to planners and decision makers in several Chinese cities (see box 10.2).

Box 10.2

Pedestrian Accessibility: Comparing Central Business and Commercial Districts in Beijing, London, and New York City

While planners agree that transit-oriented urban design is essential to attract those who have a choice in using public transport, it is not always easy to illustrate the concept of pedestrian accessibility to city leaders. Research by Torres et al. (2010), which was developed to illustrate this concept, shows the importance of coordinating urban design with public transport by looking at a basic accessibility indicator: the number of jobs and square feet of commercial floorspace accessible within a 10- or 20-minute walking radius of a major public transit station in the city's central commercial or central business district. Data were gathered in three metropolitan areas: Beijing, London, and New York (see figure B10.2.1).

Figure B10.2.1   Pedestrian Accessibility

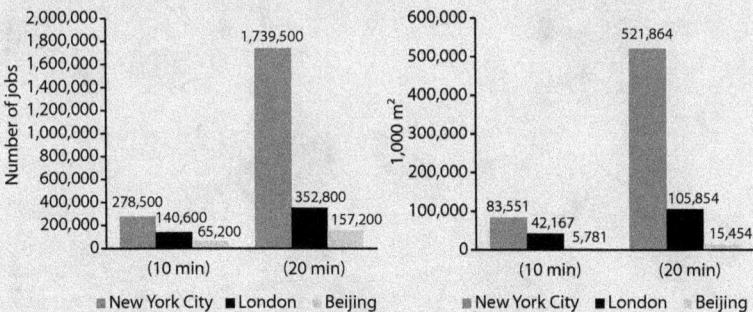

a. Number of jobs accessed within 10 or 20 minutes of walking

b. Commercial areas accessed within 10 and 20 minutes of walking (in 1,000 square meters)

Source: Torres-Montoya et al. 2010.

(continued next page)

Box 10.2 *(continued)*

The study demonstrated that a city with design characteristics like New York gives way to a much more accessible urban environment than a city with the design characteristics of Beijing, which has fewer and wider roads, large super-blocks, and widely spaced buildings set back from the road. The study highlighted the need to consider the following aspects when designing an urban area plan for high accessibility:

- High-density land use with high-rises built close together
- A dense grid network with sufficient secondary roads and small city blocks
- A pedestrian-friendly environment.

Source: Author, based on Torres- Montoya et al. 2010.

In Kunming, where the success of the World Bank–financed urban rail network in part depends on establishing high-quality urban design around stations, the focus has been on learning from global best practice.

Figure 10.3   Best Practice Urban Design across Different Scales

(a) Catchment Analysis

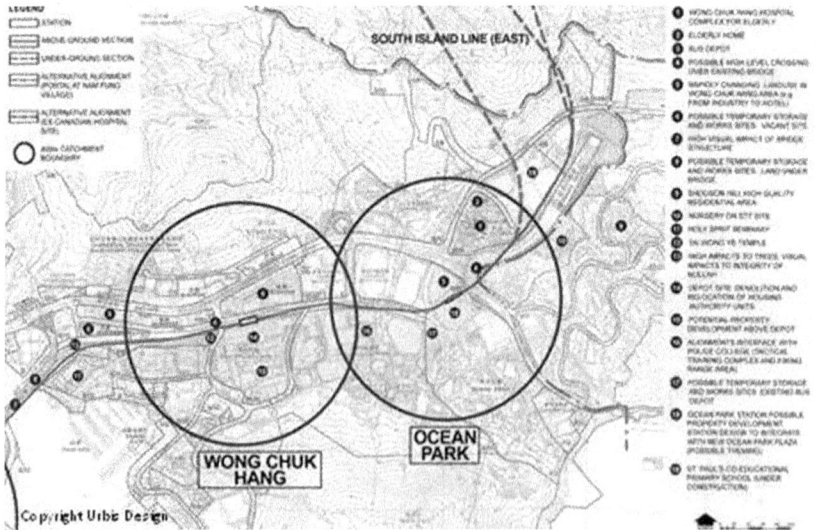

(continued next page)

Figure 10.3 *(continued)*

(b) Entrance Design

STATION DESIGN APPROACHES

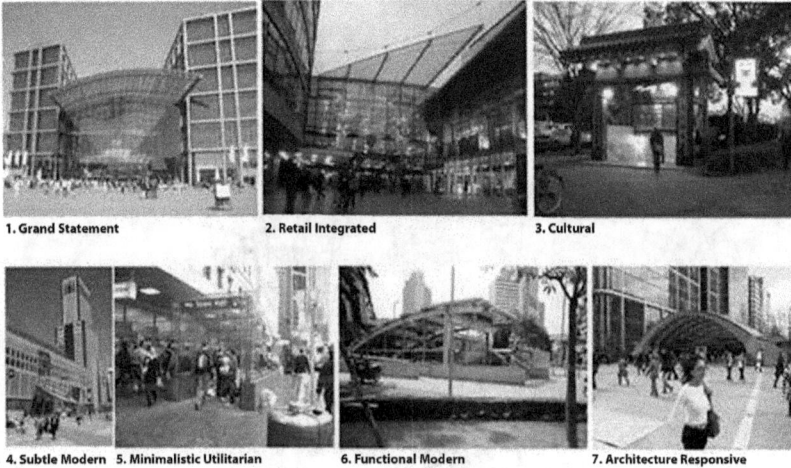

1. Grand Statement   2. Retail Integrated   3. Cultural

4. Subtle Modern 5. Minimalistic Utilitarian   6. Functional Modern   7. Architecture Responsive

Source: Urbis 2011.

The project's transport planners have used a series of analyses, from a large scale *catchment analysis* of an area within walking distance of a given station, to optimizing design details such as station entrances (see figure 10.3). As the project moves forward, the focus will shift to ensuring that design standards support the rail system and overall public transport.

Analytical work assessing the quality of pedestrian access to the Jinan Bus Rapid Transit (BRT) identified a particularly interesting insight related to pedestrian access networks (Jiang et al. 2012). Based on pedestrian interviews and a field investigation, the study found that people walk farther to BRT stations on "integrated-boulevard" corridors when the walking environment has certain "quality" features, such as a median transit way station, or when the corridor is shaded, busy, and interesting, or enables good orientation. In addition, mapping the walking paths revealed that a small network of paths accounted for a large portion of access trips (see figure 10.4). Through an unarticulated consensus, pedestrians seem to agree on a particular set of route choices due to a combination of quality, comfort, and safety. This suggests that, as with other modes, identifying and improving the quality of a relatively small pedestrian network can bring significant benefits by actively encouraging pedestrians to use the network.

Figure 10.4   Map of Pedestrian Access to the Jinan BRT System

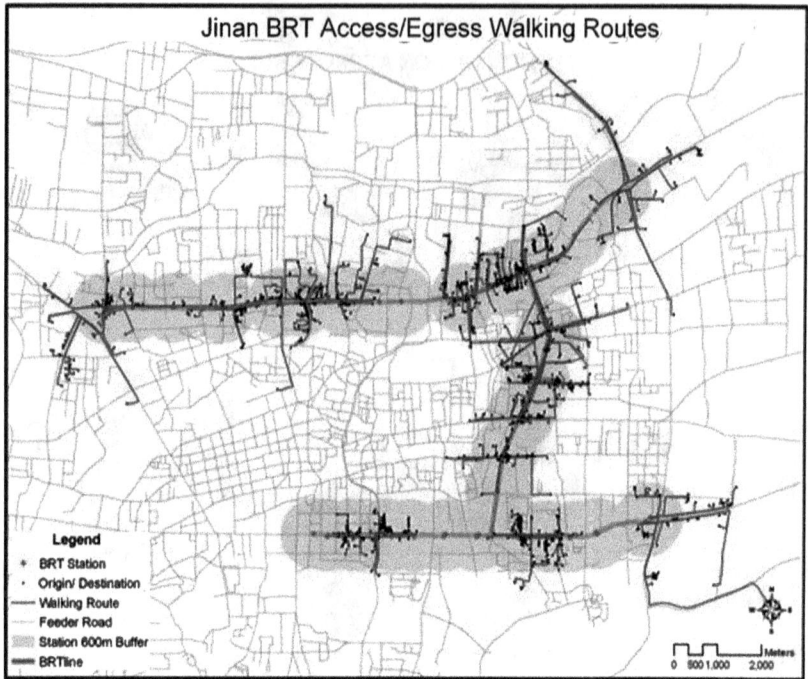

Source: Jiang et al. 2012.

Improving the Quality of the Last Mile

> The Yanhe area where I live is located in the poorest outskirts of
> Wuhan. The roads here are muddy tracks maintained by trishaw[1]
> traffic! On rainy days, we have to wear rubber boots—you just can't
> go out in one pair of shoes, they'd be ruined! It's just filthy and if you
> go out in your bare feet, you get infections. That's tough on everybody,
> but especially on women. Sometimes I put on my boots to cross the
> road, change shoes when I get to the other side and ask older relatives
> to take those filthy boots back home.
>
> *– An unemployed woman from*
> *Qinduankou area, Hanyang District*

A particular feature of the road network of many Chinese cities, related
to the gap in secondary and tertiary road systems discussed above, is the
often poor quality of the roads that provide last-mile access to residences
and work buildings, as, for example, illustrated in figure 10.5. The poor

Figure 10.5   Poor Quality of a Secondary Road in Liaoning

Source: World Bank.

quality of this network is detrimental to all trips, but particularly troublesome for bicyclists and pedestrians, who are most vulnerable to water, potholes, parked vehicles, and other barriers to access.

Structured public participation processes can be an effective way to raise awareness for the problems related to access to the last mile. Feedback from user groups—people living in a project zone and specifically targeted vulnerable groups—has, for example, been incorporated in World Bank projects in Xian, Taiyuan, and Wuhan, and the cities in Liaoning and Anhui.

In Liaoning, this public participation process has been particularly successful in influencing the investment agenda (W. Chen and Mehndiratta 2007) and much of the investments in the Liaoning Medium Cities Urban Transport Project (LMCIP) focused on rehabilitating branch, tertiary, and secondary roads. Indeed, in the US$113 million rehabilitation and maintenance component, 61 percent of the investments are targeted at tertiary roads, such as branch roads and streets in neighborhoods and alleys, and 29 percent are targeted at secondary roads. Most of this network was built in the early 1950s and has poor (if not nonexistent) drainage, and the reconstruction has significantly upgraded the quality of the cities' road network. Moreover, the public participation process related to development of primary roads even led, in some cases, to direct city investments in the branch road network. The fact that the rehabilitation of tertiary roads is a low-cost solution was certainly a determining factor.

Providing Basic Facilities and Street Furniture: The Toilets, Benches, and Trees Agenda

The structured public participation processes also highlighted the need to improve basic facilities that provide cyclists and pedestrians with some safety, security, and comfort. This includes the finish of the road, the separation of non-motorized vehicles from motorized vehicles, street furniture, greening, lighting, and clearer intersection design.

It is important that, in addition to the road itself, these road facilities are of good quality. Adequate attention must be paid to issues such as sidewalk quality or curb cuts at intersections (which are sometimes not flush with the pavement, other times not aligned with the intersection). Basic facilities, such as trees, benches, and street lights, make the difference between a road for cars and a road designed to serve a city and its residents. While all pedestrians need these basic services, they are particularly important for people with mobility impairments. Features such as textured pavements, curb cuts, safety islands, and countdown and audible crossing signals are inexpensive elements of urban infrastructure, but essential for impaired people to be able to take advantage of roads, sidewalks, and other transport facilities.

Attention to these details of road facilities is essential to ensure newly developed roads serve *all* users. Ideally, the populations that benefit the most from this attention to detail should have a role in supervising road implementation. Box 10.3 describes an interesting and potentially significant development in Jinzhou, a city participating in the Liaoning Medium Cities Infrastructure Project, where the disabled community has had a role in ensuring that roads in the city were built with adequate attention to detail. Today, Jinzhou systematically involves the Jinzhou Municipal Federation of Disabled Persons (FDP) to provide feedback on the quality of its roads and facilities.

Box 10.3

Putting "People-Centered Development" in Practice in Jinzhou, Liaoning

The cities of Benxi, Jinzhou, and Panjin in Liaoning Province all have taken a series of highly innovative steps to include residents with disabilities in the implementation of their urban transport projects. In all three cities, the local government organized seminars to increase awareness of project activities among residents with disabilities, and invited members of the disabled community to test newly constructed road facilities and provide input on their accessibility and functionality.

In Jinzhou, the local government and the Jinzhou Municipal Federation of Disabled Persons (FDP) started to jointly convene annual meetings to solicit input

(continued next page)

Box 10.3 *(continued)*

from residents with disabilities on new and rehabilitated road facilities. At the meetings, city officials present annual construction plans and summarize actions taken in response to feedback received at earlier consultations. Reporters from local newspapers also attend the meeting. Members of the Federation then test the newly built infrastructure, intersections, sidewalks, and crosswalk facilities, and provide their feedback.

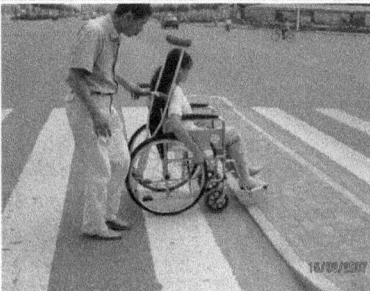

A resident of Jinzhou inspects new safety islands and curbs in a wheel chair.

A blind resident with a cane tests the textured pavements on a newly constructed sidewalk of Jinzhou.

Source: World Bank.

For cyclists, good-quality motor vehicle separators, which separate cyclists from motorized traffic, are critical (see figure 10.6). Using a "crashworthiness" assessment of different types of lane separators, cities have also been able to decide on the right vehicle separators for their situation. The assessment identified the separators that not only provided physical separation, but also had the capacity to withstand the impact of a car crashing into it at 30 kilometers per hour (figure 10.7).

Finally, street furniture can enhance a user's experience and promote more extensive use of the network. Street lighting is a basic facility and critical for providing an environment that women experience as safe. Toilets, benches, trees, and bicycling parking places are other simple facilities that benefit pedestrians and cyclists in the urban environment. Box 10.4 illustrates how the city council of Jinzhou effectively addressed public concerns related to this topic.

Figure 10.6   Lane Separators in Jinzhou, Liaoning

Source: World Bank.

Figure 10.7   Comparison of Lane Separator Displacement

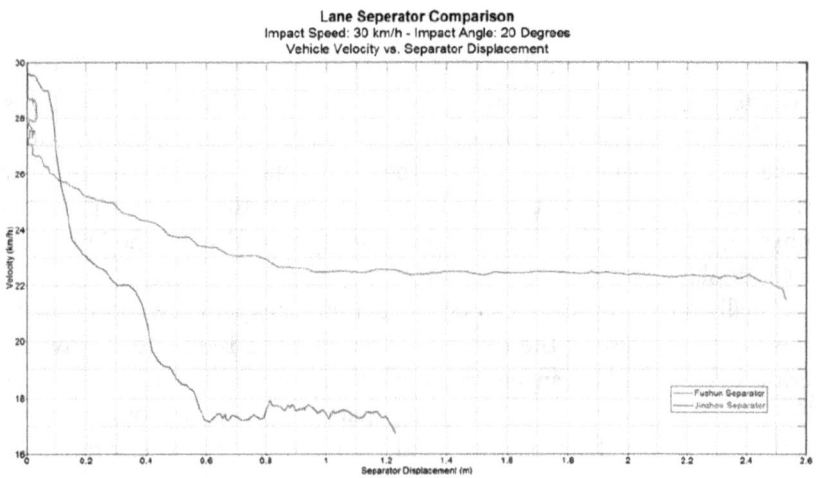

Source: World Bank, Liaoning Medium Cities Infrastructure Project.

Box 10.4

Jinzhou Picking Up on the Toilets and Benches Agenda

The Jinzhou municipal project office, after conducting an open dialogue between the public and the municipal government, reviewed the public comments and developed a responsive plan. As part of the plan, the Jinzhou municipal government has made concerted efforts to build more public toilets for people's convenience. In early 2006, the government developed a comprehensive approach to ensure that any toilet along the street, privately owned or not, must be accessible to all members of the public. Since June 2007, more than 230 toilets have changed from private to public access and many new flush and moveable toilets have been introduced. Additional public suggestions to provide street facilities, such as trash cans, benches, and trees, have also been met.

Source: Author.

Designing and Operating Safe Arterials

Data suggest that pedestrians and cyclists are disproportionately involved in traffic fatalities in China. This is unfortunately all too true within the urban context, where most fatalities occur on a few, relatively high-speed arterials.[2] To address this, cities can develop a "safe corridor" or "safe system" approach, which focuses on identifying and comprehensively treating exactly the sections of the network where the bulk of those deaths and injuries happen (Bliss and Breen 2009).

The first step of this approach is to map the location of all fatalities in the urban area using at least three years of data. Figure 10.8 is the fatality map for the urban area of Benxi in Liaoning for 2004–06. The map can be used to identify high concentrations of deaths and injuries on the network and design appropriate interventions. When used in the project cities in Liaoning and in Wuhan to identify high-risk corridors, the maps, in all cases, showed that a small portion of the urban network—just two or three corridors—was responsible for up to 40 to 50 percent of the total number of fatalities in the city. In Panjin, for example, three corridors with a total length of about 20 kilometers are responsible for 40 percent of the total number of fatalities.

The next step, building on this *Safe System* approach, is to design and implement complementary engineering, enforcement, and education

Figure 10.8   Fatality Map for Benxi (2004–06)

Legend:
- Fatalities at intersections in 2004
- Fatalities at intersections in 2005
- Fatalities at intersections in 2006
- Fatalities along corridors in 2004
- Fatalities along corridors in 2005
- Fatalities along corridors in 2006

Source: World Bank, Liaoning Medium Cities Infrastructure Project.

initiatives, along with efforts to strengthen the lead agency and include a monitoring and evaluation component. World Bank interventions also typically follow this model and include (i) an infrastructure investment program, (ii) an enforcement program, and (iii) a complementary education program for surrounding areas and schools.

The infrastructure investment program for these high-risk corridors is based on a set of countermeasures designed to achieve a realistic reduction in fatalities on the corridor. Other measures, such as the distance between safe pedestrian crossings, the number of channelized intersections, the number of kilometers of traffic separators, and the number of traffic signals, can be used as intermediate outcome measures. Box 10.5 summarizes the key features of a final "safe-corridor" plan under implementation in Benxi, Liaoning.

Network of safe crossings. The distance between safe crossings and the provision of a regular network of those crossings is particularly important for creating a safe traffic corridor. In addition to providing safe crossings at sensitive points such as schools, hospitals, and other important destinations, safe crossings should be available at reasonable and regular intervals.

Box 10.5

Benxi Safe Corridor Case Study

The city of Benxi has focused on the JieFang Road corridor as its pilot safe corridor. In 2004–08, 16 fatalities occurred on this 4.5-kilometer road corridor through the Benxi city center, representing 16 percent of the fatalities in the city.

The Benxi safe corridor plan is a comprehensive safety package that includes (i) providing safe crossings for pedestrians every 300 meters (accomplished by installing nine new traffic signals with pedestrian phases and rehabilitating eight existing ones), (ii) installing a median separator along 1 kilometer of the corridor, (iii) installing traffic signs and markings along the corridor, (iv) increasing the police capacity to provide patrols 24 hours per day, and (v) running an education campaign in neighboring schools. The plan has an estimated benefit of a 30 percent reduction in fatalities along the corridor. Figure B10.5.1 below shows the layout of the physical interventions on a portion of the corridor.

(continued next page)

Box 10.5 *(continued)*

Figure B10.5.1   Physical Interventions on the Jiefang Road Corridor in Benxi

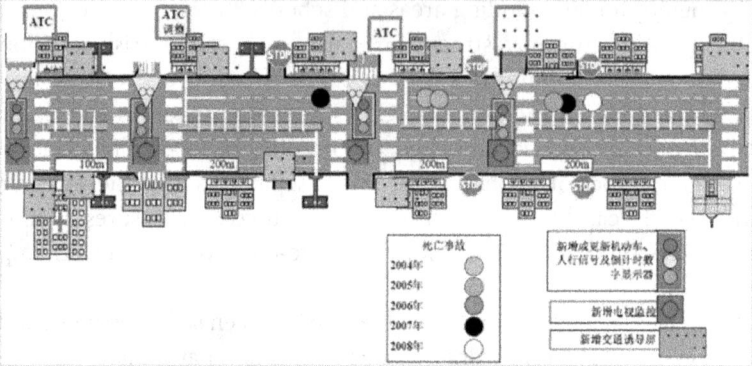

Source: World Bank, Liaoning Medium Cities Infrastructure Project.

This is a particular challenge in Chinese cities, which are built around long "superblocks" and in which it is not uncommon to go 750 meters or even a kilometer between legal, "safe" street crossings. Having about 200–300 meters between safe crossings is the international guideline. While Chinese standards actually suggest no more than 300 meters between safe crossings, this guideline is usually not observed. Finally, a concerted effort needs to be made to ensure the safety of these crossings. A current and particular aspect of Chinese road protocol is that automobiles rarely, if ever, give way to pedestrians at designated but unsignalized pedestrian crossings (zebra crossings). To create safer crossings, a variety of design elements can be used, such as mid-block signalized pedestrian-activated crossings, speed breakers (speed bumps) and other traffic calming devices, and traffic enforcement cameras (see box 10.6).

Limiting cars on sidewalks and cycle lanes. Vendors and parked automobiles often occupy bicycle and pedestrian lanes (see figure 10.9). This inconveniences bicycle users and pedestrians, which may discourage them from future walking or biking and may also force them to use the automobile lanes, which is very unsafe. For people with impaired mobility, this situation can make their life extremely difficult and unsafe. Addressing the issue of parked vehicles remains an important but difficult element of any urban transport program. World Bank projects have

Box 10.6

World Bank–Financed Pedestrian Infrastructures in Guangzhou, 2003

Figure B10.6.1   Intersection Channelization

In Tianhe New District, junction channelization has been implemented along Tianhe Bei Lu, including this good example at the intersection of Tianhe Bei Lu/Tianhe Dong Lu. The pedestrian phase runs parallel with the vehicle phase with no conflicting turns. Junction channelization islands provide protection and storage for pedestrians and bicycles, and an opportunity exists to introduce some greening.

Figure B10.6.2   Staggered Pedestrian Crossing

The concept of crossing the road in two stages with a protected pedestrian storage island in the center of the carriageway has been implemented at several locations in Guangzhou, including at this crossing of Shui Yin Lu. The pedestrian stages do not conflict with motorized vehicle traffic. For a slightly safer design, the stagger can be set the other way—whereby pedestrians face the oncoming traffic rather than look away from it as in this example—but it often means a reduction in junction capacity as the vehicle stop line has to be set farther back.

Source: Author.

Figure 10.9   Cars Parked on the Bicycle Lane

Source: World Bank.

supported many technical assistance studies of parking management systems and also focused on developing ways to create incentives for more aggressive parking enforcement and establishing a parking industry with private ownership of parking lots that would have an interest in such enforcement. In addition, bollards (see figure 10.10) can also be used at key spots, such as bus stops, to limit encroachment by cars.

Intersection design. The most stressful element of a pedestrian or cycling trip in Chinese cities is safely crossing intersections. There are often no signal phases where pedestrians and cyclists are able to cross without conflict from turning traffic. Intersections are very large and signal timings are often too short for most people to cross within a signal cycle. In addition, there are no refuges for pedestrians and cyclists and no clear paths or channels to restrict and guide automobile traffic through the intersection. Using a combination of signs, markings, traffic canaliza-

Figure 10.10   Bollards

Source: World Bank.

tion, and pedestrian refuges, however, it is possible to provide safety and comfort for pedestrians and cyclists without compromising the efficiency of the overall traffic. Because of a strong tradition of intersection design that has favored large, wide, and open intersection spaces, change is not always easy, but Guangzhou, Wuhan (see box 10.7), and other cities in Liaoning have illustrated it can be done.

Computerized traffic control systems. Computerized traffic control systems that facilitate automated and centralized control of traffic and traffic signal operations are another key element of support for pedestrian movements. Area traffic control, for example, has been used in World Bank projects to enable multiphasing of traffic signals at pedestrian crossings in Shanghai and Guangzhou or provide mid-block signalized crossings and physical junction channelization in Wuhan and in the cities of Liaoning. Area traffic control can also be used to provide traffic calming measures, such as those currently being implemented in Xian.

Box 10.7

Wuhan Implements Model Intersection Channelization

When exploring options to improve vehicle efficiency in Wuhan, Wuhan agencies were initially not in favor of designs that seemed to take road space away from motor vehicles. The city needed to be convinced that physical channelization could improve vehicle efficiency, which was in the end vividly illustrated at the junction of Jiefang Avenue and Jiefang Gongyuan Lu. The intersection was later even declared a "Model Intersection" by the mayor.

Figure B10.7.1   Model Intersection Channelization

a. Before situation: a junction similar to Jiefang Avenue/Jiefang Gongyuan Lu

b. After situation: model junction at Jiefang Avenue/Jiefang Gongyuan Lu

Before, the junction was inefficient and unsafe. There were no clear paths for vehicles to travel through the junction, and turning traffic chose their own paths under the flyover piers. Traffic signal stop lines were set far back, resulting in long clearance times for the cars. Pedestrians crossing the wide street had no safe refuge in the center and had to negotiate disorderly turning traffic. In each traffic cycle, the pedestrian phase was not long enough to cross all the way, so pedestrians became stranded in the middle of traffic.

The new design proposed by the Wuhan Traffic Police (WPSB) initially met with some resistance from local police brigades. To overcome this, the WPSB commissioned the China Management Science Research Institute to model the proposed design using a microsimulation program. This showed that the design would not only improve pedestrian safety but would also increase capacity.

The key features of the new design are as follows:

(continued next page)

Box 10.7 *(continued)*

- Physical channelization (and planting) under the flyover to provide a safe refuge for pedestrians to cross the road in two stages. The vast uncontrolled area under the flyover has been filled in to cater to pedestrians with no loss of capacity for vehicles.
- Physical islands to channel turning traffic into short, direct paths to clear the junction quickly.
- Stop lines brought forward to minimize clearance times.
- Multiphase traffic signals with special pedestrian signals (which run in parallel with vehicle signals with no conflict) to enhance efficiency for vehicles and safety for pedestrians.

Source: World Bank, Wuhan Urban Transport Project.

Challenges Going Forward

Bicycle users and pedestrians are key beneficiaries of the low-carbon mobility agenda in urban China. In the context of a bicycle and pedestrian environment that is generally deteriorating, several Chinese cities have already started to design and implement solutions that contribute to a safe and pleasant infrastructure for pedestrians and bicycle users. This chapter also has described several examples of World Bank investments and analytical work in China to support both modes of transportation.

In themselves, these various city actions are small compared to the magnitude of the Chinese cities' urban transport challenges. However, they do provide a portfolio of actions and an agenda for Chinese urban decision makers to recognize the critical role cycling and walking can play in any low-carbon growth path. In fact, there is a perfect alignment between the needs from a low-carbon perspective and the broader demands of finding sustainable solutions to the urban transport conflicts that Chinese cities are facing. To move forward, first, cities need to curtail the decline of bicycling and pedestrian trips. Second, cities have to find ways to encourage people who have stopped using these modes of transport to consider them again. International experience suggests that there is potential for significant gains in addressing congestion if people who have choices can be persuaded to use bicycles and walking as modes of transport, especially for short trips.

Box 10.8 provides examples of some initiatives within China taken by various government agencies to promote cycling. These are welcome indications of a changing mind-set and cultural attitude toward cycling. However, more can certainly be done, to go from what is now at best an attitude of tolerance toward a mode of transport for the poor, to recognizing, supporting, and promoting cycling as a valid mode of choice for everyone. To achieve this, the focus should be on the following:

- *Development:* Designing proper networks and road hierarchies to encourage and support walking and cycling
- *Execution:* Improving facilities for pedestrians and cyclists
- *Education:* Cultivating a culture of respect for pedestrians and cyclists, particularly at intersections and crossings.

Box 10.8

A Changing Attitude toward Cycling

Attitudes toward walking and bicycling are changing, and increasingly cities and higher levels of government are again recognizing the important role of those activities in urban life:

- At the national level, a car-free day was held in 2009 with the theme: "Walking and cycling: Healthy and environment-friendly ways of travel."
- In March 2010, the Beijing Development and Reform Committee released the Green Beijing Plan (2010–12) and promised to include bicycles in the municipal transport planning. Actions would include adding more demonstration areas for pedestrians and bicycling, adding more bicycle parking places, and providing a better connection between cycling and public transit, as well as more bicycle rental places. The projected proportion of bicycle travel in 2015 in Beijing is 23 percent, compared to less than 20 percent today.
- On May 1, 2008, Hangzhou initiated the first public bicycle rental system in China. More than 2,000 public bicycle stations and 50,000 public bicycles are currently for rent.

Source: Author.

Conclusion

This chapter presented a strategy and examples from World Bank programs to promote bicycling and walking and include cyclists and pedestrians in the mobility infrastructure of Chinese cities. It is obvious that the current situation is less than ideal, as cycling and walking in the modern Chinese city are often unsafe, or at best unpleasant. While cultural perceptions, noninclusive policies, and a lack of attention have contributed to the current situation, several simple measures can alleviate some of the problems. Four complementary approaches—addressing network issues, improving the quality of the "last mile," providing basic facilities, and improving the safety of critical arterials—can do much to improve the overall environment for cyclists and pedestrians. Several challenges still lie ahead, with the main one related to changing mind-sets and perceptions about the importance of supporting walking and cycling. The low-carbon mobility agenda will help focus on these issues and strengthen future programs.

Notes

1. A small three-wheeled vehicle, with pedals, either electric or motorized, with a double passenger seat behind the driver.
2. According to the *Traffic Accident Annual Report, People's Republic of China, 2007*, pedestrians accounted for 26 percent of traffic accident–related fatalities in 2007. In contrast, pedestrians accounted for about 20 percent of fatalities from traffic accidents in the European Union and 11 percent of traffic accident fatalities in the United States in that year. The absolute number of traffic-related deaths reported in China was also considerably higher, particularly when controlled for the amount of motorized traffic on the roads.

Bibliography

Bliss, T., and J. Breen. 2009. "Implementing the Recommendations of the World Report on Road Traffic Injury Prevention: Country Guidelines for the Conduct of Road Safety Management Capacity Reviews and the Specification of Lead Agency Reforms, Investment Strategies and Safe System Projects." World Bank Global Road Safety Facility, Washington, DC.

Chen, W., and S. Mehndiratta. 2007. "Planning for the Laobaixing: Public Participation in Urban Transport Project, Liaoning, China." Proceedings of the Transport Research Board Annual Meeting 2007. World Bank and PRTM Management Consultants.

Chen, Y., and S. Mehndiratta. 2007. "Bicycle User Survey in Fushun, Liaoning Province, China." Proceedings of the Transport Research Board Annual Meeting 2007. World Bank and PRTM Management Consultants.

Darido, G., M. Torres-Montoya, and S. Mehndiratta. 2009. "Urban Transport and CO_2 Emissions: Some Evidence from Chinese Cities." World Bank working paper. World Bank, Washington, DC.

Frame, G. 2004. "Thematic Review of Traffic Management in World Bank Projects in China." Unpublished working paper. September 2004. World Bank, Washington, DC.

Jiang, Yang, P., C. Zegras, and S. Mehndiratta. 2012. "Walk the Line: Station Context, Corridor Type and Bus Rapid Transit Walk Access in Jinan, China." *Journal of Transport Geography* 20(1): 1–14.

Tao, W., S. Mehndiratta, and E. Deakin. 2010. "Compulsory Convenience? How Large Arterials and Land Use Affects Pedestrian Safety in Fushun, China." *Journal of Transport and Land Use* 3(3). https://www.jtlu.org.

Torres-Montoya, M., L. Yanan, E. Dubin, and S. Mehndiratta. 2010. "Measuring Pedestrian Accessibility: Comparing Central Business and Commercial Districts in Beijing, London, and New York City." World Bank working paper. World Bank, Washington, DC.

Urbis. 2011. www.urbis.com.hk.

CHAPTER 11

Improving Public Transport in Chinese Cities: Elements of an Action Plan

Shomik Mehndiratta and Andrew Salzberg

Overview

Urban public transport can provide more energy efficient transportation than the average automobile and, because of this, urban public transport will be a key component of any low-carbon city. Realizing the benefits of urban public transport at a manageable cost, however, requires careful analysis and planning, along with communication among several government authorities, and appropriate transport policies and regulations.

This chapter summarizes the key elements of an action plan that a city could put in place to improve the quality of their urban public transport in a manner that would also lower the total carbon footprint of their transport system. The chapter address issues related to municipal institutional arrangements, including the nature and structure of the relationship between a city and its public transport operators, and provides suggestions for planning and strategic studies, as well as elements of an investment agenda. As bus systems are and will remain the backbone of public transport in Chinese cities, this chapter specifically discusses how to modernize and upgrade a traditional bus system and maximize the benefits of mass transit investments in bus rapid transit (BRT) and urban rail.

Urban Transport and Low-Carbon Growth

Public transport can be a cost-effective and efficient alternative to individual private modes for accessing urban opportunities. In addition, public transport provides a variety of benefits that private automobile transportation cannot: the efficient use of urban space, fewer traffic fatalities, and a reduction in the harmful effects of urban air pollution. This is no less true today than it was in decades past.

What has changed in recent years is that the climate change imperative has further strengthened the attractiveness of public transportation. As is shown in figure 11.1, at reasonable levels of vehicle loading, a bus or metro system can provide far more energy- and carbon-efficient transportation than the average car, per passenger kilometer.

This is the basic argument that supports public transport as an element of a low-carbon city platform—a public transport system can move more people more efficiently and with fewer negative externalities than a pri-

Figure 11.1   Life-Cycle Emissions by Passenger Kilometer

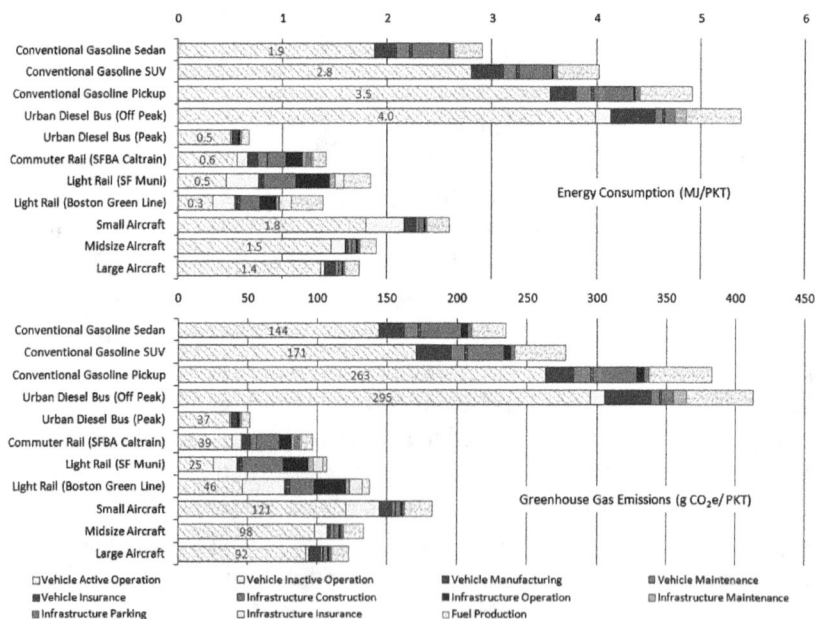

Source: Chester and Horvath 2009.
Notes: MJ = megajoules; PKT = passenger kilometers traveled; g CO_2e = grams of CO_2 equivalent.
Individual bars show energy consumption and GHG emissions per passenger kilometer for (from left to right) vehicle operation components (with number), vehicle components, infrastructure components, and the fuel production component.

vate transport system can. However, individual citizens with the freedom to choose their own mode of transport will usually not seek to maximize global environmental benefits. Rather, they will choose a mode that maximizes comfort, reliability, speed, convenience, and cost. On most of these dimensions, cars are an optimum choice for many commuters; and for reasons of status and function it is common that as incomes rise, those with financial means switch to cars. Chinese cities are currently following this pattern, and rapid economic development has led to a boom in car ownership.

The only public transport alternative for most people is a bus service steadily degraded by ever-increasing traffic congestion. Not surprisingly, for those with a choice, public transport is rarely competitive, and an overwhelming majority of public transport users in Chinese cities today are "captive" users with few alternatives. However, as economic development continues, today's captive riders will have choices tomorrow—and only a high-quality system will be able to keep them from choosing individual transportation alternatives. Ultimately, the goal is to provide public transport of quality that not only satisfies the needs of today's captive users, but also attracts customers away from cars and taxis. Such a public transport system that has the capability to attract customers from private automobiles is often a necessary political prerequisite for cities to consider restrictions on auto use.

All urban strategies for low-carbon growth will require a large share of passenger traffic to be carried by an upgraded public transport system, even as increasing income levels make auto use a viable choice for increasing numbers of people. Naturally, the definition of "upgraded public transport" will vary based on the context; a commuter in Shanghai has different expectations (and the city has different resources) than a commuter in a small city. For this reason, the appropriate program for public transport improvement will vary over time for any given place and will depend on the context. The general framework presented in this chapter, however, can be used by any city to assess and improve its public transport services.

The national government and urban public transport. In the first two decades after 1977, China's national government was not much involved in the urban transport sector, considering it a local issue best left to local municipalities. At the highest levels, these policies have begun to change. In October 2005, a State Council decision declared that urban public transport development should be a national priority.[1] Subsequently, particularly after the responsibility for urban public transport was given to the newly formed Ministry of Transport in 2007, the national government

Box 11.1

World Bank Support for the Ministry of Transport

The World Bank supports the Ministry of Transport through workshops and informal technical inputs on different models of national government participation in the public transport sector. Examples are a December 2008 workshop to provide access to experiences from the United States, France, and the Republic of Korea, and a June 2010 workshop about experiences from the United States and India. In addition, through a grant financed by the GEF, the World Bank is both supporting a strategy for national government participation and developing capacity-building tools to support the development of new regulations, standards, and codes to help national agencies exert technical leadership in the sector.

Source: Authors.

has been actively looking to define its role in this sector (see also box 11.1). The current focus is to both (i) define a national policy toward public transport and (ii) review issues related to subsidies and institutions. These developments are timely and will work well to support urban transport and low-carbon developments.

Action Plan Step One: Establishing the Correct Institutions

Creating a Unified Governmental Framework to Plan, Manage, and Monitor Urban Transport

Fragmented governmental institutions are a fundamental hurdle for Chinese cities trying to make a quantum improvement in the quality of public transport they offer. Multiple municipal government agencies, usually working with minimal coordination, are involved in the delivery of urban transport investments and services. Bus operators are usually regulated by the transport bureau (sometimes also known as the communications bureau), following a 2007 national reform. This bureau also regulates regional, interurban bus services and manages all municipal roads outside the city center. The construction, and in some cases also the management, of bus stops, terminals, and other infrastructure, however, is done by the urban-rural construction and housing bureau. Other involved agencies are the land and planning bureaus, responsible for assessing transport operator applications to use land (both for public infrastructure like bus stops and essential operator-managed infrastructure such as depots). The planning bureaus are also responsible for developing the urban and transport master plans. Moreover, the Development and Reform Commission (DRC) has a strong role in developing plans that involve significant investments—such as for urban rail. Whereas the traffic police (either as an independent agency or as a branch of the police) own and operate the traffic signals and are responsible for on-street traffic management, including bus priority and on-street parking enforcement, parking policies and public transport fare policies are within the realm of the DRC. Finally, enforcement of illegal parking on sidewalks—an unfortunately common phenomenon—is again the responsibility of an entirely different agency. This fragmentation continues at an operational level, leading to poor coordination between rail operators (usually large, national-level, state-owned enterprises reporting directly to the city mayor) and bus operators (small, private, or city-level state-owned enterprises reporting to a small division of the transport bureau). Indeed, it is even difficult sometimes for cities to coordinate planning and investment implementation for bus and rail systems along just one corridor.

This fragmentation of responsibilities takes a heavy toll on the quality of the public transport Chinese cities are able to offer. At an administrative level, it is difficult for city leadership to place clear accountability for public transport development with any one municipal agency, and at the operational level it is difficult for bus companies to operate with adequate infrastructure support. For large cities with rail systems, this multiplicity of agencies inhibits the development of seamless physical transfers across modes, or the development of seamless operations and fare strategies. International experience suggests that significant benefits accrue when cities or metropolitan regions develop unified transport authorities that are able to plan, finance, manage, and operate a municipality's transport system across modes. Hong Kong SAR, China and Singapore offer good practice examples in the region. Vancouver and London provide other good examples internally.[2] While fundamental reform and the realization of unified municipal or metropolitan transport authorities will likely require a national-level initiative, cities can improve the level of coordination across agencies involved with urban transport, for example, by placing those agencies under the responsibility of one vice mayor. This consolidation could be complemented by a standing group or standing committee with members of all relevant agencies, headed by a city leader, that meets regularly to coordinate activities.

Developing Institutional Management and Subsidies

Institutional management. Modern public transport management institutions and strategies for public transport subsidies are essential to a well-run, effective bus transport system. Both Chinese and international experiences suggest that the manner in which bus services are structured—the combination of supply arrangements, incentives for performance, fares, and arrangements to cover deficits—is critical. High-quality bus services have been provided by cities through a variety of structures. However, safe, high-quality, efficient bus services are usually found in cities where public authorities remain ultimately responsible, such as London, but where services are provided by several independent, well-capitalized bus operating companies. These companies compete for the right to operate given routes or bundles of routes for periods of five to eight years. Such a system requires strong oversight by a capable public transport authority that plays an active role in monitoring service quality and in keeping operators incentivized by retaining the right to terminate or penalize them for poor performance (see also box 11.2).[3]

Box 11.2

World Bank Support of Institutional Management of Bus Services

As the experience with institutional management of bus services has evolved in China, the World Bank has continuously provided advice and support on the topic to the Chinese authorities. In early Bank lending projects—most notably in Shanghai, Guangzhou, and Shenyang (the Liaoning Urban Transport Project)—the institutional arrangements for bus services were a key element of the World Bank's dialogue with the city, as these cities became among the first in China to introduce private capital in bus operations and use competitive tendering mechanisms to select suppliers.

More recently, while dialogue in the form of technical assistance, training programs, workshops, and seminars at the city level remains an important element of World Bank projects, the Bank has also focused on providing policy support to the national ministry responsible for public transport. Starting in the mid-2000s, the national government became directly involved in the sector. As the Ministry of

(continued next page)

Box 11.2 *(continued)*

Transport (in charge of public transport since 2007) continues to develop its own view on the national government's role in regulating and financing urban bus services, the World Bank has been providing on-request policy notes and presentations on relevant international experiences, including institutional and subsidy arrangements for bus services and the role of national governments in regulating and financing urban bus services.

Source: Authors.

In China, service is most often provided by state-owned enterprises (SOEs) that use regulated fares (the global norm for urban public transport). Bus services have evolved considerably since China's early economic transformation in the early 1980s. Initial reforms focused on creating operating companies, enterprises distinct from government. Further reforms in the 1990s focused on limiting or ending public subsidies. In many cases, these reforms resulted in a strong focus on operational efficiency and ensured relatively low staffing levels, often with little or no subsidy. However, in recent years the national mandate to "prioritize public transport" has been interpreted by some, most notably Beijing (see box 11.3), as a reason to incur large annual operating subsidies.

At the time of these earlier reforms, urban bus service was seen primarily as a local issue with little input from the national government. As a result, there were a diverse range of experiments in the use of the private sector. In a few cities, such as Guangzhou, Shenyang, and Changsha, operators independent of the municipal governments (either private operators or an SOE from another region of China) successfully obtained competitively awarded franchises to operate bus services. Other cities experimented with private owner-operators. In two notable cases, Shanghai and Chongqing, this led to fragmented on-street competition, which has since been replaced by gradual, city-encouraged consolidation (in Shanghai) or a return to public sector monopolies (in Chongqing). Generally, the most common route for the introduction of private capital in the industry has been the development of joint ventures, where the local SOE still has a majority stake and management control.

Subsidies. In many cities where public transport is regarded as a priority, economic performance is often considered secondary to improving

Box 11.3

Subsidies for Public Transport: The Differing Experiences of Beijing and Kunming

In Beijing, the operating subsidy for public transit in 2009 was over RMB 10 billion a year. Bus users pay RMB 0.4 with a transit card and rail users pay RMB 2.0, which generates revenue far below operating cost. The Beijing government subsidizes the operator, a government-owned bus SOE, for all costs above operating revenue, and it is not clear what incentives the operator has for increasing its operational efficiency. Although incomes in Beijing are among the country's highest, fares on its bus system are noticeably lower than many cities of more limited means.

Kunming, located in southwest China and with significantly lower average income than Beijing, has pursued a policy of limiting overall operational subsidies to covering specific costs such as reduced fares for elderly riders and income foregone from providing passengers with free transfers between buses. Overall, the bus system has a relatively high fare of RMB 1.00, a farebox operating cost recovery ratio of 90 percent, and overall high levels of ridership. The differing experiences of these two cities demonstrate different ways Chinese cities have used subsidies to support the development of public transport.

Source: Authors.

service and ridership, and there is limited interest in market-based institutional reform that could assure cost effectiveness. If international experience is any indicator, the appetite for reform of public transport management will change over time, particularly once ridership stabilizes and SOEs start becoming a significant burden on public expenditure. Even so, different cities have taken a variety of approaches to subsidize public transport—in some to lower fares and in others to support particular vulnerable groups and to enhance service (see box 11.3).

Action Plan Step Two: Strategy, Planning, and Operations

Developing Standards, Setting Targets, and Measuring Progress
China already has standards and national targets related to public transport, for example, specifying what percentage of trips in cities of a certain size should be done by public transportation (see table 11.1). While these high-level standards provide targets for cities that do not currently meet

Table 11.1   Chinese National Targets and Standards Related to Public Transport

Ministry of Transport targets for the end of the 12th Five-Year Plan
(Development Plan of Urban Public Transport during the 12th Five-Year Plan)

Urban population	Public transport mode share target	Average speed target	Bus ownership target (per 10,000 persons)
> 3 million	35%	15 km/h	15
1–3 million	25%	20 km/h	12
< 1 million	15%	25 km/h	10

Ministry of Construction standards: *Transport Planning and Design Standard in Urban Roads* issued in September 1995 ("Chapter 3: Urban Public Transport").

Coverage:
- No less than 50 percent of urban land area should have a functioning bus stop within a radius of 300 meters.
- No less than 90 percent of urban land area should have a functioning bus stop within a radius of 500 meters.

Density of network: 3–4 kilometers per square kilometer in the central city; 2–2.5 kilometers per square kilometer in the outskirts of the city.

Sources: Ministry of Urban Rural Construction and Housing (this Ministry was called Ministry of Construction at the time the standards were issued); Ministry of Transport.

them, standard and target setting can be improved. Specific recommendations are the following:

- *Develop and implement standards and targets that help improve services and make public transport attractive for car drivers:* This is the first strategic need, as any effort to make a city low-carbon requires that public transport attracts and displaces auto trips, more so than cycling or walking trips. It is inevitable that as cities grow spatially, many trips that used to be made by walking or cycling will transfer to public transport. The strategic goal of a city should be to increase the quality and comfort of trips in a way that public transport is able to attract trips that would otherwise be made in taxis and private automobiles.
- *Develop standards and targets that complement, not substitute, detailed planning:* The targets set forth in table 11.1 are good aggregate guides. However, they need to be seen as just that, high-level guides that need to be refined and complemented by detailed planning studies. Ultimately, the number of buses needed in a city to provide high-quality services would depend, for instance, on the spatial dispersal of the population and the demand for trips (both spatially and over the course of a day), among other factors. Similarly, quality coverage requires not

only access to a bus stop within 300 or 500 meters, but high-quality services at that stop that allow trip makers to reach their destinations of interest. Ultimately, detailed planning studies (as described in the next section) are needed to understand the nature of demand and to design a system of routes, schedules, and services that best serve that demand. These studies and plans should finally determine the location of bus stops, the number of buses, and related structures of a public transport service in a city.

- *Consider the value of creating a regular system of customer feedback:* Regular monitoring to help cities gauge if current strategies are working will be critical. International experience suggests that regular customer surveys (in the form of short on-board surveys complemented possibly with online surveys) can provide city leaders and public transport agencies with valuable feedback on performance. Such feedback can help assess trends in performance, identify any issues that trip makers are particularly sensitive to, and also provide agencies with important information on the character of their customer base. From a low-carbon perspective, cities may find it particularly valuable to identify trip makers who may have had the choice of using a car for their trip, and pay particular attention to the feedback and satisfaction levels of that segment of trip makers.

Planning—for Investments, Routes, and Coverage

While planning studies of different kinds are important for any public transport system, they are perhaps more important in Chinese cities than elsewhere, mainly due to the speed with which Chinese cities are currently undergoing change. Cities are growing spatially, and therefore population size and characteristics are changing quickly. Locations and characteristics of residential, employment, and other trip-related opportunities are also evolving rapidly. Trips are getting longer and trip demands are becoming more complex. This is a difficult environment for public transport, and to remain competitive, cities need to constantly ensure that the mix of routes, schedules, and services being offered remains relevant to the city as it is evolving. Ensuring that a system of planning tools keeps the city's transport system competitive is a key priority for any city leadership looking to improve its public transport system.

Four kinds of studies in particular are critically needed in many Chinese cities. These are as follows:

- *A current medium-term (five-year) public transport plan and strategy:* The basis of any public transport network is an understanding of travel patterns of likely customers, and the design of a system responsive to those patterns. Cities could, for example, prepare five-year rolling plans for route development. These plans, which should ideally be updated annually, include a systematic analysis of expected population and employment levels for the next five years, a study of evolving travel patterns (such as through origin-destination surveys), expected changes in car ownership and usage, a review of current levels of service on all existing bus routes, the need for new routes and adjustments to existing routes, future bus fleet requirements, future terminal and depot requirements, and expected financial performance. Such planning helps to ensure that the service level on existing routes is adequate; that plans are in place to serve new or growing areas; and that new transport facilities, such as new roads or rail lines, are taken into account. In addition, this work contributes to sound public asset investment plans that help system planners make the case for their intended use of land and resources from the city to develop depots, terminals, and other infrastructure.
- *Route adjustment and service planning:* A service planning exercise builds on the tools and data that are also required for longer-term planning, but focuses on a more detailed, almost operational analysis of the route structure. It also includes an analysis of how routes function as a network. Outputs may include suggestions on route consolidation and adjustments to route stop patterns. Such a service planning study can often illustrate the value of new special-purpose routes, such as express bus routes (with only limited stops) or commuter routes (operating only at peak times). Providing cities with the tools to make more rational decisions on bus service planning can help them make better use of scarce resources, making public transport more attractive even without major new investment. A focus on service planning is likely to improve the quality of services of most Chinese bus networks.
- *A delay analysis of current bus routes to develop a near-term program of improvements:* Door-to-door travel times remain critical to providing competitive public transport service. Delay analyses can help public transport systems systematically assess the location and nature of delays faced by their customers and allow for the development of strategies to address these delays appropriately. For instance, if delays are

being incurred in traffic, a bus-only lane may offer relief. However, if most delays are related to waiting at traffic signals, then reducing delays would require a modified traffic management plan—perhaps limiting turns at certain critical intersections. If delays are being incurred by bunching of buses at stations, then service planning approaches such as different skip-stop patterns for buses may be appropriate. Different bus stop platform designs and off-board fare collection may also contribute to solutions. A delay analysis often supplies decision makers with a systematic understanding of the nature of the issues they need to address to improve service. Such studies can be conducted citywide to identify systemwide problems, or—depending on the complexity of the system—just along key corridors. Experience shows that all kinds of cities, ranging from megacities like Beijing to relatively smaller cities like Shijiazhuang, have benefited significantly from carrying out delay analyses.

- *Mass transit plans—medium-term plans to identify and support mass transit corridors:* Ideally, cities would identify key corridors appropriate for future mass-transit investments some time ahead of when such investments are actually required. The outputs of such work could then be used as a basis for discussion with land planning agencies (to reinforce development of such a corridor, particularly focusing on nodes where future stations are envisioned) as well as investment planning agencies (to develop an appropriate financial plan in light of the possible investments) (see also box 11.4).

Action Plan Step Three: Upgrading Traditional Bus Services

Similar to the situation in other countries, traditional bus systems remain the most commonly used public transit service in China. For most commuters, the bus remains essential and is often the only mode of public transport they have access to. Despite their importance, buses are in many ways the most vulnerable element of a Chinese city's transport system. First, unless systematic efforts are made to enhance quality and preserve speeds, the competitiveness of bus systems can rapidly deteriorate as a result of increasing traffic congestion; second, many urban bus companies lack the resources to allow their services to effectively compete with cars; and third, current institutional arrangements often do not provide operators with clear incentives to deliver efficiency and performance. As a result, rapidly developing cities can quickly find themselves caught in a negative feedback cycle in which an uncompetitive bus service leads to

Box 11.4

Support for Public Transport in Beijing: An Evolving Nonlending Partnership

With a rapidly growing urban population currently numbering 13 million, a total of 4 million cars, and 2,000 new cars registered each day, Beijing epitomizes the challenges facing the adoption of low-carbon growth paths for major Chinese cities. This has not gone unrecognized; after an initial focus on primary roads, Beijing has spent considerable sums of money on building a world-class public transport infrastructure. Billions of U.S. dollars are spent each year to construct a metro system that by 2015 will include over 550 kilometers of rail (225 kilometers have already been opened) and four BRT lines.

One of the many challenges facing Beijing is to derive maximum value from these investments. For the last two years, an unusual collaboration between Beijing's Transport Bureau and the World Bank has focused on the technical underpinnings needed to address this challenge. Initiated at the request of Beijing, this donor-funded collaboration (financiers include ESMAP, AusAID, ASTAE, and the Korean TF) has focused on three key issues:

- Providing Beijing with peer city perspectives and contact with cities such as Paris, New York, and Seoul
- Detailed discussions with subject experts on technical concerns related to data and forecasting
- Technical assistance studies on selected high-priority issues, including a service-planning-oriented assessment of how to improve the performance of existing BRT lines, suggestions for developing a system of rapid commuting bus corridors, and strategies to integrate bus and rail service in corridors with newly opened rail lines.

The technical assistance studies have formed the core of this relationship. Using a hands-on approach, both partners have worked together on implementing priority corridors and developing practical tools and techniques that can be used beyond the demonstration corridors. In September 2010, Beijing Public Transport announced a 10-point priority program for 2011 that included several initiatives resulting from this partnership.

Source: Authors.
Note: ESMAP = the World Bank's Energy Sector Management Assistance Program; AusAID = Australian Government Overseas Aid Program; ASTAE = the World Bank's Asia Sustainable and Alternative Energy Program; Korean TF = Technology Foresight Center at the Korea Institute of Science and Technology Evaluation and Planning.

more commuters adopting private cars as soon as they can, further exacerbating road congestion and undermining the economics of bus transport.

Because of the importance and vulnerability of bus systems, a key focus of any city's effort in the public transport sector in China should be to modernize and improve their bus services. Efforts in this area can be categorized into three broad areas: (i) institutional management and subsidies (discussed previously), (ii) investments in bus infrastructure and planning, and (iii) improved services through bus priority schemes and integrated bus corridors, which will be discussed in more detail in the following sections.

Investing in Bus Infrastructure and Planning

In many cities, initial investments could be targeted at elements of public transport infrastructure that are crucial to day-to-day operations, but are often neglected because of their low profile. Examples of this are bus depots, passenger interchange terminals, and intelligent transportation systems.

Bus depots. Bus depots, areas where buses can be parked overnight, maintained, washed, stored, and efficiently dispatched, are essential for high-quality bus services. While bus riders do not directly interact with bus depots, they are essential to maintaining vehicles and help reduce breakdowns in service that severely impact passengers. In addition, having sufficient space to wash buses each night and properly sweep out cabins helps maintain the fleet's image and influences overall passenger perception of the service.

Most transport-related World Bank projects in China have included the construction of modern bus depots, including in the cities of Guangzhou, Tianjin, Taiyuan, Wuhan, Fuzhou, along with several cities in Liaoning and Anhui provinces. In most places, depots had long been an underfunded and ignored part of the public transport infrastructure. The new depots are not only critical pieces of bus service infrastructure, but also demonstrate international best practice in efficient and sustainable design including water retention, efficient traffic management, safety features, and noise reduction. In many cases, acquiring the requisite land has been problematic and many depots have been cancelled due to unavailability of land. In the long term, changing the incentive structure for city leadership will be essential to allow land to be regularly released for bus depots.

Passenger interchange terminals. Most Chinese cities are inadequately equipped with passenger interchange terminals. Efficient bus operations require efficient route structures, and efficient route structures require terminals throughout the service area. Terminals provide space for bus layovers, turnarounds, easy transfers between multiple routes and other modes, and space for passengers to wait for the bus. In addition, well-situated interchanges facilitate trunk and feeder systems and can improve passenger comfort. Where space for a full terminal cannot be provided, chaotic, inefficient, unsafe, and unpredictable operations can result. Terminals and interchanges, some resulting from World Bank–funded projects, have been constructed in a number of cities including Wuhan, Urumqi, and Shijiazhuang (see box 11.5).

Box 11.5

Bus Interchange Terminal in Shijiazhuang

At the bus interchange terminal at the railway station in Shijiazhuang, a well-designed bus terminal opposite the rail station allows for efficient transfer between the two modes. The new terminal, funded by the World Bank in 2005–08, alleviated a bottleneck and made public transport an appealing choice for a greater number of potential riders.

Figure B11.5.1   Bus Interchange Terminal in Shijiazhuang

Source: World Bank.

Source: Authors.

Buses. Bus fleets in China's biggest cities—Beijing, Shanghai, and Guangzhou—now are generally world class. They are modern, climate controlled, and often equipped with TV and other entertainment. However, in many other cities, bus fleets are old, functional rather than comfortable, sometimes even severely polluting, and often smaller than required. While buses in China are typically purchased and procured by bus operators, it is not uncommon for cities to support bus purchases, by way of extending credit or helping operators gain access to financing on the same terms as the municipal government. Buses are a critical part of the public transport experience, and their design can and should be customized to serve particular markets. For example, door sizes and locations can be designed to serve particular markets—with bigger doors to facilitate faster boarding and alighting, especially when off-board fare collection is possible, or doors on the left to facilitate median bus stops on priority corridors. In a World Bank–funded project in Panjin, the city focused on enhancing the overall quality of its bus fleet by enhancing the passenger experience with automatic transmission (for smoother acceleration compared to the manual transmission of the existing fleet), leaf springs for a more comfortable ride, and Euro IV diesel emission standards (figure 11.2). The upgraded buses were then put to work on bus priority corridors to provide a comprehensive upgrade in service.

Figure 11.2   New Buses in Panjin Provide Improved Passenger Services

Source: World Bank.

Intelligent transportation systems. Even at a basic level, new technology can bring great improvements in public transport efficiency by computerizing staff records, wage calculations, vehicle inventory, bus scheduling, and staff rostering. Advanced fare media and fare collection systems offer opportunities for significantly lower transaction costs, deployment of sophisticated fare strategies, and the generation of valuable trip maker data. In more advanced applications, intelligent transport systems (ITS) can directly support the operation of public transport services, including real-time monitoring of public transport vehicles using automatic vehicle location (AVL) systems. The use of global positioning system (GPS) transponders on buses with a control center monitoring the buses' position enables real-time adjustments to even out headways, avoid bunching of buses, and provide more regular service. As traffic becomes more congested and causes large variations in travel time, the ability to monitor routes and make adjustments in real time can greatly improve reliability, which is highly valued by passengers. GPS facilities also allow for real-time passenger information at bus stops, which is also greatly appreciated by passengers.

The use of these new technologies, however, should be combined with an adequate amount of training for workers and skilled support in order to maximize its impact. Experience suggests that maximizing the benefits of technology investments is not just a matter of acquiring skills to use the new system, but also often is about making fundamental transformative changes in the manner in which the bus system is operated. Technology-equipped bus systems need a different mix of staffing and skills for planning (to make use of the extensive data available), operations (a much less labor-intensive system for bus dispatching), and financial management (modern fare systems are significantly more automated but offer new financial engineering possibilities). As with any other firm investing in transformative technologies, bus companies would benefit from pairing technology procurement with complementary investments in change management support that would help them realize the potential of such technologies with minimal disruption.[4]

Improving Services through Bus Priority Schemes and Integrated Bus Corridors

While the previously described investments in an improved bus system—developing institutions, management, and supporting infrastructure—are necessary to develop quality competitive bus systems, just by themselves they are not sufficient. Particularly if the goal is to attract riders of choice, buses need to offer travel times that are competitive when compared to private modes. The experiences in China and internationally suggest that providing such competitive service often requires that buses be provided on-street priority using a series of targeted actions and initiatives that address traffic-related delays.

While the need for on-street bus priority is generally recognized by Chinese planners, implementing effective priority schemes remains a challenge. First, providing on-street priority to buses is often politically difficult because it requires explicit prioritization of buses over the alternative mode (that is, automobiles) and often requires city leaders to take away road space from auto users. Second, the experience of Chinese cities in recent years suggests that providing effective on-street priority is also a technical challenge. Initial approaches that focused on the implementation of bus-only lanes segregated from other traffic, usually targeted at individual "problem" intersections or road segments, often did not succeed (see box 11.6).

Integrated bus corridors. In response to similar experiences, cities such as London and New York developed a more comprehensive approach to bus priority that is often known as integrated bus corridors. Integrated bus corridors go beyond the first generation of bus priority by including not

---

Box 11.6

Reserved Bus Lane in Shijiazhuang

In Shijiazhuang, in 2000, a reserved bus lane in the center of a major street went into operation as a pilot. Both city and provincial government leaders, however, expressed concern about the safety of bus passengers on the narrow center-street platforms, and after five years of operation, in 2008, the central bus lanes were replaced by curbside bus lanes. Because of a lack of enforcement, the curbside lanes quickly became ineffective. Another reserved bus corridor using curbside lanes was launched in Shijiazhuang in 2005. Shortly after implementation, however, the city concluded that there were not enough bus routes to warrant the aggravation of excluding other uses and decided not to activate the reserved bus lane. These early attempts at bus priority have provided valuable lessons that have been considered during the design of more recent projects.

(continued next page)

Box 11.6 *(continued)*

Figure B11.6.1   Congested Bus Lane in Shijiazhuang

Source: Authors.

only physically segregated bus lane infrastructure (preferably located in central lanes), but also integrated bus service improvements (such as limited-stop or rapid bus services), improvements in pedestrian access to the corridor, new and better designed bus stations with real-time passenger information, new and upgraded buses with a larger capacity, traffic management to improve the flow of buses through intersections, and a distinct brand identity. Taken together, the integrated bus corridor is a comprehensive program of complementary improvements, covering an entire corridor or subarea and focusing on the passenger experience, from their front door to their destination.

Currently, this integrated bus corridor concept is being adopted in the cities of Benxi, Panjin, Jinzhou, and Liaoyang in Liaoning Province. The Liaoning project recently opened its first integrated bus corridor to positive press reviews (see figure 11.3).

Integrated bus corridors can result in improved public transport speeds between 20 percent and 40 percent, increased ridership (15 percent), and

Figure 11.3   Bus Priority Lane in Liaoyang, Liaoning Province

Source: World Bank.

fewer traffic accidents. Achieving these numbers in practice, however, requires optimal bus service planning and enforcement of parking restrictions at bus stops and in bus lanes. Often too many bus routes exist and too many small buses are operating in the dedicated bus lanes, leading to congestion at busy stops and intersections. On-board fare collection also makes bus boarding slow and inefficient, and traffic engineering, even on bus priority corridors, is often not designed to benefit transit passengers. Current signal cycles are too long, which results in bus bunching (and hence longer wait times for passengers), and too many left turns are permitted at high-volume intersections. Addressing these issues comprehensively is not merely a technical issue; it requires a great deal of political will and coordination across city agencies.

Action Plan Step Four: Investing in Mass Transit: Bus Rapid Transit and Urban Rail

While bus systems will remain the sole form of public transport in the vast majority of Chinese cities, for the largest cities, offering high-quality public transport will require significant investments in *mass transit systems*. The term mass transit systems usually refers to relatively high-speed and high-capacity systems that carry at least 5,000 passengers per direction per hour at operational speeds at and over 20 kilometers an hour.

Options for mass transit systems range from (relatively) less expensive BRT systems that cost between US$2–5 million per kilometer, to various kinds of urban rail, with the most expensive underground metro rail systems costing upwards of US$100 million per kilometer. This section summarizes the Chinese experience, challenges, and benefits, with both BRT and urban rail. However, it is critical to emphasize that cities should not assume that any one particular system is appropriate for them without a careful analysis. Indeed, whether to upgrade a bus service or develop a BRT or metro system should be decided only after a rigorous, formal, *alternatives analysis* (see box 11.7).

Box 11.7

Using a Formal Alternatives Analysis to Identify Appropriate Mass Transit Solutions

Public transport investments tend to be expensive, difficult, and high profile. In Chinese cities, as elsewhere in the world, implementing successful mass transit requires political advocacy and support. However, unless this political support is built on a solid technical analysis, cities risk suboptimal outcomes on this expensive, long-lived infrastructure.

To address this risk, formal *alternatives analysis* has emerged as a planning framework for identifying public transport investment. Unlike the traditional "feasibility study"—which determines whether a preselected alternative is technically, financially, and economically feasible according to a given set of criteria—alternatives analysis begins from a broader base. The first step in the process is a rigorous analysis of existing conditions leading to an identification of the key problems to be solved. Following this step, a group of well-thought-out alternatives is developed and compared against one another according to a series of metrics.

The key element of alternatives analysis is that these different options are not "straw men" to be compared against a preselected favored alternative, but genuine efforts to develop cost-effective solutions. The alternatives should be carefully

(continued next page)

Box 11.7 *(continued)*

tailored to the service patterns to be served, and all options should be on the table, including metro, local bus, rapid (skip-stop) bus operation, and BRT. In this context, an option not often considered in China but common elsewhere is upgrading suburban rail services for urban commuter use. In China, institutional issues and capacity constraints related to the use of Ministry of Rail infrastructure around city centers remain formidable. However, international experience suggests that in many settings suburban "commuter rail" services managed by subnational authorities can be relative low-cost, high-quality elements of a metropolitan transport system.

For each of these alternatives, a realistic financial analysis of both the upfront capital and (crucially) long-term operating costs needs to be created, and proposed sources of funds for both long- and short-term costs need to be carefully developed. In general, more needs to be done in China to move from a "feasibility study framework" to such an "alternatives analysis" framework when large and long-lived public investments are made in mass transit.

Source: Authors.

Setting Up Bus Rapid Transit

In recent years, the BRT concept has gained increasing popularity as a low-cost option to provide high-capacity, high-quality public transport. Successfully implemented BRT systems typically use a package of improvements—such as new, high-quality buses, off-board fare collection, signal priority, passing lanes at stations, and quality branding and communications approaches—to transform traditional bus systems into true "metro-on-rubber-wheels" mass transit systems.[5] At its core, BRT is a rapid, convenient, easily understandable system of public transport that functions on its own right of way with high speed and reliability.

Successful BRT systems can compete with metro and light rail transit (LRT) systems and provide mass transit services at a generally much reduced cost. However, the challenges involved in implementing such a system are significant and require sustained political leadership and collaboration among various agencies and offices not always used to working together. These include the traffic police, bus companies (often more than one in a given municipal area), the planning bureau, the communications or transport bureau, and the transport research institutes that often carry out the service planning for the bus companies.

The World Bank's involvement with BRT systems in China has developed from simply promoting the concept to eventually providing technical support and, in some cases, financial support for the development of new BRT systems. Initially, the World Bank funded capacity-building seminars and pilot projects promoting the concept, which had an impact on the development of the BRT system in Guangzhou, among other places (see box 11.8). In 2008, the Urban Transport Partnership Program, funded by the Global Environment Facility (GEF) under GEF's climate change agenda, allowed the World Bank to work directly with several cities that had expressed interest in developing their public transport systems. As a result of a collaborative effort among several national ministries and the World Bank, cities from nine provinces (including Chongqing, a municipality with provincial status) developed grant proposals for transport planning and project preparation work. The selected cities included a number interested in developing bus priority schemes, as well as seven cities requesting support to plan BRT systems: Chongqing, Jinan (Shandong), Weihai (Shandong), Changzhi (Shanxi), Urumqi (Xinjiang), Zhengzhou (Henan), and Dongquan (Guangdong). In addition, Guangzhou requested GEF support to complement its BRT development with a study on demand management strategies. The World Bank is currently financing BRT systems in some of these cities. More important,

Box 11.8

Guangzhou: China's Highest-Volume BRT System

Guangzhou recently opened the highest-volume BRT system in China, carrying as many as 800,000 daily passengers. The inception of this system took place during the World Bank–financed Guangzhou Urban Transport Project. Under the project, the Bank financed a series of seminars and workshops that helped to raise the awareness and credibility of a BRT approach. The World Bank also financed a pivotal study tour to Latin America that built institutional support for the concept in city leadership. The World Bank–financed project was closed before works could commence; however, the studies and works related to the project (financed by Guangzhou with technical assistance from the Institute for Transportation and Development Policy [ITDP]) were managed and supported by the project management office created to manage the World Bank–financed project.

Source: Authors.

since the inception of the GEF program, the cities of Chongqing, Jinan, Guangzhou, and Zhengzhou have initiated BRT service—even before GEF planning funds were released. This success indicates that national and international organizations can provide a strong incentive for the adoption of sound urban transport solutions through the promotion and support of concepts, even when not directly funding their implementation.

Supporting Urban Rail

In the last decade, China's explosive urban growth has stimulated an unprecedented boom in urban rail construction. Figure 11.4 shows the operating and approved networks as of January, 1, 2010. At that time, 10 cities were operating metros on 870 kilometers of total track, and 23 cities had approved metro plans with a total track length of 5,148 kilometers. An informal tally suggests that the total of all approved plans in China is larger than all existing mileage of metro systems in Europe and North America together. Shanghai, by some measures, is now the largest system in the world, only 15 years after the opening of its first line.

Figure 11.4   Operating and Approved Metro Networks as of January 1, 2010

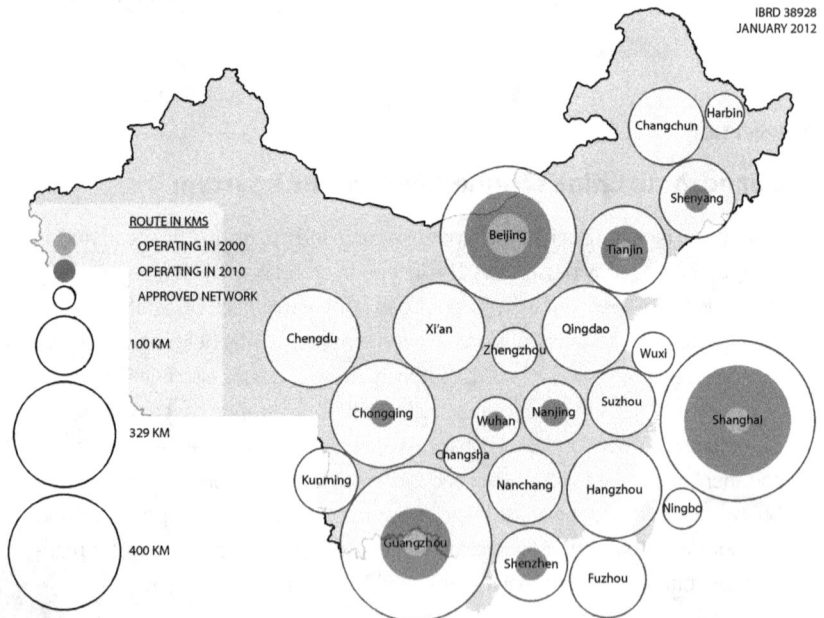

Source: World Bank.

When properly developed, urban rail is the fastest, highest-capacity form of public transport. Under the right circumstances, it can handle very high levels of passenger demand at high speeds with minimal disruption to other city traffic—thus providing a public transport alternative very competitive with the private car. In addition, urban rail has the potential to catalyze a pattern of urban growth that conserves energy, reduces carbon emission intensity, and forms the core of a public transport–oriented city. Implementing urban rail, however, can be difficult because of the exorbitant costs relative to other modes. In addition, to be successful, rail requires a supportive transport environment that restricts auto use in central cities and fosters public transport and non-motorized travel.

In 2008, a study identified areas where the World Bank could best add value to Chinese urban rail practice,[6] after which the Bank started supporting the Kunming Urban Rail Project. Experiences from this project may help inform urban rail developments in other cities. The Kunming project is currently in the early stages of implementation. The World Bank will finance the second of two lines to be opened in the initial phase of Kunming's metro development. The line stretches from east to west through the city's existing central business district, running primarily underground for 19.54 kilometers with 17 stations (see figure 11.5). It is scheduled to open in 2016.

The project experience so far has suggested three areas that Chinese cities interested in implementing rail systems may want to focus: (i) transit-oriented development, (ii) bus and rail integration, and (iii) comprehensive transport policy, including developing progressive parking and travel demand management policies.

Transit-oriented development. In Kunming, the Municipal Urban Planning Bureau is in charge of promulgating the city's urban development vision and managing the mechanisms to implement it. The Bureau is planning for significant growth in central Kunming, with the population in urban districts projected to expand from the current 2.8 million residents to about 4 million by 2020. The city's vision includes the development of compact urban centers focused around new urban rail stations.

A key issue identified during project preparation is ensuring that urban design around stations—both the design of the public domain and the restrictions and conditions placed on private developers—is carried out with attention to detail. The success of both the Singapore and Hong Kong SAR systems highlights the relationship between details of the urban environment—such as station design, entrance location, land-use mix, road widths, setbacks, and height—and ridership and the ultimate

Figure 11.5   The Proposed Kunming Urban Rail System

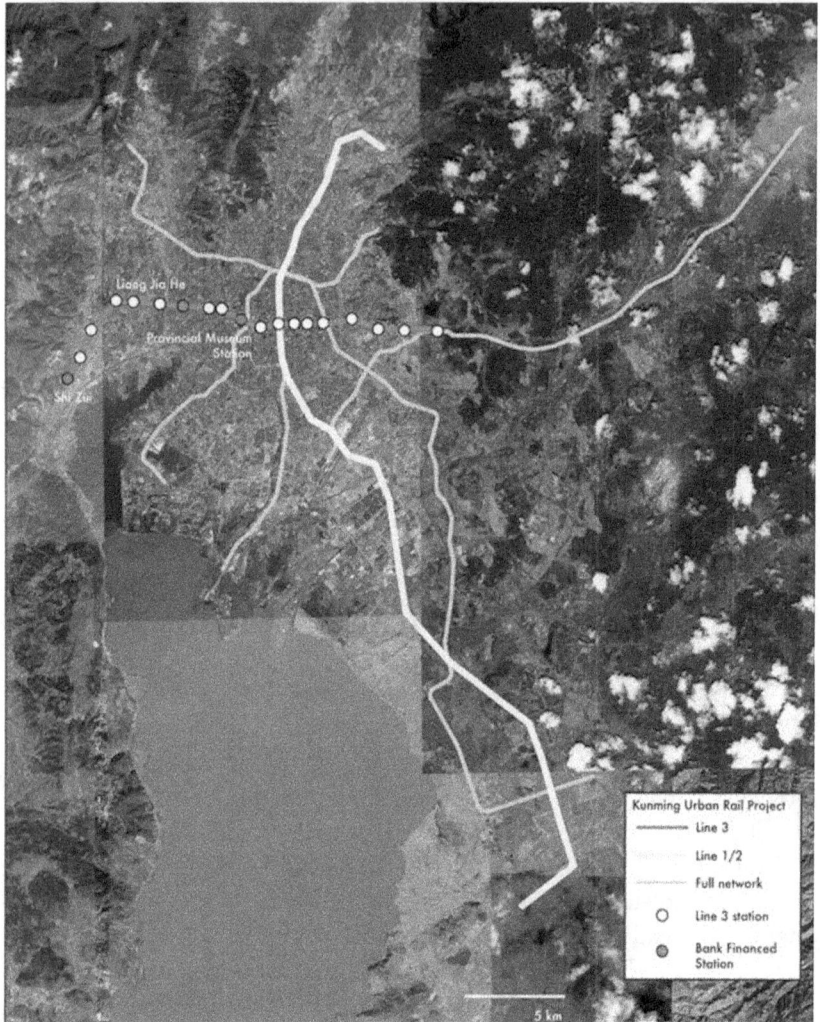

Source: World Bank.

success of urban rail systems. To date, in Chinese practice, this issue has not received the attention it deserves. Realizing this kind of compact growth will require the following:

- Hold continuous consultations between the planning bureau, developers, and the rail company on plans and design guidelines for development adjacent to any new rail line. Ideally, special design guidelines—such as those relating to building setbacks and floor-area rations—would be prepared for these developments to create pedestrian- and bicycle-friendly built environments that attract public transport riders.

- Support the rail company's own property development arm in identifying properties and developing them with appropriate connectivity to the metro system and surrounding properties.
- Support the inclusion of bicycle infrastructure at stations, including parking and easy access, to help foster inviting, safe, and attractive station environments.
- Consider the possibilities to facilitate commercial property development above maintenance depots and yards.

Bus-rail integration. Metro systems need to integrate with existing bus services to provide a comprehensive network and high-quality service to urban public transport passengers. A lack of bus-rail integration is not uncommon in recently completed Chinese urban rail systems. These problems center on the following:

- *Institutions:* In most Chinese cities, urban rail and urban bus systems are managed by two separate agencies, with no formal mechanism for integration between them.
- *Service planning:* Bus and metro services are often planned without careful cooperation between their respective services.
- *Bus interchange facilities:* Often, bus interchange facilities are omitted from the initial design of metro systems, significantly hampering operations on opening.
- *Fares and ticketing:* In many Chinese cities, bus and rail fares have not been integrated in a way that benefits both systems and limits the subsidy required from the city government.

Therefore, cities implementing rail systems should pay special attention to bus-rail integration. Issues that require particular attention in this respect include the following:

- The development of fare policies that integrate bus and rail service into a unified system, maximizing rider benefit while balancing the financial needs of both the bus and metro system. Such a policy may require, for instance, transfer discounts for intermodal trips and a discounted fare for feeder bus routes developed to "feed" passengers to the rail system.

- The inclusion of land requirements for interchange facilities into the feasibility study. Current practice in China does not include such facilities in the right-of-way or "red-line" for the rail system. As a result, these facilities are not constructed, even though most rail system planners recognize the critical need for such interchange facilities.
- A focus on institutional and operational issues related to bus-rail service integration. Issues range from creating agencies responsible for achieving effective operational integration, to the actual restructuring of bus routes and schedules to complement rail services.

Comprehensive transport policy. Experience elsewhere in the world has demonstrated that the construction of an urban rail system in the absence of a broader comprehensive transport policy that supports public transport is unlikely to achieve its policy goals.

Parking, in particular, is an area that needs attention. Parking in areas well-served by public transport, most crucially the downtown core, needs to be limited. Kunming is already ahead of national best practice on this issue. Limits have been placed on downtown parking—which is significant and rare, even around the world—and traffic impact analysis will be used for new developments to analyze parking impacts. Any city making investments in rail transport needs to consider their parking strategy and related policy so that it complements their urban rail investments and encourages passengers to use urban rail. A comprehensive parking policy to replace currently fragmented policies and agency responsibilities will support this effort.

Conclusion and Looking Forward

This chapter has summarized the range of measures a Chinese city can take to improve the quality and competitiveness of its public transport system. This starts with a focus on institutions and the character of the relationship between the city and operators. It includes a strong emphasis on planning and measuring progress. The core of the public transport system in a city is the bus network, and investing in a high-quality modern bus system should be an important priority for all cities. Finally, some cities will need to invest in mass transit systems. The choice of system should be made carefully, and implementation will need careful "systems" thinking and coordination to maximize the benefits of these expensive investments.

While improving public transport is very much in the fundamental interests of any city for reasons that have nothing to do with global climate change (reasons of productivity, efficiency, and equity for its citizens), the issue of climate change further reinforces the need to improve public transport—with a focus on attracting high-end riders who would otherwise use automobiles. The analysis in this chapter suggests that while solutions are often context-specific and every city will need to find ways to improve public transport based on detailed local needs and conditions, there are broad similarities in the strategies that almost all cities will benefit from following. The following "three-integrations" summarize the key focus areas and challenges facing Chinese cities as they work to develop public transport systems that would support a low-carbon economy:

- *Developing customer-oriented services:* Modern customer-oriented public transport enterprises can attract users of choice. This will require greater attention to the details of bus and rail transfer facilities, as well as the creation of premium services and a customer-oriented mentality.
- *Integrating schedules and fares across modes and services:* Although the use of multimodal smartcards is common, bus interchange facilities that help passengers change modes or services are systematically underused. In addition, fare policies are rarely designed to facilitate intermodal fare transfers. Integrated bus and rail services, schedules, and fares will contribute greatly to improved services for passengers.
- *Integrating land use with transport planning:* It is increasingly evident that even the most effective systems of public transport cannot be competitive if they are not carefully integrated with land-use planning and design.

The examples, framework, and action steps described in this chapter can be a starting point for cities to analyze their situation, travel demand needs, and opportunities for a sustainable, low-carbon development of their urban transport sector.

Notes

1. State Council Decision # 46. The State Council is similar to the federal cabinet in the United States.
2. For more information on institutional arrangements for urban transport and possible reform initiatives, see World Bank (2011).

3. For a full description of the World Bank's approach and a summary of international bus practice on bus system management, see Gwilliam (2007).

4. For more information on the World Bank's work supporting public transport ITS in China, see World Bank (2009).

5. A full description of BRT systems and their various elements is found in ITDP (2007).

6. The identified areas included support for the integration of new metro systems with existing and future bus service; the use of urban development tools to maximize the benefit of new infrastructure; and the development of supportive travel demand management measures.

Bibliography

Chester, M., and A. Horvath. 2009. "Environmental Assessment of Passenger Transportation Should Include Infrastructure and Supply Chains." *Environmental Research Letters* 4: 1–8. Institute of Physics, June 8.

Gwilliam, K. 2007. "Developing the Public Transport Sector in China." World Bank working paper. World Bank, Washington DC. http://siteresources.worldbank.org/INTCHINA/Resources/318862-1121421293578/transport_16July07-en.pdf.

Institute for Transport and Development Policy (ITDP). 2007. *Bus Rapid Transit (BRT) Planning Guide, 2007.* http://www.itdp.org/index.php/microsite/brt_planning_guideTDP, January 6, 2011.

World Bank. 2009. *China ITS Implementation Guidance.* World Bank Working Guide. Washington, DC: World Bank.

———. 2011. "Metropolitan Transportation Institutions; Six Case Studies. Australia, Brazil, Canada, France, Germany and the United States." World Bank working paper. World Bank, Washington, DC.

CHAPTER 12

Motorized Vehicles: Demand Management and Technology

Shomik Mehndiratta, Zhi Liu, and Ke Fang

Overview

This chapter presents options to directly address the emissions from motorized vehicles in China's cities. Previous chapters have laid out issues related to the built environment that facilitates urban trips, and discussed options to improve the quality of alternatives to motorized modes of transport. While these strategies are critical, it is inevitable that as urbanization continues and incomes rise, the number of motorized vehicles in China's cities and the demand for urban transport will continue to increase.

Indeed, as illustrated in earlier chapters, while cars account for a minority of trips in Chinese cities (figure 12.1), most of the transport-related carbon emissions in China's urban areas are generated by motorized passenger transport. Figure 12.2 illustrates that private cars have the largest transport-related carbon emissions per capita. The most direct approach to reduce these emissions is by restricting the amount of travel on these modes. A related possibility is the adoption of technologies that reduce the unit emissions from motorized travel. This group of actions—related to managing demand and technology adoption—is the focus of this chapter.

Figure 12.1   Cars Account for a Minority of Trips in Chinese Cities

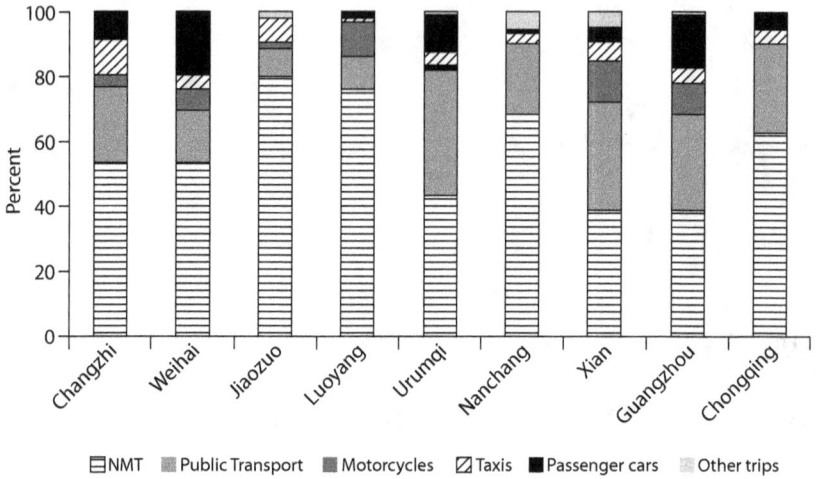

Source: Data from Darido et al. 2009.
Note: NMT = Non-Motorized Transport.

Figure 12.2   Autos Represent a Small Share of Trips but a Large Share of Transport Sector Emissions

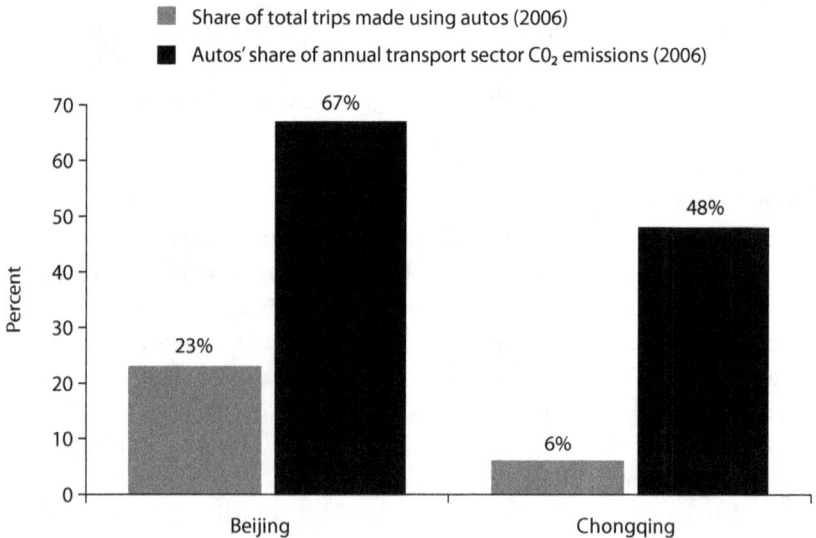

Source: Authors, based on data from Darido et al. 2009.

The chapter first discusses the range of actions governments can take to manage motorized travel. Though such policies are currently in their infancy in China, there are a number of interesting initiatives by Chinese authorities, some supported by the World Bank. These include actions related to pricing automobile ownership and use, as well as administrative measures. Next, the chapter discusses the range of technology-related opportunities to reduce emissions, in particular some initiatives related to electric vehicles and trucks.

Managing Travel Demand

In recent years urban transport professionals globally have largely acquiesced to the view that automobile demand in cities needs to be managed rather than accommodated. Rising incomes inevitability lead to increases in motorization. Even without the imperative of climate change, the physical constraints of densely inhabited cities and the corresponding demands of accessibility, mobility, safety, air pollution, and urban livability all limit the option of expanding road networks purely to accommodate this rising demand. As a result, as cities develop and their residents become more prosperous, persuading people to choose *not* to use cars becomes an increasingly key focus of city managers and planners. Improving the quality of alternative options, such as walking, cycling, and public transport, is a central element of this strategy. However, the most direct approach to managing automobile demand is making motorized travel more expensive or restricting it with administrative rules. The contribution of motorized travel to climate change reinforces this imperative. As box 12.1 illustrates, this urgency is equally true of China as it is elsewhere.

Examples of International Experience
To manage the use of motorized transport, cities use a number of complementary pricing and administrative measures that make driving more expensive and less convenient. These measures range from taxes and surcharges on vehicles and fuel to initiatives that restrict and raise the price of parking and various administrative restrictions. Economic theory strongly supports charging drivers for the cost that driving imposes on society. Economic agents (drivers) are known to "overconsume" activities (driving) when what they pay does not reflect the costs borne by the rest of society—such as the costs of climate change, pollution, or delays due to congestion. In this situation a "pigovian tax,"[1] reflecting the cost imposed on society, can help align individual incentives and costs with

Box 12.1

The Evolving Urban Transport Agenda in China: The Time for Managing Demand

The 1980s to the mid-1990s in China were characterized by urban transport infrastructure failing to keep up with urbanization and economic activity. Since that period, China has witnessed a major urban transport transformation and arrived at the era of private cars.

In 1994, the central government decided to develop the automotive industry as a "national pillar industry" and to promote a domestic market for household cars. Meanwhile, decentralization of government gave city governments a significant degree of freedom in managing local affairs, including financial resource mobilization for urban and infrastructure development. As a result, many cities underwent a dramatic transformation in spatial development and infrastructure modernization. Most cities started to widen existing streets and build more roads and new expressways for cars, sometimes by demolishing roadside trees and bicycle lanes and reducing pedestrian space.

While some cities also made significant efforts to reform the public transport sector and improve service coverage and efficiency, public transport development was dwarfed by the rapid expansion of private car ownership and the huge public investment in roads. Governments tried to avoid alienating car owners by not taking any action to appropriately price vehicle ownership and use. Petrol was inexpensive, urban road use was usually free, and parking was cheap and tolerated in public places by governments sympathetic toward car drivers. As a result, car users benefited from a range of "hidden" subsidies as urban transport investment and available capacity were oriented in their favor. This set the stage for most megacities to enter an era of severe, chronic traffic congestion.

The period since the mid-2000s has been both painful and enlightening for sustainable urban transport in China. It was recognized that in addition to the localized urban transport problems—congestion, accidents, and pollution—urban transport generates spillover effects to national and even international levels. A slow and congested transport system, for example, stifles the efficiency of the urban economy, which accounts for over 80 percent of the national economy. In addition, excessive conversion of farmland for urban development wastes scarce land resources and threatens the country's ecological systems. Excessive investments in urban transport through off-the-book borrowing by the municipal gov-

(continued next page)

Box 12.1 *(continued)*

ernments lead to heavy financial liabilities and threaten the country's financial stability. Finally, rising fuel consumption endangers the nation's long-term energy security, and growing CO_2 emissions from urban transport complicate national CO_2 emission reduction.

The recognition of the spillover effects has led to a new policy emphasis and a paradigm shift on public transport priority and sustainable urban transport development. But in itself, this is unlikely to be sufficient. As a recent opinion piece on the traffic situation in Beijing in the *China Daily* observed: "Travelers who get caught in congestion would try to find a way to escape if there are other options. Those who sit in traffic and complain aloud are right if they don't have an alternative. The job of the city government is to provide the alternative—better buses, safer bicycling, and easier access to subways. The non-pricing and pricing controls of vehicle ownership and use in congested cities are just the means to correct the long-standing policy distortions, and create the right incentive for car users to shift to other modes of transport. It is time for Beijing's car-owning group to understand this. It is time for Beijing to adopt demand-side controls" (Liu 2010).

Source: Authors.

the broader impacts on society. Box 12.2 summarizes two examples of international good practice in this area. World Bank experience with using fuel surcharges and parking restrictions for travel demand management (TDM) are described in the section below titled "Building Blocks towards a Demand Management Strategy."

TDM Design Principles

Although there are successful examples of managing demand, designing and implementing effective and acceptable demand management policies are not small tasks. In particular, the political economy of demand management schemes is complex, and to succeed a scheme not only has to be effective, but it has to be perceived as fair. As with any pricing of "public" goods that are currently enjoyed by the public for no monetary cost, it is possible the policy will be perceived as a scheme to favor the "rich" over the "poor" who would be priced out. Careful design, along with effective communication, is critical to avoid such perceptions and criticism. While any good mechanism needs to be customized to a city's travel patterns and characteristics, successful schemes are all designed to carefully mini-

Box 12.2

International Experience with Managing Auto Demand

Singapore. Singapore's system of congestion charging was, by some measures, the world's first, instituted in 1975. The early system had users purchase daily licenses that needed to be displayed in car windshields—with enforcement carried out by police officers at entry points to the controlled area. In 1998, the system was upgraded in collaboration with IBM to electronic road pricing (ERP), which uses automatic detection at entry points and has become a model for systems around the world, including London's. Overall, the system has helped reduce traffic entering the central zone (in the first year of operation by 76 percent [Spencer and Sien 1985], although this has moderated since) and helped smooth traffic flow in the downtown area.

Figure B12.2.1   Electronic Road Pricing in Singapore

Source: Wikimedia Commons 2011.

Figure B12.2.2   Use of a Congestion Charging Zone in London

Source: Wikimedia Commons 2011.

Singapore's urban geography makes it ideally suited to use congestion tools, as its dense central business district, which contains a large portion of the region's jobs, is well served by high-quality public transport. Also, aside from actual congestion charges, Singapore has instituted a series of high taxes and vehicle registration fees on vehicle ownership. The result is that in Singapore, one of Asia's wealthiest cities, only 30 percent of households has access to a car (Singapore LTA 1996). The availability of high-quality alternatives and a high percentage of auto-free commuters make the political economy of congestion charging more favorable for public policy makers.

London. In February of 2003 London instituted what has become one of the world's best-known examples of congestion charging. Vehicles were required to

(continued next page)

Box 12.2 *(continued)*

pay £5 (now £8) a day to enter the Congestion Charging Zone (CCZ)—the city's center primarily composed of employment and retail areas (now expanded). The scheme has resulted in a reduction of about 20 percent in the number of private vehicles entering the zone and a significant improvement in traffic speeds inside it, although some of this effect has diminished in recent years. A survey by Transport for London (TFL) in the first year of the program suggested that 50–60 percent of the reduction in traffic could be attributed to transfers to public transport, 20–30 percent to journeys avoiding the zone, and 15–25 percent from switching to car share (TFL 2003). Much of the revenue from the charge was directed at improving public transport, and as a result the upgraded bus system was able to adequately accommodate the dramatic increase in public transport ridership.

Source: Authors.

mize the number of people who may be disadvantaged and to maximize those who benefit. In this regard, four key principles apply:

- *Maximize benefits for public transport users:* The vast majority of people who are not using cars, but are already walking, cycling, or using public transport, have the most to gain from any kind of demand management scheme. Reducing the number of cars on the road has the potential to increase the speed of public transport and make walking and cycling safer. These gains need to be highlighted and consolidated. For instance, more public transport may need to be provided to accommodate those who move from cars to public transport. Experience also suggests that the public is favorably inclined to schemes in which revenue from demand management efforts (such as congestion charges, auctioning car ownership permits, or higher parking fees) is reinvested into improving the quality and quantity of public transport. Such mechanisms were important and high-profile elements of congestion pricing schemes in London (TFL 2003) and Stockholm (Prud'homme and Kopp 2006).
- *Maximize benefits for the general public:* Some potential benefits—such as lower levels of air pollution and more public space (if road space is reclaimed)—accrue to all urban residents, and these advantages also need to be highlighted and consolidated. Perhaps the most high-profile and successful example of this occurred in Seoul, when in 2003 the city government demolished the Cheonggye and Samil elevated highway to

restore and revitalize the then-polluted Cheonggye stream that ran under the expressway. Ultimately the stream was made the centerpiece of a successful urban park in the city center (see figure 12.3).

- *Minimize disruption for drivers:* Equally important are strategies that minimize the disruption for drivers. One approach is to package the demand management measures with simultaneous measures, such as enhanced traffic management or improvements in the secondary road system, which would minimize traffic disruption generally while still supporting the overall objectives of the city. Such actions to improve short-term traffic flow helped to build public acceptance of bus rapid transit (BRT) systems in cities like Mexico City that required the reclamation of road space from cars.

- *Provide options for those negatively affected:* Another principle is to provide those negatively affected with as many options as possible to minimize their disruption and create an opportunity for them to improve their situation. For example, if a congestion tax during peak times is accompanied by lower parking fees during off-peak, it could provide an incentive for those with flexible schedules to change their time of travel with minimal disruption. Similarly, better, more, and faster public transport may encourage drivers to consider and perhaps use public transport. Drivers could be offered incentives to modify their behavior in ways that allow them to drive but still meet the city's objectives. Examples are lowering (or eliminating) charges on carpools or particular kinds of vehicles, such as a prespecified set of low-emission vehicles.

Figure 12.3   The Cheonggye and Samil Elevated Highway (Left) in Seoul Was Demolished in 2003 and Replaced by a Restored Cheonggye Stream (Right)

Source: Kim 2008.

After a scheme has been implemented, its ultimate impact depends on how drivers respond, and how the impacts of the scheme are perceived by the public. Drivers often respond to demand management policies in ways unforeseen by the government, and the eventual impact of any demand management mechanism depends on the equilibrium reached between implementation enforcement and the actions taken by motorists (legal and illegal) to minimize the impact. Box 12.3 summarizes some recent experience in this regard in Beijing and Shanghai. Whether or not a national policy to support the car industry can be compatible with TDM and the development of cities around public transport, walking, and cycling is addressed in box 12.4.

Box 12.3

Travel Demand Management in China: Early Examples of Beijing and Shanghai

Since 1994, Shanghai has used a license bidding scheme to control the number of new vehicles. The municipality auctions a set number of new license plates annually—this number was 86,600 in 2009. The price of a license plate reflects the level of demand and in 2010 was between RMB 30,000 and RMB 40,000. As a result, each year significantly fewer cars are registered in Shanghai than in Beijing, a city of similar size and slightly lower income level. It is also likely that this scheme has contributed to Shanghai's significantly lower transport-related carbon footprint relative to Beijing. However, anecdotal evidence suggests that in many cases Shanghai's policy has resulted in a situation where many of the new cars driven in Shanghai are actually registered in neighboring provinces and cities where registration costs are lower, while Shanghai loses the possible registration-related revenue.

During the summer of the 2008 Olympics, Beijing restricted the use of automobiles to half the number of days in a week based on the license plate number (creating "odd" and "even" driving days) in what was widely seen as a successful short-term TDM scheme. After the Olympics, a variation that restricted the use of cars within the urban area two days of the workweek, also based on license plate number, was extended on a pilot basis for 18 months. Though this scheme undoubtedly has reduced the number of cars on the road, there is significant anecdotal evidence of users evading the restriction by purchasing a second car, using fake license plates, or simply driving without license plates.

(continued next page)

Box 12.3 *(continued)*

In January 2011, Beijing expanded the range of measures by restricting the number of new cars sold to 20,000 per month (compared to more than 60,000 a month in 2010), with the buyers to be selected via a monthly lottery among those who register their desire to buy a car in that period. The use of cars registered outside Beijing will also be restricted. It is reported that in January 2011, the first month of this scheme, more than 200,000 applications for new vehicles were registered (*China News* 2011). This is not surprising as economic principles would suggest that with restriction and scarcity the "right" to register a vehicle will become very valuable. If this right can be obtained at a low cost (as with a lottery), demand for it will increase and this right will be traded. If the government does not charge a fee corresponding to the value of such a "right," then a market will emerge to allow those fortunate enough to win permits to sell them to those who value them the most.

Source: Authors.

Box 12.4

Is a "Pillar" Automotive Industry Incompatible with Livable Cities Built around Public Transport, Walking, and Cycling?

In its 8th Five-Year Plan (1991–95), the government of China designated the automotive industry as one of the pillar industries of the national economy. This was followed by the promulgation of an automotive industrial policy in 1994. The policy made it clear that the development of the automotive industry should rely on the domestic market for private cars for initial growth. Within two decades, China has now become the world's largest automobile producer as well as consumer. Both annual production capacity and vehicle sales are close to 14 million units. Obviously, the automotive industrial policy is a major success in driving national economic growth and capturing the domestic market.

Is such an industrial policy fundamentally at odds with sustainable high-income cities built around walking, cycling, and public transport? While national policy makers and Chinese city leaders ultimately have to reconcile Chinese industrial auto policy with their visions for urban livability, international experience suggests that there need not always be a contradiction between these two goals. Cities

(continued next page)

Box 12.4 *(continued)*

in Germany—a country with a strong automotive sector, many iconic automotive brands, high personal incomes, and very high levels of car ownership—are one example. The same is true for Japan, which also combines a high-income population, high car ownership, and a strong automotive sector with livable, public transport–oriented cities. In both countries, with car ownership levels among the highest in the world, automobile use is significantly lower than in other, otherwise comparable, places. In Germany the average car is driven 10,500 kilometers annually, and in Japan, 5,700 kilometers—compared to about 22,000 kilometers a year for an average car in the United States. Also, the size of the cars bought by Japanese and German consumers is, on average, somewhat smaller, and their fuel efficiency is higher, than cars bought by other consumers with similar incomes. Together, these factors provide significantly lower levels of greenhouse gas (GHG) emissions and more livable cities.

Source: Authors, using data from Millard-Ball and Schipper 2010.

Building Blocks toward a Demand Management Strategy

The use of demand management tools is likely to expand in China, and approaches to TDM are expected to become increasingly sophisticated with growing experience. Some key tools for appropriate demand management mechanisms have already been established in China and are discussed briefly below. Box 12.5 describes particular initiatives the World Bank has been involved with in Beijing and Wuhan.

Box 12.5

Developing Comprehensive TDM Strategies

TDM is not a new concept for China's largest cities. Beijing and Shanghai have already introduced some initiatives that restrict automobile ownership and use. Many of the biggest cities, including Beijing, Guangzhou, Shanghai, Shenzhen, and Wuhan, have spent time and effort in recent years assessing a range of demand management options. The following examples summarize some of this work done in Beijing and Wuhan.

(continued next page)

Box 12.5 *(continued)*

Beijing: A strategic study for Beijing Municipality (Atkins 2008), financed by a Global Environment Facility (GEF) grant, has provided a comprehensive assessment and strategic options for demand management in Beijing. The study included an evaluation of current and future situations, as well as descriptions of international practice. As part of the study, objectives for TDM in Beijing were defined, which then allowed for the development of specific TDM proposals for the city—land-use strategies, alternative modes, network management, approaches to restrain car usage, and supporting measures. These strategies are interdependent in reinforcing the effectiveness of demand management. For example, restricting car use cannot stand alone as a solution without being supplemented by other measures. The report also proposed an implementation plan and potential pilot projects, and concluded that in the long term, the case for more restrictive forms of TDM should be accepted and planned for, subject to ongoing monitoring of network conditions and performance. In addition, the report recommended that early investment should be made in enhanced monitoring and analytical tools, which will allow future TDM and other proposals to be more fully assessed and planned. This includes an upgrade of Beijing's strategic and local traffic modeling capabilities and skills.

Wuhan: A strategic study of TDM options was conducted as part of the World Bank–financed Wuhan Urban Transport Project. As a follow-on to this first project, the World Bank–financed the Wuhan Second Urban Transport Project (currently under implementation), supporting a number of initiatives that can form the basis for any future TDM strategy. The project, for example, supports a comprehensive electronic toll collection (ETC) system on all river crossings within the third ring road—long identified as the key transport bottleneck in Wuhan—as a demand-side measure to address the congestion on the river crossings. This investment is also being complemented with technical assistance and support for the agencies involved, to strengthen enforcement; upgrade databases of drivers, vehicles, and traffic violations; develop monitoring systems; and support the development of specific congestion charging schemes for Wuhan.

Source: Authors.

Surcharges on fuel. Surcharges on fuel can be an effective mechanism to charge drivers for the costs their driving imposes on society, and China, since 2009, already has a fuel tax and the basic mechanism in place to be able to impose fuel surcharges. In many countries, including the United

States, subnational authorities such as cities are allowed to add additional surcharges to a fuel tax. A surcharge linked to the carbon emissions of specific fuels can closely reflect the costs of driving in terms of carbon emissions. As figure 12.4 indicates, fuel prices in China are currently significantly lower than corresponding prices in Western European countries where environmental implications are an important rationale for fuel surcharges.

Parking as a TDM tool. Most cities are not clear on their role with respect to parking provision. The general tendency is one of sympathy for those looking for parking, and a resulting policy framework that seeks to accommodate those looking for parking by (i) providing more parking facilities financed by government and (ii) laxly enforcing existing regulations in light of a perceived "inadequate" level of parking. International experience suggests that parking policies are actually a critical determinant of the sustainability of a city's transport system. In particular, a parking policy can be an important element of a city's TDM strategy. By restricting parking in the central city, enforcing those restrictions, and charging appropriately for available parking, cities can simulate congestion charges at relatively low political and transaction cost.

Perhaps the simplest and most effective intervention cities in China can make so that driving reflects its real costs on a city would be to prop-

Figure 12.4 Fuel Prices in China vs. Western Europe, India, and the United States

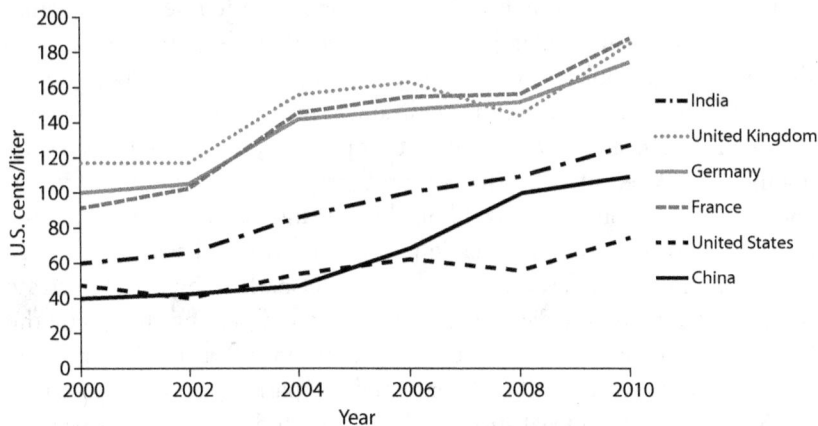

Sources: (a) For 2000–08 data: Sustainable Urban Transport Project (2009); (b) 2010 fuel prices: (i) For China: Bloomberg Businessweek (2010); (ii) For the United States: U.S. Dept. of Energy data, available at http://www.eia.gov/oog/info/gdu/gasdiesel.asp; (iii) For India: India Summary (2010); (iv) For Europe and the United Kingdom: Europe's Energy Portal data, available at http://www.energy.eu/#prices.
Note: The US$ conversion rates are those of 17–21 November 2008.

erly enforce the parking rules that already exist. In many Chinese cities, parking rules are not consistently enforced, and it is common to find cars parked on sidewalks. A general tendency to accommodate such behavior, which happens at the expense of pedestrians, cyclists, and general livability, is further complicated by institutional fragmentation with respect to enforcement. In many cities, while the traffic police are responsible for enforcing parking infractions on the street, a different division (often part of a municipal urban services management division) is responsible for sidewalks. This agency sometimes does not even have the authority to fine and penalize parking violations.

From a broader policy perspective, there are at least two parking-related issues that need to be addressed. The first relates to rules and guidelines regulating the provision of parking in new urban construction. In general, Chinese cities and building codes now specify *minimum* levels of parking that contractors need to provide in new office, commercial, and residential buildings. From a traffic management perspective, however, international experience suggests that it is equally important to consider *maximum* levels of parking provided, particularly in central city districts. In this respect, there are lessons to be learned from cities such as London in the United Kingdom and Boston in the United States that have deliberately limited the availability of parking in the central city as part of a largely successful, comprehensive strategy to manage congestion levels in the central city and to keep the urban core livable, attractive, and walkable (see Weinberger et al. 2010).

The second policy issue is linked to pricing and the role of the municipal government in parking provision. International experience indicates that in the right policy environment, parking can be privately provided by market forces. However, the tradition in most Chinese cities remains public provision; and a private market for parking provision has been slow in emerging. A recent World Bank report, based in part on project experience in Guangzhou, Liaoning, Shijiazhuang, and Wuhan, identifies three key obstacles to developing viable parking industries. These barriers are (i) parking insurance laws that deter off-street parking by leaving private operators liable for any damage; (ii) the control of parking charges by the Financial Bureau, which limits the adoption of a market-oriented approach and creates artificially inexpensive parking; and (iii) inconsistent enforcement of illegal street parking. The study also presents ways to address these barriers and provides a framework for a city to design a viable parking industry (Frame 2009).

Though much needs to be done for parking to realize its appropriate place in a sustainable transport strategy in most Chinese cities, there do exist some elements of good practice that are important to highlight. For instance, parking in Beijing is increasingly viewed as a service that can be adequately provided by the private sector, and the government has adopted the role of enforcing controls on illegal parking and setting minimum parking prices (that are gradually being increased). Kunming presents another example with elements of good practice. The city explicitly recognizes the role of parking in managing transport demand and sets three levels of differential minimum parking fees—higher in the city center compared to the broader urban and peri-urban areas. The city also has initiatives in place that supplement requirements for minimum parking provision, with advice to developers on suggested *maximum* amounts of parking to provide in central city developments.

Tolling. Collecting tolls for the use of bridges or other key elements of road infrastructure will help cities experiment and gain experience with the technology and information architecture needed to implement market-based demand management strategies. Collecting tolls also can help get drivers used to the concept of paying for the use of particular facilities. China has a rich history of using tolls to generate revenue, but most tolls are charged in inter-urban settings; the experience with tolls in urban settings has been mixed. A particular high-profile case in this respect was Beijing abandoning a strategy to toll the fifth ring road in 2004 in response to commuter protests. A number of successful tolled operations, however, do exist in Chinese cities, usually on airport access roads and on key bridges. There would be value in extending these experiences as much as possible and testing modern transponder technologies at these locations.

Vehicle registration taxes as a TDM tool. To the degree that cities have the authority to do so, there is value in reformulating vehicle purchase and annual registration charges in line with a low-carbon objective. A model in this regard could be Milan's *Ecopass* scheme, which is designed to provide an incentive to use cars with low local pollutant emissions. The scheme charges all but the cleanest vehicles a fee for entering the city center, with the option to buy daily, multiple-day, or annual (for residents) passes. A similar scheme linking vehicle taxes to a vehicle's carbon footprint could induce a shift toward vehicles with a relatively low carbon emission profile.

Technological Options for Reducing Carbon Emissions from Motorized Vehicles

Technology, in the form of better-designed vehicles, alternative fuels, or even improvements in the alternatives to travel, is expected to be an important element of a low-carbon future. This is equally true in China as it is globally. There is a strong focus globally on developing technological solutions that reduce the carbon emissions of vehicle-fuel systems. Not unexpectedly, most of these efforts are by venture capitalists within the private sector, while major automobile companies are investing significant amounts of money in developing vehicles that they believe will be in demand in a "low-carbon" environment.

In general, government is not a significant player in the area of technology development, and nor is the World Bank. The evolution and adoption of technology are mostly driven by private enterprises with significant investments and risks undertaken in search of commensurate profits. However, given the global and "public good" imperative underlying climate change, governments across the world have actively started to promote the development and use of potentially low-carbon vehicle-fuel systems. This section summarizes two ongoing initiatives in China—the New Energy Vehicles Program and low-carbon logistics initiatives—that focus on vehicle technologies and fuels. In the future, it is likely that the level of such activities will increase.

New Energy Vehicles Program and the Role of Electric Vehicles

Within the last decade, the emergence of four complementary global trends has been driving the development of electric vehicles. The first is the growing number of global climate change policies that propose significant reductions in automotive CO_2 emissions. The second trend is the rising concern over economic and security issues related to oil. A third driver for vehicle electrification is the increase in congestion, which is creating significant air quality problems. Finally, the fourth trend, rapid technology advancement, has resulted in the advancement of battery technology to a point where electric vehicles are now on the verge of becoming feasible in select mass-market applications. The industry forecasts suggest that global sales of electric vehicles will contribute between 2 percent and 25 percent of annual new vehicle sales by 2025, with most estimates agreeing this number will be close to 10 percent. This kind of transition will result in a significant shift in the car industry.

The scale of China's vehicle electrification program places China at the front of this worldwide race toward a sustainable, but also profit-generating solution. Vehicle electrification is expected to be a strategically important element for China in the areas of global climate change, energy security, urban air quality, and growth of the auto industry. In 2009, the Chinese government initiated the Ten Cities, Thousand Vehicles Program to stimulate electric vehicle development through large-scale pilots in ten cities, focusing on deployment of electric vehicles for government fleet applications. In June 2010, the program was expanded to five other cities and also started to include consumers. Significant electric vehicle technology development in China is occurring in industry as well as universities, focusing primarily on batteries and charging technology. The new electric vehicle value chain is beginning to develop new businesses and business models to provide the infrastructure, components, vehicles, and related services necessary to enable an electric vehicle ecosystem.

Challenges Going Forward

By comparing China's new energy vehicle program with similar programs worldwide across several dimensions—policy, technology, and commercial models—several challenges can be identified for China's vehicle electrification program (PRTM 2011). Going forward, particular attention needs to be paid to the following areas:

- *Policy development:* The implemented policies related to electric vehicles in China mainly focus on the promotion of vehicle adoption by introducing purchase subsidies at a national and provincial level. Meanwhile, policies to stimulate demand for electric vehicles, deploy vehicle charging infrastructure, and stimulate investment in technology development and manufacturing capacity also need to be developed. China's recently announced plan to invest RMB 100 billion in new energy vehicles over the next 10 years will need to include a balanced approach to stimulating demand and supply.
- *Integrated charging solutions:* Because the early vehicle applications have been with fleet vehicles such as buses, trucks, or taxis, charging infrastructure technology development in China has focused on the need of fleets. However, as private cars will eventually be fully involved, integrated charging solutions need to be developed to cover three basic types: smart charging, standardized/safe/authenticated charging, and networked and high-service charging.

- *Standards:* China has not yet launched its national standards for electric vehicles. The first emerging standard is for vehicle charging. The full set of such standards should not only govern the physical interface, but also take into consideration safety and power grid standards. As Chinese manufacturers intend to export their vehicles eventually, all standards should align with existing standards worldwide to minimize complexity.
- *Commercial models:* The electric vehicle value chain is beginning to develop new business models to provide infrastructure, components, vehicles, and related services. It is essential to build a commercially viable business model that bears the cost of the charging infrastructure, as the industry cannot rely indefinitely on government funding. It is also likely that revenue from services can help offset the cost of infrastructure.
- *Customer acceptance:* When government subsidies have ended, consumers will not commit to electric vehicles unless they find value in them. Even when the lifetime ownership costs become favorable for electric vehicles, the up-front vehicle cost will still be significantly higher than for a conventional vehicle and with a significantly longer payback period than most consumers or commercial fleet owners are willing to accept. While leasing could address this issue, a secondary market for batteries would have to be established, in addition to a vehicle finance market, to enable the leasing market to be viable.
- *GHG benefits:* The biggest challenge faced by China is that the current Chinese electricity grid produces relatively high GHG emissions and is projected to remain GHG-intensive for a significant period of time due to the long remaining lifetime of the coal-fired generation capacity. A new framework for maximizing GHG benefits in China has to be developed to fully realize the low emission potential of electric vehicles.

Low-Carbon Logistics Initiatives in the Transport Sector

Road-based freight transport in China, which primarily consists of trucks, accounts for 54 percent of total transport sector fuel consumption (MoT 2008). Freight traffic on roads has been increasing rapidly over the past decade due to the continuous growth of China's manufacturing-dominated economy. For example, total freight traffic (in tonnes) by trucks has increased by more than 125 percent in Guangdong Province since 2000. Over that same period, the provincial highway network grew at an average rate of 11 percent per year, and the number of registered trucks grew by 56 percent (Clean Air Initiative for Asian Cities 2010; Guangdong Province 2009).

Despite the growing importance of this sector, energy efficiency in Chinese road freight transport remains very low. This is caused by two major areas: truck technologies and logistics management.

Truck technologies. The first challenge that needs to be addressed is truck technologies. According to the Ministry of Transport (MoT), the fuel efficiency of Chinese trucks is about 30 percent lower than that of trucks in advanced Organisation for Economic Co-operation and Development (OECD) countries, largely because fuel-saving technologies and practices have not been widely adopted in China (MoT 2008). This market failure occurs because (i) carriers are unwilling to experiment with new or unknown technologies, and (ii) the market lacks information on the performance, cost, and availability of fuel efficiency technologies.

Logistics management. The second obstacle to improved energy efficiency is logistics management. The trucking industry in China is largely operated by the private sector, but in contrast with many industrialized countries, the sector is fragmented and most companies are very small—often single truck owner operators.[2] Also, a lack of modern logistics brokerage practices has resulted in a large number of annual empty back-haul kilometers—reported to be more than 30 percent of all freight vehicle-kilometers traveled in Guangdong Province.[3] A preliminary assessment of logistics management in Guangdong suggests that the low level of operational efficiency in logistics is caused by a number of factors, including (i) a lack of information sharing and operational coordination among carriers (trucking companies) and shippers (clients of trucking companies), and (ii) poor operational management within many trucking companies (including both state-owned enterprises and privately owned companies).

The following two projects—the Guangzhou "Green Truck Pilot" and the GEF Guangdong Green Freight Demonstration Project—are designed specifically to address these obstacles of truck technologies and logistics management, respectively.

Guangzhou Green Truck Pilot

Since April 2009, the World Bank, in collaboration with various donors and partners, has supported the Guangzhou municipal government in preparing and implementing a "Green Truck Pilot" project in Guangzhou. The project's purpose is to test and demonstrate energy efficient technologies in local trucks and develop a "proof of concept" before widely introducing green truck technologies in China.

The technologies used for testing have been verified by the SmartWay Program of the U.S. Environmental Protection Agency (USEPA). They included technologies such as improved aerodynamics (for example, skirts and nose cones) and improved tire systems (for example, low resistance tires, aluminum wheels, and tire pressure monitoring systems), which, as certified by USEPA, can reduce fuel consumption by more than 20 percent. Fourteen trucks from three leading truck companies registered in Guangzhou were selected. Based on the characteristics of each truck, one single technology or a combination of several different technologies was installed. In addition, drivers at the three companies received training on how to improve fuel efficiency in truck operation and maintenance.

The three-month process of monitoring and data collecting was established, managed, and supported by local coordinators; experts from Tsinghua University; and supervisors from the Clean Air Initiative for Asian Cities (CAI-Asia) Center, a nongovernmental organization (NGO) promoting better air quality management in Asia. The preliminary results show that a 6 to 17 percent reduction in fuel usage and substantial reductions in emissions of particulate matter (PM), nitrogen oxides (NOx), and CO_2 can be achieved, although the level of energy savings varies between trucks and is currently lower than levels achieved in the United States.

GEF Guangdong Green Freight Demonstration Project
Based on the Guangzhou "Green Truck Pilot," the Guangdong provincial government, with support from the World Bank, the government of China, and the Global Environment Facility (GEF), initiated a Guangdong Green Freight Demonstration Project (GGFDP). The purpose of the project is to address market failures by providing better information and building confidence in the performance of proven energy efficiency technologies and practices, increasing the awareness of and demand for them, and increasing the supply of these technologies in the Chinese market. Project implementation has started in the first half of 2011.

The project has the following key features:

- *Innovative finance arrangements:* Participating companies will receive training and incentive packages (such as a price rebate at the purchase of the technology and a performance-based award) to support the procurement, installation, and monitoring of verified energy-efficient technologies on eligible freight vehicles. The project will also assist the participating companies, which have greater financing needs than the project can provide, to access energy efficiency funds provided by commercial banks, including the China Utility-Based Energy Efficiency Finance Program (CHUEE) supported by the International Finance Corporation (IFC).

- *Green freight trade fairs:* The project will support at least two green freight trade fairs, which would be the first trade fairs in China to focus primarily on low-carbon freight technologies. The trade fairs would provide a great opportunity for more innovative technologies to enter China and spur further development of local markets for energy efficient trucking and freight management technologies.
- *Advanced logistics brokerage information systems:* To improve the logistics operation practices and significantly reduce waiting time and the empty traveling time of trucks, the project will assist development of advanced logistics brokerage information systems in Guangdong. The online-based systems will allow participating trucking and logistics services companies to better share information and better manage their operations.
- *Demonstration of "drop-and-hook":* Drop-and-hook, a transport practice that allows a tractor to "drop" a loaded trailer and "hook" onto another one,[4] has been widely used in many advanced economies. The MoT is now promoting this concept in China. This project will support Guangdong Department of Transport with the preparation and implementation of a demonstration drop-and-hook scheme in Guangdong.
- *Capacity building:* The GGFDP contains a structured capacity-building program, which includes driver training on the installation and operation of green truck technologies and smart-driving techniques, training for relevant government officials and managers of trucking companies, awareness raising and information dissemination workshops for the freight industry and general public, as well as policy research on green freight development and monitoring and evaluation studies.

Conclusion

As China's urban centers continue to expand and incomes rise, the number of motorized vehicles and the demand for urban transport will also rise accordingly. This will inevitably result in increased use of motor vehicles and consequently greater amounts of carbon emissions. As presented in this chapter, options exist to address this challenge. Demand management—through congestion pricing, fuel surcharges, or other policies—can reduce carbon emissions by restricting the amount and mode of travel. In addition, technology advances, such as electric vehicles, can reduce per-unit emissions from motorized travel. Current World Bank transport projects in Guangzhou and Guangdong illustrate that significant gains can also be made by applying existing energy-efficient technologies and better logistics for road freight transport.

Notes

1. A Pigovian tax is a term for taxes imposed on individuals or firms who are taking actions that have negative social consequences. The tax corresponds to the social burden imposed by the action, so that the total "cost" to the individual (or company) reflects the costs they impose on society. A Pigovian tax equal to the negative externality (or burden imposed on society) is thought to correct the market outcome back to efficiency. A typical example of such a tax would be to charge polluters for air or water pollution emissions.

2. For example, 78 percent of trucking companies registered in Guangdong Province consist of only one truck, and more than 99 percent of registered trucking companies in Guangdong Province own fewer than 100 trucks, according to data provided by the Guangdong Provincial Transportation Planning and Research Center in July 2010.

3. Data provided by the Guangdong Provincial Transportation Planning and Research Center in July 2010.

4. "Drop-and-hook" describes the process by which one tractor pulls a loaded trailer to a destination, immediately "drops" the loaded trailer, and then hooks to another loaded trailer that is ready to go. This process improves efficiency dramatically by using only one tractor and one driver for multiple trailers. Also, through this process, the driver spends more time on the road than waiting for trailers to be loaded. However, to implement a drop-and-hook scheme, a coordinated logistics operations center must be in place to plan and implement all the drops, hooks, routes, and loads.

Bibliography

Atkins. 2008. "Beijing Travel Demand Management Measures Study Based on Sustainable Development." Report submitted to Beijing Development and Reform Commission. October. Beijing. http://www.atkinsglobal.com.

Bloomberg Businessweek. 2010. "China Raises Gasoline, Diesel Prices by 4% on Oil Gain." Bloomberg. http://www.businessweek.com/news/2010-12-22/china-raises-gasoline-diesel-prices-by-4-on-oil-gain.html.

China News. 2011. http://www.chinanews.com/auto/2010/12-23/2743103.shtml.

Clean Air Initiative for Asian Cities. 2010. "Guangzhou Green Trucks Pilot Project: Background Analysis Report for the World Bank: Truck GHG Emission Reduction Pilot Project." Background analysis report. Manila.

Darido, G., M. Torres-Montoya, and S. Mehndiratta. 2009. "Urban Transport and CO_2 Emissions: Some Evidence from Chinese Cities." World Bank working paper. World Bank, Washington, DC.

Frame, G. 2009. "Parking as a Business: Guidance Summary Note." Unpublished paper. World Bank, Washington, DC.

Guangdong Province. 2009. *Guangdong Statistical Yearbook.* Table 14-5, Total Freight Traffic, Guangdong Province, http://www.gdstats.gov.cn/tjnj/table/14/e14_5.htm; and Table 14-12, Length of Highways and Number of Bridges, Guangdong Province, http://www.gdstats.gov.cn/tjnj/table/14/e14_12.htm.

India Summary. 2010. "Petrol Price in India Hiked Starting from Today on Dec 15, 2010 in Chennai, Delhi, Mumbai." India Summary. http://www.indiasummary.com/tag/petrol-price-in-india/.

Kim, Dr. G. 2008. "SEOUL Challenges for Sustainable Transport." Presentation at a World Bank Consultancy Workshop for "2015 Beijing Transport Development Whitebook," Beijing, December.

Liu, Z. 2010. "Time to Fix Traffic in Beijing." *China Daily,* December 20, 2010.

Millard-Ball, A., and L. Schipper. 2010. "Are We Reaching Peak Travel? Trends in Passenger Transport in Eight Industrialized Countries." *Transport Reviews.* Published on November 18 (iFirst).

Ministry of Transport (MoT). 2008. *Medium and Long Term Plan for Energy Conservation in Road and Waterway Transport in China.* http://www.moc.gov.cn/zhuzhan/jiaotongguihua/guojiaguihua/quanguojiaotong_HYGH/200811/P020081104387326543461.doc.

Prud'homme, R., and P. Kopp. 2006. "The Stockholm Toll: An Economic Evaluation." Paper presented at the World Bank on September 7. World Bank, Washington, DC. http://siteresources.worldbank.org/INTTRANSPORT/Resources/336291-1153409213417/StckhlmCngstPrudhommepaper.pdf.

PRTM Management Consultants, Inc. 2011. "The China New Energy Vehicles Program: Challenges and Opportunities." Final report available at www.eaptransport.worldbank.org.

Singapore Land Transport Authority (LTA). 1996. "A World Class Land Transport System." White Paper, Republic of Singapore.

Spencer, A., and C. Sien. 1985. "National Policy Towards Cars: Singapore." *Transport Reviews* 5(4): 301–24.

Sustainable Urban Transport Project (SUTP). 2009. *2009 International Fuel Prices Report.* http://www.sutp.org/index.php?option=com_content&task=view&id=1895&lang=en.

Transport for London (TFL). 2003. *Congestion Charge Impacts Monitoring—First Annual Report.* http://www.tfl.gov.uk/assets/downloads/Impacts-monitoring-report1.pdf.

Weinberger, R., J. Kaehny, and M. Rufo. 2010. "U.S. Parking Policies: An Overview of Management Strategies." New York: Institute for Transportation and Development Policy (ITDP). http://www.itdp.org/documents/ITDP_US_Parking_Report.pdf.

Wikimedia Commons. 2011. http://commons.wikimedia.org.

PART 4

Sectoral Action for Low-Carbon Cities: Water, Waste Management, and Urban Air Pollution

CHAPTER 13

Municipal Solid Waste Management and Low-Carbon Cities in China

Dan Hoornweg and Jian Xie

Overview

Waste management is an important and rapidly growing source of greenhouse gas (GHG) emissions in China. Global estimates suggest that solid waste accounts for 5 to 10 percent of carbon emissions generated within a city boundary, and embodied emissions—or "up-stream" impacts—associated with solid waste are even more significant. This chapter focuses on municipal solid waste management and looks at possible solutions in the context of integrated solid waste management—a holistic approach that involves all key stakeholders and addresses all components of a waste management system, including institutional, financial, regulatory, social, and environmental aspects.

For city managers interested in a transition to a low-carbon environment, the solid waste sector is of particular interest because the emissions from this sector are usually within a city's control and are relatively easy to address. In fact, solid waste sector emissions are among the biggest sources of emissions under a city's direct control—up to 30 percent in some cases—and emissions can be addressed with well-established technical solutions that lend themselves to carbon finance. The impact of methane on GHG emissions is also much more short term than CO_2 and therefore warrants particular focus. The chapter argues that optimizing solid waste management provides multiple opportunities to minimize GHG emissions, and that part of the required investments in the sector could be funded through the use of carbon markets and emissions trading schemes, such as the one being developed in Rio de Janeiro[1] and now under discussion for piloting in China.

This chapter is based on the World Bank's experience in the solid waste sector in China and elsewhere, as well as on the results of a recent analysis of China's current waste sector practices that estimated waste quantities for national planning and resource allocation purposes, and provided general recommendations for the sector (Hoornweg 2005).

Key Challenge: Reducing Emissions and Effectively Managing a Growing Amount of Waste

One of China's current challenges is to effectively manage a growing amount of waste. Urbanization, urban population growth, and increasing affluence are all contributing to rapid increases in the size of China's total waste generation. In 2005, China generated about 200 million tonnes of municipal solid waste (MSW), and by 2030 this amount is projected to be at least 585 million tonnes.[2]

This unprecedented increase in waste generation is also adding a significant financial burden to cities' budgets. Based on current solid waste plans, China faces a potential 10-fold increase in its countrywide waste management budget by 2030, going from a currently estimated RMB 50 billion to about RMB 500 billion. In 2030, if China were to provide waste management services comparable to those in Organisation for Economic Co-operation and Development (OECD) countries, annual estimated costs would be approximately US$77 billion, of which half would be used for collection and half for disposal.[3]

This growing waste generation is not only leading to greater financial burdens, but also to increased GHG emissions and other environmental impacts. Badly managed solid waste is a source of contamination for groundwater and surface water, contributes to air pollution, and has an adverse impact on public health by attracting disease vectors such as rats and mosquitoes. Uncollected garbage is also a public nuisance and aesthetically unappealing.

Urban Municipal Solid Waste

Urban residents produce two to three times more waste than their rural counterparts (Hoornweg and Thomas 1999). In part, these higher waste generation rates for urban residents result from their urban economy, including commercial, industrial, and institutional activities, but urban dwellers also tend to have higher average incomes than rural residents, and thus higher consumption patterns. Figure 13.1 shows the projected MSW composition for urban areas in China in 2030. Box 13.1 describes how MSW—the focus of this chapter—is actually only a small part of the total amount of waste that is generated.

Figure 13.1   Projected MSW Composition in Urban Areas of China, 2030 (585 million tonnes)

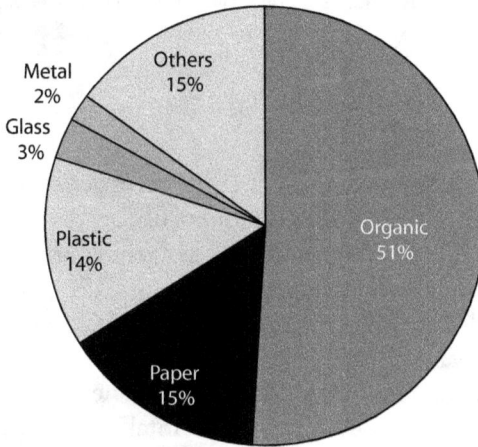

- Metal 2%
- Glass 3%
- Others 15%
- Plastic 14%
- Paper 15%
- Organic 51%

Source: World Bank 2005.

Box 13.1

Municipal Solid Waste Is Only a Small Part of the Total Generated Waste

Most MSW generation data for China are presented in three categories: municipal, industrial, and hazardous waste. "Municipal waste" usually includes residential, institutional, and commercial waste; waste from street cleaning; and nonprocess waste from industries. In some cases, construction and demolition waste is also included, which can dramatically skew the generation rate, especially in times of high economic growth and related construction activity. "Industrial waste" is usually limited to "process waste," including process byproducts like scrap metal, slag, and mine tailings. "Hazardous waste" usually refers to industrial hazardous waste

(continued next page)

Box 13.1 *(continued)*

generated as a byproduct of the manufacturing process, as well as medical waste; small-scale generation of hazardous waste from households, institutions and commercial establishments; and occasional small amounts of radioactive waste such as from smoke detectors and medical process waste. In 2002, over 1 billion tonnes of industrial waste were generated in China, which is more than five times the amount of municipal solid waste—and even this number is likely an underestimate. This industrial waste does not typically enter the municipal waste stream as industries are usually, under supervision by the Ministry of Environmental Protection, required to dispose of the waste themselves.

Source: Authors.

Emissions Associated with Current Disposal Practices

The growing amount of waste and in particular its disposal, both in landfills and through incineration, is a significant generator of GHG emissions. As in most countries, the majority of waste in China is disposed of at either a controlled dump or sanitary landfill.[4] The decomposition of the organic portion of solid waste at these locations produces landfill gas that typically consists of about 50 percent of methane, a GHG with a global warming potential 21 times that of CO_2. Total human-induced methane emissions represent about 15 percent of total GHG emissions. Worldwide, waste disposal accounts for more than 12 percent of anthropogenic methane, making it the fourth largest source of noncarbon dioxide GHGs.

With relatively simple measures, however, this landfill gas can be captured and combusted to neutralize the methane and reduce GHG emissions. China, in fact, has considerable experience with landfill gas recovery, and this process should be applied in all sanitary landfills. Landfill gas recovery can also be a major source of energy and, as such, might be eligible for Clean Development Mechanism (CDM) financing (see box 13.3).[5]

Incineration is the other common form of waste disposal. Overall GHG emissions are roughly the same as or even higher than for a sanitary landfill, but incinerators have significantly higher costs, generate pernicious air pollution, and can act as a disincentive to waste minimization. Furthermore, if China's current goal of increasing the share of waste incineration from 1 percent to 30 percent were achieved, this would likely at least double the global ambient levels of dioxin, a highly toxic, persistent organic pollutant.

Figure 13.2 illustrates the link between per capita waste generation and GHG emissions. As cities, similar to an ecosystem, have inputs, consumption, and outputs, high levels of solid waste are usually accompanied by high levels of GHG emissions and other pollutants. Controlling one output such as MSW will often result in additional benefits, such as a reduction in resource use and pollution.

Future Trends

Many of the current trends in China associated with waste generation and management mirror global trends. China's urban waste stream is undergoing a transition similar to those observed in other countries as they developed. For example, waste is increasingly put in containers for collection, which is important to reduce the addition of rainwater, reduce pests, and increase collection efficiencies. Waste volumes are also growing quicker than waste mass, as packaging materials make up a larger fraction of the waste stream. In addition, problematic waste items, such as batteries, electronic products, fluorescent light bulbs, and household hazardous waste, are having a growing and disproportionately large impact on waste management activities. Waste is becoming increasingly flammable, and fires in collection vehicles, transfer stations, and landfills are more common.

Figure 13.2   Per Capita Waste Generation Rate and GHG Emissions

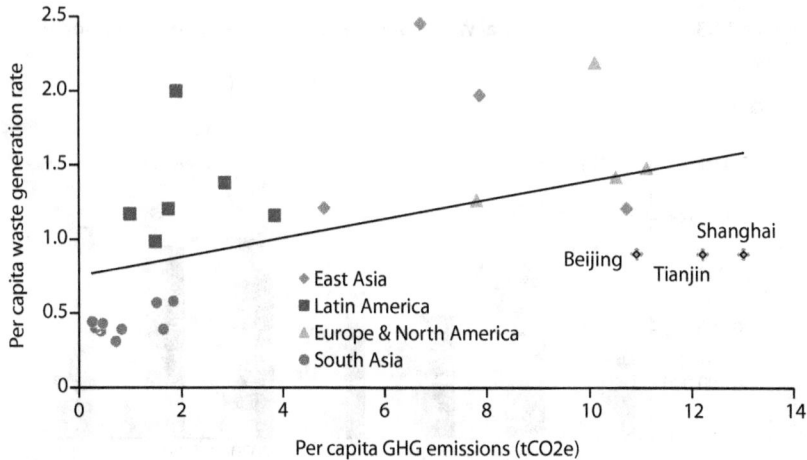

Source: Based on data from World Bank 2005.
Note: tCO$_2$e = tonnes of carbon dioxide equivalent.

While the quantity of waste will inevitably grow, various scenarios may unfold. Despite an inextricable link between GDP growth and a growth in per capita waste generation, significant variations are evident, which is illustrated by a comparison between Japan and the United States. Both countries have a similar per capita GDP, but Japan's per capita waste generation is only 1.1 kilograms per day, while each urban resident in the United States produces almost twice as much waste, 2.1 kilograms, per day. China appears to be following—and possibly surpassing—the path of the United States. Figure 13.3 illustrates the three proposed scenarios for waste generation in urban areas used in the World Bank (2005) study, assuming "low," "expected," and "high" volumes of waste. By 2030, the per capita waste generation for the three scenarios is 1.2 kilograms, 1.5 kilograms, and 1.8 kilograms per day, respectively. Over the last five years, China's rate of growth in MSW has been closest to the "high" scenario, and waste planners should anticipate a per capita waste generation rate of approximately 1.8–2.0 kilograms per day—among the highest in the world. Social attitudes and purchasing habits are considered to be the main reasons for this high rate.

Significant improvements have been made in China's waste management sector over the last 10 years; for example, the larger cities are aggressively moving toward sanitary landfilling as their main disposal option. However, the sector has been overwhelmed by the increase in waste generation. Cities have been unable to keep up with the growing

Figure 13.3   Projected Municipal Waste Generation for the Urban Population in China (in 2005)

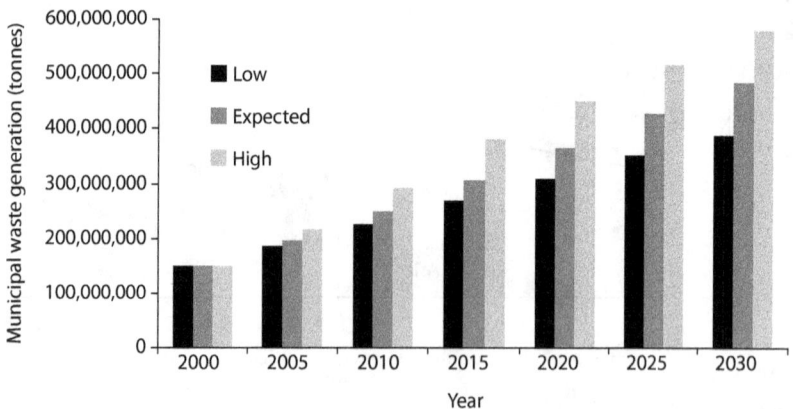

Source: World Bank 2005.

demand for waste service coverage or the environmental requirements for safe disposal systems. In addition, they are also behind in ensuring the cost effectiveness of service delivery. A lack of reliable data has further hindered effective decision making and service planning.

Way Forward—Integrated Solid Waste Management

This section presents the key characteristics of integrated solid waste management (ISWM), an approach that involves all key stakeholders in the planning of the elements of a waste management system—that is, from the point of waste generation to ultimate disposal, including waste reduction, recycling, reuse, and resource recovery. ISWM also addresses all aspects of a system, including institutional, financial, regulatory, social, and environmental (Van de Klundert and Anschütz 2001).

A key element of ISWM is also the "hierarchy of waste management," which means using an optimal combination of reducing, reusing, recycling, composting, and disposing (figure 13.4). This hierarchy implies that the best approach to waste management is to first reduce waste generation and separate recyclable materials (including organics for composting or anaerobic digestion) at the source to improve the quality of the materials for reuse. When waste cannot be reduced, materials should be reused, if possible. If not reduced or reused, materials can be recycled. If they cannot be recycled, they should be recovered, usually through bac-

Figure 13.4   The Waste Management Hierarchy

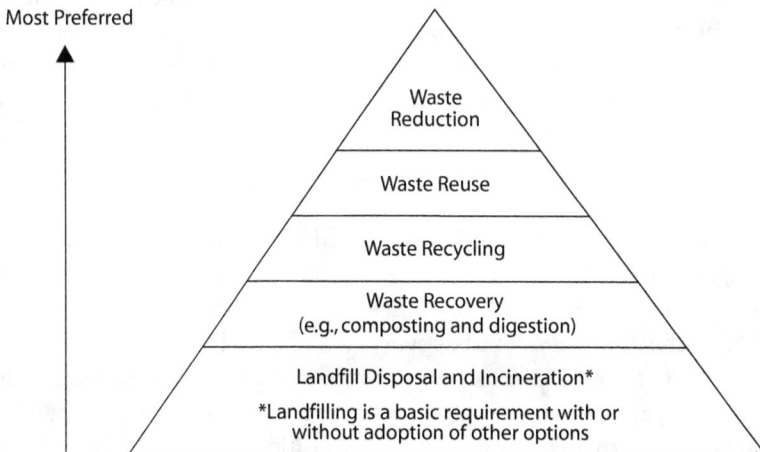

Source: World Bank 2005.

teriological decomposition. Using the waste hierarchy has multiple benefits: it reduces the amount of waste that needs to be transferred and disposed, extends the lifetime of landfills, reduces the need to extract non-renewable raw materials, generates materials for industry, reduces deforestation and GHG emissions, provides valuable resources (for example, methane gas and compost), increases employment and income, and also directly involves all waste generators in improving the environment through waste minimization and source segregation.

A successful ISWM program also typically makes use of a sanitary landfill, an up-to-date, publicly available waste management master plan, and optimized roles for recycling, composting, and possibly incineration, based on local conditions. In addition, the ISWM program will need a legal framework that ensures (i) cost recovery (fees based on waste amounts), (ii) appropriate incentives and penalties for compliance (for example, to discourage illegal waste disposal), and (iii) the application of market-based instruments. Finally, wide-scale public acceptance is essential, so that, for example, residents correctly prepare their waste for collection.

Well-designed ISWM programs are also pragmatic and recognize that there is no one single solution for the collection, transfer, treatment, or disposal of waste. Most cities, for example, benefit from having various types and sizes of collection equipment to accommodate neighborhood access and collection conditions. Having a mix of waste treatment systems can also optimize the recovery of resources based on market demand and allow a city to manage fluctuations in waste quantities and have built-in redundancy in emergency situations. A mix of public and private services to collect, transfer, and dispose of waste further enhances competition and cost effectiveness. ISWM planning also evaluates the overall system to determine the economic breakpoint for direct haul versus transfer and the number and location of key treatment and disposal facilities.

Optimizing ISWM to Minimize Carbon Emissions

While the most dramatic reduction in GHG emissions from the waste management sector depends on the way landfills are designed and operated and how methane emissions are mitigated, opportunities for minimizing carbon emissions exist at every step of a well-designed ISWM. Key components to minimize carbon emissions include waste minimization, waste segregation, composting, recycling, reducing the need for incineration, and properly managed landfills. In addition, ISWM is an ideal starting point for moving communities toward a "conserver ethic" or "circular economy" since the behavioral shifts (such as source separation and waste reduction) are generally widespread and relatively straightforward.

Waste Minimization

One of the most significant ISWM components to reduce emissions is waste minimization. Although Chinese cities may not be able to prevent the waste stream from growing, they can reduce the rate of growth by enacting effective waste minimization programs, which will reduce GHG emissions associated with waste disposal. Elements of a waste minimization program could include the following:

- *Introducing user charges:* User charges based on the amount of waste generated are a direct incentive for waste generators to reduce waste volumes and one of many possible market-based instruments to minimize waste and improve waste management. Because the introduction of disposal fees can lead to illegal dumping of waste, careful attention needs to be paid to the enforcement of illegal dumping laws.
- *Increasing awareness:* Increased awareness of solid waste–related issues can lead to process modifications, alternative disposal practices, and product changes. The government could take an active role in increasing overall public awareness of waste minimization, which could include the introduction of activities in school curricula, environmental education and awareness programs for adults, and programs that encourage a preference for products that generate less waste when making purchasing decisions.
- *Reusing products to reduce emissions from material extraction and consumption:* In some cases, waste minimization can also reduce GHG emissions from material extraction and consumption. The use of refillable beverage bottles, for example, reduces the need to dispose of bottles but also reduces the overall demand for bottles.

Waste Segregation

Waste segregation is a critical component of an integrated solid waste management strategy and the basis of any new or innovative waste management program. Although segregation brings slightly higher collection costs and requires compliance from waste generators, it significantly increases the potential to recycle waste, increases the quality of compost and recyclables, and optimizes incineration. Waste segregation usually involves requesting waste generators to separate their waste and place it out for collection in either two or three streams. Much of this segregation is already happening in China through the efforts of waste pickers.

However, as waste volumes continue to increase and disposal costs consume a larger fraction of municipal budgets, increased and more formal waste segregation will be required.

Recycling

Recycling reduces the level of GHG emissions associated with the extraction and production of goods. Less energy is usually required to recycle secondary materials such as glass, metals, plastics, and paper into new products than to make the same products from virgin raw materials. An indication of the potential importance of recycling in the reduction of GHG emissions is a recent CDM methodology (AMS-III.AJ) for the recycling of two categories of plastics—high-density polyethylene (HDPE) and low-density polyethylene (LDPE). Initially defined as a small-scale methodology by the developer, the World Bank, this methodology could be expanded to include other recyclables.

Recycling is driven by economics. Much of the waste stream can be recycled, including papers, plastics, glass, and metals, but each commodity has a market-based monetary value and it is the cost of sorting and transporting the recycled materials versus the value of the material as a feedstock in local industrial production that determines what is recycled. In addition, the feasibility of recycling is affected by avoided disposal charges. For example, every tonne of waste diverted from a landfill may save US$10 to US$25, and every tonne not incinerated may save US$50 to US$150.

China's current recycling rates are lower than those in most countries, stemming in part from the relatively low prices for secondary materials in China. Four factors contribute to this lack of attractiveness of the local secondary materials market in China:

- *Low local prices for recyclables and a lack of incentives for domestic producers to recycle:* The price for recyclables from the local waste stream is set in part by the domestic industrial market, which is currently mostly influenced by the prices of imported secondary materials. Domestic producers, such as paper mills, may have little interest in using locally sourced recycling materials, in part because of inconsistent enforcement of environmental regulations, which results in unreliable supply and material quality. While in other markets, such as the United States and Europe, regulations drive producers to more actively embrace recycling to reduce waste disposal costs, Chinese industries currently lack this incentive and their low interest in recycling and using recyclables translates to lower prices for those recyclers.

- *Thriving international market in secondary products:* At the same time, there exists a thriving and lucrative industry processing secondary materials waste (mainly paper, but also plastic and scrap metal) imported from the United States, Europe, and even lower-income countries such as India and Argentina where stricter environmental regulations and relatively low back-haul shipping rates make recycling cost effective locally. This import market sets the industry economics and reinforces the unattractiveness of the domestic waste market.
- *Relatively high domestic transportation costs:* The relative costs of domestic and international transportation mean that it can be cheaper to import and transport secondary materials by ship to a port city in China than to transport domestic materials by truck or rail to the same location.
- *Lack of industry capacity and market development:* Because of the current uncertainties around the quantities and types of secondary materials that will be provided by the municipal waste stream, industries in China have not yet developed the long-term capacity to use the materials, nor has a real long-term market been developed.

The prices for recyclables will likely change as the secondary materials industry matures, builds capacity to absorb these extra materials, and works with municipal governments to improve the overall quality of materials. Urban "mining" of materials will grow in importance—due to the size of China's domestic source of materials and the capacity to use these materials from both domestic and international sources, which will have global repercussions. Recycling programs that target a few key sectors, such as feedstock, paper, or scrap metal, could realize significant benefits:

- *Feedstock:* The use of recycled feedstock, rather than virgin resources, has large environmental benefits.
- *Paper:* Paper, because of its large and growing portion in China's waste stream and because of its relative high recyclability, should be a priority commodity for planners of recycling programs to address. If China were to set a modest target of 50 percent recycling of waste paper by 2030, over 38 million tonnes of waste paper could be diverted from disposal.
- *Scrap metal:* China's scrap metal generation will continue to grow rapidly, especially as larger waste items such as scrap cars are disposed.

Composting
Composting biodegradable organic matter will also be an important waste management tool. Even in 2030, when the waste stream will more

reflect a fully matured economy, China's urban waste stream will still contain over 50 percent biodegradable organic matter, compared to an estimated 60 percent today. Managing this biodegradable organic fraction of the waste stream is challenging, as it is both wet—well in excess of 50 percent moisture, which makes combustion impractical—and dense, which makes transportation more expensive. Biodegradable organic matter, however, is also one of the largest sources of anthropocentric greenhouse gas emissions, as well as the fraction of the waste stream that causes nuisances, such as odor and landfill leachate (high-strength liquids), and which attracts vectors like rats and flies (see also box 13.2).

Composting will eliminate all these problems, but it is particularly important in terms of reducing carbon emission and generating emission reductions. This is because composting avoids the formation of methane: the organic fraction aerobically biodegrades and no methane is generated. At current prices for internationally traded emission reductions, US$4.50 per tonne of emissions reductions under the CDM, composting could receive a subsidy of about US$12 per tonne. This is about 2.5 times the equivalent amount that would likely accrue from landfill gas recovery.

Minimizing the Need for Incineration

While incineration can be a possible component of an ISWM program in large cities where space for landfills may be limited or the siting of landfills outside of city jurisdictions may be politically difficult, overall it will be important to minimize the need for incineration. Incineration, or the

---

Box 13.2

Composting in Cairo

In 2009, the World Bank signed its first GHG emission reductions purchase agreement in the Arab Republic of Egypt, for an MSW composting project. The facility uses waste sorting to recover recyclables and aerobically compost organic waste, reducing the amount of methane and other GHGs emitted from the landfill site.

The facility is expected to receive about 1,100 tons of municipal waste per day, which would otherwise be deposited in a landfill. Under the agreement, the project developer, Egyptian Company for Solid Waste Utilization (ECARU), will sell 325,480 tCO_2e GHG emission reductions to the Carbon Fund for Europe, which is managed by the World Bank.

Source: World Bank project documents.

burning, of waste can significantly reduce the volume of parts of the waste stream and often provide sufficient heat to produce power, but also is characterized by very high costs and potentially toxic emissions. In addition, the availability of an incinerator can act as a disincentive to explore and implement other, more economically and environmentally sound, waste disposal options. Moreover, China's MSW is typically moist with high organic content and is difficult to incinerate. Most Chinese cities would have to use supplemental fuel to burn their solid waste, making incineration even more expensive.

Despite the high cost and other limitations, however, existing incentives are encouraging incineration and even run the risk of promoting excessive use of this technology. The government of China has issued a series of policies to encourage investment in incinerators. These incentives include a refund of the value added tax (VAT), prioritized commercial bank loans, a 2-percent state subsidy for loan interest, and a guaranteed subsidized price for purchase of electricity. These policies, however, are expensive and may encourage municipalities to develop more incineration capacity than is warranted.

Landfilling

Landfilling, already widely used in China, is a core element of a low-carbon ISWM program, as it is simple and inexpensive. Landfilling is always less expensive than composting, incineration, or anaerobic digestion, and these up-stream technologies also need to be carefully matched to the quality and quantity of the waste stream. However, unless landfill gas is correctly collected and combusted, a landfill can also be a significant source of GHG emissions due to the methane created from the decomposition of the organic fraction of the waste (see figures 13.5 and 13.6).

This methane, however, can be captured and combusted so that it is not emitted to the atmosphere. Under current international markets for GHG reduction (for example, the CDM that expires in 2012; see chapter 18 for more details on carbon markets), a project that collects and combusts methane from an MSW landfill, and that composts, or anaerobically digests waste, could receive payments from interested buyers for the amount of GHG not released to the atmosphere as a result of such an activity. In addition, when this methane is used to generate power such as electricity or vehicle or boiler fuel, more emission reductions can accrue from the avoided emissions of the alternative energy.

Significant scope exists to improve the quality of China's landfills. As of 2005, China's 660 cities had about 1,000 major landfills or controlled

Figure 13.5   Landfill Gas Processing Facility at the Tianjin Shuangkou Landfill

Source: Chuck Peterson.

Figure 13.6   Landfill Gas Piping on Top of the Tianjin Shuangkou Landfill

Source: World Bank.

dumps, and many of those landfills would benefit from increased oversight on operations. Specific issues that frequently need to be addressed include (i) the presence of waste pickers; (ii) inadequate slopes; (iii) overdesign and premature construction of subsequent phases (for example, synthetic liners that are exposed to the elements, thereby generating significant additional volumes of leachate); (iv) inadequate collection and treatment of leachate; (v) insufficient compaction and waste covering; and (vi) little, if any, landfill gas collection.

City managers and many municipal decision makers have a disproportionately negative view of landfilling, often perceiving it as a waste of scarce land. This attitude is often the result of the poor history of facility siting and operation and the lack of productive postclosure use of landfill sites. When developing new landfill sites, planners should anticipate its postclosure use, as closed landfills can constitute excellent green spaces and recreational spaces, such as golf courses, when adequately integrated with neighboring land uses.

The use of "controlled dumps"—legal dumping areas but with little or no control over the waste's impact on human health and the environment—will likely present a long-term liability for Chinese cities. In addition to the immediate problems of public health and nuisances, these dumps also create long-term problems, for example, because of their impact on groundwater. Over the next 50 years, China is likely to face enormous brownfield site cleanup costs. Chongqing, for example, has about 50 dump sites, of which at least 5 need urgent rehabilitation. Global experience argues strongly that China's current and new dump sites need to be operated in a manner that protects groundwater resources.

Using Carbon Markets to Support Financing Investments in Sustainable Solid Waste Management in China

The potential for packaging MSW projects in China to obtain carbon credits for reducing GHGs is significant. While major components such as CDM expire in 2012, new programs, such as city-based emissions trading systems, are under development.

The capture and combustion of landfill gas is likely the largest potential source of emission reductions from China's MSW programs. However, other large potential sources include composting, anaerobic digestion, and, to a lesser extent, vermicomposting (composting with worms). Municipalities could combine a range of technologies to raise carbon financing for projects that use solid waste. Table 13.1 summarizes indica-

Table 13.1   Estimated Savings in GHG Emissions for Various Waste Management Technologies (Compared with Landfilling with No Gas Recovery)

Waste management option	Baseline greenhouse gas emissions (tCO$_2$e/tonne of waste)	Greenhouse gas emissions (tCO$_2$e/tonne of waste)	Potential saving in greenhouse gas emissions (tCO$_2$e/tonne of waste)
Landfill with landfill gas flaring	2.46	0.74	1.72
Landfill with landfill gas utilization	2.46	0.68	1.78
Anaerobic digestion	3.54	−0.055	3.6
Composting and vermicomposting	3.54	0	3.54

Source: World Bank 2005.

tive values for various approaches of waste management and their potential savings in GHG emissions. Segregating waste at the source will contribute to significantly higher carbon emission reductions. Box 13.3 summarizes the experience of the Tianjin Shuangkou landfill, an important example of a CDM landfill project in China.

Box 13.3

Tianjin Shuangkou Landfill Gas Recovery and Electricity Generation

Every day, an estimated 4,800 tonnes of MSW (residential and commercial) are discarded in Tianjin. Construction of a new landfill, the Tianjin Shuangkou Landfill, began in 1999, and the site began receiving waste in 2001. The landfill site was financed by the World Bank, as part of a broader urban development and environment loan to Tianjin. Today, an average of about 1,000 tonnes of municipal waste is delivered to the landfill each day. The 60-hectare landfill has a design capacity of 7.4 million tonnes of waste, which means that at the current filling rate, the site has a useful lifetime of almost 17 years and will reach capacity in 2018.

The project includes the following components and characteristics:

(continued next page)

Box 13.3 *(continued)*

- *Landfill covering:* To collect more landfill gas, waste layers are covered with additional soil.
- *Gas collection system:* A total of 42 vertical gas-venting wells are installed at the site in the shape of a rectangle.
- *Gas pretreatment system:* Prior to electricity generation and flaring, the landfill is pretreated to remove its impurities and moisture and thus to prevent corrosion in the generators and flaring system.
- *Electricity generation and grid connection system:* The electricity generated with the landfill gas will be sold to the North China Power Grid. The electricity generators will be installed in different stages of the project.
- *Flaring system:* Landfill gas not used for electricity generation will be flared.
- *Financial performance:* The project entity, in June 2007, signed an Emission Reductions Purchase Agreement with the Spanish Carbon Fund managed by the World Bank for 635,000 Certified Emission Reductions over seven years. CDM revenue could improve the project's internal rate of return (IRR) from 5.87 to 15.23 percent.
- *Project progress on CDM:* Currently, the site has a 2.06 MW power generation capacity. It is projected that 3.09 MW of power generation capacity will be installed in the first crediting period (August 2008–August 2015) and an additional 1.25 MW in the second crediting period, reaching the total generation capacity of 4.34 MW.

Source: World Bank project documents (see also box 24.2).

Recommendations

As discussed in the previous sections, several urgent solid waste management issues exist in China. The following eight critical areas need attention:

- *Waste quantities:* China is currently experiencing a dramatic increase in waste generation. Furthermore, solid waste is dramatically changing in composition and waste reduction efforts are currently minimal.
- *Information availability:* A lack of reliable and consistent waste quantity and cost data makes planning for waste management strategies extremely difficult.

- *Decision-making process:* Sound decision making to ensure an optimal technology selection, private sector involvement, and cost recovery is hindered by a lack of consistent policy and strategic planning for these areas. In addition, there is inadequate public access and participation in the planning process.
- *Operations:* Facilities do not always meet design standards, particularly for pollution control. Many facility operations are deficient, and waste collection operations are often not optimized.
- *Financing:* Current cost recovery through user charges and tipping fees is inadequate to cover full costs.
- *Private sector involvement:* The government's goal of increased private sector participation in solid waste services is hindered by unclear and inconsistent "rules of engagement," nontransparent purchase practices, nonsustainable subsidies, inadequate municipal cash flows, unclear and inconsistent cost accounting practices, and an unclear regulatory framework.
- *Institutional arrangements:* The development of the sector is being hindered by inadequate decentralization of collection and transfer services; inadequate municipal capacity for technology planning and private sector involvement; inadequate clarity on mandates between government agencies—for example, between the Ministry of Housing and Urban-Rural Development (MoHURD) and the Ministry of Environmental Protection (MEP); and inadequate delineation between central and local government responsibilities.
- *Carbon finance:* Carbon finance is increasing in importance in the Chinese MSW sector. China's cities could generate significant carbon emissions reductions, which would be an important aspect of local and regional emissions trading systems.

Based on these issues and good practice examples identified in the chapter, a number of recommendations for solid waste management in China can be made:

- *Move up in the hierarchy of waste management:* China needs to move up in the hierarchy of waste management, achieving more waste reduction, reuse, recycling, and recovery (composting and digestion), and thus minimize the amount of waste that needs to be disposed.
- *Increase waste minimization:* Waste minimization should be a key priority for MSW planning in China. A particular focus is needed on the organic fraction of the waste stream, which will continue to be more

than 50 percent of the total waste stream for the foreseeable future, and on paper, which is likely the fastest growing component in the waste stream. Packaging waste should also be targeted, as it represents a large fraction of the increase in waste volume.

- *Develop an ISWM approach:* Develop and approach with the long-term objective of waste segregation.
- *Develop consistent national policies on MSW legislation:* These policies should encourage cross-jurisdiction and interagency coordination and facilitate implementation of economic instruments for improving waste management.
- *Establish targets:* Establish targets for per capita waste generation or waste reduction.
- *Consider institutional reforms to include market-based instruments and private sector involvement:* This should include issues of financing, based on a clear understanding of the actual costs of waste management.
- *Improve the recycling industry:* The industry could benefit from increased professionalism, improved product standards, market development, and better operating standards.
- *Develop product marketing for composting:* Composting may increase in importance, perhaps in part through the sale of carbon emission reductions, but product marketing of end products will require compost quality to be reviewed and marketing programs to be established.
- *Improve overall operations at landfills:* All landfills need urgent attention to improve overall operating conditions. Landfills need to be sloped to minimize leachate, developed in stages, and operated according to international standards for sanitary landfills. More attention should also be paid to the postclosure use of landfills.
- *Ensure new incinerators meet European or Japanese emission standards for dioxin and mercury:* New incinerators should also come with a sufficient level of operator training. In all cases, a complete and accurate cost-benefit analysis should be performed.
- *Focus on "special wastes":* Increased planning and service provision is needed for special wastes such as hazardous waste, demolition waste, medical waste, and disproportionately problematic wastes such as batteries, disposable diapers, single serving beverage containers, and newspapers.
- *Focus on brownfields:* The implications of brownfields, lands contaminated from inadequate disposal practices or from chemical spills, are poorly understood in China and in need of deeper review.

In moving forward with reforms in MSW management, a few cities can act as "pilot" or "model" cities to introduce replicable sustainable models. These pilots should aggressively pursue waste minimization strategies, generate credible and comprehensive waste management data (especially on costs and quantities), and serve as "centers of excellence" for waste management technologies, policies, and training in China. The pilots should also provide a venue to develop long-term management plans—that is, for the next 20 years.

Conclusion

As a result of years of rapid economic growth, China currently faces a serious challenge—a massive increase in the generation of MSW. Problems exist across a wide range of issues, including a lack of information, an inadequate decision-making process, poor operational standards, insufficient financing arrangements, and incomplete private sector involvement.

MSW management is an increasingly important component in ensuring the sustainability and low-carbon growth of China's cities, and there is a strong connection between sound solid waste management and achieving low-carbon results. The success with which China addresses this challenge will have long-term consequences for its environment, as well as any possible transition to low-carbon cities. Implementing improvements in the management of MSW will generate a number of co-benefits, such as reducing GHG emissions, generating carbon finance, and improving the overall livability and sustainability of China's cities.

Notes

1. See also chapters 24 and 25 for more details on carbon markets and the CDM process.

2. This projection is based on scenarios for "low," "expected," and "high" waste trends and volumes, as described in World Bank (2005). The high level is now the expected level for China.

3. These costs are based on an estimated 585,000,000 tonnes of waste per year in 2030 (Hoornweg 2005). Costs for collection and disposal can be calculated as follows: collection costs: 497,250,000 tonnes at US$80/tonne = US$39.8 billion (not including costs for the collection of recyclables); recycling costs: 15 percent of total waste at US$50/tonne = US$4.4 billion; costs for composting and digestion: 15 percent at US$75/tonne = US$6.6 billion; incinera-

tion costs: 15 percent at US$150/tonne = US$13.2 billion; and landfilling costs: 55 percent at US$40/tonne = US$12.9 billion.

4. A "controlled dump" includes control of site access (especially for waste pickers), record keeping, and regular covering of waste; a "landfill" typically includes enhanced site selection, daily covering of waste, and collection of leachate and landfill gas; and a "sanitary landfill" includes additional efforts on landfill gas collection and use (or flaring), as well as postclosure maintenance.

5. The first Global Environment Facility (GEF) project to pilot the collection and use of landfill gas was in China. The project tested three options for using methane: (i) combustion and conversion to electricity, (ii) gasification and use as an automotive fuel, and (iii) piping and use for heating in industrial facilities.

Bibliography

Hoornweg, D. 2005. "Waste Management in China: Issues and Recommendations." Working Paper No. 9. Infrastructure Department, East Asia and Pacific Region. World Bank, Washington, DC. http://siteresources.worldbank.org/INTEAPREGTOPURBDEV/Resources/China-Waste-Management1.pdf.

Hoornweg, D., and L. Thomas. 1999. "What a Waste: Solid Waste Management in Asia." World Bank, Washington, DC.

Van de Klundert, A., and J. Anschütz. 2001. "Integrated Sustainable Waste Management–the Concept. Tools for Decision-makers." Gouda, The Netherlands: WASTE. http://docs.watsan.net/Downloaded_Files/PDF/Klundert-2001-Integrated.pdf.

CHAPTER 14

Greenhouse Gas Emissions from Water and Wastewater Utilities

Alexander Danilenko, Takao Ikegami, Paul Kriss, Axel Baeumler, and Menahem Libhaber

Overview

This chapter summarizes the opportunities and options for reducing carbon and greenhouse gas (GHG) emissions in China's urban water and wastewater treatment sector. Although this sector is not a large contributor to GHG emissions, the chapter contends that the sector has the potential to significantly reduce energy consumption, in many cases by following well-established urban water and wastewater planning and management practices. The chapter also presents energy-saving options related to strategies that take urban expansion and integrated water management into consideration.

Introduction

The water and wastewater sector does not, at first glance, offer obvious opportunities to reduce a city's carbon footprint. Estimates suggest that even in 2020 this sector will be responsible for less than 50 million tonnes of CO_2 equivalent (tCO_2e) or about 0.66 percent of China's total (Leggett et al. 2008; see also box 14.1). Nonetheless, good reasons exist to focus on this sector:

Box 14.1

Estimates of Energy Use and Carbon Emissions in China's Municipal Water and Wastewater Sector

This table presents estimates for energy use and GHG emissions for water services within the next decade in China. The assumptions behind the estimates reflect the consensus forecast on urbanization and targets set by the 12th Five-Year Plan. The estimates also assume constant energy intensity.

	2010			2020 Forecast		
	Water	Wastewater	Total	Water	Wastewater	Total
Volume million cubic meters	50,697	37,400	—	67,964	50,137	—
Energy use *(GWh)*						
Energy use	25,349	15,708	41,057	33,982	25,069	59,051
Energy use with efficiency saving of 20% every five years	—	—	—	21,748	16,044	37,792
Carbon emissions *(million tonnes)*						
China emissions factor	20.03	12.41	32.43	26.85	19.80	46.65
United States emissions factor	14.20	8.80	22.99	19.03	14.04	33.07
China emissions factor with energy efficiency saving	—	—	—	17.18	12.67	29.86

Sources: Authors' estimate based on the World Bank/WSP Shandong (2010) water utilities benchmarking study; and International Energy Agency (2009) data on China's electricity emissions factor.
Assumptions: Average water consumption remains 165 liters per capita per day. Wastewater collection and treatment rate will increase to 90 percent and unaccounted for water will remain at the level of 22 percent on average. Current energy demand will stay the same for water and wastewater.

- *Rapid urbanization:* China's urban population is expected to increase from 690 million to 900–950 million by 2020. Inevitably, urbanization and rising income levels will lead to sharp increases in demand for water and wastewater treatment. While this will result in a higher demand for energy, significant potential exists to lessen that demand by influencing the pattern of urbanization in the coming decades.
- *Energy use for addressing water scarcity:* Some proposals to address water scarcity issues are potentially very energy intensive and need to be balanced with a significantly strengthened demand management regime.

- *Energy efficient wastewater treatment:* Multiple opportunities exist to improve the energy efficiency of wastewater treatment across China's cities, both in the construction of new facilities and in the operation of existing facilities. Improving the operation and performance of pumping, coupled with implementing appropriate sludge management schemes, can help reduce energy consumption and costs between 30 and 50 percent.
- *Overlap with established good practices:* There is considerable overlap between low-carbon solutions and established good practice in the water sector. Many of the actions that would create a lower carbon footprint are well understood and required for optimal functioning of the sector, independent of their carbon impact.

Issues and Opportunities for Low-Carbon Solutions in the Water Sector

Expanding Service with Urbanization: Integrated Approaches and Compact Growth

The pattern of urban spatial development significantly influences the energy intensity of water and wastewater treatment. During the last two decades, most new urban development has been greenfield development of formerly rural areas on the urban periphery. The resulting more dispersed pattern of urbanization with longer pipe networks to connect new developments has led to higher water pumping costs and increased energy demand for pumping longer distances and maintaining pressure in expanded water networks.

To reduce this energy demand, these greenfield sites could pilot the use of innovative low-energy water systems that integrate stormwater treatment, water supply, and wastewater treatment. These pilots could include household or community-level gray-water capturing and recycling systems; separating stormwater collection from wastewater and maximizing stormwater use; constructing wetlands; and developing small-scale wastewater treatment facilities that will generate energy for local use.

In general, an integrated and holistic approach to urban water system management is needed. Cities usually treat the challenges of providing sewage treatment, establishing flood protection along rivers, and extending wastewater collection and treatment to new developments as separate issues. In recent years, however—as interest in the concept of "eco-cities" has grown—examples of an integrated approach to urban water management have emerged. Box 14.2 provides an example of such an alternative,

Box 14.2

Philadelphia's "Green City, Clean Waters" Vision

The Philadelphia Water Department's "Green City, Clean Waters" vision is intended to unite the U.S. city of Philadelphia with its water environment, creating a green legacy for future generations while incorporating a balance between ecology, economics, and equity. This long-term goal for Philadelphia integrates combined sewer overflow (CSO) and water resources management into the socioeconomic fabric of Philadelphia by creating amenities for the people who live and work in the city. The vision includes:

- Large-scale implementation of green stormwater infrastructure to manage runoff at the source on public land and to reduce demands on sewer infrastructure.
- Requirements and incentives for green stormwater infrastructure to manage runoff at the source on private land and reduce demands on sewer infrastructure.
- A large-scale street tree program to improve appearance and manage stormwater at the source on city streets.
- Increased access to and improved recreational opportunities along green and attractive stream corridors and waterfronts.
- Preserved open space to manage stormwater at the source.
- Vacant and abandoned lands converted to open space or redeveloped responsibly.
- Restored streams with physical habitat enhancements that support healthy aquatic communities.
- Additional infrastructure-based controls, when necessary, to meet appropriate water quality.

The project is being implemented as follows:

- *First, low-cost actions:* Measures that can reduce CSO discharges and their effect on receiving waters do not require significant engineering studies or major construction and can be implemented in a relatively short time frame. Philadelphia started with a US$6.5 million project to upgrade its comprehensive system flow monitoring network.
- *Second, technology-based capital improvements:* The second phase focused on technology-based capital improvements to the Philadelphia sewerage sys-

(continued next page)

Box 14.2 *(continued)*

tem to further increase its ability to store and treat combined sewer flow, reduce inflow to the system, eliminate flooding due to system surcharging, decrease CSO volumes, and improve receiving water quality. This amounted to a
commitment of just under US$50 million.

- *Long term, watershed wide:* The long-term improvements will go throughout
  the watersheds, including identification of potential CSO controls, which would
  result in further improvements to water quality and, ultimately, the attainment
  of water quality standards.

All of these actions will reduce water pollution and focus on reduced energy
demand and overall reduction of the cost of water services in Philadelphia.

Source: Philadelphia Water Department 2009.

integrated vision. Small-scale pilot projects are or have been conducted at
Shanghai's Expo site, in Xian, and elsewhere, while large eco-city projects
like the Sino-Singapore Tianjin Eco-City also include integrated urban
water management in their design.

Water Supply: An Increasing Demand—A Shrinking Supply

A central question facing many Chinese cities is how to address the problem of water scarcity while living standards and consumption levels are
on the rise. The Ministry of Water Resources reported that annual
national water availability per capita in China is now 2,000 cubic meters,
which is one-quarter of the world's per capita average (Gleick 2011).
This annual availability is expected to drop to 1,700 cubic meters by
2030 (Anser Enterprises 2010) due to continued population growth.

In most of China, rainfall is distinctly seasonal, with 70 percent of the
rainfall occurring during the four summer months and with annual totals
higher in the south. Despite impressive investments in water supply and
wastewater treatment—as much as a trillion RMB (US$150 billion) in
2005–10 alone (World Bank 2008)—more than 400 of China's 657[1] cities already suffer from a water shortage problem, and more than 110
cities are experiencing severe water shortage.

In many cities with poor drinking water quality, households are already
incurring extra costs by having to install small-scale membrane filters in
their homes or buying bottled water. As demand grows, so does competi-

tion for fresh water, with industrial consumption of treated water continuing to be between 45 and 47 percent of the total country's water consumption. Furthermore, the central government tightened drinking water standards in 2006, which will require upgrading of most existing water treatment plants.

Parallel to the effort of raising drinking water quality is the problem that raw water sources are becoming more polluted. This issue is particularly severe in the north of China. Water-scarce cities often rely on groundwater, but pumping and treatment costs have risen due to declining water tables and groundwater quality. Pollution of groundwater is particularly disruptive since polluted groundwater aquifers require decades to recover. New types of pollutants such as medicines, micropollutants (for example, endocrine-disrupting compounds), and odor and taste pollutants (for example, 2-methylisoborneol, geosmin, arsenic, and cadmium) are now major concerns for drinking water in more developed urban centers in China.

To address this growing discrepancy between quality water supply and demand, several options exist. Each option has a different effect on overall energy consumption, and thus carbon emission intensity.

Supply-side options. Current options being considered to address the lack of available raw water for urban consumption focus primarily on enhancing the supply of water of an acceptable quality, for example, by transporting raw water over long distances or by using more intensive treatment methods. Some of these supply-side options, however, are very energy intensive.

A high-profile example of transporting high-quality raw water is Shanghai's effort to switch its water source from the city's Huangpu River—its current main water source—to an inflow point in the Yangtze estuary. Because this point is significantly farther from the city, using this cleaner water requires more pumping and thus more energy. An extreme example of transporting raw water for urban consumption is the South-North Water Diversion Project. This project, currently under implementation, transfers water from the Yangtze River in central China to Beijing, Tianjin, and other northern cities. Pumping the water alone will consume a significant amount of energy. Moreover, some observers expect the quality of the diverted water to be low and to require intensive treatment.

More sophisticated and higher levels of water treatment, requiring higher levels of energy consumption, are also becoming more common. This includes advanced energy-intensive treatment methods designed to remove some of the new kinds of pollutants; the treatment of wastewater to a standard where it can be used again for urban greening, industry, and ultimately drinking water; and desalination. A more energy efficient manner of ensuring a high-quality water supply would be to focus on protecting raw water sources. However, the required water catchment care protection is often difficult to implement in light of the complex multijurisdictional and institutional coordination challenges, not just in China but internationally.

Because of the high-energy consumption of most supply-side options under consideration, identifying alternatives to such solutions should be a priority. While some of the supply-side initiatives discussed above will be inevitable, balancing a supply-side approach with efforts to ensure that water, particularly drinking water, is properly used, valued, and not wasted, will yield significant benefits.

Strengthening demand management. Demand management can go beyond metering water consumption and using tariff corrections to also encourage the use of water-saving appliances and use public campaigns to strengthen water conservation. In the case of industrial users, apart from tariff corrections and metering, activities such as reduction of unaccounted water and optimizing pressure in water systems through hydraulic modeling, establishing pressure zones, and investing in supervisory control and data acquisition systems (SCADA) are now a norm for many utilities in Organisation for Economic Co-operation and Development (OECD) countries. Charging real production costs for water and wastewater, through tariffs, usually results in reduced consumption and at the same time generates financial sustainability. While water and wastewater tariffs in China have been increasing gradually in recent years (see box 14.3), tariff increases should be accelerated. In addition, increasing block tariffs (that is, increased unit rates charged to high-volume consumers) are not yet standard in China, and a more systematic application of such tariff policies could be a good first step for tariff demand-side management.

Wastewater Treatment and Sludge Disposal

The 11th Five-Year Plan (2006–10) contained ambitious targets to expand urban wastewater treatment, which have triggered a massive program of wastewater plant construction. A target of 70 percent coverage countrywide (from a capacity of 52 percent in 2006), with an even higher target of 80 percent in the largest cities, has resulted in the addition of more than 1,300 plants by 2010 with a further 770 plants under construction.

This rapid expansion of the sector is expected to continue. By 2015 it is estimated that 6,500 plants will be built as China expands wastewater

Box 14.3

The Shanghai Urban Environment Adaptable Program Loan, Phase 2

The Shanghai Urban Environment Adaptable Program Loan (APL) Phase 2 from the World Bank requires implementing agencies to recover costs as one of the key indicators of the project success. In Shanghai South Water Company (SWC), the tariff for nondomestic customers is currently RMB 2.00 per cubic meter (m^3), increased from the RMB 1.30 per cubic meter tariff set in November 2008 (table B14.3.1). The new water tariff for domestic customers is RMB 1.63 per cubic meter—approximately a 60 percent increase from the 2008 level.

Table B14.3.1   Water Tariff Levels for SWC

	Prior to 11/25/08	11/25/08	4/1/09	6/20/09	11/20/10
Industrial	1.30	1.50	2.00	2.00	2.00
Commercial/ Institutional	1.50	1.70	2.00	2.00	2.00
Domestic	1.03	1.03	1.03	1.33	1.63

Shanghai Municipal Sewerage Company (SMSC) increased the tariff for domestic customers from RMB 1.08 per cubic meter to RMB 1.33 per cubic meter on November 20, 2010, following the tariff increases in 2009 (table B14.3.2).

Table B14.3.2   Wastewater Tariff Levels for SMSC

	Prior to 9/20/08	9/20/08	4/1/09	6/20/09	11/20/10
Industrial	1.20	1.60	1.80	1.80	1.80
Commercial/ Institutional	1.10	1.50	1.70	1.70	1.70
Domestic	0.90	0.90	0.90	1.08	1.33

The tariff increase allows for both financial sustainability of the service providers and the proper use of water by different consumer groups, which adds to energy and water resource conservation.

Source: World Bank project documents.

treatment to all 657 cities and over 19,000 towns. Further, many existing plants are being expanded and are adding tertiary treatment to remove nutrients in order to comply with the more stringent effluent standards introduced in 2002. As this expansion proceeds, there is a benefit from focusing further on lower-energy use treatment methods—particularly anaerobic treatments and local decentralized treatments.

Increasing operational efficiency of treatment systems. Significant scope exists for increasing operational efficiency of wastewater treatment systems. In some cases municipalities have not adequately expanded collection networks to feed newly constructed plants, while other plants have remained idle or underused because local governments could not pay for their operating costs. While many of these initial issues have been or are currently being resolved, evidence suggests that significant opportunities still exist to increase the efficiency of operated wastewater plants, as the average efficiency level is just below 0.30 kilowatt hour per cubic meter, compared to 0.27 in the United States. Furthermore, pumping of wastewater requires significant amounts of energy and therefore needs to be optimized. Pumps need to be well maintained to reduce energy use. Generally, it is also preferable to use a range of pumps of different sizes or variable speed pumps to deal with flow fluctuations, rather than "over-pump" with a single large pump.

Opportunities to increase energy efficiency of aerobic wastewater treatment processes, particularly activated sludge treatment systems, also exist. Aerobic treatment processes require more energy and produce more carbon, but operate more quickly and require far less space and have therefore been widely used in urban areas in China. It is anticipated that more efficient equipment will soon become available for pumping, and good-quality instruments will assist with the correct implementation and monitoring of this equipment. Currently, however, poor understanding and monitoring of the activated sludge process lead to energy inefficiency and excess carbon production. A better-managed air injection process could potentially save significant energy in activated sludge treatment processes. In the longer term, replacing worn equipment with more flexible and energy efficient versions will enable lower carbon intensity. Box 14.4 summarizes the results of a 2001 evaluation of selected facilities in Hebei Province that identified the potential for a range of such operational improvements. A recent World Bank study estimated that potential energy savings of up to 30 percent might be achieved by optimizing operations in this manner.

Nontraditional, decentralized methods. As wastewater treatment expands to peri-urban areas, nontraditional decentralized treatment methods should be considered, as the cost of operating traditional plants will likely be high for these areas. Some Asian cities (such as Hanoi,

---

Box 14.4

Hebei Water and Wastewater Energy Efficiency Study, 2002–03

In 2001, the World Bank undertook an energy efficiency evaluation of the operation of selected water supply and wastewater treatment facilities in Hebei Province. The team worked with Beijiao Water Treatment Plant (WTP), Tangshan Running Water Company, Xijiao No. 1 Wastewater Treatment Plant (WWTP), Xinqu WWTP in Tangshan, and Qiaoxi WWTP in Shijiazhuang. The team also conducted a special study of the sludge digestion and methane recovery system at Qiaoxi WWTP and recommended the following:

- *Beijiao WTP:* Modify the backwashing process to achieve water and energy savings.
- *Tangshan Running Water Company:* Replace a number of pump/motor sets with high-efficiency units, and make improvements to the control of the pumps through the fitting of variable speed drives (VSD).
- *Xijiao No. 1 WWTP:* Convert the two coarse-bubble biological tanks to tapered fine-bubble systems, and improve the air supply system efficiency through the use of variable-speed, positive-displacement blower/motor sets. Replace the inlet effluent pumps and sludge recirculating pumps with high-efficiency units.
- *Xinqu WWTP:* Convert the single coarse-bubble biological tank to tapered fine-bubble systems, and improve the air supply system efficiency through the use of variable-speed, positive-displacement blower/motor sets. Replace the inlet effluent pumps with high-efficiency units.
- *Qiaoxi WWTP sludge digester:* Refurbish the sludge digestion unit to make it fully operational and provide training for the management and staff operating the sludge treatment plant.

Table B14.4.1 summarizes the benefits of the investment program in terms of energy savings and energy cost. The recommendations were successfully implemented between 2003 and 2007.

(continued next page)

Box 14.4 *(continued)*

Table B14.4.1   Aggregate Benefits of Recommended Investments

Project	Total investment RMB (US$)	Water savings m³/year	Water savings RMB (US$)	Energy savings kWh/year	Energy savings RMB (US$)	Payback	Financial internal rate of return (%)
Beijiao WTP	13,000,000 (1,571,946)	1,825,000	2,792,250 (337,636)	24,820	12,012 (1,452)	4.2	29.04
Tangshan Running Water Company	7,384,000 (892,865)	—	—	2,592,208	1,244,627 (150,499)	5.9	18.29
Xijiao No. 1 WWTP	2,616,713 (316,410)	—	—	1,466,091	835,718 (101,054)	3.1	38.38
Xinqu WWTP	1,158,240 (15,694)	—	—	1,227,787	699,838 (84,623)	1.7	87.50
Qiaoxi WWTP	4,135,950 (500,114)	—	—	2,000,000	1,000,000 (120,918)	4.2	27.35
Total	28,294,903 (3,421,389)	1,825,000	2,792,250 (337,635)	7,310,906	3,792,195 (458,548)	4.3	—

Source: World Bank 2006.

Vietnam, and Jakarta, Indonesia) are already selectively testing decentralized wastewater collection and treatment systems that require significantly less pumping and energy and have lower costs. This approach is also being tested in Kunming.

Anaerobic treatment. More consideration of anaerobic treatments is needed, particularly in smaller cities and towns. All wastewater treatment plants produce GHG, using electricity in the process, but anaerobic processes require less equipment and energy and produce less carbon compared to the more commonly used aerobic processes (see box 14.5). Indeed, with an anaerobic process, it is possible to largely eliminate any net energy input to the process, and thereby avoid the emissions of GHG from the use of fossil fuels. However, anaerobic treatment solutions require more space and take longer to produce good-quality effluent. Given the range of city sizes and the scale and varying topography of China, it would be useful to identify locations where these alternative, anaerobic technologies could be introduced, without compromising the quantity and quality of water and wastewater effluent. In many cases alternative decentralized anaerobic treatment options provide relevant and lower cost solutions. The implementation of these solutions, however,

---

Box 14.5

Sludge Treatment Options

The treatment and disposal of wastewater sludge is a global, environmentally challenging, and sensitive issue. This problem is continuing to grow because sludge production will increase as new sewage treatment works are built and as environmental quality standards become more stringent. It is generally accepted that sludge treatment and disposal account for about half of the total costs of sewage treatment and disposal. This makes sludge management very expensive as the volume of wet sludge accounts for less than 1 percent of sewage. In addition, the treatment of sludge is limited to a small number of options including composting, biological, and thermo conversion. Significantly, each of these options has substantial negative sides:

- Composting requires a substantial amount of space, advanced management of the landfill, and leachate control.

(continued next page)

Box 14.5 *(continued)*

- Biological treatment, or digestion, is a technically challenging issue:
  - Aerobic digestion requires large amounts of electricity.
  - Anaerobic digestion, despite reducing the amount of carbon by 50–70 percent, still results in sludge that contains a substantial amount of carbon and can generate fugitive methane if transferred to a landfill.
- Thermo conversion, while removing all carbon and also being carbon neutral, still produces dry solids which remain as ash. This ash is usually considered hazardous waste as it contains heavy metals. However, there are significant and tested opportunities for utilizing ash for construction materials, specifically when sludge is used as a fuel for cement production and ash becomes an integral part of the final product.

Engineering solutions, while bringing substantial GHG reduction from wastewater sludge treatment, can be either costly or hard to operate unless all conditions for the wastewater sludge quality are met. The appropriate choice needs to be found for each case based on comprehensive cost-benefit assessments.

Source: Authors, based on Metcalf and Eddy 2003.

is currently restricted by the high technical standards for design that are applied in China.

Sludge disposal. Increased wastewater treatment has created the challenge of treating and disposing of a growing amount of sludge. A key challenge is that current sludge disposal methods tend to be energy intensive and costly. Key issues include:

- *GHG emissions from uncontrolled sludge are significant.* Since 2000, it has been legally prohibited to dump untreated wastewater and wastewater sludge into water courses. Significant amounts of generated wastewater sludge remain unprocessed and are stored in drying beds where they produce fugitive methane. In China, GHG emissions from uncontrolled sludge management are equivalent to 11 million tCO_2e per year.
- *Potential exists to generate energy from sludge.* While some treated sludge can be applied to agricultural land, the remainder must be sent to landfills or incinerated. Excess heat from the incineration and gases from sludge digestion processes, however, can be used to generate electricity, helping to reduce the overall carbon balance of the sector and control

the fugitive methane. Several developed countries already utilize the heat generated from sludge digestion, although sludge must be dewatered before it can be burnt, which itself is an energy-intensive process, and sludge digestion is relatively expensive and economical only when government subsidies are included. It is expected, however, that over the next few years sludge digestion practices will expand, and box 14.6 describes a global good practice model in this context. Several Chinese companies and academic institutions are also already engaged in research and pilot projects to generate energy from sludge, and the Beijing Drainage Group has a pilot project at a wastewater treatment plant that generates 866,000 tonnes of sludge per year. This project experiments with drying the sludge with lime before incineration. Signifi-

Box 14.6

Singapore CDM Sludge Disposal Proposal, 2007

Singapore is seeking a low-carbon alternative to the current ultimate disposal route for treated sludge from six of its wastewater treatment plants. Presently the treated sludge (digested and dewatered anaerobically for energy recovery) from aerobic sewage treatment is disposed in a landfill after being mixed with soil. The sludge remains in an anaerobic condition in the landfill; however, methane is produced from the site.

The option proposed is to dehydrate and incinerate the sludge, reusing the heat produced in combustion for dehydration. This will reduce the volume of sludge dramatically and result in the production of an ash with no methane production potential. The exhaust gases will be treated to remove odor before being released to the atmosphere.

Incineration is CO_2 neutral and thus can contribute to CO_2 emissions reduction when energy is recovered and used (for example, for drying sludge). This would, in turn, create the external benefit of a reduction in the quantity of fossil fuel that would be burnt and, as such, would correspond to a net reduction of CO_2 emissions for this process. Also, sludge incineration, if properly designed, bypasses the formation of the potentially fugitive methane of both processes: aerobic diges-

(continued next page)

Box 14.6 *(continued)*

tion and burying wastewater sludge after anaerobic digestion. The unwanted emissions from wastewater sludge incineration can be controlled by closed or semiclosed loop heat exchangers with special scrubbers that can fully absorb dioxins and heavy metals and prevent them from escaping into the atmosphere.

Over a 10-year period the potential GHG reduction is 54,000 tCO_2e per year with an internal rate of return of 7.9 percent. Table B14.6.1 shows the reduction in CO_2e emissions, if the potential GHG reduction estimated for Singapore is applied to the 10 most populous cities in China on a pro rata population basis and with a correction factor of 0.5 to allow for differences between Singapore and China.

Table B14.6.1   Annual Reduction in Emissions, tCO_2e

City	Estimated annual reduction, tCO_2e
Shanghai	125,000
Beijing	94,000
Tianjin	77,000
Hangzhou	48,000
Hong Kong SAR	46,000
Shenyang	43,000
Changchun	42,000
Harbin	41,000
Chengdu	40,000
Guangzhou	39,000
TOTAL	595,000

Source: Authors.

cantly, projects like this might be eligible to generate carbon credits under the Clean Development Mechanism (CDM) (see also chapter 24 for more information on the CDM). A similar project of a lower scale is under implementation in Shanghai as a part of the World Bank–funded Urban Environmental APL2 Loan (see also box 14.3).

- *Transport and processing of sludge is energy intensive.* Energy is also used in thickening and transporting sludge, so processing sludge should be carefully controlled and transport distances minimized.

The Way Forward

The continuing capacity expansion in the water and wastewater sector combined with the wide range of low-carbon technical options makes this a particularly interesting sector for realizing low-carbon growth, despite its small overall contribution of GHG emissions. Furthermore, the fact that this sector still receives concessional financing from Chinese national and international sources provides an opportunity to develop an incentive program that highlights, promotes, and disseminates good experiences. This section briefly summarizes a plan of action to maximize the dissemination and implementation of good practices during the next years.

Monitoring and Carbon Accounting

Monitoring is key to any effective policy implementation and funds allocation. Programs to audit and benchmark the performance of different sectors of the urban water cycle need to be introduced quickly, especially in view of the current rapid expansion of this sector. It is important to review guidelines for upgrading and developing water and wastewater infrastructure to ensure that optimizing energy use is a key design consideration. Additional studies are needed to verify and establish efficiency levels of water and wastewater infrastructure equipment. This could be assisted by process modeling and monitoring the state of particular equipment.

In addition, the implementation of carbon accounting by Chinese water utilities should be encouraged. Carbon accounting methodologies are already in use in various parts of the world specifically for water utilities; however, their use in China is limited to a few of the largest cities. Benchmarking based on carbon accounting should help in the identification of good practice. Therefore, the two important activities that need to be considered are (i) ensuring that the equipment used is modern and in good condition and (ii) controlling the treatment process efficiently by process modeling, monitoring, and using knowledgeable, trained personnel. Box 14.7 provides an example of a good Chinese practice in this regard.

Conserving Energy in Operations and Expansions

The previous sections have discussed a wide range of technical options that can be implemented to minimize energy use and carbon production in urban water and wastewater treatment, and in distribution and collection at both operational and capital investment levels. Most of the options, if not all, are well-established good practices. However, the climate change agenda and the desire to reduce GHG emissions from the

Box 14.7

Shandong Experience

Since 2005, Shandong Provincial Water Association (SWA) has conducted annual data collection and an indicator assessment of provincial water utilities using the International Benchmarking Network (IBNET) toolkit. The performance analysis based on this assessment helps SWA to identify the needs of every company member related to performance improvements, including investment programs, technical assistance, and training of personnel.

Benchmarking has brought accountability of Shandong water utilities to the attention of SWA and its consumers. Benchmarking now has become a routine exercise and a platform for provincial utilities to share ideas as well as develop strategies and investment programs.

In 2010, SWA added energy consumption indicators for each of the utility processes in order to allow the assessment of both energy demand and costs and then help in the preparation of individual strategies for utility members targeting cost reduction and energy conservation.

Source: World Bank/WSP Shandong (2010).

urban water sector create an urgency to reintroduce these simple recommendations into the standard practices of all water companies. Box 14.8 summarizes possible action areas from water intake to wastewater sludge disposal.

Training and Audit for Utility Staff

It could be useful to develop a series of staff training courses focused on energy efficiency issues. Basic topics could be incorporated into core training programs, and more specialized courses could be developed for staff particularly interested in energy efficiency. The training program would need to encourage personnel to learn options for energy efficiency and GHG emission reductions and enable them to implement those options in their daily operations. Equally important, such a program would also benefit from energy efficiency audits, as they would reduce wasted energy and develop strategic approaches for energy conservation. Energy efficiency surveys could also help in understanding local and regional patterns in energy consumption and help to develop local goals for energy conservation.

Box 14.8

Key Action Areas for Water Companies

Urban expansion

- Consider compact development patterns to minimize infrastructure needs and pumping costs.
- Seek holistic, integrated approaches to flood protection, natural wastewater purification, and expansion of wastewater provision using natural systems such as constructed wetlands.

Water treatment

- Reevaluate raw water intake strategies and advanced water treatment methods in view of the energy use implications.
- Enhance demand management.
- Optimize pumps and other equipment in water treatment plants.

Wastewater treatment

- Consider decentralized methods as coverage is being expanded to peri-urban areas.
- Consider more use of anaerobic treatments, particularly in smaller cities and towns as coverage is expanded.
- Focus on improving operational efficiency of aerobic plant operations, including air injection processes and equipment.
- Minimize GHG emissions from sludge disposal.

Source: Authors.

Conclusion

This chapter summarizes the opportunities and options for reducing carbon and GHG emissions in three main areas in China's urban water and wastewater treatment sector. First, promoting compact urban growth and piloting integrated water management approaches can significantly lower the carbon footprint of China's water sector. Second, in terms of water treatment, energy-intensive supply-side measures, such as water transfer schemes, need to be balanced with an increased use of demand management measures. Third, in terms of wastewater treatment and sludge disposal, full consideration should be given to nontraditional decentralized treatment methods wherever appropriate, while GHG emissions from sludge need to be minimized, for example, through capturing energy generated by sludge digestion. Overall, though the water and wastewater sector is not a large contributor to GHG, it has the potential to produce savings by introducing a number of well-established good practice water management measures.

Notes

1. In 2010, China had 657 cities (Ministry of Civil Affairs).

Bibliography

Anser Enterprises Corporation, Canada. 2010. Accessed through http://water.infomine-china.com.

British Standards Institution (BSI). 2008. *Drain and Sewer Systems Outside Buildings.* BS EN 752 2008. http://www.bsigroup.com/.

Dimitriou, M. 2007. "Water and Energy: The Challenge We Are Meeting." *WaterWorld.* March 2007. Tulsa, OK: PennWell Corporation.

Gleick, P. 2011. "China and Water." In *The World's Water 2008–2009, Vol. 7,* P. Gleick et al. Pacific Institute. http://www.worldwater.org/data.html.

International Energy Agency (IEA). 2009. "CO_2 Emissions from Fuel Combustion. Highlights." Paris: IEA. http://www.iea.org/co2highlights/co2highlights.pdf.

Jensen, O., and F. Blanc-Brude. 2008. "Wastewater Sector Performance in China." Paper presented at the Wastewater Asia Summit, April 16, Shanghai, China.

Leggett, J., J. Logan, and A. Mackey. 2008. *China's Greenhouse Gas Emissions and Mitigation Policies.* Congressional Research Service report to the U.S. Congress, No. RL34659 September 10, 2008. Oakland, CA: Pacific Institute.

Means, E. III. 2004. *Water and Wastewater Industry Energy Efficiency: A Research Roadmap.* Denver, CO: Awwa Research Foundation.

Metcalf and Eddy. 2003. *Wastewater Engineering, Treatment and Reuse.* New York: McGraw-Hill.

Ministry of Civil Affairs. 2010. Social Services Development Statistical Report 2010. http://www.gov.cn/gzdt/2011-06/16/content_1885931.htm. Beijing, China.

Philadelphia Water Department. 2009. *Green City Clean Waters: The City of Philadelphia's Program for Combined Sewer Overflow Control: A Long Term Control Plan Update.* September 1, 2009. Philadelphia, PA: Philadelphia Water Department.

Quantum Consulting Inc. and Adolfson Associates. 2001. *Pacific Northwest Water and Wastewater Market Assessment.* Market Research Report #01-079. May. Portland, Oregon: Northwest Energy Efficiency Alliance.

Stephenson, T. 2009. "Municipal Sewage Treatment in 2050." Presented at The Carbon Impact of the Water Supply, Use and Treatment; Future Plans, Environment Agency Workshop on May 28. Cranfield University, Cranfield, UK.

UK Water Industry Research (UKWIR). *Carbon Accounting in the UK Water Industry: Guidelines for Dealing with Embodied Carbon and Whole Life Costing.* UKWIR Report Ref No. 08/CL/01/6.

World Bank. 2006. "Hebei Water and Wastewater Energy Efficiency Study 2002–03." World Bank, Washington, DC. http://siteresources.worldbank.org/ EXTEAPASTAE/Resources/2822887-1163788250255/China_EE_for_ Wastewater_Hebei.doc

———. 2008. *Implementation Completion and Results Report. Hebei Urban Environment Project.* World Bank Report (IBRD-45690 TF-26661) December 2008. Washington, DC: World Bank.

World Bank/WSP Shandong. 2010. "Water Utilities Benchmarking Study." World Bank, Washington, DC.

Worldwatch Institute. http://www.worldwatch.org/.

CHAPTER 15

Air Pollution Control and Carbon Reduction Co-benefits

Jostein Nygard, Jie Cao, Stefan Csordas,
Steinar Larssen, Li Liu, Jon Strand,
and Dingsheng Zhang

Overview

Climate change and air quality are closely linked. The combustion of fuels leads to emissions of carbon dioxide (CO_2), black carbon, methane, and nitrogen oxides (NOx)—all global pollutants. At the same time, this combustion also causes emissions of conventional air pollutants such as particulate matter (PM), carbon monoxide (CO), volatile organic compounds (VOC), and sulfur dioxide (SO_2), along with NOx; and some of these compounds react to create secondary pollutants, such as ozone. Therefore, most low-carbon strategies in the power and transport sector, either increasing energy efficiency or switching to renewable technologies, will also reduce emissions of air pollutants, including ozone precursors and black carbon.

This chapter reviews the recent progress made by Chinese cities to control air pollution and finds that despite considerable progress, much remains to be done to lower pollution. The chapter then examines the potential to integrate air pollution with climate change mitigation policies and programs. In the fast-growing cities of China, the rapid expansion of the vehicle fleet, as well as local energy- and heat-generation systems, provides an opportunity to address air pollution and climate change challenges simultaneously. This chapter assesses the overlap between both agendas and the potential to maximize co-benefits generated. It concludes by providing specific experiences of air quality improvement programs that can at the same time have global benefits for climate change mitigation.

Air Pollution in China: Current Status and Challenges

While air pollution is an enormous challenge in most Chinese cities, figure 15.1 illustrates the significant progress that has been achieved over the last decade. The figure tracks for the period 2000 to 2009 the number of cities classified in the different air quality categories established by the Ministry of Environmental Protection (MEP). Among the 612 Chinese cities that have established air monitoring networks by 2009, about 85 percent met the national ambient air quality minimum standards (Class 1 and 2) up from only 30 percent in 2000. About 107 cities, or 16 percent, are still classified as Class 3 air quality cities with higher levels of PM_{10} (that is, particles between 2.5 and 10 micrometers) and/or SO_2. A

Figure 15.1 PM_{10} Annual Average Concentrations for All Monitored Cities in China (2001–09)

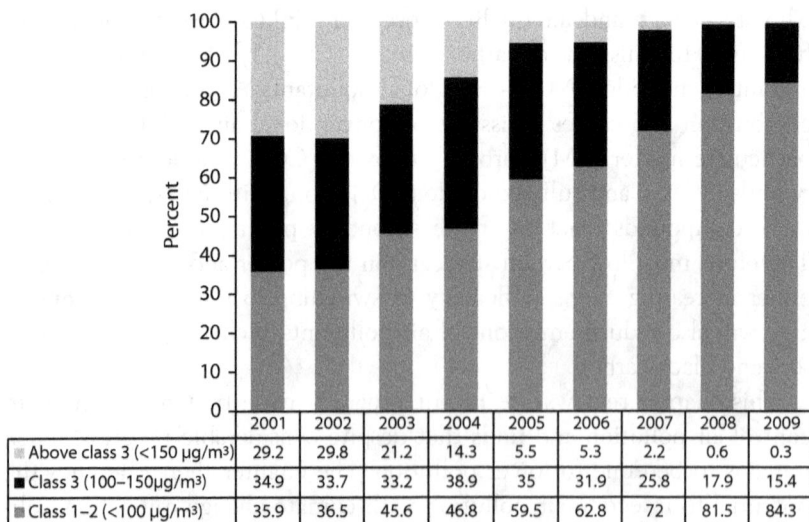

	2001	2002	2003	2004	2005	2006	2007	2008	2009
Above class 3 (<150 μg/m³)	29.2	29.8	21.2	14.3	5.5	5.3	2.2	0.6	0.3
Class 3 (100–150μg/m³)	34.9	33.7	33.2	38.9	35	31.9	25.8	17.9	15.4
Class 1–2 (<100 μg/m³)	35.9	36.5	45.6	46.8	59.5	62.8	72	81.5	84.3

Source: World Bank and MEP 2011a.

small set of cities, less than one percent of the total, do not reach even the minimal Class 3 level. At present, high annual PM_{10} concentrations are more frequent than high SO_2 concentrations and are the main reason why many Chinese cities are not reaching Class 2 or better (see also box 15.1).

It is important to note that significant additional effort is needed for Chinese cities to comply with global air quality standards. The Chinese Class 2 PM_{10} standard of 100 micrograms per cubic meter ($100\mu g/m^3$) is 2.5 times higher (that is, the standard is less stringent) than the European standard ($40\mu g/m^3$) and as much as 5 times higher than the recommended World Health Organization (WHO) standard ($20\mu g/m^3$) for PM_{10} pollution. In 2009, only 42 out of 612 Chinese cities met the Chinese Class 1 limit for PM_{10}, which is the same as the European standard. Less than one percent of the 500 largest cities in China would reach the recommended WHO standard today. As a comparison, China's average level of PM_{10} pollution today is still higher than the levels faced by many U.S. and European cities in the 1960s and 1970s.

Box 15.1

Sources of Sulfur Dioxide and Particulate Matter

In general, SO_2 sources are easier to identify than sources of PM. This is partially why control programs for SO_2 were developed about 15 years before PM control programs, which are just starting now as the implementation of the 12th Five-Year Plan unfolds (World Bank and MEP 2011a). The main sources of SO_2 are power plants, which contribute as much as 60 percent of total SO_2 emissions, with much of the rest coming from industry. Uncontrolled boilers and small-scale coal combustion for domestic heating, sources with a low emission height, are often also significant sources of SO_2. Emissions from power plants in particular are falling rapidly through the application of flue-gas desulfurization technology.

The source structure from PM is more complex. In general, the main sources include dust (generally in three forms—soil, roads, and construction); coal combustion (particularly, when considering ground-level concentration contributions, through small-scale domestic heating and uncontrolled heat-only boilers and some power plants); biomass burning; industry; vehicles; and PM in the form of sulfate and nitrate from SO_2, NOx, and ammonia (NH_3) (the sulfates and nitrates

(continued next page)

Box 15.1 (*continued*)

are called "secondary" PM). Many of these sources are also important contributors of GHGs in cities.

In the case of PM_{10}, analysis of data from 30 Chinese cities (World Bank 2010) suggests that dust contributes between 30–60 percent (of which cement and construction dust is about 5–30 percent); coal combustion between 15–30 percent on an annual average (although coal combustion can be substantively higher during the winter); biomass burning 10 percent; industry about 20 percent; vehicle exhausts about 10 percent; and combined secondary PM from sulfate and nitrate between 20 and 40 percent.

In the case of $PM_{2.5}$ (particulates 2.5 microns in diameter and smaller), the main difference from PM_{10} is that the dust content is much less important for the finer $PM_{2.5}$, while the relative contribution of coal combustion, biomass burning, industrial emissions, vehicle exhausts, and secondary PM are all higher. The linkage between $PM_{2.5}$ and GHG emissions is higher than for PM_{10}.

An even finer particulate than $PM_{2.5}$ is black carbon. It is formed through an incomplete combustion of fossil fuels, biofuels, and biomass, and is critical for both human health and climate change. The emissions that create black carbon come from a wide range of sources, including energy consumption, diesel-powered vehicles, industrial processes, and construction activities. There is much less information available about black carbon in Chinese cities and this is an area that requires further research and analysis. A preliminary analysis of the sources in China for black carbon in 2005 estimated that residential biofuel contributed about 40 percent, industrial processes 30 percent, industrial boilers 10 percent, and residential coal about 7 percent. In cities, the residential biomass contribution to black carbon would be smaller.

Source: Authors.

Moreover, these data may understate the actual situation since they do not reflect trends and concentrations of $PM_{2.5}$, the single most damaging pollutant to public health, which is not yet systematically monitored in China. $PM_{2.5}$ are the finest particulates, smaller than 2.5 microns in diameter, that penetrate deeper into lungs than typical dust or soot. While about 94 percent of China's 657 cities have established monitoring networks for air pollution in general, no city has yet established such a network or reporting responsibilities for $PM_{2.5}$. However, substantive $PM_{2.5}$

monitoring and analyses has been undertaken in some cities, and this monitoring indicates that fine particles levels significantly exceed levels allowable in countries where such standards do exist. Figure 15.2 shows data from 13 monitoring points in 7 cities that show that $PM_{2.5}$ levels exceeded a concentration of 35 μg/m³ between 50 to 90 percent and a rate of 75 μg/m³ between 10 to 45 percent of the time. These reflect annual averages that are significantly higher than annual standards set by the U.S. Environmental Protection Agency (USEPA) of 15 μg/m³. Other data indicate that annual $PM_{2.5}$ concentrations reach 80-100 μg/m³ in northern China (for example Beijing and surrounding provinces) and up to 40–70 μg/m³ in southern China. Clearly, monitoring data for $PM_{2.5}$ may well indicate a worse overall air quality situation in Chinese cities than is indicated just from the PM_{10} data monitoring.

Co-benefits between Local Air Pollution and Carbon Emission Reduction Programs

Since the combustion of fuel is a substantial source for both local air pollution and carbon emissions, there are significant linkages and co-benefits between air pollution abatement and climate change mitigation. There are two kinds of synergies. First, many low-carbon growth strategies for cities can generate significant direct cost savings associated with the health and environmental benefits of reduced air pollution (see box 15.2). These

Figure 15.2   Results from PM$_{2.5}$ Research Monitoring in Seven Cities in China

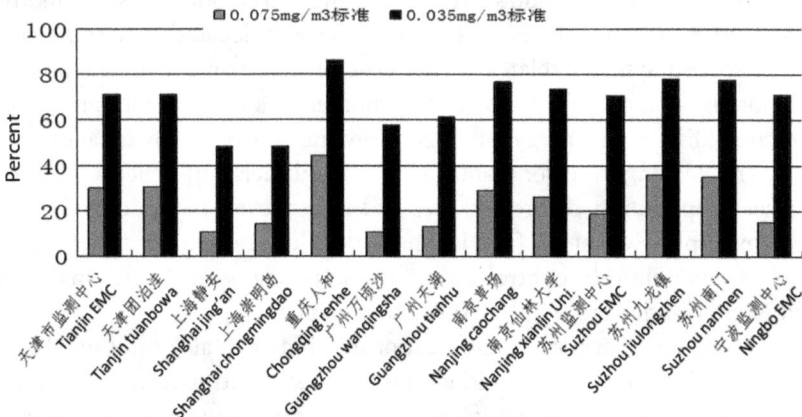

Source: CNMC database. Presented in World Bank and MEP 2011a.

Box 15.2

Local Impacts: The Health and Environmental Impacts of Air Pollution

High air pollution concentrations have a negative impact on the economy and human health. This includes the effects from SO_2 and acid rain on agriculture, forestry, and material damages. Fine particulates (PM_{10}, $PM_{2.5}$, and even finer particulate matter) have a severe impact on human health, especially the cardiovascular and respiratory systems resulting in increased mortality and morbidity. Global data from time-series analyses show a direct relation between increased mortality and short-term PM_{10} and $PM_{2.5}$ levels. Recent estimates suggest that an increase of 10 $\mu g/m_3$ in daily $PM_{2.5}$ levels can lead to an increase of 0.4 percent to 1.0 percent in daily mortality, particularly cardiovascular death (Brook et al. 2010). Other research (World Bank 2011) shows that the total estimated value of combined sickness and death associated with PM_{10} air pollution in China was RMB 700 billion (US$100 billion) in 2009. Despite substantive declines in urban ambient air pollution levels, this value is 32 percent higher compared with 2003, as a result of increased urbanization, aging population, and the statistical value of life rising with income.

Source: Authors.

co-benefits increase the attractiveness and economic return of some low-carbon strategies. A particularly good example are strategies that reduce fossil fuel consumption in sectors with a strong impact on population exposure such as domestic stoves for heating and cooking, or small industrial and district heating boilers with small stacks located in urban areas.

A second synergy relates to the cost of complying with air quality standards, which could be lower if carbon emission reductions are incorporated. Effective energy efficiency programs would lower aggregate demand, leading to fewer plants burning fossil fuels and hence a need for fewer air pollution control devices and lower levels of associated costs. For example, Syri et al. (2001), show that low-carbon strategies could reduce air pollution control costs for complying with the EU national emission ceilings in 2010 by 10 to 20 percent.

Despite these synergies, the relationship between air pollution abatement and carbon emission reductions is not straightforward. Sometimes efforts to reduce the damage from a particularly severe pollutant may not significantly impact the level of energy consumed. Conversely, the air pollution impact of climate mitigation policies depends on a variety of factors such as population exposure and quality of fuel and combustion involved. In some cases, there may even be trade-offs between air pollution and low-carbon goals. Three scenarios serve to illustrate the potential for such complexity.

Some actions, such as energy efficiency improvements and increased use of natural gas, offer significant improvements in both carbon intensity and air pollution.

However, large differences sometimes exist in the air pollution benefits of alternative strategies, which may yield similar reductions in carbon emissions. Mestl et al. (2005) show that the local health benefits of reducing carbon emissions from power plants in China are small compared to those from abating emissions from area sources and small industrial boilers, both of which have more direct health impacts through air pollution. Wang and Smith (1999) suggest that efforts focusing on sources such as domestic stoves and area sources can yield health benefits 40 times greater than a reduction in emissions from centralized facilities with high stacks such as power plants.

At the same time, some air pollution abatement strategies may actually be detrimental to low-carbon objectives. For example, desulfurization of flue gases reduces SO_2 emissions but can—to a limited extent—increase carbon emissions. Alternatively, investments in retrofitting older coal power plants and adding air pollution control equipment would lead to improved air quality, but may result in a lock-in of coal technologies that will make it more difficult to reduce future CO_2 emissions (McDonald 1999; Unruh 2000).

Given this complexity, it is important that policy options and programs for low-carbon growth include the costs and benefits associated with air pollution, particularly health benefits. This can help prioritize the activities with the biggest overall benefits (see box 15.3 for examples of such analysis in China). Sometimes, policies and programs that may not be regarded as cost-effective from a climate change or an air pollution perspective alone may be found to be cost-effective if both aspects are considered.

Similarly, there are opportunities to implement air pollution control plans to achieve cost-effective simultaneous reductions in carbon emissions. This is already a focus in the Chinese pollution control efforts under the 12th Five-Year Plan. Indeed, one of the recommendations—*"to establish and implement a voluntary climate-friendly urban air quality improvement plan"*—would require including carbon emissions into the

Box 15.3

Calculating Health Co-benefits of Improved Air Quality in Carbon Emission Reduction Programs

The co-benefits of improved health due to better air quality in carbon emission reduction programs have been calculated in several case studies in China, including Shanxi province where a World Bank supported study evaluated six different CO_2 abatement measures related to coal consumptions. Significant co-benefits of varying degrees linked to improved air quality were identified. The cheapest option to reduce carbon emissions from a GHG abatement cost-only view is co-generation of electricity and heat. However, when including co-benefit estimates due to health improvements, the most expensive measure to reduce carbon emissions—namely coal 'briquetting'—becomes the cheapest intervention, as associated health benefits are substantial. Coal washing, which at first seems to be relatively expensive carbon-reduction alternative, becomes a "no-regret" option that yields net benefits independent of carbon emission reductions, when the local health benefits are accounted for.

Another study estimates that replacing heavy-polluting stoves at a steel mill in Taiyuan with a larger arc-cast furnace is the most expensive of the analyzed interventions in terms of carbon abatement costs. However, installing the arc-cast furnace would lead to major local health benefits, which more than outweigh the total abatement costs. In comparison, a coke dry quenching project, which would reduce emissions and save coal, has abatement costs that are less than half of those associated with the arc-cast furnace project. However, the local health benefits from this project are estimated to be negligible, and thus the net costs are far higher than for the arc-cast furnace project. Other projects evaluated in the same study corroborate that accounting for health-related co-benefits can change the relative attractiveness of alternative carbon reduction options.

Source: Authors; Mestl et al. 2005.

specific improvement plans (Wang 2009). For each of the selected air pollution control options and scenarios, the associated changes in carbon emissions can be calculated, and its value entered into the multi-criteria or cost-benefit evaluations. The next section provides examples of air pollution activities supported by the World Bank in China, most of which have a concomitant benefit in reducing carbon emissions.

Lessons of Experience of World Bank Air Quality Improvement Activities in China

The World Bank has addressed urban air quality management and the interlinkages with other sectors in China through analytical work, loans, regional initiatives, and partnerships. This section presents a small sample of these practical experiences in Chinese cities in the areas of integrated air quality management assessment, air quality monitoring systems, transport, energy and heating, fugitive dust and desertification, and indoor air quality.

Integrated Air Quality Management (AQM) assessment. Developing a cost-effective comprehensive air quality management plan requires considerable analytical effort (see box 15.4). Work in Shanxi province under the World Bank financed "China Air Pollution Management Project—Particulate Matter Control" (World Bank and MEP 2011b) provides an example of such a systematic approach. This study concentrated on the PM element of the pollution. The air quality of Shanxi has suffered heavily from decades of coal mining and direct coal combustion such as power generation, coking, and metallurgy. Emissions of main air pollutants in Shanxi all far exceed the national average. Management efforts are complicated because multiple pollution sources, multiple sectors, and multiple stakeholders contribute to the pollution.

Box 15.4

Air Pollution Control Plans and China's New Regulatory Guideline Framework

MEP is developing a regulatory and technical guideline framework to support cities to develop air pollution control plans. This framework articulates a step-by-step process towards a comprehensive approach to air quality management (presented in Annex 2 in World Bank and MEP 2011a):

- The first step is to collect air quality data already available through the local monitoring system managed by the local Environmental Protection Bureau (EPB) in most of China's cities. Through this data collection, it would be possible to acquire a better understanding of the ambient air pollution situation in the city, including areas with higher pollution concentrations.

(continued next page)

Box 15.4 *(continued)*

- The second step is to determine the main sources contributing to the air pollution concentration levels. In each city in China, local EPBs maintain a pollution source inventory of the main sources that can be applied as a starting point, focusing on main point sources such as power plants and industries, as well as distributed, individual sources with low chimneys, like coal-fired domestic heating units.
- The third step is to run models that estimate contributions different sources of the pollution make to ground-level concentrations. Typically analysts use appropriate atmospheric transport and dispersion models that include meteorological, topographic, and population data as input. Such tools can also estimate the population exposure to the pollutants. Many cities are already using such tools, particularly to assess PM sources and intensities.

Finally, the calibrated model can be used to compare and select the most feasible and cost-effective options to control the key sources of air pollution. A cost-effectiveness analysis will compare the costs of each abatement measure with the commensurate pollution reduction and, more importantly, population exposure. Cost-benefit analysis goes a step further and incorporates the health effects of the pollution, by using dose-response relationships.

Solutions can be found in reducing both the supply of polluting technologies as well as the demand for total energy. The supply-side reductions generally rely on improved technologies and investments such as in replacement of inefficient industrial plants and boilers, adoption of clean coal technologies, and phase-out of small-scale coal combustion. Demand can be influenced by measures such as regulation in the form of pollution charges, taxes, or other sanctions. Market-based instruments, such as the SO_2 trading schemes already being piloted in Jiangsu province, are also highly efficient and could be scaled up.

Source: Authors.

Air quality monitoring data from the China National Monitoring Center (CNMC)/Shanxi EPB monitoring network and emissions data regularly collected through the EPB-steered emission inventory system were analyzed for the cities of Taiyuan, Lishi, and Xiaoyi. Based upon this data, as well as meteorological and topographic distribution data, an urban air quality model was developed to calculate hourly concentration and distribution within the cities. This model was then used to evaluate alternative abatement options. Figure 15.4 shows the results of two alter-

Figure 15.4   Scenario Modeling of Air Quality Abatement Options for Taiyuan

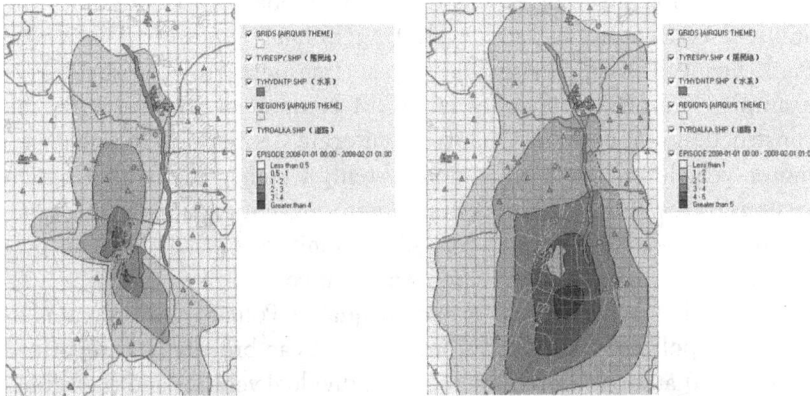

Scenario 1: Improve cleaning efficiency of PM$_{10}$ in the power sector, PM$_{10}$ emission reductions are 10,432 tonnes/year but with limited impact on population exposure and limited health benefits.

Scenario 2: Shift fuel from coal to gas in small and medium-sized industries. PM$_{10}$ emission reductions are 2,598 tonnes/year but with a large impact on concentration levels and health benefits.

Source: World Bank and MEP 2011b.

native abatement options in Taiyuan. The darkness of the colors in the figure shows the average concentration of pollutants in each square kilometer of the selected city: the darker the area, the larger the reduction in air pollution. The first modeled scenario corresponds to improvement of the cleaning efficiency of PM$_{10}$ in the power plant located in the south of the city. This control option gives substantial reductions near the sites, but does not significantly reduce the concentrations in central Taiyuan, and it does not reduce the average population exposure much over the most populated areas. Scenario 2, in which coal is replaced by gas in 50 percent of the small industries in the city, provides a more substantial reduction in PM$_{10}$ concentrations and exposure, achieving about 10 percent reduction in concentration levels in large parts of the city. These scenarios are good illustrations of how abatement options can affect smaller and larger parts of the city to a varying extent. Dispersion modeling is needed to generate such specific results (necessary for determining cost-effective abatement scenarios in an urban area) in terms of reduction of population exposure and subsequently reduction in health effects.

Air quality monitoring and assessment. A good air quality monitoring and modeling system is essential for developing air quality management plans. Attention is needed not only on monitoring hardware, but also on protocols for collecting data on ambient pollutant concentrations, developing emission inventories and dispersion modeling to determine the ambient concentrations, and evaluating human exposure. The World Bank–financed Xian Sustainable Urban Transport Project provides an example. The project includes an AQM component that supports the construction of a new Air Quality Monitoring Center; development of a motor vehicle emission inspection system; a management information system for the Xian environmental monitoring station; a data collection, transfer, and analysis platform for online monitoring of key fixed air pollution sources; and a motor vehicle emission control plan.

Sustainable transport and urban air quality. Policies and programs to reduce air pollution emissions from transport can broadly be categorized into those that target the technology of individual vehicles and their fuels, and those that are address the management of the transport system as a whole (see box 15.5). Pilots and programs that support the deployment of clean technologies—such as the GEF–supported Guangdong Green

---

Box 15.5

Lessons of Global Experience in Urban Transport and Air Quality

Institutional framework: Central governments should establish a predictable and consistent policy and regulatory framework for urban air quality management. A specific agency should be given responsibility for securing coordination in urban air quality policy within each metropolitan authority. Establishing urban traffic management centers and involving police in system design and training for traffic management can be especially effective.

Air quality action plan: Affected stakeholders—private sector participants, different levels of government, and civil society—should be engaged in developing an air quality action plan to the fullest extent possible. The incentives to comply are likely to be more powerful if the stakeholders have been involved in policy formulation.

Fuel quality and vehicle emission standards: Standards should be realistically set, progressively tightened, and stringently enforced. A targeted, well-designed, and adequately supervised emissions inspection program can foster a culture of

(continued next page)

Box 15.4 (*continued*)

proper vehicle maintenance. For two-stroke engines, it can be relatively low-cost and effective to promote proper lubrication practices for existing vehicles and to require new two-stroke engines to meet the same emission standards as four-strokes.

Public transport: Transit-oriented urban planning strategies and balanced land use should be developed to reduce trip lengths and concentrate movement on efficient public transport axial routes. Priority should be given to buses in the use of road infrastructure and the creation of segregated bus-way systems should particularly be considered, in order to improve and sustain environmental standards for buses. Competition for the market can also play an effective role in efficiency improvement and creation of incentives for raising environmental performance.

Fiscal policies: Taxes, import duties, and vehicle licensing can be designed to discourage purchase and continuing use of polluting vehicles and engines. In many countries, raising taxes on automotive diesel should be considered. Separate vehicle charges based on vehicle weight, axle loadings, and annual mileage may also be justified. Free on-street parking should not be provided in congested areas, and subsidies to public off-street parking should be eliminated.

Non-motorized transport: Provision for safe and comfortable walking, bicycling, and other forms of non-motorized transport can benefit air quality. Careful differentiation of traffic by type of road can reduce accidents and promote non-motorized transport for short trips.

Source: Gwilliam et al. 2004.

Truck Demonstration Project—are examples of a technology-based approach (see also chapter 12). Support for measures to further the development of compact cities that rely less on automobile and more on less-polluting public and non-motorized transport (see chapters 9–12) are examples of strategies that target the management of the system as a whole. Both kinds of strategies have been and will remain relevant both to pollution abatement and carbon reduction strategies.

Energy and urban air quality. Air pollution abatement is an essential element of a range of energy sector projects. As already mentioned, efficiency improvements and modernizing district heating have the maximum synergy between carbon reduction and air pollution outcomes.

- *District heating investments:* World Bank–financed district heating improvements in Liaoning, Tianjin, and Urumqi, illustrate the potential for investments to support energy efficiency and generate significant local and global environmental co-benefits by reducing emissions of particulates, SO_2, and CO_2 (see also chapter 8).
- *Energy efficiency investments:* Energy efficiency scale-up projects can reduce aggregate demand for energy and thus reduce emissions from coal fired power plants. An example is the introduction, adaptation, and scale up of energy performance contracting through the First and Second World Bank/GEF China Energy Conservation Projects. The GEF-funded China Thermal Power Efficiency Project in the provinces of Shanxi, Shandong, and Guangdong contributes to GHG mitigation *and* reduction in local air pollution by supporting the closure of small, inefficient, coal-fired power plants and facilitating investment in energy efficiency.

Fugitive dust and particulate matter. Fugitive dust is a significant source of PM, particularly in cities in the west and the drier northern regions of China. For many Chinese cities, this dust is originating from ecologically degraded areas affected by desertification and wind erosion. A new World Bank–supported program of desertification control and ecological protection in China's Ningxia Hui Autonomous Region aims to halt the shifting sand dunes and prevent the encroachment of deserts on key agricultural land, human settlements, and urban infrastructure along the Yellow River. The program supports an integrated approach to desertification control and rehabilitation that includes the establishment of straw checkerboards, the seeding and planting of indigenous grass and shrub species, tree shelterbelts, as well as grazing control and land management in the Maowusu Desert along the eastern bank of the Yellow River. Longer-term environmental and ecological benefits of such an approach include the environmental rehabilitation of entire landscapes that can sustain and regulate themselves based on natural processes; reduced silt and sand loads in water bodies, as well as reduced dust in the air and consequently the improvement of environmental quality indicators in nearby cities and towns; and, ultimately, over longer periods of time, the sequestration of carbon in soils and vegetation.

Indoor air quality. A major source of indoor air pollution in developing countries is the burning of solid fuels such as biomass (animal dung, wood, crop residues) and coal for heating and cooking (WHO 2010). Young children and women are disproportionately affected by indoor air pollution (see box 15.6). Analytical work and research studies within the

Box 15.6

Indoor Air Pollution: The Forgotten Link

Indoor air pollution (IAP) can be particularly damaging for human health. Damage from pollution increases with proximity to sources and levels of which the pollutants are inhaled; and indoor pollutants are emitted close to the ground where people spend most of their time. Consequently, they are particularly deleterious to human health. Although IAP and its health impacts are generally a larger challenge in rural than in urban areas, many urban households in China still use biomass cooking facilities and partly coal-based facilities. These households have substantively higher IAP concentration levels than households that use gas. In urban areas of northern China, about 53 percent of households use coal and biomass for cooking compared to about 35 percent in south China.

Table B16.6.1   Households' Reported Use of Various Cooking Fuels in Urban Areas in China (%)

Fuel	North	South
Gas	47	65
Coal	30	16
Biomass	23	19

Source: Mestl et al. 2007.

Using these data, it is possible to estimate the concentrations for daily PM_{10} in houses. In homes using biomass cooking, 73 percent of households in northern China reach an average population weighted exposure PM_{10} concentration level of 879 $\mu g/m^3$ per day and 87 percent of homes in southern China reach an average concentration level of 969 $\mu g/m^3$ per day. This is about 5.8 to 6.5 times higher than China's national standards. Households using gas for cooking have much lower IAP levels. These calculations illustrate that indoor air pollution is an important health issue that Chinese cities need to solve. GHG emissions from coal and biomass burning link the indoor air pollution and climate change mitigation agendas.

Source: Authors.

World Bank have focused on low-cost interventions such as improved cooking stoves, cleaner fuels, better stove placement and ventilation, behavioral modification, and other strategies for reducing exposures to smoke.

A particularly interesting project that combines the benefits of GHG emission reduction and improvements in indoor air quality is the Hubei Eco-Farming Biogas Project. This project demonstrates innovative technical and methodological approaches and a household-based Clean Development Mechanism (CDM) biogas digester program. The project reduces carbon emissions by installing and operating biogas digesters to recover methane from the livestock manure for the households' thermal energy needs, thus replacing the fossil fuel (coal) currently used to meet the households' daily energy needs for cooking and heating. In each household, the project would also support the improvement of a toilet, pig pen, renovation of the kitchen, and installation of a gas burner. Around 33,000 households in eight counties in Hubei Province have participated in the project. The establishment and use of biogas digesters by these households has led to a reduction of 59,000 tonnes of CO_2 equivalent of carbon emissions annually. This translates to revenues of around US$8.3 million to the participating farmers from selling Certified Emission Reduction (CER) credits (see chapter 24 for more detail on markets for carbon reduction). The project also improves indoor air quality and reduces the incidence of respiratory diseases and eye ailments caused by the burning of coal and fuel wood.

Conclusion

This chapter has highlighted the close link between a city's efforts to lower its carbon intensity and concurrent efforts to reduce air pollution. The combustion of fuels is the major source of local and global pollution in Chinese cities. Evidence suggests that although Chinese cities have made significant progress in improving air quality in recent years, significant additional effort is needed to reach WHO recommended standards, particularly for PM. There is also potential to further coordinate carbon and pollution reduction efforts. This chapter illustrated a range of examples where coordinated air quality and carbon reduction programs would result in different choices if only one or the other would be the goal of policy makers. The chapter called for mainstreaming coordinated air pollution and carbon reduction efforts and noted the corresponding recommendation in the 12th Five-Year Plan for the development of climate-friendly urban air quality improvement plans. Cities need to continue their efforts on air pollution abatement. The focus on reducing carbon intensity provides an opportunity to combine related objectives and scale up efforts that reduce local pollution and carbon intensity simultaneously.

Bibliography

Brook, R., S. Rajagopalan, C. Pope, III, J. Brook, A. Bhatnagar, A. Diez-Roux, F. Holguin, Y. Hong, R. Luepker, M. Mittleman, A. Peters, D. Siscovick, S. Smith, Jr., L. Whitsel, and J. Kaufman. 2010. "Particulate Matter Air Pollution and Cardiovascular Disease. An Update to the Scientific Statement from the American Heart Association." *Circulation* 121: 2331–78.

Gwilliam, K., M. Kojima, and T. Johnson. 2004. "Reducing Air Pollution from Urban Transport: Companion." Washington, DC: World Bank.

Lei, Y., Q. Zhang, K. He, and D. Streets. 2011. "Primary Anthropogenic Aerosol Emission Trends for China, 1990–2005." *Atmospheric Chemistry & Physics* 11: 931–954.

Lempert, R., S. Popper, and S. Resetar. 2002. "Capital Cycles and the Timing of Climate Change Policy." Pew Center on Global Climate Change.

Lu, Z., D. Streets, Q. Zhang, S. Wang, G. Carmichael, Y. Cheng, C. Wei, M. Chin, T. Diehl, and Q. Tan. 2010. "Sulfur Dioxide Emissions in China and Sulfur Trends in East Asia since 2000." *Atmospheric Chemistry & Physics* 10: 6311–6331.

McDonald, A. 1999. "Combating Acid Deposition and Climate Change—Priorities for Asia." *Environment* 41(3): 4–11, 34–41.

Mestl, H., K. Aunan, J. Fang, H. Seip, J. Skjelvik, and H. Vennemo. 2005 "Cleaner Production as Climate Investment—Integrated Assessment in Taiyuan City, China." *Journal of Cleaner Production* 13: 57–70.

Mestl, H., K. Aunan, H. Seip, S. Wang, and Y. Zhang. 2007. "Urban and Rural Exposure to Indoor Air Pollution from Domestic Biomass and Coal Burning across China." *Science of the Total Environment* 377(1): 12–26.

Metz, B., O. Davidson, P. Bosch, R. Dave, and L. Meyer, eds. 2007. *Contribution of Working Group III to the Fourth Assessment Report of the Intergovernmental Panel on Climate Change.* Cambridge, United Kingdom and New York, NY: Cambridge University Press.

Syri, S., M. Amann, P. Capros, L. Mantzos, J. Cofala, and Z. Klimont. 2001. "Low CO_2 Energy Pathways and Regional Air Pollution in Europe." *Energy Policy* 29: 871–884.

Unruh, G. 2000. "Understanding Carbon Lock-In." *Energy Policy* 28: 817–830.

van Harmelen, T, J. Bakker, B. de Vries, D. van Vuuren, M. den Elzen, and P. Mayerhofer. 2002. "Long-Term Reductions in Costs of Controlling Regional Air Pollution in Europe due to Climate Policy." *Environmental Science & Policy* 5(4): 349–365.

Wang, J. 2009. "Policy Recommendations for Integrating Climate-Friendly Air Pollution Control Strategy into China's 12th Five Year Plan." Chinese Academy for Environmental Planning. Presentation, November 13.

Wang, X., and K. Smith. 1999. "Secondary Benefits of Greenhouse Gas Control: Health Impacts in China." *Environmental Science and Technology* 33: 3056–61.

World Health Organization (WHO). 2010. "WHO Guidelines for Indoor Air Quality, Selected Pollutants." Geneva: WHO.

World Bank. 2007. *Cost of Pollution in China—Economic Estimates of Physical Damages.* Conference Edition. Washington, DC: World Bank.

———. 2010. "Draft Particulate Matter Control Plan for China, Supporting Research." Presentation at the Seminar on Integrated Management for Air Pollution Control in China, Beijing, December 6–7.

———. 2011. "Achieving Green Growth in China (draft)." July, forthcoming December 2011. Washington, DC: World Bank.

World Bank and MEP. 2011a. "China Air Pollution Management Project—Particulate Matter Control: Component 1: Development of a Particulate Matter Compliance Plan for China." Draft final report, July. Washington, DC: World Bank.

———. 2011b. "China Air Pollution Management Project—Particulate Matter Control: Component 2: An Air Quality Management Program for PM10 reduction in 3 cities in Shanxi Province." Draft final report, July. Washington, DC: World Bank.

PART 5

Sectoral Action for Low-Carbon Cities: Additional Approaches

Additional Approaches: Historic Built Assets, ICT, and Urban Agriculture and Forestry

Introduction

Axel Baeumler, Ede Ijjasz-Vasquez, and Shomik Mehndiratta

With a projected 300 million people being added to the urban population over the next 20 years, China is facing serious challenges. As energy demand for buildings and transport increases, CO_2 emissions are likely to triple for buildings and appliances and more than quadruple for the transport sector. The effects of such increases in emissions dictate a comprehensive approach in transitioning to a low-carbon economy. If such a transition can be implemented successfully, the rate and scale of China's urbanization in fact provide an unprecedented opportunity to dramatically change urban development and make innovative low-carbon cities a reality. China still has the opportunity to shape its future urban form—an opportunity not available to much of the rest of the world whose urban form has largely been built.

The previous chapters have described an agenda for cities that addresses climate change mitigation and adaptation, with a focus on established sectors. Some Chinese cities have already been taking action on issues related to climate change, whether dealing with industrial energy efficiency, transport technologies, or adapting to the expected changes that climate change will bring. Other cities have focused their efforts on urban management, such as municipal finance, land use and urban planning, transport, energy provision, building energy efficiencies and district heating, air pollution, waste and wastewater management, and pollution reduction. These are sectors where Chinese cities have accumulated a wealth of experience and achieved significant success in recent years. As they experiment with a range of policies and activities, Chinese cities may also consider taking advantage of additional experiences and innovations that are available internationally.

This part of the book (chapters 17–21) briefly discusses an emerging set of approaches and innovative ideas that municipal leaders potentially can use to transform their cities and direct them toward a livable, competitive, low-carbon future. Some of these ideas—such as urban agriculture—fall outside the traditional sectors along which cities are organized, and some of these approaches—such as the use of information and communication technology (ICT) in low-carbon cities—attempt to implement ideas that reflect the global frontier of knowledge. China has the potential to be a global innovator in these domains.

Other approaches presented in this part are well established in industrialized economies but have not yet been undertaken in China, such as a focus on downtown regeneration and the energy efficiency of historic built assets. This part of the book concludes with a discussion of urban forestry (chapter 21), which along with urban agriculture is an innovative approach that can enhance resilience in future cities while reducing their carbon footprint.

The following chapters illustrate that municipal leaders should not only look at traditional sectors of intervention to develop the future of their cities, but also consider opportunities to reshape a city's growth and energy efficiency in areas that are yet to be tested at an international scale.

CHAPTER 17

Energy Efficiency in Historic Built Assets

Guido Licciardi

Overview

This chapter reviews the concept of green buildings, discussing how historic buildings have already been integrating sustainability concepts. Conserving energy usually focuses on operational energy—the energy used to heat or cool buildings. Recent research, however, has focused on calculating a building's embodied energy, which has led to the conclusion that, in many cases, reusing or retrofitting existing buildings can be more energy efficient than demolishing an old building and constructing a new one with modern energy-saving features.

Embodied and Operational Energy in Buildings

Most of the current debate on energy in buildings focuses on operational energy, but buildings are actually associated with two types of energy: embodied and operational. While operational energy is easily defined as the energy needed to allow building occupancy and use, embodied energy is defined as the energy consumed by all of the processes related to the production of a building, including mining and the processing of natural resources to manufacture building materials, transport, product delivery, and final assembly at the construction site. More refined concepts con-

Figure 17.1   A Chinese Historic Cityscape: Pingyao in Shanxi Province

Source: World Bank.

sider the energy consumed in all stages of a building's life cycle, including resource extraction, goods manufacturing, construction, use, and disposal. Recent studies demonstrate that embodied and operational energies contribute to the overall energy balance of a building in almost equal shares and that their combination is responsible for about 50 percent of global CO_2 emissions. An integrated approach tackling both—embodied and operational energy—therefore is urgently needed to reduce emissions.

Conserving Energy in Historic Built Assets

The common perception is that historic buildings (that is, built in the early 20th century and before) are energy inefficient and that the environmental impacts of demolition and new construction are easily outweighed by the energy savings of contemporary, green buildings (see figure 17.1). However, studies and evidence reveal that not only can conserving and adaptively reusing historic buildings conserve the energy used for their construction (embodied energy), but that these buildings are more energy efficient than most 20th century buildings because of their site sensitivity, quality of construction, and use of passive heating and cooling (operational energy).

Embodied Energy in Historic Built Assets

The approach to embodied energy focuses on a dual objective: (i) reducing embodied energy in new buildings (that is, reducing the energy to produce and assemble their constituent materials) and (ii) conserving embodied energy in built assets (that is, adaptively reusing existing buildings). In both cases, international practice has demonstrated that the most important factor is to focus on long-life, durable buildings, in order to make them smart repositories of embodied energy. In fact, the optimal way to save embodied energy is to make buildings last longer. In the case of new buildings, a higher embodied energy can be justified only if it contributes to lower operational energy. For example, large amounts of thermal mass, high in embodied energy, can significantly reduce heating and cooling needs in well-designed and insulated passive solar houses. For built assets, priority should go to conserving embodied energy by considering the various options to adaptively reuse them, as opposed to demolition and reconstruction.

While operational energy can be easily determined by measuring what is needed to operate a building, embodied energy is less apparent because it is embedded in the various steps of building construction and material production. Various tools exist, however, to analyze embodied energy, and they are becoming increasingly refined.

Gross energy requirement (GER), for instance, is a measure of the true embodied energy of a material, which would ideally include all of the steps from mining to assembly. Research has made significant progress toward assessing GER, and a number of tools have been widely tested to measure a subset of GER, which is **process energy requirement (PER)**. PER is the energy directly related to the manufacturing of building materials (see table 17.1). It includes the energy consumed in transporting the raw materials to the factory and material production, but not the energy consumed in transporting the final product to the building site and assembling it, which are the missing steps to assess GER. In general, PER accounts for 50–80 percent of GER, and PER tables are readily available for a variety of building materials. Both GER and PER are measured in MJ/kg, that is, megajoules of energy needed to make a kilogram of product.

The consensus on PER data for a wide range of materials is extremely encouraging, and the data can already be used by stakeholders, designers, and developers to make effective decisions in urban development, especially to advocate conservation and adaptive reuse of historic built assets. As an example, PER tables suggest that producing 1 kilogram of aluminum has a PER of 170 MJ/kg, whereas producing 1 kilogram of bricks has a PER as low as 2 MJ/kg. In practice, this means that choosing materials with a lower PER dramatically reduces the embodied energy of a building. It also means that by conserving and adaptively reusing existing buildings, the PER (that is, the cumulative PER of their constituent materials) can be kept instead of being discarded, which substantially reduces CO_2 emissions.

Table 17.1   PER of Building Materials

Material	PER MJ/kg
Air-dried sawn hardwood	0.5
Stabilized earth	0.7
Concrete blocks	1.5
In situ concrete	1.9
Precast tilt-up concrete	1.9
Kiln-dried sawn hardwood	2.0
Precast steam-cured concrete	2.0
Clay bricks	2.5
Gypsum plaster	2.9
Kiln-dried sawn softwood	3.4
Autoclaved aerated concrete	3.6
Plasterboard	4.4
Fiber cement	4.8
Cement	5.6
Local natural stone	5.9
Particleboard	8.0
Plywood	10.4
Glue-laminated timber	11.0
Laminated veneer lumber	11.0
Medium density fibreboard	11.3
Glass	12.7
Imported natural stone	13.9
Hardboard	24.2
Galvanized steel	38.0
Acrylic paint	61.5
Polyvinyl chloride	80.0
Plastics—general	90.0
Synthetic rubber	110.0
Copper	100.0
Aluminum	170.0

Source: Author, based on EIA data.

The standards SBTool,[1] the UK Code for Sustainable Homes, and U.S. Leadership in Energy and Environmental Design (LEED) (the U.S. Green Building Council) already take embodied energy, along with other factors, into consideration when assessing a building's environmental impact. They are very effective tools to promote the conservation of embodied energy in historic built assets. As an example, according to U.S. LEED, projects can earn one credit for reusing 75 percent of the core and shell of an existing building. New credit points for projects in "smart-locations" and an increase in credit points for buildings at dense locations and with access to mass-transit—two adjustments currently being considered by the U.S. Green Building Council—would further support the conservation of historic built assets, as these are often located in easily accessible and dense urban cores.

Finally, a new concept, **the life cycle assessment (LCA),** examines impacts during a building's entire life, rather than focusing on one particular stage. Unlike traditional embodied energy calculations, LCA provides an assessment of direct and indirect environmental impacts associated with a building by quantifying energy, material use, and environmental releases at each stage of the life cycle, including resource extraction, goods manufacturing, construction, use, and disposal. LCA makes an even stronger case for conserving and adaptively reusing historic built assets and is the basis for the distribution of points under the updated U.S. LEED standards.

Case Study: Reusing Historic Mansions in Qufu and Zoucheng, Shandong Province

An innovative project, currently under preparation and financed by the World Bank (US$50 million) and China (US$70 million), will regenerate the two historic cities of Qufu and Zoucheng in Shandong Province. Acknowledging the importance of embodied energy, one project component focuses on the conservation and adaptive reuse of two large historic buildings that are currently underutilized. The Confucius and Mencius mansions are vast former residences, which today are mostly abandoned (see figure 17.2). The buildings will be revitalized to host a number of new productive functions, from knowledge centers to growth poles for sustainable tourism. The physical conservation of the mansions will maximize the use of low-impact traditional techniques and locally available building materials to reduce the additional embodied energy the project will create. Reusing historic assets for new functions, instead of constructing new buildings, will conserve the embodied energy and reduce the need for accumulating additional embodied energy that the construction of new buildings would require.

Operational Energy in Historic Built Assets

While CO_2 emissions result from the consumption of natural resources, activities to reduce those emissions often lead to further consumption.

Figure 17.2   The Confucius Temple and Mansion in Qufu, China

A World Bank project will finance the adaptive reuse of the temple, mansion, and other large, underutilized, historic buildings in Shandong Province, conserving their embodied energy.

Source: World Bank.

Demolishing existing buildings to construct new ones results in additional CO_2 emissions for their demolition, for debris and waste disposal, for the production of new materials, and for assembling replacement buildings. Today, the most innovative approaches are shifting toward conserving existing resources rather than consuming more.

The common perception is that existing built assets are not energy efficient. This is not exactly true: in fact, due to the low energy cost at the time of their construction, only assets built in the second half of the 20th century are energetically inefficient. In contrast, assets built in the early 20th century and before are extremely energy efficient. Indeed, energy costs in the past were very high, and building designers and developers had found very good solutions to make their buildings energy efficient.

A groundbreaking study by the U.S. Energy Information Administration (EIA), since followed by a number of similar investigations worldwide, has demonstrated the energy efficiency of historic built assets. The study concluded that contemporary, highly energy-efficient buildings require the same operational energy as historic assets built before the 1920s. The study is based on a simple analysis of the operational energy needed to operate similar categories of existing buildings, still in use, simply looking at their year of construction (see figure 17.3).

The efficiency of historic buildings is largely due to a difference in construction methods. Generally, historic buildings have thick, solid walls with high thermal mass that reduces the amount of operational energy needed for heating and cooling. Moreover, buildings designed before the widespread use of electricity feature well-designed windows for natural light and ventilation, as well as shaded porches and other details to reduce solar gain. In the past, designers and developers also paid close attention to location, orientation, and landscaping as methods for maximizing sun exposure during the winter months and minimizing it during warmer months (in other words, designers created passive heating and cooling systems).

In addition, historic buildings are mostly located in densely built areas. Compact urban development means reduced heating and cooling costs because units are smaller or are in multiunit buildings. District energy systems can be used for power generation, as China has been doing for

Figure 17.3   Average Annual Energy Consumption in U.S. Commercial Buildings, by Year of Construction (Btu/square foot)

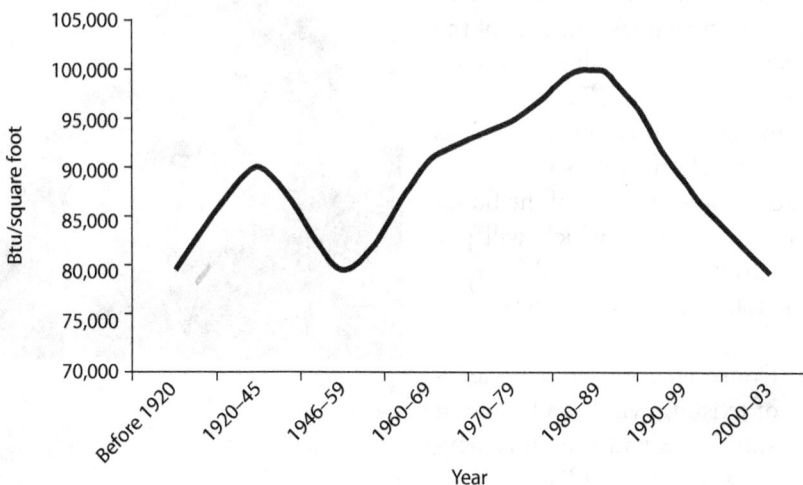

Source: Author, based on EIA data.
Note: Btu = British thermal unit.

decades, which also creates substantial carbon savings. Municipal infrastructure requirements for roads, sewers, communication, power, and water are also reduced by high-density developments, which is where most historic buildings are located.

Case Study: Reducing Operational Energy in the Empire State Building in New York City

In 2009, sustainability experts joined forces to retrofit the Empire State Building, using an innovative design process and state-of-the-art tools with one key goal in mind: using the most cost-effective measure to produce the most energy savings (see figure 17.4). After comprehensive research, it was found that replacing the windows and purchasing new ones from distant factories was not the best solution. Rather, it was more energy efficient and cost effective to conserve the glass and frames of the existing 6,514 dual-pane windows, and then upgrade them to superinsulating glass units in a dedicated processing space located onsite. As a result, 96 percent of the frames and glass of the Empire State Building were conserved and reused. The work was completed in October 2010 as one of eight measures in an innovative energy retrofit of the building. The project, which will pay for itself in three years, featured the following accomplishments:

Figure 17.4   The Empire State Building in New York City

With a recently completed retrofit project, the building's embodied energy has been conserved.

Source: World Bank.

- Conserving embodied energy of existing windows (made of aluminum and therefore having a very high PER)
- Reducing operational energy use by 38 percent
- Saving US$4.4 million per year in operational energy costs

- Saving 105,000 metric tons of CO_2 emissions over the next 15 years, equivalent to the annual emissions of 17,500 cars.

Conclusion

It has been demonstrated that historic assets can have energy efficiency comparable to newly constructed buildings. The relocation of new functions into historic buildings as well as the provision of appropriate retrofit measures can contribute to significant energy and resources conservation. With this in mind, China, with its thousands of years of history and its extensive collection of historic assets, has a great opportunity to excel in the conservation of heritage—and its embodied energy.

Notes

1. SBTool is software for assessing the environmental and sustainability performance of buildings. It is available from the International Initiative for a Sustainable Built Environment (iiSBE) at: http://www.iisbe.org/iisbe/sbc2k8/sbc2k8-download_f.htm.

Bibliography

Advisory Council on Historic Preservation. 1979. *Assessing the Energy Conservation Benefits of Historic Preservation: Methods and Examples.* Washington, DC: ACHP.

Brookings Institution Center on Metropolitan Policy. 2003. *Back to Prosperity: A Competitive Agenda for Renewing Pennsylvania.* Washington, DC: The Brookings Institution.

Brown, M., F. Southworth, and A. Sarzynski. 2008. *Shrinking the Carbon Footprint of Metropolitan America.* Washington, DC: The Brookings Institution.

Building and Social Housing Foundation and Empty Homes Agency. 2007. *New Tricks with Old Bricks.* London, UK: Empty Homes Agency.

City of New York. 2007. "PLANYC 2030." City of New York, New York, NY.

———. 2008. "PLANYC Progress Report 2008." City of New York, New York, NY.

City of San Francisco. 2008. *Building A Bright Future: San Francisco's Environmental Plan 2008.* San Francisco, CA: City of San Francisco.

———. 2008. Green Building Ordinance. City of San Francisco, San Francisco, CA.

Cole, R. 1996. "Life-Cycle Energy Use in Office Buildings." *Buildings and Environment* 31(4): 307–17.

Creyts, J. 2007. *Reducing U.S. Greenhouse Gas Emissions: How Much and at What Cost?* New York, NY: McKinsey & Company.

Elefante, C. 2007. "The Greenest Building Is ... One that's Already Built." *Forum Journal* 21(4): 26–38.

Ewing, R. 2008. *Growing Cooler: Evidence on Urban Development and Climate Change Executive Summary.* Washington, DC: The Urban Land Institute.

Foster, M. 2008. "Block of Historic Downtown Lexington May Be Leveled for Green Hotel." *Preservation Magazine,* April 16.

Frey, P. 2008. *Building Reuse: Finding a Place on American Climate Policy Agendas.* Washington, DC: National Trust for Historic Preservation.

Green Ribbon Climate Action Task Force. 2008. *Tacoma's Climate Action Plan.* Tacoma, WA: City of Tacoma.

Hammond, G., and J. Craig. 2006. *Inventory of Carbon and Energy.* Bath, U.K.: University of Bath.

Huberman, N., and D. Pealman. 2008. "A Life-Cycle Energy Analysis of Building Materials in the Negev Desert." *Energy & Buildings* 40(5): 837–48.

Katz, B., and R. Lang. 2005. *Redefining Urban and Suburban America: Evidence from Census 2000.* Washington, DC: The Brookings Institution.

Klunder, I. 2007. "Comparing Environmental Impacts of Renovated Housing Stock with New Construction." *Building Research & Information* 35(3): 252–67.

Knickerbocker, B. 2007. "China Now World's Biggest Greenhouse Gas Emitter." *Christian Science Monitor,* June 28.

Leinberger, C. 2008. "Sustainable Urban Redevelopment and Climate Change Briefing." Northeast-Midwest Institute Congressional Coalition, Washington, DC.

Ross, D. 2007. "Life Cycle Assessment in Heritage Buildings." Work Term Report. Ministry of Tourism, Sport and the Arts, Victoria, British Columbia.

Thormark, C. 2001. "A Low Energy Building in a Life-Cycle, Its Embodied Energy, Energy Need for Operation and Recycling Potential." *Building and Environment* 37(4): 429–35.

Trusty, W. 2004. *Renovating vs. Building New: The Environmental Merits.* Merrickville, Ontario, Canada: The Athena Institute.

U.S. Energy Information Administration (EIA). 2005. *Annual Energy Outlook 2005.* EIA, Washington, DC.

———. 2006. "2003 Commercial Buildings Energy Consumption Survey: Consumption and Expenditures Tables." Released June 2006. Consumption of Gross Energy Intensity for Sum of Major Fuels for Non Mall Commercial Buildings. Washington, DC: EIA.

———. 2008, *Emissions of Greenhouse Gases Report.* Washington, DC: EIA.

U.S. General Services Administration. 1999. *Financing Historic Federal Buildings: An Analysis of Current Practice*. Washington, DC: General Services Administration.

U.S. Green Building Council. 2008. *Green Building Research*. Atlanta, GA: U.S. Green Building Council.

CHAPTER 18

Benefits of Downtown Regeneration

Guido Licciardi

Overview

This chapter presents a brief overview of the objectives, sustainability, and economic benefits of downtown regeneration and cultural heritage conservation. Downtown regeneration can be part of a city's transformation to becoming low-carbon by providing access to goods and services without a need for a car, and by conserving embodied energy in existing buildings.

Objectives of Downtown Regeneration

Downtown areas in developing countries are usually surrounded by fast-growing neighborhoods. What were "the cities" in the past today have become only portions of much larger human settlements and often host poor communities.

Regenerating these downtown areas is an asset-based approach to local economic development. This regeneration has two main objectives:

- Leveraging downtown areas as service hubs for "city internal users"— the communities living in the downtown area as well as in the modern neighborhoods surrounding it

- Leveraging the downtown area as a sustainable destination for "city external users," such as people from other cities, other regions, and other countries.

Healthy and vibrant downtowns can boost the quality of life in local communities. Their regeneration conserves the character and heritage of downtown, while creating jobs, helping small businesses, reducing urban sprawl, increasing property values, and enhancing a community's access to goods and services in a walkable, low-carbon built environment. Livable downtowns are also symbols of community pride and custodians of rich history and heritage (see figure 18.1).

Sustainability of Downtown Regeneration
Downtown regeneration is a challenging process, requiring the development of a complex, well-integrated mix of uses, all within walking dis-

Figure 18.1   Chinese Historic Cityscape: Pingyao in Shanxi Province

Source: World Bank.

tance. Successful regeneration implies that existing built assets, usually of historic value, are properly conserved and adaptively reused to accommodate new functions. Regeneration facilitates the opening of small businesses adjacent to public and private services, often only a few doors down from bustling markets at the bottom floors of buildings that host low- to high-income housing. A "critical mass" of these small businesses, however, can be established only with a thriving public-private partnership, as well as an initial investment in public and private assets before the regeneration can become self-sustained. At that point, an upward spiral begins: more developers invest in real estate, more businesses open, and further investments are attracted. As a result, more people move in; rents, land, and property values increase; and the regeneration process can sustain itself.

Economic Benefits of Downtown Regeneration versus Suburban Development

Undoubtedly, one of the most tangible benefits of downtown revitalization is the steady effect it has on real estate values, which usually becomes evident seven years after the regeneration has begun. In suburban development, based on low-density models and car-friendly access and parking, benefits are generated in the short term but peak in years five through seven. Suburban development is built cheaply to help drive early financial returns. Downtown regeneration shows an opposite trajectory. The combination of a longer project design and implementation, conservation of built assets of historic value, higher complexity of civil works, upgrading of public spaces, improvement of services, as well as the existence of fragmented property, make the initial investment for downtown regeneration higher than suburban development. However, once the initial investment is made, downtown revitalization has the advantage of becoming self-sustaining by attracting further investments faster than suburban development and for a longer period of time. Ultimately, the rewards for downtown development are significantly greater than for suburban development, as shown in figure 18.2.

Conclusion

Despite the high-level investments required to revitalize the center of a city and conserve its cultural heritage assets, downtown areas have the potential to become economic drivers of a city. Ultimately, downtown

Figure 18.2   Comparison of the Financial Characteristics of Downtowns with Critical Mass (Dotted Line) with Suburban Development (Solid Line)

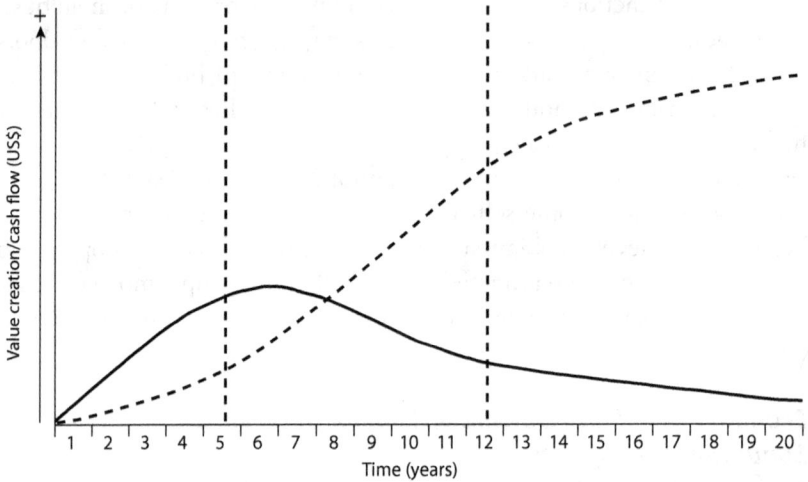

Source: Leinberger 2005.

development will change not only the physical design of a city and urban fabric, but also change the city's vitality and atmosphere and improve the quality of life for its citizens

Bibliography

Florida, R. 2002. *The Rise of the Creative Class.* New York, NY: Basic Books.

Lang, R. 2003. *Edgeless Cities: Exploring the Elusive Metropolis.* Washington, DC: Brookings Institution.

Leinberger, C. 1995. *The Changing Location of Development and Investment Opportunities.* Washington, DC: Urban Land Institute.

———. 2005. *Turning Around Downtown: Twelve Steps to Revitalization.* Washington, DC: Brookings Institution.

Urban Land Institute. 1997. *America's Real Estate.* Washington, DC: Urban Land Institute.

CHAPTER 19

ICT and Low-Carbon Cities

Junko Narimatsu and Randeep Sudan

Overview

Studies indicate that information and communication technology (ICT) solutions have the potential to reduce global carbon emissions by up to 7.8 gigatonnes (Gt), or 15 percent of total business as usual (BAU) emissions, by 2020 (Boccaletti et al. 2008). While energy efficiency of the ICT sector itself—which was responsible for 2 to 3 percent of global carbon emissions in 2007 (Gartner 2007)[1]—must be actively pursued, ICT's largest influence will be by enabling energy efficiencies in other sectors, an opportunity that could deliver annual carbon savings five times larger than the total emissions from the entire ICT sector in 2020 (The Climate Group 2008). This contribution includes enabling ICT solutions for climate change *mitigation*, such as the use of smart grids, smart motor systems, smart logistics, and smart buildings, which—especially when combined—can contribute to a significant reduction of global carbon emissions from other sectors. ICT can also play a major role in many *adaptation* measures—for example, in early warning and response systems for disasters such as typhoons, or in the form of sensors for optimizing water use in urban agriculture and forestry.

Working across multiple sectors, ICT-enabled developments such as high-capacity broadband, dematerialization, mobile services, development of common standards, climate monitoring and analysis, as well as citizen feedback and participation using digital tools will be key cross-sector enablers to realize these potentials. Furthermore, forging partnerships with the private sector will be critical for cities to adopt cutting-edge solutions and implement schemes that would make them sustainable. Therefore, it is important for Chinese cities to integrate innovative ICT solutions in their climate change policies and consider interdisciplinary partnerships for a collaborative transition to a low-carbon economy.

Smart Solutions to Green Other Sectors

At the Organisation for Economic Co-operation and Development (OECD) Technology Foresight Forum 2010, OECD countries acknowledged that "smart" ICT applications are the key enablers of "green growth" in all sectors of the economy (OECD 2010). Top application areas in reducing carbon emissions include manufacturing (use of smart motor systems), transport (smart logistics), buildings (smart buildings), and power (smart grids). Table 19.1 presents the sectors and application areas in which these smart technologies are considered to have the greatest impact on carbon emissions, based on global analyses. A selection of smart technologies is presented in this section.

Smart Grids

Smart grids are electricity networks that use digital technology to promote energy and cost efficiencies. The potential for ICT to reduce carbon emissions through smart grid technology could be substantial, with a possible 2.03 Gt of reduction in 2020 (The Climate Group 2008). Smart grids along with consumer energy management systems that are linked up with advanced metering infrastructure (AMI) can help optimize home energy use.

In 2007, the United States established a national policy for grid modernization, and its "Modern Grid" initiative is currently a world leader. Other countries, however, are also actively engaging in projects to transform old power networks into smart electric grids. In 2005, the European Commission launched the "SmartGrids European Technology Platform for Electricity Networks of the Future" to create a joint vision for the European networks; and in Australia the government has committed US$100 million and is developing its first commercial-scale smart grid in Newcastle. In addition, the Republic of Korea is embarking on a smart-grid demonstration project on Jeju Island, as part of its US$24 billion initiative to cut national energy consumption by 3 percent by 2030 (Kim

Table 19.1 ICT-Enabled CO$_2$ Equivalent Reductions across Sectors

	ICT sector	Power sector	Manufacturing sector	Transport sector	Buildings
Carbon emissions	2% of global CO$_2$ equivalent (CO$_2$e); (2007 data)	24% (of 2002 data)	23% (2004 data)	14% (2004 data)	8% (2002 data)
ICT-enabled reductions	—	2.03 GtCO$_2$e in 2020	0.97 GtCO$_2$e in 2020	1.52 GtCO$_2$e in 2020	1.68 GtCO$_2$e in 2020
Enablers	Green IT	Smart grids	Smart motor systems	Smart logistics	Smart buildings
Application descriptions	**PCs** • Hosted virtual desktops; Solid state hard drives; OLED screens; PC labeling **Telecoms** • Solar power mobile devices; Silicon anode batteries **Data Centers** • Delocalization; virtualization; cloud computing; data de-duplication; thin provisioning; data center infrastructure management software; cooling management software	• Grid management systems (e.g., supervisory control and data acquisition, output management) • Smart meters • Smart thermostats and appliances • Smart billing software (e.g., IP-based billing) • Energy accounting software • Protocols for gridwide system interoperability	• Lean manufacturing systems • Process control and automation • Variable-speed drives (VSD) and intelligent motor controllers (IMC) • Digital meters and components for real-time information • Simulation and optimization software • Wireless communication between systems	• Adaptive traffic signal control • Real-time status for public transit systems • Electronic freight exchanges (EFX) • Radio frequency identification (RFID) for asset tracking • Global positioning systems (GPS) • IT-enabled transportation pricing systems, e.g., congestion pricing, vehicles miles traveled (VMT) usage fee systems	• Building management systems (BMS) • Building automation solutions (e.g., occupancy-based lighting) • Building design and simulation software (e.g., temperature modeling, fluid dynamic modeling) • Building integrated photovoltaic solar • Appliance interconnectivity and networking and remote appliance control

(continued next page)

Table 19.1 *(continued)*

	ICT sector	Power sector	Manufacturing sector	Transport sector	Buildings
Smart initiatives	• "Green Grid" Global Consortium; Electronic Product Environmental Assessment Tool (United States)	• Modern Grid (United States); SmartGrids (Europe); Jeju Smart Grid Demonstration Project (Republic of Korea)	• Energy Smart (Australia); Power Smart (Canada); Motor Decisions Matter (United States)	• Smartway (Japan); T-money (Republic of Korea); iTransport (Singapore); Kilometerprijs (the Netherlands)	• New Houses (Canada); Green Building Council (Australia); Building Research Establishment Environmental Assessment Method (BREEAM) (United Kingdom); Leadership in Energy and Environmental Design (LEED) (United States); Comprehensive Assessment System for Built Environment Efficiency (CASBEE) (Japan)

Sources: Gartner 2010; The Climate Group 2008; Ezell 2010.

2010). In Japan, the government announced a US$1.1 billion smart grid trial in four major cities, and in China, General Electric (GE) is partnering with the city of Yangzhou to build a smart grid demonstration center to demonstrate how the city can draw its required power while reducing environmental impact (BusinessWire 2010).

Light Emitting Diode (LED)
LED technology used for street and area lighting can contribute to energy savings of more than 50 percent. Such lights are also dimmable and can be turned down at times of limited activity, resulting in further savings of energy.

Smart Motor Systems
Smart motor systems, such as variable-speed drives (VSD) and intelligent motor controllers (IMC), present promising opportunities for ICT to contribute to mitigating carbon emissions in the manufacturing sector. Industrial activities contributed to 23 percent of global emissions in 2002, but with the adoption of smart motor systems and industrial process optimization it is expected that global carbon emissions can be reduced by 970 megatonnes (Mt) by 2020. "Energy Smart" in Australia, "Power Smart" in Canada, and "Motor Decisions Matter" in the United States are programs working with businesses to identify optimal use of smart motor systems in their processes. As cities in China contain a large number of industries, this is a particularly important area on which to focus.

Smart Logistics
Smart logistics, such as geographic information systems (GIS), real-time route optimization (RTRO) software, and electronic freight exchanges (EFX), can enable the monitoring, optimizing, and managing of operations, particularly in the transport sector, which accounts for 14 percent of global carbon emissions (The Climate Group 2008). Smart logistics may be able to reduce global emissions by up to 1.52 Gt. Japan, Korea, and Singapore have been leading the world in this area. Japan's Smartway system offers drivers real-time traffic flow information, accident reports, and navigation suggestions to avoid congested roadways. In Korea, T-money, an electronic money smart card, makes 30 million contactless transactions per day on public transit. Singapore's i-Transport system is at the cutting edge of predictive traffic flow modeling based on historic and real-time traffic data. In Europe, the "kilometerprijs" (price per kilometer) system in the Netherlands is the world's first nationwide vehicle miles

traveled (VMT) fee system, which charges both passenger vehicles and heavy vehicles by their annual distances driven (Ezell 2010).

Smart Buildings

Smart buildings also offer major opportunities for ICT solutions to contribute to a transition to a greener economy. Globally, smart building technologies have the potential to reduce emissions by as much as 1.68 Gt in 2020 (The Climate Group 2008). In China—which has nearly half of the world's current construction—smart buildings with building management systems (BMS) hold great potential for drastically reducing global carbon emissions. In addition, intelligent lighting in buildings that combines LEDs with motion, time, and other sensors can further significantly reduce energy consumption.

The next generation of building integrated photovoltaic (BIPV) systems might also be able to better use solar energy. Thin-film technology may be able to capture solar energy from windows and skylights while polymer coatings could be applied to building exteriors as paint, converting the entire building into a solar energy system.

In 2010, at the China Green Building Forum, government and industry leaders sought collaborative opportunities to advance the smart building agenda. Other countries have also set up national schemes to promote smart buildings, such as "New Houses" in Canada, the "Green Building Council" in Australia, and "BREEAM"[2] in the United Kingdom.

Greening the ICT Sector

While ICT has great potential to enable energy efficiency in other sectors, greening the ICT sector itself cannot be dismissed, especially in countries like India and China where demand for computers and mobile phones is rapidly growing. In 2008 only 5.7 percent of the population in China owned a personal computer (World Bank 2010), but this number is estimated to rise to 70 percent by 2020, with half of all households connected to broadband services. In 2007, the total carbon emission footprint of the ICT sector was 830 Mt, which accounted for 2 percent of global carbon emissions from human activity that year. ICT emissions are currently estimated to grow at an annual rate of 6 percent until 2020.

While the use of personal computers and telecommunication devices continues to expand, data centers will grow faster than any other ICT technology, largely driven by the explosion of web traffic including mobile Internet traffic, which is foreseen to increase 26-fold between 2010 and 2015 (Couts 2011). If this growth continues, by 2020 the world will be using 122 million servers, up from 18 million today. ICT solutions such as virtualization[3] and low-energy cooling systems can reduce emissions by up to 27 percent—the equivalent of 111 Mt of carbon emissions in 2020 (The Climate Group 2008). Additionally, server consolidation by providing "cloud computing"[4] services across sectors is expected to enable further efficiency by increasing utilization rates and reducing energy required for power and cooling.

Cross-Sector ICT Contributions to Emission Reductions

ICT developments will also play an important role across sectors. The use of high-capacity broadband, dematerialization (for example, through electronic documentation), mobile services, the development of common standards, and climate monitoring, as well as online citizen participation (e-participation) are cross-sector enablers that have huge potential in contributing to carbon emission reductions.

High-Capacity Broadband
Characterized by the next generation networks (NGN), high-capacity broadband is important to enable fast, interoperable, redundant, and converged "smart" solutions. NGN, which consolidate voice, data, and media into one core IP-based network, are seen as central for powering many of the ICT solutions essential to supporting climate change mitigation and adaptation. National broadband diffusion rates also reflect the extent of dematerialization that can take place in the economy.

Dematerialization
Advances in ICT and other technologies facilitate the replacement of carbon-intensive products and processes such as face-to-face meetings and paper documentation by low-carbon alternatives (for example, telecommuting, videoconferencing, e-paper, e-commerce, e-government, and online media). According to studies, dematerialization has the potential to reduce emissions in 2020 by as much as 500 Mt (The Climate Group 2008). The largest opportunity for dematerialization might be teleworking, with a potential to reduce global emissions by as much as 260 Mt. In the European Union, around 13 percent of employees were estimated to have teleworked in 2002, based on private data sources (OECD 2010).

Songdo, an experimental, newly built city in Korea, has telepresence systems installed in every household, delivering services such as education and health and government services.

Mobile services. The delivery of government services using mobile phones can reduce the need for citizens to travel to government offices, thus reducing carbon emissions. Further, mobile applications could help monitor the carbon footprint of individuals with location-aware, GPS-equipped mobile phones that can stream data. Such phones would allow urban planners to determine the use of various modes of transportation, whether walking, biking, driving, or even flying.[5]

Common Standards

Creating common standards to collect, collate, and analyze energy consumption and carbon emission data across cities is important for developing a comprehensive roadmap to address climate change. For instance, the Green Digital Charter by EUROCITIES (a network of major European cities) has brought together 22 cities to coordinate efforts and build benchmarks of good practices to realize a low-carbon society. Similarly, GreenTouch is a global consortium of leading ICT industry, academic, and nongovernmental research experts dedicated to transforming communications and data networks and significantly reducing the carbon footprint of the ICT sector. Members of the consortium include prominent institutions such as AT&T, Bell Labs, CEA-Leti, China Mobile, Huawei, and MIT (GreenTouch 2010).

It will also be important to adopt smart appliance standards, which can improve integration with advanced metering infrastructure systems. This will provide homes with pricing information and improve management of home appliances as part of a home area network (HAN).

Climate Monitoring and Analysis

Modern geographic information system (GIS) techniques such as vector mapping, aerial surveys, and remote sensing can provide valuable information for measuring, monitoring, and analyzing carbon emissions, as well as for the study of the human dimensions of global climate change. In December 2010, Google launched the Google Earth Engine, a cloud computing–based platform that, at an unprecedented scale, draws together satellite imagery and data, including measurements dating back more than 25 years (Google 2010). Such applications will likely be vital tools to collect and analyze environmental data.

Citizen Participation

E-participation such as online consultation with residents, politicians, and council officers on sustainable strategies can become a powerful tool to collaboratively generate innovative ideas to reduce carbon emissions. In 2010, Coventry City Council in the United Kingdom launched "CovJam," which successfully engaged more than 800 stakeholders in a three-day interactive online forum, generating over 2,000 posts from participants (IBM 2010). These online tools, together with social networking applications and the use of mobile devices, can give rise to innovative, community-oriented approaches that can help cities to effectively brainstorm and collaboratively create solutions with stakeholders.

Public-Private Partnerships

The private sector, especially large multinational information technology (IT) corporations with their abundant resources and expertise, has a key role in the agenda to realize a "smart" low-carbon economy. Companies like IBM and Cisco have been highly committed to realizing this agenda. In September 2009, Cisco, in support of China's long-term strategy of "green growth," signed a memorandum of understanding with Chongqing to advance the city's IT manufacturing industry and spur innovation in green technologies (Cisco 2009). Furthermore, Cisco's Connected Urban Development (CUD) program, launched in 2006, explores how innovative ICT applications can reduce carbon emissions in urban cities across the globe. Projects in three partnering cities are leading this work: Green ICT in San Francisco, Smart Transportation in Seoul, and Smart Work in Amsterdam. In particular, the "connected bus" in San Francisco, with its mobile hotspot and GPS tracking features that help reduce costs and monitor maintenance needs, has great potential to be replicated in public transportation systems worldwide (Mitchell and Wagener 2009).

In 2009, IBM launched the Smarter Cities Challenge, a grant program in which IBM will award US$50 million worth of technology and services to help 100 municipalities across the globe make themselves "smarter." Currently, IBM has launched pilot programs in Austin, Baltimore, and Charlotte in the United States and continues to invite cities to learn about the program and apply for grants. In China, IBM is also collaborating with the city of Dongying to build a cloud computing center that would help establish a smarter city through dematerialization of government services and businesses (Babcock 2009). These initiatives illustrate the critical roles the private sector, together with governments, can play in realizing a sustainable low-carbon economy while still maintaining economic growth.

ICT and Environment Framework Principles

In 2010, the OECD Council established 10 framework principles to support efforts to establish, improve, and review policies on ICT and the environment (OECD 2010). The principles provide a general framework for enhancing the contribution of ICT in improving environmental performance. These principles include:

- Coordination of ICT, climate, environment, and energy policies across governments
- Adoption of life-cycle perspectives that promote environmentally efficient R&D, design, production, use, and disposal of ICTs
- Support for research and innovation in green technologies and services
- Development of skills in the area of "green ICT"
- Increase in public awareness of the role of ICTs in improving environmental performance
- Encouragement of best practices to maximize diffusion of ICTs and "smart" ICT-enabled applications
- Promotion of green ICT concepts, with governments leading by example
- Accounting of environmental criteria in public procurement
- Measurement of environmental impacts
- Set up of policy targets, monitoring compliance, and improving accountability.

Conclusion

The opportunities for ICT to support the development of low-carbon cities in China are substantial. While reducing carbon emissions in the ICT sector itself is critical, given the dramatic growth in the use of the Internet and mobile technology, exploring opportunities where ICT can enable energy efficiencies in other sectors will likely have a far greater impact on carbon emission reductions. Smart technologies such as smart motor systems, smart logistics, smart buildings, and smart grids present huge opportunities for carbon emission reductions and should continue to be aggressively explored as part of collaborative efforts among city administrations, the private sector, academia, and civil society. ICT's potential contribution to energy saving by working across sectors—through improvements in high-capacity broadband, dematerialization, mobile services, common standards, climate monitoring and analysis, and citizen e-participation—is also substantial, and could be explored and used by cities as an integral part of their successful transition to a low-carbon economy.

Notes

1. This widely cited estimate is based on research published in 2007 but carried out in 2005, and is, in turn, based on data from the Intergovernmental Panel on Climate Change (IPCC) third assessment report. These reports are carried out at intervals of approximately five years, and the IPCC is currently working on the fifth assessment report, suggesting the estimate is in urgent need of updating.

2. The Building Research Establishment (BRE) Environmental Assessment Method (BREEAM) sets the standard for sustainable design of buildings by assessing their environmental performance. See http://www.breeam.org/page.jsp?id=66.

3. A number of concepts can fall under the broad definition of "virtualization." One example of virtualization is the ability to share hardware resources by a number of operating systems simultaneously.

4. Cloud computing is defined as location-independent computing, whereby shared servers provide resources, software, and data to computers and other devices on demand, as with the electricity grid.

5. An example of an application is described in the "New Mobile Phone App to Track Carbon Footprint" article, available online at http://cleantechnica.com/2008/09/29/new-mobile-phone-app-to-track-carbon-footprint/.

Bibliography

Babcock, C. 2009. "IBM Building Smarter City Cloud in China." *Information Week*, September 25. http://www.informationweek.com/news/services/saas/showArticle.jhtml?articleID=220200250.

Boccaletti, G., M. Löffler, and J. Oppenheim. 2008. "How IT Can Cut Carbon Emissions." *The McKinsey Quarterly*, McKinsey & Company, October. http://www.mckinsey.com/clientservice/sustainability/pdf/how_it_can_cut_carbon_missions.pdf.

BusinessWire. 2010. "GE Bringing State-of-the-Art Smart Grid Efficiency, Reliability and Productivity Technologies to China." *BusinessWire*, January 8. http://www. businesswire.com/portal/site/home/permalink/?ndmViewId=news_view&news Id=20100108005613&newsLang=en.

Cisco. 2009. "Cisco Signs MoU with Chongqing to Foster Economic, Social and Environmental Sustainability." September 11. http://newsroom.cisco.com/ dlls/2009/prod_091109d.html.

The Climate Group and Global eSustainability Initiative (GeSI). 2008. "SMART2020: Enabling the Low Carbon Economy in the Information Age." A report by The Climate Group on behalf of the Global eSustainability Initiative (GeSI). http://www.smart2020.org/_assets/files/02_Smart2020Report.pdf.

Couts, A. 2011. "Cisco: Mobile Web Traffic Growing at a Staggering Rate." *Digital Trends*, February 1. http://www.digitaltrends.com/mobile/cisco-mobile-web-traffic-growing-at-a-staggering-rate/.

Ezell, S. 2010. *Explaining International IT Application Leadership: Intelligent Transport Systems*. Report of ITIF, The Information Technology & Innovation Foundation. January. http://www.itif.org/files/2010-1-27-ITS_Leadership.pdf.

Gartner. 2007. "Gartner Estimates ICT Industry Accounts for 2 Percent of Global CO_2 Emissions." http://www.gartner.com/it/page.jsp?id=503867.

Google. 2010. Google Earth Engine, http://earthengine.googlelabs.com/#intro.

GreenTouch. 2010. http://www.greentouch.org/index.php?page=about-us.

IBM. 2010. "Coventry Launches First UK City's Mass Online Brainstorm: CovJam." http://www.ibm.com/smarterplanet/global/files/gb__en_uk__cities__covjam. pdf?ca=content_body&met=uk_smarterplanet_sustainable_cities_ideas&re=spc.

———. n.d. "Smarter Cities Challenge." https://smartercitieschallenge.org.

Kim, Tong-hyung. 2010. "Smarter, Greener Power." *The Korea Times*, February 24. http://www.koreatimes.co.kr/www/news/tech/2010/02/133_61390.html.

Mingay, S., B. Tratz-Ryan, and S. Stokes. 2010. "Hype Cycle for Sustainability and Green IT." Gartner, July 29. http://www.gartner.com/.

Mitchell, S., and W. Wagener. 2009. "The Connected Bus: Connected and Sustainable Mobility Pilot." Cisco Internet Business Solutions Group. http:// www.connectedurbandevelopment.org/pdf/toolkit/tcbprojectcud0617final-090618114521-phpapp01.pdf.

Organisation for Economic Co-operation and Development (OECD). 2010. "Greener and Smarter. ICTs, the Environment and Climate Change." http:// www.oecd.org/dataoecd/27/12/45983022.pdf. September.

World Bank. 2010. *The Little Data Book on Information and Communication Technology*. Washington, DC: World Bank.

CHAPTER 20

Urban Agriculture Is Climate-Smart

Anjali Acharya, Dan Hoornweg, and Marielle Dubbeling

Overview

Rising food prices and the impending impact of climate change are placing the health and quality of life of the world's poor under greater threat. Increasing urbanization and the prevalence of poverty in urban areas have combined to make this threat most severe in the cities of the developing world. Escalating food prices—due to increasing fuel and fertilizer costs and higher purchasing power of the growing middle class—are expected to push more people into poverty, increasing their vulnerability and food insecurity. In the long term, the urban poor with their lower adaptive capacity will be most affected by the growing frequency of extreme weather events and the impacts of changes in temperature and rainfall patterns on agricultural productivity.

Cities are major players in the effort to establish low-carbon growth while simultaneously helping their populations prepare for climate uncertainty and natural disasters. Environmentally sustainable solutions for food, water, energy, and transport are needed as integrated components of a disaster risk-management plan. Urban agriculture is a potential "outside-the-box" solution. It can play a strong role in enhancing food security for the urban poor, greening the city, and improving the urban climate, while stimulating the productive reuse of urban organic wastes and reducing the urban energy footprint.

Urban Agriculture Promotes Food Security

Modern conventional agriculture systems are threatened by shifts in climate zones. Climate change will reduce water sources, raise sea levels, and dry the interiors of the northern continents. This will stress agricultural systems and likely cause food shortages. An expected increase in the frequency of natural and human-induced disasters will also cause disruptions in food-supply chains, thus further reducing food security. Meeting the needs of a burgeoning urban population with its increased affluence and desire for more resource-intensive foods, such as meat products, in an era of increased climate insecurity requires adopting more sustainable methods of food production.

Although cities continue to largely depend on rural agriculture, urban agriculture in some cases already provides a large part of a city's food supply for vegetables (especially fresh leafy vegetables), as well as for fresh milk, poultry, eggs, and—to a lesser extent—pork and fruits. Depending on the city, between 10 and 60 percent of food in poor urban households is self-produced (De Zeeuw et al. 2011). In Harare, 41 percent of poor households normally rely on homegrown food at least once a week, as do 12 percent in Maputo (Crush et al. 2010). Other data indicate the total percentage of urban demand for specific food types that are covered by urban agriculture: 58 percent of Havana's vegetables (Gonzalez Novo and Murphy 2000) and about 70 percent of Dakar's poultry are produced within city limits (Mbaye and Moustier 2000). In China, this is true for as much as 90 percent of Shanghai's eggs and almost all of its milk (Yi-Zhang and Zhangen 2000). Vegetables, fruits, meat, eggs, and milk are produced in community gardens, private backyards, schools, hospitals, window boxes, vacant public lands, and on rooftops. New innovations of "vertical farms" in which crops are grown in tall buildings using state-of-the-art hydroponics and other techniques could provide high-density population centers with year-round access to fresh and safe produce, thus enhancing public health through better nutrition.

Urban Agriculture Reduces Ecological Impacts

Cities encourage consumption, and their "food-print" accounts for a large portion of greenhouse gas (GHG) emissions. The current food system in many industrialized countries uses more than four times the energy to transport food from the farm to the plate than is used in the farming practice itself. For conventional agriculture, the need for fossil fuel–

intensive transportation along with refrigeration results in considerable energy usage.

Cities can include urban agriculture in their GHG mitigation strategies, since moving the farm closer to the kitchen helps to reduce their ecological impacts, including CO_2 emissions. Urban agriculture requires less transport and less refrigeration and therefore uses less energy than conventional production. It also enables cyclical processes and efficient use of wastes through a variety of methods, including using urban organic wastes as compost and using excess heat from industries to warm greenhouses. Locally grown and prepared food also reduces fuel use for transportation (known as "food miles") and is less likely to be associated with the GHG emissions from land conversion to agricultural land. For example, if the 350,000 citizens of Almere in the Netherlands buy 10 percent of their food from local sources, emission reductions would equal the energy use of 2,000 Dutch households. Meanwhile, market costs will likely be significantly reduced because of the reduced transport and energy consumption.

Urban Agriculture Greens Urban Spaces

The growth of cities exerts significant pressure on natural resources, resulting in a reduction of green open spaces, depletion of trees, increased heat island effects, floods, and other natural disasters, all of which are further aggravated by the effects of climate change. In addition, air quality worsens as vehicle use grows exponentially in many cities.

The use of productive urban greening to grow food improves the urban environment. Other ways to green the city include the use of green rooftops, which adjusts the built environment in response to climate change. In addition, tree planting can build a city's green "lungs" and contribute to improved air quality. In 2007, Brisbane, Australia, became the first city in the world to include both urban agriculture and green roofs in its municipal action plan to meet predicted global climate change challenges. Since 2008, the municipality of Ethekwini, Durban has promoted rooftop gardening for temperature and stormwater benefits, biodiversity protection, and food production (City of Durban 2011). Such green spaces contribute to lower costs and energy savings by improving a city's microclimate through the significant cooling effect due to direct shading and increases in evapotranspiration. Green spaces also help control stormwater flows by increasing infiltration.

Urban Agriculture Optimizes Water Use

Declining rainfall in many areas, aggravated by climate change, has resulted in surface water gradually drying up and the levels of groundwater falling. With increased water scarcity, cities and their growing populations require innovative solutions such as more efficient water use and decentralized reuse of wastewater.

Rainwater harvesting systems are currently promoted in residential areas and for peri-urban agriculture. Stormwater collected in roadside gutters and stored in local retention ponds can be used to irrigate city green areas and urban agriculture. In addition, using recycled, treated wastewater for urban farming is an innovative adaptation measure. Porous pavement and other similar measures can also lessen the effects of flooding.

Urban Agriculture Helps Mitigate Disaster Risk and Flooding

As discussed in chapter 22, city populations in low-elevation coastal areas will be exposed to hurricanes and storm surges. These storms and resultant floods are expected to contribute to a rapid increase in the number of urban poor, as these weather events will be more destructive in squatter settlements and slums.

Urban agriculture can contribute to proper land management and land use for urbanized areas, and can even serve as an innovative way of keeping environmentally sensitive and dangerous urban lands from illegal residential development. The use of micro-gardens can provide an emergency food source in the aftermath of natural disasters, including extreme weather events resulting from climate change. Hillsides and valleys prone to flooding and landslides can be planted with trees, providing added value as agro-forestry, while preventing erosion and creating flood buffers for the existing housing areas.

Conclusion: Integrating Urban Agriculture in City Planning

In their efforts to identify low-carbon growth paths, cities and local governments in both developed and developing countries are paying greater attention to building codes, urban transportation, and urban form. Given its potential, city officials could also more comprehensively incorporate urban agriculture into their cities' action plans to build climate-resilient cities that can provide affordable, safe, and healthy food for residents.

Bibliography

City of Durban. 2011. http://www.durban.gov.za/services/epcpd.

Crush, J., A. Hovorka, and D. Tevera. 2010. *Urban Food Production and Household Food Security in Southern African Cities.* Urban Food Security Series No 4. African Food Security Urban Network (AFSUN).

De Zeeuw, H., R. Van Veenhuizen, and M. Dubbeling. 2011. "The Role of Urban Agriculture in Building Resilient Cities in Developing Countries: Foresight Project on Global Food and Farming Future." *Journal of Agricultural Science* 149: 153–63.

Gonzalez Novo, M., and C. Murphy. 2000. "Urban Agriculture in the City of Havana: A Popular Response to a Crisis." In *Growing Cities, Growing Food: Urban Agriculture on the Policy Agenda,* ed. N. Bakker, M. Dubbeling, S. Guendel, U. Sabel Koschella, and H. de Zeeuw, 329–47. Feldafing: German Foundation for International Development (DSE).

Mbaye, A., and P. Moustier. 2000. "Market-Oriented Urban Agricultural Production in Dakar." In *Growing Cities, Growing Food, Urban Agriculture on the Policy Agenda,* ed. N. Bakker, M. Dubbeling, S. Guendel, U. Sabel Koschella, and H. de Zeeuw, 235–56. Feldafing: DSE.

Wenhua, J., and C. Jianming. 2008. "Adapting to Water Scarcity: Improving Water Sources and Use in Urban Agriculture in Beijing." *Urban Agriculture Magazine* 20 (September). Resource Centres on Urban Agriculture and Food Security (RUAF).

Yan, W., C. Jianming, X. Liou, and J. Liu. 2009. "Resilient Chinese Cities: Examples from Beijing and Shanghai." *Urban Agriculture Magazine* 22 (June). RUAF.

Yi-Zhang, C., and Z. Zhangen. 2000. "Shanghai: Trends Towards Specialised and Capital-Intensive Urban Agriculture." In *Growing Cities, Growing Food, Urban Agriculture on the Policy Agenda,* ed. N. Bakker, M. Dubbeling, S. Guendel, U. Sabel Koschella, and H. de Zeeuw, 467–76. Feldafing: DSE.

CHAPTER 21

Urban Forestry

Leticia Guimarães and Monali Ranade

Overview

Urban forestry is defined as the planned, integrated, and systematic approach to managing trees in urban and peri-urban areas to allow them to contribute to environmental health and the socioeconomic well-being of urban society. Urban forestry encompasses woodlands, groups of trees, and individual trees in areas where dense conglomerations of people live. Urban forestry also covers a wide variety of habitats, including streets, parks, and derelict corners, and is concerned with a great range of benefits and problems (FAO 1995).

China's Early Involvement with Urban Forestry

The Chinese government has been involved in urban forestry since 1950 when Chairman Mao Zedong initiated a campaign to promote tree and flower planting in areas near cities. In 1981 the National People's Congress adopted the "Resolution on the unfolding of nationwide voluntary tree planting campaign," determining that citizens should plant three to five trees per year or do the equivalent amount of work in seedling, cultivation, tree tending, and other related services. It is stated that at least 1,000 million trees were planted in China between 1982 and 1992 (Dembner 1993). In the 1990s, in response to the increasing pressure

from population growth and urbanization and to improve urban environmental conditions, long-term planning of urban forestry was included in
China's National Development Strategy. The goal was to expand the
coverage of urban forests and trees to 45 percent in 70 percent of all cities by 2050 (Liu et al. 2004).

Potential Benefits from Urban Forestry for China

A significant amount of progress has been achieved in advancing urban
forestry in China. In 2004, cities such as Changchun, Guangzhou, and
Nanjing already had more than 40 percent of their total area covered by
trees (Konijnendijk and Gauthier 2006). Nevertheless, much remains to
be done. Air quality in the main Chinese cities in the first half of 2010
decreased for the first time from one year to the next since 2005 (Jacobs
2010). During the last quarter of 2008, the average concentration of particulates in Beijing's air violated the World Health Organization's standards more than 80 percent of the time (WHO 2008). Further, China is
currently the largest emitter of greenhouse gases (GHG) in the world[1]
and will also be one of the countries impacted the most by climate
change. Air pollution and GHG emissions continue to grow in China due
to the numerous construction and infrastructure projects in the cities,
combined with an increasing number of private cars and poor road infrastructure. In this context, urban forestry offers significant opportunities
to mitigate air pollution and GHG emissions and promote multiple environmental and social co-benefits in China. Those benefits include carbon
sequestration, improvements in air quality, and microclimate regulation.

Carbon Sequestration

Trees have the ability to sequester and store carbon in trunks, leaves, and
roots and, in the long term, recycle nutrients in the soil. Forest composition and the age structure of urban forests influence their carbon storage
and sequestration. A study on carbon storage in the city of Hangzhou
(Zhao et al. 2010) showed a higher rate of carbon storage in the oldest
city center trees, even though these older trees had a lower carbon
sequestration rate than younger trees in other districts.

Selecting the proper native evergreen species can improve the carbon
sequestration potential of urban forests throughout the year, while at the
same time contributing to urban forest biodiversity. As properly managing green spaces in urban and peri-urban areas may also increase carbon

storage (Zhao et al. 2010), urban forestry projects can be eligible to benefit from the sale of GHG emission reductions in the regulatory (that is, the Clean Development Mechanism or CDM) and voluntary carbon markets.

The CDM methodology AR AMS0002 (Version 2) covers small-scale afforestation[2] and reforestation projects in urban areas resulting in GHG removal of up to 16,000 tonnes of CO_2 equivalent (tCO_2e) per year. The applicability condition of this methodology requires projects to be implemented in lands along the transportation infrastructure (for example, strips along streets, highways, and train tracks) or in human settlements (for example, residential and commercial lawns or parks within the cities). In the voluntary market, the Voluntary Carbon Standard (VCS) and the Chicago Climate Exchange (CCX)[3] also have methodologies regulating the development of urban forestry projects.

Air Quality Improvement

Urban forests improve air quality by removing nitrogen dioxide (NO_2), sulfur dioxide (SO_2), carbon monoxide, ozone, and particulate matter, as trees capture airborne particulates on foliage, which is then washed off by rainwater, blown off by winds, or recycled into the soil through leaf fall. This function is particularly important in Chinese cities where air quality is quickly deteriorating due to rapid urbanization and industrialization. China has the highest level of SO_2 emissions in the world and acid rain has become a problem in nearly 200 of the 440 cities monitored in China (Jacobs 2010). Recently, nitrogen oxide (NO_x) has also emerged as a major air pollutant in many cities due to a rapid increase in private cars and resulting traffic congestion (Jim and Chen 2008). Smog during the summer months is a serious threat to local people's health.

The environmental services provided by urban forests in improving air quality can be fostered by planting more trees closer to areas with a large concentration of pollutants. This has been established as a key factor for determining tree pollutant removal efficiency in a study developed in Guangzhou (Jim and Chen 2008). Trees in more polluted industrial lands were more efficient than trees in less polluted recreational lands in removing pollutants, even though the total removal of pollutants was larger in the recreational areas because of their higher concentration of trees. Chinese cities could benefit from prioritizing tree plantations in polluted areas, such as along busy roads and in industrial districts. The study also showed that the benefits of urban forestry could be promoted by systematic green space planning.

For positive results, it is important to select diverse species with a higher tolerance to pollutants. The size of the leaf, the growth rate of the tree, and the health condition of individual plants can also affect the amount of pollutant removal (Jim and Liu 2001b). In Chinese cities, since the pollution levels are aggravated during the winter, planting evergreen species that grow throughout the year is also an important strategy (Jim and Chen 2009). Overall, it is important to provide sound urban forest management, from identifying the locations for planting and the design configuration of the space to maximizing the trees' environmental benefits (for example, planting two or three rows of trees, high plant density, and adequate ventilation) and providing sufficient maintenance and protection.

Microclimate Regulation

In Chinese cities, most of the population resides in multistory buildings. As a result, the shading provided by trees does not have the same effect as in some cities in Western countries, but the trees' evapotranspiration still affects the microclimate. Trees absorb heat from the atmosphere and vaporize it into water, a natural air conditioning process that can significantly decrease ambient temperature, creating an oasis effect (Jim and Chen 2009). By lowering air temperature in summer, urban forests may reduce energy demand for cooling purposes and make the ambient temperature comfortable for pedestrians, cyclists, and outside activities.

Other Socioeconomic Benefits

The revitalization of cities through the promotion of urban forestry can have direct effects on the welfare of the residents. Urban and peri-urban forestry can provide local residents with recreational alternatives, create local jobs, and, when developed in residential areas, even enhance property values. The shade of urban forests may also contribute to the longevity of road infrastructure. A healthy urban forest is a major municipal capital investment, but the value of its benefits is between two and six times the costs of tree planting and care (McPherson et al. 2005).

Urban Forestry Initiatives in China

Over the last two decades, Chinese cities of all sizes have become involved in urban forestry. In 1989, Changchun, Jilin's capital, started a program called "Forest City," and became the first city in China to have urban forestry as a city development goal. In 2001, Shanghai commenced planning its urban forest development with the goal of reaching 35 percent forest coverage by 2020. In 2002, the capital of Huaining county initiated a plan for urban forest development (Liu et al. *2004*) and in 2003, Guangzhou launched the "Beautiful Mountain, Green Land, Blue Sky and Clean River" project, which included an urban forestry component, to improve people's living standards. In Beijing, the 2005 Eco-Cities strategy fostered research for the development of an urban forestry plan even though it was eventually not put into practice (see also box 21.1).

While urban forestry is slowly becoming more popular in China, a particular challenge in this sector is the fact that many different agencies are involved with decisions related to urban greening. Land resources in urban and peri-urban areas, for example, are state property managed by various levels of government and public institutions rather than by private individuals (Jim and Liu 2001a). Small streets and lanes are the responsibility of the local bureau, and the larger roads fall under the City Park Bureau. Species selection and decisions related to the choice of planting are done through the City Planting Office in consultation with the District Bureau and the Institute of Landscape and Gardening (Knuth 2005). Improved cooperation and coordination between these different authorities will lead to more successful urban and peri-urban forestry.

Box 21.1

Integrating Urban Greening into Beijing's Urban Master Plan

In 2002, the Beijing Municipal Institute of City Planning and Design asked the scientific community for support in revising the Beijing Urban Master Plan. A strategic conceptual framework was developed to be part of China's Eco-Cities strategy for 2005. Among other things, the plan identified the potential for compensation schemes as a strategy to reflect the real value of green spaces. Although the plan itself was never implemented because of problems related to budget and project preparation, the ideas are still useful for future projects.

For the sustainable development of Beijing, the plan encompassed an integrated ecological network at three levels:

*   *Regional level:* Protecting the environmental quality of Beijing and habitats for wildlife by establishing a big natural and seminatural forest area in the north-

(continued next page)

Box 21.1 *(continued)*

west and an ecological buffer belt (including forest parks, forest belts, nurseries, farmlands, vegetable lands, orchards, and shelterbelts against sandstorms) in the southeast.

- *City level:* Improving urban environmental quality and providing habitats and migration routes for wildlife by creating a green network system of green wedges, parks, and green corridors to help limit future urban expansion; and forming an integrated ecological network by connecting the urban center, forest parks, mountains, and the outer regional space.
- *Neighborhood level:* Providing green areas in the neighborhoods by vertical greening (for example, roof gardens and wall greening) and by creating green extensions and connections of riverside greenways, road greenways, and public parks to permeate into the built-up areas.

The built-in green space provided by the ecological network was also designed—especially at the city and regional levels—to protect existing green space and prevent both industrial development and municipal infrastructure from invading and occupying green areas.

Source: Lia et al. 2005.

To create an effective urban forestry approach, city and municipal officials should also devise an urban forestry strategy for the next 20 to 40 years and incorporate this strategy in municipal environmental initiatives, city-level climate action, and sustainability plans. The plan must be based on the principles of watershed and landscape management, using trees and forests to protect soil, land, biological diversity, and water. It must also develop or support a multifunctional network of urban green spaces and trees to respond to the food, energy, and income needs of the poor (Gauthier 2006).

Programs supporting urban tree planting should focus on incentives for growing trees in residential and public lands, integrating trees in mixed land use and along transit corridors, training in tree care practices, implementing tree care agreements, and involving communities in enforcing tree protection. To implement all activities, urban forest management plans need to have adequate budget and personnel, such as forestry managers, field operations staff, technical and administrative personnel, and nursery crews.

One final challenge to be overcome is that in China the government is still the major funder of urban forestry. The private sector has no incentives to invest in it as there are no direct short-term economic benefits. This presents a great challenge for scaling up urban forestry in China because government investments alone are not sufficient to satisfy the urgent need for planting new trees in many cities (Liu et al. 2004). The city and municipal governments should encourage or partner with the private sector and local nonprofit groups to supplement volunteer tree planting and maintenance. Initiatives such as the one in Shanghai to increase incentives for private sector involvement in urban forestry could potentially be replicated in other cities across China (see box 21.2).

Conclusion

Urban forestry presents an important opportunity for mitigating climate change and air pollution while improving the quality of life for the urban population in China. It also contributes to landscape enhancement, local wildlife protection, erosion control, and protection of catchments for urban water supplies. This strategy nevertheless comes with a price. Urban forestry projects compete for land with other construction and infrastructure projects that have greater rates of return and therefore are more attractive to private sector investments. To foster the development of urban forestry initiatives, the Chinese government should consider

---

Box 21.2

Motivating Private Investments in Urban Forestry

For a significant period, the Shanghai government has been renting out land for urban forestry purposes to private companies. According to the contract between the government and a company, 60 percent of the land rented by the company must be used to grow forest, and the remaining 40 percent can be used for establishing a tree seedling and flower nursery, which can bring commercial benefits to the company within a short period of time. In addition, to even further support the companies in establishing urban forests, the government provides them with certain economic supplements according to the area of the rented land. After 10 years, the forests are returned to the government. This initiative has successfully fostered an increase in urban forestry in Shanghai.

Source: Liu et al. 2004.

advancing policies that motivate private sector investments and foster public participation, not only in planting activities but also conserving green areas. The different sectors related to urban forestry, which currently constitute the fragmented and complex institutional framework that oversees urban forestry activities in Chinese cities, need to be systematically integrated.

Urban forestry is already included in China's National Development Plan. The goal to expand forest cover to 45 percent of cities' total surface in 70 percent of the Chinese cities by 2050 should be supported by specific goals at the city level. This may include targets for GHG emission reductions and improvements in air quality. This means not only increasing the overall tree cover in cities, but also choosing the right plant species for different areas and investing in management practices that ensure the long-term presence of forests in cities.

Notes

1. Total GHG emissions in China are the largest in the world, while per capita emissions are about 33 percent of that of Organisation for Economic Co-operation and Development (OECD) countries. For more information, visit http://cait.wri.org/, last accessed on October 12, 2010.

2. Afforestation refers to establishing a forest or stand of trees in an area where the preceding vegetation or land use was not forest.

3. The first urban forestry project approved by the CCX was developed by Michigan State University in 2009 at its East Lansing Michigan campus. For more information please see CCX 2009.

Bibliography

Chicago Climate Exchange (CCX). 2009. *Offsets Report* 1(5), September. http://www.chicagoclimatex.com/docs/offsets/Reports/CCX_Offsets_Report_Vol1No5_Sept_Dec.pdf.

Dembner, S. 1993. "Urban Forestry in Beijing." *Unasylva* 173, 44(2): 13–18.

Food and Agriculture Organization of the United Nations (FAO). 1995. *The Potential of Urban Forestry in Developing Countries: A Concept Paper.* Forestry Department, FAO, Rome. http://www.fao.org/docrep/005/t1680e/t1680e00.htm.

Gauthier, M. 2006. "Urban Forestry and Greening. Towards Achieving the Millennium Development Goals." European Tropical Forests Research Network, *ETFR News* 47/48. Winter 2006–2007. Forests and the Millennium Development Goals. http://www.etfrn.org/etfrn/newsletter/news4748/nl47_oip_26.htm.

Jacobs, A. 2010. "In China, Pollution Worsens Despite New Efforts." *New York Times*, September. http://www.nytimes.com/2010/07/29/world/asia/29china.html.

Jim, C., and W. Chen. 2008. "Assessing the Ecosystem Service of Air Pollution Removal by Urban Trees in Guangzhou (China)." *Journal of Environmental Management* 88(4): 665–76.

———. 2009. "Ecosystem Services and Valuation of Urban Forests in China." *Cities* 26(4): 187–94.

Jim, C., and H. Liu. 2001a. "Patterns and Dynamics of Urban Forests in Relation to Land Use and Development History in Guangzhou, China." *The Geographical Journal* 167(4): 358–75.

———. 2001b. "Species Diversity of Three Major Urban Forest Types in Guangzhou City, China." *Forest Ecology and Management* 146(1): 99–114.

Knuth, L. 2005. *Legal and Institutional Aspects of Urban, Peri-urban Forestry and Greening: a Working Paper for Discussion.* Food and Agriculture Organization (FAO) of the United Nations, Legal Papers Online # 48. FAO, Rome.

Konijnendijk, C., and M. Gauthier. 2006. "Urban Forestry for Multifunctional Urban Land Use." In *Cities Farming for the Future. Urban Agriculture for Green and Urban Cities*, ed. R. van Veenhuizen. Published by RUAF Foundation, IDRC and IIRR. http://publicwebsite.idrc.ca/EN/Resources/Publications/Pages/IDRCBookDetails.aspx?PublicationID=111.

Lia, F., R. Wang, J. Paulussen, and X. Liu. 2005. "Comprehensive Concept Planning of Urban Greening Based on Ecological Principles: A Case Study in Beijing, China." *Landscape and Urban Planning* 72(4) 325–36.

Liu, C., X. Shen, P. Zhou, S. Che, and Y. Zhang. 2004. "Urban Forestry in China: Status and Prospects." *Urban Agriculture Magazine* 13: 15–17.

McPherson, G., J. Simpson, P. Peper, S. Maco, and Q. Xiao. 2005. "Municipal Forest Benefits and Costs in Five US Cities." *Journal of Forestry* 103(8): 411–16.

World Health Organization (WHO). 2008. *Health in Asia and the Pacific.* Geneva: WHO. http://www.searo.who.int/biregional/linkfiles/Biregional_Publication.pdf.

World Resources Institute (WRI). n.d. Climate Analysis Indicators Tool. http://cait.wri.org/login-main.php?log=7andpostlogin=cait, last accessed on October 12, 2010.

Zhao, M., Z. Kong, F. Escobedo, and J. Gao. 2010. "Impacts of Urban Forests on Offsetting Carbon Emissions from Industrial Energy Use in Hangzhou, China." *Journal of Environmental Management* 91(4): 807–13.

PART 6

Beyond Mitigation:
Cities' Adaptation to Climate Change

CHAPTER 22

Adapting to Climate Risks: Building Resilient Cities in China

Paul Procee and Henrike Brecht

Overview

Cities are hotspots of disaster and climate risks. The risks are linked to the high concentrations of people, resources, and infrastructure in urban areas. In fact, the ongoing process of urbanization is one of the main reasons for the staggering increase in disaster death tolls and economic losses over the past decades. Across the world, only 1.5 percent of the total land area is estimated to produce 50 percent of worldwide GDP, while accommodating about a sixth of the world's population. Risks also stem from poverty, inequalities, failures of governance, and residential neighborhoods in hazard-prone areas. Cities therefore play an important role in tackling disasters and climate change; they are a major part of the problem but also a major part of the solution. Cities share the global responsibility to respond to these changes. They face both the challenge of mitigation in a carbon-constrained economy and the challenge of adaptation to climate change and its associated effects, including water and food scarcity, storm and flood events, sea-level rise, and environmental migration.

This chapter explores how cities can adapt to the ongoing climate changes and argues that a city's adaptation strategy needs to build on sound risk management practices for disasters, including a systematic process of risk and vulnerability assessments, building codes reflecting climate risks, emergency preparedness, and financial risk transfer mechanisms. It makes the case that cities will be better off if they evaluate their risks related to climate change, develop action plans to deal with potential hazards, and, ultimately, reduce their vulnerability to the adverse impacts of climate change.

Why China's Cities Need Climate Risk Management

China ranks among some of the most vulnerable countries exposed to meteorological hazards. China has about 70 percent of its land area, 50 percent of its population, and 80 percent of its industrial and agricultural areas at risk (Meiyan 2010). Projections show that the country will be vulnerable to more frequent and intense rainfall and floods in the southwest, and while typhoons are predicted to decrease in number, their intensity and potential impacts are projected to increase (see also box 22.1). At the same time, China's water scarcity problems are expected to become more severe, with the arid areas at risk of increased desertifica-

---

Box 22.1

Typhoons and Climate Change: Adaptation through Risk Management and Risk Transfer

Typhoons are heat engines that gather strength from warm seawater. The associated windstorms and floods can wreak devastating effects on human populations. China is particularly vulnerable to destructive typhoons, which can have a significant impact on both urban and rural communities. In 2005, for example, typhoon Talim killed 110 people in eastern China after unleashing torrential rains and triggering floods and landslides. More than 150,000 people were evacuated and thousands of homes were damaged or destroyed. The Ministry of Civil Affairs in China reported that the typhoon caused RMB 12.19 billion in damages. Nearly three weeks later, typhoon Damrey flattened houses, damaged crops, and forced more than 170,000 people to flee their homes in Hainan. In 2010, eight storms affected China, including typhoon Megi, which struck Fujian Province in the form of a severe tropical storm with an impact on 729,800 people. A total of 36,050 hectares of crops and 530 houses were destroyed, with overall losses of RMB 2.8 billion.

(continued next page)

Box 22.1 *(continued)*

While these damages are already substantial and underscore the need for adaptive measures to mitigate the impact of these rare and extreme catastrophic events, preliminary evidence suggests that the intensity of typhoons and their ability to cause widespread flooding will increase in the future as a result of climate change. Figure B22.1.1 illustrates the strong link between the Power Dissipation Index (PDI), a measure of a typhoon's intensity, and sea surface temperature (SST) over the main development region for typhoons, suggesting that with rising sea surface temperatures, this destructive capacity will increase. Climate models agree that recent trends in sea surface warming will not cease in the foreseeable future, and while the 20th century witnessed an approximately 0.6°C warming of the tropical sea surface temperature, substantially greater warming of about 2°C is anticipated for the 21st century due to anthropogenic forcing. These rising surface water temperatures and the potential increases in the intensity of typhoons indicate that coastal communities are likely to be exposed to even more intense storms. The increase in coastal population and the growing number of buildings in disaster-prone areas will further accentuate economic damage caused by typhoons.

Figure B22.1.1   Tropical North Pacific SST over the Period of July–November and Locations 1N–15N to 160E–150W, versus Smoothed Total PDI

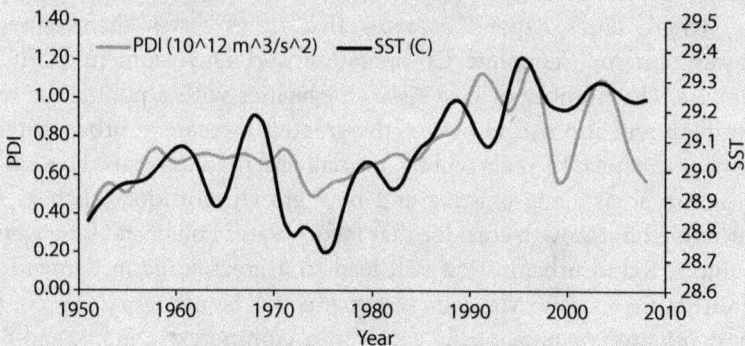

Source: Data provided by Prof. Kerry Emanuel from the Massachusetts Institute of Technology.

The failure of a city to manage this risk associated with typhoons and tropical storms has direct repercussions for their communities and can cause debilitating economic effects. Cities at risk should act quickly to implement adaptation mea-

(continued next page)

438   Sustainable Low-Carbon City Development in China

Box 22.1 *(continued)*

sures, including strengthening building codes, increasing the capacity of storm-water collection systems, building structures to protect against storm surges, and—of paramount importance—creating institutions that are skilled, dynamic, and flexible to respond to potential disasters. In addition to risk management, prevention, and mitigation, it is also essential to devise risk transfer instruments in order to transfer the risk of disaster-related damages to the international capital market. Building the resilience of cities and provinces to withstand the likely impacts of climate change will require a comprehensive adaptation framework that covers the spectrum of risk management approaches.

Source: Contributed by Abed Khalil, World Bank.

---

tion. The 130 million residents of China's coastal cities are particularly vulnerable to sea-level rise. Additional consequences of climate change include water and food scarcity; a more rapid spread of respiratory, vector, and water-borne diseases; greater population displacement; and conflicts over scarce resources.

In the next 15 years, the urban population in East Asia will double. The fastest rates of urbanization will take place in China and Southeast Asia, where cities expand at rates five times faster than those in Organisation for Economic Co-operation and Development (OECD) countries. The number of East Asian megacities with a population over 10 million will also rise. However, the greatest increase in urban population over the next 15 years will be in small and medium-size cities and in peri-urban areas along existing and new growth corridors, such as the Southern China growth corridor that incorporates Fujian and Guangdong provinces. Rapid urbanization will lead to a great surge in demand for infrastructure services. Massive investments will be necessary to serve the export-oriented manufacturing economies, commercial centers, and burgeoning populations. Similarly, demand for electric power, telecommunications, rails, highways, seaports, and modern water and sanitation facilities will continue to rise. With staggering growth at present and in the near future, decisions need to be taken now to change building practices and to climate proof infrastructure. Sustainable development can be achieved only if actions are taken to make infrastructure more resilient and resistant to anticipated scenarios of long-term climate change and other hazards.

Prevention pays. Although the costs of implementing policies on climate change adaptation can initially be high, the costs of delaying action to integrate climate risk management into investments and ensure climate-smart growth will be significantly higher. Costs will result not only from direct damages but also from indirect impacts, including disruptions of supply lines, losses in productivity, and relocation costs. Prevention is cost-effective and there are measures that governments can undertake to build safer cities. The challenge for city governments is to stop viewing policies in a merely short-term view and adopt a long-term cost-benefit outlook favoring measures for climate change adaptation and disaster prevention.

China's Cities and Climate Change

Climate change increases the existing exposure and vulnerability to natural hazards. Every year, natural disasters from climate-related hazards already cause substantial loss of life, produce economic damage, and reverse gains from past economic and social development. Increased extreme events, heat and cold waves, sea-level rise, and water scarcity are some of the impacts that Chinese cities will face. China's cities are particularly vulnerable to some specific risks:

- *Extreme events:* Climate change is expected to lead to an increased intensity of storms, typhoons, droughts, and flooding. This will have impacts throughout China but specifically at risk are many of China's economic centers located on the eastern coast, which are likely to be adversely affected by more intense storm surges. The increase in precipitation in some areas is expected to result in an increase in the intensity and frequency of flooding events. In 2010, floods, long a major hazard in China, killed more than 700 people, causing US$20.9 billion in economic losses.
- *Heat and cold waves:* According to China's *National Assessment Report on Climate Change*—which was jointly issued in December 2006 by six governmental institutions, including the Ministry of Science and Technology and the Chinese Academy of Sciences—it was estimated that, compared to 2000, nationwide average temperatures would increase between 1.3 and 2.1°C by 2020, 1.5 and 2.8°C by 2030, and 2.3 and 3.3°C by 2050 (Government of China 2006). Increasing temperatures will contribute to heat island effects, and heat waves can have severe consequences, as witnessed, for example, in 2003, when 40,000 people died as a result of the European heat wave. Cold waves also have dev-

astating costs, as experienced by China in 2008 when the worst snow storm in half a century affected China's economy, destroying crops and livestock, paralyzing transportation, and disrupting operations at countless factories and companies with costs of several billion U.S. dollars.

- *Sea-level rise:* China's coastal zone represents just 2 percent of the total land area, but is home to 23 percent of the urban and 14 percent of the total population. As figure 22.1 shows, China has the largest number of people living in the low elevation coastal zone. The Intergovernmental Panel on Climate Change (IPCC) predicts that average sea levels will increase 18 centimeters by 2040 and possibly by as much as 48 centimeters by 2100 (IPCC 2007). Guangzhou, Hong Kong SAR, Ningbo, Qingdao Shanghai, and Tianjin are among the top 20 cities ranked in terms of population or assets that would be exposed to coastal flooding in the 2070s, taking into account both climate change and socioeconomic changes. Salt water intrusion due to sea-level rise poses another challenge to Chinese coastal economies. For example, salt water has intruded into Shanghai's water supply and has greatly reduced the quality of groundwater. Box 22.2 describes adaptation strategies useful for coastal cities.

Figure 22.1   Countries with Highest Urban Populations Living in the Low-Elevation Coastal Zone, 2000

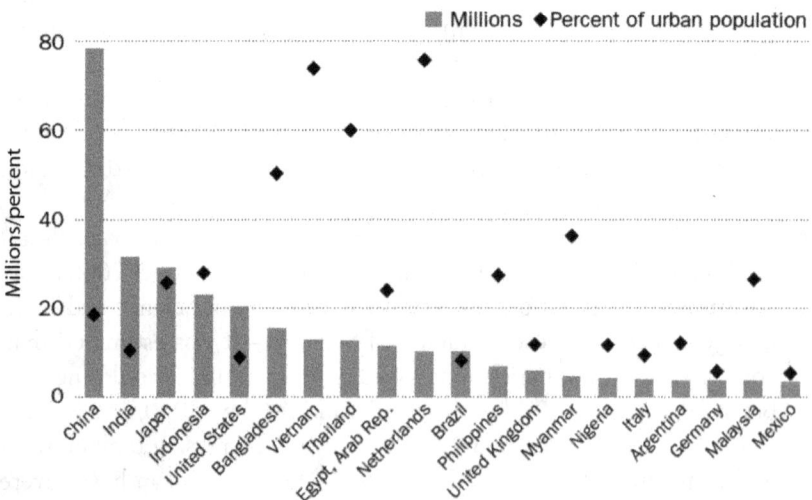

Box 22.2

Adaptation Strategies for Coastal Cities

Adaptation strategies that a coastal city will have to implement include a combination of (i) upgrading flood protection infrastructure, (ii) managing subsidence (in susceptible cities), (iii) adjusting land-use planning by restricting development on floodplains, (iv) selectively relocating away from high-risk areas, and (v) developing flood warning and evacuation systems.

Relocation of valuable city infrastructure is extremely difficult but might be necessary to reduce risks to acceptable levels. Cities in locations prone to human-induced subsidence could reduce future exposure and risk by having and enforcing policies to minimize future human-induced subsidence, as is already the case in the Netherlands and major cities in Japan and China. In addition, all port cities should use a combination of spatial planning and enhanced defenses to manage the increasing risk of sea-level rise and storm surges from climate change.

Source: Prasad et al. 2009.

- *Water scarcity:* Climate change is expected to aggravate China's water scarcity problems. While the total annual precipitation will increase partly as a result of climate change, higher evaporation together with a spatially uneven distribution of precipitation will certainly worsen the already serious water scarcity situation, especially in the north of China. The major river basins in this part of China are already experiencing decreases in precipitation and water flow. Over the last 100 years, inter-regional differences in precipitation have increased, with rainfall gradually declining in the north at a rate of 20–40 millimeters per decade, and rising in the south at a rate of 20–60 millimeters per decade. Similarly, over the past 20 years, water flows have declined by 41 percent in the Hai River basin, 15 percent in the Huang River basin, 15 percent in the Huai River basin, and 9 percent in the Liao River basin (Xie et al. 2009). For these "3-H basins," the current water shortage—about 30–40 cubic kilometers per year—is projected to rise to 56.5 cubic kilometers by 2050 (NDRC et al. 2007).

Vulnerable groups. Already vulnerable groups will often be the most severely affected. Groups that are already vulnerable will likely face some of the most serious exposure to climate change risks. Such groups are often at the highest risk in the event of natural disasters due to the location of their low-income settlements. These settlements are often on sites subject to floods and landslides, infrastructure is weak or lacking, and housing is substandard and prone to fire damage or collapse. Low-income and vulnerable groups thus face threats to their lives, assets, and future prosperity because of the increased risk of storms, floods, landslides, and extreme temperatures. The same groups are also more likely to suffer from an unequal distribution of scarce assets, such as water, energy, and urban infrastructure, thereby increasing their vulnerability. Recovering from disasters is also particularly difficult for the poorest and most vulnerable population as they do not have resources or adequate safety nets, and public policies often prioritize rebuilding efforts in key economic regions and areas of the city.

Building Resilient Cities

Resilience is the capacity of a society, city, or community to adapt when exposed to a hazard. It does this by either defending against or adapting to change in order to reach and maintain an acceptable level of functioning and structure. A resilient society can withstand shocks and rebuild itself when necessary. A resilient city is one that is able to sustain itself through its systems by dealing with issues and events that threaten, damage, or work to destroy it. The resilience of communities, finally, is the resilience of individual households, which depends both on the assets (capital, labor, social, and knowledge) they possess, as well as on the services provided by external infrastructure and institutions (such as all elements of urban governance, including flood control, coastal protection and protection of other infrastructure, transport and communications, access to credit and financial systems, access to markets, and emergency relief systems). Resilience is greatly influenced by the quality of urban governance and the level of infrastructure and services provided by the public institutions.

Climate change adaptation and disaster risk management. Climate change adaptation and disaster risk management have similar strategic aims. Both are approaches for reducing the vulnerability of natural and human systems to natural hazards and disaster effects, including climate change. They exist in the framework of sustainable development and share the ultimate goal of reducing people's vulnerability and increasing their ability to cope with the impact.

Key differences between the two approaches are in dealing with weather related risks and long-term effects. On the one hand, disaster risk reduction addresses not only weather-related risk but also geophysical hazards. Because weather-related events and epidemics dominate disaster statistics, however, only the small subset of disaster risk reduction dealing with geophysical disasters fails to overlap with climate risk. On the other hand, climate change adaptation also addresses longer-term impacts of climate change, such as those related to biodiversity, ecosystem services, stress-resistant crop and animal varieties, and spread of diseases. But while adaptation to climate change covers long-term adjustments to gradual changes in average conditions, most of the impacts will indeed occur through variability and extremes. Therefore, disaster risk management is the first line of defense in adapting to climate change and a no-regrets climate change adaptation strategy. Both fields should largely be managed as one agenda to avoid overlaps and duplication.

Building resilience to natural hazards essentially embodies four steps:

- Assess the risks and consider them in development planning.
- Reduce the risks and adapt to climate change.
- Prepare for and manage residual risks.
- Transfer risks through financing and insurance.

These four steps represent the core framework for climate risk management and adaptation. Depending on the circumstances, the extent of risks present, and resources available, the four steps can be undertaken in a number of different ways and the case studies throughout this chapter give examples for each of them. All four steps, however, have common principles and approaches that are highlighted in the sections below.

Step 1: Assess the Risks and Consider Them in Development Planning

Understanding risk is critical to building more resilient communities. Risk is the probability of harmful consequences. Gaining a better understanding of the expected risks and of the main drivers of vulnerability is a key challenge for city authorities. A better knowledge of risks helps local actors communicate with decision makers, mobilize political will for assessing available policy options, and design cost-effective and timely responses.

Quantifying risk and expected future losses is the first step in a disaster risk reduction program. Three factors need to be considered to measure risk:

$$\text{Risk} = \text{Hazards} \times \text{Exposed Elements} \times \text{Vulnerability}$$

Assessment of hazards, including climate change. The hazard assessment identifies the location, severity, and probability of hazards in an area. It quantifies past and future risks. First, it assesses hazards by analyzing the historic frequencies and severities of past events in the area of interest. However, it must not stop at only quantifying the usual risks derived from historic data, but also identify risks that may be induced or exacerbated by climate change. Climate scenarios need to be incorporated in the hazard module to ensure that climate change is taken into account in decision making. The indirect climate change impacts, such as health and food security, are based on international and national data applied to local climate conditions. Indirect, second-, and third-order impacts are less obvious, but can create devastating chain reactions that undermine a city or region's ability to function and recover. Understanding both direct and indirect climate change impacts and their risk to a region or city is critical in building resilience. Box 22.3 describes a climate change impact and adaptation study for three selected Asian coastal megacities. Hazard maps assist in visualizing the results of hazard modeling.

Box 22.3

Assessing Climate Risks in Asian Coastal Megacities

Recognizing the importance of addressing urban adaptation and major vulnerabilities in the East and South Asia region, the World Bank, the Asian Development Bank (ADB), and the Japan International Cooperation Agency (JICA) undertook an analysis in three coastal megacities, Bangkok, Ho Chi Minh City, and Manila. The objectives of the studies were to strengthen the analysis of climate-related risks and impacts in these cities and to convey to national and municipal decision makers (i) the scale of climate-related impacts and vulnerabilities at the city level, (ii) estimates of associated damage costs, and (iii) potential adaptation options.

Key findings for Bangkok included:

- **Major risks are posed by increased temperature and precipitation:** Temperature increases between 1.9°C and 1.2°C are estimated for 2050. A flood that currently occurs once in 50 years may occur as frequently as once in 15 years by 2050, highlighting the potential for an increase in the frequency of extreme events.

(continued next page)

Box 22.3 *(continued)*

- **Flood-prone areas will increase due to climate change:** Under the conditions that currently lead to a 1-in-30-year flood, there will approximately be a 30 percent increase in the flood-prone area.
- **The population exposed to flooding will increase:** By 2050, the number of persons affected (flooded for more than 30 days) by a 1-in-30-year event will rise sharply.
- **Costs of damage are likely to be substantial:** The increased costs associated with climate change from a 1-in-30-year flood are approximately two percent of the gross regional domestic product (GRDP) plus additional costs associated with climate change. Over 70 percent of flood-related costs in all scenarios are a result of damage to buildings.
- **Impact on the poor and vulnerable will be substantial:** The study estimates that about 1 million inhabitants will be affected by climate change conditions in 2050. Of the total affected population, approximately one-third may have to encounter more than a half-meter inundation for at least one week, marking a twofold increase in the vulnerable population.

The policy implications resulting from the analysis are relevant to other cities assessing climate risks and identifying adaptation options. Policy implications include:

- Climate-related risks should be considered as an integral part of city and regional planning.
- Targeted, city-specific solutions combining infrastructure investments with zoning and ecosystem-based strategies are required.
- Better management of urban environment and infrastructure will help to manage potential climate-related impacts.

Source: World Bank 2010d.

Assessment of exposed elements. To determine exposure, an inventory of main assets at risk is created, including population, physical assets, economy, and environment. Inventories of assets at risk are developed using traditional techniques of data collection and databases (for example, a cadastral database) or innovative techniques (for example, remote sensing). If a risk assessment is conducted for a specific sector, the databases can be sector specific. For example, a risk assessment in the agricultural sector would need to create a geographical atlas of major crops.

Assessment of vulnerability. Vulnerability is defined as the capacity to anticipate, cope with, resist, and recover from the impact of a natural hazard. The goal of the vulnerability assessment is understanding the region or city's ability to cope with or adapt to natural hazards including existing climatic variability and future climatic changes. Different kinds of vulnerabilities can be assessed. A social vulnerability assessment, for example, will identify living conditions and vulnerable groups, such as those in poverty or homeless and with the least ability to adapt to climate change. A physical vulnerability assessment evaluates the ability of buildings, roads, and other infrastructure to withstand threats. The qualitative evaluation is based on existing and future plans, infrastructure conditions, economic growth strategies, and other development policies. In the case of Ningbo (see box 22.4), the vulnerability of the city is compared to similar, selected regional and competing Chinese cities, and against the national average. The assessment for Ningbo uses five indicators—people, infrastructure, economy, environment, and government—to illustrate the city's vulnerability to climate change impacts and natural disasters.

Box 22.4

Comprehensive City-Based Climate Adaptation: The Ningbo Local Resilience Action Plan

The city of Ningbo, Zhejiang Province, China, has made it a priority to develop a disaster prevention and reduction plan. The city has invested in climate-proofing infrastructure, integrated watershed management approaches, and strategies for urban disaster management. To improve its understanding of risks and vulnerabilities related to climate change and natural disasters, the city, supported by the World Bank, is preparing a Local Resilience Action Plan (LRAP). The plan will be based on assessments of climate change risk and city vulnerability, as well as spatial assessments. The plan will also review options to mitigate these risks and consists of a strategic set of short (less than one year), medium (one to three years), and long-term (more than three years) structural and nonstructural measures to increase the city's resilience. While the action plan outlines a set of discrete activities, developing the plan requires disaster risk reduction to be integrated in day-to-day city planning and management operations.

(continued next page)

Box 22.4 *(continued)*

Stakeholder involvement and priority setting: Developing the LRAP involves gathering input from various stakeholders at all stages of the planning process. In particular, stakeholders have been engaged at the very beginning of the program implementation and are periodically consulted—for example, at the launch of the program, to identify target areas, or to discuss drafts of the plan. Involving stakeholders also enhances resilience by raising general awareness of factors that contribute to a city's vulnerabilities and risks.

Focus areas and time frame: The plan identifies focus areas such as assets, infrastructure, sectors, geographic areas, and communities in the city, as well as expected activity time frames (short, medium, and long term) and the institution responsible for its implementation. The package and sequence of activities should be appropriate for the city's financial and technical capacities, its planning and budgeting cycles, and its political and cultural environments. In addition, it would reflect the city's and stakeholders' priorities and be consistent with local and national policies and institutions that might be involved in the implementation.

Difficult choices: Many steps in the development of an LRAP require the city to make difficult choices among competing priorities, as no city can afford every option immediately. Continuing to involve a wide variety of stakeholders will help build support for decisions.

An ongoing effort: An LRAP illustrates that building resilience is proactive, not reactive, and therefore needs to be integrated into master planning and urban development strategies. Like any urban plan, an LRAP is not a static document but a process—a series of activities, which, over time, reduce a city's vulnerabilities to natural disasters and make its citizens, businesses, and infrastructure safer. As the plan is being implemented, results should be evaluated and used to update the action plan. Ningbo municipality, for example, is well aware that the completion of its LRAP is only the first step in understanding vulnerabilities and identifying sound urban planning measures that will build resilience.

Source: Contributed by Federica Ranghieri, World Bank.

The outputs of a risk assessment need to be incorporated into sustainable development planning. The results of the assessment provide summaries of risk from future hazards and answer questions on the expected average annual losses per year. They identify the key risk factors that need to be addressed to reduce losses from climate change. The outputs of a risk assessment are visualized in risk maps. Maps are powerful tools to illustrate vulnerabilities and risks and assist in decision making. The assessment maps play a key role in choosing sites, land-use planning, visualizing distribution networks, and planning for and responding to climate change impacts, natural hazards, and other emergencies. Cities and regions must identify the geographic areas with the highest disaster risk potential and adapt accordingly. Successful development, implementation, and integration of the risk assessment will deliver high value through risk reduction, efficiency improvements, and better decision making and planning. A number of World Bank projects integrate the development of risk and vulnerability assessments.

Step 2: Reduce the Risks and Adapt to Climate Change

Risk reduction and climate adaptation include actions that reduce the severity of future disasters and the impacts of climate change. Options to reduce risks from disasters and climate change include building institutions and developing a policy framework. They also broadly entail structural mitigation works, such as sea defenses, drainage retrofitting, or reinforcement, and nonstructural means such as drain maintenance activities, establishing incentives for climate risk management, breeding resilient seeds, and organizing awareness campaigns. The costs of adaptation measures vary. While physical flood protection measures, such as dikes, are costly, other measures can be implemented with small investments. For example, minor investments in storm drainage and trash removal can greatly reduce flood risks.

Building institutions and developing a policy framework. The adaptive capacity of cities is mediated through institutions and policies. As part of the design of a comprehensive resilience strategy, cities and national governments need to systematically invest in building institutional and research capacity in areas like early warning systems, emergency preparedness, and infrastructure planning and construction. At the same time, adaptation approaches must be integrated into policies. A high-level policy framework that addresses the drivers of risk and is supportive of innovative approaches is crucial to gain traction. Box 22.5 is an example of good practice.

Reducing underlying risks. Ways to reduce underlying risks can include the use of housing and building codes, land-use planning and zoning, adaptation strategies to address sea-level rise, and mainstreaming adaptation efforts into regular planning and activities. Box 22.6 gives an overview of measures that the city of Bogota, Colombia, has undertaken to reduce its risks.

Box 22.5

Singapore: Developing a Strong Institutional Basis for Action

Because climate change actions cover many sectors of the economy and society, Singapore has developed its National Climate Change Strategy through a consultative, multistakeholder approach, involving various stakeholders and the public at large. Leadership is provided by a ministerial committee on climate change, chaired by the deputy prime minister of Singapore. All the main departments and ministries are included in the ministerial panel, which ensures that the national strategy will have strong institutional support and that policies will be fully supported by the government and other stakeholders. Because most programs involve several ministries and departments, Singapore has also established four subcommittees (for buildings, households, industry, and transportation) and four working groups (for electronics, silicon wafer fabrication, pharmaceuticals, and research and development), which operate under the national committee.

Source: Prasad et al. 2009.

Box 22.6

Bogota Disaster Vulnerability Reduction Project, Colombia

The Bogota Disaster Vulnerability Reduction Project was launched by the World Bank in 2006 to strengthen the capacity of the Capital District (DC) in Colombia to manage disaster risks and reduce the district's vulnerability in key sectors. This project is the second phase of a program that supports interventions in key regions that combine a high vulnerability to natural disasters with a high level of economic activity and contribution to the country's GDP. In particular, the Bogota project works to:

- Enhance the capacity of the Bogota, DC to identify and monitor risks by upgrading hydrologic, seismic, and volcanic detection and forecasting systems, as well as conducting vulnerability assessments that will help the city better target its investments and identify potential calamities before they occur.
- Continue the city government's existing risk reduction efforts to ensure the functioning of critical facilities and lifeline infrastructure in the event of a natural or technological catastrophe.

(continued next page)

Box 22.6 *(continued)*

- Strengthen, through training and provision of equipment, the district administration's effectiveness and capacity to prepare for and respond to significant emergencies.
- Increase awareness at the community level about the importance of risk mitigation and disaster preparedness through, among others, disaster management education and the preparation of local emergency response plans.
- Develop a risk financing strategy for losses due to natural disasters, which will provide Bogota, DC with a financial strategy that guarantees the appropriate resources for disaster reconstruction or rehabilitation will be available when needed.

Source: Prasad et al. 2009.

- *Housing and building codes:* Flood proofing of infrastructure is effective, especially where warning times are short. Appropriate codes can reduce the debilitating impacts of floods on the economy. The World Bank has assisted in defining regulations and codes intended to control the design, construction, material use, and maintenance of infrastructure that are necessary to ensure human safety and welfare.
- *Land-use planning and zoning:* Land-use planning and water management should be combined in one synthesized plan since water quantity and quality are inherently linked to the use of land. Controlling development in floodplains combined with providing incentives for development to take place elsewhere is crucial for effective adaptation. The relocation of vulnerable populations away from flood plains and landslide-prone slopes is a common adaptation response. Relocation, however, may have extremely adverse social consequences if not planned as a part of an adaptation strategy and may lead to social and political instability, for example, when people are forced to relocate from their livelihoods and social support system.
- *Adaptation strategies to address sea-level rise:* Measures combining slope protection with shore protection and combining engineering measures with biological approaches have to be taken to protect China's coastal cities. The protection and restoration of the coastal shelterbelt systems and marine ecosystem—with emphasis on cultivation, transplanting, and recovery of coastal mangroves; protection of coral reefs; and protec-

tion of coastal wetlands—will reduce the vulnerability to coastal flooding and storm surges. Countermeasures also include preventing the overexploitation of groundwater and land subsidence in coastal areas.

- *Mainstreaming:* The actions and programs for disaster risk management are most effective if they are suitably integrated with the corresponding programs of all actors in a city. For example, a structural mitigation program to improve building codes is effective only if the building permit department incorporates the modifications as a part of its routine activity. The integration of programs in the regular activities of the various functions of the cities and other stakeholders is known as "mainstreaming." It is recognized that mainstreaming is essential for effective and sustainable disaster risk management programs. Table 22.1 presents examples of mainstreaming adaptation measures into the water, infrastructure, health, tourism, transport, and energy sectors. It also presents key constraints and opportunities that these measures, policies, and instruments may cause when applied at the city level.

Synergies exist between successful climate change adaptation and successful local development. The concept of "integrated climate risk management" captures this link and promotes the integration of climate risk management strategies in development planning. In urban areas, poverty reduction, including housing upgrades and basic civic infrastructure and services, is central to adaptation. Successful, well-governed cities greatly reduce climate-related risks for low-income populations. Box 22.7 describes the approach of New York City to reduce risks through its PlaNYC.

Step 3: Prepare for and Manage Residual Risks

A critical element of disaster risk management is a quick response system to minimize casualties in the event of a disaster. Preparedness refers to activities and measures taken in advance to ensure an effective response to the impact of hazards, including the issuance of timely and effective early warnings and the temporary evacuation of people and property from threatened locations. It includes such efforts as a city's contingency plans for flexible deployment of staff, hospital preparedness, and creating fully equipped emergency response teams. In the event of a disaster, the region and city have to quickly respond and maintain security of the city and try to resume its basic functions for all of its citizens as quickly and as fully as possible.

Early warning systems. Weather services support efforts to prepare for disasters. Hydromet networks, like the Hong Kong Observatory, have

Table 22.1   Key Sectoral Adaptation Opportunities Used in Urban Areas

Sector	Adaptation option or strategy	Underlying policy framework	Key (–) constraints and (+) opportunities to implementation
Water (e.g., King County/ Seattle, Singapore)	Expanded rainwater harvesting; water storage and conservation techniques; water reuse; desalination; water-use and irrigation efficiency	National water policies and integrated water resources management; water-related hazards management	(–) Financial, human resources, and physical barriers (+) Integrated water resources management; synergies with other sectors
Infrastructure and settlements (including coastal zones) (e.g., Venice, London, New York)	Relocation; seawalls and storm surge barriers; dune reinforcement; land acquisition and creation of marshlands/wetlands as buffer against sea-level rise and flooding; protection of existing natural barriers	Standards and regulations that integrate climate change considerations into design; land-use policies; building codes; insurance	(–) Financial and technological barriers (+) Availability of relocation space; integrated policies and management; synergies with sustainable development goals
Human health (e.g., Singapore, New York)	Heat-health action plans; emergency medical services; improved, climate-sensitive disease surveillance and control; safe water and improved sanitation	Public health policies that recognize climate risk; strengthened health services; regional and international cooperation	(–) Limits to human tolerance (vulnerable groups) (–) Knowledge limitations (–) Financial capacity (+) Upgraded health services (+) Improved quality of life

(continued next page)

Table 22.1 *(continued)*

Sector	Adaptation option or strategy	Underlying policy framework	Key (–) constraints and (+) opportunities to implementation
Tourism (e.g., Switzerland)	Diversification of tourism attractions and revenues; shifting ski slopes to higher altitudes and glaciers	Integrated planning (e.g., carrying capacity, linkages with other sectors); financial incentives (e.g., subsidies and tax credits)	(+) Appeal/marketing of new attractions (–) Financial and logistical challenges (–) Potential adverse impact on other sectors (e.g., artificial snow-making may increase energy use) (+) Revenues from "new" attractions (+) Involvement of a wider group of stakeholders
Transport (e.g., King County/ Seattle, Albuquerque, Rockville, Singapore, Tokyo)	Realignment/relocation; design standards and planning for roads, rail, and other infrastructure to cope with warming and drainage	Integrating climate change considerations into national transport policy; investment in R&D for special situations (e.g., permafrost areas)	(–) Financial and technological barriers (+) Availability of less vulnerable routes (+) Improved technologies (+) Integration with key sectors (e.g., energy)
Energy (e.g., King County/ Seattle, Albuquerque, Rockville, Singapore, Tokyo)	Strengthening of overhead transmission and distribution infrastructure; underground cabling for utilities; energy efficiency; use of renewable sources; reduced dependence on single sources of energy	National energy policies, regulations, and fiscal and financial incentives to encourage use of alternative sources; incorporating climate change in design standards	(+) Access to viable alternatives (–) Financial and technological barriers (–) Acceptance of new technologies (+) Stimulation of new technologies (+) Use of local resources

Source: Adapted from IPCC 2007.

Box 22.7

PlaNYC: A Greener, Greater New York City

In 2007, the New York City Mayor's Office released an innovative strategic plan to create a greener, greater, and more resilient city. The plan, PlaNYC, focused on nine key issues: housing, open space, brownfields, water quality, water network, transportation, energy, air quality, and climate change. To increase the city's climate change resilience, the approach included the following steps:

- Quantify the impacts of climate change.
- Identify the impacts of climate change on the city and develop strategies to mitigate these risks.
- Launch a citywide strategic plan, addressing infrastructure and buildings.
- Engage with vulnerable communities.

To develop the plan, the City of New York involved stakeholders from the public and private sectors, think tanks, and academia, securing cooperation between the Mayor's Office, prestigious universities, NASA, and the insurance industry. The NYC Climate Change Adaptation Task Force was the first of its kind to include city, state, and federal agencies along with private companies to work together on climate change adaptation issues. So far, the city has:

- Planted over 380,000 trees as part of the MillionTreesNYC program and planted over 280 "Greenstreets," garden areas set in median strips and traffic triangles.
- Released the NYC Green Infrastructure Plan and secured citywide high-resolution LiDAR elevation data.
- Coated 1 million square feet of rooftops white as part of the NYC °Cool Roofs program to reduce heat island effects.
- Launched three Solar Empowerment Zones where the development of solar power systems is encouraged.
- Implemented the NYC Department of Environmental Protection's (DEP) Climate Assessment and Adaptation Plan. The Plan outlines specific steps that the DEP is taking to better understand and plan for the potential impacts of climate change and refine the climate change projections for New York City and its watershed region, better quantify risks to existing systems, integrate climate change data into departmental planning for new projects, and develop both short- and long-term adaptation strategies for critical infrastructure.

(continued next page)

Box 22.7 *(continued)*

- Developed a Comprehensive Waterfront Plan, which includes specific strategies to increase the city's resilience to climate change and sea level rise. Proposed actions include further research to better understand risks and design effective measures to increase the city's resilience; regulations such as building codes, insurance, and emergency preparedness planning to reduce flood damage; and information sharing and outreach to engage communities in resilience planning.
- Launched a public awareness campaign on Emergency Management, and enhanced New York's emergency response and preparedness programs.
- Advocated for national and international action on climate change and the need to engage cities.

Source: City of New York, Mayor's Office 2010.

been successful in providing vital information for advance warnings that save lives and reduce damage to property and the environment. Studies have shown that, apart from the incalculable benefit to human well-being, every dollar invested in meteorological and hydrological services produces a significantly greater economic return. For example, a recent World Bank study in the Eastern Europe and Central Asia Region suggested that each 100 euros spent on meteorological systems yields at least 200 euros in avoided damages (World Bank 2008).

Disaster risk management plans. Disaster risk management plans are prepared for an optimal utilization of resources in the context of an expected disaster. Developing and implementing disaster risk management plans provide an opportunity to better understand a city's disaster history and capacities, as well as enable shared learning and establishing a joint understanding with other government agencies. The changing hazard profile due to climate change has to be considered in disaster risk management plans and requires new and more flexible approaches to address uncertain future risks.

Step 4: Transfer Risks through Financing and Insurance

There is a critical need for cities and national governments to design comprehensive catastrophe financing strategies and transfer mechanisms. Insurance and other ex ante risk financing mechanisms form a critical part of a comprehensive disaster risk management strategy and have the potential to play an important role in disaster risk management and climate change adaptation. Financial products are not enough on their own, however, and must be tied to efforts and incentives for investment in risk reduction.

Ex ante financial programs. Ex ante financial programs meet several needs. They can provide immediate liquidity to governments for postdisaster relief and reconstruction of damaged government properties and infrastructure, and offer insurance to homeowners and businesses to mitigate the financial impact of disasters. The World Bank has been exploring opportunities for the gradual implementation of effective risk financing and transfer mechanisms to reduce, pool, and share climate-related disaster risks. The Disaster Risk Financing and Insurance (DRFI) Program of the Global Facility for Disaster Reduction and Recovery (GFDRR) assists countries in increasing their financial resilience to natural disasters. The DRFI Program partners with countries in a variety of ways, from establishing natural disaster micro-insurance programs to acting as an intermediate between governments and international financial markets, seeking innovative ways to mitigate the financial impacts of natural disasters on individuals, small- and medium-size enterprises, agricultural sector participants, and governments.

Comprehensive catastrophe financing strategies. Comprehensive catastrophe financing strategies should consist of multiple sources of financing. On the one hand, financing strategies should include "on-balance sheet" financing, such as the design of rapidly disbursing postdisaster social safety nets and other funds, including contingent lines of credit. On the other hand, there should be sources of "off-balance sheet" financing, such as risk transfer to the private sector through mandatory insurance programs like the Turkish Catastrophe Insurance Pool (see box 22.8), and catastrophe-linked securities like the World Bank platform for a multicountry, multiperil cat bond that transfers diversified risk to private investors.

Disaster risk financing and insurance. Disaster risk financing and insurance can be classified into four broad categories: sovereign disaster risk financing, property catastrophe risk insurance, agricultural insurance, and disaster micro-insurance. Activities for each include:

- *Sovereign disaster risk financing:* Develop financial strategies to increase the financial response capacity of governments in the aftermath of natural disasters, while protecting their long-term fiscal balances.

Box 22.8

Turkish Catastrophe Insurance Pool

The Turkish Catastrophe Insurance Pool (TCIP) was established in the aftermath of the Marmara earthquake in 2000, with assistance from the World Bank. Turkey has a high level of exposure to earthquakes. As Turkey's private insurance market has traditionally been unable to provide adequate capacity for catastrophe property insurance against earthquake risk, the government of Turkey faced a major financial exposure in postdisaster reconstruction of private property. The government's objectives for TCIP were to:

- Ensure that all property tax–paying dwellings have earthquake insurance coverage.
- Reduce government fiscal exposure to recurring earthquakes.
- Transfer catastrophe risk to the international reinsurance market.
- Encourage physical risk mitigation through insurance.

Key features of TCIP include:

- *Providing insurance through a public sector insurance company:* TCIP is a public sector insurance company, which is managed on sound technical and commercial insurance principles. The company's initial capital was supplemented by a World Bank contingent loan. TCIP purchases commercial reinsurance and the government of Turkey acts as a catastrophe reinsurer of last resort for claims arising out of an earthquake with a return period greater than 300 years.
- *Providing an attractive and affordable insurance policy:* The TCIP policy is a stand-alone property earthquake policy with a maximum sum insured per policy of US$65,000, an average premium rate of US$46 and a 2 percent of sum insured deductible. Premium rates are based on the construction type (two types) and property location (differentiating between five earthquake risk zones) and vary from less than 0.05 percent for a concrete reinforced house in a low-risk zone to 0.60 percent for a house located in the highest-risk zone.
- *Policy marketing:* The policy is distributed by about 30 existing Turkish insurance companies, which receive a commission.
- *Achieving market penetration:* To achieve market penetration and overcome traditional resistance to property insurance, the government invested heavily in insurance awareness campaigns and also made earthquake insurance compul-

(continued next page)

Box 22.8 *(continued)*

sory for homeowners on registered land in urban centers. Coverage is voluntary for homeowners in rural areas.

- *Reinsurance:* The program is reinsured by international reinsurers.

Since its inception in 2000, TCIP has achieved an average penetration rate of about 20 percent of domestic dwellings (about 3 million dwellings). Romania is about to set up a similar pool for earthquakes and floods.

Source: Cummins and Mahul (2009) in World Bank 2010a.

- *Property catastrophe risk insurance:* Develop competitive catastrophe insurance markets and increase property catastrophe insurance penetration among homeowners and small and medium enterprises.
- *Agricultural insurance:* Develop agricultural insurance programs for farmers, herders, and agricultural financing institutions (for example, rural banks, microfinance institutions) to increase their financial resilience to adverse natural hazards.
- *Disaster micro-insurance:* Facilitate access to disaster insurance products to protect the livelihood of the poor against extreme weather events and promote disaster risk reduction in conjunction with social programs such as conditional cash transfer programs.

Property risk insurance and micro-insurance. Property risk insurance and micro-insurance can help city dwellers protect themselves against the impacts of climate change. Property risk insurance products insure a defined property, economic activity, or other entity (such as a business) against specific hazards like earthquakes, wind events, or floods. In the event of the insured item being lost or damaged as a result of a covered hazard, the policyholder is compensated for their financial loss. Insurers pay claims based on actual losses. The intent of micro-insurance is to provide easily accessible insurance coverage for small-scale assets at affordable premiums by keeping transaction costs low. Micro-insurance holds great potential to protect the poor from disaster shocks. Existing schemes are securing livelihoods and supporting reconstruction and recovery for poor households. Index-based schemes have demonstrated their value in improving the creditworthiness of farmers. Some schemes are attempting to couple insurance with capacity building and incentives for risk reduction.

Spotlight on Integrated Flood Management

Building resilience in flood control. Integrated flood risk management programs increase the resilience of communities potentially affected by this specific type of disaster. The World Bank has extensive experience with flood management projects that take into account both current and future risks due to climate change. The World Bank has assisted governments in dealing with the impacts of more than 250 floods since 1984, focusing not only on reconstruction but also on the development of integrated flood risk management programs. In China, 17 projects either fully focused on or with components related to flood management have been implemented since 1995, with a total investment of US$1.9 billion. The strategy in most of these projects has been to apply a systems approach that balances structural measures (for example, levees, dikes, drainage systems, pumps, and retention ponds) with nonstructural measures based on the socioeconomic context and a cost-benefit analysis. Structural measures, while necessary, need to be carefully assessed before implementation because they often are expensive and have the potential to provide short-term protection at the cost of long-term problems. Flood control systems, for example, have exacerbated rather than reduced the extent of flooding when sediment deposits have decreased the depth of the river channels and put pressure on dike systems. Now when floods occur, they tend to be of greater depth and more damaging than in the past. In addition, structural measures often provide a false sense of security with people being unaware of the risks that remain. The damages from the 1993 flooding of the Mississippi River in the United States were made worse by misplaced confidence in structural mitigation measures that had encouraged development in high-risk areas.

A recent policy note prepared by the World Bank on integrated flood risk management[1] provides specific recommendations for China to strengthen its flood risk management strategies and protect human lives as well as properties and infrastructure. The note suggests adopting cost-effective strategies that focus less on controlling floods and more on the concepts of living with floods, protecting key assets, and minimizing losses. To further strengthen China's flood disaster management capacity, eight specific recommendations were offered:

- Mainstream flood risk management into national flood control regulatory, policy, and investment frameworks for flood prevention. Integrate flood risk management, particularly nonstructural measures, into government-financed investment programs, by adopting early risk identification (for instance, by applying a quick and simple risk-screening tool) and following up throughout the design process if necessary.

- Implement integrated flood risk management strategies at the river-basin level, taking into account the current and future climate risks and vulnerabilities and designing the most cost-effective measures to protect or respond to floods and other disasters, incorporating locally acceptable and adequate techniques.
- Develop a comprehensive understanding, analysis, and assessment of flood risks and vulnerabilities that will guide river basin flood disaster risk management strategies, urban development, and land-use plans.
- Develop integrated flood risk management strategies that balance disaster risk reduction and prevention through structural and nonstructural control measures and preparedness plans, by defining minimum or optimal levels of acceptable risk.
- Continue improving and strengthening the management of small/rural dams and develop operation and maintenance procedures for dams, as well as emergency preparedness plans.
- Strengthen capacity and coordination mechanisms, especially at the local government and community level, to build resilience and more effectively respond to future disasters.
- Improve flood forecasting systems and the implementation of emergency preparedness and response mechanisms based on community participation.
- Gradually implement effective risk transfer mechanisms to reduce the impacts of disasters and help individuals to recover more quickly from flood events by providing postdisaster financial assistance.

Conclusions

Resilient cities are capable of withstanding and recovering from shocks without severe upheaval or permanent harm. Designed in advance to anticipate, weather, and recover from the impacts of natural hazards, resilient cities are built on the known principles of prevention.

Cities in China are already experiencing an increased frequency and intensity of weather-related disasters that are affecting their economies and citizens' quality of life. In addition to helping mitigate climate change impacts by becoming low-carbon, cities urgently need to build resilience to be ready for the likely impacts of climate change. The first step is to determine a city's particular climate risks and vulnerabilities, followed by developing and implementing action plans to manage the risk of disasters and, ultimately, reduce vulnerability to climate change. Rapid urban growth combined with weak regulatory and planning regimes aggravates the already existent high incidence of natural disasters. Cities disproportionately face the brunt of climate change impacts due to their concentration of people and physical assets, as well as their geographic location. The current historically unprecedented rate of urbanization implies that exposure to hazards in China is increasing on concentrated and economically important space. This may translate into heavy loss of life and property unless proactive measures are mainstreamed into urban planning processes to create resilient cities.

Adaptation to climate risks in essence builds on elements of sound urban planning, and successful adaptation and effective regional and local development are linked. The concept of "integrated climate risk management" captures this link and summarizes key areas around which to organize adaptation measures that are flexible, spread the risk, and are integrated in city planning. Flexibility and resilience are particularly important for cities as impacts at the local level are expected but not well defined. For all sectors of a city's economy, ample international experience with adaptation strategies and relevant policy frameworks exist. As cities in China continue to grow and lock down their urban form, it is important that adaptation becomes integrated in city planning today.

Box 22.9

Glossary

Hazard	A potentially damaging physical event, phenomenon, or human activity that may cause the loss of life or injury, property damage, social and economic disruption, or environmental degradation.
Disaster risk management	The systematic management of administrative decisions, organization, operational skills, and capacities to implement policies, strategies, and coping capacities of the society and communities to lessen the impacts of natural hazards and related environmental and technological disasters. This comprises all forms of activities, including structural and nonstructural measures to avoid (prevention) or to limit (mitigation and preparedness) adverse effects of hazards.
Exposure	Exposure is the total value of elements at risk. It is expressed, for example, as the number of human lives, and value of the properties, that can potentially be affected by hazards.

(continued next page)

Box 22.9 *(continued)*

Resilience	Capacity to recover normal functioning and development after being hit by a disaster.
Risk	The probability of harmful consequences, or expected losses (deaths, injuries, property, livelihoods, economic activity disrupted, or environment damaged) resulting from interactions between natural or human-induced hazards and vulnerable conditions.
Risk assessment	A methodology to determine the nature and extent of risk by analyzing potential hazards, exposed elements, and evaluating existing conditions of vulnerability.
Risk transfer	Insurance and reinsurance for both physical damage and business interruption, coverage that would provide cash compensation immediately after a disaster.
Vulnerability	Physical, social, economic, and environmental factors that increase susceptibility to the impact of hazards. Vulnerability engages resistance and resilience.

Notes

1. This is an internal note prepared by the World Bank in August 2010 for the Ministry of Finance and the Ministry of Water Resource Management to advise the government on strategies to reduce risks and vulnerabilities from floods, focusing on secondary rivers. This note was not officially published but is available on request.

Bibliography

City of New York, Mayor's Office. 2010. Presentation at the World Bank. Information also publicly available in the PlaNYC Report, 2007, and the PlaNYC Report, 2008, available at: http://www.nyc.gov/html/planyc2030/html/downloads/download.shtml.

Government of China. 2006. *National Assessment Report on Climate Change.* December. Beijing: Government of China.

Information Office of the State Council of the People's Republic of China. 2008. "China's Policies and Actions for Addressing Climate Change." Beijing. http://www.gov.cn/english/2008-10/29/content_1134544.htm.

Intergovernmental Panel on Climate Change (IPCC). 2007. *Climate Change 2007: Synthesis Report. Contribution of Working Groups I, II and III to the Fourth Assessment Report of the Intergovernmental Panel on Climate Change* [Core Writing Team, Pachauri, R.K and Reisinger, A. (eds.)]. Geneva, Switzerland: IPCC.

McGranahan, G., D. Balk, and B. Anderson. 2007. "The Rising Tide: Assessing the Risks of Climate Change and Human Settlements in Low-Elevation Coastal Zones." *Environment and Urbanization* 19(1): 17–37.

Meiyan, J. 2010. "Meteorological Disaster Prevention and Mitigation: Practice & Progress." Presentation delivered by the Deputy Administrator of the China Meteorological Administration at the World Bank Beijing Office, on October 22, 2010.

National Development and Reform Commission (NDRC), MWR (Ministry of Water Resources), and MOC (Ministry of Construction). 2007. *The 11th Five-Year Plan of National Water Resources Development.* Beijing: Ministry of Water Resources.

Prasad, N., F. Ranghieri, F. Shah, Z. Trohanis, E. Kessler, and R. Sinha. 2009. "Climate Resilient Cities: A Primer on Reducing Vulnerabilities to Disasters." Washington, DC: World Bank.

World Bank. 2008. "Weather and Climate Services in Europe and Central Asia. A Regional Review." World Bank Working Paper No. 151. June. World Bank, Washington, DC.

———. 2010a. "Weathering the Storm: Options for Disaster Risk Financing in Vietnam." World Bank, Washington, DC.

———. 2010b. "It Is Not Too Late: Preparing for Asia's Next Big Earthquake With Emphasis on the Philippines, Indonesia and China; What East Asia and the Pacific Can Do to Prepare for the Next Big Earthquake: Developing and Implementing Regional and Countrywide Strengthening Program for Vulnerable Structures." *Policy Note,* October. World Bank, Washington, DC.

———. 2010c. *Natural Hazards, Unnatural Disasters.* Washington, DC: World Bank.

———. 2010d. "Climate Risks and Adaptation in Asian Coastal Megacities. A Synthesis Report." September. World Bank, Washington, DC.

———. 2010e. *Cities and Climate Change: an Urgent Agenda.* Washington, DC: World Bank.

Xie, J., A. Liebenthal, J. Warford, J. Dixon, M. Wang, S. Gao, S. Wang, Y. Jiang, and Z. Ma. 2009. "Addressing China's Water Scarcity: Recommendations for Selected Water Resource Management Issues." World Bank, Washington, DC. Available at http://go.worldbank.org/QNHD1TGXX0.

PART 7

Financing a Low-Carbon City

CHAPTER 23

Financing a Low-Carbon City: Introduction

Axel Baeumler and Shomik Mehndiratta

Achieving the right balance of financing tools and incentives will be critical in creating low-carbon cities. Although a crucial area, China's experience with financing tools and incentives focused on supporting low-carbon development is very limited and a significant amount of work is required to develop new approaches. The following two chapters summarize a range of financing issues based on experience gained from carbon finance (chapter 24) and World Bank projects (chapter 25). However, it is important to note that the emerging, important agenda on how to effectively finance low-carbon development can be seen only as complementary to—and dependent on—changes to the underlying manner in which Chinese cities are financed.

From a municipal finance perspective, as is argued in chapter 4, the current financing of China's cities needs fundamental rethinking. While municipalities have a significant responsibility for local economic development and the provision of a range of urban public services, they have very limited options to mobilize financial resources: cities' share of the total tax base is not commensurate with their responsibilities and municipalities are not allowed to directly mobilize debt. Further, even if cities were allowed to take on debt, more would need to be done to establish transparent, credible, and stable local revenue streams to effectively tap the capital market. While isolated instances of project finance exist, particularly in the case of energy efficiency projects, the bulk of urban financing is structured by off-balance sheet government platforms that heavily depend on land sales and redevelopment for their revenue base. Chapter 4 describes how the alignment of municipal incentives, lack of diverse financing mechanisms, and the use of land sales as a financing tool create a socially and financially unsustainable situation in which municipalities appropriate the land of rural residents on the urban periphery, land is overused and overdeveloped, and car-oriented urban sprawl is encouraged.

Supporting the development of an alternative financing paradigm for Chinese cities will be an important focus of World Bank work in the near future. While it is too early to present specifics, and such details would also be outside the scope of this book, we anticipate that developing and considering new options, as well as implementing pilot approaches to alternative financial paradigms, will lead to a wealth of new and relevant experiences. Future editions of this book will be able to focus on these experiences and emerging lessons, and offer more detailed and sustainable city financing solutions for developing low-carbon cities.

From a project finance perspective, the energy section of this book, chapters 5 through 8, describes a range of tools and practices that have been tried in China and internationally to finance transition to a low-carbon energy future. This wealth of experience in the energy sector will likely serve as the basis of future approaches to green financing for projects. In chapter 5, a range of options to mobilize funds is presented, from using government sources through tax incentives to allowing consumers to directly pay for the incremental costs of the green energy they choose to buy. Chapter 6 highlights the importance of specialized energy conservation funds, targeted concessional financing programs, tax rebates, and necessary pricing reforms to incentivize industrial energy efficiency. Chapters 7 and 8, on energy efficiency in buildings and district heating, respectively, highlight, in addition to the above-mentioned incentive schemes, the importance of establishing appropriate standards, such as green building standards and introducing consumption-based billing for all municipal services. Generally, energy efficiency—and by extension low-carbon financing—must overcome different sets of barriers depending on which specific issue and subsector is being addressed. Box 23.1 provides an initial framework that can help categorize these different barriers.

Box 23.1

Typology of Barriers to Financing Energy Efficient and Low-Carbon Investments

Barriers to financing energy efficient and low-carbon investments can be grouped into three broad categories, each of which implies a distinct subset of solutions.

Category A: Investments have positive returns, but access to up-front capital is limited. A large number of energy efficiency and greenhouse gas emission reduction activities ultimately generate fiscal benefits sufficient to re-cover initial investment costs, for example, in the form of direct energy savings or through the generation of byproducts that can be monetized or used to reduce expenditures in other areas. An example of the latter would be the use of cap-tured methane from landfills for energy generation. (It should be noted that use of methane captured from landfills for power generation is not always a net rev-enue generator; in many cases, these activities in China are supported through car-bon finance.) Since these energy efficiency and greenhouse gas emission reduction activities generally fall outside the typical purview of commercial lending practices or budgeted municipal expenditures, the greatest obstacle in financing these ac-tivities tends to be limited access to up-front financing at reasonable terms.

Category B: Investments have positive returns, but the party that bears the costs is not the recipient of the returns. Some energy efficiency invest-ments generate sufficient energy savings to offset costs, but these savings do not necessarily accrue to the investor. This is especially true in the building sector. For example, an apartment building owner may install green retrofits in all units, but it is the apartment tenants who would benefit from lower utility bills—not the building owner. In this case, the obstacle is finding mechanisms through which incentives of the tenant and the owner can be aligned.

Category C: Investments have negative or unknown returns, but also have other, nonfiscal benefits. Some low-emissions technologies are not yet commercially competitive with technologies responsible for higher greenhouse gas emissions, while others generate returns that are difficult to predict or quan-tify. For example, small-scale solar power facilities and wind farms, which emit fewer greenhouse gases than traditional fossil fuel–based power plants, tend to cost more per kWh of energy generated and thus are not competitive. To support this type of investment through subsidy (whether grant, tax incentive, rebate, con-cessional finance, or other paid-incentive program), it must be determined whether the long-term benefits (social, environmental, economic) outweigh the costs.

Source: Contributed by Holly Krambeck, East Asia and Pacific, World Bank.

In this context, it is worthwhile to focus on the experience with and potential of carbon finance mechanisms, financing instruments specifically created to facilitate low-carbon solutions. Chapter 24 discusses the basic concepts related to carbon finance, as well as the experience with the Clean Development Mechanism (CDM), the carbon market based on the Kyoto Protocol. The chapter also discusses the emerging range of possibilities for carbon markets outside of the Kyoto Protocol, focusing on experiences particularly relevant to China's cities in the near term. Finally, chapter 25 describes the range of financial instruments and experience that international financial institutions like the World Bank Group can offer to support Chinese cities with the transition to a low-carbon growth path.

CHAPTER 24

Cities and Carbon Finance

Monali Ranade and Marcus Lee

Overview

Carbon finance involves the sale and purchase of emission reductions in carbon markets. Various instruments exist to finance the incremental cost of reducing carbon emissions emanating from cities. One such mechanism is the Clean Development Mechanism (CDM). The CDM is the dominant form of carbon finance found in developing countries, and China has an extremely strong track record in reducing emissions in a wide range of sectors, including waste, energy, transport, and forestry, through the CDM. This chapter reviews current and potential future uses of carbon finance, along with other carbon market instruments, to reduce emissions in China.

Instruments governing carbon markets have largely developed as part of the Kyoto Protocol of the United Nations Framework Convention on Climate Change (UNFCCC), which sets legally binding greenhouse gas (GHG) emission reduction obligations for developed countries. Developed countries can meet these obligations through domestic actions, such as carbon taxes and subsidies, and market-based mechanisms, such as emissions trading. In addition, they can meet part of their GHG emission reduction obligations by acquiring Certified Emission Reductions (CERs) generated by projects that are implemented in developing countries and registered under the CDM.[1]

The Kyoto Protocol is defined only until 2012, after which the future of the CDM, which is linked to the Kyoto Protocol, and of the international market for carbon credits generated in China is uncertain. Nonetheless, this chapter reviews the practical and successful experience China has had with the CDM, as it is expected that a carbon finance mechanism with some characteristics similar to the CDM may be in place after 2012 as part of a future global accord to combat climate change.

Carbon Finance and the Clean Development Mechanism in China

Over the last few years, China has built the largest and most dynamic CDM program in the world.[2] Overall, Chinese CDM projects are expected to generate total carbon finance resources in excess of US$9 billion through 2012 (Nygard et al. 2011). As of April 2010, China had more registered CDM projects (751 projects, or 36 percent of the world's total), and more registered CERs (205 million tonnes of carbon dioxide [CO_2] equivalents, or 60 percent of the world's total), than any other country. The breakdown of the projects is 49 percent hydro, 22 percent wind, and 10 percent energy efficiency projects. The leading provinces in terms of the number of registered projects are Yunnan (93 projects, mainly hydro), Sichuan (73 projects, mainly hydro), and Inner Mongolia (56 projects, mainly wind). Figures 24.1 and 24.2 summarize the key data on CDM projects in China.

The types of CDM projects that support low-carbon investments in and around urban areas include energy efficiency, landfill gas, and potentially such renewable energy sources as solar, biomass, and wind, if located in proximity to cities. As can be seen in figure 24.1, these categories of CDM projects account for slightly less than 10 percent of all CDM projects in China. It is important to note that investment in low-carbon technologies in industries located in and around cities is also likely to have strong socioeconomic benefits, in terms of employment and reduced local air pollution.

For projects to be registered with the CDM, a set of specific conditions has to be fulfilled. In China, a project first has to be approved by the Designated National Authority (DNA). As of April 2010, there were 2,400 DNA-approved projects, far more than the 751 projects registered under the CDM. This means that 1,649 projects were still in the CDM registration process. CDM rules specifically require a project to demonstrate that it (i) reduces GHG emissions when compared to a baseline and (ii) is additional to activities in the baseline. The CDM regulatory system reviews and approves methodologies for the quantification of

Figure 24.1   CDM Projects in China by Sector, 2010

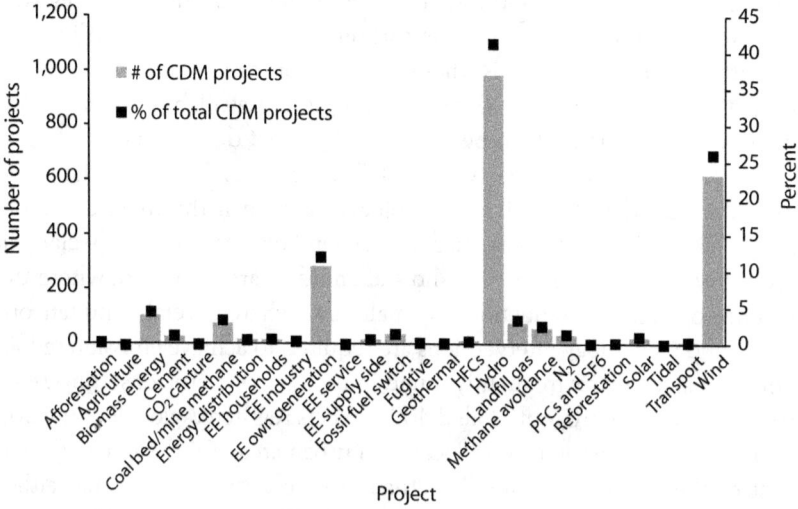

Source: Nygard et al. 2011.
Note: EE = energy efficiency; HFCs = hydrofluorocarbons; N_2O = nitrous oxide; PFCs = perfluorocarbons; SF6 = sulfur hexafluoride.

Figure 24.2   CDM Projects in China by Region, 2010

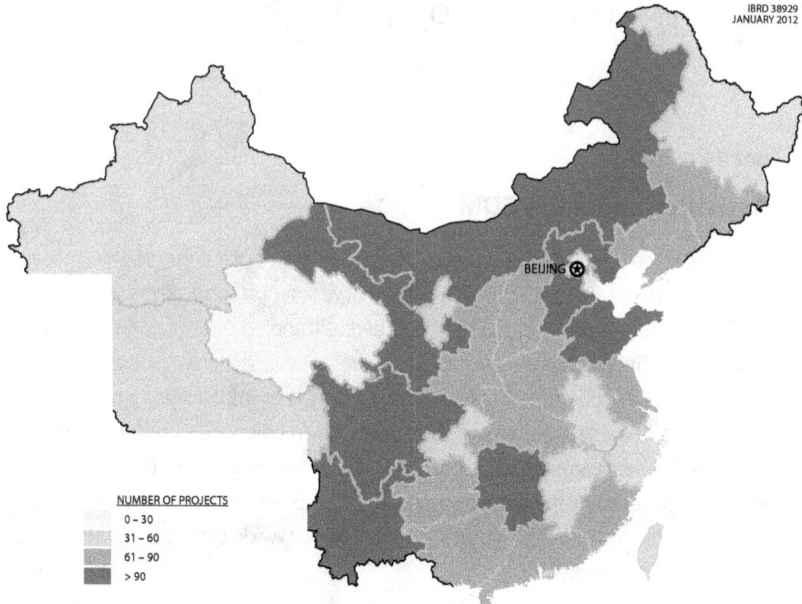

Source: Nygard et al. 2011.

emission reductions, provides tools for assessing additionality and other technical requirements, and establishes rules and procedures for registering projects and issuing CERs or carbon credits. A CDM baseline and monitoring methodology is the standard for calculation of emission reductions, and all approved methodologies are available on the CDM website as a public good to be used by all project developers.[3]

To date, there are three types of CDM projects (see box 24.1), and over the past decade, individual projects have been the most common. However, single-project activities have several disadvantages, especially in sectors where emission sources and stakeholders are dispersed, where the volume of emission reductions is small, and where several simultaneous policy and technology interventions are required to achieve emission reductions—characteristics frequently found in urban CDM project settings. As a result, in March 2010, out of all 2,400 projects registered globally, only 203 (8.5 percent of the total) were located in urban areas. Of these, 164 (7 percent of the total) were landfill methane gas recovery projects that either flare the gas or utilize it to generate electricity. The remaining projects were in building energy efficiency, renewable energy, and urban transport.

Single CDM projects in medium-size cities, such as energy efficient streetlights and energy recovery in nonindustrial wastewater treatment projects, yield a very low volume of emission reductions—approximately an average of 5,000 tonnes of CO_2 equivalent (tCO_2e) per year—and are

---

Box 24.1

Activities under the CDM

There are three types of CDM projects: those that consist of a single activity, those that have "bundled" activities (that is, groups of very similar subprojects submitted together), and programmatic activities. Whereas bundled project activities share common technological or operational features, CDM program activities are defined by their Program of Activities (PoA), which is an initiative by a private or public entity to generate emission reductions via an unlimited number of similar activities. The programmatic approach was developed in an effort to enable scaling up of project activities. A proposed extension of the PoA would consolidate and integrate individual CDM projects under one citywide program, but this approach is not yet approved.

Source: UNFCCC, http://cdm.unfccc.int.

generally not considered to be sufficiently attractive to be developed as CDM projects in their own right. Bundling projects across sectors or creating PoAs across cities to aggregate energy savings may be more attractive, but both these approaches also introduce new complexities, since they require decision making and data collection by multiple city authorities. Bringing together multiple cities also requires significant administrative complexity. Unfortunately, therefore, current CDM procedures do not encourage city authorities to take a holistic view of their development plans and identify GHG emission reduction opportunities across different sectors.

There are additional reasons for the small number of CDM projects in cities. Climate change mitigation has largely been viewed as the responsibility of national governments. Cities tend to focus more on local and immediate benefits in terms of environmental quality, economic growth, and social development. The direct local benefits of GHG emission reduction projects may be difficult to quantify, and as a result city authorities are unable to justify expenditures on these projects. Also, the administrative and transaction costs of setting up individual CDM project activities in cities have been very high compared to the transaction costs of other larger, private sector–led CDM projects.

Citywide Approach to Carbon Finance

Given the above barriers for cities to access carbon finance, a modified approach to developing CDM projects in cities is being developed. The "citywide approach" to carbon finance (World Bank 2010a) is designed to address the concerns mentioned above, particularly the difficulty of looking across sectors to locate emission reduction opportunities. The idea is to better align CDM project planning with normal urban planning and management processes, which are focused on the provision of urban services. A citywide CDM program would essentially be an expanded PoA that consolidates and integrates different CDM projects—thereby limiting transaction costs and optimizing the total carbon finance revenue generated. This approach recently received support at the 6th meeting of the Parties to the Kyoto Protocol in Cancún in December 2010, where the decision-making international body under the UNFCCC requested the Executive Board of the CDM to simplify programmatic CDM to explore the possibility of allowing citywide programs (UNFCCC 2011b).

Through cross-sectoral or citywide approaches for financing under a programmatic CDM, cities could be encouraged to change many business-as-usual practices into newer, lower GHG emission practices. For example, many cities currently replace equipment only when it is broken beyond repair, do minimal maintenance (only when reported broken), and strictly purchase the lowest-cost equipment (due to budget constraints). For these cities with limited budgets, carbon finance resources can help justify the extra effort and cost of purchasing and maintaining lower-emission technology.

Opportunities for GHG Mitigation in Cities

GHG mitigation opportunities in cities broadly fall under four sectors: energy, transport, solid waste, and water and wastewater—all sources of GHG emissions. Within these generally, energy consumption for transport and in buildings constitute the largest share of emissions and therefore offers the greatest potential for emission reductions. In addition to these four sectors, urban forestry, as a carbon sink, can also help achieve significant GHG emission reductions. Sectorwide and spatial planning approaches, such as integrated waste management or urban densification, can also be effective in harnessing both local benefits and GHG reduction benefits as part of a single comprehensive intervention. Figure 24.3 illustrates the interlinkages that exist between the different sectors, which can

Figure 24.3   Opportunities for GHG Mitigation in Cities

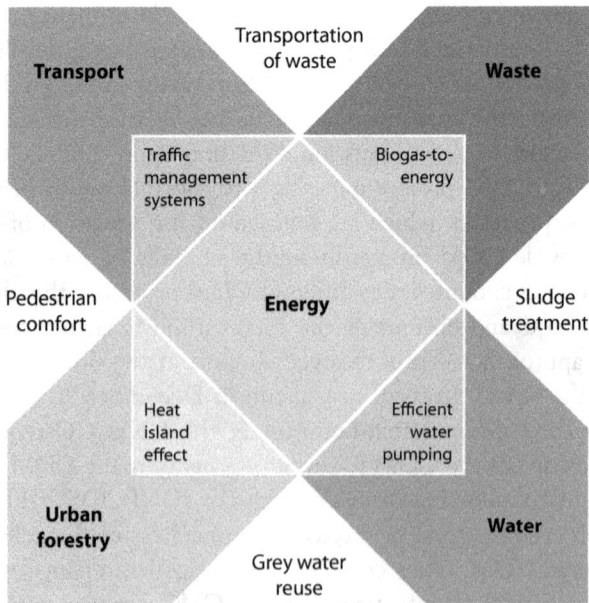

Source: World Bank 2010a.

be captured and capitalized upon only at the overall urban planning level. An integrated approach is the key to promote cost efficiency, energy efficiency, and, ultimately, emission reductions and avoidance.

Waste management. Globally, waste management is among the most attractive options for CDM projects in urban areas (see box 24.2; also see chapter 13 and box 13.3). Waste management projects constitute 23 percent of all CDM projects as of March 2010. Of 751 registered projects in China, 61 are methane avoidance activities in the waste management sector. This indicates that CDM is helping countries find supplemental finance to address their growing waste management challenges, even though this is largely restricted to the capture of landfill gas and avoidance of methane, which has a high global warming potential, sometimes referred to as the "methane kick." With the exception of recycling, all waste sector projects involve avoidance of emission of methane into the atmosphere, by flaring and transforming it into CO_2 which has only 5 percent of the global warming impact as compared to methane.

Energy. Emission reduction activities in the energy sector are broadly categorized as (i) renewable energy and (ii) energy efficiency. In urban settings, renewable energy investments can range from larger perimeter wind, waste-to-power, or solar installations, to highly decentralized sources of power generation, such as rooftop solar power installations. Energy efficiency initiatives fall into demand side and supply side. Supply-side energy efficiency includes technological improvement in power plants, combined heat and power (CHP) generation, and transmission and distribution (T&D) of heat and electricity. Demand-side energy

---

Box 24.2

Tianjin Shuangkou Landfill Gas Project

Located 137 kilometers southeast of Beijing, the project is Tianjin's first modern sanitary landfill, including impermeable liners and a collection and treatment system for liquid runoff. The state-of-the-art landfill gas collection system captures methane and other gases, such as carbon dioxide and non-methane organic compounds. By 2017, the project is expected to reduce GHG emissions by an average of 155,822 tCO_2e per year and produce a total of 218,509 megawatt hours (MWh) of electricity.

Source: http://cdm.unfccc.int/Projects/DB/JQA1193375340.58/view.

efficiency could include reductions from the provision of urban services, district heating, buildings, and households. China has 14 CDM district heating projects that involve the use of waste heat to supply heating or hot water to residential and commercial consumers (see box 24.3). However, developing CDM projects in the building sector has been a challenge because of the dispersed and varied nature of the individual projects, which include houses, offices, and apartments, as well as the difficulty in measuring the actual energy savings.

Transport. Activities that reduce emissions from the transport sector fall into one or more of three categories: (i) reduced emissions per kilogram of fuel combusted, (ii) reduced fuel combusted per kilometer traveled, or (iii) reduced vehicle kilometers traveled. Currently, there are few CDM-financed activities in the transport sector, even though the fastest growth in emissions in most urban areas in the developing world comes from private vehicles. While there are a few approved methodologies for this sector, transport projects account for only about 0.1 percent of the total number of registered CDM projects. Successful examples include public transport systems such as bus rapid transit (BRT), fuel efficiency, and transport system energy efficiency improvement. In China, no projects have been registered in the transport sector, although two BRT projects, in Chongqing (see box 24.4) and Zhengzhou, are currently undergoing the CDM process.

Creating a Citywide Program

A well-designed, citywide program would typically emerge from a traditional city-led initiative, such as a city development plan, master plan, or climate change action plan. A citywide program builds on the existing

---

Box 24.3

Southern District Heating Network in Urumqi

Located in Tianshan District, Urumqi City, this new primary district heating system replaces the existing inefficient and dispersive coal-fired boilers. The project improves the thermal energy efficiency, supplying heat to 17.45 million square meters of residential, commercial, and public buildings. This project is under validation and by 2018 is expected to reduce GHG emissions by 8.17 million tCO_2e.

Source: http://cdm.unfccc.int/Projects/Validation/DB/H1BYZ2UEIVYE999VGCLRII7KDWW7VT/view.html.

Box 24.4

BRT Chongqing Lines 1–4

Located in Chongqing municipality, the project establishes an efficient, safe, rapid, and effective modern mass transit system. The project involves new infrastructure including 81 kilometers of dedicated bus lanes, transporting more than 600 million passengers per year on the system. The project is expected to reduce GHG emissions by 1.76 million tCO_2e over the first seven years of project operation.

Source: http://cdm.unfccc.int/Projects/Validation/DB/15LY3XDSSI94R1U0BJBCXZRTN7TI1J/view.html.

administrative structure of the city to allow the head of the municipal authority—the mayor or city manager—to enable, encourage, and support individual departments that are responsible for the provision of urban services (such as water or public transport) and for enforcement of local, regional, or national regulations (such as building codes or subsidy programs) to continuously and systematically identify lower-carbon alternatives. A citywide program has the potential to act not only as the coordinator of projects and aggregator of carbon finance, but also as the unified effort of the city to raise much-needed financing to implement all the identified projects. A city or municipal area is also the more appropriate scale for interventions in spatially integrated sectors like transport. Program development can follow a very simple process, as given in figure 24.4.

The first pilot operation based on a citywide approach is currently being prepared for Amman, Jordan. This program emerged from the city's master plan 2025 (Greater Amman Municipality 2011). This plan looks at the holistic development of the city from a socioeconomic and environmental perspective. Based on this broad objective, the municipal authority, under the direct guidance of the mayor and city manager, was able to identify technological interventions across the sectors. These interventions include activities from BRT and streetlighting by the transport department to wastewater treatment by a private operator and installation of solar water heaters by residential consumers (see box 24.5).

The citywide approach is being considered by other cities as a potential carbon finance–based strategic program to access finance from various sources, including CDM, the voluntary market for carbon credits, the Global Environment Facility (GEF), and other emerging domestic and international carbon market mechanisms.

Figure 24.4   Citywide Program Development Process

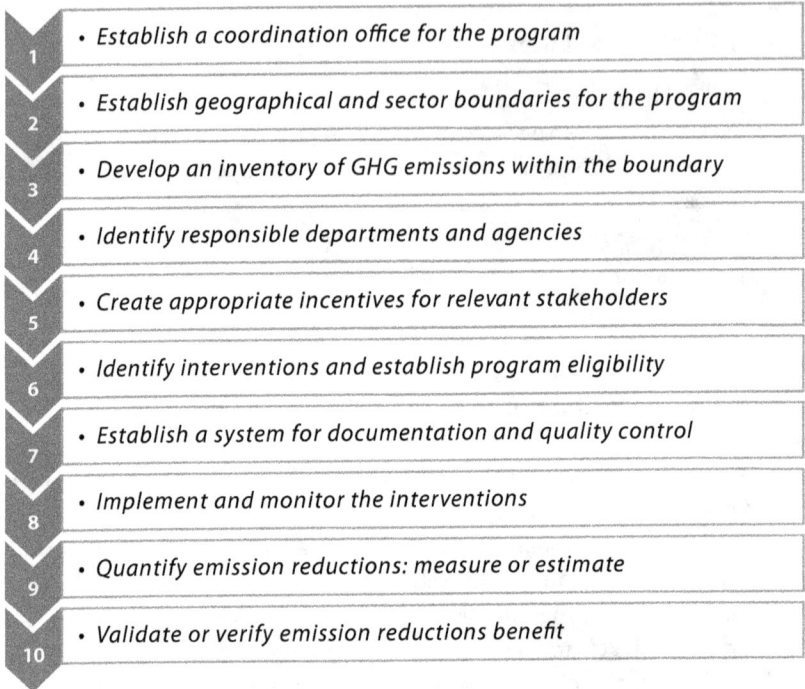

1	• Establish a coordination office for the program
2	• Establish geographical and sector boundaries for the program
3	• Develop an inventory of GHG emissions within the boundary
4	• Identify responsible departments and agencies
5	• Create appropriate incentives for relevant stakeholders
6	• Identify interventions and establish program eligibility
7	• Establish a system for documentation and quality control
8	• Implement and monitor the interventions
9	• Quantify emission reductions: measure or estimate
10	• Validate or verify emission reductions benefit

Source: Authors.

Box 24.5

Amman Green Growth Program

Greater Amman Municipality is in the process of developing its first citywide Green Growth Program in collaboration with the World Bank's Carbon Partnership Facility (CPF). This program, to be implemented over 20 years, is based on the Amman master plan 2025 and will include projects in water, solid waste, energy, transport, and urban forestry sectors. The first set of eight projects across various sectors is expected to require investment of US$2 billion, with GHG emission reduction in excess of 10 million tCO_2e over a 10-year period. The program framework includes financing, interdepartmental coordination, implementation, and monitoring mechanisms.

Source: World Bank project documents.

Scaling Up GHG Mitigation

The need to scale up GHG mitigation efforts is now widely accepted worldwide, by developed and developing countries alike. This may require the global community to look beyond the current efforts, including the CDM and the Kyoto Protocol. This section discusses Nationally Appropriate Mitigation Actions, the World Bank's Carbon Partnership Facility, and the Partnership for Market Readiness.

Nationally Appropriate Mitigation Actions (NAMAs)

As part of efforts to scale up and accelerate GHG mitigation activities, under the Copenhagen Accord, the concept of Nationally Appropriate Mitigation Actions (NAMAs) was introduced. NAMA refers to voluntary plans proposed by developing countries to limit the growth of their emissions, with appropriate and adequate support from industrialized countries in the form of technology cooperation, finance, and help in capacity building. In this context, capacity building means strengthening the national institutional and personnel resources needed to achieve developing-country adaptation and mitigation objectives. NAMAs are grounded in the overall objective of ensuring sustainable development, and are aimed at achieving a deviation in emissions relative to what would otherwise be "business as usual" emissions by 2020 (UNFCCC 2011a).

Many countries have submitted NAMAs to the UNFCCC and are in the process of identifying new cost-effective mechanisms to implement and achieve their national development objectives, while reducing their GHG emissions (UNFCCC 2011c). Voluntary domestic mitigation goals have been established in some countries, while new domestic mechanisms for cost-effective implementation and achievement of national targets are also being identified. Application of domestic market instruments, such as emission trading schemes as voluntary initiatives to achieve emissions reduction, is increasingly attracting interest in various countries, including Brazil, China, and Mexico. Therefore, performance-based payments for GHG emission reduction, or carbon finance, are expected to continue to play an important role in climate change mitigation, even if under different market regimes than the CDM (see box 24.6).

Over the past decade, the CDM has made important contributions to mitigation efforts through the bottom-up approach of learning-by-doing. To enable scale-up of mitigation efforts, it is necessary to build on the current knowledge, technologies, and experience to develop simplified and innovative approaches for large-scale mitigation programs. Future

Box 24.6

Carbon Market Growth

Global carbon markets have witnessed spectacular growth, with overall transaction volume increasing from 100 million tCO_2e in 2004 to 8.7 billion tCO_2e in 2009. Between 2002 and 2008, about 1.9 billion CERs worth US$23 billion were contracted. However, in 2009, the primary CDM market declined 48 percent from its 2008 volume—a dramatic 62 percent fall from 2007. This downturn can be largely attributed to the global economic crisis, negatively impacting both the demand and supply sides of the market, as well as post-2012 uncertainty.

Source: World Bank 2010c.

market-based mechanisms are expected to take the experience gained from the CDM into account. As instruments for accelerating and scaling up GHG mitigation, which require significant financial commitments, NAMAs may become the vehicle for countries to access global funds, governed under the framework of UNFCCC. However, given the current uncertainty in international climate change negotiations, this is only a future possibility.

The World Bank's carbon finance unit continues to develop forward-looking carbon finance instruments to encourage large-scale, transformational initiatives closely linked with the CDM, and to support countries in developing market mechanisms suitable to their needs and priorities. Two of the latest initiatives are discussed here.

Carbon Partnership Facility (CPF)

The Carbon Partnership Facility (CPF) is a new World Bank initiative designed to support programs that generate emission reductions and support their purchase over long periods after 2012. The facility brings buyers and sellers together in a partnership forum to focus on national priorities and strategies and to develop carbon revenue streams around projects and programs of interest to both. Its objective and business model are based on the need to prepare large-scale, potentially risky investments with long lead times, which require durable partnerships between buyers and sellers. It is also based on the need to support long-term investments in an uncertain market environment, possibly spanning several carbon market cycles.

A preparation fund (the Carbon Asset Development Fund) finances the development of the emission reduction programs and the related due diligence by, among other methods, providing grant resources. A portion of the carbon credits generated by the emission reduction programs can be purchased by a carbon fund (the CPF Carbon Fund) using financial contributions from developed-country governments and the private sector. The remaining credits can be sold to the market by the sellers.

The World Bank acts as trustee of the CPF, contributing its expert knowledge and capacity in not only carbon finance but also sustainable economic development, policy advice, and finance. "Learning-by-doing" is an essential aspect of the CPF as it supports the development of new CDM methodologies and programmatic approaches. Programs under the CPF are expected to expand and broaden the scope of the CDM, while generating a flow of CDM-eligible carbon credits for up to 10 years after 2012. As one of its innovative efforts, the CPF is supporting the development of the citywide approach to CDM, which was discussed earlier in the chapter.

Partnership for Market Readiness (PMR)

As parties to the UNFCCC negotiating process seek workable strategies for global GHG mitigation efforts post-2012, various proposals for new market instruments and reform of the CDM have been discussed. To inform the design process for these new instruments, there is a need for developing countries to improve their knowledge and capacities. To support this development, the World Bank, in December 2010 at the United Nations Climate Change Conference in Cancún, launched the Partnership for Market Readiness (PMR), a fund for capacity building with a target size of US$100 million. Market readiness is defined as having the technical, policy, and institutional frameworks that are needed to enable a country to put in place market mechanisms to mobilize private and public sector financing for GHG mitigation and low-carbon development. Objectives of PMR include (i) contributing to global GHG mitigation efforts post-2012 via market instruments; (ii) facilitating country-led capacity building and piloting that builds on country priorities and leverages existing reduction efforts; and (iii) providing a platform for technical discussions, South-South exchange, and collective innovation on new market instruments in developing and emerging market countries.

PMR-supported activities will be country specific and will build on countries' existing initiatives to meet nationally defined priorities for GHG emission reductions. Based on a country's initial expression of interest, PMR funding could support the setup or scale-up of market mechanisms for GHG reduction, such as domestic emissions trading schemes and crediting for NAMAs; the strengthening of technical capacity, such as data collection and management, and the establishment of reference levels and measuring, reporting, and verification (MRV) systems; and the strengthening of legal and compliance policy frameworks.

Emissions Trading

Emissions trading—also known as "cap-and-trade"—is driven by a country, province, or city setting a limit on the total quantity of pollutants (for example, GHG emissions) over a given time period. If a city decides to adopt a GHG emission reduction target, a citywide program could provide a framework for an emission trading platform to be created within the city. Emissions trading is successful when market participants have an incentive to reduce their emissions, due to the cap, and are then provided the option of buying emission reduction credits generated by others to achieve a portion of their own reduction targets. At the beginning of the trading system, each participant in the scheme receives an individual allowance under the overall cap. Individual allowances may be determined in a number of ways, including from historical baselines, or by auctioning allowances to participants.

The price for carbon credits is determined by the market. Those who are able to reduce emissions cheaply, for instance, by investing in more efficient technology, have the incentive to sell their unused allowances to others. Conversely, those who find it difficult or expensive to reduce emissions may find it cheaper to purchase allowances from others.

An emissions trading system (ETS), when designed and implemented well, is economically efficient and results in overall emissions remaining within the cap. ETSs already exist (see table 24.1). Two examples are the European Union's ETS and the Regional Greenhouse Gas Initiative (RGGI) in the northeastern United States.

Even before carbon emissions trading systems started, several cities, such as Chicago, Los Angeles, and Santiago, developed air pollution trading systems designed to reduce local air pollutants. The world's first city-level carbon cap-and-trade program, with the primary objective of mitigating climate change, was launched in Tokyo in April 2010. Tokyo's ETS covers approximately 1,340 large installations including industrial factories, public facilities, educational institutions, and commercial buildings. With this ETS, the Tokyo Metropolitan Government (TMG) aims to

Table 24.1   Emissions Trading Systems around the World

Administrative level	Name of ETS	Target pollutants	GHG	Target participants
International ETSs				
European Union	EU-ETS	CO_2, CH_4 (methane), N_2O (nitrous oxide), HFCs (hydrofluorocarbons), PFCs (perfluorocarbons), SF_6 (sulfur hexafluoride)	Yes	Electricity generation and energy-intensive industries
Country-based ETSs				
United Kingdom	CRC Energy Efficiency Scheme	Energy-based CO_2	Yes	Large organizations with high energy consumption (although exempts those covered by climate change agreements or the EU-ETS)
Subnational ETSs				
Northeastern and Mid-Atlantic United States	Regional Greenhouse Gas Initiative (RGGI)	Energy-based CO_2 from power plants	Yes	Electricity generators
New South Wales, Australia	Greenhouse Gas Reduction Scheme (GGAS)	GHGs from electricity production	Yes	Energy producers and highly energy-intensive users
City-based ETSs				
Los Angeles, United States	Regional Clean Air Incentives Market (RECLAIM)	Nitrogen oxides (NOx), sulfur oxides (SOx)	No	Facilities emitting more than 4 tonnes a year of either gas
Chicago, United States	Emissions Reduction Market System (ERMS)	Volatile organic materials (VOMs) (particularly tropospheric ozone)	Partly	Stationary sources emitting more than 10 tonnes per season (2 seasons per year)
Santiago, Chile	Emission Offset Program of Supreme Decree No. 4	Total suspended particles (TSP)	No	Stationary combustion sources with a rated exhaust gas flow rate greater than 1,000 cubic meters per hour
Tokyo, Japan	Tokyo ETS	Energy-related CO_2	Yes	Large facilities using more than 1,500 kiloliters crude oil equivalent per year

Source: World Bank 2010b.

reduce CO_2 emissions by at least 6 percent during the first compliance period (2010–14), and by 25 percent below 2000 levels by 2020.

A number of key enabling conditions in Tokyo were critical for the implementation of its ETS (World Bank 2010b). First, mandatory reporting of emissions from at least 2002 provided a solid baseline for designing the ETS and setting compliance targets as the system relies on existing data from electricity and fuel bills and equipment inventory lists. Second, a process of stakeholder consultations was integral to the development of the ETS. Stakeholder engagement provided a means of receiving feedback and technical input that strengthened the design of the ETS while helping to build confidence and increase acceptance of the ETS more widely. Third, the regulatory and legislative framework was conducive to the implementation of its ETS. Although Tokyo had initiated a program for voluntary reductions in 2002, it had a very limited effect. Later, the necessary legislative provisions for the ETS were enacted by the Tokyo Metropolitan Assembly, thus institutionalizing the ETS in a legally binding and enforceable framework.

In China, considerable progress has been made in the area of emissions trading since the late 1980s for both air pollution (mainly SO_2) and water pollution (mainly chemical oxygen demand, COD) (Wang et al. 2008). More recently in 2008, three domestic carbon emissions trading systems were established in Tianjin, Beijing, and Shanghai (see box 24.7). The Tianjin Climate Exchange has been set up as a joint venture among China National Petroleum Corporation (CNPC) Asset Management Co. Ltd., the Tianjin Property Rights Exchange, and the Chicago Climate Exchange. This exchange, as with the Beijing Environmental Exchange and the Shanghai Environment and Energy Exchange, is intended to facilitate trading in a wide range of environmental rights and interests. However, in the absence of mandatory carbon "caps," the demand for domestically produced carbon emissions credits is very low and relies only on voluntary trades (Bloomberg 2010). The further development of carbon emissions trading systems in China could rely on both (i) the establishment of carbon "caps" to motivate demand, and (ii) the promulgation of policies addressing such issues as initial allowances, pricing, market supervision, and MRV activities.

Conclusion

Cities are essential to achieving sustainable development from economic, social, and environmental perspectives. Carbon finance offers an opportunity to access financial resources to reduce the higher cost of imple-

Box 24.7

Domestic Emissions Trading: China's First Three Carbon Exchanges in Beijing, Tianjin, and Shanghai

In 2008, three voluntary environmental exchanges were established in Beijing, Tianjin, and Shanghai through private sector collaborations with approval from municipal governments. All three can be considered pilots for testing the use of domestic emission trading as a tool to support China's climate change mitigation efforts, even though none involve the central government.

The China Beijing Environmental Exchange (CBEEX) provides a platform for trading various environmental commodities, including CO_2. Its current operations include developing the voluntary "Panda standard" for creating domestic GHG offset assets in the agriculture and forestry sectors. Panda standard carbon credits are designed to also bring social co-benefits, typically related to rural development. The CBEEX also conducts CDM transactions, as well as voluntary transactions through the China Carbon Neutral Alliance. It supports a Voluntary Emissions Reduction Carbon Fund of RMB 0.5–1 billion, capitalized by member companies.

The Tianjin Climate Exchange (TCX) is China's first integrated exchange for the trading of environmental financial instruments. Its focus is similar to the CBEEX, but also promotes energy efficiency through intensity-based emissions trading, particularly for heating suppliers. The first transaction occurred in February 2010. After its pilot phase, the Tianjin plan may be extended to cover all public, commercial, and residential buildings and their heating suppliers.

The Shanghai Environment Energy Exchange (SEEE) provides a platform for trading environment and energy-related asset rights, creditor's rights, stock rights, and intellectual property rights. It is exploring ways to reduce CDM transaction costs and bring more transparency to CER pricing.

Sources: Nygard et al. 2011 and Norton Rose 2010.

menting projects that mitigate GHG emissions in cities. Carbon finance also provides a unique incentive for cities to assess, reduce, and monitor their GHG emissions. In addition, most GHG emission reduction projects provide significant ancillary local benefits, such as improved air quality, reduced commuting times, more sustainable natural resource use, reduced pollution, financial savings, and improved satisfaction for users of urban services. Mitigation efforts require the establishment of a baseline of emissions, followed by the measuring, reporting, and verifying of performance compared against the baseline levels. City-level baseline information and comprehensive monitoring and verification systems are critical basic requirements for financing GHG mitigation activities.

The concrete steps required to set up a citywide GHG emission reductions program were presented above in the section "Citywide Approach to Carbon Finance." City trading platforms can decide if they want to trade local credits only, or try to integrate across larger geographic markets. Integrated markets may be national or even, over time, international. They could also decide if they want to trade either CDM-registered CERs or low-priced credits traded in voluntary markets (such as voluntary efforts that promote carbon-neutrality for conferences, sporting events, and other public activities). Finally, flexible citywide GHG mitigation programs could provide the enabling framework to promote low-carbon investments from a range of different sources of carbon and climate finance that may be developed in the near future as a result of both domestic and international policy decisions.

Notes

1. For further information on CDM, refer to http://cdm.unfccc.int/.
2. For further information on CDM in China, refer to http://www.euchina-cdm.org/.
3. For CDM methodologies, refer to UNFCCC 2010.

Bibliography

Bloomberg News. 2010. "China May Start Its First City-wide Carbon Market (Update 1)." http://www.bloomberg.com/apps/news?pid=newsarchive&sid=arHr7BXpQIfQ.

Carbon Partnership Facility. http://carbonfinance.org/cpf.

Greater Amman Municipality. 2011. http://www.ammanplan.gov.jo/english/index.asp.

Norton Rose. 2010. "UN Climate Change Negotiations, Tianjin, October 2010, Day 4." http://www.nortonrose.com.

Nygard, J., C. Brandon, and H. Yang, eds. 2011. *Clean Development Mechanism in China, Five Years of Experience (2004–2009)*. Washington, DC: World Bank.

United Nations Framework Convention on Climate Change (UNFCCC). 2010. UNFCCC Clean Development Mechanism (CDM). *CDM Methodology*

Booklet. Information including EB 56. November. http://cdm.unfccc.int/
methodologies/documentation/meth_booklet.pdf.

———. 2011a. "The Cancun Agreements. Decisions Addressing Developing
Country Mitigation Plans." UNFCCC Website. http://cancun.unfccc.int/miti-
gation/decisions-addressing-developing-country-mitigation-plans/#c178.

———. 2011b. "CMP.6 Guidance relating to the Clean Development Mechanism,
paragraph 4(b)." UNFCCC Website. http://unfccc.int/files/meetings/cop_16/
conference_documents/application/pdf/20101204_cop16_cmp_guidance_
cdm.pdf.

———. 2011c. "Compilation of Information on Nationally Appropriate Mitigation
Actions to be Implemented by Parties Not Included in Annex I to the
Convention." Ad Hoc Working Group on Long-term Cooperative Action,
Note by the Secretariat. March 18. UNFCCC Website. http://unfccc.int/
resource/docs/2011/awglca14/eng/inf01.pdf.

Wang, J., Z. Dong, J. Yang, Y. Li, and Y. Gang. 2008. "Practices and Prospects of
Emission Trading Programs in China." Beijing: China Academy for
Environmental Planning.

World Bank. 2010a. *A City-wide Approach to Carbon Finance*. Washington, DC:
World Bank. http://siteresources.worldbank.org/INTCARBONFINANCE/
Resources/A_city-wide_approach_to_carbon_finance.pdf.

———. 2010b. "Tokyo's Emissions Trading System: A Case Study." *Directions in
Urban Development*, Issue 5. World Bank, Washington, DC.

———. 2010c. *State and Trends of the Carbon Market 2010*. May 2010, Washington,
DC:WorldBank.http://siteresources.worldbank.org/INTCARBONFINANCE/
Resources/State_and_Trends_of_the_Carbon_Market_2010_low_res.pdf.

CHAPTER 25

World Bank Financial Instruments to Support Low-Carbon Cities in China

Frederic Asseline

Overview

This chapter presents the respective uses of World Bank Group financing instruments in support of low-carbon cities. The World Bank Group's traditional investment lending instruments—International Bank for Reconstruction and Development (IBRD) and International Development Agency (IDA) loans—can be used to provide long-term financing for the capital costs of low-carbon projects, while grants from the Global Environment Facility (GEF) can be used to set up an enabling environment, build capacity, and share transaction costs and risks associated with early investments in low-carbon solutions. Climate Investment Funds (CIF) provide concessional financing to buy down the incremental costs and risks of low-carbon technologies, while carbon financing (also discussed in chapter 24) could add an additional revenue stream to improve the financial viability of innovative, riskier projects.

The chapter illustrates how these various instruments can be blended for stronger impact and financial leverage by presenting case studies from projects implemented in China. Projects developed by the International Finance Corporation (IFC) and the Multilateral Investment Guarantee Agency (MIGA), the institutions within the World Bank

Group working directly with the private sector, will also be discussed. In China, IFC has played a key role in building the capacity of local commercial banks and in providing innovative guarantees to finance low-carbon ventures.

The chapter concludes with a presentation of some innovative financial products developed by the World Bank Group to finance climate change adaptation measures, in particular the Global MultiCat Bond.

Introduction

The World Bank Group has a wide range of concessional financing instruments that can cover the incremental costs and risks associated with low-carbon investments. Today, the World Bank Group offers instruments that range from traditional investment lending (IBRD and IDA loans) and GEF grants, to innovative solutions such as Green Bonds or risk guarantees. The World Bank also offers specific carbon financing instruments and financing via the newly established CIF such as the Clean Technology Fund (CTF).

The World Bank has developed a rich experience applying these instruments worldwide and, over the last three decades, in China. Investment loans from the IBRD have been used in China to develop projects across a wide range of sectors, and GEF grants have helped develop innovative solutions notably in the urban, energy, and transportation sectors. Figure 25.1 presents an overview of the World Bank's current lending portfolio in China. Sixty-seven percent of projects in the current portfolio have environmental, climate change, or low-carbon objectives. Experience gained over the last decade in China and elsewhere has evidenced that the integration of new and existing financing sources (IBRD, IDA, GEF, CTF, and carbon financing) can increase the magnitude and speed of the shift to a sustainable urban development path. In the

Figure 25.1 The World Bank Lending Portfolio in China by Sector, 2010

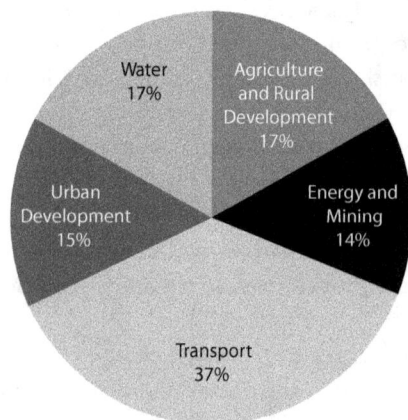

Source: World Bank.

Chinese context, where the financial architecture to support low-carbon investments is still evolving, the expertise the World Bank has developed and its ability to blend different instruments to finance low-carbon projects represent a unique opportunity.

World Bank Group Financing for Low-Carbon City Development

World Bank Lending Products

World Bank loans fund two basic types of operations: investment operations and development policy operations. Investment operations provide funding (in the form of IBRD loans in China) to the government to cover specific expenditures related to economic and social development projects in a broad range of sectors. Development Policy Loans (DPLs) provide untied, direct budget support to governments for policy and institutional reforms aimed at achieving a set of specific development results. To date, the DPL instrument has not been used in China.

Investment loans, credits, and grants can provide financing for a wide range of activities aimed at creating the physical and social infrastructure necessary to reduce poverty and create sustainable development. Over the past two decades, investment operations have, on average, accounted for 75 to 80 percent of the World Bank's portfolio worldwide. The large majority of investment loans are either Specific Investment Loans (SILs) or Sector Investment and Maintenance Loans. New instruments, such as Adaptable Program Loans and Learning and Innovation Loans, have recently been introduced to encourage innovation and provide more flexibility in how funds can be used.

Other World Bank instruments tailored to borrowers' specific needs are Technical Assistance Loans (supporting primarily consulting services, capacity building, and training), Financial Intermediary Loans (focused primarily on financial institutions), and Emergency Recovery Loans (to support recovery in the aftermath of natural disasters).

The Global Environment Facility (GEF) was established in 1991 at the time of the Rio Convention on Sustainable Development to provide incremental cost financing for projects with global environmental benefits. This grant program was originally a partnership between the United Nations Development Programme (UNDP), the United Nations Environment Programme (UNEP), and the World Bank, but now provides its support through 10 agencies. In recent years, the GEF has been committing about US$250 million per year, largely in the form of grants to eligible countries as the financial mechanism of the UN Framework Convention on Climate Change (UNFCCC).

GEF projects are designed to support energy efficiency, renewable energy, new clean energy technology, and sustainable transport projects. Its approach focuses on removing barriers to "win-win" climate change mitigation projects by providing support for technical assistance, policy reform, capacity building, piloting, and partial risk guarantees. GEF grants implemented by the World Bank average between US$8 million and US$25 million and are intended to be combined with larger investment engagements. From 2000 to 2008, a total of US$490 million in GEF grants was approved to support activities in China.

Carbon Finance Products

Traditional carbon finance refers to financing generated through the trade of emission reductions in carbon markets. Projects registered under one of the flexible mechanisms of the Kyoto Protocol, among others, reduce greenhouse gas (GHG) emissions in developing countries or economies in transition and obtain Certified Emission Reductions (CERs), which can be traded in the market, thereby providing a performance-based revenue stream to the project. Carbon finance, in principle, can increase the bankability of projects and leverage new private and public investment for projects that reduce GHG emissions; as such, it constitutes an essential green finance instrument.

The World Bank has demonstrated global leadership in the development of the carbon markets and continues to play a leadership role in the development of Clean Development Mechanism (CDM) projects and methodologies. One of the latest initiatives of the World Bank's expanded program on carbon finance is the Carbon Partnership Facility.

The Carbon Partnership Facility (CPF) is designed to support programs that generate emission reductions by purchasing carbon credits through and beyond 2012.[1] Its objective and business model are based on the need to prepare large-scale, potentially riskier investments with long lead times, which require durable partnerships between buyers and sellers to support longer-term contracts in an uncertain market environment. Programs under the CPF are expected to expand and broaden the scope of CDM, while generating a flow of carbon credits for up to 10 years after 2012.

Chapter 24 in this book provides more information about carbon finance. See also box 25.1.

Box 25.1

Climate Finance in Cancún and Beyond

There is significant international debate on how to best finance climate change mitigation and adaptation measures. The UN Climate Change Conference in Cancún, Mexico, concluded in December 2010 with the adoption of a package termed the "Cancún Agreements" designed to set all governments more firmly on the path toward a low-emissions future. Among other elements these agreements strengthened the Kyoto Protocol's Clean Development Mechanisms to drive more major investments and technology into environmentally sound and sustainable emission reduction projects in the developing world.

The agreements also launched a set of new initiatives and institutions including US$30 billion in fast-start finance from industrialized countries to support climate action in the developing world up to 2012. The intention to raise US$100 billion in long-term funds by 2020 was also included in the decisions.

In the field of climate finance, a process was established to design a Green Climate Fund under the Conference of the Parties, with a board with equal representation from developed and developing countries. The Green Climate Fund will initially use the World Bank as a trustee. At the recent UN Conference of the Parties in Durban, South Africa, from November 28 to December 9, 2011, further agreement on the broad design of this Fund was reached.

Source: Author.

Climate Finance Products

The Climate Investment Funds (CIF) are a new pool of climate funds created in 2008 as a collaborative effort among the multilateral development banks and countries to bridge the financing and learning gap between now and a potential post-2012 global climate change agreement. The CIF are governed by a balanced representation of donors and recipient countries, with active observers from the United Nations, the GEF, civil society, indigenous peoples, and the private sector. China is part of the CIF Board but did not participate in the first part of project funding via the CTF funds.

The CIF consists of two trust funds, each with a specific scope and objective and its own governance structure. The first, **the Clean Technology Fund (CTF),** promotes investments to initiate a shift toward clean technologies. Through the CTF, countries, the multilateral development banks, and other partners agree upon country investment plans for programs that contribute to the demonstration, deployment, and transfer of low-carbon technologies with significant potential for GHG emissions savings. The CTF is meant to be transformative, taking clean technology investments and markets to scale in the participating recipient countries. Between 15 and 20 countries will participate as recipients during the initial phase, which will run until 2012. The CTF provides limited grants, concessional loans, and partial risk guarantees of between US$50 million and US$200 million per project to help countries scale up clean technology initiatives intended to transform a country's development path.

The second, the **Strategic Climate Fund (SCF)**, serves as an overarching fund to support targeted programs with dedicated funding to pilot new approaches with potential for scaled-up, transformational action aimed at a specific climate change challenge or sectoral response. Targeted programs under the SCF include the Forest Investment Program (FIP), the Pilot Program for Climate Resilience (PPCR), and the Program for Scaling-Up Renewable Energy in Low Income Countries (SREP).

To date, neither of the CIF funds (CTF or SCF) has been used in China. See table 25.1 for a summary of lending and finance products.

International Finance Corporation Instruments for Low-Carbon Cities

International Finance Corporation (IFC), a member of the World Bank Group, is the largest global development institution focused on the private sector in developing countries. IFC provides direct debt and equity financing, mobilizes capital from other sources through syndication, and delivers advisory services.

Tackling climate change is a strategic priority for IFC. IFC's specific work on climate change includes (i) investments in sectors such as renewable energy and clean technology, (ii) donor-supported concessional finance to help reduce the perceived risks and costs that often deter private investors from environmentally friendly projects, (iii) advisory services to help implement more climate-friendly operations, and (iv) establishment of sustainability standards through IFC's environmental and social policies. IFC also advises governments on creating an investment climate that promotes low-carbon growth.

In China, IFC focuses on the following specific climate change and low-carbon development programs:

- *Market-driven solutions*: creating and demonstrating the viability of local bank financing of climate change mitigation, such as the China

Table 25.1 Summary of Key GEF, CTF, and CPF Features

Attribute	GEF	CTF	CPF
Objective	To transform the market development paths of eligible countries into trajectories with lower GHG emissions in the energy, industry, and transport and land-use sectors	To provide scaled-up financing to contribute to demonstration, deployment, and transfer of low-carbon technologies with a significant potential for long-term GHG emission savings	To target long-term emission reductions; to scale-up low-carbon interventions; and to support strategic, transformational interventions in key sectors
Overall approach	Removing barriers for sustainable market development and growth, including through pilots and demonstration—includes reduction of risks and support to innovation	Scaling up low-carbon development through support to investments	Increasing the scope and scale of verifiable GHG offsets and generation of carbon revenues by reducing GHG emissions through output-based approach
Determination of funding requirements	Initial resource allocation through resource allocation framework; incremental costs of each project, including costs of barrier removal	Financing gap necessary to make project viable	Payment made upon certification of emission reductions at prenegotiated or prevailing market rates
Financial tools	Grants and limited nongrant instruments	Loans and risk mitigation instruments at concessional (IDA) rates; limited grants available	Emission reduction purchase agreements (ERPA) typically payment upon delivery; pricing based upon market prices for CERs
Scale of financing	US$250 million per year over four years of GEF (2007–10)	US$4.4 billion over four years (2009–12) or US$1.1 billion per year	CDM primary transactions in 2008 totaled US$6.5 billion
Typical project size	From US$5 million to US$40 million GEF allocation per project, linked to larger World Bank projects (average size = US$8 million)	Between US$50 million and US$100 million, linked to larger client project including World Bank loan resources	CPF aims to scale up the size of the transactions significantly, typically at least one million emission reduction units (ERUs)

Source: Hosier 2010.

Utility-Based Energy Efficiency Finance Program (CHUEE). The next generation of the program will focus on energy efficiency (EE) financing by small and medium-size enterprises, supporting small renewable energy projects, and promoting industrial water use efficiency improvement and wastewater recovery.

- *Renewable energy*: supporting the sustainable energy sector through investment in renewable energy producers and their manufacturing supply chain to reduce the cost of electricity generated by these sources.
- *New energy management technology services*: facilitating the deployment of new technologies where commercial sources typically perceive high risks.
- *Policy promotion of lower-carbon approaches*: complementing the World Bank's climate change program and strengthening incentives to choose lower-carbon options through policy and regulatory reform.

The Multilateral Investment Guarantee Agency

The Multilateral Investment Guarantee Agency (MIGA) encourages foreign direct investment (FDI) in developing countries by providing political risk insurance (guarantees) to foreign private investors against the risks of expropriation, transfer restriction, breach of contract, and war and civil disturbance.

In China, MIGA's strategic focus is on providing guarantees in sectors that are government priorities, such as infrastructure. The agency is eager to facilitate more investments in support of China's western and northeast regional development strategy and is working closely with Chinese partners on outward investment. Since 2000, there has been rising interest in MIGA guarantees, particularly for projects that involve sub-sovereign risk, such as those in the water, wastewater, and solid waste management sectors (see also box 25.2).

Examples of World Bank Group Investments in Low-Carbon Growth in China

Examples of IBRD Investment Loans for Low-Carbon Projects

IBRD investment loans have played an important role in the development of the Chinese urban, energy, and transportation sectors. IBRD loans have been used to develop innovative projects—such as the Kunming Urban Rail and Shandong Energy Efficiency Project—that have introduced new low-carbon solutions.

Box 25.2

Additional Resources for Financial Instruments for Mitigation Funding

The following websites provide additional information about the financial instruments available for low-carbon projects in China.

- World Bank Financing Instruments: www.worldbank.org
- The Global Environment Facility: www.thegef.org
- The Climate Investment Funds: www.climateinvestmentfunds.org
- Carbon Finance Instruments: www.carbonfinance.org
- International Finance Corporation: www.ifc.org
- Multilateral Investment Guarantee Agency: www.miga.org

Source: Author.

The Kunming Urban Rail Project

As elsewhere in China, Kunming municipality has witnessed a significant increase in the use of motor vehicles in the last two decades. With the rapid growth of the city's extent, population, and motorization, Kunming is now confronting a rapid rise in traffic congestion. In response, the city has planned, and gained approval for, a massive investment in urban rail.

The project's objective is to achieve compact, transit-oriented development in Kunming by supporting the construction of high-quality, integrated public transport on a main east-west corridor. The total project cost is estimated to be US$1.711 billion, composed of US$1.411 billion of local counterpart financing and a US$300 million World Bank loan. The World Bank–supported Kunming Urban Rail Project consists of the construction of the 19.54-kilometer Kunming Metro Line 3. The project includes construction of the line including maintenance and stabling facilities for the trains, traction, signaling, communication, fare collection, train control systems, procurement of the train sets, and all other works related to the implementation of the line (see also chapter 11).

The IBRD investment will finance civil works (US$210 million), equipment (US$87 million), and technical assistance (US$3 million). The project will be implemented by the Kunming Rail Transit Company (KRTC), which will have responsibility for managing and coordinating the implementation of the project. The Ministry of Finance will on-lend

World Bank loan funds to the Yunnan provincial government, after which the provincial finance department will on-lend to the Kunming municipal government. The municipal finance bureau will then on-lend these funds to KRTC.

The Shandong Energy Efficiency Project

The objective of this project is to improve energy efficiency in industrial enterprises in Shandong Province, particularly through energy efficiency leasing and an increased use of biomass for power and heat generation. The total estimated project cost is RMB 2.2 billion (US$311.25 million) with an IBRD loan of US$150 million (48 percent of the total estimated project costs).

The energy efficiency leasing component (IBRD loan financing of US$134 million) will support financial leasing of energy efficiency investments in industrial enterprises. This IBRD loan will be on-lent to two leasing companies: a US$84 million sub-loan to the Shandong Rongshihua Leasing Company, Ltd., and a US$50 million sub-loan to the Guotai Leasing Company, Ltd. These companies are 2 of the 37 pilot enterprises permitted to engage in financial leasing by the Ministry of Commerce and the State Tax Administration and are major leasing companies in Shandong currently interested in supporting energy efficiency investments.

Examples of GEF Grants for Low-Carbon Projects

The GEF has provided grants to remove investment barriers, condition markets, provide partial risk guarantees, and demonstrate innovative technologies and approaches for low-carbon projects.

At the market level, GEF support has been used to help create the proper enabling environment and investment frameworks. At the project level, GEF resources have covered the incremental costs of barrier removal and market preparation.

The Energy Conservation Projects in China (I and II)

China's first three energy service companies (ESCOs) were created in 1997 in Beijing Municipality, Shandong Province, and Liaoning Province. Startup financing was provided by a GEF grant of US$22 million and European Commission grant assistance of US$4.5 million. The project was scaled up via a loan from the World Bank (US$60.5 million) setting China on a decade-long course to develop its ESCO industry. A number of new ESCOs replicated the business model that had been successfully pioneered by the three original entities created under the project.

The Second Energy Conservation Project of the World Bank and the Chinese government was launched in 2003 to develop the ESCO industry further. The project included support for a loan guarantee program for ESCO projects and the development of the Energy Management Company Association (EMCA). A second GEF grant of US$26 million, which included a risk guarantee of US$20 million, has enabled approximately US$100 million in energy efficiency lending by local banks. One of the most important contributions of the loan guarantee program has been to help many small and medium-size companies jumpstart energy performance contracting, establish their first credit records, and develop their first borrowing relationship with a bank. During the subsequent three years, China's ESCO industry grew at an astonishingly fast pace, with investments in energy efficiency projects based on energy performance contracting of approximately US$1 billion in 2007. (See also chapter 6 and boxes 6.4 and 6.9 for more information about this project.)

The Housing Reform and Building Energy Efficiency Project
This US$18 million GEF grant was approved in March 2005 and supports improvements in building energy efficiency through demonstrations of better building design, improved construction, and new materials, and through new building codes and standards and their implementation. The project uses the GEF grant to cofinance incremental investments in energy efficiency innovations in residential buildings and heat supply systems and also supports the implementation of heat reforms that will reduce coal consumption, which is the primary fuel used for heating residential buildings in northern China.

The project is city based and nationally coordinated. It has adopted a general implementation framework under which each participating city carries out a comprehensive Heat Reform and Building Energy Efficiency (HRBEE) program. The GEF grant supports critical demonstration projects and capacity-building activities essential to the implementation of the local HRBEE program. A subproject approval process has been adopted in order to determine eligibility for GEF grant financing in each of the cities—Chengde, Dalian, Tangshan, Tianjin, and Urumqi—participating in the project.

Examples of IFC-Supported Projects in China
Renewable Energy
Notable recent examples of IFC interventions in the Chinese renewable energy sector include the financing of Suntech, a solar manufacturing

company; Goldwind, a wind turbine manufacturer; and China WindPower (CWP), China's leading wind farm developer in Gansu Province.

IFC has financed CWP's 201-megawatt plant in Guazhou, in China's northwestern Gansu Province, one of the country's poorest regions (see figure 25.2). IFC provided a US$45 million loan for the project and mobilized an additional US$95 million from leading foreign commercial banks. The Guazhou plant on its own is expected to offset more than 421,000 tonnes of carbon emissions annually over the next 20 years—the equivalent of taking more than 85,000 cars off U.S. roads every year. IFC also took a US$10 million equity stake to help CWP at the corporate level explore opportunities outside China, such as in India and Africa.

New Energy Management Technology Services
One recent example of an IFC investment in the area of new energy management technology services in China is Shuoren Energy High-Tech Co., an energy efficiency business geared toward carbon abatement for heavy industries.

Figure 25.2   China WindPower's 201-Megawatt Plant in Guazhou, Gansu Province

Source: China WindPower 2011.

Shuoren designs and implements blast furnace dehumidification technology for major steel manufacturers in China. The company's proprietary technology is designed to improve energy efficiency, both from reduced energy consumption and from improved performance. Shuoren is an energy management company (EMC, or also ESCO; see chapter 6) that designs, finances, installs, operates, and maintains equipment that supports energy efficient manufacturing and thus reduces carbon emissions.

Shuoren's proprietary technology extracts humidity (water) from air before the air passes through the blast furnace, at the initial melting phase of the steel manufacturing process. By reducing humidity, Shuoren's technology eliminates the energy that would otherwise vaporize water in the blast furnace, thereby reducing the overall energy required to melt iron ore. Shuoren's technology has the potential to save about 15,000 tonnes of standard coal per year per steel company. As 90 percent of China's steel production employs the blast-furnace method and blast furnaces consume approximately 60 percent of the energy required in the steel production process, this can lead to large energy savings and efficiency gains.

IFC committed US$3 million in straight equity in September 2009 and US$5 million in convertible loans in December 2009. The US$8 million commitment was part of a total funding round of approximately US$56 million, to expand Shuoren's technology solutions to 17 steel plants, primarily in the less-developed southern and southwestern provinces of China.

IFC is also collaborating with the China Banking Regulatory Commission (CBRC) and the Ministry of Environmental Protection (MEP) in the development and implementation of China's Green Credit Policy. The CBRC, MEP, and the Central Bank jointly issued a policy in 2007 requesting all banks to incorporate environmental and energy efficiency considerations into lending decisions—widely known as the Green Credit Policy.

IFC has provided policy input in the policy development stage, as well as technical assistance to facilitate its implementation, along with a wide array of capacity-building activities for both bankers and regulators. Activities, for example, have included the introduction of international best practices in standards development and financial innovation based on an understanding of regulator concerns and local market development. Specifically, this has involved extensive policy dialogues with the Chinese regulatory counterparts; sharing IFC experiences on developing the Performance Standards; releasing a joint handbook with MEP on international experience in promoting green credit (IFC and MEP 2008); introducing the Equator Principles[2] to China's financial market; and providing energy efficiency financing and other financial innovation as technical tools for banks' implementation of the policy. Capacity building has also included regional support for South-South collaboration and project demonstration, for example, through a Vietnam regulator and banker study tour to the CBRC.

IFC support also extends to capacity building at the market level and includes a series of workshops for bankers and regulators ranging from knowledge transfer on general sustainability issues to provision of technical tools on managing environmental and safety risks. In addition, IFC has targeted its support at the individual bank level. A notable example is the Industrial Bank, which became the first Equator Bank in China and also the first in the Asian emerging market. The bank is now sharing its experience with banks in both China and the region.

Example of a MIGA-Supported Project

The Expansion of Istanbul Metro Project

The Kadikoy-Kartal-Kaynarca Metro Project, which will be the first underground metro system on the Asian side of Istanbul and which will eventually connect with the European side of the city, is expected to reduce traffic and congestion problems in the Kadikoy-Kartal-Kaynarca corridor and reduce automobile trips and their associated emissions.

In 2011 MIGA insured €280 million of a loan provided to the Metropolitan Municipality of Istanbul by West LB of Germany and a consortium of banks—the proceeds of which will be used exclusively for the financing of the metro project. The project uses MIGA's new authority to provide a guarantee to cover a large infrastructure project in the event that sovereign financial obligations are not honored.

World Bank Investment Packages Blending Low-Carbon Finance Instruments

Some low-carbon development projects require additional financial support to become financially and economically attractive. Climate financing instruments, including those discussed in previous sections, help to make these mitigation activities feasible. However, their reach, in isolation, remains insufficient to translate many expensive, largely precommercial low-carbon technologies or other innovative low-carbon development approaches from the drawing board into reality. Combining resources from different climate financing instruments provides support to climate change mitigation projects in a way that can create synergies and increase their joint development and low-carbon impacts.

In China, the World Bank has worked with the government to design projects that blend some of these different instruments to create financing leverage. Some examples highlighting the experience of such blended projects, and illustrating their impact, are described below.

Case Study 1: China Renewable Energy Scale-Up Project (CRESP)

In 2005 the World Bank helped the Chinese government obtain resources from both the GEF and the Asia Sustainable and Alternative Energy Program (ASTAE) to evaluate international experiences and best practice with respect to policy options for renewable energy and to develop its own renewable energy policy framework. In response, the government of China developed and passed a renewable energy law that was the basis for sustainable renewable energy development—one of the first outside the Organisation for Economic Co-operation and Development (OECD) countries.

This technical assistance laid the foundation for an IBRD Specific Investment Loan (US$173 million) which provided support for co-financing two 100-MW wind farms, a 25-MW biomass power plant, and a bundled package of small hydro projects. The World Bank loan was viewed not only as investment support, but also as a conduit for international best practices in private sector renewable power development.

Despite IBRD financing, the terms of the investment program were still insufficient to make the targeted investments feasible. However, when carbon finance was added, the project was elevated over the private sector's rate of return hurdle, making the project sufficiently profitable to function independently. By combining its own resources with those of the GEF and carbon finance, the government of China was able to create a sustainable policy environment that successfully led to rapid growth in the wind market, making it the largest in the world today. Table 25.2 presents an overview of the financial package of CRESP.

Case Study 2: China Energy Efficiency Financing Program

The China Energy Efficiency Financing Program was launched in 2007 as an on-lending operation. The World Bank extended a US$200 million loan to the Ministry of Finance, which was then on-lent via commercial banks party to the project to large industrial enterprises and ESCOs in order to finance energy efficiency investments. A GEF grant was provided to increase the local financial institutions' confidence in jump-starting energy efficiency financing through practical experience. The GEF funding (US$14 million) has been used to assist the participating banks in preparing a project pipeline and building their capacity.

Table 25.2   Financial Package for CRESP

Project financing need	Financial instrument	Targeted outcome
Create enabling conditions and capacity building: • Implementation of mandated market policies at national and provincial levels • Technology improvement (local manufacturing) • Resource assessment • Project development fund • Cost-shared pilot or demonstration • Capacity building/training	GEF grant: US$40 million ASTAE grants	• Successful implementation of renewable energy law • Local manufacturing industry created • Resource information available • A bankable project pipeline built • Local capacity strengthened
Investment resources: • 2 wind farms: 2 x 100 MW • 1 biomass power plant: 25 MW • Bundling small hydro plants < 10 MW	IBRD loan: US$173 million	In addition to investments implemented, the wind and biomass power projects are the first large wind farms (100 MW) in China. CRESP introduced international best available technologies through international competitive bidding.
Revenue enhancement: • An additional revenue stream from carbon financing enhances the financial viability of the Inner Mongolia wind farm	Carbon finance: US$15 million	For the Inner Mongolia wind investment of 100 MW, the carbon financing proved instrumental in improving the project's financial viability from a marginal 7 percent to a financial internal rate of return of 9 percent, which made the project attractive to developers when the feed-in tariff would not.

Source: Hosier 2010.

In the process of developing an energy efficiency project pipeline under the Energy Efficiency Financing Project, a World Bank carbon finance deal was reached with the Baotou Iron and Steel Company. This project, with a total investment of US$67 million, contracted to sell 900,000 tCO$_2$e valued at approximately US$12 million (€8.5 million). The carbon revenues have raised the financial internal rate of return of this project from an unsatisfactory 11.5 percent to over 14.3 percent—a rate considered financially attractive.

This project remains the largest energy efficiency lending operation of the World Bank in China and has contributed to an increased capacity of participating Chinese commercial banks in extending loans to the more risky energy efficiency sector. Table 25.3 presents an overview of the financial package for this program.

Table 25.3   Financial Package for the China Energy Efficiency Financing Program

Project financing need	Financial instrument	Targeted outcome
Create enabling conditions and capacity building: • Assistance for participating banks in capacity building, marketing, due diligence, and pipeline development • Assistance for other banks and overall banking sector to begin investing in EE • Preparation of pilot projects • Monitoring and verification • National policy and institutional support to National Energy Conservation Center	GEF grant: US$14 million	• A project pipeline built • Increased capacity of local banks to develop and evaluate EE projects and to incorporate carbon finance in their operations • National Energy Conservation Center fully operational
Investment resources: On-lending through two selected domestic banks to medium- and large-scale EE investments (US$5–25 million per subproject)	IBRD loan: US$200 million	Energy saved and CO_2 reduced
Risk mitigation:	Loan guarantee program operated by China National Investment and Guarantee Company (I&G)	Enabled ESCOs to expand financing
Revenue enhancement: An additional revenue stream from carbon financing enhances financial viability of the Baotou Iron and Steel EE project.	Carbon finance €8.5 million for 900 kilotonnes of CO_2e	Enhanced financial viability of waste-heat utilization project—for Baotou Iron and Steel Co., the financial internal rate of return jumped from 11 to 14 percent.

Source: Hosier 2010.

Case Study 3: The Beijing Environment Phase II Project
A US$25 million GEF grant and a World Bank loan of US$349 million
were approved in 2000 for the Beijing Environment Phase II Project. This
supports the Beijing municipal government's efforts to alleviate air and
water pollution by converting scattered coal-fired boilers to natural gas,
improving the efficiency of coal-fired heating systems, providing wastewater collection and treatment to the Liangshi River basin (which covers
over a quarter of the city), and strengthening environmental management. In addition, the project is also assisting the Beijing municipal government in developing a low-carbon development study in preparation
for a new project for energy efficiency and carbon emissions reduction.

These financing efforts are complemented by other bilateral and multilateral investments, including for the development of Beijing's Green
Finance Development Strategy (see box 25.3).

Box 25.3

The Beijing Green Finance Development Strategy

The Beijing municipal government has an ambitious strategy to position Beijing
as an international financial center for green finance with the proposed development of a Beijing pilot carbon finance district that will be a hub for carbon finance and
green finance transactions in China. The pilot carbon finance district is to be located in
Beijing's Dongcheng district, which has been designated a low-carbon economic zone.

The Beijing municipal government plan also calls for the expansion of CBEEX
into a major exchange for carbon finance products. The creation of the pilot district and a major exchange will promote the growth of the environmental finance
business. Increased financial transactions and innovations, in turn, will finance
activities that will lead to reduced GHG emissions.

The Asian Development Bank (ADB) is assisting the Beijing municipal government in achieving its emission reduction target through the development of carbon finance. The ADB is conducting a study on the state of carbon finance in China.
The study will make recommendations on enabling policies, and will recommend
a road map for the establishment of the carbon finance center in Beijing. The results of the study will form the basis for discussions and policy recommendations
to relevant government agencies, such as the National Development and Reform
Commission, China Banking Regulatory Commission, China Securities Regulatory
Commission, the People's Bank of China, and the Ministry of Finance.

Source: World Bank project documents.

Case Study 4: The IFC CHUEE Program

The IFC China Utility-Based Energy Efficiency Finance Program (CHUEE) is a market-driven solution proposed by IFC to create and demonstrate the viability of local bank financing for climate mitigation. CHUEE is supported by grant funding from the GEF, Finland's Ministry of Employment and Economy, and the Norwegian Agency for Development Cooperation, and operates under the IFC Private Enterprise Partnership for China.

Responding to a request from the Ministry of Finance to support the implementation of energy efficiency (EE) and renewable energy (RE) projects in China, the IFC CHUEE Program was designed to reduce GHG emissions by creating a sustainable financing mechanism that provides financial support to EE and RE projects. IFC offers risk sharing with Chinese commercial banks for their qualifying EE and RE loans by covering a percentage of the potential loan losses. It also provides technical assistance on marketing, engineering, project development, and equipment financing services to banks, project developers, and suppliers of EE and RE products and services (see figure 25.3).

Figure 25.3   CHUEE: China Utility-Based Energy Efficiency Finance Program

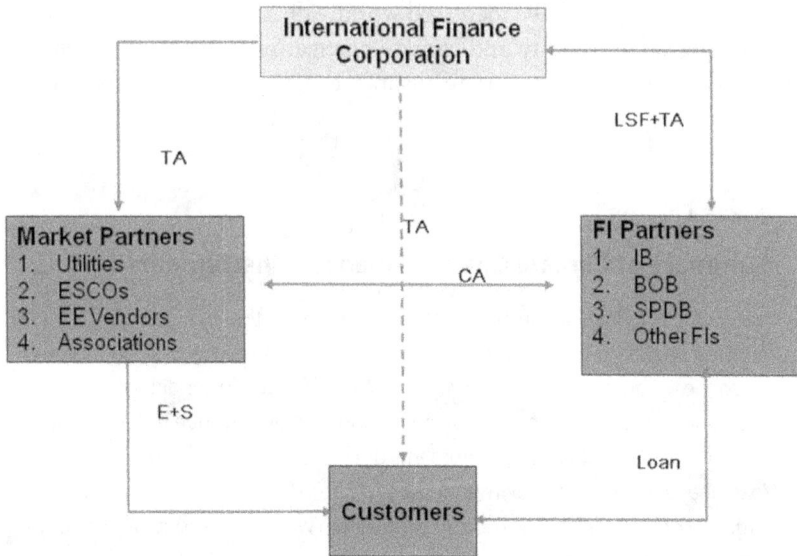

Source: IFC project documents.
Note: FI = Financial Institutions; IB = Industrial Bank; BOB = Bank of Beijing; SPDB = Shanghai Pudong Development Bank.

The program was launched in May 2006 with support from the Finnish and Norwegian governments and is currently working intensively with three partner banks, the Industrial Bank (IB), Bank of Beijing (BOB), and Shanghai Pudong Development Bank (SPDB). As of September 30, 2010, the CHUEE Program's partner banks provided EE and RE loans totaling US$570 million to 142 projects to reduce GHG emissions by 16 million tCO_2e per year, and there are no delinquent loans and no defaults in the existing portfolio. CHUEE also provides seminars and workshops on EE/RE financing opportunities for the wider banking community, as well as market analysis of areas with a strong potential for energy savings, such as district heating and pulp and paper manufacturing.

In the future, a CHUEE SME facility will focus more on assisting small and medium-size enterprise (SME) borrowers, adding up to six commercial banks to the initiative. CHUEE is working with the Hangzhou city government to implement the CHUEE model with locally active banks. IFC also plans a pilot program using the CHUEE model in the water sector, targeting heavy industrial users of water to upgrade their water use efficiency and wastewater treatment capacity.

Financing for Climate Change Adaptation

Natural catastrophes have increased worldwide in frequency and cost due to growing urban density and climate change. Yet most governments do not have access to appropriate insurance against such events. Various

---

Box 25.4

Summary of Climate Change Financing Instruments

Many different financing instruments are presented in this chapter. Matching financing needs with specific instruments could be categorized into four broad categories as outlined in table B25.4.1: (i) creation of enabling conditions, (ii) provision of investment finance, (iii) risk mitigation, and (iv) revenue enhancement. While the different financing instruments discussed may occasionally fulfill more than one role, each has its own appropriate niche in financing a low-carbon infrastructure project and can be used in combination with other existing and emerging sources of finance.

(continued next page)

Box 25.4 *(continued)*

Table B25.4.1   Matching Financing Needs with Specific Instruments

Project financing needs in climate change mitigation projects	Available financing instruments to fill identified need
Creation of enabling environment:	
• To initiate and/or continue a relevant policy dialogue • To make adjustments to policy or regulatory framework • To provide project development funds • To undertake technology piloting and demonstration • To build capacity and train personnel • To increase awareness	• GEF • Multilateral Fund (Montreal Protocol) • Trust funds, such as ESMAP, ASTAE, PPIAF (Public-Private Infrastructure Advisory Facility) • Bilateral donor funds • Foundation funding • IBRD resources also available
Investment resources:	
• Private sector resources: To invest in those projects that have a favorable risk-return profile for private sector financiers	• International private sector resources • National private sector resources
• Multilateral development bank (MDB) resources or government resources: To invest resources for short- to medium-term investments with a rate of return at or near market levels	• IFC resources • IBRD (SIL or possibly DPL) • Government resources
• Concessional resources: To provide significant investment resources to blend with MDB, government, or private sector resources for medium- to long-term investments to fill a financing gap for marginal investments	• IDA (SIL) • CTF or CIF • Government resources • GEF (limited incremental investment resources)
Risk mitigation:	
• To cover risks or enhance credits associated with new technology, business models, resource certainty, and country or currency risks	• CTF (partial risk guarantees) • GEF (limited resources for nongrant risk coverage) • Carbon finance (may help defray currency risks as ERPA are normally hard-currency denominated) • MIGA
Revenue enhancement:	
• To provide additional revenue streams to improve financial viability of investment	• Carbon finance (CPF and other CF funds) • Output-based aid (Global Partnership for Output-Based Aid—GPOBA) • Non-World Bank carbon funds • Voluntary carbon markets

Source: Hosier 2010.

financial instruments have been developed for this purpose, but for many countries they are technically complex and expensive. However, appropriately structured, the international capital markets, with over US$100 trillion in assets, do have the capacity to absorb these risks.

The World Bank MultiCat Program

In response to demand from its member countries, the World Bank has developed a catastrophe bond issuance platform—the MultiCat Program—that allows governments to use a standard framework to buy parametric insurance on affordable terms. Parametric insurance pays shortly after a natural disaster event based on its measured severity. The MultiCat Program (see box 25.5) comprises the following key elements:

- Facilitates access to international capital markets for insurance against the risk of natural disasters
- Ensures access to immediate liquidity to finance emergency relief/reconstruction post disaster

---

Box 25.5

The World Bank's Global MultiCat Bond

The Global MultiCat catastrophe bond pools together a large number of countries and perils and thereby considerably reduces insurance costs through diversification. Instead of individual countries looking for their own insurance, the World Bank selects a pool of insured countries, regions, and risks, with identified donors paying the insurance premiums.

Capital market investors buying the Global MultiCat are paid an insurance premium for providing coverage to the entire pool. The unique risk return profile associated with the pool attracts interest from a wide variety of investors. Estimates show that a three-year US$250 million Global MultiCat placed in capital markets could provide US$50 million in insurance against earthquakes, hurricanes, or floods to each country in a group of 40 countries.

The insurance premiums embedded in the Global MultiCat are paid by a group of donors. If triggered, the insured amount is paid to donors, who could use it to provide immediate assistance to the affected governments. Prior to a disaster, the presence of such insurance provides a concrete starting point to engage with governments on a disaster risk management framework and policies.

Source: World Bank.

- Supports a wide variety of structures, including the pooling of multiple risks (earthquakes, floods, hurricanes, and other wind storms) in different regions.

The Caribbean Catastrophe Risk Insurance Facility

As a result of their experiences during the 2004 hurricane season, governments of Caribbean countries requested World Bank assistance in improving access to catastrophe insurance. The Caribbean Catastrophe Risk Insurance Facility (CCRIF) is the result of two years of collaborative work between the region's governments, key donor partners, and a team of experts from the World Bank.

The CCRIF will allow Caribbean countries to purchase coverage akin to a business interruption insurance that will provide them with immediate liquidity in case of a major hurricane or earthquake. Because of the financial structure of the insurance instrument used, the CCRIF will provide participating countries with coverage tailored to their needs at a significantly lower cost than if they were to purchase it individually in the financial markets (box 25.6).

Box 25.6

The Caribbean Catastrophe Risk Insurance Facility

The CCRIF functions as a mutual insurance company controlled by the participating countries. It was initially capitalized by the participating countries themselves, with support from donor partners. The CCRIF is essentially a system through which several countries agree to combine their emergency reserve funds into a common pool. If each individual country were to build up its own reserves to sustain a catastrophic event, the sum of these country-specific reserves would be much larger than the actual needs of the pooled countries in a given year.

Considering that, on average, a hurricane or an earthquake affects only one to three Caribbean countries in any given year, a pool holding only the reserves for three potential payouts should be sufficient for the entire group of countries participating in the pool. Each year as the pool is depleted, participating countries would replenish it in proportion to their probable use of the funds in the pool.

The CCRIF then expands this concept by combining the benefits of pooled reserves from participating countries with the financial capacity of the interna-

(continued next page)

Box 25.6 *(continued)*

tional financial markets. It retains some of the risks transferred by the participating countries through its own reserves and transfers some of the risks to reinsurance markets when this is cost effective. This structure results in a particularly efficient risk-financing instrument that provides participating countries with insurance policies at approximately half the price they would obtain if they approached the reinsurance industry individually.

This risk insurance method could be adapted to China, where cities on the southern coastline regularly suffer from the passage of South China Sea typhoons. The Chinese Meteorological Administration has been active in developing modeling to predict typhoons and has engaged international partners in piloting climate adaptation insurance schemes. The World Bank-supported CCRIF provides a possible approach to structuring future insurance programs for Chinese coastal cities.

Source: World Bank.

Conclusion

Existing financial instruments supporting low-carbon investments in China include traditional asset financing, public market financing, and limited but growing financing through private equity and venture capital markets.

China has also been trading CERs on international markets for many years, most notably via the CDM, and is in the process of developing pilot municipal carbon trading exchanges. Environmental asset exchanges have been established in Beijing, Shanghai, and Tianjin, but there is no cap-and-trade currently in place to facilitate trading on those markets (see also chapter 24). Looking ahead, one option could be for Chinese cities to issue green bonds in support of low-carbon city development (see box 25.7).

During the transition to the establishment of a mature green finance framework in China, the World Bank Group has been acting as a catalyst by providing its experience in a number of green financial instruments. These range from stand-alone traditional investment lending and GEF grant projects to more innovative structures that blend various financial instruments into one, in particular blending GEF grants and carbon finance with IBRD or IFC financing.

Box 25.7

World Bank Green Bonds: An Example of an Instrument to Mobilize Funds from the Market for Low-Carbon Projects

The World Bank Green Bond raises funds from fixed-income investors to support World Bank lending for eligible projects that seek to mitigate climate change or help affected people adapt to it. The Bond was designed to respond to specific investor demand for a triple-A-rated, fixed-income product that supports projects that address the climate challenge. Since 2008, the World Bank has issued over US$2 billion in Green Bonds.

Many investors are concerned with the effects of climate change, and, with their investments, want to make a difference by supporting projects related to climate change. The urgency of this issue has led to the emergence of a climate asset class to which institutional and retail investors are increasing allocations. For investors, World Bank Green Bonds are an opportunity to invest in climate solutions through a triple-A-rated, fixed-income product. The credit quality of the Green Bonds is the same as for any other World Bank bonds. Repayment of the bond is not linked to the credit or performance of the projects, and investors do not assume the specific project risk. Investors benefit from the triple-A credit of the World Bank, as well as from the due diligence process of the World Bank for its activities.

Green bonds can support a variety of projects for climate change mitigation and adaptation.

- Examples of eligible climate change mitigation projects include solar and wind installations; funding for new technologies that result in significant reductions in GHG emissions; rehabilitation of power plants and transmission facilities to reduce GHG emissions; greater efficiency in transportation, including fuel switching and mass transport; waste (methane emission) management and construction of energy efficient buildings; and carbon reduction through reforestation and avoided deforestation.
- Examples of eligible climate change adaptation projects include protection against flooding (including reforestation and watershed management); food security improvement and stress-resilient agricultural systems (which will slow down deforestation); and sustainable forest management and avoided deforestation.

As Chinese cities begin to explore municipal finance reform options, including through the issuance of municipal bonds, the World Bank Treasury can offer technical assistance in the development of Green Bonds. For Chinese cities, issuing Green Bonds would present an opportunity to signal to the financial markets a city's commitment to sustainable and low-carbon development.

Source: World Bank Treasury.

However, going forward, financing low-carbon cities will require significant additional innovation in terms of developing suitable financing instruments. The instruments reviewed in this chapter can only provide an initial basis for cities to address the low-carbon financing challenges. Effective scaling up of low-carbon deployment will require expertise on how to utilize these instruments in the most effective manner—as well as finding ways to go beyond them.

Notes

1. The mandate of the Kyoto Protocol terminates in 2012. At present no agreement exists that guarantees the existence of a global market for carbon credits after that.
2. The Equator Principles (EPs) are a voluntary set of standards for determining, assessing, and managing social and environmental risk in project financing (http://www.equator-principles.com/).

Bibliography

China WindPower. 2011. http://www.chinawindpower.com.hk.

Hosier, R. 2010. "Beyond the Sum of Its Parts: Combining Financial Instruments to Support Low-Carbon Development." World Bank, Washington, DC.

International Finance Corporation (IFC) and Ministry of Environmental Protection (MEP). 2008. "International Experience in Promoting Green Credit: The Equator Principles and the IFC Performance Standards and Guidelines." Washington, DC: IFC; Beijing: MEP.

McKinsey & Company. 2009. "China's Green Revolution: Prioritizing Technologies to Achieve Energy and Environmental Sustainability." March. http://www.mckinsey.com/locations/greaterchina/mckonchina/reports/china_green_revolution_report.pdf.

The PEW Charitable Trust. 2010. "G-20 Clean Energy Fact Book: Who's Winning the Clean Energy Race?" http://www.pewtrusts.org/uploadedFiles/wwwpewtrustsorg/Reports/Global_warming/G-20%20Report.pdf.